Teaching from a Research Knowledge Base

Teaching from a Research Knowledge Base

A Development and Renewal Process

JERRY J. BELLON
The University of Tennessee

ELNER C. BELLON
Bellon & Associates, Knoxville

MARY ANN BLANK
Tennessee State Department of Education, Knoxville

Merrill, an imprint of
Macmillan Publishing Company
New York

Maxwell Macmillan Canada
Toronto

Maxwell Macmillan International
New York   Oxford   Singapore   Sydney

Editor: Linda James Scharp
Production Editor: Linda Hillis Bayma
Art Coordinator: Vincent A. Smith
Photo Editor: Gail L. Meese
Cover Designer: Russ Maselli
Production Buyer: Pamela D. Bennett

This book was set in Galliard by Carlisle Communications, Ltd. and was printed and bound by Book Press, Inc., a Quebecor America Book Group Company. The cover was printed by New England Book Components.

Macmillan Publishing Company
866 Third Avenue
New York, NY 10022

Macmillan Publishing Company is part of the
Maxwell Communication Group of Companies.

Maxwell Macmillan Canada, Inc.
1200 Eglinton Avenue East, Suite 200
Don Mills, Ontario M3C 3N1

Library of Congress Cataloging-in-Publication Data

Bellon, Jerry J.
    Teaching from a research knowledge base : a development and
renewal process / Jerry J. Bellon, Elner C. Bellon, Mary Ann Blank.
        p.   cm.
    Includes bibliographical references (p.   ) and indexes.
    ISBN 0-675-20639-1
    1. Teaching.   I. Bellon, Elner C.   II. Blank, Mary Ann.
III. Title.
LB1025.3.B45   1992
371.1′02 — dc20   91–30128
                                                              CIP

Printing: 1   2   3   4   5   6   7   8   9   Year: 2   3   4   5

Photo Credits: Photos courtesy of Aurora East School District, Aurora, IL; Knox County Schools, Knoxville, TN; Libertyville High School District, Libertyville, IL; Nashville Metro Schools, Nashville, TN; Shelby County Schools, Memphis, TN; Thornton High School District, Harvey, IL; and Valley View School District, Romeoville, IL.

This is a book about teaching and teachers. Although the title accurately represents our emphasis on teaching research, the real world of teaching is captured in over one hundred scenarios that help to bridge the gap between research and practice. The scenarios are descriptions of actual classroom events that have taken place during the past several years. The teachers in the scenarios range from those still in preservice programs to those who are considered to be peak performers. We believe that teachers, from novice to expert, can benefit from insights provided by examining the relationships between the findings from the research on teaching and the instructional interactions described in the scenarios.

There are several important reasons for our decision to write this book. We have been teachers and teacher educators for nearly four decades. Early in our teaching careers we relied on conventional wisdom or practical knowledge to guide our instructional decisions. We were not aware of any credible research on teaching that could serve as a frame of reference for improving our own instruction. When we became involved in teacher preparation programs, we could not find an organized body of research knowledge we could use to help us prepare and develop aspiring teachers.

For more than 20 years we have had the good fortune to work on instructional improvement programs with school systems across the country. These programs have included: helping administrators and supervisory personnel develop and strengthen their instructional evaluation skills, establishing peer coaching and mentoring programs, and conducting research into practice workshops with teachers. Over and over again, the participants in these programs voiced the need for an up-to-date instructional research reference. Our first attempt to respond to this need was a research synthesis we wrote and published that we titled *What Really Works: Research Based Instruction*. We were quite surprised but pleased with the response to our initial effort. We gained several insights from these experiences. Contrary to what we have often heard, teachers are eager to be aware of and understand the research that can help them to be more effective. With rare exception, they are committed to professional development and renewal—if it meets their needs and makes sense to them. Teachers and administrators, however, no matter how committed they are, simply do not have the time or resources necessary to identify the research that can be beneficial to them.

Even though there are many external influences that teachers must deal with, and many new challenges facing teachers at all stages in their careers, we have been struck by the desire of nearly all of the teachers we have known to help students reach their full potential. It is to these teachers—past, present, and future—that we dedicate this book.

We also want to thank our many good friends and colleagues in school systems and preparation programs who have provided us the opportunity to work with them and who have been, in many cases, the inspiration for our own renewal efforts. They are too numerous to mention individually, but they know who they are and they know how much we appreciate their commitment to teaching and learning.

Sincere thanks go also to our reviewers: Robert Eaker, Middle Tennessee State University; Ruth Ferguson, Pace University–New York City; Dwane M. Giannangelo, Memphis State University; Gloria McFadden, Western Oregon State College; John McIntyre, Southern Illinois University–Carbondale; Theona McQueen, University of Miami; Donna J. Merkley, Iowa State University; James Reardon, University of California–Riverside; Eugene Schafer, University of North Carolina–Charlotte; Elizabeth Stimson, Bowling Green State University; and Dixie M. Turner, Olivet Nazarene University.

There are four people who provided us with invaluable assistance in the preparation of this text. Joseph Bellon edited and proofread our first manuscript. Mark Perkins was our primary research assistant who spent countless hours locating and retrieving critical research information. Mark and Dave Brown worked with us as we proofread and prepared the final manuscript for publication. They have our deepest appreciation.

We also extend our gratitude to our editor Linda Scharp, production editor Linda Bayma, art coordinator Vince Smith, and free-lance copy editor Martha Morss.

Contents

Unit Two

Instructional Management

Conclusion

13. Developing and Renewing— A Career-Long Process

Introduction

1.

Building a Research
Knowledge Base

INTRODUCTION

We have spent over 25 years learning about teachers and teaching. We have learned from our experience with preservice programs, from observing teachers at work, and from the research literature on teaching. We have worked with novice teachers, mature teachers, and teachers who are considered to be experts or peak performers. We have had the opportunity to work with teachers in more than 20 states and several foreign countries. Our knowledge base about teaching continues to expand, and we are pleased to have the opportunity to share with others what we have learned up to now about the complex process of teaching. It is our belief that the insights we have gained can be helpful to those who are preparing to enter teaching as well as those who are career teachers.

Some of the past insights that we developed about the challenges facing those who want to become effective classroom teachers come from our experience with intern teachers. There was a teacher shortage at the time (the early 1960s) so every effort was being made to recruit potential candidates to the teacher workforce. The internship program was considered to be one of the most effective approaches available for inducting potential candidates into the teaching profession. The interns had been identified through a careful screening process. They were well grounded in their specific content areas, but they had not had any courses or experiences that focused on the process of teaching. All of the interns had expressed their desire and commitment to become teachers even though nearly all of them had been successful in other occupations.

The internship program was organized so that prospective teachers would have early opportunities to work in classrooms with master teachers who would serve as their mentors. The university sponsoring the internship program provided supervisors who were expected to observe the interns and help them develop their teaching repertoires. The supervisors were also responsible for conducting seminars that addressed the problems being experienced by the interns and to examine other educational and pedagogical issues. For the most part, the internship program developed teachers who were at least as effective as those graduating from traditional preparation programs. They also suffered from many of the same problems as other beginning or novice teachers. In retrospect it is easy to understand the reasons for their problems and concerns.

When the interns were observed carrying out their instructional responsibilities, the quality of the feedback they received varied a great deal. Neither the master teachers nor the university supervisors were able to support their recommendations for improvement with a solid research knowledge base. The research available during that period of time was limited and difficult to access. Much of the feedback given to teachers was based on conventional wisdom and "folklore." This situation was not as bad as it may seem because many of the common sense recommendations were consistent with current research on effective teaching. For example, asking interns to involve as many students as possible in the interactive process and to monitor and give feedback to students while they were doing seatwork were recommendations that would be consistent with today's research findings. Because of the limited amount and quality of available research, many of the recommendations given to interns were based on each supervisor's experience as a classroom teacher. It is no surprise that many of the interns, when they had completed the program, expressed the need for more assistance and information about how to teach.

Since the initial experience with the internship program, the quality and quantity of research on teaching has increased to the point that it has become a tremendous challenge to stay abreast of the information. Hundreds of documents have been published since the early 1970s reporting findings from school-based research. We have had the good fortune to have a team of associates help us identify and collect the most relevant research on teaching. Because we have used a team approach, we have been able to conduct a comprehensive analysis and synthesis of the research. We have extrapolated the most critical findings from the research syntheses as a basis for this book.

In addition to attempting to stay up to date with the research, we have continued to work with prospective and experienced teachers. Although many preservice programs are incorporating more and more of the research into their classes and field experiences, it has been difficult to develop a solid research knowledge base with all teacher candidates. Different programs have different emphases, so prospective teachers may be well grounded in some areas but have significant knowledge gaps about other aspects of research on teaching. We understand the problem, especially in light of the time limitations that are being placed on professional education programs. The emerging alternative certification programs further limit the amount of time that can be spent helping prospective candidates develop a credible research knowledge base.

For many reasons, staff development programs for teachers are receiving more and more attention and support. We have had the opportunity to be involved in a number of these programs. The programs have included teachers from all grade levels and from a wide spectrum of schools. Our involvement in these professional development activities has helped us understand the needs and aspirations of experienced teachers. There are several patterns or themes that we believe reflect the attitudes of teachers who have been involved in staff development programs.

Many experienced teachers are not conversant with the recent research on teaching. They may have had workshops on specific areas of the research such as questioning techniques, but they have not had the opportunity to be involved in in-depth explorations and applications. Most teachers, however, are interested in the research and would like to make selected applications of research findings. In the final chapter of this book, we have presented necessary conditions and actions that can be taken to provide professional development activities that will assist teachers who want to apply research findings in their own instruction.

We have found that the most able teachers do not want simple prescriptions that are intended to help them be more effective. They know teaching is a complex process that is individual and highly contextual. They have experienced alterations in learning contexts when their student population changes and when environmental influences shift. Successful teachers want to have a broad knowledge base that will help them make the most appropriate instructional decisions. They resent having to follow a teaching script that is promoted as being effective for all teachers without regard to the learning context.

Because teachers, from novice to expert, want to make improvements that will have a positive impact on their students, it is easy to promote new ideas or strategies without providing a solid research base. Teachers will adopt new approaches without understanding the underlying principles and assumptions. It is fortunate, however, that most experienced teachers will screen new ideas against their own knowledge about what will work with their students. Unfortunately, beginning teachers do not have a practical knowledge base that will help them evaluate the efficacy of new teaching strategies that are widely promoted.

Many current professional development programs emphasize the need for teachers to be mentored by their supervisors or by their more experienced colleagues. Conceptually this sounds like a reasonable approach. We have found a number of professional development programs to be ineffective because neither the supervisor nor the teacher mentor had an adequate research knowledge base. When asked to give assistance, mentors often have to rely on their own contextual experiences. We are pleased to find that many of those who have accepted mentoring responsibilities soon become interested in expanding their knowledge of the research on teaching.

We believe that nearly all teachers are interested in developing teaching strategies that will have the most positive impact on their students. We know that many teachers have not had the opportunity, in their preparation programs or in professional development activities, to develop an adequate research knowledge base. When

FIGURE 1−1. Impact of practical knowledge and research knowledge on teaching strategies

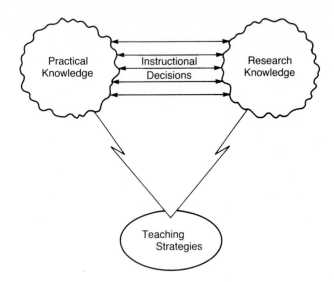

teachers have a limited knowledge base, their teaching and decision-making repertoires are also limited. When this is the case, learning opportunities for students are adversely affected. When both practical knowledge and research knowledge are the basis for instructional decisions, teaching strategies will be more effective. The impact of these knowledge bases on teaching strategies is portrayed in Figure 1−1.

EVOLUTION OF RESEARCH ON TEACHING

Research on teaching is a relatively new field of inquiry. While teaching has been a topic of scholarly thought for centuries, it has been a subject of scientific research for only several decades. Lanier (1978) has suggested that the debate over whether teaching is an art or a science may have been a hindrance to the empirical research on teaching. Because there was so much support for the position that teaching is an art, it was believed that there was little room for scientific inquiry. Recent thinking about teaching supports the contention that it is both an art and a science. Figure 1−2 illustrates how the art and science of teaching interact to influence student learning.

Even though teaching is both an art and a science, it can be systematically studied. Jaeger (1988) has taken the position that "education is a field of study, a locus containing phenomena, events, institutions, problems, persons, and processes, which themselves constitute the raw material for inquiries of many kinds " (p. 5). Researchers can probe in many directions in an effort to understand the field of education and to develop a reliable knowledge base that informs practice. A primary assumption about education research efforts is that the quality of teaching practice varies greatly and that research can identify what accounts for the differences (Medley, 1987). Researchers over the years have used a wide range of questions, designs, and methodologies to document important differences in effective and ineffective teaching practice.

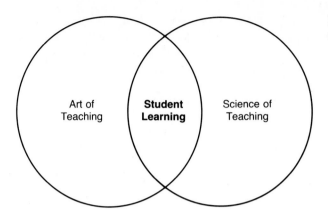

FIGURE 1–2. Teaching and student learning

In the early 1900s most of the research efforts and resources were used to investigate learning processes which, to a large extent, ignored the scientific study of teaching. It was assumed that research on learning would provide adequate information for constructing models of teaching behavior without having to directly investigate the teaching process.

When studies of teaching were conducted, they focused on the teacher rather than on teaching and learning interactions. Research efforts were aimed at finding personal characteristics or qualities that made for effective teaching (Medley, 1987). Studies compared the personal qualities of teachers, such as concern for children and knowledge of subject matter, with their perceived ability to teach. Results from these studies had little impact on teaching.

During the 1960s, researchers began to focus specifically on teacher and student interactions. This research was based on the belief that effective teacher behaviors could be identified and taught to others. A number of instruments were developed for measuring teacher-student classroom interactions (Simon & Boyer, 1970). The instruments were designed to measure the frequency of teacher-student interactions based on a set of predetermined categories. The amount of teacher talk and student talk was the focus of one aspect of the interaction research. Other focuses included the number and types of questions used during instruction and the number of times students were called on to respond. Although these studies did not yield the results that were to have a long-term positive impact on teaching, researchers had begun visiting regular classrooms to gather their data. More important, the studies began to shift their focus from teachers' personal characteristics to teacher and student behaviors in order to identify causal links and variables that are not fixed but alterable (Bloom, 1981).

Brophy (1979a) noted that research methodology improved significantly during the 1970s. Among the improvements were the inclusion of enough teachers to allow for statistical analyses, collection of many hours of data per classroom, rational sampling of teachers rather than random or convenience sampling, and the development of classroom coding instruments that accounted for context and sequence of interaction rather than just frequency of behavior. Also, the studies began to use the individual teacher as the unit of analysis rather than groups of teachers. These studies produced findings that differentiated between the behaviors of more and less effective teachers using student achievement as the criterion for success. The studies also produced findings which gave teachers specific target areas for improving their instruction (Doyle, 1981).

The changes in the research were rather dramatic. More attention was given to subject matter, grade level, and characteristics of students as factors which influence effective teaching. The changes in the research reflected movements in psychology and the involvement of scholars from the social sciences. Doyle (1981) noted that research on classroom contexts would contribute to the improvement of teaching as it focused on understanding "the natural rhythms of classroom life" (p. 4). This type of research is characterized by:

1. An emphasis on long-term observation using narrative accounts primarily, rather than preestablished categories or rating sheets
2. A focus on describing classroom processes in such a way that behavior is viewed within the framework of surrounding events
3. A concern for participants' perspectives on classroom events and for how teachers and students make sense of classroom realities

Context research has provided insights into the distinctive nature of settings which influence the interpretation of data on teaching effects. The research addresses the complexities that teachers face and acknowledges the role of teacher and student mediation in the teaching-learning process. The research is beginning to reveal that a discrepancy exists between what teachers think students are learning and what they are actually learning (Hallden, 1988).

Some important shifts in research on teaching occurred during the 1980s. Researchers recognized that it was not enough to study a single teacher to identify behaviors that might affect student achievement. One major shift was to study the context of teaching and learning. Researchers looked at teaching patterns in context, as influenced by numerous classroom processes and relationships. The research focuses included teacher roles, thoughts, and actions; the enduring problems of practice; and teacher planning, thinking, and decision making (Porter & Brophy, 1988). The outcome of this research was an expanded base of general pedagogical knowledge and content-specific pedagogical knowledge. The knowledge base was strengthened by the identification of underlying principles and integrated theories that explained teacher effects on student behavior (Porter & Brophy, 1988).

Attempts were made to tap the practical pedagogical knowledge possessed by teachers by involving them as collaborators in research studies. This has resulted in findings that make sense to teachers (Clark, 1988). A clearer understanding of teacher knowledge and the structure of that knowledge can aid teacher education program designers. Teaching practice can be improved by focusing on what teachers need to know and finding the best method for them to acquire the knowledge.

Helping teachers build an adequate research knowledge base is a formidable challenge. It is, however, a possibility that did not exist 20 years ago when there was a paucity of credible research on teaching. It is ironic that now there is so much current research available that we have to carefully select findings that are consistent across studies and which are based on sound research techniques. Certainly this is a much better situation than not having reliable information to serve as a basis for instructional decision making.

Graduates from teacher education programs have often voiced their concerns about too much theory and not enough practice. A recent study (Darling-Hammond & Barnett, 1988) reinforced these concerns and also pointed out the need to link theory more effectively to practice. Teachers in preparation programs do not want to be steeped in practices that do not have a solid research base any more than they want to be immersed in research that does not lead to practical applications. The study also pointed out that those who have gone through alternative certification programs are less satisfied with their preparation than graduates of traditional programs. Alternative programs usually provide less pedagogical coursework and fewer practicum experiences. The concerns expressed by teachers in all types of programs clearly emphasized the need for them to have an adequate research knowledge base when they begin their teaching.

Acquiring a research knowledge base is a developmental process. As a minimum, preservice teacher candidates should be well versed in planning, classroom management, and instructional management. They can build their interactive decision-making repertoires in areas such as verbal interaction and higher level learning as they engage in the process of teaching. The developmental process should begin during clinical experiences and expand as preservice teachers gain more experience. The acquisition of a research knowledge base should continue throughout teachers' careers and be supported and facilitated by appropriate professional development opportunities.

Current efforts to improve the schools are focusing on what can be accomplished at a single school site. Teachers are once again being expected to meet the needs of their students creatively. New assessment measures are being developed and implemented to evaluate student learning as a developmental process. More and more emphasis is being given to providing higher level learning experiences for all students. In order for teachers to respond to current and future expectations effectively, they will need to have a range of teaching strategies they can draw on to provide the best possible learning opportunities for their students. It is essential for these teaching strategies to be well grounded in research.

THE CONTEXT FOR TEACHING: PROPOSITIONS FOR CONSIDERATION

We believe that teachers must be aware of the context of their work, especially the conditions that influence teaching and learning. To be truly effective, people must not only be aware, but they must make every effort to master their contexts (Bennis, 1989). We present the following propositions for consideration as being central to current and future teaching conditions. Taken together, they help define the context of teaching. The first step in mastering context is to understand those conditions and influences that have the greatest impact on organizational life. This is especially important for those in the teaching profession where the context is seldom in steady state, but constantly changing and evolving in response to social and environmental conditions.

Proposition 1: The role and structure of the school is changing and will continue to change.

This proposition may be closer to a law or a fact of educational life. Anyone who has been involved in schooling for a period of time is fully aware of the many role and structure changes that schools have undergone, especially in response to political and social concerns. If we are to understand future demands and expectations, we need to be reminded of some of the recent external influences that have had a significant impact on schooling in this country.

In 1957 the Russians launched their satellite *Sputnik* and thereby demonstrated they were ahead of the United States in the race to control outer space. The response was immediate and new demands were placed on schools. American schools were criticized because their students were not equal to or better than Russian students in mathematics and science. The federal government provided funds to upgrade teaching in math and science, especially in secondary schools. Summer institutes for teachers were funded to upgrade instruction in these subjects. Academicians became involved in restructuring math and science curricula. Unfortunately, many teachers did not receive adequate staff development so that the new curricula could be effectively enacted.

During the 1960s a number of political and social changes took place that had a significant impact on schools. The civil rights movement caused a major restructuring of schools through the desegregation process. The war in Vietnam and the student movement caused important changes in attitudes about educational expectations. For several years test scores were deemphasized and attempts were made to humanize the educational process. Curricula became more process oriented and teachers attempted to meet the needs of the whole child.

The total school population began to shrink during the 1970s. Concerns were expressed about declining school populations and the abundance of teachers. Efforts were made to establish greater teacher and school accountability. Evaluation of programs and people was emphasized in an attempt to improve the quality of education. In spite of these efforts, a report issued by the federal government in 1983 called *A Nation at Risk* emphasized the "rising tide of mediocrity" in the nation's schools. Although the report was criticized for not having a solid research base, many citizens and educators accepted its conclusions. The report was one of many in the early 1980s that focused on schooling in America. The political response quickly led to numerous educational reform measures that were enacted across the country.

An increased emphasis on standardized testing was one of the most important reform actions supported by state legislators in the 1980s and, in many cases, by state departments of education. The federal government highlighted the efforts of the National Assessment of Educational Progress (NAEP). Comparisons were made between the test scores of students in the United States and those in foreign countries. The comparisons helped to support the contention that education in this country was mediocre when compared to other industrialized nations. Teachers were under a great deal of pressure to raise student scores on standardized tests, especially those that could be compared nationally. The idea that "that which is tested is taught" was widely embraced by educators and others involved in reform efforts. The testing and accountability movement was having a significant impact on teaching and learning activities.

In concert with the testing movement, teacher proof curricula were developed to assure that all students would be provided opportunities to learn the same basic material. Administrator proof evaluation procedures were also developed to hold teachers accountable for instructional sequences and activities that were expected to provide maximum learning gains (Wise, 1988).

A number of states enacted, or attempted to enact and implement, merit pay and career ladder programs for teachers. It was expected that these programs would reward the most effective teachers and enhance education for their students. Another anticipated benefit was to attract more able candidates into the profession. Several proponents of the programs also stated that perhaps those who were not worthy of merit pay might decide to leave the profession to pursue other occupations.

There has been increasing pressure from the business world to prepare students with the skills and competencies to perform effectively in their work assignments. It has been stressed over and over again that we must compete with foreign countries, especially Japan, if we are to have a healthy economy. Nearly all major businesses and industries have been calling for a literate work force. Students are expected to develop technological skills while they are in school so that they can use technology effectively when they enter the work force. Schools are also expected to help students develop and refine interpersonal and social skills so they can work effectively with colleagues in their job assignments. Business leaders are seeking entry-level workers who are problem solvers capable of working without close supervision. Some educators have accepted the idea that the central mission of schools is to prepare students for the world of work.

Our changing social structure is placing other demands on the schools. The concern for the health of the country is reflected in the emphasis being given to AIDS, family life, and alcohol and drug abuse in the curricula. Schools also have students who come to school hungry and suffering from different forms of nutritional deficiencies. Many students live in homes where there is very little adult supervision or contact. Very often these youngsters are expected to take care of themselves from the time they are in preschool programs. Recently, a considerable amount of attention has been given to at-risk youth. Nearly all of the conditions described above contribute to the expansion of the at-risk student population.

For some years schools have been expected to attend to the needs of handicapped youngsters. These handicaps range from mild to severe. In many cases handicapped students are expected to be in the regular classrooms or in what is known as the least restricted environment. As a consequence, teachers are expected to meet a wide range of needs as they attempt to provide optimal learning opportunities for all students.

The dropout rate continues to be a concern of educators and citizens. Many causes for the consistently high rate of student dropouts have been identified. The causes range from student and parent apathy to charges that students view much of what goes on in schools as irrelevant to their lives. More and more students are working 20 or more hours a week while attempting to go to school. Because of the growing shortage of qualified workers, students are actively recruited to fill part-time and full-time jobs. It does not take long for young wage earners to decide that their work, and the money they make, are more important to them than staying in school.

The role of the school continues to expand and change. Instead of just providing a basic education for all students, schools are now expected to attend to the needs of those who are very young (such as three-year-old preschool students) to adults who are not functionally literate. Schools are also held accountable for meeting the intellectual, social, and health needs of all of their students. Students are expected to score well on standardized tests and at the same time develop higher level thinking and problem-solving skills and competencies. Schools are supposed to help students develop positive self-concepts so that they will be productive, healthy members of society. Helping students to become lifelong learners is viewed by many to be one of the most important functions of schools.

To respond to the myriad demands being placed on education, attempts are being made to restructure schools so that they can be more responsive to the needs of their specific client groups. State mandates are giving way to broad guidelines that place the responsibility for quality education on individual schools. Governors and legislators have taken the position that statewide mandates and reforms enacted in the 1980s have not produced the desired results. The current consensus of opinion is that the single school site should be the locus of control and the organizational unit most responsible for improving education.

The emerging structural changes have several common patterns. Teachers are expected to take part in schoolwide decisions. They are being involved in leadership and management activities that go beyond their classrooms. Individual schools are involving their communities in key educational decisions. Community governance boards are being established to work with administrators and teachers to improve local education. Parents are being asked to become more actively involved in school programs and to play a larger role in the education of their children. In some states and school systems, parents may choose the schools they want their children to attend. The school choice process is being supported by many citizens and government officials, including the President of the United States.

There has been considerable debate about the knowledge that students should acquire while they are in school. Schools are shifting from focusing on basic information, which often seems to be fragmented, to teaching underlying principles and concepts. More and more attention is being given to the structure of the subjects being taught and conceptual relationships that should be understood.

With the changes taking place in knowledge acquisition, related assessment practices are also being refined and adjusted. Less attention is being given to assessing recall of unrelated facts and bits of information and more to determining how well students can engage in higher level thinking processes. Assessment practices will need to be altered considerably if educators accept the contention that human beings have multiple intelligences (Gardner, 1983) that can be identified and further developed. In the future, less attention may be given to assessing lower levels of cognitive learning.

The instructional delivery processes being developed are consistent with recent information about knowledge acquisition. Teachers are expanding their instructional repertoires so that they can effectively address a range of student learning needs. Although direct instruction continues to be the predominant mode of instruction in middle schools and high schools, many teachers are using alternative structures such as cooperative learning and peer tutoring. Some of the emerging instructional delivery systems are well grounded in research while others are not.

Schools will continue to be the focus of social needs and political concerns. As a consequence, teachers and administrators will be expected to respond to a wide range of external influences and at the same time provide students with optimal learning experiences. Many recommendations are being made about restructuring schools to meet these diverse demands and expectations. An especially compelling recommendation is for schools of the future to be viewed as communities of learners (Barth, 1990). In these schools, teachers would be learners as well as teachers. Principals would also be both teachers and learners and, perhaps most important, students would be expected to play both roles. The central purpose of schools would be to prepare students to be lifelong learners.

Proposition 2: Teaching is a complex process that cannot be reduced to simple prescriptions.

This proposition may seem obvious to anyone who has taught or who has carefully observed and analyzed teaching. Anytime there is a move to reform education, the focus is on what teachers know and do. As Shulman (1987) pointed out, "The investigations, deliberations, and debates regarding what teachers should know and know how to do have never been more active" (p. 19).

Some policy makers, thinking they can improve teaching by administrative fiat, have decreed that all teachers should exhibit a particular set of teaching behaviors as they teach their classes. It is their position that when teachers exhibit these behaviors student achievement will be improved. For example, in some school systems (and states) teachers are expected to ask higher level questions during each lesson without regard to the purpose and appropriateness of the questions. If teachers do not exhibit this behavior while they are being observed, their evaluations will be adversely affected. This type of teaching prescription does not take into account the complex nature of the teaching-learning process.

Teaching is a multifaceted process consisting of preactive, interactive, and reflective decisions. During the preactive process, teachers must plan their instruction to meet a wide range of student needs and at the same time assure that the curriculum is being properly enacted. It is not enough for teachers to understand the cognitive needs of their students, they must be prepared to enhance ego needs and to develop positive student attitudes about schooling.

If teachers are to be effective in classrooms, they must have a deep knowledge and understanding of the content to be taught. They are expected to know their subjects well enough to make the information understandable to students whose prior knowledge and experience are limited. Teachers must also be well grounded in pedagogy so that they can make the most appropriate decisions about instructional organization and delivery. It is not enough for teachers to have strong knowledge bases, they must have repertoires of teaching strategies that will allow them to attend to the learning needs of all of their students.

A staff of teachers is seldom at the same point in the development of pedagogical knowledge. Novice teachers may be strong in content knowledge but have a limited repertoire of instructional strategies. As teachers mature professionally, they develop strategies and routines that help them reduce the complexity of the teaching and learning processes.

Interactive decision making is the most challenging aspect of teaching. Decisions must be made in a constantly changing environment. Teachers must be alert to cues from their students and respond in the most appropriate manner. At times the cues may indicate that students do not understand what they are supposed to be learning. Students also give cues that indicate that they are turned off, or not motivated to learn. Teachers must then attend to the affective needs of their students as well as to cognitive and psychomotor learning. They face the challenge of helping all of their students reach their full potential while they are addressing the educational goals of the school. At the same time, teachers have personal needs that must be met if they are to function effectively throughout their careers.

Teachers are expected to exercise judgment-in-action throughout the interactive process. They know that the actions they take are going to have a significant impact on student learning and development. They are supposed to create and maintain learning environments where students can function as independent learners. This is a difficult task. When procedures reduce the complexity of interaction, independent learning may be inhibited. A quiet, orderly classroom, for example, may meet teacher needs but may reduce the teacher-student and student-student interactions that can contribute to higher level learning. It is clear that if the interactive process is to be effective teachers must be thoughtful decision makers who attend to a myriad of needs. The experiences and opportunities teachers provide should be well grounded in research and effective practice. The challenge is for teachers, as knowledgable professionals, to integrate research and practice to enhance the learning of all students. This is not a role that can be played by technicians.

The reflective process is essential for teacher growth and development. Teachers must be reflective during the interactive process. They must make decisions, adjust what they are doing based on student responses and their own insights, and continue the search to accomplish their most important goals. After they have taught, it is important for teachers to reflect on what took place and plan for future instruction. Unfortunately, most teachers have very little time to reflect during the school day. The reflective process usually takes place at the end of the teaching day when energy levels are relatively low. Because reflection is an important aspect of the instructional process, many teachers find that they must set aside time to consider what took place during the day and refine and adjust their plans accordingly. The process of reflection, leading to desired action, is one of the most important aspects of a teacher's career development.

For novice teachers, of course, the reflective process is constrained by both their inexperience and limited knowledge. As their experience and knowledge bases are expanded and enriched, reflection becomes more valuable to them. The importance of reflection never diminishes for those who desire to become peak-performing teachers.

It is impossible for effective teaching to be reduced to scripts and prescriptions. In order to be effective, teachers must view their work as being highly contextual, requiring them to make decisions in action, so that they can integrate their knowledge of content and the needs of their students with the most appropriate instructional processes. This is a difficult and complex task, but when successfully carried out the rewards for students and teachers are immeasurable.

Proposition 3: The role of the teacher is changing and will continue to change.

Whenever attempts are made to reform or improve education, teachers are the center of attention. Perhaps this is the way it should be. Student learning is most often influenced, guided, and facilitated by teachers. The transactions that take place between students and teachers are really the heart of the educational process. Even though the overall structure of education may not appear to change very rapidly, teachers make many changes and accommodations to respond to external influences. These changes often influence the nature of instructional transactions.

A number of changes have been taking place that affect entry into the teaching profession. These changes will very likely influence the instructional approaches used by beginning teachers. An organization known as the Holmes Group has emphasized the need for a five-year preparation program for all teachers. Because the members of this group represent teacher preparation programs in a number of major universities, their recommendations carry substantial weight. The recommendation for a five-year program was based to a large extent on the group's belief that beginning teachers need stronger preparation in their academic fields. Professional education courses in this program would be taken, for the most part, during the fifth year in college. Proponents of five-year programs contend that graduates of these programs would have a better understanding of their disciplines which would result in qualitative improvements in the knowledge they transmit to students.

Alternative certification programs are at the other end of the preparation spectrum. These programs are designed to induct into the profession candidates who have college degrees in academic disciplines but who have not had any courses in professional education. Alternative certification programs have been popular whenever there has been a teacher shortage. The current programs, however, are gaining popularity as an acceptable alternative for certifying teachers in all subject fields. Beginning teachers in these programs are expected to acquire their pedagogical expertise while they are teaching. A variety of approaches are used to fulfill this requirement. Staff development programs, mentoring by experienced teachers, and specifically designed college courses are all examples of strategies used to meet certification requirements. The lack of pedagogical knowledge can have an adverse impact on the instructional delivery process. Participants in alternative certification programs do not have extended clinical or practical experiences. Their first year of teaching is, in fact, their practicum. As noted earlier, graduates of these programs are not as satisfied with their preparation as graduates from traditional programs.

Changes continue to be made in the so-called traditional preparation programs. Many of the programs have been expanding their clinical activities such as field experience, student teaching, and intern teaching. The programs have become increasingly field based with a number of the professional education courses being offered in the schools. The programs are attempting to draw a closer relationship between instructional theory and the practice of teaching. The number of methods courses is being reduced in some preparation programs to give students time to engage in additional clinical experiences. In some cases, generic courses on teaching have been developed to provide information on teaching research to all candidates. Subject-specific pedagogy is incorporated during clinical experiences. Graduates from these programs are expected to benefit by having both a sound knowledge of their respective subject areas and the ability to transmit their knowledge to their students.

Teachers have always been held accountable for the progress of their students. Recently the emphasis has been on how well students perform on standardized tests. Elementary teachers have been expected to demonstrate that their students are mastering basic skills, while secondary teachers are expected to improve students' scores on college entrance exams. The current reform movement places a high priority on teaching higher level thinking and problem solving. Rather than focusing on the recall of information, the teacher's role is to help students develop higher level thinking skills, improve their problem-solving skills, teach them to work cooperatively, and develop a commitment to lifelong learning. Thus the role of the teacher is becoming more and more complex.

Teachers are filling roles outside of the classroom that have long been the sole responsibility of administrators. Recommendations made by the Carnegie Forum on Education and the Economy (1986) have been a major influence on the changing role of teachers. Two of their recommendations have especially shaped the teacher's role. First, they recommended that schools be restructured "to provide a professional environment for teaching, freeing [teachers] to decide how best to meet state and local goals for children while holding them accountable for student progress" (p. 3). Another one of their recommendations was to "restructure the teaching force, and introduce a new category of Lead Teachers with the proven ability to provide active leadership in the redesign of the schools and in helping their colleagues to uphold high standards of learning and teaching" (p. 3). A number of interpretations of and responses to the recommendations appeared in the forum's report, *A Nation Prepared: Teachers for the 21st Century.*

Some school systems have begun to restructure their schools by having lead teachers assume many of the duties and responsibilities of supervisors and administrators. Lead teachers make major curriculum and instruction decisions as well as supervise and evaluate other teachers. Other school systems have moved to school-based management with teachers involved in schoolwide decision making. Teachers in these schools play a major role in establishing school policies that are implemented and monitored by the administrative staff. Teachers in some schools find themselves involved in committees that do not make important policy decisions, only minor operational recommendations.

Several problems have resulted from the restructuring process. Most teachers have not had formal training in leadership and management processes. They may not be familiar with different decision modes and processes. Professional development programs are needed to help teachers acquire the skills and competencies necessary to function effectively in schoolwide leadership roles. Very often schools have not been able to provide teachers with the time to be involved in meaningful schoolwide leadership responsibilities. Freeing teachers to play significant leadership roles is a costly and time-consuming process.

Restructuring, however, has been a positive experience for a number of schools. Teachers have developed practical knowledge about leadership as a result of their classroom experience. In carrying out their teaching responsibilities, they have been expected to communicate effectively, manage conflict, use good judgment in making decisions, and engage in effective planning. Many teachers also model trans-formational leadership behaviors; that is, they help their students achieve higher level goals and work to reach their full potential. Given the time and opportunity, teachers can function effectively as schoolwide leaders. When teachers are involved in devel-oping important school policies, they are more likely to be committed to the success-ful implementation of policy-related activities.

Teachers' roles continue to change as a result of social, political, and cultural influences. In the future, schools will continue to be expected to respond to the needs of all client groups. When structural changes are made, the roles of key personnel also change. If schools of the future become communities of learners, teachers in these schools would act as both teachers and learners. They would serve as role models for their students, encouraging the development of knowledge, skills, and attitudes nec-essary for lifelong learning. These actions may not be very different from the roles many teachers play in their current positions.

Proposition 4: Teachers can establish conditions that enhance the quantity and quality of student learning.

During the 1960s, several researchers contended that student achievement was influenced primarily by socioeconomic status and home conditions. The influence of teachers on student learning was viewed as being minimal. Since that time, credible researchers and well-qualified practitioners have demonstrated that teachers do make a difference in student achievement and learning. There is no question that students' environmental influences play a major role in their development, but the actions that teachers take do have a direct influence on student learning.

Patterns of teacher behavior have a strong influence on student performance, whereas individual behaviors may have little influence. For example, when teachers are consistently well prepared for class and demonstrate that they expect class time to be used for learning, students tend to respond to the expectations by being more work oriented while in class.

Patterns of teaching behavior express the expectations teachers have for their students and the inferences teachers make about the potential of their students. The inferences are based on a variety of factors such as teacher knowledge about previous student performance, the cultural background of the students, and their socioeconomic status. Much of the research on teacher expectations has focused on the differential behavior of teachers toward high- and low-achieving students. This research provides a framework for identifying patterns of teacher behavior that can have the most impact on student learning.

Good (1981) identified several differential behavior patterns teachers have used with high- and low-achieving students. These patterns are

- Seating slow students farther away from the teacher, making it more difficult to monitor these students or treat them as individuals
- Paying less attention to slow students, by smiling and making eye contact less often
- Calling on slow students less frequently to answer classroom questions
- Waiting less time for slower students to answer questions
- Failing to provide clues or ask follow-up questions in problem situations with slower students
- Criticizing slower students more frequently for incorrect answers
- Praising slower students less often for correct or marginal responses
- Giving slower students less feedback and less detailed feedback
- Demanding less effort and less work from slower students
- Interrupting the performance of slower students more frequently. (p. 417)

When teachers categorize students, formally or informally, they are more likely to display differential behavior toward them. It is also clear that teacher expectations are the basis for differential treatment of students. However, not all teachers base their differential behavior on achievement expectations. Differential treatment is acceptable if it is based on informed educational judgment but not if it reflects bias with regard to race, sex, cleanliness, or socioeconomic background.

Teachers can design their instruction to emphasize student learning. The first step is for teachers to communicate the expectation that all students are capable of learning. Although teachers are expected to attend to curriculum goals and objectives, they should also assess their students to determine their prior knowledge with respect to curriculum expectations. They should take the responsibility to adjust learning goals and objectives so that their students can be successful learners. It may be necessary to adjust the objectives upward for those students who have a rich knowledge base as well as make provisions for students who do not have an adequate knowledge and experience background. Learning expectations for all students should be high but attainable.

After teachers have carefully assessed their students and established appropriate learning objectives, they are in a position to determine which instructional strategies would facilitate optimal learning. It may be most effective to use large group direct instruction to develop a knowledge base for all students, or it may be appropriate to have students work in small groups to help one another attend to learning objectives. Teachers can enhance student learning by using strategies that will help all of their students experience academic success.

Task structures used by teachers can also enhance student learning. Teachers who believe that students can learn from one another, as well as from the teacher, will organize and structure the classroom to promote student involvement and interaction. Although cooperative learning is currently one of the most popular structures for facilitating student to student learning, other structures have proven to be equally beneficial. Peer tutoring used at appropriate times to accomplish specific learning objectives has been successful. Because many students tend to model their behavior after other students, providing positive student models can help unlock the desire to learn among lower achieving students. When teachers develop and use task structures that help students experience success, the learning environment is more positive and productive for all students.

Whatever task structure is used, student learning should be carefully monitored. It has been demonstrated repeatedly that teachers who monitor the work of their students and give corrective feedback strengthen the learning process. This is especially helpful when students are working independently while engaged in seatwork and similar task structures. Teachers who assign homework that is closely related to learning objectives and give timely feedback about the homework tend to enhance student learning. Careful monitoring of student learning communicates positive expectations about academic progress. Teachers who effectively monitor learning are using behavior patterns that have a favorable impact on student academic success.

Teachers exhibit other behaviors that can have a powerful influence on learning. The behaviors teachers model will affect students' attitudes about school. Teachers who are genuinely enthusiastic about teaching and the subjects they teach tend to develop student enthusiasm for learning. Teachers must also demonstrate that they really know and like their students. When students feel positive about their teachers and are enthusiastic about learning, they are more likely to succeed. When students enjoy success in school, their attendance rates improve, their test scores are better, and their self-concepts are enhanced.

Proposition 5: School factors and conditions have a significant influence on teaching and learning.

The quality of leadership may be the single most important influence on overall school effectiveness. Many studies have emphasized the relationship of leadership to the quality of school life. Principals and other school leaders are responsible for establishing school cultures that promote and support positive attitudes about teaching and learning. Teamwork and cooperation, for example, will more likely be evident in classrooms when school leaders demonstrate that they value cooperative working relationships.

Schools have been shown to be more effective when clearly defined missions and goals unify the efforts of administrators, teachers, students, and support personnel. It is the responsibility of those in leadership positions to provide the mechanisms and direction to guide the development of appropriate missions and goals for their schools. After the goals have been developed, they should be clearly communicated to all personnel, students, and parents. Schoolwide expectations should be consistent with the school mission and goals. Expectations should be positive and help motivate everyone to be the best that they can be. Properly developed and implemented, goals and expectations can provide a unity of purpose for an entire school.

School leaders have the responsibility to model the behaviors they expect of teachers and students. If teachers are expected to develop positive, caring relationships with their students, leaders must develop the same kind of relationships with teachers, students, and other personnel. Studies of leadership have supported the contention that leaders who are positive and enthusiastic tend to foster similar attitudes through-out their organizations. Studies of schools demonstrate that pervasive attitudes found in a school are often a reflection of the attitudes of those in leadership positions.

Several nonmonetary factors affect teachers' work satisfaction which, in turn, has a major impact on student learning. These factors can be strongly influenced by those in leadership positions. When teachers are given recognition for having done high-quality work, they are more likely to feel that they are valued by their organizations. These positive feelings can be reinforced if teachers are involved in schoolwide decisions that have an impact on their responsibilities. Schools that promote cooperation and teamwork will develop a sense of belonging and inclusion rather than isolation. Recognition, in-volvement, cooperation, and inclusion are all factors that school leaders can, to a great extent, control and use in ways that will foster positive attitudes in teachers. When teachers feel that their work is valued and that their contributions are important, they are more likely to be effective in their instructional interactions.

Schoolwide policies and procedures often have a direct impact on instruc-tional practice. Decisions about grouping, tracking, and student placement will affect teachers' decisions about classroom and task structures. Grading, promotion, and attendance policies have to be translated into classroom practice. If policies are pos-itive and flexible, student learning can be enhanced. Negative, restrictive policies tend to lock rather than unlock the motives of students and teachers. School leaders have an important responsibility to ensure that school policies are designed to enhance, rather than demean, teaching and learning.

Procedures used to evaluate teaching and learning can lead to improved performance or can create negative attitudes and adverse responses. Student learning should be assessed by using a range of formal and informal processes. Assessment measures that provide students with helpful ongoing (formative) feedback about their work are the most useful. This feedback should provide direction and guidance for their improvement activities. The evaluation of teaching performance should also be a positive, formative, interactive process that generates helpful recommendations for future practice. Evaluation policies should be the basis for procedures that are posi-tive, helpful, and growth promoting.

If teachers and students are to be successful, they must have the resources necessary to do quality work. Basic resources such as adequate materials, supplies, and equipment, should be available to all teachers. In spite of all the attention being given to reforming education, many schools still do not have the resources necessary to carry out their instructional programs. In addition to resources, time is necessary for learning. School personnel should ensure that learning time is not interrupted or diminished by unnecessary activities. The quality of teaching and learning can be improved by reducing class size and having specialists available to enrich the standard curriculum. It is likely that very few schools will ever have an abundance of resources; nevertheless, every effort should be made to provide sufficient resources to support quality education.

Teachers and students do not work in isolation from the total school. What takes place in the classroom will be influenced by a number of factors and conditions that exist throughout the school. All school personnel should work together to provide the best possible environment for teaching and learning. Certainly, there are factors and conditions that are beyond a school's control, but those that can be controlled should become the basis for developing school cultures that enhance teaching and learning.

ORGANIZATION AND USE OF THE TEXT

The primary purpose of this book is to provide an up-to-date useable reference for those interested in teacher development and renewal. We believe that it is imperative for readers to understand the organization, structure, and rationale of the text so they can make the best use of the information.

For the past 20 years we have been collecting, reviewing, and analyzing the research on teaching. We have studied hundreds of research reports, publications, and presentations. After reviewing the material, we used content analysis procedures to establish major domains and categories. The domains were crosschecked with the work being done by others who were also attempting to synthesize the research on teaching. We were pleased to find that the domains and categories that we had established were consistent with those developed by colleagues in other institutions. The major domains became the organizing centers for the chapters presented in this text. The chapters are presented, we believe, in a logical order, but each chapter is a self-contained unit so that readers can address the chapters in an order that fits their instructional needs.

The text will assist the reader in attending to the following goals:

1. Developing a sound, current, pedagogical knowledge base
2. Understanding a common research on teaching vocabulary
3. Identifying important research on teaching themes
4. Understanding how teachers have integrated the research knowledge base with their practical knowledge
5. Developing insights from the research that can be applied to improve current practice
6. Engaging in collegial problem-solving and improvement activities to strengthen and enhance student learning

Audience

The text was written for all those involved in teacher development and renewal programs. Certainly, first and foremost, students in certification and preparation programs should develop a research knowledge base. This includes students in traditional programs, internship programs, and alternative certification programs. We believe that all preservice teachers should develop a research knowledge base. They need information that can help them develop teaching repertoires that are well grounded in research so that they will be prepared to make sound instructional decisions.

The material included in this text has been the basis for a number of professional development and renewal programs. Teachers at all stages of career development have been participants in programs that have included activities such as peer coaching and mentoring. Mature and expert teachers have found the research findings especially useful in refining and improving their instructional strategies. Many teachers in these programs reported they had not had any previous exposure to recent research on teaching.

Those responsible for supervising and evaluating teachers and teaching are expected to provide substantive recommendations for instructional improvement. Administrators and supervisors representing school systems in over 15 states have used our initial research syntheses and findings to improve their supervisory programs. They have reported that teachers are much more likely to take their recommendations for improvement seriously if they know that the recommendations are based on credible research.

Previous versions of the material in the text have been used by professors of graduate and undergraduate courses on instruction and teaching. Student teaching supervisors have used the material in seminars and in providing individual student teachers feedback about their clinical experiences. In all cases responses to the information, and to the format used to present and discuss the research, have been positive. We believe this new and expanded version of the material can be helpful to all of those who are seriously interested in improving teaching and learning.

Organization

The body of the book is divided into three units emphasizing instructional planning, management, and delivery. Each chapter in these units focuses on a specific area of the research on teaching. The chapters are based on the research domains that we extrapolated from our research review and analysis. Although the information is presented in what we believe to be a logical sequence, each chapter can be considered an independent learning module. The information in each of these research-focused chapters is presented in seven sections, as described in the following paragraphs.

Commentary.   Each chapter begins with our commentary, or perceptions about, the particular area of research. The perceptions are based on our experiences in schools and classrooms as teachers and supervisors. They are also based on our work with teachers and administrators at all stages of their careers. The commentaries are primarily advance organizers that summarize the research presented in each chapter. Major themes derived from the research are introduced as they relate to the practical world of teaching and learning.

Rationale.   The rationale sections point out the need for knowing and understanding the research domains. Educators at all stages in their careers should be interested in the underlying reasons for the presentation and discussion of each area of research. If there is sufficient support for the need to know, it is more likely that close attention will be paid to the research discussions. Those who understand the relevance of the information will be in a position to appropriately integrate research findings into their own instructional activities.

Research Synthesis.   Each research synthesis represents a comprehensive review of a research domain. The information is presented in a straightforward manner without extensive elaboration. Graphic organizers are provided to emphasize and clarify key concepts and major ideas. The topics discussed under each domain have been selected for their impact on effective teaching and learning. The citations are up to date and represent the most credible research available. Every attempt has been made to ensure that the information presented is supported by several research studies. Any research findings that appeared to be biased and were not supported by convincing data have been excluded from the syntheses.

Primary References.   The primary references include articles, book chapters, and research reports that have a high degree of utility and are relatively easy to access. These references have been briefly annotated to guide readers in their selection of materials for in-depth reading and analysis.

Research in Practice.   The key findings are derived from the research syntheses and represent the most obvious and important research themes. The scenarios are synopses of the real-life experiences of teachers and students that are directly related to the key findings. The scenarios help to explain what happens when teachers, from novice to expert, purposefully or inadvertently engage in instructional activities that are either consistent with or contrary to the research findings. The scenarios describe the experiences of teachers and students in a variety of geographic regions, school settings, and grade levels.

Guide to Observation, Analysis, and Reflection.   These guides relate the research knowledge base to classroom events and interactions. The major goal of the activities in this section is to provide a structure for translating the research into practice so that students of teaching will have a common base for their observation, analysis, and reflection experiences.

Initial activities suggested in the guides are designed to help participants focus on, and accurately observe classroom interactions. The observation phase targets specific behaviors and interactions to be objectively described. We offer strategies and techniques that can be used to collect objective data and make suggestions about the information observers need to collect prior to classroom observations.

The analysis process takes place when the observer shares observation data with the teacher. The first phase of analysis is for the observer and teacher to review the observation data to reach a common understanding and agreement about what took place. Once this has been accomplished, the participants are in a position to analyze the data to identify patterns of teacher or student behavior related to the observation focus. At this point in the analysis process, it is important to understand those influences that guided the teacher's interactive decision making. Analyzing the relationship of patterns to instructional decision making can provide meaningful insights for teachers and observers. The analysis should conclude with an assessment of the effect of the patterns of behavior on desired student learning. Teachers should have the opportunity to reflect on the perceived effect of the patterns and through the reflection process decide which patterns to continue, which to strengthen, and which to discontinue.

The reflection process should take place after the discussion with the teacher. At this point the observer is in a position to relate the observation and discussion results to the research as well as to practical knowledge. As a result of the reflective process, you should be able to suggest actions that will improve future instructional interactions. Reflection should also help teachers and observers become proactive in conceptualizing future instruction.

Development and Renewal Activities.   The activities in this section are designed especially for those who would find it difficult to conduct K–12 classroom observations. They provide opportunities to interact with other professionals in exploring and analyzing the application of research knowledge in selected instructional settings. The information generated by the activities should provide a basis for personal reflection and future instructional decision making. The insights gained through the process should assist students of teaching in developing and expanding their research-based knowledge and teaching repertoires.

Content

In this section we present brief summaries of the material found in each chapter. The summaries should help readers understand the focus of individual chapters as well as acquire a sense of the scope of the book.

Chapter 1: Building a Research Knowledge Base.   In this chapter we have presented background information about our work that led to the development of this text. A short retrospective review of the research on teaching was included with special attention given to the changes that have taken place during the last two decades. Five propositions about the context of teaching have been submitted for consideration. We contend that for teachers to be effective they must understand and master the context of their work. The final section of the chapter describes the content and organization of the text. Readers should find the chapter summaries helpful in focusing their thinking about developing a research knowledge base.

Unit 1: Instructional Planning.   The three chapters in this unit address the important aspects of planning and motivation. Although the planning process involves an interrelated set of decisions, it is important to examine the conceptualization process independently from the steps necessary to develop instructional plans. As teachers conceptualize and develop their instructional plans, they should take into consideration the conditions that affect students' motivation to learn.

Chapter 2: Conceptualizing Instruction.   This chapter focuses on how teachers conceptualize instructional planning. Conceptualizing the instructional plan is the foundation of preactive teaching. Planning decisions, types of planning, and the relationship of teacher experience to planning are all factors that influence the conceptualization process. The belief that effective planning meets teacher needs as well as student needs is a key planning concept. Planning does not start and stop but is an ongoing process that incorporates preactive, interactive, and reflective processes. Planning decisions and processes are affected by a number of variables including grade level, subject matter, and teachers' belief systems and prior experience.

Chapter 3: Planning Instruction.   Specific steps involved in developing instructional plans are discussed in this chapter. The effects of a well-planned, articulated curriculum on instructional planning are described. Using appropriate preassessment and postassessment strategies is one of the most important planning activities. The instructional plan should be the basis for developing classroom and task structures. The relationship of classroom activities to teacher expectations for student learning is described. As teachers develop their instructional plans, they should select instructional materials that support learning expectations and that are at the appropriate level of difficulty for their students.

Chapter 4: Motivating Students to Learn.   Unlocking student motivation is a major challenge for teachers at all levels of schooling. This chapter includes a description of the conditions that affect motivation such as student characteristics, the climate within the school and within the classroom, expectations, the degree of control students and teachers have over learning, and the ways students are rewarded for their efforts. Motivation is a complex concept, but teachers can develop strategies that will help them motivate students such as using appropriate reward structures and incentives, knowing when and how to use praise and criticism, and communicating positive expectations about the ability of students to learn.

Unit 2: Instructional Management.   Effective instructional management is based on the planning and preventive strategies used by teachers. The three chapters in this unit describe actions that teachers can take to prevent misbehavior, correctives that are appropriate responses to misbehavior, and routines that can reduce the complexity of the management process.

Chapter 5: Developing Classroom Management Strategies.   Teachers can develop a classroom climate that promotes and facilitates learning. In this chapter, the effects of management practices on classroom climate are discussed. The importance of schoolwide management practices on individual classrooms should be understood and accepted by all personnel. A positive classroom climate is characterized by teachers and students working together to accomplish learning goals and objectives. Students in these classrooms are able to meet both academic and social needs. Teachers can take actions that will prevent student misbehavior and limit the amount of time used for behavior management. Effective classroom management takes into account students' needs and levels of maturity.

Chapter 6: Responding to Misbehavior.   Responding to student misbehavior is a challenge that faces all teachers. The causes of and influences on misbehavior as well as actions that can be taken to manage misbehavior are discussed in this chapter. Teachers who successfully employ preventive strategies spend less time managing student behavior. Corrective strategies must be based on student needs, characteristics, and an understanding of the conditions that cause misbehavior. Teachers must be in a position to employ a wide range of appropriate corrective measures. The role and function of punishment in behavior management must be clearly understood by all teachers and administrators. Long-term behavior management programs are much more effective than unplanned reactive interventions.

Chapter 7: Making Instructional Decisions.   Teachers make hundreds of instructional decisions each day. This chapter examines the actions that teachers take during the instructional decision-making process. Teachers who are effective at organizing instruction have taken actions to protect academic learning time and to assure that task and grouping structures are most consistent with student needs and teachers' learning expectations. The routines they establish help them to make more effective interactive decisions as they monitor student learning and manage instructional transitions. Teachers have many contacts with their students each school day. It is important for these contacts to focus on and promote student learning. The cues that teachers give about their learning expectations play an important role in student achievement, as do their decisions made about the pace of instruction.

Unit 3: Instructional Delivery.   As teachers make instructional delivery decisions, they must take into account their own competencies as well as the needs and characteristics of their students. When to use whole-class direct instruction, how to manage discussions, and which questioning strategies to use are examples of instructional delivery decisions made by most teachers. The five chapters in this unit are designed to provide a frame of reference for teachers as they give instruction.

Chapter 8: Providing Direct Instruction.   Direct instruction is the dominant instructional mode used by teachers at all grade levels. Lectures and presentations are two of the most common forms of direct instruction and under certain conditions can be highly effective strategies in building a knowledge base. When teachers lecture, they have opportunities to use a variety of approaches to clarify and reinforce the information being presented. They also have the opportunity to develop positive student attitudes about learning. Teachers can use specific structuring behaviors to enhance student learning during direct instruction. They can also take steps to ensure that lectures are clear and that students will be able to comprehend the information. Effective explanations depend on several factors that teachers can control.

Chapter 9: Conducting Recitations and Providing Feedback.   Teachers may believe that conducting a recitation is a relatively simple and straightforward process. Because recitations are so frequently used by teachers, care should be taken to ensure that they are properly structured and used to achieve specific learning objectives. There is a tendency to overuse recitations, which may limit the options for student learning. Feedback, as a part of the recitation process, has a powerful effect on student achievement and the development of students' self-concepts. Teachers can be more effective when they use multiple forms of feedback and when the feedback is appropriate for each student.

Chapter 10: Questioning and Responding.   Effective questioning techniques are the basis for much of the interaction between teachers and students. Teachers can improve their questions if they keep in mind the purpose of the questioning and monitor verbal interactions to keep their questions at a level consistent with their learning objectives. Developing effective questioning strategies is a complex task that must take into account several important variables. It takes a considerable amount of patience and insight to adjust the pace of the questioning process so that students will gain maximum benefit from verbal interactions. It is also important for teachers to help students develop the ability to ask good questions. When two-way questioning techniques are effective, the quality of the discussion improves and attitudes about learning become more positive.

Chapter 11: Adapting Instruction for Small Groups and Individuals.   More and more teachers are moving from whole-group direct instruction to alternative task structures. Changing from single to multitask structures requires teachers to be well versed about the options available and to have the time and resources to make the changes. Several grouping strategies can promote student learning, especially higher level thinking and problem solving. Cooperative learning groups are being used extensively to address a variety of learning goals. Adaptations can also be made to provide individualized instruction to meet the specific needs of students. Teachers should be aware of the options and when these adaptations are most appropriate. Independent study and homework, under the right conditions, can also help produce positive results.

Chapter 12: Moving to Higher Level Learning.   Helping students engage in higher level learning is a challenging task. What students bring to higher level learning experiences, in the form of prior knowledge, is a major influence on the success of the learning experience. By using a variety of cognitive organizers, teachers can facilitate student learning of complex information. Students can learn to monitor their own thinking processes, which in turn will assist them in becoming self-regulated learners. Teachers can design instruction to focus on and strengthen concept formation so that students can organize information in a meaningful manner. It is difficult, however, for teachers to change previously learned misconceptions. Teachers can teach higher level thinking skills through direct instruction. They can reinforce the thinking skills they want students to acquire by modeling higher level thinking as they engage in the instructional process.

Conclusion.   The concluding chapter emphasizes the need for all teachers to engage in lifelong professional development and renewal.

Chapter 13: Developing and Renewing: A Career-Long Process.   Teachers need to be aware of the research on teaching and have the opportunity to develop research-based teaching strategies. For preservice teachers clinical experiences can provide them with opportunities to develop insights and strategies that will help them make a successful entry into the profession. Experienced teachers should also have the opportunity to keep their research knowledge base up to date and incorporate new information into their teaching repertoires. Those responsible for preparation and renewal programs should carefully assess the conditions and influences that affect teacher professional development and renewal at various career stages, from novice to expert. There are a number of effective approaches for translating research into practice. Whatever approach is used, it should be consistent with the needs, characteristics, and career stages of the participants.

Instructional Planning

2.
Conceptualizing Instruction

COMMENTARY

Successful teachers usually acknowledge the importance of sound instructional planning. It is sometimes difficult, however, for teachers to explain how they conceptualize the planning process. For the most part, they have never been asked to explain how they think about planning prior to teaching. Most experienced educators will agree that instructional planning goes well beyond the development of daily lesson plans and that effective planning is a complex process.

Conceptualizing and planning for instruction should consist of three distinct but interrelated processes. The planning that takes place before class begins is referred to as preinstructional planning, or the preactive process. Any changes teachers make during instruction are considered to be part of the interactive process. After instruction takes place, most teachers reflect about what happened and then make future instructional decisions based on what they have learned. This postinstructional planning is commonly referred to as the reflective process. Even teachers who regularly engage in the preactive, interactive, and reflective processes seldom refer to all three of these processes when they explain how they plan. They tend to describe their planning in terms of daily, weekly, or unit lesson plans. In this chapter we are interested in examining planning as a holistic process.

When we visit with preservice or intern teachers, we hear some interesting comments about how they view the planning process. They know that they are supposed to have detailed lesson plans to show to their college supervisors. Many of these teachers say they learned to write lesson plans in their methods classes. They tell us, however, that these are not the plans they use when they actually teach. They are more likely to develop their real plans by following the lead of their cooperating teachers. Cooperating teachers have usually developed their own unique and somewhat idiosyncratic approaches to planning. Their written plans may be as informal as notes written on the margins of their textbooks or a few main ideas listed on the chalkboard. It does not take long for novice teachers to replicate the processes modeled by their more experienced colleagues. Because many beginning teachers do not know what questions to ask about planning, they neither find out what the cooperating teachers were thinking about when they formulated their plans nor do they ask about interactive and reflective decisions that may affect future planning.

School administrators may also have a somewhat limited view of the planning process. When we ask administrators about the importance of planning, we usually get answers about the need for lesson plans, especially when teachers miss school and need substitutes. Seldom do we hear anything about the complexity of the planning process, the need to deal effectively with the three interrelated processes, or how schools should provide teachers adequate time before the year begins to do comprehensive instructional planning.

It appears to us that the actual practice of planning for instruction leaves much to be desired. What preservice teachers learn about planning may have little relevance to the real world of teaching. When teachers have the experience and insight necessary for effective planning, they may have little time or support from their schools to develop the best possible plans. Many schools schedule some time before school begins for teachers to work on long-range planning, but very often other activities take precedence over the planning process. It is ironic, to say the least, that even though most teachers and administrators acknowledge the importance of being effective planners little training, support, and guidance is provided to ensure that the planning process is properly conceptualized and implemented.

RATIONALE

Today's schools are complex organizations that place many demands on teachers and administrators. Student populations are representative of the diversity found in the general population. Secondary schools often have so many students and classes that schedules have to be generated by computers. Elementary schools have pull-out programs that keep students moving in and out of classes throughout the day. Individual classrooms are laboratories of human interaction. Some researchers estimate that most teachers have several thousand interactions with their students each day.

There is constant pressure on teachers to have their students do well on standardized tests. It is very important for the schools to do well on these measures so that parents will be satisfied and will support the schools. More and more politicians are saying that schools are a high priority, even when they neglect to support legislation to increase support for the schools. The constant pressure on teachers to satisfy multiple constituencies makes teaching a highly demanding profession.

Although effective planning is not an antidote for all the ills that face schools, it can help teachers keep their energies focused on helping students learn. When teachers have the time to conceptualize the planning process properly and engage in comprehensive instructional planning, they are more likely to be effective instructional managers. They are better able to predict how to make the best use of time, space, and materials to achieve learning goals and objectives. They can make conscious decisions about instructional priorities in order to make the best use of scarce resources.

When there is a lack of careful, systematic planning, instructional problems are likely. Teachers may not pace instruction properly or give sufficient time to addressing key concepts. Allocated learning time can be lost when materials and equipment are not available when needed. Students who are not actively engaged in instructional tasks may become apathetic or disruptive. Planning should be seen as an enabling process, one that helps teachers attend to a myriad of responsibilities. For beginning teachers, planning is a survival technique, a process that can give them enough security to attend to the learning needs of their students. Experienced teachers plan so they will have the time to address the various learning needs of their students.

There does appear to be a planning paradox. Experienced educators agree about the importance of both long-term comprehensive planning and day-to-day incremental planning. At the same time, many school activities that have less impact on student learning are allowed to take away time and resources that are badly needed to support high-quality planning. Just as important, current research on the planning process does not appear to be widely used in preservice and inservice programs.

RESEARCH SYNTHESIS

The Concept of Planning

Planning is an important activity whenever people are involved in attempting to achieve goals in a complex environment. As Clark and Yinger (1987) pointed out, planning is both a psychological process and a practical activity. It is important for teachers to engage in planning that will help to guide them in their day-to-day activities; they manage a wide range of activities and need to organize their thinking so that they can successfully achieve their instructional goals. They must also be prepared to solve the problems that occur during instructional transactions. Planning is not only practical for teachers, it is an essential component of effective teaching. Unfortunately, planning cannot always be a rational, carefully thought-out process. This is especially true when teachers are immersed in the instructional process.

Classrooms are complex environments where teachers must deal with a wide range of abilities, interests, motivations, and goals (Doyle & Carter, 1987). Many activities are happening at once and many of the events are unpredictable. Although teachers may know students well and understand most of their needs, it is nearly impossible for them to be prepared for changes in attitudes that may be the result of external influences. Many factors that affect students' motivation and attitude toward learning are beyond the control of teachers. It is imperative, therefore, for teachers to plan carefully so they will be in a better position to manage as many of the predictable events as possible and to solve unexpected problems that may arise.

Planning is largely a process of thinking about situations that will be encountered, goals that need to be achieved, and problems that will need to be solved. It begins as a futuristic process that depends on teachers being able to forecast, predict, and imagine what will be taking place during an instructional sequence. Planning is a mental process which depends on teachers' ability to conceptualize what should take place before being engaged in the highly interactive process of instruction. They must develop lesson images which will be a part of the activity flow in the classroom (Clark & Yinger, 1987). Teachers' images are the cognitive representation of how a particular activity ought to unfold. Teachers want their images to become reality (Parker & Gehrke, 1986).

Several basic propositions about teachers and planning have been posed by Clark and Yinger (1987). These propositions help to establish a frame of reference for thinking about planning:

1. Teachers do not just act spontaneously; what they do is influenced by what and how they think.
2. Teachers have implicit and explicit knowledge about students, content, environments, and instructional processes.
3. Effective teachers are able to translate and adapt curricula to create learning activities that are appropriate for diverse groups.
4. Teaching is a complex interactive process involving communication, negotiation, and the construction of shared meaning.
5. Teachers must integrate a large amount of information and knowledge into idiosyncratic contexts.

Taken together, these propositions express the complexity of planning and the need for teachers to be able to conceptualize the total planning process.

The Planning Process

Planning has been described as formulating a course of action for a period of time (Shavelson, 1987b). Planning decisions affect the content covered, the materials to be used, the social structure of the classroom, and the success of the learning activities. Plans essentially become scripts for the interactive phase of teaching. Plans for teaching have also been compared to maps that provide information about the entire route but allow for occasional detours (Calderhead, 1987).

Planning involves a wide range of activities throughout the year. It has been estimated that teachers spend about two hours a day in some aspect of planning (Calderhead, 1987). The time is spent not only before instruction but also during instruction and in reflections that take place after instruction. Some teachers have estimated that they spend 10 to 20% of their time in planning (Clark & Yinger, 1979). The amount of time spent varies greatly with individual teachers and is influenced by factors such as the complexity of the teaching assignment, the range of pupil needs, materials available to the teacher, adequacy of the facilities and equipment, the experience level of the teacher, and the teacher's attitude toward planning.

The primary function of planning is to provide the best possible learning opportunities for students, but planning must meet important teacher needs as well. Beginning teachers especially need to feel secure and confident when they enter their classrooms. Their overwhelming need is to survive (Borko & Niles, 1987). These important needs can be partially met through careful instructional planning that includes establishing a set of classroom routines. Routines help teachers manage their classrooms effectively (Shavelson, 1983). The routines most often reported are those that help teachers move an activity toward completion. Some routines focus on student learning while others are used simply to complete the activities (Parker & Gehrke, 1986). Both beginning and experienced teachers feel more confident and secure when their plans include routines that will help them effectively manage their classes.

A number of important student needs can also be met through the planning process. Students who have special learning needs will have an influence on teachers' planning. Mainstreaming has made it imperative for teachers to make adjustments in their plans to accommodate a wide range of learning and behavior needs. The adjustments may be reflected in the organizational arrangement of the classroom, the grouping of students, the pacing of instruction, the allocation of time for learning activities, and in classroom routines.

One of the most common functions of planning is to provide direction and guidance for substitute teachers. Teachers are usually expected to have plans available in case something unexpected happens that requires someone else to take their classes. All too often the plans that are available are inadequate and do not meet the needs of either the substitute teacher or the students.

Perhaps the most important planning function is to provide appropriate coverage of the learning expectations. Some teachers have expressed concern about long-range planning because they feel it may prevent them from being flexible and making day-to-day adjustments to respond to student needs. Careful planning can accommodate such adjustments and at the same time ensure that the content will be covered within the expected time frame.

The allocation of time for instructional activities is a critical element in the planning process. Teachers make important daily decisions about the allocation of time for specific learning activities. This is especially true for elementary school teachers. Some teachers allocate as much as seven times more time to certain instructional activities than do their colleagues. In some cases these differences are deliberate and in other cases they are unintended (Karweit, 1983). The way time is allocated not only affects what happens during a given day but has a major impact on long-range content coverage.

While there are at least three planning phases in instruction, in practice these phases often blend or blur together (Clark & Peterson, 1986). Instructional planning is cyclical rather than linear. It is a continuous process that integrates planning, teaching, and reflection, as depicted in Figure 2–1.

Planning Decisions

Berliner (1982) described the decisions that are made during the three planning phases. During the preinstructional (preactive) phase decisions are made about content, pacing, allocation of time, and structuring activities. Interactive phase decisions include use of time, transitions, success rate, monitoring, and responses to spontaneous incidents. Postinstructional (reflective) decisions are concerned with feedback, praise, use of ideas, criticism, and student response to the instructional activities. It is easy to see how the decisions during the three phases are interrelated and blend together to affect the entire instructional process. While specific instructional decisions are made on a daily basis, overall planning involves broader decision making. For example, teachers make long-range planning decisions about structural and social features of the classroom as well as content coverage, opportunities to learn, grouping, scheduling, and routines (Clark & Yinger, 1987).

Teachers' theories and belief systems affect both the preactive and interactive processes, which in turn influence their thinking (Clark & Peterson, 1986). It is important for teachers to understand how their belief systems affect their decisions. They should also pay attention to student behaviors that can give them information for improved decision making. The reflective process gives teachers the opportunity to think about what they have done, what they value, the problems and success they have experienced, and what improvements they can make (Schon, 1983).

Planning involves making decisions about instructional means based on knowledge of students, content, resources, outcomes, and other factors that influence classroom events. Teachers must consider the social structure of the classroom as well as the academic tasks before them (Doyle & Carter, 1987). Planning decisions will vary with the time of the year. Students are more often the focus of planning decisions at the beginning of the year (Shavelson, 1987b). The composition of the class often affects which activities are selected (Doyle & Carter, 1987). The majority of teachers make their planning decisions based on the activities they want to take place during instruction. Very often the activities are scheduled to fit the available time. To a large extent these activities are aimed at managing students so that classrooms will be orderly. Planning decisions are seldom based on learning expectations or how students will be evaluated.

When making decisions about content, teachers rely heavily on textbooks and published materials. Curriculum guides and testing programs also influence content de-

FIGURE 2–1. Instructional planning process

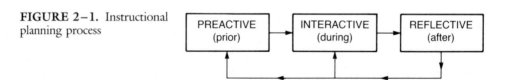

cisions. The content to be taught is more often a concern of teachers in the upper grades. With the increased emphasis on standardized testing in the lower grades, content decisions are assuming greater importance for elementary school and primary grade teachers.

Many teachers develop their plans based on the needs of their students. The ability of teachers to assess their students' knowledge and skills correctly is a critical aspect of planning that enhances student achievement. Activities that focus on student needs can also foster engagement and motivation to learn. When the plans include grouping students for in-class instruction, they have an even greater impact on student learning and achievement. It has been found that students placed in the highest reading group may be working at an instructional pace that is 13 times as fast as children in the lowest reading group, and test scores reflect the differences in pacing (Shavelson & Borko, 1979).

The physical arrangement of the classroom also often affects planning decisions. Teachers may have classrooms that lend themselves only to total-group instruction, especially when classrooms are overcrowded. In some classes, teachers have to consider the location of book shelves, electrical outlets, sinks, and other fixtures that may be needed for a lesson. They may also need to consider distractions caused by traffic patterns if desks or tables are in close proximity to instructional centers. Creative planning is often needed to make the best use of the physical characteristics of each classroom so that a stimulating learning environment can be developed. Planning in the primary grades often focuses on the physical arrangement of the classroom. When instruction does not go well, teachers respond by reorganizing their rooms and making adjustments to their physical facilities and resources (Clark & Peterson, 1986). The various influences on planning decisions are summarized in Figure 2–2.

Types of Planning

The type of planning most often taught in preservice and inservice programs is a sequential process based on clear goals and objectives. The model for this linear

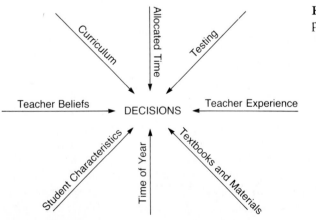

FIGURE 2–2. Influences on planning decisions

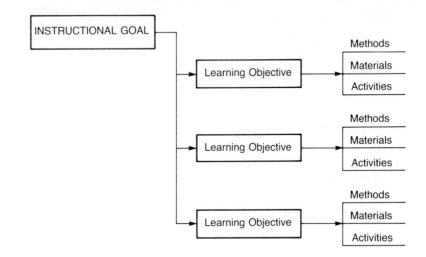

FIGURE 2–3. Linear planning process

approach to planning was developed from the work of Ralph Tyler (Clark & Peterson, 1986). This is the type of planning least used by teachers (Gage & Berliner, 1984). In the linear approach a set of goals and objectives is expected to give direction to the selection of methods, materials, and activities, as shown in Figure 2–3. Yet, when teachers do engage in planning, they seldom emphasize goals and objectives. They are more apt to focus on activities necessary to manage students more effectively during the instructional process (Tursman, 1981).

The activity or task has become the structural unit for planning (Shavelson, 1987b). Beginning teachers often find this type of planning most attractive because it does not require as much information about student needs or the content to be learned. They may also be attracted to this process because it is very often the type of planning used by the more experienced teachers with whom they work. Many times the learning objectives are identified by teachers during the interactive phase of teaching (Clark & Yinger, 1987). Although planning is most often not a linear process, teachers should be aware that, when students know and understand the goals and objectives prior to being engaged in instructional activities, their learning is enhanced and their motivation to learn is improved. However, when objectives are used to structure student learning experiences, incidental student learning may be limited. If not carefully monitored, this type of planning may limit teachers' flexibility in meeting student needs (Zahorik, 1970).

Comprehensive planning and incremental planning are the two major types of instructional planning. The elements of each type of planning are shown in Figure 2–4. Comprehensive planning is based on longer-term decisions and is goal oriented. Incremental planning is based on day-to-day decisions that are consistent with the current status of the students and their learning (Clark & Yinger, 1987). Incremental planning may be effective for specific lessons but may not help in achieving long-term goals. Comprehensive planners tend to use a more detailed and thorough framework for their decisions. They take into consideration the content to be covered, student needs, time allocation, and the pacing of instruction. Comprehensive planning is more effective in achieving student learning expectations. For example, Rosenshine (1983–84) and others have shown that content coverage and pacing are important determinants of student achievement.

Teachers use a variety of different plans. The daily lesson plan is the most common type of instructional plan. Beginning teachers are often expected to have very detailed daily plans. Daily plans can be quite helpful, but too often they are designed only to meet administrative expectations and not to attend to student needs or address specific learning expectations. Daily plans are often required, and the format is usually designed to give attention to specific elements of instruction. Weekly plans are also developed by many teachers and have many of the same characteristics as daily plans.

Unit plans cover a series of lessons and generally focus on longer-term goals. When unit plans are carefully formulated to achieve specific goals and objectives that are based on the content to be covered and the needs of students, there is usually a better payoff in terms of student learning. Well-developed unit plans would be good examples of effective comprehensive plans.

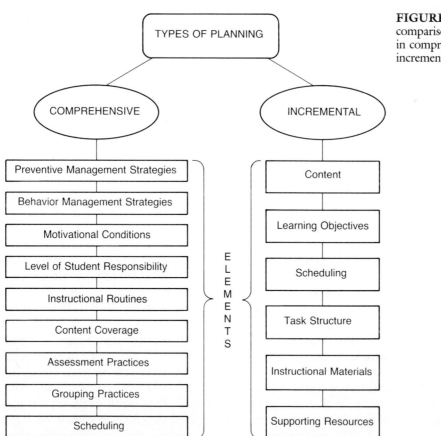

FIGURE 2–4. A comparison of the elements in comprehensive and incremental planning

Year-long plans provide the overall direction for the other types of plans that have been described. Many teachers have found that year-long plans are critical if they are to cover the required content adequately. Year-long plans should be developed before school begins so that all of the known school-year factors can be taken into consideration. These factors include the availability of materials, planned holidays and vacations, times that are the most conducive to learning, and times that may be the most unproductive. At a minimum, year-long plans should include the major goals to be achieved, target dates for the completion of the work to achieve the goals, and the materials needed for the related learning activities.

Teacher Experience and Planning

Experienced teachers think about and approach teaching differently than do novice teachers. Experienced teachers usually have better-developed knowledge structures or schemata than do beginning teachers. These differences are reflected both in teachers' ability to recall classroom events and their analysis of classroom situations (Peterson & Comeaux, 1987). Experienced teachers often have plans in memory from previous teaching experience, while novice teachers may have plans that are superficial and not carefully thought out (Calderhead, 1987). Both types of teachers most often base their planning on activities, materials, and objectives that are included in the teachers' editions of their textbooks.

Because of their prior knowledge of students, experienced teachers are more likely to plan for contingencies, rules and regulations, and how to assess and give feedback (Gagne, 1985). They know what to expect in terms of student behavior, and so they are able to develop plans that will more likely motivate students to learn. Novice teachers are more likely to be involved in trial-and-error planning until they have developed the background and experience that will help them predict student responses to the planned activities.

Experienced teachers who have been identified as experts are likely to have developed sophisticated planning processes. Their plans build on prior student learning, allow for fluid movement within the lesson structure, include lesson agendas, and meet goals with well-rehearsed actions. Novice teachers, on the other hand, often teach lessons that are fragmented, give unclear signals, have ambiguous goals, do not access knowledge well, and do not do a good job of integrating topics (Leinhardt, 1986). Experienced teachers who have not reached the expert level may not be using what they do know about the teaching act when they formulate their instructional plans.

Berliner (1986) identified several characteristics of expert teachers. These characteristics include having different schemata from novice teachers, making inferences rather than viewing events literally, recognizing patterns, taking time in problem solving, attending to social structure, using materials in more nontraditional ways, and being self-regulatory (metacognitive) in planning and using time. Expert teachers also plan for contingencies and adaptations, and derive goals from student work.

As experienced teachers engage in the interactive process they are significantly more responsive to cues from students than are novice teachers (Berliner, 1988). As a result of these cues, teachers make adjustments to their plans that help them improve the effectiveness of their lessons. These adjustments may include changing the pace of the lesson, adjusting learning expectations, and changing the time allocated for selected activities. Overly rigid planning that is not adapted to student progress may have a negative effect on learning (Calderhead, 1984). Furthermore, when teachers monitor the implementation of their plans, there is a positive effect on student learning (Neely, 1986).

All teachers must be responsible for their own planning. Novice teachers can learn a great deal about planning from teachers who exhibit the characteristics that are most often associated with their expert colleagues. They should, however, learn to develop their own comprehensive plans including daily, weekly, and unit plans. When teachers are given specific plans to follow, they tend not to be as sensitive to the needs of their students. This approach to planning can be counterproductive for both students and teachers (Shavelson, 1983).

Planning for instruction is a critical element in the instructional process. Teacher and student needs should be given careful consideration during preactive decision making. Effective comprehensive plans will have a positive effect on student learning. When gains in student achievement are realized, the attitudes of students are improved and teachers are more confident about their instructional decisions.

 ## PRIMARY REFERENCES

Clark, C. M., & **Peterson, P.** (1986). Teachers' thought processes. In M. Wittrock (Ed.), *Handbook of research on teaching* (3rd ed., pp. 255–296). New York: Macmillan.

This book contains a comprehensive synthesis of the research on teaching. Chapter 9 by Clark and Peterson is an excellent discussion of teachers' thought processes. Included in this chapter is a well-documented summary of the research on teacher planning.

Clark, C. M., & **Yinger, R. J.** (1987). Teacher planning. In J. Calderhead (Ed.), *Exploring teachers' thinking* (pp. 84–103). London: Cassell.

This chapter summarizes studies of how experienced teachers plan and how teachers link instruction to curriculum. The complexity of the design process is highlighted, with a focus on the types and functions of planning, the models used, and the effect of planning on classroom interaction.

Doyle, W., & **Carter, K.** (1987). Choosing the means of instruction. In V. Richardson-Koehler (Ed.), *Educators' handbook: A research perspective* (pp. 188–206). New York: Longman.

The chapter analyzes the decisions teachers make in selecting appropriate means of instruction. The focus is on planning and managing classroom activities which involve decisions about the way students are organized, the social structure of the classroom environment, and the academic task.

Shavelson, R. J. (1983). Review of research on teachers' pedagogical judgments, plans, and decisions. *The Elementary School Journal, 83,* 392–413.

Shavelson's article in this special issue of the journal presents the research on teachers' judgments, plans, and decisions. A comprehensive model of interactive decision making helps clarify this complex area of study.

 RESEARCH IN PRACTICE

Finding 1: Because teaching is a complex process, planning for instruction should begin with teachers conceptualizing what is likely to take place during the interactive process.

The research on planning and teacher thinking reinforces the notion that teaching is a highly complex activity. Teachers must be prepared to orchestrate a wide range of activities while they are attempting to help students attend to different learning expectations. Experienced teachers usually have the knowledge base to conceptualize what will take place during the interactive process. It is likely that their images about what will happen during instruction are reasonably accurate. They may have encountered enough situations in their careers to prepare them mentally for almost any event. When experienced teachers are faced with situations that are unexpected or do not fit their images about what will occur during instruction, they use a variety of contingency management techniques. These techniques may include changing the management of the classroom, redirecting the instructional process, or changing teaching strategies and student activities.

Beginning teachers do not have the experience base to help them accurately conceptualize what will happen during the interactive phase of instruction. They may even have false images about what to expect. This can happen when their experiences during their preparation program are quite different from their first teaching assignments.

Scenario. An elementary teacher told us about how different her images were for her first teaching assignment compared to those she had developed during her student teaching experience. She had been a student teacher in a small, rural, all-white elementary school. She was employed by a city school system and assigned to an inner-city elementary school. The total environment was so different that she felt she had no way to predict what would happen in the classroom each day. She lacked the experience to understand the needs of the students; the effect of the physical facilities on teaching and learning; and the expectations of parents, students, and administrators. She was not able to envision what would be likely to happen during the interactive phase of instruction. Her first year of teaching was traumatic for both the teacher and her students.

It took several years for the teacher to really understand her school and community culture and the impact of the culture on classroom expectations and behavior. She was gradually able to develop images that were consistent with the real world of her students. Her planning for instruction began to pay dividends in terms of student performance and she was better able to attend to the important learning needs of her students. She had fewer and fewer unexpected classroom situations to manage that would detract from instructional activities. Because there were fewer unexpected situations, she felt capable of coping with those that did occur.

Finding 2: Planning for instruction helps teachers meet their security needs, establish management routines, and organize resources to meet a range of student needs.

Effective planning does help teachers meet their security needs. This is especially true at the beginning of the year when many teachers plan to develop classroom routines that will help them more effectively manage the myriad activities that will be taking place. Once these routines are established, attention can be paid to the learning tasks. The routines developed are closely related to the conscious or subconscious needs of teachers. For example, some teachers function most effectively when the majority of the classroom tasks are performed by the entire group in an orderly manner with very little individual deviation. Other teachers whose students perform equally well may have a higher tolerance for idiosyncratic student behavior. Before teachers plan their classroom routines, they should be sure they know and understand their own needs and the tolerance they have for individualistic behavior.

Teachers must also know how to identify and understand student needs. A variety of sources for information can help them clarify individual and group needs. Teachers should access all of the available information and then carefully analyze it for possible bias. The images and predictions that teachers make about classroom interactions require an accurate picture of student needs. This is essential if instructional resources, including time, are to be appropriately allocated to the planned learning activities.

Scenario.   We know that many teachers want to involve their students in some form of small-group learning. They have experimented with both cooperative learning and team learning. Teachers who have been successful in moving from a single task structure to a multitask structure attribute their success to careful planning. They realize that they have to plan to teach new management routines to their students before they begin the group work. This requires spending some time to prepare students to assume new roles and responsibilities. Teachers must also organize their resources differently so that little time is lost in transitions and in providing instructional support. When they first move into new task structures, some teachers report that they feel like they have lost control. Once the routines are well established, they become more secure about what is happening and once again feel that they have control of the instructional process.

One teacher felt that she had done all of the necessary preparation and planning in order to use cooperative learning groups, but when it was time to make the transition she became so insecure that she did not go through with her plan. She realized that even though her students' needs might be better met through a multitask structure she would feel so insecure that her effectiveness would suffer. It was probably better for her and her students to stay in a task structure that would enhance rather than weaken the instructional process.

Finding 3: Instructional planning should be an ongoing process consisting of three interrelated components: preactive decisions, interactive analysis, and reflective evaluation.

Many teachers may not consciously make the link between preactive, interactive, and reflective decisions. However, the majority of teachers go through these three processes as they plan and replan their instruction. Teachers who carefully plan during the preactive process have a solid frame of reference for interactive analysis and decision making. Because their expectations are clear, they can make thoughtful interactive adjustments that will support their learning objectives. Teachers often reflect during the interactive process. The reflection may be subconscious but they tend to use the information generated from the reflective process when they plan future instruction. Unfortunately, most teachers do not have time during the teaching day to carefully reflect on their instruction and take corrective action. For most teachers, reflective evaluation that may lead to action takes place at the end of the day, in the evening, or the next day before school starts. School administrators need to provide teachers with time and support to attend to all three important phases of the planning process.

Scenario.   A number of school systems have begun peer coaching or mentoring programs. The central purpose of many of these programs is to have teachers help one another improve and strengthen their instructional interactive processes. One of the additional benefits of several of these programs is that teachers have the time and opportunity to engage in the reflective evaluation process. The programs are structured so that teachers observe each other during some phase of instruction. When the observer has developed a comprehensive written description of what takes place during instruction, the teacher and observer are in a position to analyze the interactive process. This cooperative analysis leads to reflective evaluation. Teachers have reported that this is an invaluable experience. Being able to review what happened during instruction is beneficial, but the real payoff has come from reflecting about what took place and using the insights gained to plan future instruction. Teachers say that the time provided to carefully analyze their own instruction is one of the most important aspects of peer coaching and mentoring programs.

Finding 4: The focus for instructional planning depends on the grade or subject taught and the belief system of the teacher.

It has been well documented that teachers in the elementary grades approach planning differently from secondary teachers. Elementary teachers tend to focus heavily on activities, while secondary teachers more often emphasize the content to be covered. Nearly all teachers, however, make planning decisions based on their personal belief systems. For example, expectations about student success may have a heavy influence on the planning process. Teachers who believe that all students can succeed plan differently from those who believe that some students will not be able to accomplish the learning tasks. Another belief that can have a major influence on planning has to do with student motivation. Teachers who believe that extrinsic rewards are more important than intrinsic rewards will plan and organize their instruction differently from teachers who value and believe in the power of intrinsic motivators. The belief about who should control learning is another important factor in the planning process. Those who believe that students can and should be responsible for their own learning will structure the learning tasks differently from teachers who believe that the teacher should direct and control all of the learning tasks.

Scenario.   Several years ago the leaders of a city school system decided to change the system's organizational structure and replace the junior high schools with middle schools. The philosophy of the middle schools was to focus the educational programs first and foremost on student needs. The middle schools were expected to facilitate student learning in positive supportive environments. The administrative team responsible for staffing the middle schools found that teachers who had been prepared to teach in elementary schools had belief systems that were most compatible with the system's middle school philosophy. These teachers planned their instruction based on student needs and communicated their expectations of success. Although the teachers had high expectations, they were more concerned about student success than with the amount of content coverage. The teachers were also willing to structure the learning environment so that students took greater responsibility for their own learning. They expected to use different task structures to accomplish their objectives.

The scenario presented in the previous paragraph supports the research finding that teachers at different grade levels tend to plan instruction differently. It is incumbent on school systems to understand how their teachers plan and their underlying belief systems. This understanding can lead to improved compatibility between teacher and school expectations which should result in improved learning experiences for students.

Finding 5: Planning decisions vary depending on the time of the year, class composition, content to be covered, facilities, and the availability of equipment.

Planning at the beginning of the year tends to focus on how to manage students effectively. This is the time when many teachers attempt to establish routines that they will follow for the balance of the year. Very often students in preservice programs do not have the opportunity to observe teachers planning for the year, and they may not be in schools during the early part of the year when the routines are established. Lacking this experience, first-year teachers find themselves inadequately prepared to plan and establish important management routines.

The composition of a class may change during the year because of a mobile population. Any important changes in class composition will have an influence on the planning process. Teachers are also finding that with the heavy emphasis on testing, content coverage has to be carefully planned and structured.

Teachers who share facilities and equipment with other teachers find it necessary to take into account the availability of these resources when they plan. This is especially important for teachers who share laboratories, special equipment, and physical facilities.

Scenario.   A group of elementary teachers who were working in a state that mandates standardized testing in the early grades found that a number of important concepts in their curriculum were tested before they were scheduled to be taught. The teachers were in the process of reviewing and refining their curriculum, so they mapped out all of the major concepts to be taught in grades K through 6. Then they analyzed the state tests to determine which concepts would be tested at each grade level. As a part of the curriculum review, they adjusted their curriculum so that it would be congruent with the testing program. This caused them to adjust the timing for teaching certain elements of the curriculum.

There are those who question the ethics of making curriculum and instruction adjustments in order for students to perform more successfully on state-mandated tests. In this case the adjustments were made as a part of an overall curriculum review process. The process of developing curriculum and test congruence caused teachers to take a very close look at the concepts they were teaching and the sequence for teaching them. It was their collective judgment that the adjustments did not conflict with appropriate developmental learning activities. The process also caused the teachers to engage in group planning activities that have proven to be beneficial for students at all grade levels in the school.

Finding 6: Although the planning process most frequently taught in preservice programs focuses on goals and objectives, activities and tasks are usually the basis for teacher planning.

Many teachers begin their planning by deciding which activities they want to take place during instruction. The activities are often selected to fit available time frames, to keep students actively involved, or to maintain positive classroom interactions. Novice teachers, as well as their more experienced colleagues, often find it difficult to begin their planning by identifying learning goals and objectives that give direction to instructional strategies and activities. They may have in mind what they want their students to learn, but they do not take the time to explicate goals and objectives during the preactive process.

There are several reasons why teachers take the activities approach to planning. In some cases teachers are not teaching from a well-formulated and articulated curriculum that includes clearly delineated goals and objectives. Even when curriculum guides include helpful information, teachers may not use them. They may not have been involved in the development of the guides and do not feel committed to using them. They may also lack important background information that would encourage them to use the guides. Furthermore, textbooks and materials available to teachers may not be consistent with the curriculum guides. Finally, past practice may have to be changed if teachers decide to use the guides as a basis for instructional planning.

Scenario. We interviewed a number of teachers to determine how they acquired the instructional strategies they use most often in their teaching. As a part of the interview process, we attempted to identify the most commonly used planning processes. A discussion with a novice teacher about her planning was fairly consistent with the information we received from the majority of the teachers. She said that she had learned to plan during her coursework by specifying goals and objectives first and then deciding upon the appropriate activities and materials to be used. She said that when she was student teaching she wrote her plans the way she was taught so that her college supervisor would give her a good rating. These plans, however, were not the plans she actually used. She observed the experienced teacher with whom she worked do her planning by making notations in her textbooks about what activities she would use for each lesson. These notations seemed to be sufficient for her supervising teacher, so the student teacher used the same process for her planning. She was quite satisfied with this approach to planning because it saved her a considerable amount of time.

This teacher, as well as others we have interviewed, agreed that it is probably important to focus on student learning during the planning process, but it is not something they normally do. Consequently, they tend to measure their success in terms of the activities they plan and implement. This situation makes it very difficult to develop assessment measures that determine student readiness for learning and student success in achieving specific learning objectives.

Finding 7: Comprehensive planning that is focused on learning goals and objectives will have a positive effect on student achievement.

The emphasis on incremental plans, usually in the form of daily lesson plans, has contributed to teachers' tendency to develop activity-oriented plans. Many teachers who have been required to turn in their lesson plans regularly for review have done so quickly without investing a significant amount of time and energy in planning. Effective comprehensive planning begins with identifying learning goals and objectives that are consistent with the needs of the students. Teachers make decisions about the amount of time to be spent on each area of study and the most appropriate pacing to ensure that the desired content will be covered. An important requirement for comprehensive planning is to provide teachers the time necessary to do this type of detailed planning. It is especially important to see that teachers have adequate time to plan before the school year begins.

Scenario. A principal in a junior high school was working with a teacher he was going to observe and evaluate. During the first conference with the teacher, the principal asked the teacher what he wanted his students to learn during the current unit of study. The teacher carefully explained what he wanted the students to do and he described the instructional strategies that he would be using. Several times during the conference the principal attempted to get the teacher to state his learning goals and objectives for the unit. The teacher was not able to articulate what he wanted the students to learn.

The principal observed several lessons taught by the teacher. During each observation he carefully recorded what took place during instruction. His written observations were objective descriptions about what took place and did not include any value judgments. The principal shared the observation information with the teacher and asked the teacher to analyze what took place in terms of the teacher's expectations. The teacher began to realize that he did not have a frame of reference for determining the effectiveness of his own instruction. After reflecting on the analysis process, the teacher told the principal that for the first time in his several years of teaching he began to understand the importance of identifying his learning expectations, communicating them to his students, and assessing their performance against the expectations. The teacher began to consider these elements during planning. Both he and his students reported that his instruction was more clearly organized and structured and that his lessons were much more coherent and meaningful to the students. As a result, student performance improved considerably.

Finding 8: Daily, weekly, and unit plans should be carefully integrated with year-long plans.

This finding is based on the assumption that most teachers develop year-long plans. Long-term planning is more likely to take place when time has been provided before the school year begins. Short-term planning cannot take into account important variables that can have a significant impact on student achievement. It is virtually impossible to make the best possible use of time and other key resources when planning is a day-to-day process that does not take into account what should be learned over the course of a semester or school year.

Scenario. Teachers in an elementary school were told that, instead of attending the traditional back-to-school orientation sessions and meetings conducted by the administrators, they could use the time to do their year-long planning. They were expected, at a minimum, to identify when they would be teaching each of the major goals in their curriculum and how much instructional time they would allocate to achieving these goals. The planning went so well that the teachers were able to establish the framework for their unit plans as well as complete their year-long plans. They reported that their weekly and daily plans were much easier to formulate as a result of the comprehensive planning. Even more important, they felt much more secure about their ability to meet the needs of their students as they proceeded through the year. They had a plan that would give them direction and at the same time provide the flexibility for them to make adjustments in their weekly and daily plans. As a result of their planning efforts, they felt they would be able to concentrate on seeing that their students were fully engaged in the appropriate learning tasks.

At the end of the year the teachers were so pleased with the results achieved by the comprehensive planning that they met with the principal and reached agreement about expanding the amount of time that would be set aside for long-range instructional planning. When other schools in the system heard about what was happening in this school, many of them began to allocate time for long-range planning.

Finding 9: Knowledge from prior teaching experience is an important determinant in how teachers plan for instruction.

It is not uncommon to find experienced teachers spending a considerable amount of time doing comprehensive planning and less time doing incremental planning. Because beginning teachers do not have an extensive teaching background, it is important for them to develop detailed lesson plans that will help them effectively manage the varied and complex transactions that occur during daily instruction. Novice teachers should not be expected to develop their instructional plans in isolation and without the guidance of their more experienced colleagues. These teachers have much to gain from the insights their peers have acquired from their years of experience. Conversely, experienced teachers are likely to develop a better understanding of the planning process if they are expected to provide guidance to their less experienced coworkers. Teachers at different stages in their careers often find that reviewing and analyzing their instructional approaches can lead to improved practice.

Scenario.   After being involved in a teaching research workshop, a high school mathematics teacher and department chair analyzed the teacher's approach to instructional planning. He had been a classroom teacher for 13 years and was considered one of the better teachers in his school. He reported that during the first few years of his teaching career he developed detailed lesson plans to guide his daily instruction. He said that he needed to concentrate on his daily planning in order to do more than just survive. He aspired to be a successful teacher and was willing to work extra hard to do a good job in the classroom. During this period of time he did not spend any time developing long-range comprehensive plans.

After this teacher was appointed to head the mathematics department, he worked with his faculty to develop semester-long instructional plans. The long-range planning process had become institutionalized and was considered to be a major factor in improved student performance throughout the department. The department had not hired any new teachers for several years so less attention was being given to developing daily lesson plans. The department head told us that several members of his department would be retiring and he would need to employ new teachers for the first time during his tenure as department head. He was already making plans with members of the department to orient new teachers to the long-range planning process. He was also instituting a program to provide support and assistance to new faculty that would help them develop high-quality daily instructional plans. The department head was convinced from his practical knowledge and from the research on teaching that attention to all phases of instructional planning would bring positive results in his department.

GUIDE TO OBSERVATION, ANALYSIS, AND REFLECTION

The focus of these activities is on how teachers conceptualize instruction within the total planning process. The observation and analysis components can be accomplished by interviewing teachers rather than through actual observations. Insights into teachers' thinking can be gained by talking with teachers about how they think students learn and how teachers' personal and instructional needs influence their planning decisions. Reflecting on the information gained from the teachers will help you become aware of different approaches to conceptualizing instructional planning.

1. Planning influences: Beliefs about learning

Observation: What beliefs about students and the way they learn influence your planning? It is important to understand the teacher's perspective on the conditions that promote learning for a particular group of students. Ask about the teacher's expectations concerning students' ability to learn, the degree of freedom and choice students should have, and the degree of responsibility students should take for their own learning.

Analysis: How do teachers' beliefs about students and how they learn influence planning? Try to determine whether teachers' plans are consistent with teacher beliefs. For example, if teachers believe that students learn well from each other, the plans should include opportunities for small-group work, cooperative learning, or peer tutoring. Teachers may also share the ways they adapt the curriculum to be more consistent with their beliefs.

Reflection: What assumptions do I hold and how will those beliefs guide my planning? Examine your educational beliefs about the conditions that promote learning in your students. Reflect on the congruence between your beliefs and the instruction you plan. If you are an inexperienced teacher, your belief system may be in a formative stage. If you are an experienced teacher, periodic examination is a helpful practice.

2. Planning influences: Personal and instructional needs

Observation: What personal and instructional needs influence your planning? Ask the teacher what the personal benefits of planning are. Since personal areas of competence or expertise influence planning, have the teacher assess his or her knowledge of the content, level of experience, and ability to organize and manage instructional activities and student behavior.

Analysis: *How effective is planning in helping meet personal and instructional needs?*   Ask teachers how planning helps them capitalize on their strengths or learning opportunities and how it enables them to adjust to external constraints or areas of personal insecurity. Teachers may share ways that their ability to plan has changed with experience or in response to changing conditions.

Reflection: *How will my personal and instructional strengths impact my plans?* Reflect on your skills and competencies as a teacher. Think of ways you can use planning to capitalize on your strengths and minimize weaknesses. Determine how planning can help you take advantage of instructional opportunities and overcome constraints.

3. Planning format

Observation: *What planning format(s) is used?*   Ask the teacher about his or her approach to daily, weekly, unit, and yearly planning. If written plans are available, notice the level of detail and the areas addressed in the plans. Discuss with the teacher curriculum considerations and administrative requirements for written plans.

Analysis: *What are the advantages and disadvantages of the different planning formats?*   As teachers share their plans, ask them why they use particular formats and choose not to use others. Administrative requirements may be one area for discussion. Try to determine if specific formats tend to be used in certain subject areas or grade levels or if formats vary with the teacher's experience in teaching the subject or topic.

Reflection: *What planning format(s) will I use?*   Consider whether the different formats you have observed or used could be incorporated in your planning process. Think about administrative requirements and the need for accountability. In many situations, certain types of plans are required (by the administration or by supervisors) and must be turned in on a designated day. Some type of standardized planning may also be required to help substitute teachers. Written plans are a means of documenting learning objectives covered and the instructional materials incorporated.

 ## DEVELOPMENT AND RENEWAL ACTIVITIES

1. Talk with teachers or college instructors about how they find time to plan. Experienced colleagues have developed some time-saving approaches to cope with the ever-present demands of planning. Encourage teachers to share information about how they organize and file plans, how they note adjustments or special reminders, how they plan with other teachers, how far ahead they plan, and how they plan for alternatives and supplementary activities.

2. Arrange to observe a teacher or college instructor. Talk briefly with the teacher prior to the observation session to gain an understanding of what the teacher has planned and what is anticipated. Be sure to ask about the sequence of events, estimated times, methods, and materials. While observing the lesson, make notes on the events and on any deviations from what was planned.

Following the lesson, discuss with the teacher any adjustments that were made and the reasoning behind them. For example, were the adjustments made because of time, level of student understanding, or unexpected responses or events? As part of postinstruction reflection, find out if the teacher was satisfied with student progress. If not, inquire about changes the teacher would make if the lesson were taught again. Think about what you have learned from the teacher that could enhance your planning if you were to teach a similar lesson.

3. If you are currently involved in teaching, visit with several colleagues in your same grade level or content area and in different levels and areas to talk about how the images they have of their students and classes influence their planning. You might want to visit with both experienced and inexperienced teachers and to compare the differences and similarities in the images they describe.

4. At the beginning of a year, term, or unit, develop a comprehensive plan, by yourself or with colleagues. Use the following strategies in your planning process. Obtain a calendar, mark out holidays, test days, special days, and any other days where instructional time will be limited. Using available curriculum guides, identify the major goals that need to be addressed during this time period. Establish a time line and a schedule for each goal and related learning objectives. Review your plan to see if it is feasible and consistent with the needs and characteristics of your students. As a result of the review, make any adjustments in the plan that seem to be appropriate.

5. What are the characteristics of a successful lesson? After you have planned a lesson or series of lessons, identify the characteristics that would indicate that the lesson(s) was successful. Think about the patterns of student or teacher behavior that would suggest that students had made progress and that the teacher had achieved the desired objectives.

3.
Planning Instruction

COMMENTARY

There are several elements that ought to be common to unit, weekly, and daily instructional plans. While the format may vary, the content of the plans should systematically address student learning needs. Many of the instructional plans that we have reviewed include some but not all of the elements needed for effective planning.

Many educators, both practitioners and theorists, agree that the formal (explicit) curriculum should be the basis for individual instructional plans. We often ask teachers during preinstructional conferences how the lessons we will be observing relate to the curriculum. In some cases, especially when we are working with primary and elementary teachers, the relationship is clear. In other cases, teachers will tell us the curriculum is out of date or not relevant to what they are doing. Secondary teachers usually tell us that the textbook is really the curriculum, so their plans are based on getting through the material in the book. Many teachers for a variety of reasons do not develop instructional plans based on formal curricula.

Instructional plans should include specific learning objectives or expectations. Ideally, learning objectives should be derived from, or at least be consistent with, the curriculum goals. We have found, however, some confusion about the difference between goals, objectives, and activities. For example, a number of teachers have told us that their objective for the day was to get through a certain amount of material.

When we ask them what the students will learn as a result of getting through the material, the responses have often been ambiguous. It is difficult for some teachers to delineate clearly between the means (activities) and the ends (objectives) of their instructional plans.

Teachers and researchers have known for years that assessing student readiness for learning is a prerequisite for effective instruction. Yet we have found this to be one of the weakest elements in instructional planning. Prior to observing teachers' classes we asked how they have determined that their students have the prerequisite skills and knowledge necessary to achieve the learning objectives. We have received some interesting responses. Sometimes the level of student readiness is clearly described. When this happens, we usually find that teachers have carefully preassessed their students. It is not uncommon, however, for teachers to tell us that they are not really sure which students will be successful and which students will have problems with the lesson. In most cases, this uncertainty occurs because of inadequate assessment of previous learning.

A variety of classroom and task structures can be used to address learning goals and objectives. We hope that decisions about how to structure and organize the classroom are made *after* the learning objectives have been determined. When the objectives are not clear or have not been made explicit, it is very difficult for teachers to make decisions about the most appropriate classroom or task structure.

Beginning and experienced teachers should be knowledgeable about the essential elements of an instructional plan. Even more important, they should be able to see how the elements interrelate so that the plan will have the greatest impact on teaching and learning.

RATIONALE

A well-organized and integrated instructional plan can be the most important component of an educational delivery system. When the curriculum serves as the frame of reference for unit, weekly, or daily plans, teachers and others have regular opportunities to evaluate how well the curriculum meets the needs of all of the students. They can analyze curriculum content for adequacy, accuracy, utility, and relevance. They can also evaluate how well the curriculum is articulated from grade to grade or throughout a sequence of subjects and courses.

Sound instructional plans focus on clear learning objectives that have been derived from the curriculum and written to address the needs of a specific group of students. Teachers with well-developed plans are in a position to clearly communicate learning objectives to their students. It is helpful to both teachers and students to differentiate between what students are supposed to do during class and what they are supposed to learn. When students understand what they are expected to learn, they are much more likely to have successful learning experiences.

Both preassessment and postassessment procedures are important elements of the instructional plan. Assessment activities can be used to ascertain students' knowledge and skill levels at the beginning of instruction. Effective teachers carefully monitor student learning throughout the school year. They are, in effect, regularly assessing student learning so that they can make appropriate instructional decisions. They use postassessment measures to determine how well students have achieved learning objectives.

All teachers, from those in preservice programs to those who have a wealth of experience, should have the necessary skills and knowledge to develop thorough instructional plans. They should understand how each of the elements of a plan plays an important role in effective instruction. They should also appreciate the positive impact instructional plans can have on the learning of all students. Experienced teachers should make every effort to develop and communicate positive attitudes about instructional plans so that beginning teachers understand their value.

RESEARCH SYNTHESIS

The Concept of Instructional Plans

An instructional plan is usually based on the content or knowledge to be transmitted. The knowledge may be in the form of textbooks and other educational materials or from other sources of information available to teachers. When knowledge is organized to provide a framework for teaching and learning, it is usually referred to as a curriculum.

The characteristics and needs of the learners must be taken into consideration if the instructional plan is to be effective. Assessment practices used by teachers help to determine the knowledge, skills, and attitudes that their students have acquired prior to instruction. Assessment after instruction provides important information about the effectiveness of the instruction and gives direction to future planning.

The structure or organization of the classroom is another important planning consideration. At some point in the planning process, teachers make decisions about how they will organize instructional tasks and activities, including the amount of time to be spent in various task structures and the role of the teacher and students for each structure.

An instructional plan will, at a minimum, address curriculum expectations, needs and characteristics of the learners, assessment procedures, structure and organization of the classroom, learning activities, and instructional materials to support the learning process. The essential elements of an instructional plan are presented in Figure 3–1.

Curriculum

Teacher planning is the process that links the curriculum and instruction (Clark, 1988). Teachers' personal preferences and differences in their conceptions about curriculum are important planning influences (Brandt, 1988). Planning for

---

Curriculum goals (desired curriculum outcomes)

Learning objectives (specific learning expectations)

Learner needs and characteristics (knowledge, skills, competencies, and attitudes of learners)

Assessment procedures (determining level of readiness and evaluating progress)

Classroom structure (organization or framework for student learning)

Learning activities (processes used to direct learning behavior)

Instructional materials (textbooks, resources, and materials used to support learning activities)

FIGURE 3–1. Essential elements of an instructional plan

instruction, however, is a process that should go well beyond individual classroom teachers. Effective schools have a curriculum planning process that is consistent at the district, school, and classroom levels (Northwest Regional Education Laboratory, 1984). Curriculum planning should be the basis for effective instructional planning.

Curriculum content decisions should be based on several considerations. An important factor in the selection of content should be the nature of society and current social priorities. The nature of the learners and the relevance of the content to meet their needs is a critical curriculum consideration. The nature of the knowledge to be transmitted and the instructional processes to be used must also be considered (Brandt, 1988). When the curriculum is carefully formulated, properly articulated, and appropriate for learners, those engaged in instructional planning have a clear frame of reference. It is impossible to separate curriculum content from the delivery system. Processes must be employed that will ensure meaningful acquisition of the content (Brandt, 1988). Teachers' beliefs and expectations about how students learn and what they ought to learn appear to have the greatest impact on curriculum implementation (Tobin, 1987a).

Shulman (1987) pointed out that we engage in teaching to achieve educational purposes, to accomplish ends having to do with student literacy. These ends or outcomes are often stated as the educational goals that give direction to curriculum development activities. They have been defined as timeless and nonmeasurable statements of desired outcomes that give direction to program planning (Bellon & Handler, 1982). The scope of the educational program, the broad design of the curriculum, and the nature of the learning opportunities are embodied in the curriculum goals (Saylor, Alexander, & Lewis, 1981).

Learning goals and objectives, properly developed and sequenced, provide the basis for courses and units of study. They are the ingredients needed for sequential, articulated learning experiences. When instruction is planned from a well structured and articulated curriculum, student achievement improves (Rosenshine, 1983).

Poorly structured curricula may result in fragmented learning experiences. Pacing and content coverage problems are more likely to occur when there is a lack of understanding about what is to be taught within and across subject areas and grade levels. Tobin (1987a) pointed out that one of the major impediments to achieving curriculum goals and objectives is the relatively large amount of content teachers feel they must cover. However, teachers, he maintained, would find it difficult to change even if there were less content and more time because they feel they are doing what is right for the learner.

Each learning goal is the basis for several specific learning outcomes that can be assessed during a predetermined time frame. These specific learning outcomes are usually referred to as objectives. Effective schools identify a limited number of important objectives and use them to clarify what students are expected to learn (NREL, 1984). The objectives are sequenced by grade or learning level, reviewed for specificity and clarity, and targeted for students according to their developmental level. Gronlund (1985) developed guidelines that are useful to those engaged in instructional planning. He pointed out that instructional objectives should direct attention to the students and to the types of behaviors they are expected to exhibit as a result of their learning experiences. A common mistake is writing objectives that focus on teaching activities rather than on student learning outcomes.

Instructional planning that includes a balance of cognitive and affective objectives will promote optimal student learning. When the emphasis on affective objectives is at the expense of cognitive expectations, student learning will suffer (Rosenshine, 1983–84). When cognitive objectives are overemphasized, learning gains may be made but student attitudes toward learning may be adversely affected. Instructional planning should aim for an appropriate balance of learning objectives.

Teachers base their instructional planning decisions on several important factors. They decide what to teach based on what will be tested, the difficulty of the content, and their personal attitude toward the content (Squires, Huitt, & Segars, 1983). Standardized tests are having more and more influence on what will be taught. Aligning the curriculum with the test has become commonplace, especially in those school systems and states that place a high priority on test scores. Teachers also make planning decisions based on their values and capabilities. However, when instructional planning is heavily influenced by the needs of teachers, student learning may suffer (Berliner, 1984).

Comprehensive instructional planning is most effective when the curriculum framework includes appropriate content that has been carefully structured and clearly articulated. Teachers' instructional planning decisions will more likely focus on learner needs when the total learning context has been clearly described by the curriculum goals and objectives. For some years a number of teachers have engaged in comprehensive planning by "postholing" the curriculum. The major curriculum goals become the posts or foundations for the comprehensive plan, and specific learning objectives are the strands that connect the posts. The posts help to establish curriculum sequence, while the objectives provide depth and scope. Using this approach, teachers can establish target dates for achieving curriculum goals. Figure 3–2 represents comprehensive planning using the postholing process.

FIGURE 3–2.
Comprehensive planning

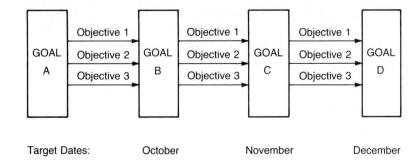

Assessment of Student Progress

Assessment of student knowledge, skills, and understanding is a basic component of instructional planning. Across the country there is a preoccupation with standardized test scores and accountability. The heavy dependence on standardized testing communicates the lack of confidence in teacher assessment practices and judgments (Stiggins, 1985). Assessment, however, is a much broader concept than testing. All of the actions that teachers undertake to collect, record, and interpret information about students before, during, and after instruction are a part of assessment. Assessment is the process of finding out what students know before instruction, how well they do during instruction, and what they have learned from instruction (North Carolina State Department of Public Instruction, 1985). Assessment data provide teachers with information for instructional decision making. Assessment activities may consume as much as 20 to 30% of a teacher's time (Stiggins, 1988b). Clearly, time is needed to design, develop, and administer useful assessment processes. The information generated can then be used to adjust and revise teaching and learning activities. Components of the assessment process are depicted in Figure 3–3.

Hawley and Rosenholtz (1984) identified assessment as one of the practices that has a sizable impact on achievement. Providing information on student performance and using that information to improve teaching has a powerful effect on learning. Properly designed and administered procedures affect self-concept and motivation as well as achievement (Stiggins, 1985). Assessment data also give teachers a means for considering instructional alternatives and their potential effectiveness. Teachers need to make assessment of student learning a major component of instruction. It should be an ongoing process as students proceed through the curriculum.

There are several prerequisites for an effective assessment program. Teachers must have some expertise in the field of evaluation, experience with the subject they are teaching, and an understanding of student and school characteristics. For assessment to be most effective, teachers must have the ability and willingness to adapt instruction to meet student needs (Janssens, 1986).

Assessment is a complex activity that places heavy demands on teachers, and assessment programs vary depending on grade level and the subject matter. Teachers are expected to measure affective behaviors in addition to knowledge and skill acqui-

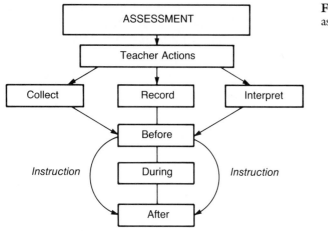

FIGURE 3–3. The assessment process

sition. They need to have assessment information readily available so that they can make instructional adjustments as they move through the curriculum.

Assessment Purposes.   In order to make the assessment process an integral part of instruction, teachers must plan their data gathering so that they obtain information about the important knowledge and skills that students should acquire. Brophy and Evertson (1976) found that many elementary teachers do little formal testing. They know what students should learn and they watch for evidence of those skills and understandings. When skills have not been acquired, these teachers use remedial exercises and corrective procedures. High school teachers in Haertel's (1986) study used three kinds of assessment for each unit of instruction. Quizzes were used to make sure students did the assignments, written work was evaluated to check for successful practice or application, and unit examinations served as summative measures. If teachers are really to determine what students have learned, they will have to use assessment modes that help them probe for understanding (Rogers & Stevenson, 1988). Tests alone will not provide this information.

Rudman (1980) found that teachers need four kinds of assessment information: (1) data that relate directly to the appropriate instructional treatment, (2) data that highlight relative strengths and weaknesses, (3) information about conditions that enhance or inhibit performance on specific tasks, and (4) data that are cheap and efficient. The beginning of the year is a crucial time for gathering and using student information. Many important decisions about students' instructional levels are made at this time as teachers identify specific student strengths and weaknesses.

During the first few weeks of school, elementary teachers often check for retention of information and skills in basic subjects. Bloom (1984) found that first-of-the-year assessment was most helpful in high school subjects that are sequential and require mastery of prior skills and knowledge. Teachers also gather data about each student's personality, perseverance, motivation, and physical and mental health (Rudman, 1980; Tursman, 1981). This analysis leads to the identification of students who have exceptional needs. Most teachers do not have the training or time to do a detailed diagnosis of learning problems. Stallings (1982) pointed out the disadvantages of waiting until the school year starts to identify students for further diagnosis. By the time the diagnosis is completed and the students have been appropriately placed, the classes or instructional groups are already in full swing. In order to avoid losing this important instructional time, diagnostic activities should be completed before the school year begins.

Decisions about instructional grouping are also usually made during the first weeks of school. Student assignment to groups affects the pacing of instruction and therefore students' opportunity to learn. Teachers should have adequate student assessment data when they organize their groups. Students placed in the wrong groups may have little opportunity to move to groups that would be more consistent with their ability.

During the school year effective teachers use ongoing assessment activities as a basis for their planning. They identify prerequisite skills at each new step in instruction and evaluate student readiness with respect to each skill. This information is used to refine instruction. It helps teachers make decisions about the difficulty of assignments and when to go on to the next step.

Determining the pace of instruction is one of the most important reasons for assessing student learning. Effective teachers plan to teach differently, depending on the skill levels of their students. They repeat, review, reteach, or adjust the pace of instruction based on their assessment activities (Gagne, 1985; Bloom, 1984; Squires et al., 1983).

Teachers often use assessment activities to motivate students. They see this as one of the major purposes of the assessment program. They refer to grades on homework, tests, and examinations in order to keep student attention focused on the content to be learned. This kind of assessment is the most common form of extrinsic motivator in classrooms (Tobin, 1987a).

Marking or grading is the most frequent purpose for assessment. And yet assigning grades does not tell students what they have learned or still need to learn. For low-ability students, or those in remedial classes, grading can result in lower motivation. Regular negative feedback creates a negative attitude toward learning. Teachers need to understand the complex relationship that exists between grades, motivation, and achievement.

Assessment Strategies.   Effective teachers know how to develop and use assessment instruments. Their tests and other data-gathering devices demonstrate a high degree of overlap with instruction (Rudman, 1980; Squires et al., 1983). They identify key concepts and skills and devise methods to measure student progress on each item. They avoid the practice of teaching one skill and evaluating another (Haertel, 1986). They are careful not to limit their data gathering to a few, easily measured skills. Once they acquire information about student learning, they analyze it to see which concepts or skills have been mastered and which need to be reviewed or retaught. The best assessment devices are often the most effective teaching devices (Rogers & Stevenson, 1988). Both formal and informal assessment measures generate important student data. Formal assessment includes a variety of tests. Standardized tests usually produce information that can be used to determine how local students compare to those in other school systems. Standardized tests in specific content areas generate more precise information, but they do not necessarily test what has been taught at the local level. Teachers in schools with students of low socioeconomic status must monitor the use of standardized achievement test data carefully so that the information is not misused in making comparisons with other groups (Popham, 1982; Brophy & Evertson, 1976).

Criterion-referenced instruments, designed to measure student achievement of specific skills, are useful for day-to-day instructional planning. Teachers can use criterion measures to identify specific instructional strengths and weaknesses. Good criterion-referenced tests assess a manageable number of skills that subsume lesser skills (Popham, 1982). Criterion-referenced tests provide teachers information they need without sacrificing instructional and planning time. Effective teachers adjust criterion tests that accompany their textbooks to be sure that the tests measure what is being taught. However, many schools depend too much on objective tests as indicators of student learning. There are problems associated with using objective tests, especially those not developed by teachers. In some cases knowledge is trivialized and important concepts are not tested. When the tests used have been developed by professional test makers, local information may be missing and, in effect, curriculum decisions are made by people far removed from the actual instruction (Berlak, 1985).

Although teachers use commercially prepared tests, the majority prefer to use their own tests and rely heavily on their own judgments (Stiggins, 1988b). Haertel (1986) found that teachers at the high school level use 10 to 15% of their class time on paper-and-pencil tests. When the time spent returning and discussing the tests was included, it rose to about 20%. Tests are an important part of classroom life because they punctuate the flow of instruction. They are used to signal transitions from one unit to another and to bring closure to a concept or topic. Effective tests mirror each segment of the curriculum and give students an opportunity to demonstrate what they have learned. Test items that measure recall should be included so that all students can demonstrate a degree of content mastery. Tests should also include items that require problem solving, application of skills, and higher level thinking. Unfortunately, many standardized and teacher-made tests do not assess higher level thinking. As Nickerson (1989) pointed out:

> A major criticism of both standardized tests and tests constructed by teachers for purposes of determining students' grades is that they tend to emphasize recall of declarative or procedural knowledge and provide little indication either of the level at which students understand subject matter or of the quality of their thinking. (p. 3)

When higher level thinking skills are not tested, less instructional time and effort is allocated to engaging students in complex cognitive operations. Testing higher level thinking may cause instruction to emphasize higher cognitive learning (Tobin, 1987a). In such cases the influence of tests on teaching and learning could have positive effects.

FIGURE 3–4.
Assessment strategies

Informal	Formal
Teacher questions	Diagnostic pretests
Teacher observations of student performance	Teacher-made tests
Student comments	Standardized tests
Student questions	Quizzes
Skill inventories	Homework assignments
Checklists	Seatwork assignments
Interviews	Portfolios of student work

Many teachers do not have the training or background to develop high-quality assessment instruments. Teachers often report that they learned their assessment strategies from colleagues or from their experiences as students. Very few perceived the training they received as helpful (Stiggins, 1988b). Teachers do seem to be concerned about the quality of their assessment practices and their lack of training in this important area of instruction.

When formal test information is overused, it has an exaggerated influence on instruction. Informal measures often yield more helpful information. Teachers should make systematic use of informal sources of information on student progress such as writing assignments, lab reports, and homework. Other informal measures include class participation and responses to questions during teacher-led discussions (Haertel, 1986; North Carolina State Department of Public Instruction, 1985). Additional informal assessment devices may include small-group interviews, discussions related to concepts being studied, and learning logs in which students write about what they have learned and points that are still confusing to them (Rogers & Stevenson, 1988).

Student feedback is an important source of information for teachers. When teachers solicit and use student feedback, they can alter and improve their teaching. Individual discussions with students who are having trouble can help teachers adapt instruction to meet student needs. Adjustments may be made by adapting materials, varying cues, changing the sequence of instruction, adjusting timing and transitions from one activity to another, or developing more appropriate expectations (Weinstein, 1983).

Several problems are associated with the use of assessment data. In some schools, teachers get so much information about their students that they are in a state of information overload. Many of them do not have a full understanding of the value and use of the data. Rudman (1980) found that teachers integrate assessment data into a few best guesses about students' cognitive, affective, and behavioral states. Effective teachers are more analytical because they know that it is possible to focus on the wrong information or to ignore important influences on instruction. Formal and informal assessment strategies are summarized in Figure 3–4.

Structure

Structure is the organization or framework for student interactions (Levin & Long, 1981). Effectively structured classrooms put students in contact with the curriculum, maintain the contact, and keep the students engaged in appropriate academic activities (Rosenshine, 1983–84).

When teachers plan instruction, they organize a mix of activities that make up the school day or class period. This is referred to as task structure (Slavin, 1980). Task structure influences the nature of the teaching task and also shapes the behaviors of teachers and students (Doyle, 1986b). Instructional expectations for both teachers and students will vary with the task structure.

When teachers are engaged in the preactive process, they structure tasks by determining the goals or end results and by attending to the problem of space or behavioral setting. Teachers' preactive actions should address both components. Activities, conditions, and resources should be carefully planned and organized to work within the behavioral setting to accomplish instructional goals.

According to Doyle (1986b), teaching requires that task structures address the goals of learning as well as order. Learning is the instructional function of content coverage, mastery, and motivation to learn. Order is the managerial function of organizing, establishing limits, reacting to misbehavior, monitoring, and pacing. These two goals are intertwined.

When classrooms are properly structured, students understand the content expectations as well as the rules and routines necessary for optimal learning. In examining learning task structures, teachers focus on the group or the social system. Effective teachers plan these structures based on information about students' abilities, needs, and interests.

In general there are two types of task structures: single-task and multitask. Lectures or recitations are examples of a single-task structure. All students are expected to participate in teacher-directed instruction. This requires a greater degree of teacher control and rewards that are usually based on individual performance in the group. When students make mistakes or fail to conform to behavior expectations, sanctions are given publicly. When teachers use a single-task structure, they attend to individual differences within the total group (Slavin, 1986b; Bossert, 1977).

Other single-task structures include reading an assignment, completing a written paper, and teacher-assisted practice. The distinguishing characteristic is the requirement that all students work on the same task. Teacher control in this format can be somewhat relaxed. Students can be given some choice of pace or sequence as long as the task is completed. The reward structure is still based on individual effort, but sanctions for lack of effort and misbehavior can be less public. Teachers can plan to address individual needs through one-on-one interaction.

Multitask classrooms include a mix of group and independent work, use of learning stations, small-group work, and many forms of experiential or individualized instruction. Cooperative learning strategies fit this category. Multitask structures must be carefully planned to accommodate the changing roles and responsibilities of teachers and students.

Task structure is important because it greatly influences how teachers control and reward students. In addition, task structure influences not only the social relationships in the classroom but also the kind of learning that can take place. Cooperation, responsibility, and many higher-order thinking skills are not easily learned with a lecture or recitation format. Therefore, teachers must plan to use task structures that foster interaction and thinking. Although recitations foster acquisition and recall of information, critical thinking may require some form of large- or small-group discussion (Brophy & Good, 1986).

Teachers who structure their classrooms based on learning goals, organize to maintain order, and select appropriate methods and materials reap great benefits. Students are more apt to pay attention when they understand the goals of the lesson. Clear, well-communicated goals and objectives have a positive influence on student learning in both the short term and the long term.

Teacher expectations influence the structure of their classrooms and, most important, the level of student learning. Successful classrooms reflect high expectations that are challenging and attainable. Students are expected to succeed, not fail. When the success rate increases, students tend to be more motivated to achieve (Berliner, 1984). On the other hand, inappropriate expectations are detrimental to teachers as well as students. When teacher planning reflects low expectations, the major influence on learning may be student conduct rather than ability. Teacher expectations need to be both accurate and flexible (NREL, 1984).

Communicating expectations is often indirect and subtle. Teachers need to be aware of their expectations, how they were developed, and the effect they have on all students. They need to monitor their expectations to assure that they are accurate and promote success rather than failure (Rohrkemper, 1982). The monitoring process is greatly facilitated by careful instructional planning.

The characteristics of students should be the basis for setting expectations and planning classroom structures. Younger, less-skilled students need more structure, while more-skilled students can assume increased responsibility for their learning (Tursman, 1981). The socioeconomic status (SES) of the students should also be considered. Students in lower SES groups benefit from more control while higher SES students seem to function effectively with less control and structure (Borich, 1979).

It is possible to overstructure a classroom. For example, overstructuring occurs when teachers perform tasks that students can perform for themselves (Tursman, 1981). Teachers should also recognize that lower cognitive objectives are achieved best in highly structured classrooms, while higher cognitive objectives are more likely to be achieved in flexible environments.

Activities

In planning task structures, teachers also make decisions about the activities that will facilitate instruction. An activity is a distinctive pattern of behavior of students and teachers in the classroom. Activities involve several components including the way the participants are arranged, information sources, the way students are involved, how the action is controlled, and the amount of time allocated. When teachers plan activities, they integrate the behavioral setting, the curriculum or content, and teacher actions that are both managerial and instructional (Gump, 1987).

Activities occur in some planned sequence throughout the school day. Yinger (1986) noted that nearly all classroom action occurs during activities. Activities usually last between 10 and 12 minutes. Berliner (in Doyle, 1986b) has identified common types of elementary classroom activities: reading circles, seatwork, one-way presentations, two-way presentations, mediated presentations, silent reading, construction, games, play, and housekeeping. Transitions connect the activities (Gump, 1987). Other researchers have identified similar activities with some lists being more extensive. In secondary schools, activities show less variety in format. Although time spent in particular activities varies by content area and student characteristics, researchers estimate that 65% of class time is spent in seatwork, 35% in recitation or whole-group presentations, and 15% in transitions or housekeeping (Doyle, 1986b).

All activity formats require teacher actions. Gump found that, overall, about 50% of teacher actions involved instruction, 23% involved arranging, organizing, and orienting students to instruction, 14% involved handling misbehavior, and 12% involved dealing with individual problems and social amenities (Doyle, 1986).

As previously noted, studies have shown that teachers focus on activities as they plan. Researchers have discovered several reasons for this tendency. Teachers often feel that they must focus on student cooperation and involvement instead of learning. Doyle (1986b) emphasized that the level of complexity of the task has an influence on the degree of student cooperation and participation. Teachers know that the best plans are useless if students do not cooperate. Therefore, teachers base their choice of activities and objectives on what they know about student behavior. They know that activities organize and direct the behavior of students. Experienced teachers seem to have an intuitive sense about how well students will cooperate in different activities and task structures. Being able to predict student behavior reduces the complexity and difficulty of the activity and the amount of time it takes to get students settled down to work. Easy, familiar tasks run smoothly. With this in mind, teachers select activities they know they can implement successfully, which helps them maintain a smooth flow of instruction with few interruptions and a minimum of frustration (Doyle, 1979).

Effective teachers structure activities so that students can work without difficulty. Timing and organization are important. Time constraints require activities to match the length of the class session (Doyle, 1985). The necessary materials are available, and the classroom is arranged so that the teacher has a clear view of students. Seating is arranged to foster the desired interaction. Activities are planned to give students adequate time to learn without too much time left over; alternate activities are available for early finishers (Doyle, 1979; Gage & Berliner, 1984).

If activities are to promote student achievement, there must be a direct relationship between learning objectives and activities. The most successful activities are neither too hard nor too easy. The teacher knows the prerequisite skills and knowledge required to accomplish each activity and plans so that there is enough challenge to maintain student interest. Successful teachers also increase student motivation by varying the kinds of activities (North Carolina State Department of Public Instruction, 1985; Doyle, 1985; Tursman, 1981). Planning for activities requires decisions about student engagement, grouping, seating arrangements, variety of activities, materials, reward structure, and type of independent practice.

Instructional Materials

Teachers plan to use printed instructional materials during 90 to 95% of class time and use textbooks 70% of the time (Komoski, 1985). In secondary classrooms, teacher presentations incorporate textbook information, while in elementary classrooms teachers primarily use seatwork activities provided by publishers. Instructional time is spent on topics provided by those materials (Lindheim, 1982). The ways students interact with the materials also influences their willingness to learn. Recent research provides important information that helps teachers integrate materials with instruction, analyze materials for appropriateness, and align materials with tests.

Teachers often use materials they believe to be appropriate without carefully checking them to see if they align with learning expectations and student ability. Doyle (1983) reported 61% of one group of students were assigned materials easier than their ability level and 85% of another group of students were required to use materials that made inappropriately high cognitive demands. Recent studies have demonstrated a lack of congruence between local curriculum and instructional materials. A study of high-SES districts revealed that 60% of the students had already mastered 80% of the objectives addressed by the instructional materials when they were tested in September. It is interesting to note that their scores had regressed by June. Teachers need to examine materials and make careful adaptations to address the learning expectations for their particular classes (Komoski, 1985).

Teachers should be aware of the wide variations in content covered in textbooks published by different companies (Institute for Research on Teaching, 1982). The textbooks may vary in the topics or skills introduced, the sequence of skills, and the depth of coverage. Perceptive teachers know that different companies may give the same label to two quite different skills. They examine the materials carefully to see how the authors conceptualize skills and how difficult the content is (Lindheim, 1982; Farr & Tulley, 1985). The choice of textbooks greatly affects what is learned by students.

Teachers also need to give attention to the congruence between textbooks and the accompanying tests. In some cases authors have not worked closely with those responsible for developing the tests. This results in discrepancies between what is taught and the information tested. One study found the best match to be only 50% agreement, and the worst was 21% (IRT, 1985a). Instructional plans should include assessment activities that are congruent with skills and content that have been taught. Performance modes required by tests should be consistent with modes used in the learning process (Lindheim, 1982).

Appropriate textbooks and materials should meet several additional criteria. They should be accurate and clear. Directions should be easy to understand and the language should be appropriate for the grade level. The materials should be well organized and focus on clear instructional objectives. Text divisions, headings, and subheadings should be appropriate, and charts, pictures, and visual aids should be well placed (Farr & Tulley, 1985; Hawley & Rosenholtz, 1984).

While problems exist, in general, high-quality published instructional materials promote high-quality instruction (IRT, 1987b). Teachers feel comfortable using carefully selected materials to serve as a reference for their teaching. Most teachers do not have the time, money, or training to develop good materials. The effort may be better spent using published materials and enriching instruction in other ways.

Many teachers have access to computers as instructional aids. Computer-assisted instruction (CAI) is used for repeated drill and practice with immediate feedback, for tutorials that develop according to student responses, and for simulations that usually involve discovery and higher level learning. Computers can be used for educational purposes other than CAI such as word processing, analyzing data, programming, studying technology, and managing classroom information.

Roblyer (1985) reported the effects of computer use in instruction. Computer use with elementary students produces higher achievement than with older students. Computer-based instruction results in higher achievement, but the effects are only small or moderate when compared to other instructional approaches. When computer-based instruction is supplemented by other forms of instruction, the effects are higher than with a computer alone. Computers can reduce instructional time. Students have positive attitudes toward computers and like to use them, and positive social interactions and cooperation among students develop if they enjoy working together at computers. Given these advantages, computer instruction should be carefully integrated into the curriculum.

More research is necessary to assess the instructional gains from using CAI. Some of the cognitive gains made with CAI may be due to the opportunity for self-instruction. Computer-based methods can produce increased student achievement, but there is some evidence that gains may be less than what is obtained with other instructional approaches. Long-term retention of content may be better promoted with traditional methods (Hawley & Rosenholtz, 1984). An additional concern is the problem of uneven distribution and use of the technology.

 PRIMARY REFERENCES

Brandt, R. S. (Ed.). (1988). *Content of the curriculum*. Alexandria, VA: Association for Supervision and Curriculum Development.

> Of particular interest in this ASCD publication is Brandt's introductory discussion of what schools should teach. In addition, content area specialists propose discipline-specific concepts that could be useful to curriculum designers.

Doyle, W. (1986). Classroom organization and management. In M. C. Wittrock (Ed.), *Handbook of research on teaching* (3rd ed., pp. 392–431). New York: Macmillan.

> Doyle provides a synthesis of the research on the organization and management of the classroom environment. This in-depth review provides information helpful in studying how classroom life is organized for learning and order.

Hawley, W. D., & **Rosenholtz, S. J.** (1984). Good schools: What research says about improving student achievement. *Peabody Journal of Education, 61,* 15–52.

The authors present a comprehensive summary of the research on improving student achievement. One highlight of the article is the discussion of single- and multitask classrooms. An excellent presentation of resources that support teaching and learning is included.

Popham, W. J. (1982). Basic skills and measurement basics. In D. G. Wallace (Ed.), *Developing basic skills programs in secondary schools* (pp. 105–116). Alexandria, VA: Association for Supervision and Curriculum Development.

Popham's chapter looks at the shortcomings of norm-referenced achievement tests and the advantages of criterion-referenced tests. Because tests have assumed so much importance in education, he makes several recommendations to improve assessment practices in schools.

Rudman, H. (1980). *Integrating assessment with instructional review (1922–1980).* East Lansing, MI: Michigan State University, Institute for Research on Teaching.

This IRT monograph includes a review of the research on assessment and teaching from 1922 to 1980. Four important questions about the link between testing and teaching are addressed. Of special interest is the description of the gap between teachers and test developers.

Squires, D. A., Huitt, W. G., & **Segars, J. K.** (1983). *Effective schools and classrooms: A research-based perspective.* Alexandria, VA: Association for Supervision and Curriculum Development.

The authors of this ASCD publication have reviewed the research on effective schools and classrooms and present the information in an easy-to-read format.

Stiggins, R. J. (1988). Revitalizing classroom assessment: The highest instructional priority. *Phi Delta Kappan, 69,* 363–368.

This article is a brief summary of research related to current classroom assessment practices. Stiggins's main concern is that overemphasis on standardized measurements has kept teachers from becoming more proficient in designing and using teacher-directed assessments. Included in the article are recommendations for training teachers and administrators.

Tobin, K. (1987). Forces which shape the implemented curriculum in high school science and mathematics. *Teaching and Teacher Education, 3*(4), 287–298.

Tobin investigated factors that influence the implementation of the curriculum. His synthesis provides insight into the ways the actual curriculum implemented differs from the intended curriculum.

RESEARCH IN PRACTICE

Finding 1: A well-planned, structured, and articulated curriculum helps ensure that student needs will be the focus of instructional planning.

Carefully planned and organized curricula should be the basis for instructional planning. Curricula should be developed by teachers and supervisors who are knowledgeable about what students should learn. The curriculum should give direction to specific learning expectations within a school or school system. Clear goals and learner objectives should be included in curriculum documents or guides. The guides should provide an up-to-date frame of reference for teachers' instructional planning.

Teachers will, of course, make adjustments in the curriculum in order to provide the best learning experiences for their students. Any curriculum changes should be dictated by the needs and characteristics of the students. By using the curriculum as the basis for instructional planning, teachers can make better use of allocated learning time, ensure content coverage, and sequence instruction to provide optimal learning opportunities.

Scenario.   A high school English teacher was about to be observed by his principal. During the preobservation conference the teacher said that he was teaching a unit on death and dying. After the conference we asked the principal if this unit was part of the curriculum. The principal said he was not sure but would check to see if this was the case. He was not able to locate the English curriculum, so he asked the teacher during the postinstruction conference how this unit related to the goals of the English program. The teacher said he did not believe there was a relationship but that he had developed an interest in the topic while taking a summer workshop at the local university. He enjoyed the information so much that he wanted to share what he had learned with his students. By the way, the data from the classroom observation indicated that the lesson was well organized and the instruction was effective. It was clear, however, that influences other than a curriculum guided the teacher's instructional planning. Most important, the needs of the students in the English class were not considered in selecting this unit of study.

About the same time that the instruction described above was taking place, a group of K–12 teachers and a districtwide subject area coordinator in another school system were revising a language arts and English curriculum. They met regularly for more than a year to establish the major goals for this area of study, identify specific learning objectives, and agree upon responsibilities for each grade level and subject area. The entire curriculum was developed to meet the specific needs of the students in that school system. They did not, however, ignore the learning expectations addressed by the various state and national tests that were administered in their schools. When the curriculum was completed, teachers were able to develop their daily plans so that students would be engaged in activities that addressed all of the important learning goals and objectives for their particular grade level or subject area. The learning objectives were well balanced in terms of cognitive and affective expectations.

Finding 2: Effective instruction emphasizes lower and higher cognitive expectations with appropriate attention to the affective domain.

A number of influences such as standardized testing and assessment practices have caused teachers to focus their instruction on lower cognitive learning. Teaching for comprehension and higher level learning has been given less attention, and in some cases little emphasis has been given to the affective domain. Properly developed curricula can help to alleviate this one-dimensional approach to teaching and learning. Teachers also have the responsibility to ensure that their instruction properly balances different levels of learning. They must also promote positive attitudes about learning. Although it is difficult to assess affective learning, it is an important learning domain. It is difficult, if not impossible, to clearly differentiate between cognitive and affective learning. Teachers, therefore, should plan their instruction to emphasize a range of learning outcomes and use instructional strategies that will generate enthusiasm for learning.

Scenario.   An outstanding elementary school teacher was very upset when her school shifted from a balanced educational program to almost exclusive emphasis on lower cognitive objectives. This shift was intended to prepare her students for the state competency tests, even though they had always done well on these tests. Prior to this change she had taken the time to develop critical thinking skills, cooperative group work, and positive attitudes about learning and school in general. She found that the recent emphasis on test scores had little effect on her students' development of basic skills, and at the same time students did not perform as well in the areas of critical thinking and problem solving. Fortunately, she recognized the problem and on her own is moving back to a balanced instructional program.

This teacher is not going to ignore the curriculum expectations of the school system. She is, however, going to make adjustments to provide her students with a range of learning opportunities. She will continue to develop a strong knowledge base in each of the content areas, but she will use a portion of her allocated learning time to focus on higher level learning. She will also use instructional strategies that promote higher rates of student engagement in their own learning. She expects that the changes she is making will help her students become more enthusiastic learners. Although the teacher is making her own commitment to a balanced instructional program, she knows that she is taking some risk in paying less attention to student performance on standardized tests.

Finding 3: Assessment practices have a critical influence on teachers' decisions about learning expectations and instructional activities.

Perhaps the most important assessment practice is to determine student readiness for new learning experiences. Preassessment helps teachers know if the students are going to be successful when they engage in new learning experiences or, equally important, to determine how well they already know what is to be taught. Proper assessment provides information that helps teachers make the best possible preactive and interactive decisions and, at an appropriate point, determine how well instructional objectives have been achieved. Oftentimes, teachers make instructional decisions without the necessary assessment data. This can lead to pacing problems, inappropriate use of learning time, and the increased possibility that students will be off task. The research is clear; the best instructional decisions are based on adequate data about student performance.

Scenario. A high school physical education class had just begun a unit on tumbling in a coeducational class of approximately 80 ninth grade students. On the first day of the unit the teachers had all of the students line up single file to go through the first exercise, a simple front roll with the assistance of two spotters. The line was long, movement through the activity was slow, and the students who were waiting in line soon became bored and began to misbehave. At the end of the first class, the teachers were asked by an observer if they had preassessed the students to determine their level of tumbling proficiency. They had not made any attempt to do this but decided to check students' tumbling skills as the first activity on the following day. Their assessment strategy was based on the sequence of skills to be mastered.

The next day the teachers spent the class period conducting the assessment and found that they could divide the class into four different groups based on their skill levels. They had beginners, intermediate, advanced, and demonstration groups. A number of the students were gymnasts who could serve as peer tutors to other students. By the next day the class was well organized, students stayed on task, and the behavior problems all but disappeared. It should be noted that students in the most advanced group (demonstration level) had created most of the problems on the first day. As the unit progressed, these students helped the teachers by working with other students, and the motivation of the entire class was excellent. A positive unintended outcome occurred when the class developed a tumbling and gymnastic show to present to parents for open house night at school.

Finding 4: A range of assessment practices should be used to provide data necessary for making important instructional decisions.

Teachers often need information about student achievement very quickly in order to make instructional decisions about pacing and reteaching any students who have not mastered the concepts that have been taught. Standardized tests cannot be used for this type of decision making because they do not address teachers' specific learning expectations and because it takes so long to get the tests scored and the results back.

Informal assessment techniques, such as class discussions and questions about the material to be learned, prior to instruction can yield helpful information about the students' current level of knowledge and understanding. Similar techniques can be used after instruction to determine if the majority of the students have reached the desired level of achievement. Teacher-developed tests can also provide readily accessible information about the level of student learning, and the results used to make decisions about whether to reteach certain concepts, slow the pace to increase the success rate, or move more quickly through the curriculum to challenge and motivate the students.

Scenario.   A high school science department was concerned about the low overall achievement of its students. None of the members of the department felt that they had a sound background in tests and measurements, so one teacher agreed to take an evening class on assessment techniques. After taking the class he served as a resource person for the rest of the department to help develop better assessment strategies. The department members began by reviewing their curriculum and identifying key concepts that would have to be mastered in each class. Each concept was broken down into specific components to be taught. Tests and other assessment strategies were developed to determine the level of learning after instruction on each concept. The assessment strategies were specific to the learning expectations established by the department and provided data very quickly so that teachers could make instructional decisions to meet the needs of their students.

There was almost an immediate payoff for teachers and students. Instructional planning became an important priority for all members of the department. Their plans included strategies that attended to the learning needs of all of their students. Interactive decision making was improved because of the new emphasis given to assessment during the preactive process. Student success on teacher-made tests improved within a short span of time. At the end of the first year, student performance on departmental exams was much better than in preceding years. Members of the department realized they had made some important gains but that they needed to give continued attention to student assessment and instructional planning.

Finding 5: Assessment practices should generate information about higher level thinking, problem solving, progress on assignments, and other expectations that may not be included in a formal testing program.

Standardized tests can yield important information about student performance in comparison to the population against which the tests were normed. These tests are not constructed to assess what is taught in a single school system. Teacher-made tests and criterion-referenced instruments are needed to evaluate how well students have achieved local objectives. Also, formal testing procedures often do not generate the best information about complex learning processes.

Discussions with students can provide important insights about their thinking processes and their ability to perform at higher levels of learning. Student explanations can also yield information about their levels of understanding and their ability to assimilate diverse information. Homework assignments, class projects, and research activities that are clearly integrated with learning expectations can provide assessment data that are invaluable in planning future instruction.

Scenario.   Several years ago a school system decided to provide special schools for their gifted and talented students beginning at the middle school (sixth grade). Administrators and teachers decided to use a range of assessment strategies to help them make decisions about which students should be given an opportunity to enroll in these special schools. They used all of the standardized test data that had been generated during the first five grades as well as data from teacher-made tests and other pertinent information from the cumulative folders. They also asked elementary teachers to identify students they thought would be most successful in meeting the challenges provided in these schools.

After the schools had been in existence for several years, a study was conducted to determine the best predictors of success for the students selected. Teacher judgment was found to be the most accurate and reliable predictor. These judgments were based, of course, on a wide range of both formal and informal data that teachers had about the students' classroom performance. Interestingly, a number of students who were considered to be marginal candidates based on their standardized test scores were more successful than some of the students who had very high scores. These students were admitted because teachers recommended them based on attributes that could not be measured by formal testing procedures.

Finding 6: Effectively structured classrooms focus on learning expectations in an environment that places a high priority on enhancing the learning process.

Teacher expectations are the primary determinant in structuring classrooms and instructional environments. Both learning and orderliness are affected by structuring decisions. The best decisions are made when they are based on students' characteristics and needs, teachers' learning expectations, teachers' needs for control, and necessary management routines. When appropriate structuring decisions are made, academic and social environments are aligned and teachers are in a better position to attend to learning instead of spending an inordinate amount of time on behavior management. Positive expectations that are translated into instructional decisions have a beneficial impact on student learning.

Scenario.   A science teacher whose primary responsibility was to teach biology was also responsible for a general science class. In a conference before the general science class, she did not appear to have a well-defined plan for the lesson. She said that many of the students would be late to class, not have their textbooks with them, and would not participate very much in the class discussion. When she was asked about what she expected them to learn and what her teaching strategies would be, her answers made it clear that very little thought had been expended in the planning process.

Our observation of the class was consistent with her discussion about what to expect. A number of the students drifted into class late without their books and materials. They did not pay much attention to the teacher, who tried to involve them in a discussion by writing several science terms on the board and asking the students for definitions. After this proved unsuccessful, she asked the students what they would like to discuss and they said they did not want to talk about science. They spent the rest of the class time visiting in small groups and talking about their social lives.

We also observed a mathematics teacher on the same day in the same school. She told us before the observation what her students were like, the high expectations she had for them, and how she had structured the instructional tasks so that there would be very few disruptions. Her students all arrived on time or early, went to their seats, and reviewed the day's learning objectives and assignment that had been written on the chalkboard. They were all working while she quickly took roll and collected assignments. She began her presentation within a few minutes and had the full attention of nearly all of her students. She moved briskly through the lesson with a great deal of student interaction and comments that reflected a high level of enthusiasm. At the end of the class the students copied the next day's assignment that was posted on the front chalkboard. This caused several of them to be late leaving the room. A number of positive comments were exchanged with the teacher as they left.

The expectations of these two teachers were reflected in the structure and environment of their classrooms. The differences in student behavior and attitudes were remarkable. It was not surprising that the assessment data provided to us by the school reflected the excellent mathematics instruction that was taking place. We should note, however, that the science teacher's biology classes were very different from her general science class. She had a clear structure, high expectations, and very successful learning experiences in these classes.

Finding 7: Instructional activities should be based on the most appropriate task structures, the needs and characteristics of the students, and teacher expectations for student learning.

Instructional activities should be used to involve students, facilitate information sharing, provide social interaction, and achieve specific learning objectives. When too many activities are used, confusion may result. Allocated learning time may be lost and students may not have enough time to complete their learning tasks. Too few activities, however, may lead to student boredom, apathy, and misbehavior. In order for activities to facilitate learning and unlock student motivation, they must be carefully planned and organized and congruent with the needs and characteristics of the students. Materials and equipment must be accessible, and the physical arrangement of the instructional setting should be adequate to accommodate the desired activities.

Scenario.   A sixth grade intern teacher wanted to increase student interaction when he was teaching social studies. He had attended a seminar on using small groups in the classroom and decided to implement the strategy immediately. He did not know the students well and had not established classroom routines that were consistent with his expectations. Needless to say, his first venture into group work was not very successful. He did make a commitment to understanding how to create a multitask structure in the classroom. Later in the year, he again organized his students into small groups for a social studies unit. This time he based his structure on what he wanted the students to learn, which students would work together most effectively, and an assignment that clarified the responsibilities of both the individual and the group. His second attempt was very successful in improving learning gains, student involvement, and attitudes about social studies.

The teacher said that the year had been a valuable learning experience. He wanted to engage his students in group work, but he had not taken into consideration all of the factors that would need attention when he changed the task structure. Because he was a learner who wanted to become a more effective teacher, his persistence paid off. Most important, his students benefited from his commitment to mastering a different instructional approach.

Finding 8: Instructional materials should be carefully selected to ensure that the information is clearly presented, accurate, timely, and consistent with the learning expectations and ability levels of the students.

It is not unusual to find that instructional materials available to teachers are a major influence on the interactive instructional process. Materials can have a significant impact on what students learn as well as their attitude toward learning. Materials must be up to date and at the right level of difficulty. Materials that are too easy do not promote learning, while those that are too difficult may cause frustration which can lead to behavior management problems. Materials should be used that will support the scope and sequence of instruction as well as give adequate attention to information and concepts that will be tested.

Scenario.   The third grade teachers in an elementary school were very concerned about the match between the mathematics materials and their curriculum goals and objectives. They decided to analyze the problem to see what needed to be done to improve mathematics instruction and student achievement. They began by writing their mathematics curriculum objectives on large empty envelopes. Each envelope represented one objective. They arranged the envelopes on library tables so the objectives would be sequenced in the order that they were expected to be taught. They made copies of pages from their textbook and supplementary materials and placed them in the envelopes with the objectives that were most closely related to the materials. When they finished this process, they had some envelopes that were full and overflowing while others were empty. They quickly realized that if the textbook and materials were going to guide instructional planning curriculum goals and objectives would receive uneven emphasis during instruction.

The process used by these elementary teachers points out how important it is for teachers to analyze the relevance of the materials they use in terms of local learning expectations. The mismatch between materials and local curriculum goals can cause major problems for teachers and create serious learning deficits for their students. The work done by the third grade teachers led to a long-range curriculum development and evaluation program for their entire school. The results have been gratifying to teachers, students, and parents.

GUIDE FOR OBSERVATION, ANALYSIS, AND REFLECTION

The purpose of these activities is to focus on planning for a specific lesson rather than on the total planning process. One way to understand how teachers plan lessons is to ask them to share their thoughts about elements they consider when they plan. Additional insight into planning can be gained by arranging a follow-up observation of those teachers you have interviewed. Analyze the relationship among preactive planning, interactive decisions, and the reflective process, focusing on the information gained in the preinstructional interviews and during the observations. Analysis is most effective when the teacher and the observer cooperatively analyze the data. Reflect on what you have learned and incorporate your insights into your teaching approach.

1. Learning context

Observation: *What is the overall unit or area of study?* Gather information about the larger instructional unit such as overall topic, theme, and goals. Have the teacher describe where this lesson falls in the instructional sequence for the unit or area (i.e., introduction, development, or summary). You may also want to ask what occurred in previous lessons and what will occur in subsequent lessons. Ask teachers about the total time allocated for the unit.

Analysis: *How well did the lesson relate to the larger unit or area of study?* Decide if this lesson was closely related to the unit or area and to the curriculum. Discuss whether the sequencing of the lesson and the time allocated were appropriate. Together, discuss what adjustments could be made to improve planning.

Reflection: *What preactive steps will you take to ensure a logical relationship between this lesson and the overall unit of study?* Incorporate what you've learned from others about how they design well-connected lessons that relate to the learning goals. Be sure to consider ways to delineate specific objectives for a series of lessons, to sequence the lessons, and to allocate instructional time.

2. Learner characteristics

Observation: *What are the learning characteristics of the students?* Teachers should share information about a particular group of students or a specific class. Have the teacher talk about the group in general but also about individual students. Teachers could identify students with particular abilities and talents and those with learning or behavioral problems. Teachers may share special planning considerations based on class composition.

Analysis: Was the lesson consistent with student needs and characteristics?   Determine the relevance of the lesson for the students. Decide if the lesson was suitably adapted for the students, collectively and individually. Discuss the possibility of other adaptations that could have been made.

Reflection: What can I do to assure that this lesson will be appropriate for my students?   Based on the characteristics and needs of your students, think about the adaptations that may be necessary to make this lesson as appropriate as possible for all of the students. Be sure and consider those students who have special needs and those who may already know most of the information to be presented.

3. Learning objectives

Observation: What are the learning objectives for the lesson?   The discussion should cover the specific content objectives (cognitive, affective, and psychomotor). Find out how students are to be involved when they are learning the content.

Analysis: Were the learning objectives clearly communicated and consistent with the stated curriculum?   The analysis could address the appropriateness of the academic and content expectations. Also explore the relationship of the objectives to the goals of the unit or area, the balance of cognitive, affective, and psychomotor objectives, and whether the level of the expectations was reasonable. Consider how well the expectations were communicated to the students. Decide if the ways the students were engaged while processing information were effective in helping them achieve the learning objectives. Discuss other ways that students could have been engaged during the lesson.

Reflection: What do I want my students to learn from this lesson?   Identify the specific learning outcomes and level of mastery expected for this lesson. Determine how the outcomes will be communicated to the students and what the students will be expected to do during the lesson.

4. Assessment practices

Observation: What assessment procedures are used before, during, and after instruction?   Focus the discussion on the formal or informal strategies the teacher used to assess students' level of readiness for the learning activities. Also ask about the formative and postassessments that will occur during and after the instructional sequence. This discussion will show how teachers plan to gain feedback about students' levels of understanding and their progress in achieving the learning objectives.

Analysis: How effective were the assessment strategies?   Determine whether the evaluative strategies used provided adequate information about student progress.

Decide if preassessment information and interactive evaluations were adequate and if the lesson was adjusted based on assessment information. Suggest other assessment practices that might be beneficial.

Reflection: *What assessment strategies will I use for this lesson?* Identify the preassessment strategy you will use to ascertain the level of student readiness. Also consider how you can use this information to modify the lesson or add remedial or enrichment activities to meet individual student needs. Determine the critical points in the lesson when student understanding should be assessed and how overall progress should be evaluated.

5. Instructional strategies and materials

Observation: *What instructional strategies and materials will be used during this lesson?* Teachers should discuss the specific events that will take place during the lesson. Be sure to ask about management activities as well as instructional activities. The teacher should describe the task structure including how the students will be organized, teacher and student materials to be used, and the estimated time for each component of the lesson.

After the preinstructional conference, observe the lesson. Focus your attention on the areas discussed during the conference. Record any references to the preceding or following lessons that establish context. Note how learning expectations are communicated, verbally and visually. Record the assessment and instructional strategies, materials, how students are engaged, and time allocations. Look for teacher actions that indicate preparation for the lesson, such as the use of special visuals, handouts, room arrangements, manipulatives, equipment, calendar, assignment sheets, and student notebooks.

Analysis: *To what degree did the instructional strategies and materials promote student learning?* Examine the specific instructional and noninstructional events that occurred during this lesson. Decide if the task structure was consistent with curricular and student needs. You might discuss the appropriateness of materials used and the instructional sequence. Determine if the time allocated for this lesson was inadequate, adequate, or excessive. Identify any additional strategies that could have been used to enhance learning.

Reflection: *What instructional strategies, learning activities, and materials will I use to best promote student learning in this lesson?* Identify all management and instructional events that need to occur during the lesson and the best sequence for those events. Develop several ways students could be organized to accomplish learning tasks. Determine which approach could be most appropriate for achieving the learning objectives. Identify appropriate instructional materials that would reinforce important concepts to be learned.

 ## DEVELOPMENT AND RENEWAL ACTIVITIES

1. Obtain several daily lesson plans in different formats. Examine the elemens included and how they are organized. Experiment with the various formats to determine which works best for you.

2. Refer to Figure 3–5. Which sources of information (listed along the left side of the chart) would be the most appropriate for each of the eight critical assessment events? Copy the chart and mark an X in the appropriate boxes.

3. If you are currently teaching, examine your own plans for a unit of instruction and the related postassessment instruments. Determine the match or congruence between what is planned and what is tested.

4. Give yourself a grade as you evaluate your assessment practices. Respond to each of the items on page 80.

	Student Profiles, Guidance Folders	Achievement Tests	Diagnostic Tests	Inventories, Checklists	Observation	Projects, Work Samples	Teacher Tests of Knowledge	Criterion-referenced Tests
1. Beginning of the Year								
2. Classifying/Grouping of Students								
3. Diagnosing								
4. Instructional Pacing								
5. Evaluating/Grading								
6. Retention/Promotion								
7. Parent Conferences								
8. Curriculum Planning								

FIGURE 3–5. Strategies for eight critical assessment events

My Assessments:

▪ Provide students with regular feedback	A	B	C	D	F
▪ Give the students the opportunity to show what they have learned	A	B	C	D	F
▪ Are motivating to students	A	B	C	D	F
▪ Emphasize student progress	A	B	C	D	F
▪ Are based on students' characteristics and needs	A	B	C	D	F
▪ Are closely related to instruction	A	B	C	D	F
▪ Evaluate a broad range of knowledge and skills	A	B	C	D	F
▪ Incorporate both formal and informal sources of information	A	B	C	D	F
▪ Are based on test items which reflect several levels of thinking	A	B	C	D	F
▪ Guide planning of future instruction (e.g., alternative instructional approaches, pacing decisions)	A	B	C	D	F

4.
Motivating Students to Learn

COMMENTARY

Concern about student motivation is not a recent phenomenon. Before the advent of compulsory attendance laws many educators took the position that motivation was largely the student's problem. If a student did not have the right attitude, the best solution was for the student to leave school. As young people have been required to stay in school, teachers have had the challenge of working with students whose attitudes about school range from apathetic to hostile.

Although disruptive behavior is a problem in many classrooms, nearly every teacher with whom we have worked has been just as concerned about students who are turned off about learning. For some of us apathy has been more of a challenge than any other single student behavior. It is easy to place the blame for apathy on the students, or on their homes and environmental conditions over which teachers have virtually no influence. On the other hand, students generally begin school with positive attitudes about learning and are usually excited about being in school. Over a period of time, however, some students begin to display negative attitudes about school and make little or no attempt to engage in the learning process.

Many factors of course, influence and shape student attitudes. Some of these factors are beyond teachers' control. For example, students who are hungry and who are operating at the survival level may not view learning as one of their highest priorities. There also appears to be a relationship between parent education and student attitudes about school. Parents who have realized benefits from being educated often expect their children to benefit as well. These positive expectations, often communicated to children when they are very young, tend to have a sustained effect on children.

Even though teachers do not have control over out-of-school influences, they do have a significant role in establishing and maintaining positive attitudes about learning and school success. First, they must know what motives the students have when they come to school and what influences have shaped those motives. It is critical for teachers to really get to know their students to understand how students feel about themselves. Students who come to school feeling worthless need to have caring teachers who can help strengthen and improve their self-esteem. Second, teachers need to know which students really feel positive about school and want to learn. School and classroom conditions are most likely to enhance student motivation when they are based on a thorough understanding of student needs and characteristics.

RATIONALE

Motivating students to learn is a major challenge for all teachers. They are expected to teach all of their students certain information that will very often be assessed through the use of standardized tests. The information to be learned may or may not be meaningful to students, who are essentially a captive audience. Teachers are also expected to meet the diverse learning needs of their students. All of this is supposed to occur in an environment that may not always be conducive to effectively meeting the personal and educational needs of the students. In spite of such constraints, however, teachers can take actions that will have a positive impact on student motivation.

Considerable evidence supports the contention that the majority of students do have positive motives about learning, that they do really want to learn and be successful in school. If teachers accept this position, they can focus their attention on unlocking the positive motives that students have about learning, growing, and developing. No single strategy is effective for motivating all students. What may be effective for one student may not make much difference to other students. However, conditions can be established that will have a positive impact on attitudes toward learning.

Students need to develop a sense of personal efficacy, the belief that they can become capable learners. They need to understand that if they apply the right amount of effort to attainable learning tasks they can be successful. Teachers play a critical role in the development of student efficacy. They must know how their students feel about themselves, what they have learned previously, and what they are capable of achieving. When they have solid information to guide them, teachers are in a position to establish individual and group learning conditions that promote student efficacy. Teachers must keep in mind that some of their students may have previously rejected the notion that effort equates with success. If this has happened, extra effort and attention should be given to helping these students believe that they too are capable of becoming successful, independent learners.

Learning tasks can be structured for greater appeal to students. Some students may feel more comfortable about learning if they have the opportunity to work with their peers. Many students have a strong need to be included in a group, to feel a sense of belonging. It is difficult to accommodate this need in a single-task structure such as large-group direct instruction. Having the opportunity to engage in small-group problem-solving activities, or to work with one other peer, may help motivate those who have a need to be included. Some students, on the other hand, function quite well as independent learners. Knowing and understanding the personal needs of students is a prerequisite for establishing the most favorable learning conditions.

The types of rewards students receive also has an important effect on motivation to learn. Negative feedback does not promote learning and positive feedback can enhance attitudes toward learning. Keep in mind, however, that not all students respond well to the same type of positive feedback. Some students have a need for public praise while others benefit most from private feedback. Many students benefit from cooperative reward structures, while other students respond best to individual or competitive structures. Once again, teachers can provide a range of rewards that will have a positive influence on nearly all of their students.

Motivating all students to learn is clearly one of the most formidable and complex tasks facing teachers. To be successful, teachers need to have a firm grasp of the research on motivation to learn. They also need to have the opportunity to establish the most appropriate conditions for enhancing student motivation and to develop a repertoire of strategies that can be used to meet the different needs of their students.

Teachers have found it difficult to find information about student motivation in any single source book or reference. There are, of course, journal articles that focus on some aspect of motivation and there are textbooks (very often used in psychology classes) that present motivation research and theory. Here we provide a synthesis of the work on motivation for teachers and administrators to use as they plan and organize their work.

RESEARCH SYNTHESIS

The Concept of Motivation

Students motivated to learn are attentive and eager to be engaged in learning activities. They are persistent in their efforts and show a high level of interest in their learning tasks. They do not need external reinforcement to perform at an acceptable level of performance. They appear to value what they are learning and are pleased with their efforts. Students tend to behave in ways consistent with their self-perceptions. There is a clear and positive relationship between positive self-regard or self-esteem and academic success (Kearns, 1988; Hansford & Hattie, 1982; Wlodkowski, 1977). Students who feel that they will succeed make different choices than students who act out of anxiety and the fear of failure. Students can learn to be helpless or independent (Seligman, 1975).

The knowledge base about the relationship of motivation to learning has been greatly expanded by recent research efforts. One finding of this research is that student motivation may account for differences in student achievement beyond those resulting from differences in intelligence or scholastic aptitude. According to Gage and Berliner (1984), "Motivation is one factor that determines the degree to which a student will understand or gain knowledge and skill" (p. 374). Motivation can drive performance and underlies covert activities which occur during learning, such as attending and processing information (Brophy, 1987).

Good and Brophy (1987) examined several factors that are related to students' motivation to learn. They define motivation to learn as a "student tendency to find academic activities meaningful and worthwhile and to try to get the intended academic benefits from them" (p. 328). Student motivation to learn can be conceptualized as a general trait or as a situation-specific state. As a general trait, students exhibit an enduring disposition to learn content or knowledge or to master skills. When motivation to learn is situation specific, students may only intend to master a particular skill or learn specific content. In either case, as Brophy (1987) contended, motivation to learn can be acquired. Gage and Berliner (1984), along with others, also supported the idea that the need to achieve or to be successful is an "acquired motive" (p. 389). Once motivation is activated, it can function as a scheme or script that includes affective and cognitive elements involving goals and strategies (Brophy, 1987).

Although developing self-starting, intellectually curious students is an important outcome of schooling, it remains one of education's most elusive challenges. Even those schools recognized as outstanding are actually ineffective in reaching a significant segment of their total population (Brookover, 1984). Teachers are responsible for numerous students with motivational problems. These problems are reflected in behaviors such as defensiveness, hopelessness, anxiety, and apathy (Stipek, 1988). Students may be inattentive and pursue an activity of their own interest rather than assigned tasks. Many do not persevere to complete tasks successfully or they need external support to stay engaged. Some students play it safe by not attempting challenging work or do not perform to their ability level. Many students also exhibit failure-avoiding behaviors which prove to be counterproductive and self-defeating in the long term (Stipek, 1986).

For many researchers and educators, schools are not as successful as they should be in motivating students to learn. Studies of at-risk students have pointed to excessively high dropout rates. In many states up to one third of the children who enter school will not continue in school until graduation. Other studies have documented the difficulty of providing a stimulating, satisfying learning environment. Brophy and Kher (1985) noted that students may begin school with enthusiasm but soon settle into an unenthusiastic state. Stipek (1988) reported that nearly every kindergarten student feels he or she is the "smartest child in the class" (p. 16). Children appear to be self-confident learners in those beginning years but begin to lose that confidence as they go through the primary grades.

Glasser (1986) has urged the restructuring of secondary schools to meet his definition of a good school. A good school is "a place where almost all students believe that if they do some work, they will be able to satisfy their needs enough so that it makes sense to keep working" (Glasser, p. 15). Glasser pointed out that in most secondary schools half of the students do not do the work even though they could, and they say they hate school. Glasser advocated creating less frustrating schools and working to satisfy students' basic needs.

Conditions Affecting Motivation

Several important characteristics of students determine their willingness and ability to learn from academic activities. The climate of the school as well as the classroom are strong determinants of students' attitudes toward schooling and learning experiences. A supportive, orderly environment promotes a sense of security and risk taking in students. Teachers' feelings of efficacy, their expectations for students' learning, and their instructional expertise are equally significant influences on students' attitudes toward learning. Teachers can establish instructional tasks that encourage learning and engagement. They can also incorporate research-based instructional strategies and provide conditions that promote student motivation. The most important conditions affecting student motivation to learn are presented in Figure 4–1.

Student Characteristics

Children come to school with personal characteristics, such as interest, need, value, attitude, aspiration, and incentive, that affect their motivation (Gage & Berliner, 1984). Childhood factors related to home background also affect motivation.

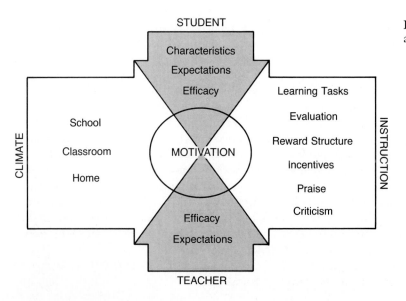

FIGURE 4–1. Conditions affecting motivation

These factors include actual achievement, independence and self-reliance, and aspirations that have been communicated to youngsters by parents and others (Gage & Berliner, 1984).

Motivational problems differ by grade level. Underachievement in early grades could be due to immaturity or poor socialization (Stipek, 1988). Students may not yet be convinced that what teachers assign will be useful. Students may be more intent on doing what pleases them rather than on doing what pleases their teachers. Secondary educators have additional obstacles to motivation. Adolescents may view school not as a novel experience but as an unpleasant routine. Very often teenagers do not seek adult approval, but they do have a need for peer recognition and acceptance. Also, high schools tend to focus more on curriculum demands than on student needs (Sava, 1987).

Students' actions are usually goal oriented and are influenced by a variety of factors. Some students exhibit apathy and disinterest in performing to an acceptable level in an attempt to protect their feelings of self-worth. One study reported that nearly 40% of ninth graders failed two or more courses. Students chose to be apathetic and uninvolved. They avoided failure and preserved their self-worth by not trying. These students seemed to believe, "Nothing ventured, nothing failed" (Raffini, 1986, p. 54). The students exhibited anxiety and apprehension rather than confidence.

School and Classroom Climate

School climate characteristics have been shown to affect student achievement. Few of the differences in student achievement can be explained by students' socioeconomic status alone. Brookover, Beady, Flood, Schweitzer, and Wisenbaker (1979) found that 75% of the variance in mean student achievement could be explained by school climate characteristics. These characteristics were also found to affect student self-concept, self-reliance, and sense of futility in academic settings. Rutter, Maughan, Mortimore, and Ouston (1979) reported similar relationships between student attitudes and behaviors and the school's social system or ethos.

A supportive learning climate is a precondition to promoting student motivation to learn (Brophy, 1987). Students must feel valued and secure in a predictable environment before positive outcomes can occur. Communicating positive regard for each student encourages students to take academic risks (Stipek, 1986). For high school students another important factor influencing the amount of effort they expend is respect for the teacher. "Basic respect" is a necessity (Stipek, 1986). Not all schools or classrooms provide a supportive, respectful climate with the appropriate academic emphasis, positive teacher and student interactions, and a reward structure that promotes and encourages effort. According to Alderman and Cohen (1985), "Motivational inequity is pervasive in today's classrooms" (p. 1). The research shows that teachers are the primary determinants of the classroom environment (Anderson, Stevens, Prawat, & Nickerson, 1988) and that administrators also control a number of environmental factors that affect students' motivation to learn.

In classrooms teachers frequently demonstrate that academic accomplishments are highly valued. However, accomplishments in extracurricular programs should also receive recognition. Teachers can provide opportunities for students to demonstrate competence and excellence both in and out of the classroom (Stipek, 1986).

Teacher Expectations

Teacher expectations have been defined as inferences that teachers make about the future academic achievement of students (Good & Brophy, 1980). Some researchers differentiate between two types of expectations—sustaining expectation effects and self-fulfilling prophecies (Cooper & Good, 1983).

The sustaining expectation effect reinforces and maintains existing behaviors and can be an important aspect in preventing change. Self-fulfilling prophecies, on the other hand, can encourage change rather than prevent it. In self-fulfilling prophecies, once expectations are expressed, individuals tend to behave according to those beliefs. Eventually, the behavior may cause the expectations to become a reality (Rosenthal & Jacobson, 1968). While self-fulfilling prophecies are the more dramatic and visible form of expectations, they may occur infrequently in classrooms (Cooper & Good, 1983). Sustaining expectation effects are more subtle, but they occur quite frequently.

Good and Brophy (1991) emphasized that it is not merely the existence of expectations that causes the self-fulfilling prophecy effect. They described the process as working in the following manner:

- The teacher expects a specific behavior and achievement from particular students.
- Because of these different expectations, the teacher behaves differently toward different students.
- This treatment tells the students what behavior and achievement the teacher expects from them and affects their self-concept, achievement motivation, and level of aspiration.
- If this treatment is consistent over time, and if the students do not resist or change it in some way, it will shape their achievement and behavior. High-expectation students will be led to achieve high levels, while the achievement of low-expectation students will decline.
- With time, students' achievement and behavior will conform more and more to original expectations. (p. 115)

Much of the research on expectation effects has focused on the differential behavior of teachers toward high- and low-expectation students (Good & Brophy, 1987; Cooper & Good, 1983). Studies have shown that there are a number of common ways that teachers treat high-achieving and low-achieving students differently. For example, teachers may call on low-expectation students less often and give them less time to answer questions, while high-expectation students are given more personal attention (Good & Brophy, 1980). Because researchers have focused on the differential behavior of teachers toward high- and low-expectation students, many teachers have become aware of the problem and have attempted to correct the situation.

Student Expectations

Students need to expect that with reasonable effort they can succeed at a learning task and that they can gain value from accomplishing their tasks. The effort expended on tasks will be the product of the expectation for success and the perceived value of the learning. Students need both to expect success and to feel the task is worthwhile. Students will exert less than maximum effort on tasks they expect to fail or on tasks which hold no meaning for them (Stipek, 1988). Successful experiences enhance students' self-concepts. Enhanced self-concept in turn encourages students to be more persistent and confident in approaching learning tasks (Wlodkowski, 1977).

Effective teachers plan learning experiences that ensure student success. They are skillful in assessing students' abilities and challenging students with learning objectives at the appropriate level. Vygotsky (1978) referred to this area where challenge and success come together as the zone of proximal development; it is "the distance between the actual development level as determined by independent problem solving and the level of potential development as determined through problem solving under adult guidance or in collaboration with more capable peers" (p. 86). Instruction should focus on clear, reasonable objectives which are within the zone of proximal development. If students put forth sufficient effort, they should expect success.

Meaningful learning tasks are those that are intended to teach knowledge and skills students perceive as worth knowing. The task could be an end in itself or part of a sequence leading to a more complex skill. Students do not generally see repeating activities dealing with skills and knowledge previously mastered as worthwhile. Having students memorize information without clearly communicating the rationale is also not usually perceived as meaningful.

Glasser (1986) described teaching students relevant material they want to learn as a process of student empowerment. Forcing students to learn something that is not relevant is not enabling the students. Glasser also stressed the need to promote a deeper knowledge of the material rather than accepting superficial knowledge. The structure of secondary schools and the time allocated for each class often limits opportunities to thoroughly comprehend a subject.

Teacher Efficacy

Teachers who have developed a high sense of efficacy feel that they have the capacity to positively affect student performance (Alderman & Cohen, 1985). Researchers have investigated the premise that high-efficacy teachers promote high efficacy in their students (Ashton, 1984). The assumption that they can make a difference underlies the instruction of high-efficacy teachers. Development of teacher efficacy is depicted in Figure 4–2.

Teachers with a high degree of commitment to excellence in teaching tend to take personal responsibility for student failure (Gage & Berliner, 1984). There are teachers, however, who generally attribute failure to lack of student preparation, low ability, home conditions, and test difficulty (Bar-Tal, 1979). Teachers do not tend to blame themselves for student failure, although they attribute student success to teach-

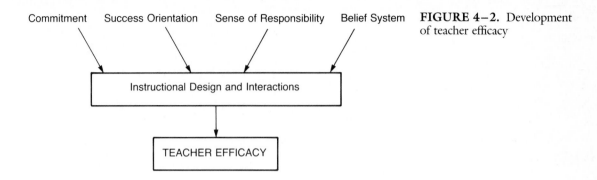

FIGURE 4–2. Development of teacher efficacy

ing skill. This sense of responsibility affects teachers' selection of strategies and efforts to persist in attempting to motivate students (Ashton, 1984; Brophy & Rohrkemper, 1981; Rohrkemper & Brophy, 1983). Brophy and Kher (1985) recommended intense teacher training to change negative teacher beliefs, attitudes, and expectations. Teachers must first believe that developing motivation to learn in their students is a realistic goal.

Teachers who are effective at motivating students to learn have an ongoing commitment to helping students succeed. They regularly monitor and assess student behavior in order to appropriately diagnose motivational problems and devise successful remedies. Teachers should be encouraged to carefully evaluate the intended and unintended effects of their strategies. Teachers who monitor their own behavior may find that well-intentioned actions may actually be promoting dysfunctional motivation patterns in students (Brophy & Rohrkemper, 1981; Rohrkemper & Brophy, 1983). Systematic observation can uncover productive and counterproductive effects of motivational strategies, but it is difficult to accurately observe students' attention to a task. Even a trained observer can be fooled by students looking busy.

Student Efficacy

As with teacher efficacy, certain factors promote the development of student efficacy. These factors are summarized in Figure 4–3. Students need to connect their success at a task with the cause of that success. Attempting to attribute success or failure to a cause is one process students use to mediate their instructional experiences. The way students interpret their learning experiences determines learning behavior (Stipek, 1986). Students who believe that they have some control over positive outcomes approach learning tasks with more effort and persistence. These students are generally higher achievers who accept more responsibility for their learning (Anderson & Prawat, 1983). One of the important findings of the Coleman et al. study (1966) was that the "mean verbal achievement of believers in the importance of hard work was higher than the mean of *all* children who believed in luck as the cause of success, regardless of race or geographic region of the country" (p. 320).

Theories of attribution and self-efficacy provide insight into motivational consequences. Attribution theory deals with how the individual perceives the causes

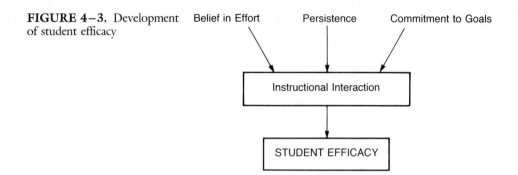

FIGURE 4–3. Development of student efficacy

of achievement (Ames, 1985). It looks at what students believe is important. For most students, there are four causes or explanations for success or failure: effort, ability, luck, and task difficulty (Anderson & Prawat, 1983). These factors can be viewed on three continuums of locus, stability, and controllability (Weiner, 1979).

Bandura (1977) defined efficacy expectation as a "conviction that one can successfully execute the behavior required to produce the outcomes" (p. 193). Effort is the behavior necessary to produce positive outcomes. Effort is a preactive action that can dispel the feelings of helplessness or hopelessness some students feel. If success is attributed to effort, it can positively affect subsequent effort on similar tasks. Individuals high in achievement motivation persist longer even when experiencing failure as they tend to view failure as caused by lack of effort (Weiner & Kukla, 1970). Attributional patterns tend to be stable over time and across situations. The learner's self-concept is also affected by his or her attributional patterns (Gage & Berliner, 1984). Early academic success is an important influence on long-term motivational patterns. Developing a positive view of personal competence promotes more effort and persistent behavior (Stipek, 1986).

Researchers have suggested several ways teachers can encourage students to attribute outcomes to effort (Anderson & Prawat, 1983; Ames, 1985). Teachers can make the relationship between effort and success clear by encouraging statements such as "I really tried hard" or "I listened well and followed directions." Teachers should discourage statements which connect success to the easiness of the task ("It wasn't hard"), to luck ("I was lucky—I guessed"), or to innate ability ("I'm just smart in math"). They should also make appropriate verbal statements about their own learning efforts ("I can do it if I try") and communicate the importance of effort. Teacher modeling of effort and persistence when attempting to solve problems and expressing statements for students are also powerful strategies. Students can be instructed to do their best work and to improve their efforts rather than get all the answers right. Teachers can promote positive task-related beliefs in students (Anderson et al., 1988). Schunk (1985) noted the motivational impact of directly informing students of their capability to do the task. Success that follows the statement "You can do it" can increase feelings of self-efficacy. Bar-Tal (1982) likewise reported that teachers have a great influence on the causal perceptions of students regarding their successes and failures on achievement tasks.

We offer some words of caution about applying attribution techniques. First, young children do not have the cognitive development necessary to understand the cause-and-effect relationship between effort and outcome. Second, if students are attempting tasks beyond their abilities frustration and lowered self-esteem may develop. Therefore, the relevance of attributions becomes important only when students possess the required skills but are not putting forth enough effort in applying those skills (Anderson & Prawat, 1983).

Goal setting and making a commitment to accomplishing goals has been shown to increase student performance and feelings of efficacy (deCharms, 1976). Students can learn how to set goals, assess their progress, and develop self-reinforcement skills. Good and Brophy (1987) suggested that effective goal setting involves goals that are short term rather than long term, specific rather than global or too general, and challenging but reasonable. For students to become independent, autonomous learners, they need experience in setting realistic, personal goals and developing skills of self-evaluation. Giving students an appropriate degree of freedom and choice in determining learning goals as well as in organizing tasks and setting completion dates can result in more student involvement, effort, and self-direction (Stipek, 1986).

Commitment can be enhanced when students have input into goal setting through contracting or informal negotiation. As they pursue their goals, students need feedback about their performance (Wlodkowski, 1977). Progress should be measured against previous performance or a preset standard, not in comparison with classmates. Teachers can provide feedback to help students assess their progress. As students reach goals, teachers should help them take credit for their accomplishments. For some students, internal reinforcement, such as pride in doing well, is enough. For others, external reinforcement is needed.

Learning Tasks

Incorporating learning tasks which are perceived to have intrinsic interest to students can increase motivation. The major components of motivational learning tasks and their characteristics are depicted in Figure 4–4. According to Brophy (1987), "Intrinsic motivation usually refers to the affective aspects of motivation—liking for or enjoyment of an activity" (p. 41). When students show energy and effort and need no external encouragement, they are intrinsically motivated (Gage & Berliner, 1984). Some learning activities are intrinsically more appealing to students than others. Teachers who know students' interests and needs can select and design activities that are challenging and worthwhile.

Appropriately designed learning tasks encourage students to actively process information and integrate new information with familiar knowledge. It is important to apply information that has been previously learned in some meaningful way. Using unique or unexpected contexts for this application can be helpful and appealing (Gage & Berliner, 1984). Developing competence or engaging in complex, higher order thinking is generally satisfying to students. Focusing on progress or finished products is a way to increase motivation (Brophy, 1987). Engagement can be sustained by

FIGURE 4–4. Learning tasks that increase motivation to learn

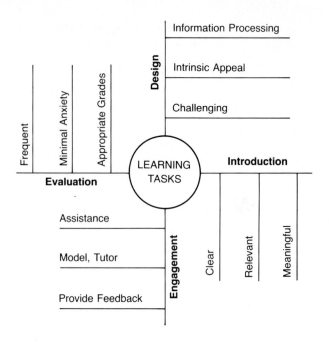

providing the opportunity to interact with peers and provide activities that directly involve students in hands-on experiences. Learning activities such as simulations, games, or carefully structured competitions, can also produce positive cognitive and affective outcomes.

The way a learning task is introduced can influence student motivation (Stipek, 1988; Huhnke, 1984; Brophy & Kher, 1985). Effective task introductions set a positive note by stressing the purposes, intended outcomes, and possible future uses for the activity. Students are more easily engaged initially if their curiosity is aroused, if they are hooked by an apparent contradiction, or if they have the opportunity to explore and discover some unknown on their own. Introductions should be delivered with enthusiasm, intensity, or with emphasis on the unusual. According to Stipek (1986), "The teacher's own enthusiasm for teaching . . . affects students' enthusiasm" (p. 216).

Brophy, Rohrkemper, Rashid, and Goldberger (1983) found that teachers rarely incorporated task introductions that could inspire students: "Teachers do not systematically take advantage of opportunities to present tasks in a positive light, and sometimes even present them in a negative light" (p. 547). In their study introductions tended to be vague and not detailed enough to be memorable or meaningful to the students. For about one fourth of the tasks presented, teachers made statements about liking or enjoying the subject or activity. Only a few task introductions addressed the importance or relevance of the learning. None of the statements addressed the personal satisfaction that could be derived from the learning.

Once students are actively engaged in learning tasks, teachers should ensure that students do not become confused. Confusion and frustration can diminish student learning. To avoid undue frustration, teachers should offer feedback about students' progress. The appropriate amount of assistance allows students to be successful but still allows students to take credit for completing the tasks (Stipek, 1988). This strengthens students' feelings of control over academic outcomes.

Using students as models and tutors can be an effective instructional practice. Modeling involves students observing peers attempting instructional tasks. Their motivation can be increased if peers try and succeed at their tasks. Since modeling is a form of social comparison, it is important to choose models wisely (Schunk, 1985). Models who are perceived by the observers as similar in ability, experiences, or personal characteristics promote social comparisons. If observers view comparisons positively, motivation can be enhanced. Caution is advised in using peer models who are perceived as superior in capability to the observer. Low-ability students could become particularly discouraged. Schunk (1985) noted the possible ineffectiveness of teacher modeling for the same reason, since students perceive the teacher to be more competent.

Models are of two types: mastery and coping. Mastery models complete the tasks to perfection without hesitation, whereas coping models encounter difficulties and make typical mistakes. When coping models exhibit persistence and positive problem-solving behaviors, student observers are encouraged and become more confident in their subsequent efforts (Zimmerman & Ringle, 1981).

Using students as tutors is a way to increase feedback to learners (Wagner, 1982). As with peer modeling, social comparison can be positive if student tutors are carefully selected. Learners will feel more confident and able to do their tasks if tutors are seen as similar in capability. In terms of fostering self-efficacy through favorable social comparison, the use of adults and high-ability students to tutor less able ones may not be the most productive arrangement (Schunk, 1985).

Learning tasks should be tested and graded in a way that minimizes negative effects on motivation. Tests and grades provide useful feedback on student progress or mastery, but they generate emotion. Tests and grades are used as the basis for various social rewards, such as approval, promotion, graduation, and jobs, and therefore have motivational power. Tests and grades can have a positive effect on student motivation, but teachers must be sure that the feedback is growth promoting and does not create an aversion to learning. Knowing that a test will be given affects students' study habits and the amount of effort they expend (Gage & Berliner, 1984).

Anxiety can adversely affect the performance of some students. There appears to be an optimal level of anxiety; performance can be inhibited when the level of anxiety is too high or too low (Gage & Berliner, 1984). Many students succeed at learning tasks in relaxed situations but perform below their ability at more stressful times. Teachers can lower the anxiety level by placing minimal emphasis on external evaluations. They can help students develop test-taking skills and emphasize the positive aspects of evaluation such as the opportunity to show progress and get feedback. Pressure is lessened too when no time limitation is placed on students (Plass & Hill, 1986). Students should be allowed to work toward mastery without time constraints. Students may be less anxious if they know that some test items may be beyond their ability and they should not be concerned about missing those items (McCombs, 1988).

Frequent evaluations are advised. They provide more opportunities for feedback and can have a positive effect on student achievement. An unintended side effect of frequent testing may be the student's negative attitude toward the teacher. Teachers should show consideration when students experience special circumstances such as being overly fatigued, nervous, or caught unprepared. Accountability produces positive effects. Tests should be fairly administered to prevent the possibility of cheating. Allocating conventional letter grades also results in more student effort than when students are given either a pass or fail grade (Berliner, 1982).

Student motivation can be enhanced if grades are used appropriately. Grades should be kept private and not used for social comparison. Grades can be based on different performance standards and tasks of different levels of difficulty (Stipek, 1988). Grades can be negotiated by allowing students to select the sources for their grades. Grades can also be based on a variety of sources, not solely on teacher judgment. Some teachers employ the practice of eliminating the lowest grade thus giving the students an advantage. Severity or leniency of grading practices has motivational consequences. If students perceive grading to be too strict in a particular subject area, they may choose to avoid that subject (Gage & Berliner, 1984).

It is important to interpret errors as indicators of growth and learning rather than as indicators of failure. Students need to know when they are wrong and receive suggestions for improvement, but the absence of errors may show that students are not challenged enough (Stipek, 1986). Learning from errors can be reinforced by providing opportunities for students to check and correct their own work (Stipek, 1988).

Standards of performance can have an impact on student motivation. By setting standards of performance, teachers let students know what behavior is required to achieve a specific grade. Standards should be high; when the teacher sets mediocre or low standards, students will perform at that level. But standards set unrealistically high can prove to be dysfunctional. Students "who aspire too high and degrade their own accomplishments will constantly live in a state of anxiety and depression" (Gage & Berliner, 1984, p. 347). Driscoll (1986) suggested students' feelings of self-efficacy as an intervening variable. If students believe that they can achieve high standards, they are likely to modify their behavior to meet those standards and achieve higher grades. Individuals, other than teachers, set standards of performance. The standards set by parents and peers affect student effort and achievement (Natriello & McDill, 1986).

Reward Structure

The reward structure in a classroom affects student attitude, achievement, and motivation to learn. Student motivation can be significantly affected by the way students work at accomplishing a learning task (Wlodkowski, 1977). Hawley and Rosenholtz (1984) defined reward structure as "the rules under which students are rewarded for academic performance" (p. 27). There are three basic reward structures: individualistic, competitive, and cooperative. Each structure specifies the type of interdependence among students (Johnson, Johnson, Holubec, & Roy, 1984) and influences social comparisons among students (Schunk, 1985). The important components of reward structures and their influence on student motivation are presented in Figure 4–5.

With an individualistic reward structure, one student's achievement is unrelated to achievement of other students. Each student's performance is judged against a predetermined set of criteria. Rewards for one student are not tied to rewards for other students. Under individualistic structures, students are not motivated to help or hinder one another since there may be little or no interaction among students. In individualistic reward structures, social comparisons are deemphasized and rewards are based on each student's self-improvement. Success is viewed in terms of "exceeding one's own standard . . . rather than in terms of surpassing the performance of others" (Stipek, 1986). Student motivation to learn is likely to be enhanced as long as the student is progressing (Schunk 1985). For teachers, an individualistic structure is the easiest to manage.

In a competitive reward structure, one student's success depends on another student's failure. A negative reward interdependence exists. Because there are winners and losers, not all students earn rewards. Performance is evaluated by comparing the performance of students to one another (Stipek, 1986). Competitive situations are

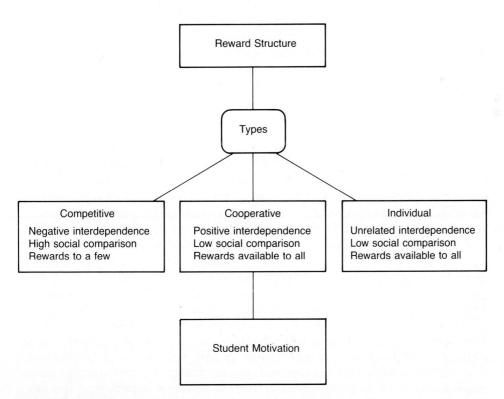

FIGURE 4–5. Reward structure

more likely to sustain the motivation of high achievers and inhibit the efforts of lower ability students. (Schunk, 1985).

A cooperative reward structure depends on positive reward interdependence. Students work together to achieve mutual learning goals. In cooperative structures, students are usually organized into small heterogeneous groups that facilitate supportive student interaction. Because evaluation is based on a preset standard, rewards are available to all students. Social comparison is reduced as differences in student motivation and ability are not as evident (Schunk, 1985). For teachers, cooperative structures require different approaches to planning and management which may require them to relinquish some control of student interaction.

All three reward structures have an appropriate role in instructional practice. Teacher decisions about which structure to use will depend on student characteristics, the objectives to be accomplished, and teacher needs. Some insight into the effectiveness of different reward structures is provided by Hawley and Rosenholtz's (1984) analysis of the research. Competitive reward structures appear to be most effective for students in the top one third of the class. When objectives require simple drill so that students can develop speed and increase the quantity of work, a competitive structure can be helpful (Johnson & Johnson, 1974). Competition between individuals of equal ability can optimize student effort (Stipek, 1986). Cooperative reward structures appear to be most appropriate when teachers want to promote problem solving, retention, application, transfer of concepts, verbal ability, cooperation, viewing issues from the perspective of others, and productive controversy (Johnson & Johnson, 1974). Higher order cognitive skills are best learned in cooperative reward structures (Okebukola, 1985). Individual reward structures are most effective for learning factual information, simple mechanical skills, and for producing individual projects.

Extrinsic Incentives

Motivational strategies that depend on using externally applied incentives are consistent with reinforcement theory. Reinforcement theory is based on the assumption that the frequency of a behavior will increase if it is positively reinforced, and, conversely, that the frequency of the behavior will decrease or stop if it is negatively reinforced. Operant psychologists contend that appropriate learning behavior is achieved when the desired behavior is reinforced early in the learning process.

Reward systems can have a positive impact on student motivation, but rewards affect individuals in different ways. Student responses to a reward system depend on factors such as students' prior learning and experiences, their developmental level, and the task characteristics (Alderman & Cohen, 1985). Giving rewards is a form of extrinsic motivation that "emphasizes the value an individual places on the ends of the action and the probability of reaching those ends" (Wlodkowski, 1977). Good and Brophy (1987) noted that rewards are more effective in "stimulating level of effort rather than quality of performance" (p. 39).

Although applying rewards in classroom settings is considered appropriate practice, certain characteristics of rewards make their use problematic. The most evident difficulty is determining an individual's preference for reinforcers. Effective reinforcers are those that students perceive as important and those that result in an increase in the desired behavior (Cohen, 1985).

Teachers must be careful to use rewards that are congruent with students' characteristics (Brophy & Evertson, 1976). For example, in the lower grades, and especially in low socioeconomic schools, symbolic rewards taken home and shared with parents have been associated with learning gains. Conversely, the practice of allowing students to perform housekeeping or monitoring duties as a reward has had a consistent negative effect on learning outcomes (Brophy & Evertson, 1976). Grades are not effective with students in early elementary grades since they do not yet understand the importance placed on high grades (Stipek, 1986). For symbolic rewards to be effective, parents and peers need to reinforce the value teachers place on grades (Stipek, 1986). In general, many middle school and high school students are more concerned with nonacademic pursuits. Used appropriately, grades, adult approval, competition, consumables, peer approval, independence, and special privileges or responsibilities are all potential reinforcers for academic performance (Stipek, 1988). Students generally rate getting good grades and free-time privileges as desirable rewards (Martens, Muir, & Meller, 1988).

Teachers also find it difficult to apply reinforcers so that the desired learning behavior is in fact rewarded. Observable behaviors are the ones most often noticed and reinforced, and yet learning is covert and not easily observed. Some students are masterful at appearing attentive and on-task while they may actually be mentally unengaged and off-task.

Giving extrinsic rewards may have an unintended negative effect on student motivation. Rewards can stimulate learning during less exciting, routine tasks such as memorization and drill and practice. However, rewards can be detrimental to motivation when learning tasks are more challenging and appealing. One unintended negative effect of rewarding students for correct responses on easier tasks is that students may choose less challenging work.

Giving students extrinsic rewards may undermine existing intrinsic motivation. Offering rewards for engaging in a task the person finds interesting may result in less interest in performing the task (Cohen, 1985). Lepper and Greene (1978) found that this effect occurs when the student is initially stimulated by the complexity or novelty of the task. Another caution in applying extrinsic rewards is that they may have only a short-term impact. When a reward has been given for a behavior and is then withdrawn, the behavior will occur less frequently (Stipek, 1988). Frustration can result when the student is no longer reinforced (Gage & Berliner, 1984).

There are several factors to consider in using rewards to motivate students. Because all students should have the opportunity to earn rewards, using grades as extrinsic rewards is generally ineffective. With normative grading systems, good grades are limited and are not available to all students. Older students may have such a long history of failure that they do not believe that they can ever earn high grades. Rewards for young children are generally given immediately, while teachers of older students may delay the delivery of rewards until students have completed a series of tasks. Some teachers deliberately use delayed rewards to develop persistence. In all cases, each student should know what the reward will be and what must be done to receive it (NREL, 1984).

Problems associated with the effective use of extrinsic rewards suggest judicious application and careful monitoring (Wlodkowski, 1977). The challenge is to use rewards to promote rather than undermine existing motivation. External rewards should not be used as a means to control student behavior. Students should not see rewards as the reason for achieving learning goals or exhibiting appropriate behavior. They should see the learning activity or the process as rewarding in itself.

Praise

Verbal praise can be a form of extrinsic reward. Brophy (1981) defined praise (and criticism) as "teacher reactions that go beyond simple feedback about appropriateness or correctness of behavior" (p. 6). Teacher praise conveys more than corrective feedback; it provides information about the student's status in relation to the teacher (Hawley & Rosenholtz, 1984). The purpose of praise can be reinforcement, but praise can also be used to maintain a positive climate or control student behavior (Zahorik, 1987).

Teachers may intend to use praise in ways that will positively affect student learning but may find it has inadvertent negative consequences. Praise is used infrequently in classrooms, although teachers use praise twice as often as negative statements. Ornstein (1988) reported that praise was used less than five times per hour in elementary classrooms and considerably less in secondary classes. Furthermore, praise for good conduct was rare. Brophy (1981) found that praise was not always contingent on great effort or good performance. In addition, a teacher's praise can lack credibility if such verbal statements are not consistent with the teacher's nonverbal actions. Praise has been found to be general and determined by students' personal qualities or teachers' perceptions of students' need for praise (Gage, 1986).

Several guidelines have been suggested to ensure that praise promotes motivation (Brophy & Evertson, 1976). Praise should:

1. Be individualized, rather than be equally applicable to all students
2. Focus on the effort of and the meaning of the accomplishment to the student
3. Be delivered privately or less noticeably
4. Not relate to students' personal qualities or status
5. Be specific to the accomplishment, rather than global
6. Be contingent, clearly tying the behavior to the reinforcement
7. Be credible and genuine
8. Be spontaneous and varied, rather than bland and perfunctory
9. Be of appropriate magnitude
10. Reward attainment of a specific performance outcome
11. Express the student's present progress relative to past performance

12. Describe the student's accomplishment on its own terms, not in comparison with classmates
13. Orient students toward appreciating their own task-related behaviors

Several factors affect the power of verbal reinforcement, among them timing and circumstances. When students are engaged and enthusiastic, verbal rewards may be counterproductive (Rohrkemper, 1982). Verbal praise is effective when used with well learned, algorithmic tasks but ineffective and possibly detrimental with skills that are in the process of being learned. Students' intrinsic motivation may be increased if praise provides information about the level of knowledge or competence. Praise should focus on students' attention, on their enjoyment of tasks, and on their desire to develop skills rather than on pleasing the teacher or winning a reward. Praise should not distract students from task-relevant behaviors before an assignment is completed.

When teachers offer praise to students who are working, positive effects occur. More specific praise and a more even distribution of praise is usually found during these interactions than when teachers give praise on demand to dependent students. Praise given during student-initiated private interactions is negatively related to achievement (Brophy & Evertson, 1976). Teachers can become conditioned by praise-seeking students. Competitiveness, jealousy, and overconcern with teacher praise can result.

In some situations, praise has been found to be unrelated to student learning (Zahorik, 1987). Students interpret praise differently; some students are encouraged by praise, while others are not. The effect of praise and rewards on learning gains needs to be considered within the total instructional context.

Students respond differentially to praise depending on grade level and individual differences. Children in the early grades accept praise and tend to let the praise shape their success expectations, even though the verbal praise may not be consistent with their numerical scores (Stipek, 1988). Young children accept praise at face value. Older elementary students are more discriminating and desire objective feedback. Some children may be unaccustomed to praise because it is rarely given in home and play situations (Green & Smith, 1983). The influence of praise also depends on the source of the praise. Young children are especially sensitive to the source of praise. Praise from high-status adults has more effect than praise from peers or other adults (Brophy & Evertson, 1976).

The effect of praise is also related to students' socioeconomic status. Praise with low-SES students, and with students who are accustomed to failure, is associated positively, but weakly, with learning gains. Praise is usually encouraging to students who are hesitant and fearful. These students are usually motivated through gentle, positive encouragement. Praise with independent learners (those accustomed to success) and high-SES students may negatively affect learning gains and motivation. It may contribute to students' passivity and withdrawal (Zahorik, 1987).

Praise conveys powerful information. It is important not to praise adolescents for what all students are able to do. The message may have a detrimental effect if success has resulted from little student effort. It is also important not to be sympathetic to failure since this reaction conveys the feeling that the student is not capable (Ames, 1985). Praise is usually public and student peers tend to analyze why praise has been given to others. They may perceive students who are overpraised as being low in ability and students whose teachers expect more of them as being high-ability (Hawley & Rosenholtz, 1984).

Criticism

Criticism is not always negatively related to student achievement or motivation. Research does not support strong and consistent relationships among criticism, achievement, and motivation (Gage & Berliner, 1984). For criticism to be productive, it should be given for inadequate performance, such as insufficient effort or lack of concentration, on academic tasks. This has been found to be true of able students who are accustomed to success (Brophy & Evertson, 1976). Effective teachers of high-achieving students attempt to motivate by providing challenge and communicating high expectations. With less able, failure-oriented students, teachers have achieved positive results with praise and encouragement, while using criticism has proved to be detrimental.

Other conditions must exist for criticism to increase learning and motivation. It must occur within a general context of warmth and interest in the student. It should match the situation and communicate what behavior is expected. There appears to be an optimal level of criticism (Silvernail, 1986). Learning can be promoted through criticism up to a certain point. Beyond that point, student progress is hindered. Teachers should be aware that criticism can have a strong effect on a student's self-concept. Ornstein (1988) noted that "it is not only what you say that counts, but how you say it, why you say it, and how you follow it up" (p. 80).

Criticism in the form of scolding, ridicule, or sarcasm does not produce positive effects. Silvernail (1986) cautioned, "Extreme criticism is negatively related to student gains under all circumstances" (p. 20). Fortunately, the use of criticism in classrooms has not been found to be a frequent practice. Dunkin and Biddle (1974) found that criticism occurred at a low rate (less than 6% of the total time). Good and Grouws (in Zahorik, 1987) concluded that "neither praise nor criticism should be used to any extent for most effective learning" (p. 421).

 PRIMARY REFERENCES

Alderman, M. K., & **Cohen, M. W.** (1985). *Motivation theory and practice for preservice teachers* (Teacher Education Monograph No. 4). Washington, DC: ERIC Clearinghouse on Teacher Education.

These articles address extrinsic reinforcers, intrinsic motivation, attributions, social comparison, self-efficacy, and achievement motivation. The aim of the presentation is to synthesize the expanding knowledge base on motivation in a way that will promote the dissemination of the information to preservice teachers.

Brophy, J. (1987). Synthesis of research on strategies for motivating students to learn. *Educational Leadership, 45*(2), 40–48.

The article summarizes important findings from a review of the literature on motivation. The concept of motivation to learn is clarified. The main focus is on identifying strategies educators can apply during instructional activities to stimulate students to learn.

Cooper, H. M., & **Good, T. L.** (1983). *Pygmalion grows up.* New York: Longman.

The authors synthesize studies in the communication of expectations that were conducted after the original *Pygmalion in the Classroom* research was published by Rosenthal and Jacobson in 1968. Concepts related to communicating expectations are thoroughly explained. Studies addressing the different components of the process are presented and analyzed.

Gage, N. L., & **Berliner, D. C.** (1984). *Educational psychology* (3rd ed.). Boston: Houghton Mifflin.

Section E deals with the concept of motivation, the relationship of motivation to learning, types of motivation, and factors that influence motivation. Also included are suggestions for designing teaching approaches that make classes more interesting to students.

Glasser, W. (1986). *Control theory in the classroom.* New York: Harper and Row.

Glasser advocates restructuring classrooms using learning teams to engage unmotivated students and presents a well-grounded, persuasive argument. Glasser points out that implementing team learning is an effective way to satisfy the needs of secondary students and to access the power of knowledge. The research efforts of D. W. Johnson, R. T. Johnson, and R. Slavin are referenced. Classroom examples and suggestions for getting started are also included.

Hawley, W. D., & **Rosenholtz, S. J.** (1984). Good schools: What research says about improving student achievement. *Peabody Journal of Education, 61*(4), 15–52.

The presentation on effective teaching includes research findings on practices that promote student achievement. Included is information on rewarding achievement, communicating high expectations, and using interactive teaching practices.

Stipek, D. J. (1988). *Motivation to learn: From theory to practice.* Englewood Cliffs, NJ: Prentice-Hall.

Important motivation theories are reviewed and explained. The emphasis is on how theory and research can be productively applied in classroom settings. The examples and strategies address the broad range of motivational problems teachers encounter and provide positive approaches in dealing with these problems. This is a readable and comprehensive presentation on motivation to learn.

Wlodkowski, R. J. (1977). *Motivation (What research says to the teacher).* Washington, DC: National Education Association.

> This concise, nontheoretical presentation includes research findings from some relatively early studies of motivation. The emphasis is on helping teachers apply the most relevant findings in everyday instruction.

Wlodkowski, R. J. (1986). *Motivation and teaching: A practical guide.* Washington, DC: National Education Association.

> This book is what it purports to be—a practical guide. Wlodkowski asserts that teachers should plan for conditions that promote student motivation and provides numerous strategies that can be incorporated in classrooms. This is an excellent resource book.

 ## RESEARCH IN PRACTICE

Finding 1: Although motivation is a complex concept, recent research provides important insights about conditions that affect motivation to learn.

Establishing school and classroom conditions that enhance motivation is especially important in light of recent research showing that student motivation may have more effect on student achievement than intelligence or scholastic aptitude. Teachers can establish conditions that will enable students to develop positive attitudes toward learning. The conditions should be based on a thorough understanding of students' backgrounds, interests, and needs. Classroom conditions should reduce anxiety and apprehension about failure and help to enhance students' self-worth. Teacher expectations should be the basis for actions that encourage and support success for all students. Students should view learning tasks as meaningful and applicable to their own lives.

Scenario. A small city school district had a student population that came from high-SES families where education was a high priority. Virtually all of the students came to school wanting to learn and excel in their studies. Parents were very supportive, provided their children with a wide range of out-of-school learning opportunities, and were willing to tax themselves to have the very best schools. Over a period of time demographic changes began to take place and lower SES families began to move into the community. These families could not provide the academic support that had been traditional in the community. Over a period of years the student population became bimodal, with almost an even distribution of lower and higher SES students in the schools.

Many of the teachers in this school system were not successful in working with the children who did not come to school motivated to learn. They cited home conditions that were not conducive to learning and the lack of parent concern about children being successful in school. When the population shift began to take place, school personnel made no concerted effort to examine the relationship of school and classroom conditions and expectations to the characteristics of the new students. The schools did not change or adapt to the changing population. When students were unsuccessful, much of the blame was placed on home conditions.

As problems with students increased, administrators and teachers began analyzing the situation and attempted to identify appropriate improvement activities. It became clear, very early in the analysis process, that the majority of the professional staff was not willing to accept responsibility for creating conditions to motivate the lower SES students. For years they had been successful with students whose background and characteristics were consistent with teacher and school expectations. Very few students had not responded well to the school culture that had gradually developed.

After a considerable amount of study, the professional staff decided to launch a systemwide staff development program that would focus on motivating all students. The major challenge of the program was to convince teachers and administrators that they could create conditions in their schools and classrooms that would unlock the learning motives of students whose home conditions were not supportive of school success. Over a period of time the attitudes of the professional staff began to change and they took more and more responsibility for student attitudes about school success. As attitudes began to change, teachers and administrators began to examine a range of strategies they could use to enhance students' willingness to learn. The staff development program was successful because it was a long-term systematic project that began with changing attitudes and then focused on developing the most appropriate learning conditions. The schools did not lower their standards; they adjusted conditions and expectations to improve the performance of all of their students.

Finding 2: Even though student characteristics and background are important influences on motivation to learn, a school's climate can be one of the most important factors in developing positive attitudes about learning.

Virtually all students have goals that guide their behavior. The goals differ depending on age, grade level, and home background. The wide range of values, needs, and aspirations of the total student group presents a major challenge to schools. It would be impossible for any single school to respond to varied expectations of all students and parents. It is possible, however, for a school to develop an overall learning climate that supports the values of those who have positive expectations about the role of a school in providing opportunities for success.

The research on effective schools, conducted over the past decade, places a high premium on a positive school climate. Schools that have a positive school climate are able to improve students' self-concepts, which in turn improves student achievement. Schools have used a variety of strategies to improve climate. In some cases it has been necessary to establish clear schoolwide behavior expectations and carefully monitor and enforce them. Once a school has become a safe and orderly place for learning, action can be taken to improve affective factors that influence student learning.

Scenario.   A school system made the development of a positive climate the highest priority for all of its schools. The administration and board of education began by making a public commitment to improving school climate throughout the system. Each school was asked to make the same commitment and develop strategies to assure that climate would be improved. Students were involved with teachers and administrators in devising plans of action. It was not long before the entire community was involved in promoting positive expectations about schools and supporting the need for student success. The effort paid important dividends for students, teachers, administrators, and parents. As attitudes about school improved, there were fewer absences, students felt better about going to school, and academic performance improved. It is important to note that students from all SES groups and from all grade levels felt better about school and were able to benefit from the positive school climate.

As student attitudes about school and attendance improved, there was a noticeable gain in student learning. Student performance on both standardized tests and teacher-made tests improved. Although improving test performance was not the primary motive for changing the school climate, gains in student learning were reflected in these measures.

Finding 3: Teacher expectations that are translated into specific classroom behaviors have an important influence on student achievement.

Teachers make a number of inferences about the academic potential of their students. They often make conscious inferences based on student characteristics. In some cases teachers may not be fully aware of some of the inferences they have made about certain students. These inferences shape teacher expectations and teacher actions. Because teachers hold different expectations for different students, teacher behavior toward students tends to vary. Many students quickly understand the expectations a teacher has for them and tend to behave accordingly. When this happens, the self-fulfilling prophecy becomes a reality. The self-fulfilling prophecy can raise students to higher levels of performance or give them an excuse for not succeeding in school. Therefore, teachers should be aware of the inferences they make and how they affect their instructional interactions. Self-monitoring can help teachers eliminate behavior that may have a negative influence on student learning.

Scenario.   Several years ago we interviewed a number of students representing different high schools in one of our most populous states. In each school we interviewed three different groups of students: those who were very successful in school, those who seemed to be apathetic about school, and those who had a history of behavior problems. We asked the students a number of questions that focused on school success and failure. In almost all cases, the students who were having problems reported that they began to dislike school in the early grades. They often cited instances of teachers telling them they were dumb, that they would never succeed in school, or that they did not have the right attitude. The students were also able to give specific examples of being treated differently from the more successful students.

It is interesting to compare what we learned from this study to an incident that occurred during one of our staff development sessions. We were conducting an instructional improvement workshop in a large comprehensive high school in a metropolitan school system. The workshop was in August and included teachers from all grade levels and administrators with whom the teachers worked. We were walking behind one of the women teachers in the group one day as we were returning from lunch. As she started to cross one of the corridors, a young man in his early twenties saw her, and they embraced and began an animated conversation. As we came up to them, she introduced him to us as one of "her boys" that she had taught in the fifth grade. He explained to us that up to the fifth grade no one believed that he would ever learn to read and that he was totally negative about school. He went on to say that this teacher told him she would not allow him not to learn to read and that she would help him meet her expectations. She evidently spent many hours tutoring him and working with him so that he would be proficient in all of his subjects. He told us that he had graduated from high school and community college and that he had earned a technology degree. He was in the building to supervise the work on the heating and cooling equipment. Obviously, because this teacher's expectations were translated into action, she had a powerful and lifelong influence on this student.

Finding 4: Teachers who take the responsibility for student success monitor their own behavior to ensure that they use instructional strategies that will be most effective in unlocking the learning motives of their students.

The most effective teachers really believe that they are responsible for developing positive student attitudes toward learning. They plan their teaching on the basis that all students will succeed. Teachers with a strong sense of efficacy carefully monitor their own instructional behavior so that they can be sure that what they are doing will produce desired outcomes. They never stop searching for ways to improve their teaching. They spend a significant amount of time getting to know their students so that they understand their learning motives. These teachers also carefully assess their students so they know what skills and knowledge they have acquired in their prior learning experiences. As a result of their previous successes, effective teachers really believe that they can help all students learn. Because these teachers have developed a strong sense of personal efficacy, they can usually convince students that they too can be successful.

Scenario.   An English teacher in a city high school is an exemplar of a high-efficacy teacher. Many of the students in this school perform poorly in their academic subjects. In this teacher's classes, however, a high percentage of the students perform much better than their peers in other sections of the same subject. This has happened in virtually every year of this teacher's rather long tenure in the school. A great deal can be learned about effective teaching by observing the teacher and talking with her about her role as a teacher. She feels strongly that she is the person responsible for her students' success in her English classes. If they fail, she believes that she too has failed. She attributes her success to the fact that over the years she has mastered a wide repertoire of instructional strategies. For example, she knows when to use large-group direct instruction, when to provide individual tutoring, and when to have the students work in small groups. She uses peer tutoring when it is appropriate, and she works with individual students to develop projects that are meaningful to them.

Some people believe that teachers like the one described in this scenario are just naturally gifted teachers. This may be partially true, but what sets this teacher apart from many of her colleagues is her deep belief that she is responsible for helping all of her students succeed. She continually seeks to develop new insights about what works with different students. Her success is due, in large part, to her commitment and her willingness to work long and hard to help her students reach their full potential.

Finding 5: Teachers can use strategies and model behaviors that will improve student efficacy.

Students who have not experienced much success in school may believe that they are not capable of performing well. When they do get something right, they are apt to attribute it to luck or to a good guess. They have lost faith in the value of hard work and in being persistent. These students do not have a strong sense of efficacy. Teachers can help to strengthen student efficacy by carefully structuring tasks that low-efficacy students can accomplish. They can verbally assure students that they are capable of accomplishing the learning tasks. They can provide students with the help they need to succeed rather than leave them to sink or swim. Just as important, teachers can model high-efficacy behaviors such as persistence and positive self-talk. Over a period of time students can develop the belief that they are competent. When this becomes a consistent belief, students are more likely to put extra effort into the learning process.

Scenario.   A number of inner-city families were relocated from a large city to smaller suburban communities in the same general locale. This was a cooperative project between the state and federal government. Some of the inner-city students found themselves in schools where academic expectations were much higher than in their home schools. One city high school student, whose family had been relocated, was scheduled by his counselor into several classes that the student thought would be too difficult for him. Mathematics was one of those classes. When he went to class the first day, he told his teacher that he was probably over his head in this particular class. The teacher responded by telling him that he would give him plenty of help and that with hard work he was sure the student could be successful.

In addition to the extra help given the student during class, the teacher had an after-school study group for all students having problems in any of his mathematics classes. The teacher also used peer tutors and small cooperative groups during class so that students could help one another. The new student was also assured by other students in the class that anyone who was willing to work would be successful in this teacher's classes. It took a considerable amount of conditioning and persistence by the teacher and students to help the new student develop the belief that if he worked hard and was persistent he could be successful. Although it took time, and there were occasions when things did not go well, the student gradually began to develop a sense of efficacy and slowly became an independent learner.

Both the counselor and the teacher knew that the boy had the ability to do the work but that he simply did not have confidence in his ability to perform well in school. The teacher used a range of strategies to provide support and to demonstrate that effort can pay off. The teacher was a person who believed that he could help students succeed and communicated his own sense of efficacy to all of his students.

Finding 6: Reward structures should be used that are most consistent with student characteristics and learning objectives.

Classroom reward structures strongly influence student attitudes toward learning. Individualistic reward structures are easy to manage and tend to be most effective with students who have a good sense of personal efficacy. Demonstrating individual improvement is easy when learning criteria and expectations are clear. Cooperative reward structures work very well with students who feel a sense of achievement when they are a part of a successful group or team experience. This type of reward structure is often especially helpful with students who are not sure of their individual ability to perform well. Competitive reward structures should be used with caution. When the competition is between individuals, rather than between groups, the winners will very likely be motivated toward further learning while losers may quit trying to succeed.

Scenario.   Many teachers have successfully incorporated a variety of reward structures into their instructional programs. One elementary teacher has been especially effective in using different reward structures. She uses individualistic rewards when her students are learning basic mathematics skills. She has very specific criteria for assessing mastery of the skills. Each student is rewarded according to the criteria. When she engages the class in higher level problem solving, she usually has the students work in cooperative groups. Each group works together to solve the problems, but she does allow competition between groups. This keeps the interest high and students stay on task during group work so they will be competitive with the other groups. She changes the composition of the groups every few weeks so that some students are not always in winning groups and others are not always in losing groups. She also is very careful to structure the groups so that each group is representative of the range of ability within the total class.

The teacher described in this scenario has demonstrated that it is possible to use several reward structures to enhance the motivation of all of her students. She carefully plans and organizes each structure to help her students achieve specific learning objectives while responding to the specific needs of her students.

Finding 7: When used properly, praise and criticism can have a positive effect on student attitudes toward learning.

Teachers should understand the conditions necessary for the effective use of praise and criticism and the impact these forms of feedback have on student performance. Some teachers have been led to believe that there is a direct relationship between the amount of praise they give and how well students perform. Many teacher evaluation forms (including statewide instruments) reward teachers with better ratings if they are observed giving a great deal of praise. If teachers are observed criticizing students, they may be given poor evaluations. Yet there are instances when praise should be withheld and students should be constructively criticized.

Praise can provide corrective feedback as well as reinforce appropriate behavior. When praise is overused or used inappropriately, attitudes toward learning may be adversely affected. Students respond differently to praise. Age, grade level, and background are examples of factors that can influence students' responses to praise. Criticism can be effective if given in a supportive environment and if it is clearly intended to help students improve their performance. Criticism is counterproductive when it is used to demean students' efforts or when it causes students to feel that they are being put down.

Scenario.   A principal of a medium-size rural high school was having problems with schoolwide discipline. Although the students were generally well behaved in their classes, they tended to create disturbances in the hallways and during lunch hour. The principal decided to have weekly assemblies as an incentive to improve school discipline. The first assembly was held at the end of a typical troublesome week. During the assembly the principal praised the students for their good behavior and told them that he would have assemblies and other school activities to reward them for their improved behavior. After the assembly the students were rowdier than ever. They knew that they had not earned the praise and that they were getting phony rewards. Several more assemblies were held with the same result before the principal was willing to admit that the students were not responding well to his form of reward. Praise was being used in an inappropriate manner by this principal.

In contrast to this situation, one of the most successful basketball coaches in the history of the sport regularly used criticism to improve the performance of his players. When one of his players did not do what was expected, practice was stopped and the player was immediately told what he was doing wrong. The coach then carefully explained or demonstrated what he expected the player to do. The player was then given the opportunity to try as many times as necessary to correct his performance. Further criticism was not usually necessary. When the player met the coach's expectations, the coach gave praise that was related specifically to his improved performance. The coach clearly communicated his expectations, gave criticism specific to a behavior without being sarcastic, never ridiculed a player, and knew how and when to use praise. This coach, who had also been an excellent classroom teacher, had carefully integrated the use of praise and criticism in his teaching and coaching.

GUIDE TO OBSERVATION, ANALYSIS, AND REFLECTION

The following activities are designed to increase the awareness of conditions, factors, and actions that enhance student motivation to learn. Although motivation is a difficult concept to understand and describe, observations of classrooms and discussions with teachers about the observations can provide important insights about what actions can be taken to unlock student motives.

1. Schoolwide conditions

Observation: *What evidence indicates a schoolwide emphasis on developing and maintaining student motivation?* Look for visible signs that schoolwide attention is being given to promoting student motivation. Your notes could include descriptions of banners, posters, bulletin boards, buttons, pins, or slogans. You may also find that student handbooks include information concerning expectations, incentives, and recognition.

Find out how student accomplishments are recognized through announcements, pictures, assemblies, and the like. Find out the percentage of students recognized and why they are recognized—for academic, athletic, or extracurricular excellence, for improvement, for participation, for honorary awards, and so on.

Also check into student information such as the number of student dropouts, transfers, and requests to attend the school. You may also want to note failure or retention rates, and numbers of students on the honor roll or enrolled in honors or advanced classes. Identify the opportunities that exist for students to get extra help or to be involved in enrichment activities or special programs.

Analysis: *What is the schoolwide level of attention given to promoting student motivation to learn?* In examining all of the information gathered, determine the degree of importance the school places on student achievement. Analysis could focus on how well these schoolwide actions positively affect student effort, motivation, and attitude. Determine what actions should be continued and what additional actions could be taken to establish norms of achievement, improvement, and involvement.

See what conclusions you can make about the consistency of the classroom conditions and reward structure with teacher expectations, student characteristics, and learning goals. You may need additional information from the teacher. You may find that different reward structures are used for specific reasons and do vary over a period of time.

Reflection: *What schoolwide actions should be taken to promote student motivation and effort in my own school setting?* Identify actions that should be implemented in your school setting to promote student motivation. Give consideration to those actions which would positively affect the greatest number of students and those directed to high-achieving, average, low-achieving, and special need students. Suggest ways these actions could be incorporated in the day-to-day schedule.

2. Classroom conditions

Observation: *What classroom conditions and reward structures are related to student motivation?*   Observe the ways in which the teacher emphasizes student effort, improvement, achievement, and involvement. In particular, note the ways the teacher recognizes and rewards individual student efforts and accomplishments. Describe bulletin boards, any displays of student work, student leadership roles, use of stickers, tokens, symbols, and so on.

Focus on how the students are organized as they do their learning tasks and how they are rewarded for their effort. Describe any conditions that are individualistic, competitive, or cooperative. Note the degree of independence, opposition, or interdependence that appears to exist in the classroom.

Analysis: *In what ways do classroom conditions and reward structure promote student motivation?*   In analyzing your notes, determine the level of attention given to recognizing student achievement, improvement, and attitude. Decide what actions should be continued and suggest other actions that could be incorporated.

See what conclusions you can make about the consistency of the classroom conditions and reward structure with teacher expectations, student characteristics, and learning goals. You may need to obtain additional information from the teacher. You may find that different reward structures are used for specific reasons and do vary over a period of time.

Reflection: *What classroom conditions and reward structures can I use to promote student motivation and positive attitudes toward learning?*   Identify those classroom conditions that seem to support and enhance student motivation. Select specific actions you would take and plan ways to incorporate them in the classroom. Consider how you will find out what students' interests are and what is rewarding to your students, how you will recognize effort and improvement in your students, and how you will enhance their self-esteem, encourage peer support, and set goals with your students.

In planning future lessons, think specifically about the type of reward structure you will use. Regularly monitoring the effects of the reward structure on student motivation can help ensure optimal benefits.

3. Communicating expectations

Observation: *What teacher behaviors communicate the teacher's expectations to the students?*   Record teacher messages that express what is expected in the class. Listen for and record statements such as:

"You can do this. Do the first three, then we'll talk."

"Let's do our R-A-H cheer—everybody did better today than yesterday!"

"The reason we are learning about lab techniques now is so we can use these techniques with our experiments later this week."

"It doesn't matter if you're not sure of the answer. Try or venture an educated guess."

"Studying our state's geography is a topic I find particularly interesting, and I know you will too."

"It's okay to make mistakes—mistakes mean you're learning!"

"We'll be working in our teams as we learn how to do these problems. Teach each other well! I'll be available to help you if your team has trouble."

"Although this may seem contradictory at first, we'll think through this together and figure it out."

These examples communicate a positive message, but you should also record any statements that might communicate a different message, such as:

"Now be quiet and get busy. You need to do this work on your own."

"Let's all make 100s."

"We've only got 10 minutes left—you may talk quietly with your neighbor as long as you don't disturb anyone else."

"Let's skip this one—it's too difficult."

"I never really liked insects, but they're the topic of our next chapter."

Analysis: *To what extent are the communicated expectations congruent with the teacher's intended expectations?* Identify patterns in the recorded statements. For example, several statements about interest or enjoyment might indicate the expectation for those outcomes. Determine if there is more emphasis on improvement, perfection, or excellence. Does the teacher communicate the idea that learning is a continuing process and that mistakes are acceptable and seen as a sign of growth? Messages that say it's okay to learn from others communicate the expectation that students can learn together rather than learn only from the teacher. Determine if there is emphasis on helping students attribute success to effort, or if luck, ability, or task difficulty are emphasized. You may notice that the teacher's most important expectation is for students to finish a task rather than learn from it.

To determine if the teacher's expressed expectations are congruent with intended expectations, find out what learning or behavioral goals the teacher perceives to be important. You might ask what the teacher's goals are for the students during the year or for this unit of study. Try to focus on the broader aims the teacher has for the students.

Reflection: *In what ways can I communicate expectations consistent with my beliefs?* The first step is to identify your expectations for student learning behaviors and attitudes. Once you know what is important to you and your students, plan direct and indirect methods for communicating and reinforcing those expectations. Periodic tape recording and self-analysis, or peer observation, can help you monitor the expectations you communicate to your students.

4. Task conditions

Observation: *How are learning tasks planned and implemented to promote student motivation?*   Observations could be made over a period of several days or of a single lesson. Focus your observations on the conditions of the learning task that are related to student motivation. Describe the way the task is introduced. For example, listen for a connection between this lesson and previous or future lessons and for the use of cognitive organizers, curiosity or cognitive dissonance, or the unique or unexpected. Note the general tone of the delivery.

Describe the ways students are mentally or physically involved such as watching, listening, writing, and orally or physically responding. Note if the tasks involve lower level skills (such as drill and practice) or higher level skills (such as discovery or problem solving).

Notice the techniques the teacher uses to make the task appealing such as hands-on activities, gamelike elements, working with others, and addressing intrinsically interesting topics. Also describe teacher attempts to minimize the students' level of anxiety. Note the use of flexible time limits, the giving of adequate assistance and feedback, the grading structure, and opportunities to redo the task.

Analysis: *What learning task conditions appear to promote student motivation?* Describe which ways of introducing tasks seem to engage the students more readily. Identify the information that should be included in a task introduction. Describe the introductions that seem to have little positive effect on student motivation.

List the ways students are actually involved in accomplishing the task. If their involvement is relatively passive, think of ways to replan the activity so students could be more actively involved. Determine if the task could be redesigned to incorporate elements that are more appealing to the students while still addressing the learning objectives.

Examine the conditions defining the task. Consider the consistency of the conditions and the expected outcomes. Identify possible ways in which the conditions—time limits, feedback to students, assistance from the teacher, the grading structure—could be adjusted to lessen performance anxiety.

Reflection: *How can I plan and conduct learning tasks to promote student motivation?* From observations and your own teaching experiences, identify those learning task conditions that appear to promote student motivation. Think about the elements that should be included in task introductions and plan how to incorporate those elements in future lessons. Look for ways to design tasks for more active student involvement and for more intrinsic appeal. Specify task conditions that are necessary and those that could be adjusted to lessen student anxiety. Remember that it is difficult and possibly undesirable to incorporate these conditions with all learning objectives and tasks.

5. Praise, reward, and criticism

Observation: *What praise, criticism, and rewards are given in the classroom?* Record all instances of praise, criticism, and the use of rewards that occur during the observation period. Write down the specific statements or rewards used and the circumstances (why given, how given, which group or individual was addressed, and the reaction). Notice whether students other than the target student react in an apparent positive or negative manner and describe the reaction. If the action is rather fast paced, it might be helpful to tape-record the lesson and add any additional information to your classroom log.

Analysis: *What impact does the use of rewards, praise, and criticism appear to have on student motivation?*   Summarize your observation information to identify patterns in the use of rewards, praise, or criticism. Determine how frequently rewards, praise, and criticism are used. Note patterns related to how the rewards, praise, and criticism were given, whom they were given to, and apparent student reactions. Your analysis can provide some insights into the immediate effect of the use of praise, criticism, and rewards.

Reflection: *How can I use praise, criticism, and rewards to promote student motivation?*   Based on your observations and on the research findings, suggest guidelines for working with your students or a group of students you know best. Try to determine when praise, criticism, and rewards may be appropriate and when their use may be counterproductive.

 ## DEVELOPMENT AND RENEWAL ACTIVITIES

1. Reflect on your own efficacy as a student or compare your own feelings of efficacy with those of your classmates. Think about the degree to which you attributed success to effort, your persistence in accomplishing tasks, and your commitment to achieving goals. Also consider the influences teachers and significant others (adults or peers) had on your sense of efficacy. These reflections should have implications for your instructional practice. What conclusions can you draw about how independence, maturity, confidence, the need for peer or adult approval, the willingness to take risks, and self-directedness affect performance?

2. Identify one (or several) of your college professors who appears to exhibit a high degree of teacher efficacy. Interview the instructor(s) about his or her sense of control over student outcomes. You might ask about:

- Their assumptions concerning motivation to learn
- The level of commitment they feel toward motivating students
- The ways they help their students succeed
- Their sense of responsibility in providing conditions that foster positive learning attitudes

3. Talk with teachers or college professors about how their assessment practices relate to student attitudes toward learning. Have the instructors tell you about assessment procedures related to a particular lesson or series of lessons. Address such questions as:

- How did you preassess your students' level of readiness for the learning task(s)?
- How did the preassessment information influence your planning? What specific adjustments did you make?
- How did you structure your lesson to accommodate the individual or special needs of your students (through remedial or extension activities)?
- What differentiation between students, if any, do you make with your postassessment standards?
- In order to ensure adequate opportunities for students to demonstrate what they know, how do you determine the appropriate number of items to include on your assessments?

After talking with several instructors about their assessment practices, determine which practices seem to be especially helpful in fostering student success.

4. Make developing student motivation a high-priority professional goal. If you are currently teaching, begin by identifying a student with motivational problems. Follow a systematic plan for addressing that student's problems. The following steps should be included in your plan:

- Observe and record the specific behaviors exhibited by the student. Be sure to note times and conditions of the learning activity or intervening factors.
- Analyze your information to determine the conditions that seem to positively or negatively influence the student's level of motivation. Pay special attention to the antecedent conditions that seem to either promote or interfere with appropriate learning behavior and attitude.
- Interview the student to learn which needs, goals, and strategies are important to the student.
- Read the suggested annotated references in this chapter for ideas.
- Enumerate feasible strategies that you could use to capitalize on the conditions that seem to promote motivation.
- Plan to implement the strategies you consider to be the most promising.
- Continually assess the impact of the strategies, looking at intended and unintended consequences.

- If the strategies are working well, maintain them and recycle through the plan to identify strategies that might address other motivation problems of your target student or other potential target students.

5. Organize a small group of teachers who are interested in developing and sharing strategies for helping students experience success and develop greater self-esteem and positive attitudes about school. Use the following guidelines to give direction to the work of the group:

- Schedule definite meeting times. The group might enjoy meeting at a relaxed atmosphere away from school.
- For each session, each participant should be ready to share one example of a positive approach in helping a student succeed. It does not matter how encompassing the strategy is (it could apply to one student or all students). The presenter should provide enough information so other teachers can use the approach.
- In discussing, "Yes, but . . ." is not allowed, as in, "*Yes,* I understand how that could work for you, *but* it just wouldn't work for me." Openmindedness should be a criterion of membership.
- Giving up is definitely not allowed. There is always another approach to try.

6. If you are a faculty member, you could enlist other faculty members in a project to assess the school climate as it impacts student motivation. Instruments are available that can be used to evaluate the perceptions of groups involved in the entire school culture (e.g., students, teachers, parents, and support staff). Such an assessment can give a realistic picture of *what is* in order to set priorities for *what ought to be.* Targeting certain areas for change can promote a norm for achievement and effort.

7. Develop an interest inventory to give to students you work with (your own or your supervising teacher's). The inventory could cover short-term and long-term goals; school and leisure activities; favorite things such as possessions, books, TV, music, food, movies, and heroes; dislikes such as things they tend to put off or avoid; and past accomplishments. Be sure to include school-related and home-related areas. One of the easiest response formats is the open-ended or fill-in-the-blank question. You may want to give some personal examples from your own inventory to get things started and to let the students know about you.

After students have completed the inventory, if some have not been filled out to your satisfaction, follow up with an informal interview. Keep the approach nonthreatening, conversational, and supportive. What you learn from the inventory can help you incorporate topics of interest and develop more appealing rewards and incentives.

8. Teacher efficacy is based on the belief that the teacher can affect student outcomes. One way to develop a sense of efficacy or confidence in dealing with students with motivational problems is to track your progress. Begin a process of systematic, periodic reflection on the positive strides students have made. You can look at individual students or groups of students, but look carefully. Focus on the small steps forward; giant leaps are seldom observed. Describe specific changes you have noticed in the students collectively or individually. The changes in attitude and behavior will be incremental and need to be noticed, reinforced, and celebrated.

In general, it is a good idea to stop periodically and reflect on your current efforts in providing conditions that encourage student motivation. Providing those conditions takes analysis, thoughtful planning, and careful assessment.

9. Think about a group of students you know fairly well. Reflect on three of the most able students and three of the least able students. Write down all the adjectives that describe these two groups of students. Focus on the gender of the students, the physical attributes, personality traits, friends, intellectual, verbal, and athletic abilities, manners and demeanor, family status, and any personal association you have had with the family such as prior contact with brothers, sisters, or relatives.

In examining your list of descriptors, look for patterns in the qualities or characteristics that may influence your expectations about these students. Knowing what influences your expectations can help you monitor these influences.

10. Help students develop goals that are realistic and attainable and will help them achieve self-efficacy. The goals could be related to one subject area or to learning behavior in general. Guide students in setting goals that are important to them. Decide on appropriate check points and ways to determine if progress is being made. Be sure that success is measured against preset standards and against students' previous performance. Remember to allocate time for checking student progress in your plan book. Reflect on how effective goal setting can disrupt or reverse the failure orientation of the students.

11. Rehearse or role-play ways to help students develop self-efficacy. The things teachers do and say are powerful influences on students' attributional patterns. Be sure to address:

- What teachers can say or demonstrate to the entire group, such as modeling effort, using a systematic approach, and showing persistence
- What teachers can say to individual students, especially when giving feedback, cuing, or reinforcing
- What teachers can do, such as giving the right amount of assistance and helping students set attainable goals

Instructional Management

5.
Developing Classroom Management Strategies

COMMENTARY

We have found that many people have difficulty differentiating between the concepts of managing classrooms and disciplining students. When we talk with administrators about prospective teachers, they often say that they want teachers who can effectively manage student behavior. When we ask about the managerial behaviors that the administrators value, the focus of the discussion often shifts to classrooms with "good discipline." Student teachers regularly lament that they have not had enough training in discipline and management. They, too, fail to differentiate between these two important interactive functions.

In this chapter we have concentrated on the research and strategies that are the basis for effective management. The following chapter focuses on responding to student misbehavior and includes those factors that are most often associated with discipline. We believe that it is important to separate these two teaching responsibilities so that teachers can study, analyze, and put into practice strategies that will create school and classroom environments that are most conducive to student learning.

Although teachers often work in isolation, they tend to have many common concerns. They want to do everything possible to help their students learn and develop so that they will feel successful and develop positive attitudes about school. It is difficult, however, for individual teachers to create a climate that is positive and productive without support and assistance from administrators and colleagues. With the changing social structure, it has become even more imperative for parents to be involved in establishing and supporting policies and procedures that will lead to effectively managed schools.

With the demands and expectations placed on teachers, it is surprising that so many elect to stay in the classroom. Beginning teachers enter the profession enthusiastic about the difference they can make in the lives of their students. They soon realize that much of their time, especially early in the school year, has to be devoted to managerial tasks. Class sizes continue to be large and numerous interruptions must be dealt with every day. New materials and equipment provide exciting learning options for students but must be carefully managed and integrated into required instruction. Teachers are usually delighted to have computers in their classrooms and materials that will help meet individual learning needs, but with new opportunities come additional management responsibilities.

Teachers who stay in the profession have usually been successful at managing the complex environments in which they work. They have established rules and routines that help their classrooms run smoothly and effectively. They have spent considerable time teaching and monitoring the routines that help to keep students on-task and minimize the amount of time lost due to transitions and interruptions. They have been effective in developing students who can work independently and who feel responsible for their own behavior. Successful, experienced teachers often tell us that they have developed most of their effective management strategies intuitively, through trial and error.

Beginning teachers generally are expected to start their teaching careers with the same level of management proficiency as their more experienced colleagues. All too often they find they do not have the background, training, and experience to effectively manage their classrooms. Unfortunately, they may be left to sink or swim because their colleagues do not have the time to assist them and their administrators and supervisors may not be available to give support and assistance. In spite of the adversity faced by novice teachers, the majority, over a period of time, do develop classroom management strategies that work well enough for them to feel they are successful teachers. Unfortunately, some novice teachers who have the potential to be excellent leave the profession because they have not been able to cope with the myriad activities they are expected to manage while providing the best possible learning experiences for their students.

RATIONALE

More and more expectations are placed on schools and individual teachers without any substantive changes in the organization and structure of education. Schools are expected to have the best possible test results so they can remain competitive both in our own educational system and with school systems in other countries. This form of accountability continues even when schools go through different phases and stages of educational reform.

In keeping with the accountability movement, the number of prescriptions from state educational agencies has increased. These prescriptions include what to teach, the amount of time to be allocated to certain subjects, and even how to teach the required curriculum. Demands have increased without any corresponding increase in the amount of time in the school day or school year and, in most cases, without any additional resources.

At the school level other factors complicate the management task. The majority of schools have increased the number of pull-out programs over the past few years. These special programs are designed to help students needing different kinds of remediation, students with special talents, and to provide opportunities to use new technology such as computer laboratories. Although they provide important educational opportunities, these programs make it virtually impossible for classroom teachers to keep their students on-task while they maintain a smooth instructional pace.

Within the classroom more and more attention is being given to multitask arrangements to accomplish learning goals and objectives. For years elementary teachers have used reading groups so they can give close attention to the learning needs of each child. Now it is not uncommon to observe classrooms at all levels in some form of multitask arrangement throughout most of the school day. Cooperative learning groups have become especially popular and are used by teachers at all grade levels and in most subject areas.

For classroom management to be effective, several important decisions have to be made at the school level. The number and types of pull-out programs should be agreed upon. Every attempt needs to be made to minimize the interruptions caused by these programs. The scheduling of all programs and activities should protect the amount of learning time allocated to teachers. Administrators should establish school-wide rules and procedures that demonstrate the importance of the quality use of school time.

Successful teachers know they must quickly establish rules and routines that will help them make the best use of allocated time. They know the time spent doing this early in the year will have important payoffs throughout the year. Beginning teachers who have not had the background and experience of their more experienced colleagues face additional challenges. They may not have had the opportunity to work closely with their supervising teachers at the start of a school year when they were involved in their preparation programs. In many cases, preparation programs provide very little experience in organizing and managing multitask classroom structures. The majority of the professional courses in this area offer lecture and discussion with very little modeling of how to organize and teach in multitask structures.

Students in preservice programs and beginning teachers can benefit from a clear understanding of the classroom management research and from suggestions on how to develop effective classroom management programs. Experienced teachers, no matter how successful, can improve their programs by reviewing the research, analyzing what they are doing that may or may not be consistent with research findings, reflecting on the similarities and differences, and refining their approaches to ensure that they are making the very best use of their allocated learning time.

RESEARCH SYNTHESIS

The Concept of Classroom Management

Teachers commonly view classroom management as synonymous with discipline. Classroom management is a broad concept while discipline is much narrower. Classroom management is defined as "the provisions and procedures necessary to create and maintain an environment in which teaching and learning can occur" (Duke, 1987, p. 548), while discipline is "the treatment of misbehavior in classrooms and schools" (Doyle, 1986b, p. 394). A comprehensive school and classroom management system attends to both preventive management practices which are intended to promote a positive learning climate and corrective management practices which deal with instances of misbehavior.

According to the research evidence, in every process-product study, effective management skills are positively related to student achievement (Hawley & Rosenholtz, 1984). Effective management practices increase the time students are engaged in academic tasks. Student performance and achievement are higher when behaviors incompatible with achievement are reduced (Hawley & Rosenholtz, 1984). Management strategies must address ways to increase student engagement.

Although research provides insights into effective strategies and practices, management is a complex process. Classroom management is both an art and a science; it has an intuitive dimension, as teachers relate to students, as well as a technological dimension, as they apply management skills (Lasley, 1981). Teachers must consider the custodial and socialization needs of students as well as learning concerns (Evertson & Emmer, 1982). They play an important role in developing work and social responsibility in students in addition to helping them achieve academic goals. Teachers also must attend to contextual factors. Successful management strategies must be appropriate to student needs and characteristics, teacher needs and characteristics, and organizational constraints (Duke, 1982).

Effective classroom management practices are built on the following underlying assumptions:

1. The teacher is the final authority and instructional decision maker.
2. Good classroom management is related to sound instructional practices.
3. The focus is on preventing problems from occurring rather than on re-acting to problems.
4. A comprehensive management system attends to both preventive and corrective management.

The teacher manages the classroom by acting on these assumptions. The teacher is responsible for managing the classroom in a positive manner and should clearly be in charge. It is important for teachers to know that they can be in charge and positive at the same time (Brandt, 1984). Classroom management decisions often parallel instructional decisions. During both the preactive and interactive phases of teaching, decisions are made that affect the students' level of engagement, motivation to learn, and performance. Teachers who are effective classroom managers place a high priority on planning management procedures that prevent inappropriate behavior. The preventive procedures used by teachers help to determine the management strategies used during the interactive phase of instruction. The conditions and actions that influence classroom management are depicted in Figure 5–1.

Preventive management practices encourage appropriate behavior and increase students' desire to be involved in learning activities. Management is a dynamic phenomenon which is embedded in an unpredictable context. Teachers and students must jointly maintain order in an environment where many immediate concerns and demands arise (Doyle, 1986b). Individual classrooms are strongly influenced by the total school environment. Although many teachers can independently develop productive classroom environments, classroom management is most effective when the total school works from the same management assumptions and toward the achievement of common learning goals. Schoolwide management systems should guide the work of teachers as they plan and implement their management programs.

Schoolwide Management

Schoolwide management should be the concern of all participants. Attention should be given to learning expectations, school policies, and the physical environment. School administrators, teachers, students, and parents should be involved in the development of management expectations.

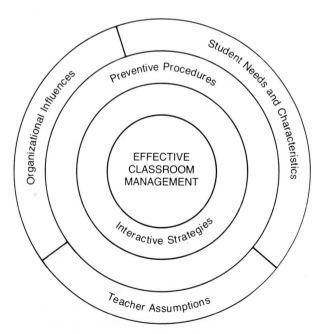

FIGURE 5–1. Conditions and actions affecting classroom management

Parents can play a significant role in establishing behavior expectations. They can provide important information about their values and the commitment they will make to support school policies and procedures. Their involvement is needed in developing preventive management practices, not just when problems have occurred. Parents should also be consulted when changes in school policies are being initiated.

School administrators can provide the leadership necessary for establishing effective school policies and procedures. They can establish links between the school and community that can be instrumental in promoting appropriate student behavior (Swick, 1985b).

As the school leader, the principal is a major force in setting the overall climate. The climate should be pleasant, positive, goal driven, and work oriented, with a strong emphasis on academic excellence. The principal should take a problem-solving approach to management problems which looks at causes rather than symptoms (Lasley & Wayson, 1982). The principal models commitment to promoting the school as a place for learning and as a place that rewards and recognizes effort, improvement, and outstanding performance and behavior.

Specific actions by school principals can promote appropriate student behavior. The way principals interact with teachers, staff members, and students is a powerful influence on how teachers, staff members, and students interact with one another. The pervasiveness of this influence is reflected in a collegial and supportive school climate. Principals can work to limit the number of classroom interruptions such as announcements over the intercom and messages sent from the administrative offices. The number of school assemblies and the frequency of students being taken out of class also make it difficult for teachers to attend to learning and effectively manage student behavior. Disruption of learning time reduces student achievement and increases management problems for teachers (Hawley & Rosenholtz, 1984).

School administrators are also responsible for maintaining a physical environment that is conducive to learning and on-task behavior. The noise level of a school may be distracting to students and affect their performance (Arends, 1988). Orderly movement through the school, logical use of space, and efficient use of equipment and materials are all factors that need to be properly managed by the school administrator. School cleanliness and a pride in the physical appearance of the school are examples of conditions that can provide a positive environment for teachers and students (Ainley, 1987).

Teachers and support staff should be involved in developing and maintaining schoolwide management policies and procedures. It is important that they assist in the formulation of policies they will be expected to support. The policies should be clear but flexible enough to allow for teacher autonomy (Cangelosi, 1988). Expectations must be clearly communicated and carefully monitored. Too often, schools spend little time developing and communicating expectations but a good deal of time enforcing them (Englander, 1986).

Students should also be involved in establishing schoolwide expectations. The degree of involvement depends, of course, on their level of maturity. Older students can be active participants in developing policies, procedures, and expectations for behavior. Younger students can make suggestions that should be given thoughtful consideration by teachers and administrators.

Establishing a Positive Climate

Each classroom has its own unique climate. Establishing a positive climate for learning with good working relationships between teachers and students is more important than any specific management technique (Brophy & Putnam, 1979). Although it is difficult to describe what constitutes a positive classroom climate, specific, observable teacher behaviors can help create such a climate. Students need to have the feeling of being treated equally by teachers. Teachers should show sincerity, concern, positive expectations, cooperation, respect, credibility, tolerance, and consistency in words and actions (Brophy & Putnam, 1979). The primary management task for teachers is to maintain maximum cooperation within the total classroom environment. Cooperation occurs when most students are willing to be active participants in the program of action. Cooperation is a jointly constructed phenomenon between teachers and students (Doyle, 1986b). Teachers' managerial skills affect the quality and quantity of cooperation. A neutral climate has also been found to be productive. A warm, social-emotional climate is not a necessity; however, a negative environment is almost always counterproductive.

A learning environment characterized by student cooperation and taking responsibility in academic pursuits is associated with higher achievement (Anderson & Prawat, 1983). Teachers need to give responsibility to students and also teach students how to deal with that responsibility. Responsible behavior is exhibited by students showing self-regulation and self-control during academic tasks and social interactions. These students have internalized the standards of behavior; the teacher does not have to force compliance. Students with an internalized locus of control devote energy to academic tasks, are concerned about grades, and are responsible (Maples, 1985). Throughout the school adults should foster students' independent work behavior with a minimum amount of supervision. Although it is not desirable for students to work regularly without supervision, at times they will have to be self-sufficient or work with very little assistance from their teachers.

On the secondary level, student-delegated work responsibility is associated with higher achievement, although achievement is affected by the socioeconomic status of the students. Higher SES students achieve more when students schedule their own work. Lower SES students are engaged more when teachers assign the tasks (Hawley & Rosenholtz, 1984). Students accept greater responsibility for their achievement when they have a strong sense of personal control over outcomes.

Effective teachers develop leadership styles that build cohesiveness and consensus between teacher and students. Their styles encourage students to work toward consensus and develop greater cohesiveness with other students. An authoritative approach may be more efficient but may not be as successful as a democratic style in terms of the affective quality of the experience (Brophy & Putnam, 1979). Teachers should be the dominant leaders in their classrooms with students being active participants. Classrooms should be teacher directed with the responsibility for learning divided between teachers and students (Levin & Long, 1981). When there is too much pupil freedom, student learning and creativity are adversely affected (Soar & Soar, 1979). The responsibility for developing positive classroom environments, however, is a joint responsibility of teachers and students. Their respective responsibilities are summarized in Figure 5–2.

Establishing a positive classroom environment is a challenging task due to the complexity of life in a classroom. Doyle (1986b) identified several classroom variables that influence teachers' ability to establish positive environments: multidimensionality (many people doing numerous tasks), simultaneity (many events occurring at the same time), immediacy (numerous interactions needing quick attention), and unpredictability (unexpected events occurring). These variables occur in all classrooms and make up some of the constant pressures of teaching (p. 395).

Classroom climate affects student motivation. A supportive, encouraging, organized environment is a necessity for students to feel motivated. Anderson et al. (1988) pointed out the need for teachers to employ effective management techniques to make the classroom environment predictable and reasonable for students. This helps students understand how to control outcomes.

Teacher Characteristics and Skills

Teachers need strong interpersonal skills in order to establish positive classroom climates. They also need skill in managing groups. If teachers only dealt with one student at a time, there would be little need for group-processing skills (Doyle,

Responsibility	Teacher	Student
Establish Cooperative Climate	Organize environment Support, encourage all students Treat all students equally	Come to school with a positive attitude
Maintain Cooperation	Employ effective managerial techniques	Participate willingly in classroom activities
Foster Student Responsibility	Delegate responsibility Teach students how to deal with responsibility	Accept responsibility for learning Regulate attention Control social interaction
Develop a Cooperative Leadership Style	Build cohesive relationships Work for consensus Balance teacher control and student freedom	Develop cohesive relationships with peers and teacher

FIGURE 5–2. Responsibilities for building a positive classroom environment

1986b). But teachers must deal with diverse student groups, which requires information processing and decision-making skills based on a knowledge of effective management practices. They need skill in conflict resolution and problem solving. They also need to develop techniques to deal with individual students' personal and adjustment problems.

Teachers are active classroom managers who establish and maintain order by planning, organizing, orchestrating, and reacting to individual students and the total group (Doyle, 1986b). They make preactive decisions that help them focus on academic tasks. Effective classroom managers analyze classroom tasks, teach students the going-to-school skills, see the classroom from the students' perspective, and monitor student behavior (Duke, 1982).

Kounin (1970) identified several managerial behaviors that teachers use to prevent student misbehavior, known as withitness, overlapping, and group alerting. *Withitness* is a process whereby teachers are aware of what is happening at all times. They monitor to detect inappropriate behavior early and accurately. Timing errors (waiting too long) and target errors (reprimanding the wrong student) are avoided. Withitness is a teacher behavior that is strongly related to student engagement.

Effective teachers are able to do more than one thing at a time. They handle routine tasks and individual demands simultaneously without disrupting the focal activity. This phenomenon is referred to as *overlapping*. Overlapping is especially important in classrooms that have multitask arrangements. A related management strategy is known as smoothness and momentum, meaning the class moves through the instruction at a brisk pace with few interruptions. Classroom activities are maintained when teachers exhibit a continuous academic signal or focus. Teachers direct students with relevant stimuli or cues which help them to be more attentive to academic tasks.

Group alerting is the process of keeping students attentive to presentations and holding them accountable for learning. Group alerting techniques include deliberately managing the response opportunity for students (e.g., selecting responders randomly and having a broad response distribution by including choral responses, calling on volunteers and nonvolunteers, and redirecting responses to other students), pausing before calling on a student, and alerting students to challenges. Occasional use of contextually appropriate group alerting and accountability techniques is recommended. The technique of calling on students randomly and unpredictably is not positively related to student learning in all cases. If teachers notice they are overusing group alerting, they should reexamine their total classroom management systems.

Kounin's study of teachers' managerial behavior emphasized the importance of the role of teachers in helping students make academic progress. Teachers should exhibit purposeful behaviors and demonstrate that they want to use instructional time constructively (Brophy, 1982). They hold students accountable for their work, review at appropriate times to monitor and provide help, actively monitor during independent work, and return completed work promptly.

Teachers must be alert to student needs, but they must also meet their own needs (Brandt, 1984). Teachers' belief systems play a significant role in the total management system. Teachers who have a clear identity, ego strength or self-confidence, poise, and a pleasant, well-adjusted personality usually establish a reciprocal relationship with students. Effective managers are able to see the classroom from the students' perspective. They listen to students and are in tune with them. These teachers have tolerance and respect for student individuality and develop and maintain a rapport with their students. Their verbal statements are positive rather than negative, expressing what students can do rather than what students cannot do. They provide more descriptive, corrective messages than judgmental statements. They use socialization and positive problem solving instead of punishment (Weber, 1984). They are willing to use instruction and persuasion rather than simply assert their power. Last, they respond supportively and empathetically to students, accepting their feelings, calming frustration, and defusing conflict.

Student Characteristics and Needs

Teachers must attend to the individual and collective needs of their students and at the same time manage instructional transactions. This is a challenging task, especially when classes are large and when programs are departmentalized, with many teachers having well over a hundred student contacts each day. However, teachers who understand the needs of their students are in a better position to prevent misbehavior and help students achieve their academic goals.

The research provides several frames of reference for understanding student needs. Maslow (1943) has done some of the best-known work in this area. Maslow's hierarchy of needs demonstrates that lower level survival and security needs must be satisfied before ego needs can be met. Many teachers have found that Maslow's work helps them understand the behavior of their students.

William Schutz (1966) postulated that individuals have three important interpersonal needs: inclusion, control, and affection. People, he said, need to feel a part of a group if they are to function effectively in a group or classroom. This need for inclusion parallels the belonging need in Maslow's hierarchy. The control need is satisfied when people feel they have the right amount of control in a situation. The affection need is satisfied by having caring relationships with others.

Other theories may help teachers understand the behavior of their students. All teachers should have a frame of reference for understanding their students' psychological and physical needs so they can use the most appropriate management and instructional strategies.

At times students resist teacher work demands in order to meet their own needs (Doyle, 1986b). When teachers engage students in activities that require higher order thinking, or more complex cognitive processing, they create situations that have a higher level of ambiguity and risk. Students use a variety of approaches to adjust the risk and ambiguity to levels they can tolerate. They may do this by quietly negotiating for less demanding expectations or they may simply give up and not respond to teacher demands. Teacher responses, in turn, take a variety of forms but frequently teachers reduce work demands so that the challenge is not so great. This helps to preserve order in the classroom and maintain teacher and student cooperation.

Allen (1986) investigated classroom management practices from the perspective of high school students. He found that one of the most important needs of high school students is the desire to socialize with their friends. At the same time, students expressed a need to pass their courses. The strategies that students used to meet these two primary needs depended on the task demands, the teacher's academic and behavioral expectations, and the overall classroom environment. Students use a variety of strategies to ascertain the teacher's limits and find ways to minimize work so they have more opportunity to socialize. Allen's study suggests that the best classroom learning environment is one that provides students with a good balance of work and opportunities to socialize with their peers while they are engaged in academic activities.

Student characteristics also have a strong influence on classroom management practices. For example, students from rural areas have different characteristics from those of urban students. Suburban students may have characteristics that are different from their rural and urban counterparts. Classroom management concerns will be different for students from different types of community environments (Kohut & Range, 1986).

The intellectual and social developmental stages of students should be considered as teachers devise management strategies (Brophy & Putnam, 1979). Primary grade students are oriented to adults; they want to please and are compliant. The teacher's role is to teach appropriate behavior for children to be socialized into school roles and expectations. Students in the elementary grades are generally receptive to teacher expectations and possess going-to-school skills. Teachers spend less time socializing students. As students progress through the middle grades, they become more peer oriented and in some cases resent authority. Thus management demands are heavy and time-consuming. At this stage, private, positive student-teacher interactions can be satisfying. Older high school students tend to be more settled, academically focused, and have more mature attitudes. The management demands for teachers usually decrease during the later high school years (Brophy, 1982).

Grouping practices also influence classroom management expectations and procedures. When groups encompass a wide range of student needs and characteristics, the teacher must give close attention to organization and management practices. More planning is needed, and student progress has to be carefully monitored (Emmer & Evertson, 1981).

Most teachers have students in their classrooms who have very special needs or characteristics that are related to physical and emotional problems. Although few management prescriptions will work for all students, teachers can be guided by several general principles. They need to understand why students exhibit behavior that may differ from the norm (Steere, 1988). Whatever the special need, each student should be accepted in a supportive manner. This is especially true for students who have been victims of abuse. In all cases teachers should have appropriately high but attainable academic and behavioral expectations. Teachers tend to be more tolerant of behavioral disturbances from low-ability students (Hawley & Rosenholtz, 1984). However, if some students are allowed to be disruptive, the opportunity to learn for all students is adversely affected.

The research leaves little doubt that student characteristics and needs have a significant impact on classroom climate. Teachers must have the skills and understanding necessary to take student needs into account as they work to establish positive classroom climates. Teachers' belief systems also influence how they respond to student needs. The influences brought to bear on the classroom environment by teachers and students are presented in Figure 5–3.

Beginning the Year

Prevention is the key to effective classroom management. At the start of each new year teachers should have plans for creating orderly, predictable environments that are based on the needs and characteristics of the students. It is easier to teach appropriate behavior than it is to correct inappropriate behavior.

Proactive classroom management begins prior to the first day of school. Time spent on management during the first few weeks of school provides additional time for instruction later on. The amount of time students are off task during the first few days of school will be indicative of the amount of off-task behavior during the year (Association for Supervision and Curriculum Development, 1988). Teachers need to

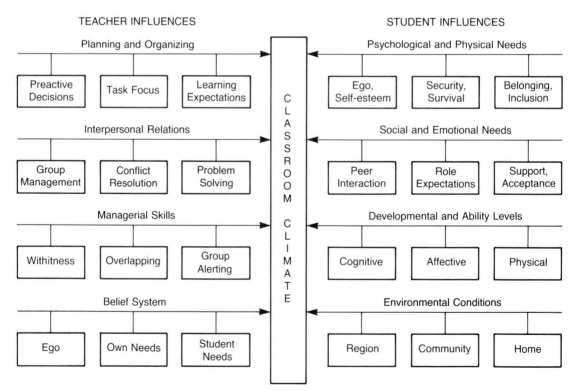

FIGURE 5–3. Teacher and student influences that affect classroom climate

help students feel secure and prevent early problems from happening (Evertson, Emmer, Clements, Sanford, & Worsham, 1984). A total classroom management system helps to prevent many of the most common management problems. The components that should be included in a comprehensive management system are depicted in Figure 5–4.

The first phase of the management system is to determine appropriate expectations based on students' developmental level, amount of self-control, degree of independence, and readiness to assume responsibility. The behaviors that are expected and monitored become the norm for the classroom. Norms greatly influence student behavior since individuals are socialized to these norms.

Expectations are translated into rules and procedures. Rules and procedures communicate expectations and are basic to the organization of the classroom. Rules indicate general behaviors that are acceptable and unacceptable. They are standards for behavior that are not related to a particular activity (Evertson et al., 1984). Students need guidelines for appropriate behavior; they need structure. The guidelines may vary, but every productive classroom has rules and procedures.

Component	Definition	Function	Source
Expectations	Assumptions teachers make about future student behavior	Create underlying foundation of classroom management system	Values and philosophy of the school and community
Rules	Statements that communicate general expectations and standards of behavior	Provide guidelines for behavior Promote and sustain desired behavior	Expectations, adapted to meet student characteristics and needs
Procedures	Routines for specific activities	Help accomplish specific objectives Increase efficient use of time Act as support system for the teacher	Expectations, rules, student characteristics and needs
Consequences	Rewards and penalties for appropriate and inappropriate behavior	Support management and instructional processes Deter inappropriate behavior and encourage compliance with rules and procedures	Expectations, rules, procedures, student characteristics and needs

FIGURE 5–4. Essential components of a comprehensive classroom management system

Every classroom rule should have a purpose, such as encouraging on-task behavior, promoting courteous behavior, providing safety and comfort, and preventing disturbance to other classes. If a rule does not address an important purpose, it may not be necessary (Cangelosi, 1988). The following guidelines are helpful in developing and implementing effective rules:

1. Have only as many rules as necessary to address specific management purposes.
2. Rules should clearly state and communicate expectations.
3. State rules in positive terms that emphasize what students should do rather than what they should not do.
4. Involve students in developing rules whenever appropriate.
5. Thoroughly discuss the rules and the rationale for them.
6. Post rules as reminders of what is expected and refer to them as needed.

High school teachers often establish rules differently from elementary teachers. They may not hand out a list of rules or explicitly teach the rules; rather, the rules seem to be a part of the common knowledge shared by teachers and students. They become clear as problems occur and teachers respond with appropriate actions. In junior high classes, teachers appear to focus more on rehearsing academic work routines rather than on teaching rules and procedures (Doyle, 1986b).

Procedures differ from rules. Procedures are developed for particular activities such as turning in assignments or being excused from activities. Used repeatedly, procedures become routines that increase efficient use of classroom time and decrease the need for teacher direction. Procedures are support structures or subroutines that help instruction continue in an uninterrupted fashion (Doyle & Carter, 1987, p. 203). Classroom procedures are useful in the following areas (Evertson et al., 1984):

1. Using room facilities such as learning centers, teacher and student desks, and storage areas
2. Communicating expectations for what students should do during seatwork and teacher-led activities
3. Beginning the day and transition activities during the day
4. Organizing for small-group activities and returning to the normal classroom structure
5. Responding to interruptions such as students leaving the room and schoolwide drills

Adequate time should be allocated for teaching procedures, modeling behavior, and student practice with corrective feedback. For elementary teachers up to one third of the time during the first few days of the school year is spent teaching, monitoring, and reinforcing rules and procedures (ASCD, 1988). Teachers should teach, rehearse, and monitor rules and procedures until they are followed automatically. Reteaching may be necessary. Teachers should view noncompliance with rules and procedures or instances of inappropriate behavior as an indication that learning is incomplete.

Teachers need to monitor adherence to rules and procedures systematically. Adherence should be reinforced until it becomes automatic. Effective classroom managers use rules to sustain desired behavior. Whole-group activities requiring less complex management procedures should be used while rules and procedures are being implemented. Teachers should impose firm but flexible limits that may be adjusted as students mature and become more independent and responsible.

Consequences for appropriate and inappropriate behavior need to be identified and should evolve systematically from expectations and related rules and procedures. A logical relationship should exist between misbehavior and penalties (Emmer & Evertson, 1981). Planning which consequences to use ahead of time allows teachers to act promptly, but not emotionally or hastily. Prior thought helps formulate reasonable consequences and helps teachers avoid inconsistencies which lead students to perceive teachers as being unfair.

Researchers are not in total agreement as to whether or not teachers should explicitly state the identified consequences. Communicating the consequences of misbehavior deters students from misbehaving in order to discover the consequences for themselves (ASCD, 1988). On the other hand, prior knowledge of consequences may not discourage students from the inappropriate behavior if they are willing to "pay the price."

Consequences have three components: clearly identified desired behavior, student feedback about the behavior, and contingent and consistent application (Emmer & Evertson, 1981). Positive and negative consequences should address behaviors that are critical to the management and instructional functions of teaching. Positive consequences should occur when students follow rules because it is important for teachers to reward effort and conduct in addition to achievement (Evertson et al., 1984). The reinforcer may be internal (within the student), which is the ideal, or external (provided by the teacher). Rewards need to be feasible and can include symbols, recognition, activities, or physical materials. Negative consequences should occur when students behave inappropriately in order to discourage the reoccurrence of the misbehavior. The use of consequences is discussed in detail in Chapter 6.

Structuring Physical Space

Prior to the students' arrival in the classroom, teachers should structure the room so they can effectively accomplish their instructional goals and manage their classrooms efficiently. The physical arrangement of the classroom does reflect the teacher's need for control and managerial style. Room arrangements can have a significant impact on student behavior and attitude (Arends, 1988). For example, students' attention can be increased if they have an unobstructed view of the teacher. Desks should be arranged so students can be easily monitored during instruction and when they are doing seatwork. Traffic patterns should allow students to move about the classroom without distracting others.

Research on seating arrangements is limited and sometimes contradictory, but seat location does appear to affect student achievement (Steere, 1988). Action zones tend to form around the teacher where student participation is greatest (Adams & Biddle, 1970). There is generally more teacher-student interaction at the front of the classroom and down the center, in an area referred to as the *T* zone (Weinstein, 1987).

There are strong indicators that where students choose to sit reflects their attitude about school. Students who sit near the front tend to have more positive attitudes about learning and their potential for success. Students who prefer to sit in the back generally have more negative attitudes about school and their ability to succeed (Weinstein, 1987).

A teacher's choice of seating arrangement, such as rows, clusters, or a horse-shoe, should promote the accomplishment of the learning goals and objectives. For example, traditional rows may be more appropriate when students are receiving information or are doing independent work. More students can have direct eye contact with the teacher. Row arrangements seem to promote more on-task behavior and inhibit student talking. Horseshoe or circle arrangements are helpful during student discussions. The opportunity for direct eye contact and nonverbal communication makes it more likely that students will speak to those directly across from them rather than to those beside them (Weinstein, 1987).

The research provides guidelines for consideration in planning room arrangements (Weinstein, 1987; Doyle, 1986b). Because their position in the classroom determines the action zone, teachers should be able to move throughout the classroom so that they can interact with all students. There should be a home base for everyone to return to if management becomes a problem. Seat assignments should be changed occasionally. Seating arrangements should facilitate interaction and the development of student leadership potential. Figure 5–5 shows a checklist that teachers can use to evaluate the physical arrangement of their classrooms.

My classroom is organized so that

☑ Student behavior is easily monitored.

☑ Traffic patterns are not distracting.

☑ The total classroom is a learning action zone.

☑ Maximum attention can be given to learning goals and tasks.

☑ Students can interact appropriately.

☑ Task structure can be changed quickly with minimum disruption.

FIGURE 5–5. A checklist for organizing classrooms

Classroom Monitoring

Effective teachers know that they can prevent misbehavior, reduce the number of management incidents, and maintain a high level of task involvement by systematically monitoring the classroom. Monitoring usually involves the teacher's physically moving around the classroom to observe student behavior and give appropriate feedback. Monitoring is especially important when students are doing seatwork, working independently, or working in small groups.

Monitoring increases engagement and improves student achievement. When students work without teacher supervision, achievement is usually affected negatively. All students need to be actively supervised by teachers if monitoring is to have maximum effect. Teachers need to be careful not to spend an inordinate amount of time monitoring a few students and neglecting the remainder of the class. They should position themselves appropriately, circulate, look beyond individual students or a small group, avoid becoming absorbed with one student for too long, and on a routine basis check students' progress (Evertson et al., 1984).

Specific techniques teachers can use to monitor student behavior include maintaining eye contact with as many students as possible, periodically scanning the room, staying alert to minor problems, and positioning themselves to prevent misbehavior. When teachers use these behaviors, they communicate withitness (Kounin, 1970). They help teachers maintain a businesslike environment with a high level of task engagement.

PRIMARY REFERENCES

Allen, J. D. (1986). Classroom management: Students' perspectives, goals, and strategies. *American Educational Research Journal, 23*(3), 437–459.

> Allen's unique investigation looks at classroom management from the perspective of high school students. The findings are enlightening and will be helpful to teachers as they develop management practices.

Cangelosi, J. S. (1988). *Classroom management strategies: Gaining and maintaining students' cooperation.* New York: Longman.

> Part 1 discusses what causes students to be cooperative and uncooperative. Part 2 describes how to get students to cooperate and how to keep discipline problems from occurring. Research information and detailed scenarios that will help teachers think about proactive management systems are provided.

Emmer, E. T., Evertson, C. M., Sanford, J. P., Clements, B. S., and **Worsham, M. E.** (1984). *Classroom management for secondary teachers.* Englewood Cliffs, NJ: Prentice-Hall.

Evertson, C. M., Emmer, E. T., Clements, B. S., Sanford, J. P, and **Worsham, M. E.** (1984). *Classroom management for elementary teachers.* Englewood Cliffs, NJ: Prentice-Hall.

These are excellent resource books for novice and experienced classroom teachers. Both books include specific information on planning, implementing, and maintaining positive management systems. Attention is also given to instructional areas that affect management. Detailed examples, checklists, activities, and self-assessment questions for improving classroom management are especially helpful.

Good, T. L., & Brophy, J. E. (1987). *Looking in classrooms* (4th ed.). New York: Harper and Row.

Chapter 6, "Management I: Preventing problems," presents research findings and practical examples of preventive actions teachers have taken to minimize inappropriate student behavior. The focus is on specific management activities, such as rules and room arrangements, and instructional activities, such as the use of praise, cues, and holding students accountable. Observation guides are useful in examining specific areas.

Swick, K. J. (1985). *A proactive approach to discipline: Six professional development modules for educators.* Washington, DC: National Education Association.

Each of the six modules provides definitions, contextual issues, and challenge tasks for teachers to reflect on or discuss with colleagues. The modules address preventive management efforts and guide teachers in clarifying and rethinking their strategies.

RESEARCH IN PRACTICE

Finding 1: Planning for classroom management is a major factor in preventing student misbehavior.

It is much easier to prevent problems than to correct them. Many beginning teachers hear this often in theory classes but do not make the connection to their first teaching experience. Planning for classroom management is a complex task that requires as much understanding and attention as instructional planning. It is not a skill that teachers acquire intuitively but one that comes from considerable thought and careful analysis of effective management practices.

The prevention process begins before school starts each year or even at the end of the previous year. Knowledgeable teachers plan to communicate their behavior and management expectations during the first few days of school. These teachers also try to learn as much as possible about their incoming students prior to the start of the school year. Once they become familiar with the needs and characteristics of their students, they can plan prevention measures that will be more effective.

Scenario.   An experienced primary grade teacher was notified that she would be on a remediation plan the following school year. She was informed that parents were upset with her instruction because students were not performing well in her classes.

Parents also reported that her classes were disorganized and disorderly. The notice reminded her that the principal had earlier asked her to work on improving the management of her classes and that there was no evidence that she had improved. (The principal had not given her any specific assistance with her management problems.)

The teacher's school system acquired the services of an outside consultant with expertise in primary education and instructional research. The consultant and teacher worked together during the summer to develop detailed plans for the next school year. They became familiar with the students who would be in the teacher's class and gave special attention to the unique needs of several students. They spent a considerable amount of time developing classroom expectations and rules that would be consistent with the expectations. They planned the procedures that would be used for managerial tasks such as taking roll, distributing materials, and organizing into groups for specific learning activities. They also took the time to organize and structure the physical arrangement of the classroom so that it would be easy to monitor the behavior of all the students. This planning took place during the summer when there were no teaching demands and pressures to interfere with the planning process.

The planning did not solve all the teacher's problems instantly, but the beginning of the school year was moderately successful, and the teacher began to experience some improvement in managing her class. Students were on task the majority of the time. The teacher stayed in touch with the consultant to make adjustments in her management system to accommodate unforeseen problems. As the year progressed, the teacher experienced fewer and fewer problems and student performance continued to improve. By the end of the year the teacher had been successful enough to be taken off the remediation plan. During the following summer she carefully planned for the upcoming school year using the strategies she had developed the previous year. The second year of this cycle became the best year of her career. Not only was her performance better, but her self-concept improved to the point that she was having a positive impact on her students and her colleagues. The attention to planning was beneficial to both the teacher and her students.

Finding 2: Effectively managed classrooms have a positive impact on student achievement.

Numerous studies and many classroom examples support this finding. When classrooms are effectively managed, students will be more likely to stay on task. Disruptions and distractions are kept to a minimum, and students and teachers are able to concentrate on learning tasks and activities. When students feel that they are successfully achieving what is expected of them, they develop positive attitudes about their performance. As a result, they tend to perform well on a variety of measures of student achievement.

Scenario.   Not long ago we had the opportunity to observe an auto mechanics teacher in a vocational high school. Although the teacher did not have a strong educational background, he had given a considerable amount of thought to which classroom procedures would be most effective with his students. He explained that nearly all of his students were considered failures in their academic high schools. Most of them were not used to succeeding in school and had very poor self-concepts. He pointed out, however, that all of the students in the class we would be observing were successfully mastering the information that they needed prior to using the auto shop. It was clear that the teacher had taken the time to really get to know his students, and he understood that it was important for him to deal with their special needs and characteristics.

We were in the classroom a short time when we realized why the teacher was successful. When the students came into the room, he reminded them about the assignment for the day that was posted on the front chalkboard. He stayed near the door until all of the students were in the room and seated. He moved into the lesson with very little time spent on taking roll and dealing with managerial tasks. As he made his presentation, he moved about the room monitoring all of the students and giving gentle reminders if they got off task. One loud disturbance occurred outside his room during the period, but he quickly responded to it without leaving the room or interrupting the flow of the lesson. One message for a student which could have distracted the class was brought in by an office worker. The teacher took the message to the student without interrupting the lesson. The students were able to maintain their attention on the learning tasks for the entire class period. After observing his class, we understood why this teacher's students meet or exceed their performance expectations.

Finding 3: Schoolwide management policies have a significant effect on individual classroom management programs.

Schoolwide management should focus on developing a pleasant, positive, goal-driven, work-oriented climate that emphasizes academic success. Schoolwide policies should clearly communicate management expectations, and school personnel should monitor them consistently to see that they are implemented. When there are no schoolwide management expectations, or when they are not in harmony with classroom teachers' expectations, it is very difficult for teachers to develop and maintain effective classroom management programs. The lack of management consistency throughout a school is frustrating to students, parents, and teachers. When frustration levels are high, maintaining effective management systems is even more difficult.

Scenario. A large urban school system demonstrated what can happen when improving school and classroom management becomes a high priority. Numerous complaints had been received about the lack of discipline and order in the schools. As a result, the board of education and the superintendent made "improving order in the schools" the highest priority for the entire system. All of the schools responded positively, and plans were made at each school site to improve discipline and classroom management. The plan developed at one high school demonstrated the success that can be achieved when everyone works together to improve the schoolwide management program.

The principal of the high school launched the plan by working with faculty members and students to establish specific improvement objectives which, when achieved, would demonstrate that schoolwide management had improved. One of the objectives was to establish schoolwide discipline and management policies that everyone would understand and accept. In order to achieve this objective, a committee of parents, students, teachers, and administrators was formed. The committee spent many hours discussing school problems and needs and listening to presentations on effective management practices. The committee stayed in close contact with the groups it represented. The groups were eager to give their input about what ought to be included in school management policies. The development process took a good part of the school year, but by the time the policies were ready to be implemented, they had a significant amount of support.

The schoolwide management program was an instant success. There were fewer problems in the hallways and in out-of-class activities. Just as important, classroom management practices improved throughout the school. Teachers developed or adjusted their management expectations so they would be consistent with the total school expectations. As a result, teachers made fewer discipline referrals to the office and students spent more time on task in the majority of the classrooms. One of the most important effects of the new program was improved student achievement. This was partially attributed to improved working relationships between administrators, teachers, parents, and students.

Finding 4: Teachers, parents, students, and support staff should work with appropriate administrators in establishing schoolwide management expectations and procedures.

Research findings from organizational studies consistently show that those who are expected to carry out important policies should be involved in the development process. In addition, many studies demonstrate the powerful effects of group work over individual effort. In too many instances schools and other organizations expect staff to carry out policies that they have not helped develop. If teachers, students, and parents are expected to support schoolwide management procedures, they should be represented in the development process.

Scenario.   Recently a new principal was appointed to a school where the previous principal had taken the responsibility for all schoolwide management activities. The teachers did not involve themselves in the business of the total school and concentrated on managing their own classrooms. The new principal soon realized that a number of schoolwide discipline and management problems needed immediate attention. She called a faculty meeting to discuss her perception of the problems and quickly found out that the majority of the teachers did not feel they should be involved in solving problems outside their classrooms. The principal got the same response from parents, who did not feel they were welcome at the school and who had been conditioned by the previous principal not to express their concerns.

The new principal made the decision to involve the teachers and parents in establishing schoolwide discipline and management policies in spite of resistance (mostly from the teachers) to her leadership style. She was not able to move very rapidly with her approach. Several teachers indicated that she was shirking her responsibility by involving others in solving what they considered to be administrator problems. They were not able to see that if they could work from a common philosophy their individual classrooms could be managed more effectively.

The problem this principal faced has been addressed by several organizational psychologists in their research about leaders and followers. They point out that when any group has been dependent on a strong leader who is willing to make all of the decisions for the group, the group becomes more and more dependent. This dependency tends to weaken the initiative of the followers to solve organizational problems. This phenomenon often occurs in classrooms where teachers have made students so dependent on them that the students will not try to solve many of their own problems. When people have become dependent on others, it takes time and patience for them to accept greater responsibility. The principal of the school described in this scenario had to be patient and persistent in her efforts to get the faculty to work cooperatively to improve the total school.

Finding 5: Well-managed classrooms provide opportunities for students to meet both academic and social needs.

Teachers who attend to the academic and social needs of their students are in a better position to prevent and respond to misbehavior. Management decisions based on an understanding of student characteristics, developmental needs, and behavioral norms are more likely to promote achievement of important academic and social goals. This finding has important implications for beginning teachers. Without a clear understanding of student characteristics and needs, novice teachers may follow general advice they have been given to be tough at the beginning of the school year and gradually ease up as the year progresses. This approach, however, may cause teachers to be viewed as not caring about students and worrying too much about their own needs. Also, these teachers may tend to focus entirely on academic goals and neglect the social needs of students. Considerable evidence supports the view that when teachers' interactions with students are positive and based on mutual respect academic performance is enhanced.

Scenario. A high school physical education student teacher who had been an outstanding basketball player at a nearby university had an unfortunate student teaching experience. He was a physically imposing person who was taller and larger than any other person in the high school. He had been advised by his university coordinator to really start out tough and let the students know who was boss. He followed his coordinator's advice and quickly established that he was in charge and that he would not allow any fooling around in his classes. It did not take the students long to realize that the teacher had unreasonable expectations, especially in his attempt to keep them from socializing with one another when there were natural opportunities for this during games and activities. They responded by doing everything they could to cause him to lose his temper and make irrational threats.

The supervising teacher had to take over the classes and ask the student teacher to observe for a few weeks so that appropriate norms and expectations could be reestablished. It was a tribute to the student teacher that he was willing to observe, take some helpful feedback, and develop a more realistic attitude about how to work with high school students. The supervising teacher also had very high performance expectations, but he was able to balance what he wanted to accomplish with the needs of his students. Because he gave the students the opportunity to achieve some of their personal goals, they were much more positive about performing well in class.

Finding 6: A positive classroom climate promotes cooperative working relationships which help to prevent management problems.

Classrooms that have positive climates have similar observable characteristics. Students in these classrooms respect and cooperate with one another. They often engage in activities that give them opportunities to work together in problem solving and related academic activities. Teachers who have developed positive classrooms demonstrate that they care about their students, and their classroom interactions are based on mutual respect. The work in these classrooms is based on positive expectations. The emphasis is on success rather than on failure. Students know that they will be treated fairly and that teachers really care about them. Thus, cooperative working relationships are common, and there are fewer classroom management problems.

Scenario.   Two high school English teachers in the same school system developed totally different classroom climates. One teacher's classes included some of the most able students in the school. She began each school year by letting the students know that she was totally in charge, that they would do exactly what she told them, and that they were not nearly as bright as they thought they were. Feedback given to the students was often demeaning and used to keep the students in their place. As the school year progressed, the students became hostile and negative toward the teacher, their performance suffered, and by the end of the year many of them verbalized their distaste for English. The teacher left teaching fairly early in her career because she was so unhappy with her work. It is interesting to note, though, that when this teacher was not in the classroom she genuinely seemed to like the students and was quite personable with them.

Another English teacher in the same school system who has always had extraordinarily positive classrooms uses a totally different approach. She begins each school year by letting the students know that she really cares about them and that she wants them to succeed. She treats all of the students with a great deal of respect, and all of her students receive equal treatment. Students are given the opportunity to work together in teams and cooperative learning groups. The academic performance in her classes is excellent, with many of the students achieving beyond their own expectations. The students obviously enjoy their work and have positive attitudes about the teacher and the subject matter. The teacher is positive in and out of the classroom and is a model for other teachers in the system. She is regularly asked to work with student teachers and first-year teachers as a part of their induction process. She is a career teacher who intends to work in the classroom until she retires.

Finding 7: The use of specific managerial skills can prevent student misbehavior.

Recent studies of teachers in action consistently support this finding. Effective teachers carefully plan, organize, and orchestrate their instructional activities. They appear to know what is happening with their students throughout the instructional process. They monitor students' behavior as they manage the complexities of the classroom and keep instruction moving at an appropriate pace. These teachers use a variety of techniques to alert students to ongoing instructional expectations. Because the teacher maintains the flow of instruction and monitors the process, students have fewer opportunities to misbehave.

Scenario.   We have found that teachers can learn the withitness behavior described by Kounin. Simply asking teachers to move about the room and monitor student behavior, especially when the students are doing seatwork, is a helpful first step in developing withitness. Teachers can also be coached to observe and monitor student behavior during recitations and discussions. It is not uncommon for inexperienced teachers to become so engrossed in what they are saying that they forget to monitor what students are doing.

A first-year mathematics teacher asked us to observe one of her more advanced classes because she was concerned about the lack of student participation. She said that participation had been good earlier in the year but that there was less and less as the year went on. The situation proved to be interesting. The teacher, who wrote left-handed, spent most of the period at the front chalkboard demonstrating how to solve complex problems. She had virtually no eye contact with the students because she was facing the board most of the time. When she asked questions, she turned slightly to her right so she could see the students on that side of the room. Students on the left side of the room appeared to be observing what she was doing, but they were not actively engaged in the discussion. It would have been difficult for them to volunteer information without calling out or interrupting what the teacher was doing. The teacher was, in fact, inadvertently discouraging student involvement by not maintaining eye contact with them.

When these observations were shared with the teacher, she was truly surprised that she had been losing contact with her students because of her work at the chalkboard. We agreed that it was fortunate that they were good students or there could have been a number of managerial problems. She said that she had begun to develop this pattern during recent weeks and was not aware of the students' disengagement. She began to make plans to change this aspect of her instruction.

Finding 8:   Classroom management systems must be based on teacher and student needs and take into account students' levels of maturity and socioeconomic needs.

Teachers' needs and belief systems play a dominant role in shaping their approaches to classroom management. Some teachers can operate effectively without having their classes tightly structured, while others must have complete control at all times. Although teacher needs give direction to classroom management procedures, student needs and characteristics must also be taken into consideration. Students come to school with a variety of needs. Some may be hungry and at a survival level, while others may have all of their basic needs met and are capable of functioning at a higher level. Students' levels of maturity must also be taken into consideration when teachers develop their classroom management expectations. At a minimum, classroom management systems should not exacerbate student problems, and generally they should facilitate positive student and teacher relationships.

Scenario.   An intern teacher nearly quit teaching because her supervising teacher expected her to be very informal with the students and impose very little structure in the classroom. The supervising teacher was very effective using this approach because it was consistent with his personality. The intern, however, was a much more structured and formal person who found his approach to be contrary to her needs and belief system. Fortunately, she was able to convince her supervisor that she could be much more successful when her management style was consistent with her personality. He relented, and she went on to become a successful teacher.

Teachers must also be able to adjust their management systems to accommodate the needs of their students. Several years ago, teachers in a middle school were having serious discipline and management problems with students from migrant families. The families worked and lived in what is known as a "migrant stream." They worked on farms and ranches and moved from the south to the north as the seasons changed. The children moved from school to school, seldom staying more than six weeks at a time in any one school. Teachers in this particular school expected the migrant students to understand and adhere to their rules, which had been developed over a period of time with local students. They did not take into account the fact that the migrant students did not feel a sense of inclusion or belonging. The result was confusion, a good deal of hostility from the migrant students, and an increase in the number of management problems.

As management problems continued to increase, the teachers decided to develop a better understanding of the needs, characteristics, and culture of the migrant students. Gradually they were able to adjust their management expectations so that they would be more realistic for these transient students. The climate of the entire school improved and the number of problems significantly decreased.

Finding 9: Establishing rules, routines, and consequences for behavior are critical beginning-of-the-year management activities.

The first few days of school set the stage for the entire year. Successful teachers know that they must carefully plan and put into practice rules and routines they expect students to adhere to during the year. Primary and elementary teachers must spend considerable class time actually teaching rules and routines so that their students understand how to behave in their new environments. This is especially important for kindergarten students, who are going to school for the first time. They do not understand the school culture and norms. They need to go through a socialization process, which should be initiated the first day of school and continued as long as needed. Young children must learn the language patterns and signals that are used to manage group behavior. They may have never been told how to line up with other children or how to take turns when they are using facilities or materials.

Scenario.   A second grade teacher was observed by her principal attempting to teach her students the rules and routines they would be expected to follow when she conducted reading groups. She started off each morning reminding the students about the rules and then enumerated her expectations for seatwork. This process was observed several weeks after school had begun. The principal was surprised when the teacher took 17 uninterrupted minutes to describe what the students were supposed to do during the first part of the morning. By the time she finished, the students were totally confused about what she wanted them to do and asked her to repeat much of what she had told them earlier. The teacher restated what she said, but the students appeared to remain confused when the teacher began working with a reading group. Not only was the teacher poorly organized, she failed to take into account the maturity level of her students. It took a considerable amount of time and effort for her and her principal to restructure her approach to developing and communicating her expectations.

Finding 10: Rules should be based on appropriate expectations, have clear purposes, and state in positive terms how students are to behave.

Rules should help students learn what is considered appropriate behavior. For this to happen, teachers should use a limited number of rules that are consistent, easy to understand, and based on rational expectations. Young students usually need to be taught school and classroom rules, while older students need to have them clearly communicated so that the students and the teacher have a common understanding. Rules are also more effective when students understand why the rules have been developed or why they are needed. When students are faced with long lists of rules that describe what they are not allowed to do, a considerable amount of time and energy may be spent in enforcement activities. When rules become the focus of school life, management problems and misbehavior may increase.

Scenario. A new high school was opened in a rapidly growing school system. Students from the feeder schools were fairly representative of all of the students in the area. They ranged from the very well behaved to those who were known to have serious self-control problems. The faculty agreed to have very few rules, and their rules would emphasize positive expectations.

The short list of rules and expectations was shared with the students on the first day of school during the first assembly. The students could not believe the brevity of the expectations and the positive attitude exemplified by the faculty and administration. During the first few weeks, student behavior was carefully monitored throughout the school. At the first sign of any misbehavior, students were reminded about the way they were expected to behave. As the year progressed, the school climate became very positive and the number of school and classroom discipline and management problems was minimal. One of the most important outcomes was the excellent performance of the students in academic and co-curricular activities.

The positive high school experience described above was in sharp contrast to a middle school that took a different approach. In this particular school, the majority of the teachers had long lists of rules posted that consisted of unacceptable behaviors. The lists were so long that students would find it impossible to remember all of the things that they should not do. One teacher in the building had a rule stating that unless students kept their feet flat on the floor while seated in their desks they would have to do their work standing up. It was not uncommon to see the majority of the students in this teacher's classes standing in awkward positions rather than sitting at their desks. Because students found it difficult to concentrate on their work while they were standing, they were off task most of the time. Management problems continued to increase until the teacher finally realized that the rule was based on inappropriate expectations and was creating havoc in her classroom.

Finding 11: Procedures and routines should facilitate independent work behavior and assure the best use of allocated time.

More and more teachers are using multitask classroom structures. They have found that they can more effectively meet the individual needs of their students when they organize the classroom into several learning activities. Multitask arrangements, however, require more planning and greater attention to management systems. Without this, valuable learning time can be lost both during transitions and when students are not sure what they are supposed to be doing. Procedures and routines should be developed and implemented that will help ensure that learning time is not lost when the task structure is changed.

Scenario. A fourth grade teacher in a local school system made a strong commitment to the use of learning centers. This was at a time when many teachers were experimenting with the use of various kinds of centers and multitask arrangements. This teacher was one of those who thoughtfully analyzed the pros and cons of using the learning center approach. She carefully organized her centers to meet specific learning objectives. She then took the time to prepare her students to use the centers. Some observers may have thought that she took too much instructional time to organize and prepare her students for this new approach. She was, however, one of the few teachers in her school to improve student success rates while spending the majority of the instructional time in multitask activities. Even when she completely changed the materials in the centers, students did not lose any time adapting to new expectations. The procedures and routines established early in the year had been thoroughly ingrained, and were carefully monitored, so that students were very seldom off-task. Transition time was kept to a minimum and it was evident that nearly all of her students had become responsible, independent learners.

Finding 12: Consequences should be carefully planned and clearly linked to classroom expectations, rules, and procedures.

By carefully planning consequences for appropriate and inappropriate behavior, teachers are able to respond rationally to unexpected occurrences. When teachers have not given thoughtful consideration to consequences that will be used to respond to misbehavior, they are more likely to use consequences that may be inappropriate or appear to be unfair. When consequences are carefully planned, students should be able to see a logical relationship between consequences and behavior expectations. Positive consequences should be used to reinforce desired behavior, while negative consequences should discourage students from misbehaving.

Scenario. A high school band teacher required band members to do push-ups when they misbehaved. The misbehavior could range from hitting the wrong notes during practice to not paying attention and engaging in horseplay. It became a game among the students to see who would have to do the most pushups during practice. Every time the pushup penalty was assigned, the entire band got to stop and watch. Needless to say, the band's musical performance suffered (but the students were in better physical condition at the end of the year!).

Planning consequences for appropriate behavior can have a beneficial impact on students, teachers, and the total school climate. This has proven to be the case in one large midwestern high school. The principal and the teachers have an agreement that when a student does something especially worthwhile, in or out of the classroom, the principal is notified. The principal finds the student and gives a personal commendation specifically related to what the student has done. The principal then contacts the parents, usually by telephone, to share the good news with them. He often has to wait until late evening to make his calls for the day.

It is easy to see why this school has such positive relationships with students and parents. Teachers and administrators have found that sharing positive consequences has improved their own attitudes and strengthened their commitment to their work. They have also found that over a period of time teachers have had to use fewer and fewer consequences for inappropriate school or classroom behavior.

Finding 13: The physical organization of the classroom can have a significant effect on student behavior.

Carefully planning the organization of the classroom is such an obvious good practice that it is hard to believe poor arrangements still exist in many classrooms. Sometimes poor physical organization creates minor nuisances such as poor traffic patterns. At other times, however, inattention to planning and organizing the classroom results in management problems that interfere with student learning. Teachers should regularly review and assess the physical arrangement of their classrooms to ensure that they are making the best use of their space and facilities and that the physical organization is not contributing to student misbehavior.

Scenario.   A third grade teacher in a northeastern school had the desks for her reading groups organized so she could have close contact with the students in the group, but she was not able to see one corner of the room where students were supposed to be doing their seatwork. During a reading group one of her students, who could not easily be seen by the teacher, left the room three times to look in on other classes in the building. He had been doing this for several days before it was brought to the teacher's attention. It did not take long for her to change the classroom so she could visually monitor all the students while she was working with her reading groups.

At times the physical arrangement of the classroom has a direct effect on student academic performance. A foreign language teacher in California typically had large numbers of students in her first-year Spanish classes. For several years she organized students in a standard room arrangement of six rows with six or seven desks in a row. The students were allowed to select their own desks, so several of those having problems learning the language sat in the back of the room. When the teacher asked the students to give choral responses in Spanish, the students in the back either did not respond or made halfhearted attempts to respond.

Her classes were observed several times with special attention given to student behavior. The teacher analyzed the observation data and made the decision to reorganize her classroom. She arranged the desks in a large half circle with no more than two desks behind each front desk in the half circle. She was able to move quickly across the half circle and maintain eye contact with every student in her class. She was also able to hear the choral responses from all of the students. It did not take long to improve the performance of the students who previously had attempted to disengage themselves from the learning process.

GUIDE TO OBSERVATION, ANALYSIS, AND REFLECTION

The focus of these activities is on preventive management practices. While observing in another teacher's classroom, pay special attention to management procedures. Many practices can be inferred from watching teacher and student interactions. As you observe, take notes that describe student and teacher behavior or map teacher and student movement. A record of teacher or student verbal statements may also yield important information about management practices. It is most effective when the teacher and observer have the opportunity to review and examine observation data together. The observation and analysis activities should provide valuable information for the reflection process. It is beneficial for teachers to reflect on their own behavior and expectations after they have had opportunities to observe and analyze the work of others. Once this has been done, decisions can be made about developing, improving, or revising teaching and management strategies.

1. Classroom rules

Observation: What rules appear to be in effect?   Recording information about student and teacher behavior (statements or actions) related to rules will help answer the question. For example, rules may be posted, or students may be required to keep them in their notebooks.

Analysis: Are the rules that are in effect consistent with the teacher's expectations?   Analyze your observations describing student behavior patterns to determine if there are clear links among behavior patterns, rules, and classroom expectations. Teacher input is necessary to confirm that the rules have been communicated to the students. Together, assess the extent to which the rules and expectations are realistic in terms of the students' characteristics (e.g., age, SES, special needs). Further analysis can determine the degree of consistency between classroom and schoolwide rules and expectations.

Reflection: Are my rules consistent with my expectations for student behavior? List your own rules and compare them to a written list of your expectations. Analyze any discrepancies that may exist between the two sets of information. Decide what adjustments you will make to eliminate the discrepancies.

2. Classroom climate

Observation: What observable teacher and student behaviors contribute to the classroom climate?   Examples could include the use of humor, encouragement, or sarcasm and criticism. In addition, teacher statements showing concern for student needs and descriptions of student-student interactions could provide relevant information. It is also helpful to note the time the statements were made, the events before and after the statements, and the names of the targeted students.

Analysis: *Is the classroom climate positive, negative, or neutral?* Summarize teacher and student behaviors that appear to have an influence on the climate of the classroom. Try to determine how the behaviors affect the classroom. Find out the teacher's rationale for the preferred climate. Analyze your data to identify any behaviors you did not record that have an effect on the climate. For example, an absence of negative statements could be an indicator of a positive climate.

Reflection: *How would I describe the climate that I desire for my classroom?* You may have observed classrooms that have the type of climate you think of as highly desirable. If so, decide what you have to do to develop a similar environment. If you have not observed such classrooms, describe in detail what you would have to do to develop an ideal classroom climate.

3. Preventive management

Observation: *What teacher behaviors indicate a preventive management approach?* Actions that communicate behavioral expectations, such as the use of rule reminders, verbal and nonverbal cues, and teacher movement, are examples of preventive management strategies. Observation notes could include descriptions of teacher-student interactions, teacher concern about staying on-task, and teacher attention to student concerns. From these notes, describe the modeling behaviors and preventive actions of the teacher.

Analysis: *How effective was the teacher in preventing management problems?* Analyze the observation data to see if any management problems could have been prevented by better planning, a more appropriate physical arrangement, or improved instructional management. If there did not appear to be any problems, assess the preventive actions the teacher used to promote effective classroom management.

Reflection: *What management problems have I encountered that could have been prevented?* Reflect on your use of preventive management strategies. Determine if any preventive actions that you have observed could have been helpful to you. Review your approaches to planning, classroom organization, and instructional management to see if you have gained additional insights that could help prevent future classroom management problems.

4. Classroom routines

Observation: *What routines seem to facilitate the management process?* Look for consistent student behaviors that require little or no teacher direction. Student behaviors after finishing an activity or when they need help from the teacher or another student are indicators of classroom routines. In activity or laboratory classes, describe student behaviors during transitions between activities and when obtaining and returning materials and equipment.

Analysis: What impact did the routines have on the preventive management system?   Summarize the routines you can identify from the observation data. Decide to what extent the routines influenced student behavior during activities when there was little teacher supervision (e.g., seatwork or independent practice). Assess the impact routines have on the use of allocated time. For example, were the transitions efficient and orderly? Evaluate students' ability to get and use instructional materials without interrupting the work of others. Are there additional routines that could be used to prevent management problems?

Reflection: What management routines would be most desirable in my classroom?   Identify the routines you have observed or are familiar with. Decide how these routines would influence the management of your classroom. Select beneficial routines that you will emphasize at the beginning of the school year and decide how you will monitor them throughout the year.

5. Student responsibility

Observation: What indicators show that students work independently in a responsible manner?   Describe students' opportunities to interact, move around the room, and work cooperatively with others. Note teacher comments that encourage or discourage independent behavior. Also note whether students comply with teacher requests. It may be easier to note examples of noncompliance, nonengagement, and lack of self-control. Observe whether leadership roles have been delegated to the students. Information describing the behavior of the students, individually or collectively, will indicate the extent of their leadership responsibilities.

Analysis: How did independent student work behavior affect learning opportunities?   Determine the extent to which students were responsible for their own actions and learning. Responsible independent learning can occur when students work by themselves or as small-group members. Your analysis of the data can provide insights about the relationship of independent student behavior to classroom learning expectations. Make suggestions for additional opportunities that will help students develop responsible behavior. Have teachers share their thinking about how responsibility can be developed throughout the year.

Reflection: What are the independent behaviors that I want to foster in my students?   Enumerate examples of independent student behavior that you have observed. Which of the behaviors would you like to see your students exhibit? Describe strategies you would use to develop the desired behaviors in your students.

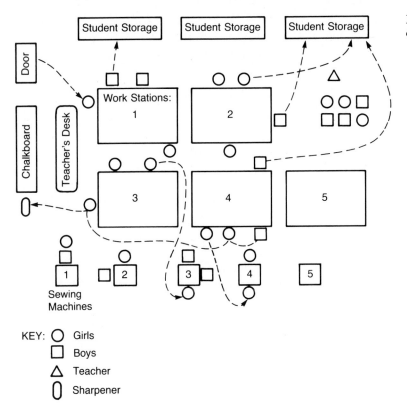

FIGURE 5–6. Family living classroom

★ DEVELOPMENT AND RENEWAL ACTIVITIES

1. Observe a videotaped teaching episode or a simulated activity. Focus your observations on classroom climate and rules, routines, level of student responsibility, and preventive management actions. Discuss your notes with other observers.

2. Observe and diagram the physical arrangement of several classrooms. Try to map a variety of room arrangements. If students are not present, sit in several areas of the room to understand how they will perceive the classroom structure. Include in your diagram the location of the pencil sharpener, materials storage, teacher and student desks, and designated instructional areas. If students are present, develop a classroom map of student movement.

Figure 5–6 shows the physical arrangement of an eighth grade family living class. Students are assigned to work groups. Notice that the students from table 5 are in the lecture area (at upper right) for direct instruction. Students in the other groups are working at their tables, sewing, or waiting to use a sewing machine. The dotted lines indicate student movement around the room.

3. Develop rules appropriate for the age group with which you will be working or are now working. Developing and evaluating classroom rules may be a productive collegial activity. Assess your rules to be sure they are

- Clearly stated
- Stated in positive terms
- Purposeful
- Reasonable and practical
- Limited in number

After you have reviewed and evaluated the rules, make any changes you feel would be appropriate. When you are satisfied with your rules, develop related consequences. Be sure that there is a clear and logical link between the desired behaviors and the consequences.

4. Developing an effective management system is a personal undertaking. Management practices should be congruent with one's own beliefs and skills. To analyze how your beliefs and capabilities influence your management system, think about your position on each of the beliefs presented on the continuum below. Write each pair of statements below a horizontal scale on a separate sheet of paper, and mark an *X* on each line to indicate where you stand.

$$\longleftarrow \qquad\qquad\qquad\qquad\qquad\qquad\qquad\qquad \longrightarrow$$

Students can learn alone.	Students can learn together.
Students must be quiet to learn.	Students can interact and also learn.
Students need to be controlled by the teacher.	Students can control their own behavior.
Students are lazy and uncooperative.	Students are eager and cooperative.
I am realistic in what I expect.	I may expect too much (or too little).
I am confident in my ability to manage students.	I am not confident in my ability to manage students.
I can be assertive and decisive.	I find it difficult to be assertive and decisive.
I am comfortable as the authority figure.	I am uncomfortable using my authority.
I am reciprocal in relationships with students.	My relationships with students are adversarial.
I want to help students with personal problems.	I avoid getting involved.

To what extent is your classroom management system consistent with the beliefs enumerated above?

5. Develop lesson plans for the first week of school or for the first week that you will be teaching. Review your plans to see if the following areas are satisfactorily addressed. Copy the checklist onto a separate sheet of paper, and check off each item you have addressed. After you have completed the review, revise your plans as needed.

Initial Socialization Activities

_____ Welcome students.
_____ Provide opportunity for students to get to know each other.
_____ Provide opportunity for students to get to know the teacher.
_____ Share information about the school and the classroom.
_____ Communicate norms for student-student and teacher-student interactions.
_____ Give overview of the year and describe normal daily schedule.
_____ Communicate expectations for student role and for teacher role.

Getting-Started Activities

_____ Allocate appropriate time to teach and practice rules and procedures.
_____ Arrange for beginning-of-the-year activities (e.g., initial seat assignments, locker assignments, book and materials distribution, fee collections, collecting required information).
_____ Communicate behavioral expectations to parents.
_____ Initiate positive incentive system.
_____ Initiate monitoring practices.

Instructional Activities

_____ Arrange whole-group activity and home-base format.
_____ Prepare academic assignments at appropriate level of challenge.
_____ Prepare time fillers and supplementary activities.
_____ Introduce procedures as necessary.
_____ Communicate grading standards.
_____ Allow time for interaction with individual students.

6.
Responding to Misbehavior

COMMENTARY

Responses to misbehavior are often considered disciplinary actions. We would like to believe that teachers, administrators, and parents are more concerned about how to manage the behavior of students effectively than they are about how to be disciplinarians. The concept of discipline creates unpleasant images in the minds of many people. It also tends to be an emotional term that gets considerable attention, especially from the media. National polls and surveys have identified school discipline as a major concern of parents across the country. Parents are concerned about the safety of their children, but when questioned about the discipline in their schools, many parents say it is other schools they have heard about that have major discipline problems.

In everyday use the term *discipline* can cause some confusion. Some people use it to refer to orderliness. They may refer to a school or classroom as having good discipline if students are orderly and well behaved, there is a minimum of noise, and there are very few distractions or disruptions. Others perceive discipline as a form of punishment that may involve inflicting pain. Parents and teachers may say that they are going to have to discipline a child. There has been an ongoing debate about the use and effect of corporal punishment in schools. This is usually the most intense form of discipline that schools use to manage student behavior. As a side note, for the most part corporal punishment is no longer used in prisons and other institutions where young people are incarcerated.

At times discipline and self-management are seen as being nearly synonymous concepts. Someone may be referred to as being a very disciplined person. People are perceived as good self-managers when they take responsibility for their own behavior. A disciplined adult may be a person who stays on task until a project is finished, while a well-disciplined student may be viewed as one who is willing to conform to teacher and school expectations.

Responding to misbehavior is the process of helping individuals become effective self-managers so that they can function effectively and productively in a group setting. The process requires identifying and communicating what constitutes acceptable behavior in classrooms and schools. Usually standards, either implicit or explicit, help to establish the boundaries for acceptable or unacceptable behavior in a group.

Both beginning and experienced teachers are most effective when they use appropriate responses to misbehavior as their frame of reference for providing safe, orderly, and productive classroom environments. We have been concerned for a number of years because many of the teachers with whom we have worked have communicated their desire to develop fail-safe discipline techniques that will solve a variety of behavior problems. Some of these teachers want to have recipes for correcting misbehavior without regard to special student needs and circumstances.

When teachers are engaged in some form of behavior management, they must consider the context in which the behavior is taking place. Many different influences cause people to behave the way they do. We must attempt to understand the cause of the behavior before we attempt to take corrective action. The use of correctives is most effective in the context of a positive, caring relationship. When such a relationship does not exist, even the most subtle correctives may be viewed as being punitive and behavior problems may be exacerbated.

RATIONALE

Experienced teachers do not have to be told about the behavior management problems they deal with on a regular basis. Not too long ago the most serious student management problems included smoking on the school grounds, being tardy to class, and being absent without an excuse. Today teachers must deal with students who are chemically dependent, young children suffering from some form of abuse, students who are not a part of a family structure, and drug dealing on school grounds. Unfortunately, these are just a few of the more common behavior management challenges facing teachers and school administrators.

In many cases, norms for acceptable behavior are not established by families or other social institutions, so schools are expected to fill this vacuum. When appropriate behavior norms are not established and adhered to, it is extremely difficult (if not impossible) to have productive work groups. Almost without exception, schools operate on the expectation that students will be engaged in some form of group work throughout the school day. The group may be as large as a total class or as small as two students working together on an assignment. One individual whose behavior is not under control can have a detrimental effect on a large group. Teachers are held accountable for both individual and group behavior, which affects how well learning goals and expectations can be achieved.

Beginning teachers often do not have an adequate background in behavior management. The great majority of the students in college have conformed fairly well to the expectations of their teachers throughout their school years. In most cases they have not had a great deal of experience in behavior management.

Preparation programs usually include one or two courses dealing with some approaches to discipline and classroom management. Seldom is there a comprehensive program for attending to behavior management problems. Even when students are adequately exposed to theories about how to appropriately respond to misbehavior, they have little opportunity for actual involvement in dealing with student misbehavior. Simulations and videotapes have been used to give preservice teachers an opportunity to review and analyze potential behavior management problems, but many teacher candidates do not perceive these experiences as realistic.

Student and intern teachers are usually fortunate enough to work under the direction of successful mentor teachers. The mentors typically have fewer behavior management problems because of the preventive strategies they have developed over the years. Also, these teachers often have fewer students with behavior management problems. Preservice teachers, although they may be getting expert assistance and helpful mentoring, may not have many opportunities to deal firsthand with challenging behavior management problems. Their experience in identifying and using appropriate corrective measures may be very limited. We believe that teachers, both beginning and experienced, must regularly evaluate their approaches to behavior management and make adjustments or revisions that will help them work effectively with their students.

RESEARCH SYNTHESIS

The Concept of Behavior Management

The actions that make up effective management strategies (addressed in Chapter 5) include: developing, implementing, and monitoring rules and routines; managing resources, especially time, to achieve learning objectives; and organizing the classroom so that students will not disrupt others and the teacher can easily monitor student work.

Behavior management focuses on individual students and what can be done to keep them productively engaged in learning activities. Cangelosi (1988) reported that in some classrooms up to 50% of allocated instructional time is lost due to off-task behavior (p. 19). Some teachers spend as much as 80% of their time and effort managing student behavior (Englander, 1986). When teachers spend a large percentage of their time dealing with misbehavior, student learning suffers and negative attitudes about school are developed. Teachers tend to become discouraged about their lack of impact on student learning. Many teachers have based their behavior management approach on intuition and experience but do not use a carefully integrated and articulated system of intervention (Brophy & Rohrkemper, 1988). With few exceptions, teachers without a sound behavior management system spend an inordinate amount of their allocated learning time attempting to correct student misbehavior.

Effective teachers know that it is easier to prevent inappropriate behavior than it is to correct misbehavior. (A number of preventive actions that teachers can take have been discussed in Chapters 2–5.) In spite of the very best preventive measures, however, some students will not stay on task or will otherwise misbehave. Curwin and Mendler (1988) reported that 80% of students are generally cooperative and well behaved, while 15% misbehave with some regularity and 5% may be chronic behavior problems. These percentages will, of course, vary based on the teaching situation and the composition of the class. When good preventive measures have been taken, most teachers will have a smaller percentage of students whose behavior requires corrective action.

What constitutes acceptable student behavior depends on several important variables. The variables and their relationship to behavior management are presented in Figure 6–1. Student needs and developmental levels should be given careful consideration when teachers establish behavior expectations. Teachers must also understand their own tolerance levels for student activity, movement, and off-task behavior. What teachers view as unacceptable classroom behavior should be clearly communicated to students. Students in departmentalized settings often have to make major adjustments in their behavior patterns when they change classes and have different teachers. Teachers must also try to understand the cause and influences of any student misbehavior that occurs. Finally, teachers must plan and use the most appropriate corrective measures.

Misbehavior

A discussion of misbehavior most often focuses on problems created by students. In some cases, however, teacher behavior may be responsible for inappro-

FIGURE 6–1. Variables affecting behavior management

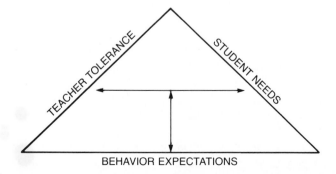

priate student behavior. Many teachers find it difficult to acknowledge that this may be true (Brophy & Rohrkemper, 1988). They tend to see student misbehavior as being entirely the responsibility of the students. Sylwester (1971) identified four principal ways that teachers cause misbehavior: inadequate preparation, special relationships with students (favorites or enemies), verbal abusiveness, and unfair punishment.

Inadequate preparation is usually more of a problem for new teachers. They tend to structure fewer and more passive activities per period, which leads to student restlessness (Moskowitz & Hayman, 1976). Special relationships with students often develop without teachers being aware of what is happening. Students, however, know who the favorites are and who the teacher does not appear to like. Students may also perceive verbal abusiveness when teachers engage in what they believe is friendly sarcasm. Once again this may be a problem that teachers are not aware of, and they may not realize the negative impact they are having on their students.

Using inappropriate consequences to correct unacceptable behavior is usually more of a problem for beginning teachers. Through trial and error, most experienced teachers develop correctives that work and that students believe to be fair. They use correctives when they are needed in a uniform and evenhanded manner.

Student misbehavior can include any actions that teachers perceive as disrupting the established order of the classroom. Inappropriate behavior occurs when students do not respond properly to academic tasks or when they cannot control their impulsiveness and work cooperatively with the teacher and their peers. Appropriate student behaviors expected by the teacher may require social action and communication that is beyond the ability of students (Trenholm & Rose, 1981).

Student misbehavior ranges from very subtle actions to those that are very aggressive. Doyle (1986b) gave examples of subtle misbehavior such as faking involvement, whispering, passing notes, blocking the teacher's view, and avoiding individual performance situations by remaining bystanders (as in physical education classes). Students also try to meet their own needs and reduce the level of academic demands by asking many questions and feigning nonunderstanding. One of the more serious subtle misbehaviors occurs when students are inattentive, quietly withdrawn, or disengaged from the learning activities (Gage & Berliner, 1984).

The most commonly exhibited classroom misbehaviors in primary and secondary schools are inappropriate talking (e.g., in excess, out of turn, unnecessarily) and inappropriate movement (e.g., without permission, clowning) (Calderhead, 1984; Cangelosi, 1988; Steere, 1988). Other common misbehaviors include tardiness, cutting class, not bringing supplies and books, inattentiveness or daydreaming, and mild verbal and aggressive acts (Doyle, 1986b). Bellon, Doak, and Handler (1979) found in a statewide study that the six most frequent disciplinary concerns were inattention to lessons, talking out of turn, overactive behavior, ongoing apathetic behavior, abusing property, and abusing other students. Brophy and Rohrkemper (1988) identified 12 typical elementary student problems that are consistent with the previously identified inappropriate behaviors. They divided these behaviors into the four categories of achievement, hostility, student role adjustment, and peer relationships.

In addition to the more common problems enumerated above, teachers may encounter other special management problems such as crying, lack of control of bodily functions, fighting and arguing, and stealing and cheating (Steere, 1988). Although misbehavior from narcotics and alcohol use occurs less frequently, teachers must be prepared to deal with these more serious problems (Bellon et al., 1979).

While knowing the kinds of misbehavior that may be encountered in classrooms is important, understanding the causes and influences of inappropriate behavior is even more important. Glasser (1986) contended that discipline is only a problem when students are forced into situations where they do not experience satisfaction: "To focus on discipline is to ignore the real problem. We will never get students (or anyone else) to be in good order . . . if we try to force them to do what they do not find satisfying" (p. 12).

Although a lack of satisfaction is an important factor in student misbehavior, there are a number of potential causes and influences. Behavior is complex and not explained by a simple cause-effect relationship. Students who misbehave may be trying to reduce their frustration, tension, and anxiety. Misbehavior may be a defense mechanism to help preserve self-esteem. Students may also act inappropriately because they perceive school as boring and are not motivated to become involved. Students may be rebelling against the imposition of rules and authority. They may be testing the limits or boundaries of authority and checking teachers' willingness to be assertive in handling misbehavior. Students who act out may be attempting to fulfill a need for attention, power, or belonging, or they may misbehave because they have a difficult time differentiating between what is expected at home and what is expected at school (Doyle, 1986b).

The structure of the classroom may contribute to inappropriate patterns of behavior. When students are expected to be quiet and passive for long periods of time, the potential for misbehavior increases. This can also occur when students are presented with too many activities and transitions between the activities. When teachers spend an inordinate amount of time working with one or two students, other students may tend to get restless and misbehave.

Misbehavior may be more directly related to influences in the home than they are to the school or classroom. Hyperactivity, shyness, aggressiveness, and anxiety may be the result of malnutrition, lack of sleep, abuse or neglect, excessive television watching, or violence in the home (Swick, 1985; Romney, 1986). Many teachers believe that improper training at home is by far the most important influence on student misbehavior (Bellon et al., 1979). Other influences perceived to be important are the undesirable effects of television and other media, parental noninvolvement in school experiences, overcrowded classrooms, and physiological and psychological problems.

Teachers need to be alert to problems that may be developing with students who do not normally misbehave. Sudden changes in students' behavior, such as instances of extreme behavior, being unprepared and disorganized, and inability to accept authority, are warning signs of potential problems (Swick, 1985). Teachers should seek to identify the conditions that are causing such sudden changes in behavior. By understanding the causes and influences, they will be better prepared to take corrective action.

Teachers should keep in mind that they, as well as their students, are responsible for misbehavior in classrooms. The most important influences on misbehavior are summarized in Figure 6–2.

Managing Misbehavior

Effective classroom managers are also effective decision makers. Their judgments are reflected in their behavioral expectations for students, their ability to respond to behavioral cues, the use of preventive measures to anticipate problems, and the interventions they select to respond to misbehavior. The student-teacher interaction cycle can sometimes become a downward spiral; negative student behavior leads to negative teacher reaction which leads to further negative student behavior (Swick, 1985). The cycle can be broken when teachers make appropriate intervention decisions. The effects of teacher intervention decisions on student behavior are depicted in Figure 6–3.

In deciding when and how to intervene, the overriding concern should be the effect on instruction. Teachers have to decide to what extent the intervention will promote or inhibit instructional activities. When misbehavior occurs, teachers must decide what intervention will be effective in restoring order without disrupting the flow of instruction. Teachers make decisions to intervene based on specific information, such as the nature of the misbehavior, the student(s) involved, and when the misbehavior occurred (Doyle, 1986b).

In general, teachers' responses vary with the degree to which the student behavior is perceived to threaten order (Brophy & Rohrkemper, 1988). Teachers have to make accurate judgments about the probable consequence of student behavior in different situations. Reprimands occur in classrooms at a very high rate. White (1975)

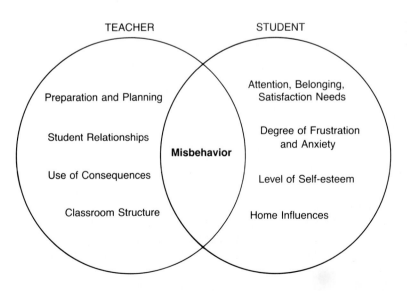

FIGURE 6–2. Influences on misbehavior

TEACHER

Preparation and Planning

Student Relationships

Misbehavior

Use of Consequences

Classroom Structure

STUDENT

Attention, Belonging, Satisfaction Needs

Degree of Frustration and Anxiety

Level of Self-esteem

Home Influences

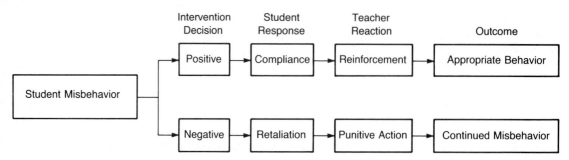

FIGURE 6–3. Effects of intervention decisions on student behaviors

found the rate of teacher reprimands in all grades was one every two minutes. Reprimands exceed praise in every grade after second grade.

Doyle (1986b) reported that acts of misbehavior that usually draw reprimands from teachers include not listening, violating schoolwide rules, and creating noise that is audible beyond the classroom. Beyond these few inappropriate behaviors, it is not quite so clear as to what misbehaviors elicit reprimands. Whether reprimands occur appears to be highly situational. Minor misbehavior occurring after the lesson is over or during the last few minutes of the period is generally tolerated. If the misbehavior is judged to be insignificant, brief, and not likely to escalate, teachers may notice but decide not to intervene. This is especially true if the offending students are usually well behaved.

Other factors may influence teachers' decisions to intervene. Because interventions are reactive and considered risky, they may cause more disruption to the instruction than the misbehavior itself. Doyle (1986b) reported that most teachers intervene at a rate of 16 times an hour. Kounin (1983) studied successful and unsuccessful managers. He found that the most successful teacher kept the children on task 98.7% of the time, while the least successful one intervened 986 times a day, which resulted in student engagement only 25% of the time. A ripple effect (Kounin & Gump, 1958) occurs when interventions interrupt instruction and affect other classmates.

In managing misbehavior, teachers need a broad range of skills and techniques in order to increase the possibility of making effective intervention decisions. Numerous strategies have been found to be effective. In general, effective managers want to be seen as leaders who can solve their own problems. They are determined not to allow the misbehavior of a few students to interfere with the learning of other students. Brophy and Rohrkemper (1988) identified three main characteristics of teachers who are effective in dealing with problem elementary students: a willingness to become personally involved with the students, the confidence to bring about significant improvements, and the use of longer term prevention techniques.

Teachers effective in managing student behavior generally rely on positive strategies. They tend to be nonpunitive, supportive, and encouraging (Lasley, 1981). Teachers who communicate positively with all their students using "we" statements and supportive comments have fewer discipline problems (Swick, 1985b). In addi-

tion, teachers help students understand how the consequences of their disruptive behavior are detrimental to themselves and other students. They focus on the behavior,
not on the child's personality. They view misbehaviors as instances when appropriate
behavior was not learned (Emmer & Evertson, 1981) and as something to be corrected
rather than endured (Porter & Brophy, 1988). Effective teachers actually teach students the appropriate behaviors. They respond to misbehavior with explanations and
reorientation rather than with punishment (Kounin & Gump, 1961). It is interesting
to note that teachers may feel confident of their ability to get positive results with
certain types of student problems, such as failure, perfectionism, passive-aggressive
behavior, distractibility, immaturity, and shyness, while less confident in dealing effectively, for the long term, with other types of problems, such as low achievement,
hostile-aggressive behavior, and defiance (Brophy & Rohrkemper, 1988).

Practices of ineffective behavior managers differ markedly from those of effective managers. They may stop the misbehavior, but they generally elicit more
inappropriate behavior. They tend to control student behavior through demands and
threats (Porter & Brophy, 1988). They have not learned that while reprimands,
corporal punishment, and other punitive actions may stop misbehavior temporarily
they are ineffective in the long term because they do not teach substitute constructive
behavior (Goldstein, 1989).

Punitive teachers generally have students who are more aggressive, more
unsettled, and less concerned with learning (Kounin & Gump, 1961). Negative
responses such as criticism, shouting, scolding, ridicule, and sarcasm are not productive approaches in dealing with misbehavior (Kounin & Gump, 1961; Weber, 1984;
Swick, 1985).

Nonpunitive teacher responses are necessary to bring about positive changes
in student behavior (Swick, 1985). Threats, nagging, and overdwelling on misbehavior should be avoided. Some inexperienced teachers are ineffective managers because
they tend to ignore problems and continue teaching even though misbehavior continues and escalates. They then intervene by overreacting, causing the situation to
degenerate more (Moskowitz & Hayman, 1976).

Corrective Measures

Corrective measures include a wide range of teacher actions. Whatever measure is used, it should result in a consequence that is appropriate for the type of
student misbehavior. For example, many teachers use unobtrusive corrective measures
to manage minor behavior problems such as making eye contact with students who
are talking. More serious behavior problems require correctives, or interventions, that
may require the support and involvement of others, such as parents, counselors, and
administrators, to reach an appropriate solution. Teachers in one study identified
21 actions that they would recommend for dealing with student misbehavior. The
actions ranged from unobtrusive responses, such as nonverbal communication, to
expulsion from school. The four most frequently recommended actions were meeting
with parents, conferring with students, admonishing students privately, and restricting individual privileges (Bellon et al., 1979). Clearly, teachers should have a full

repertoire of corrective actions they can use to deal with misbehavior. Corrective actions that can be included in a teacher's repertoire are enumerated in Figure 6–4. Common forms of misbehavior are also presented. Each of the lists is presented in a hierarchy from the least serious misbehaviors and most subtle correctives to those that are more serious and may result in stronger corrective responses.

The corrective measures employed by teachers were found to be mediated by teachers' perceptions of the misbehavior. In Brophy and Rohrkemper's study (1988), elementary teachers generally reacted more sympathetically when students were seen as victims (exhibiting behavior beyond their control), or when the behaviors were nondisruptive or nonirritating. In contrast, teachers were more controlling and punitive with irritating, disruptive behaviors or when the behavior was perceived to be caused by the student's lack of self-control or poor decision making.

Overt responses to student misbehavior are often referred to as desists. Effective calls to desist are delivered calmly, firmly, with intensity, promptly, and to the responsible offending student. Delivery of desists is important in establishing a teacher's competence with the students. The orientation should be prochild or neutral. Private, individualized, and brief orders to desist that invite no response from the student and do not disrupt instruction are found to be effective (Erickson & Mohatt, 1982).

Calls to desist can be observable, forceful actions, or they can be unobtrusive interventions such as using eye contact, touching or gesturing, moving closer, giving low-key directives, using cues, and redirecting attention. It is important to demonstrate or reteach the rule and to direct students' attention to the corrective behavior or rule when necessary. Teachers should withhold attention and reinforcement of inappropriate behavior and also encourage peers to ignore the behavior (Gage & Berliner, 1984).

FIGURE 6–4. Common forms of misbehavior and potential correctives

Range of Misbehavior	Repertoire of Correctives
Talking in class	Eye contact
Minor misbehavior	Nonverbal communication
Using bad language	Redirecting attention
Verbal putdowns	Call for desisting
Persistent disobedience	Changing the activity
Hitting, fighting	Private conferences
Destroying property	Parent conferences
Stealing	Group conferences
Persistent truancy	Social isolation
Refusing to obey	Detention
Using a controlled substance	Loss of privileges
Carrying a weapon	Corporal punishment
Physical violence	Expulsion

If unobtrusive interventions do not produce a desired behavioral change, more forceful strategies may need to be employed. The teacher may need to alter the environment by removing the stimulus for misbehavior or separating the student from the stimulus by using isolation, in or out of the room. Teachers may find it necessary to change instructional activities. It is generally effective to offer students dignified ways to stop their misbehavior (Cangelosi, 1988). Another option is to allow students to resolve their conflicts or to provide time for students to regain self-control (Swick, 1985).

For minor offenses, calls to desist and unobtrusive interventions may stop inappropriate behavior. For more serious offenses or persistent problems, teachers need to use interventions that have longer-lasting effects. Brophy and Rohrkemper (1987) found that teachers can directly instruct aggressive students in ways to handle frustration, control their tempers, and express anger verbally rather than physically to resolve conflict. Teachers can hold private conferences with the offending students to discuss problems and resolutions. Glasser (1969) pointed out that great care must be exercised when involving parents in a behavior management conference. They may make matters worse if they want to punish the student rather than improve the situation. Glasser suggests that students should always be present at their conferences.

For some teachers, group counseling techniques such as values clarification or problem solving are productive in resolving or preventing group conflict. Teachers occasionally face problems for which they do not have positive options or solutions. They must know when to seek help from trained personnel such as counselors, psychologists, social workers, and nurses. Teachers cannot be expected to be equipped to deal successfully with all student problems on their own.

Punishment as a Corrective

No matter what the offense, the most common reaction to misbehavior in the schools is punishment (Englander, 1986). In nearly 80% of the cases Englander examined, teachers reacted punitively. In most schools the corrective measures most often used are verbal reprimands and corporal punishment. Teachers and administrators make few attempts to help students learn constructive, positive ways to deal with the problems they encounter (Goldstein, 1989).

Punishment is often defended as an effective means for inhibiting undesired behavior, but it does not teach desired behavior (Brophy & Putnam, 1979); nor is the effect long term (Steere, 1988). Punishment also does not remove the underlying causes of behavior problems (Englander, 1986).

Punishment can suppress inappropriate behaviors but may also produce anxiety which hinders learning. Punishment may result in negative outcomes and further withdrawal from learning if it is viewed as excessive or unwarranted (Steere, 1988). Children find ways to avoid punishment, but these ways may be counterproductive to learning (Stipek, 1988).

Types of punishment include social isolation (time out), loss of points or tokens, detention, having the student write sentences about the misbehavior as a repetitive activity, withholding privileges, and corporal punishment (Emmer & Evertson, 1981; Gage & Berliner, 1984). Mild punishment that gives the student information about the behavior and how to change it is more effective than extreme punishment (Brophy & Evertson, 1976). Appropriate punishment is brief, mild, involves restitution, and allows students to regain normal status. Assigning regular school work for punishment is negatively related to learning gains (Brophy & Evertson, 1976). Physical punishment and group punishment have not proven to be effective techniques (Brophy & Putnam, 1979).

Teachers who use group punishment to modify the behavior of individual students should proceed with caution. Sherviakov and Redl (1956) have proposed one basic law to guide the disciplining of individuals and groups, the law of marginal antisepsis. According to this law, "a technique which is right for the child's problem must at least be harmless to the group. A technique which is rightly chosen for its effect upon the group must at least be harmless to the individuals involved" (p. 25).

Punishment is complex and situational. Teachers need to be aware of the context and how punishment will be interpreted. The effectiveness of certain forms of punishment differs according to the socioeconomic status of the students (Brophy & Evertson, 1976). What teachers perceive as punishment may not be perceived as negative by students. Some systems of penalties require complex recordkeeping and, even if they are somewhat effective, may be too complicated to be practical.

Corporal punishment is an issue in schools and is not an uncommon practice. It is currently legal in 43 states, while 7 states have outlawed its use (Goldstein, 1989). The option of using corporal punishment is usually a local system decision in states where it is permitted. Rose (1984) reported that corporal punishment is widely used in the nation's schools. Seventy-four percent of principals surveyed in 18 states confirmed the use of corporal punishment for various offenses with varying degrees of seriousness.

Limited research has been conducted on the effects of corporal punishment. Negative findings suggest that corporal punishment results in more misbehavior and is an ineffective practice (Steere, 1988). According to Cangelosi (1988), "All corporal punishment is abusive because of its deleterious effects on both the long-term welfare of students and on the educational environment of the school" (p. 205). Schools that are punitively oriented are not judged to be effective schools (Englander, 1986). Avoiding the need to punish is much more effective than using punishment to correct misbehavior.

Long-Term Correctives

More and more educators have begun to use long-term behavior management strategies such as teaching social skills and self-control strategies. These approaches help students learn to cope rather than requiring teachers to implement behavior modification approaches (Doyle, 1986b). Self-control strategies are effective in managing behavior and in fostering achievement (Brophy, 1982). Many young children develop their own strategies for controlling themselves, while others must be taught how to control their behavior.

There are several basic approaches to developing self-control. The approaches involve devising ways to think differently about situations, but they all require predictable classroom environments with clear behavioral expectations. Self-control approaches include monitoring one's own behavior, intervention through self-talk, and applying problem-solving routines. Assisting children in developing routines for problem solving can help them control their behavior and also enhance their feeling of being in control in social situations (Anderson & Prawat, 1983).

Cognitive behavior modification strategies that have been applied successfully in clinical situations have also proven to be viable in regular classrooms (Manning, 1988). Group counseling interventions focusing on cognitive behavior techniques have been found to be effective with hostile, aggressive students (Omizo, Hershberger, & Omizo, 1988). Relaxation training applied in the classroom setting can improve student self-management skills and lessen discipline problems such as fighting and cutting classes (Matthews, 1986). Students learn to employ relaxation strategies when they begin to feel tense or anxious. Collectively, these strategies are effective in controlling impulsiveness and aggressiveness (Stipek, 1988).

Contingency contracting is another corrective method that emphasizes self-monitoring and developing self-control. Contracts have been successful with students who are resistant, less motivated, and easily distracted. Contracts have several advantages: reinforcement is not externally controlled (which is impractical in large classes), responsibility for improving behavior lies with the child, and the effects seem to generalize to other settings (Brophy, 1982).

In addition to behavior modification, several other large-scale intervention programs have been developed, including reality therapy, assertive discipline, management training (using body language, proximity, and incentives), teacher effectiveness training, and transactional analysis. With the exception of behavior modification approaches, most intervention strategies have not been heavily researched (Doyle, 1986b). The behavior modification principles of extinction, reinforcement, substituting alternative behavior patterns, shaping, cueing, and so on, have to be systematically applied if they are to change behavior patterns. Doyle (1986b) reported that behavior modification approaches are not practical in classroom settings. It is difficult to determine what is reinforcing to individual students, and reinforcers may not be stringent enough or have a long-term effect (Tursman, 1981). Evidence is also mounting against the use of extrinsic rewards because of their detrimental effect on existing intrinsic motivation.

Lasley, Lasley, and Ward (1989) examined the use of assertive discipline, which they considered to be a high-profile intervention system. They concluded that the use of assertive discipline caused more, not fewer, incidents of inappropriate behavior. The effective managers in the study used more low-profile techniques, such as proximity and holding students accountable.

Weber (1984) suggested that most management strategies can be categorized into the following eight groups: authoritarian, behavior modification, cookbook, group process, instructional, intimidation, permissive, and socioemotional climate. He found that the use of group process and socioemotional climate was positively related to students' on-task behavior. In both approaches, the teacher attends to aspects of the classroom such as the social system, positive interpersonal relationships, shared leadership, group morale, cooperation, and student involvement.

In applying any strategy to manage student behavior, a systematic, long-term approach is preferred. Teachers can develop plans for managing behavior as they do for managing instruction (Weber, 1984). The major advantage of well-planned procedures is that teachers can be less reactive and more proactive. In general, the following procedures can be used in developing a long-term behavior management system:

1. Identify desired (and reasonable) classroom conditions and student behaviors.
2. Analyze existing conditions by observing and accurately describing student behaviors.
3. Target specific behaviors for change and decide on priorities.
4. Select and apply intervention strategies.
5. Evaluate the effectiveness of the strategies and make adjustments.

With any intervention strategy, teachers must use their professional judgment. Teachers can systematically arrive at strategies that are consistent with their skills and their teaching situation. The intervention strategies should lead to the positive resolution of conflicts while maintaining a high level of student cooperation.

Periodic monitoring and systematic assessment of management practices is necessary in maintaining a system of corrective and preventive procedures (Evertson et al., 1984; Swick, 1985). Maintaining a successful management system or bringing about beneficial changes in a less than effective one requires concentrated attention and effort. Teachers live in highly reactive and isolated worlds, which makes reflecting on practice difficult. Teachers also may have a limited perspective on what standards of behavior are reasonable and may not know what specific student behaviors could indicate success.

Changing ineffective management practices requires identifying specific actions for change. The most important actions to be taken and the sequence that should be followed are shown in Figure 6–5. It may be that changing teacher behavior patterns is less complex than changing student behavior patterns (Evertson et al., 1984). Regardless of the target, modification takes commitment and continued, periodic assessment. A problem-solving orientation focusing on strengths and weaknesses in plans for action keeps improvement efforts going in a positive direction. Deficiency-oriented assessment can have a negative effect on student self-concept and teacher perception of students (Swick, 1985).

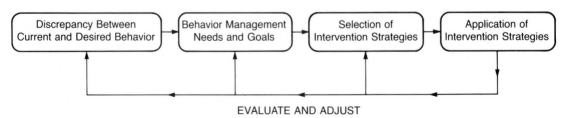

FIGURE 6–5. Development of a long-term behavior management plan

PRIMARY REFERENCES

Brophy, J. E., & **Rohrkemper, M.** (1988). *The classroom strategy study: Summary report of general findings* (IRT Research Series No. 187). East Lansing, MI: Michigan State University, Institute for Research on Teaching.

The study is a large-scale investigation involving approximately 100 elementary teachers nominated as outstanding or average in their ability to deal with problem students. The findings provide insight into effective strategies teachers use in working with these students.

Doyle, W. (1986b). Classroom organization and management. In M. C. Wittrock (Ed.), *Handbook of research on teaching* (3rd ed., pp. 392– 431). New York: Macmillan.

This comprehensive review focuses on ways teachers promote order and learning in the classroom. Of particular interest is the discussion of student misbehavior and teachers' interventions to stop the misbehavior.

Englander, M. E. (1986). *Strategies for classroom discipline.* New York: Praeger.

The book is based on the premise that punishment is the way teachers most frequently react to misbehavior. Research findings document the ineffectiveness of punishment in decreasing the frequency and severity of misbehavior in the classroom. Strategies that have been shown to be effective are presented.

Good, T. L., & **Brophy, J. E.** (1987). *Looking in classrooms* (4th ed.). New York: Harper and Row.

Chapter 7, "Management II: Coping with problems effectively," presents appropriate and inappropriate interventions for dealing with minor and more prolonged misbehaviors. Ways to punish effectively and to cope with more serious inappropriate behavior are addressed. Excellent suggestions and examples are provided.

Steere, B. F. (1988). *Becoming an effective manager: A resource for teachers.* Albany, NY: State University of New York Press.

Of particular interest is the presentation of several management models. This information may be helpful for teachers creating or reestablishing a management system. Also included are practical suggestions and useful resource ideas.

Swick, K. J. (1985). *Disruptive student behavior in the classroom.* Washington, DC: National Education Association.

The influences and possible underlying causes of student behavior are described in this publication. Swick emphasizes that understanding the influences on students' behavior is an important step in understanding and dealing with the behavior. Suggested teacher responses to student misbehavior are provided.

RESEARCH IN PRACTICE

Finding 1: When teachers have not employed appropriate preventive strategies, behavior management can consume a large percentage of allocated learning time.

It is interesting to observe different classrooms and see how much time is spent on behavior management. In some classrooms teachers seem to spend little if any time correcting misbehavior; in others teachers seem to spend the majority of the time giving reprimands and intervening to correct misbehavior. More effective teachers are able to describe rather specifically how they teach students their expectations for behavior. Teaching, rehearsing, monitoring, and reinforcing appropriate behavior most often takes place at the start of the school year. Teachers who spend a great deal of time dealing with misbehavior are usually not able to describe what they have done to prevent misbehavior. Instead, they attribute behavior problems to the kind of students they have and do not believe they can do anything to prevent misbehavior.

Scenario.   Teachers in an elementary school had a student population that was largely from families who placed a high priority on quality education. The students were generally well behaved, and most of the instructional time was used to facilitate student learning. The teachers, however, were upset about one situation in the school. When they sent their students to work with the art teacher, the students would return to class unruly and hyperactive. It would take the classroom teachers several minutes to settle the students down and get them back on task.

The principal asked one of us to visit the art teacher's class with him to help assess the situation. The teacher told us during a preobservation conference that she would have the students engaged in a large-group activity for the entire 40 minutes. She was able to describe in some detail what would be happening for the class period. We were in the room when the class arrived. The students were not in assigned seats and sat where they wanted to at the art tables. Some tables were crowded while others just had one or two students. The class got started without any major problems, and the teacher followed the plan she had outlined to us in the conference. Approximately 10 minutes into the class two boys seated at one of the crowded tables began hitting each other. The teacher did not seem to notice and continued with the lesson. When the principal moved toward them, they stopped. Less than half way through the class the teacher suddenly told the students that she did not have anything more to say and that they could work on art projects.

The second half of the class was chaotic. Students did not appear to follow any procedure for getting materials. Some of them simply wandered around the room and bothered those who were attempting to work. Several students went out into the hallway and played around. The teacher spent the entire time trying to get individual students on task but was generally unsuccessful. The class ended without any apparent attempt to get the students back together and prepare them to return to their regular classroom. They left at different times and in various states of excitement or hyperactivity.

A conference with the teacher after the class revealed that she had not communicated any expectations for student behavior to her class. She thought that the students would behave appropriately because that is what their regular teachers expected. She had not done anything to prevent misbehavior, had not established rules and routines for her classes, and had made faulty assumptions about how the students would work in her classes. Unfortunately, all of this took place well into the school year so it was very difficult to establish preventive strategies and expect students to respond in an appropriate manner.

Finding 2: Behavior management systems are most effective when they are based on teacher and student needs and on an understanding of the conditions that cause misbehavior.

It is easy to overlook the importance of understanding teachers' needs in the behavior management process. Teachers become accustomed to organizational factors that have an impact on their work, and they learn to make adjustments so they can work effectively in their classrooms. Students also learn to adjust their behavior as they work under the direction of several teachers who have different behavior expectations. Students' needs and developmental levels should be carefully considered when teachers institute behavior management systems. Expectations should be appropriate for the students and consistent with the teacher's own level of tolerance.

Scenario.   An elementary school in the southeast was closed when a new school was built to accommodate a growing population. The new school, however, was an open-space building with no interior walls between classes and nothing to separate learning and activity centers. The teachers and students had previously been in a building with totally self-contained classrooms. Teachers were not prepared for the difference in the noise level when they were trying to teach, and the amount of student movement throughout the building was disconcerting to both teachers and students.

One of the first teacher responses to the new environment was to create artificial walls by using bookcases and movable chalkboards to separate the classes. Teachers who had a low tolerance for noise and movement when they were teaching found the new environment difficult. One teacher was fairly successful in creating her own self-contained classroom within the open-space setting. Students were more active as a result of the new setting. Many of the teachers used whole-class, direct instruction as their predominant task structure. This helped them to have better control over their students than when they were allowing students to work in small groups and in activity centers.

It was not long before the teachers realized they would have to make some adjustments in their management practices. They gradually accepted the fact that there would be more student movement than in their previous school and that they would have to adjust to the new situation. They also realized that they would have to expect more noise than there had been in their self-contained classrooms.

Students needed help learning to respond to the new behavior expectations. The biggest change for the students was the expectation that they could work independently and still stay on task. They had to learn to ignore the movement of other students and to make as little noise as possible when they were working in small groups.

Needless to say, it took a considerable amount of time for everyone to work effectively in this new setting. Fortunately, the teachers began to solve the problem because they were willing to look at what was bothering them and make adjustments in their behavior before they established new expectations for the students. The teachers knew it would take time to adjust their behavior and the behavior of the students so that everyone could function effectively. Over a period of time, adjustments were made and the school became a cohesive organization with teachers and students working together as well as, and in some cases better than, they had in their previous school.

Finding 3: Inappropriate teacher behavior can be one of the most important causes of student misbehavior.

Teachers' actions can cause students to misbehave. In the majority of cases, teachers are not aware that their behavior may be creating conditions that lead to student misbehavior. When teachers are not well prepared to teach their classes, students may decide that they do not need to pay attention and they may become disengaged from the instruction. Teachers who show favoritism to certain students may make others feel they are not receiving equal treatment and cause some acting out in order to get attention. Sometimes teachers give negative feedback that may be perceived by students as verbal abusiveness. Students often respond by being verbally abusive to the teacher or to other students. It is important for teachers to be aware of their own behavior so they do not stimulate or contribute to student misbehavior.

Scenario.   A high school foreign language teacher was always well prepared for his classes and was exceptionally strong in his content area. When his students did not perform as well as he expected, he would become verbally abusive. The majority of his students did not react to his tirades, and eventually he would calm down. The students in his advanced classes, who were mostly juniors and seniors, began to respond to his abusiveness with negative and sarcastic comments. When they did not respond to his calls to desist, he used one intervention over and over; he sent students to the office. It was not long before some of the best students in school were spending a good deal of time in the administrative offices.

The teacher in this scenario was creating insubordination among students who had gone through school without any instances of serious misbehavior. In spite of visits with parents, counselors, and administrators, the teacher refused to believe that he was causing the problem. The situation deteriorated completely when the best student in the advanced language program was sent from the room during one of the teacher's emotional outbursts. The student reported to his counselor who immediately went to the teacher's room to resolve the conflict. The teacher was sitting at his desk distraught, and the students were trying to find something to do to keep themselves occupied. He was devastated by his own behavior because the boy he had just sent out of class was one of his favorite students.

The school provided the teacher with support and assistance to help him change a behavior that was on the verge of ending his teaching career. He finally accepted the fact that he had reacted negatively largely because he could not tolerate any response that was not almost perfect. He did work very hard to adjust his level of tolerance for imperfection and tried to substitute neutral or positive responses when he was tempted to be negative or abusive. Over a period of time the teacher improved his relationships with his students, and the misconduct in his classes decreased in direct proportion to his own improvement.

Finding 4: Student misbehavior may range from frequent nondestructive actions to occasional aggressive, hostile behavior.

Teachers are challenged daily by a broad spectrum of student misbehaviors. They range from subtle forms such as faking involvement, appearing to be disinterested, and acting confused about teacher expectations to more disconcerting and destructive misbehaviors such as emotional outbursts, physical abuse, and hostile actions. These overt misbehaviors generally occur less frequently. Misbehavior of all types demands teacher attention and can negatively impact the learning environment.

Scenario.   An elementary school teacher had a rare gift for dealing with almost any student misbehavior. She was a picture of equanimity in virtually all of her interactions with students. She remained calm when others would become upset and lose their composure. She was able to prevent most potential behavior management problems by planning well and being proactive. She was diligent about getting to know her students and understanding their special needs. When students did misbehave, she carefully and calmly intervened so that she did not exacerbate the situation. She asked questions such as "What can I do to help you?" when other teachers would have given reprimands. Her presence usually helped everyone settle down, and then she could resolve the problem.

A number of teachers wondered what would happen if this teacher was ever involved in a hostile, aggressive conflict. Some thought she would lose her composure and respond with hostility; they could not believe that she would remain her calm, cool self. One day a fourth grade boy became very emotional about a problem that he had on the playground. When the teacher tried to reason with him, he became more and more upset and in a fit of anger kicked her as hard as he could. She was obviously stunned and in considerable pain. In spite of this, she calmly put her arm around the boy and asked him what she had done to upset him. By then he had realized what he had done and began to cry and apologize to the teacher. She continued to talk with him and shortly thereafter he was able to go to class and function reasonably well. She had put his needs and well-being ahead of her own and as a consequence was able to help him work effectively in the classroom. Some believed the boy should have been punished, but the teacher took the position that her responsibility was to help all students succeed in school and that the boy needed her help.

Finding 5: Before appropriate corrective measures can be taken, teachers must understand the causes and influences of misbehavior.

New teachers are especially prone to dealing with the symptoms of misbehavior rather than attempting to determine the cause of the problem. It is much easier to use corrective measures without taking into account why students are acting out. Secondary school teachers, especially, have trouble getting to know all of their students well enough to know why they behave the way they do. It is also easier to identify school influences that can be a factor in creating problems than it is to find out what kind of pressures a student may be experiencing at home. If teachers take the time to get to really know their students, they will be in a better position to use behavior management strategies that will help to solve problems rather than make them worse.

Scenario.   A high school American history and government teacher had six classes a day with more than 35 students in each class. One of his history students was a girl who seemed to have a good personality and functioned well in school most of the time. She was, for the most part, well liked by her peers, and because she was physically attractive, she received the attention of many of the boys in class. There were days, however, when she would become very loud and obnoxious in class. She appeared to want to have conflict with someone, especially the teacher. He usually responded with a mild reprimand and ultimately she would settle down enough to get through class.

The teacher met with the girl's counselor and shared his concerns. The counselor could not shed any light on the matter, and the girl refused to discuss it with the counselor. One day the young woman became very loud and profane in class. The teacher was on the verge of removing her from class when he noticed that she had a large bruise on the side of her face that she had tried to cover with her make-up. He managed to quiet her down and asked her to meet with him after class. She stayed after class and agreed to talk with him further after school. During a rather lengthy and tearful discussion, she told her teacher that she was physically punished at home for seemingly minor problems and at times received severe beatings from her father. The school psychologist and other support personnel became involved and worked with the girl and her family to resolve the problems at home. The parents were told at one point that they would lose custody of the girl unless they stopped the abuse. The psychologist told the teacher that the girl had probably been trying to get someone's attention with her inappropriate classroom behavior in hopes that she would get some help. Whatever the reason, it was fortunate that the teacher was able to identify the cause of the misbehavior before using corrective measures that might have caused the girl to feel that she was also being abused at school.

Finding 6: A number of factors influence teachers' decisions about how and when to intervene to correct student behavior.

The most effective teachers seem to be able to use good judgment as well as intuition when they make decisions to correct student behavior. Truly expert teachers seem to make intervention decisions almost automatically. They do not appear to be very deliberate in the decision-making process. If student misbehavior is hostile or aggressive, these teachers know they must act quickly to prevent others from being harmed. When the misbehavior is relatively passive and will not be harmful to other students, the teacher's primary consideration is the effect the intervention will have on the total instructional process. Sometimes teachers intervene because the behavior is bothersome to them, even though it has little or no effect on the other students. When this happens, valuable instructional time can be lost and the learning of all of the students can be negatively affected.

Scenario.   Two teachers intervened very differently when one of their students would sleep in their classes. A high school science teacher observed that one of the students in the back of the classroom went to sleep during his lecture. None of the other students appeared to notice, and most of them were generally attentive to the lecture. Suddenly the teacher stopped his presentation, walked to the back of the room, and with a great deal of fanfare awakened the student. He then chastised the student and threatened to kick him out of class if it happened again. The entire episode took only several minutes, but a considerable amount of time elapsed before the class got back on task. The teacher had to find out where he was in his presentation, and the students had to get their attention off of their friend's plight and back on the lecture.

A fourth grade teacher handled a sleeping student very differently. When one of the boys in her class kept falling asleep, she used out-of-class time to visit with him and find out why he was always so tired. After some discussion he told her that his parents were heavy drinkers and that almost every night they had a loud argument or fight. Because this usually happened late at night, it kept him from sleeping. He was obviously upset about the situation, which also contributed to his insomnia. The teacher told him that she wanted him at school each day no matter how tired he was, and if he got too tired he could sleep. She also offered to work with him after school to help him stay up to date with his work. The teacher did have the boy sit at a desk where the other students would not notice him if he went to sleep. She also explained to the class that because of special circumstances his school day would be a little different from theirs. As a result of this teacher's extra effort, and her consideration of the needs of the boy, he was able to have a successful school year. Furthermore, the rest of the class did not lose any instructional time because of one student's problems.

Finding 7: Teachers manage behavior most effectively if they employ a wide range of corrective measures.

Teachers need to use a range of corrective strategies to deal effectively with different types of student misbehavior. It is especially important for teachers to use correctives that are appropriate for the misbehavior. For example, punishing students severely for minor infractions can lead to further misbehavior. Teachers are most effective when they have a plan for dealing with misbehavior so that they know which correctives they will use when misbehavior occurs. Some teachers have found that it helps to work with other teachers to identify corrective measures that are deemed to be most appropriate for various behavior problems. Although there is no right strategy for every situation, teachers can respond more effectively to problems when they have several options available.

Scenario.   A junior high school principal was to observe a second-year mathematics teacher who was having discipline and management problems. When he observed the class, the teacher repeatedly used the same corrective in response to student misbehavior. Whenever a student misbehaved, the teacher would put the student's initials on the chalkboard. If the student misbehaved a second time, a check would be put next to the initials. Soon many of the students wanted to have their initials on the board, and they thought it was an honor to have the most checks next to your name. Before the class was over, the chalkboard was covered with initials and checkmarks. More time was spent making this tally than working on mathematics problems.

During a visit with the teacher after class, she said that she had picked up this management technique from a workshop and had used it ever since. She said it seemed to work at first but had become less and less effective. Originally she told the students that after so many marks they would have to stay after school. Pretty soon she realized that most all of her students from nearly all of her classes would have to be kept after school. She would have had to use the auditorium or cafeteria to seat all of them. The students realized that having their names on the chalkboard would have no effect on them and used it as a way of keeping the teacher off task. It took the teacher a long time and a considerable amount of help from her colleagues before she developed an effective repertoire of behavior management strategies.

Finding 8: Corrective measures should be viewed by teachers and students as being appropriate consequences for misbehavior.

At every grade level most students seem to have a sense of what is fair and what is overly punitive. They tend to be supportive of corrective measures that seem appropriate to the misbehavior. On the other hand, students will take exception to their classmates' being corrected too harshly for what they feel are minor offenses. They also get quite upset when they see one student being "picked on" by a teacher or administrator. Inappropriate teacher responses to a student's misbehavior tend to elicit additional misbehavior from other students.

Scenario.   A junior high school principal decided that he was going to shape up his school. He announced that in the future any student sent to his office for any reason would receive a minimum of five swats with a paddle. At first this new edict seemed to work and there were fewer and fewer referrals. It was not long, however, before several popular and generally well-behaved students were sent to his office for relatively minor offenses. They received their swats and did not complain too much. When several of the other students found out why their friends had been paddled, they became upset and organized an unusual type of rebellion against the principal. They made an agreement that they would do things that would get them referred to the principal until he would have to paddle most of the student body. Even some of the teachers were sympathetic to the students and began to send students to the office for almost any misbehavior. The principal had a waiting line most of the day and as a result he spent most of his time and energy administering the punishment.

The principal soon realized that his edict had backfired and was creating a significant amount of student misbehavior. Although he had lost credibility and trust with the student body, he did rescind the "swat rule." With the help of the teaching staff and some of the student leaders, a policy for handling referrals based on individual circumstances was agreed upon. A range of corrective measures was identified as appropriate, but paddling was not included. Discipline in the school improved as the students responded in a positive manner to the new program. They liked to tell the story about how they had improved the principal's health. All the paddling, they said, had helped him lose some weight and improve the muscle tone in his right arm.

Finding 9: The use of punishment to correct misbehavior does not have a long-term positive effect nor does it teach students the desired behavior.

Any action that causes physical or psychological pain may be considered a form of punishment. Punishment most often used in schools ranges from social isolation and withholding privileges to corporal punishment, suspension, and expulsion from school. Inflicting pain on students may help them understand what they should not do, but it does not teach them how to behave. Punishment may deter some students from misbehaving, but it does not produce long-term constructive changes in behavior.

Scenario.   A number of junior high and high school students were interviewed to find out how they viewed discipline in their schools. Students who had very few problems in school described discipline as a form of good self-control. Students who had experienced numerous problems in school described discipline as punishment. They associated discipline with some form of pain. Students in this category continued to have frequent behavior problems. The punitive, painful actions they experienced did not seem to have a positive effect on their behavior.

A second grade teacher in a small city school district had a transfer student in her class who had already been identified as a discipline problem. His previous teacher reported that no matter how she punished him he continued to misbehave. She also noted that after she conferenced with his parents about his behavior they paddled him. It was apparent that the boy had not been taking any responsibility for his own behavior and that he was not responding well to being punished. His new teacher decided that she would try a different approach. She talked with the boy privately about how she expected him to act and told him that he was going to be responsible for his own behavior. She did not threaten to punish him, she simply began to teach him how to behave. The teacher had to spend a lot of time with the boy talking to him about how to behave and getting him to use self-talk to coach himself. She met with him after school whenever he did not have a good day. They talked about what he had done and ways to avoid repeating negative experiences. The teacher stressed any evidence of progress. Over a period of time the boy began to behave appropriately throughout most of the school day. He was learning how to behave and had fewer and fewer problems. This teacher's patience and her belief that the student had experienced enough pain had a positive payoff for the student as well as for the teacher and other members of the class.

Finding 10: Teachers can use specific procedures to develop long-term behavior intervention programs.

Long-term intervention strategies generally help students learn to manage their own behavior. If long-term intervention procedures are to be effective, they have to be carefully planned, appropriate for the students, based on sound principles of human behavior, and regularly assessed. Long-term intervention strategies need to be based on consistent and predictable expectations. It is extremely difficult, if not impossible, to be successful with any program if the rules or expectations keep changing, or if they are not applied uniformly. Students want to be able to predict how teachers and administrators will respond when they are faced with problems. Adequate structure and security must be provided so students can function effectively in a group environment.

Scenario.   Several years ago a number of schools were experimenting with a long-term behavior management program. Several features of the program seemed to be especially helpful in prompting and sustaining behavior changes with unruly students. One of the most effective aspects of the program was developing behavior contracts with students. Contracts were used with students whose misbehavior tended to persist when less formal measures were used. Students were expected to describe their misbehavior and to develop a list of consequences that would be appropriate for dealing with the misbehavior. They signed the contracts, and in some cases parents were asked to read the contracts and sign off on them. Not all contracts were successful, of course, but when the teachers persisted in using this strategy, students were always fully aware of the consequences if they misbehaved.

A number of elementary teachers also used class meetings to talk about problems and seek appropriate solutions. When there was chronic misbehavior during recess, at lunch, or within the classroom, teachers might decide to hold a class meeting to discuss the problem. At first, some students thought the meetings were a lot of fun and did not seem to be serious about solving behavior problems. When teachers systematically used this approach, students began to see the meetings as problem-solving sessions where their opinions were valued, and the approach became more and more effective.

 ## GUIDE TO OBSERVATION, ANALYSIS, AND REFLECTION

Arrange to observe teachers in regular classrooms and, if possible, in classes especially for children who often exhibit inappropriate behavior or are considered to be difficult to manage. The observations should focus on the events before, during, and after misbehavior. Prior to observing, try to obtain a seating chart and find out which students tend to behave inappropriately. Observation notes should describe teacher and student verbal and physical behavior with direct statements, anecdotal descriptions, or charts, maps, and tallies. After making observations, review your records with the teachers to analyze what is occurring and possibly why the behaviors occurred. Observing and analyzing the behavior management practices of other teachers provide a framework for formulating and adapting approaches to deal with student misbehavior.

1. Student misbehavior

Observation: What student misbehaviors are occurring? Record information about student actions and statements that you believe indicate inappropriate behavior. Note the time the incidents take place and which students are involved. Remember to look for the subtle forms of inappropriate behavior as well as more overt misbehaviors. It may be appropriate to focus your observations on a few key students.

Analysis: To what extent do the identified student misbehaviors interfere with the learning process? Begin by summarizing the observation information. Include the most frequent, moderately frequent, and least frequent misbehaviors, the number of students, and the amount of time involved in each case. With the teacher's help, determine if and how the learning process was hindered by student misbehavior. Look at individual students and compare the amount of time spent engaged in learning activities versus the amount of time they did not seem to be involved.

Compare your perceptions of student misbehavior with the teacher's perceptions. It is important to understand whether the misbehaviors are typical of the students and whether these misbehaviors denote improvement or regression in self-control.

Reflection: *What student behaviors would I consider inappropriate for my students?*   Based on your knowledge of the students and the time of the year, decide if the misbehaviors observed are appropriate for students you teach or expect to teach. Identify the behaviors that are unacceptable, those that represent improvement or regression, and those that have little negative impact on student learning and on the teaching process.

2. Antecedent conditions

Observation: *What is the teacher doing prior to the student misbehavior?*   Focus specifically on the teacher. Consider what the teacher is doing but also what the teacher may not be doing. Observation notes could include any negative or verbally abusive comments and the ways behavioral expectations are communicated. Look for a lack of preventive actions, such as actively monitoring, using verbal and nonverbal cues, and modeling on-task behavior.

Analysis: *In what ways are teacher behaviors contributing to student misbehavior?*   Look for patterns in the teacher's physical and verbal behaviors. Also, try to link teacher behaviors to student misbehaviors. If certain teacher behaviors consistently lead to student misbehavior, discuss strategies for modifying those teacher behaviors. If specific teacher behaviors seem to promote appropriate student behavior, suggest ways to continue or strengthen those behaviors.

Reflection: *What teacher misbehaviors do I want to avoid in my teaching?*   From your observations or your own teaching experiences you may have identified teacher actions that seem to provoke or at least allow student misbehavior. Identify several critical teacher misbehaviors. Devise ways to eliminate or prevent those behaviors. For example, if relating poorly to certain students is a problem for you, think of specific steps you can take to develop positive relationships with target students. Also reflect on those specific behaviors you model for your students. Are those behaviors consistent with the behaviors you expect from your students?

3. Instructional conditions

Observation: *What instructional conditions are present when student misbehaviors occur?*   Note the type of instructional activity, such as seatwork, group work, or recitation that is occurring when misbehavior occurs. Include a description of the students' expected behavior, such as their level of involvement in the lesson. Also note the time span of the activity. Record indications of whether the level of challenge is appropriate, such as the students' ability to do the task, their level of frustration, or failure to attempt the task. It may be advantageous to observe the same group of students in several different task structures.

Analysis: *What instructional conditions appear to contribute to student misbehavior?*   Analysis should address the productive and nonproductive outcomes of various instructional conditions. Determine which factors are linked to student misbehavior, such as the way the students are organized, the degree of engagement required, the perceived relevance of the task, the students' expectations of success, and the duration of the activity. Discuss possible ways that nonproductive instructional conditions might be changed.

Reflection: *In thinking about planning for instruction and planning to maintain order, what are the important conditions to consider?*   In reflecting on the group of students you know best, describe the aspects of instruction that best fit your needs and the characteristics of your students. Consider the content to be covered and how the students can most effectively process the material. For example, if the students are older, insecure learners who exhibit minimal self-control, they may need to work independently in short spurts spread over the week rather than participate in a full class period of lecture and recitation.

4. Corrective measures

Observation: *What corrective measures are used?*   As misbehavior occurs, record the actions the teacher takes to correct the misbehavior. Note the number of times correctives are used and the specific correctives used. Teacher actions could range from no overt response to unobtrusive responses and more forceful actions. If there are any indications of long-term behavior management systems, such as the use of contracts or behavioral checklists, these should be cited.

Analysis: *What influences the teacher's use of corrective measures?*   Categorize the corrective measures used as unobtrusive or obtrusive and instructional or punitive. With the teacher's assistance, assess the relationship among the specific student misbehaviors, the correctives used, and the target students. Ask the teacher to share his or her rationale for using particular correctives and the sequence that guides the use of the correctives. Find out if particular student characteristics influence the use of correctives.

Reflection: *What corrective measures will I use in my behavior management system?*   You may have identified corrective measures that address common, minor misbehaviors and measures that address more serious misbehaviors. Plan ways to incorporate constructive interventions in your management system. If punitive measures were used, pose more constructive alternatives.

5. Outcome of the intervention

Observation: *After correctives are used, what is the resulting student behavior?*   Focus on the degree of compliance the students exhibit and their apparent attitude.

Record student statements or behaviors that indicate their level of compliance. Descriptions of student attitude will be subjective but may provide relevant information.

Analysis: *What impact does the use of correctives have on subsequent student behavior and attitude?*   Synthesize a description of the student's reactions to corrective measures. Decide if the reactions were consistent with the teacher's expectations. Assess the ultimate effectiveness of the correctives used in terms of both individual and group student behavior and attitude, and positive resolution of the conflict. If the corrective measures were judged to be ineffective in eliciting the desired student reaction, suggest alternative actions.

Reflection: *What behavior management strategies produce positive resolutions to teacher-student and student-student conflicts?*   In reflecting on your observations and analyses, think about those teachers who were effective in dealing with students who have behavior problems. List the strategies these teachers use to deal with challenging students. Think about how you can develop strategies that will be most effective for you.

It is important that teachers have an image of the desired result of their intervention strategies. From a teacher's viewpoint, describe what would constitute a positive resolution of typical problem situations. Also think about the end result from the student's perspective. Decide which corrective measures effectively stop the misbehavior but also allow students to regain normal status and promote self-controlled, responsible action.

 ## DEVELOPMENT AND RENEWAL ACTIVITIES

1. If there are opportunities to observe simulated incidents involving misbehaving students, describe specific student misbehaviors, inappropriate teacher actions and instructional conditions, interventions used, and the resulting student behavior.

2. After your behavior management system has been planned and implemented, regular systematic observation and assessment should occur. Observing student behaviors is the best method for gaining information about the effectiveness of your behavior management strategies. Focus your observations, enlisting the help of a colleague as needed, on these areas:

- Regularity of student misbehavior
- Severity of student misbehavior
- Number of students off task and uninvolved
- Effectiveness of correctives

If the level of student misbehavior is unacceptable, make the necessary changes in your management system.

3. The way in which teachers regularly communicate with students is a powerful influence on how students respond and behave. Observe college instructors and other teachers or have a colleague observe you to note important communication patterns. Verbal and nonverbal actions such as the following should be listed:

- Using judgmental terms (as opposed to objective descriptions)
- Nagging or pleading
- Berating a student in front of other students
- Using "we" statements, humor, and individual students' names
- Acknowledging students' accomplishments and interests
- Modeling appropriate listening skills
- Using supportive body language

After the observation, decide which communication patterns promote positive student attitudes and responses and which patterns interfere with effective teacher-student interactions.

4. List the misbehaviors you have experienced as a teacher or an observer from the least severe to the most severe. Then make a parallel list of consequences you have used (or would use) from the least severe to the most severe. Respond to the following questions:

- Is the range of consequences consistent with or adequate to address the range of misbehaviors?
- Are consequences logically related to misbehaviors?
- Are consequences specific and clear?
- Are consequences punitive or instructional?
- Could consequences be easily applied regardless of time and place?

5. Teachers need to develop success expectations for difficult students and confidence in dealing with them effectively. If you are currently teaching, target one challenging student, perhaps not the most difficult but one you feel is capable of improving. If you are not currently teaching, identify a particular student about whom you are knowledgeable. For either case, develop a plan to modify that student's behavior. Address the following steps in your plan:

- Identify specific misbehaviors and prioritize the misbehaviors from the most to least disruptive.
- Develop possible strategies to address the problem.
- Decide on internal and external influences that might be modified. Think about factors you could change in your behavior in addition to changes the student needs to make. Also consider environmental changes you could make in seating arrangement, scheduling, grouping, and so on.
- Apply and evaluate the strategies (if possible). In assessing the outcome of the intervention, identify beforehand the desired student behaviors that

would indicate progress. Small steps are significant and can add up to great changes over the long term.

- Plan ways to maintain the appropriate behavior once it has been established.

If a generalized behavior problem exists, such as students being rude or using abusive language, develop a plan to address the situation. Be sure to include your plan for providing instruction on desired behaviors, modeling of appropriate behaviors, reinforcing students who exhibit the appropriate behavior, and providing opportunities for students to practice appropriate behaviors.

6. If you have experienced confrontation from a student, assess your reactions during the incident. (As an alternative, view simulated, videotaped incidents.) Analyze your response using the following questions:

- Did you react emotionally or remain cool and calm?
- Were you responding to a specific misbehavior or "history"?
- Did you view the misbehavior as a personal affront?
- Did you identify the responsible offending student?
- Did you respond in a timely manner?
- Did you provide a way for the student to stop the misbehavior in a dignified way?
- What other corrective actions did you consider using? What would have been your next step?
- What will you do differently the next time you experience conflict with a student?

7.

MAKING INSTRUCTIONAL DECISIONS

COMMENTARY

Teachers do make a difference in how students learn. This may seem like an obvious statement to anyone who has ever taught, but there has been a considerable amount of debate about the amount of influence teachers have on student learning. Some years ago a study was released that concluded that teachers had little effect on student learning. The major influences, according to this study, were the child's socioeconomic background and environmental conditions beyond the control of teachers. Certainly these are powerful influences and they do affect all aspects of a child's life. The evidence from current research and practical knowledge, however, clearly supports the position that what teachers do has a profound effect on student learning.

The decisions teachers make in organizing and managing instructional tasks have a significant impact on student outcomes. Oftentimes teachers are not aware of the many instructional decisions they make each day. When we have observed teachers and have given them feedback about their preactive and interactive decisions, they are often amazed at the number of decisions they make as they organize and engage in the instructional process. For example, the decisions made about task structure create instructional conditions that have a direct effect on student learning. Because each structure demands certain behaviors of students and teachers and each task requires certain cognitive skills, teachers' selections of learning tasks and structures can greatly limit or expand opportunities to learn. In some cases, task structure decisions are made to increase and enhance student cooperation with the teacher or with other students. Whatever the reasons for these decisions, there is no question that they are critical.

There are a number of schoolwide organizational decisions over which teachers have very little control and not much involvement or input. This is beginning to change with the current emphasis on participatory management and teacher empowerment. For the time being, however, teachers must make their classroom instructional decisions within the context of school or systemwide conditions. For example, the amount of time allocated to instruction is often dictated by factors such as bus and cafeteria schedules. Because time is such an important resource, decisions about allocated time have a major impact on the instructional program.

The routines established by teachers directly influence the quality and quantity of learning opportunities. Most teachers select specific classroom routines they will establish and monitor so that they can make maximum use of learning time. When routines have been established, teachers can concentrate their efforts on interactive instructional decision making. We regularly observe classes that flow so smoothly it's as if invisible rules were guiding the interactions of students and teachers. In these classrooms learning and positive attitudes are greatly enhanced because teachers can concentrate their efforts on attending to student needs.

Teachers who are expert in making instructional decisions have a positive influence on the quality of student learning. We believe that these experts, who in many ways are very different from one another, have several similar characteristics and behaviors. Virtually all of them have established classroom routines and patterns that are so well developed and managed that students know exactly what to expect and how to behave. Expert teachers are skillful at orchestrating physical and mental moves from one topic or task structure to another. They also are more likely to monitor the learning progress of all of their students as well as their compliance with expectations. Alterations in the flow of events, the cues used to signal important points, and the pacing of instruction are made when these teachers see the need to improve student success rates. Expert teachers seem to intuitively understand the importance of interacting with each student, and they devise creative ways to ensure maximum participation in the learning process.

RATIONALE

Teachers, over a period of time, tend to develop patterns of behavior during interactive instruction. Some of these patterns are conscious while others appear to be subliminal. Certain patterns of behavior have a significant and positive effect on student learning, while others have a negative effect. In some cases, teachers' behavior patterns will have little or no influence on student performance.

All teachers should be aware of their instructional interaction patterns and the effect these patterns have on student behavior. By being aware of their interactive behavior, teachers can make conscious decisions about which interactive patterns will have the most positive influence on their students. For example, a solid research base supports the position that teachers should carefully monitor student behavior during seatwork and other independent learning activities. Teachers should be aware of their monitoring patterns and, if necessary, make adjustments to ensure that they are effectively monitoring students.

There has been a considerable amount of research on the use of allocated learning time. The studies done in this area point out that the amount of time that students are academically engaged in classrooms varies widely depending on teaching patterns and expectations. Some teachers expect class to start on time and students to be engaged in learning tasks throughout the class period. Other teachers do not appear to make efficient use of learning time a high priority. Less organized and focused, they may allow a good deal of class time to be used for noninstructional activities. When teachers are aware of how they use their allocated time, they are more likely to plan and organize their instruction to make the best use of the time available to them and their students.

Pacing a lesson is an important instructional process that is closely related to the use of learning time. If teachers are not aware of the pace of instruction, they may end up cramming in important points at the end of a lesson, or they may never get to the critical information. Some of the most significant interactive decisions are related to pacing instruction. Teachers must know when to slow down, when to reteach important points, or when to increase the instructional pace to keep students on task.

Teachers, especially in elementary schools, must manage many transitions during the school day. These transitions can use up a significant amount of the allocated learning time. Teachers at all levels need to be able to manage transitions so that a minimum amount of instructional time is lost. This is especially critical in activity and laboratory classes where student movement is the norm and where materials and equipment must be organized to support instruction.

Teachers are expected to foster substantive interactions focusing on the content to be taught, but there are times when it is important to attend to the personal needs of students. This does not mean that teachers should ignore the curriculum, but they must make instructional decisions that will develop positive attitudes toward learning as well as focus on content expectations. The more teachers know about the instructional decision-making process and how their own patterns of behavior affect instructional interactions, the better prepared they will be to make decisions that benefit their students.

RESEARCH SYNTHESIS

The Concept of Organizing Instruction

Classrooms are workplaces where teachers have instructional management responsibilities. Berliner (1982) identified the executive functions teachers perform as they plan and manage instruction:

- Planning the work, which includes selecting content and activity or task structures, scheduling, and assigning groups
- Communicating instructional goals
- Regulating instructional activities by pacing, sequencing, monitoring success, and controlling behavior

Teachers have control over these executive functions, and the ways teachers perform them affect the achievement of their students and their attitude toward learning.

Determining the task or activity structure is an important aspect of instructional planning. This process is illustrated in Figure 7–1. Instructional tasks can be classified. Eleven activity (task) structures commonly occur in elementary classrooms. Reading circles, seatwork, two-way presentation, and one-way presentation are examples of activity or task structures. Each instructional activity can be described in terms of its duration, number of students involved, the public or private nature of student responses, the role of the participants, the locus of control (teacher or students), the stability of the group, the degree of student attending, evaluation, and feedback (Berliner, 1983; Doyle, 1986b). Each activity structure will have different combinations of these conditions. Doyle (1986b) noted that secondary classrooms have less variety in activity structure and that some differences in structure can be attributed to the nature of the subject matter.

Instruction is a series of tasks and routines carefully defined and sequenced. Teachers present tasks to students and furnish the necessary external resources to accomplish the tasks (Marx, 1983; Posner, 1982). These resources include a goal and a set of operations that are necessary to achieve the goal (Posner, 1982). Of critical importance to the quality of student thinking and learning that occurs are the operations or cognitive strategies required to complete the instructional tasks (Mergen-

FIGURE 7–1. Making decisions about task structure

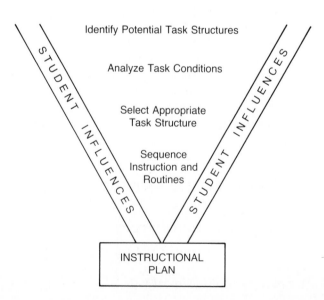

doller, Marchman, Mitman, & Packer, 1988; Marx, 1983). Tasks influence the learning processes and determine what students will practice and subsequently learn.

Analyzing task or problem structures and response formats to determine the level of cognitive challenge is another significant teacher planning activity. Several frameworks are helpful in conducting this analysis. Doyle (1986a) identified four types of instructional tasks based on the cognitive challenge they offer: memory, procedural, comprehension, and opinion. Memory tasks require recognizing and recalling previously learned information. Procedural or routine tasks involve applying a set of predictable solutions to questions or problems that have one correct answer. Comprehension or understanding tasks challenge students to decide on an appropriate solution and apply it to new information. Opinion tasks engage students in defending a point of view. Common instructional tasks can be categorized by the level of mental challenge required.

From a teacher's perspective, several factors tend to influence the choice of instructional tasks. One factor is the anticipated degree of student cooperation. Teachers generally incorporate instructional content, arrangements, and activities they know they can implement successfully (Doyle, 1981). Doyle (1986) noted, "The decisions teachers make to enhance order affect the quality of academic work and thus the quality of what students learn" (p. 417). A tension exists between classroom management considerations and instructional considerations; a high value is placed on the appearance of a well-managed, productive classroom.

Related to concerns for student cooperation are concerns about the demands of different instructional formats. These demands depend on the size of the group, cognitive level, risk, and ambiguity. Teachers tend to assign tasks with lower cognitive demand because these tasks lead to more student cooperation and fewer management demands for teachers (Mergendoller et al., 1988; Doyle, 1986). One study reported that 60% of the tasks assigned involved familiar content and context (many times involving specific skills, memorization, and following procedural directions) (Mergendoller et al., 1988).

Common instructional tasks demand certain teacher and student behaviors. During whole-class recitations, which are two-way presentations, the demands on the teacher are high. Teachers must attend to content development, pace, and student behavior. Teachers provide a continuous academic signal and appropriate support materials. Recitations require teachers to have situational awareness and memory. During successful recitations, teacher actions result in a high student engagement rate of 80 to 90% (Doyle & Carter, 1987). In contrast to recitations, discussions are mutually constructed situations in which more equal demands are placed on both students and teacher.

Student ability level appears to influence teachers' selections of instructional tasks. In general, teachers tend to use shorter presentations with lower ability groups, taking less time on particular topics and being less explicit in their instructions. Lower ability groups are usually required to complete fewer assignments and do more busy work (Tobin, 1987b). Gamoran and Berends (1987) found that lower track students experienced simplified, slower paced instruction. These students appeared to be more comfortable with less taxing, more routine, independent written work. Tobin (1987b) noted that films were used more often with lower ability students. Very often these films had not been previewed and contained content beyond the ability level of the students.

Students attend to instructional tasks differently depending on their previous knowledge and experience, the amount of effort that is required, the expectation for success, the anticipated benefit, and the degree of risk and ambiguity involved (Posner, 1982). Students who lack experience and feel uncomfortable or defeated by certain content or structures may respond differently than students who have previously been successful and tolerate a higher level of ambiguity. Accountability measures influence completion and accuracy. If students believe that the work will influence their grade, they give it more significance (Doyle, 1986b). Feedback about the adequacy of the work affects engagement and effort (Marx & Walsh, 1988). Comments about what has been accomplished and what is left to do help students stay involved.

An important consideration in task structure decisions is the impact on students' motivation to learn. The expectation for responding publicly produces anxiety in some students. Marx and Walsh (1988) found that teachers differ greatly in the degree to which they expect students to respond publicly. Task and classroom structure influences students' perceptions of their own abilities and the abilities of others (Marx, 1983). If all students are required to attempt the same tasks, the teacher has a high degree of control and students are readily able to compare their academic and social status to other students. If students engage in different tasks, teacher control is reduced because students have some control over instructional decisions, and social comparison is less easy (Marx & Walsh, 1988). Engaging in group work with peers may require students to develop new engagement styles (Marx & Walsh, 1988).

Academic Learning Time

Numerous research studies have focused on the relationship of student learning to the amount of time spent on instructional tasks. Many findings suggest that the reason time is only a modest predictor of school achievement is that several other factors intervene. According to Gettinger (1989), "How much time a learner needs to spend in learning . . . depends largely on what goes on during the learning time" (p. 74).

In recent years a great deal of attention has been given to the management of time in schools. The amount of time given to overall instructional activities (allocated time) is controlled at the school or system level. Teachers then allocate class time based on their goals and priorities. The amount of time students appear to be engaged in learning activities is referred to as time on task. However, it is not enough for students just to be on task. It is important for them to have a high rate of success while engaged in activities or using materials that are directly related to the learning outcomes. This is referred to as academic learning time (ALT) (Berliner, 1984). Figure 7–2 shows how the amount of allocated time relates to the potential amount of academic learning time.

It has been reported that the maximum estimate of daily instructional time is about 60% of the school day. This is the time actually used for planned instructional activities (Karweit, 1983). The total amount of engaged time is estimated to be about

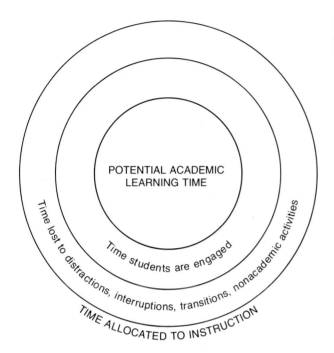

FIGURE 7–2. How academic learning time relates to allocated instructional time

40% of the time allocated for classroom instruction. There are, of course, wide variations in engaged time within and across classrooms. Rosenshine (1980) estimated that in elementary classrooms students spend 30% of their time in teacher-directed activities and 50 to 70% of their time doing seatwork. Student engagement rate is higher when students are working directly with a teacher or another adult.

The percentage of academic learning time is usually considerably less than the amount of engaged time. Berliner (1984) contended that a positive example of ALT for 100 minutes of allocated time would be when students pay attention 85% of the time and are at a high success level about 67% of that time. This would yield about 52 minutes of learning time.

Both standardized and criterion-referenced tests show that teachers and schools that allocate more time to academic activities improve academic learning. Although the total time allocated to classroom instruction may be difficult to change, teachers can set priorities for instructional time that help them increase ALT in their classrooms and, therefore, student achievement. Teachers who spend a minimum amount of time on nonlearning activities increase ALT and the opportunity for their students to learn. Decisions that alter ALT change student learning opportunities and priorities (Porter, 1989). For example, when teachers focus on academic instruction that is curriculum related, they will have greater gains in achievement than when the instruction is not curriculum based (Brophy & Good, 1986).

Critics have raised a number of concerns about the attention given to increasing engaged time. They point out that more time does not necessarily mean more learning. The quality of the time and the instruction, rather than the quantity, is the critical variable. Mandating more time for academic activities could have negative results if the instruction or resources are not appropriate (Karweit, 1988).

Another concern is that students may be denied opportunities for socialization when the major focus is on the amount of time on task. Learning does not occur in single episodes without interaction between learning activities. Squires, Huitt, and Segars (1983) contended that the amount of time necessary to produce expected achievement is greater than might be predicted.

Teacher Awareness and Influence.   If ALT is to be increased, teachers need to be aware of how instructional time is lost. This can help them to make adjustments and in some cases learn how to cope with the influences that reduce instructional time. Levin and Long (1981) pointed out that teachers need to "observe" and analyze their instructional patterns to spot nonacademic activities that do not contribute to learning. For example, in many classrooms large amounts of instructional time may be lost to transitions. In one study, one fourth of the instructional time in a multistationed classroom was lost to student movement between stations (Berliner, 1984). Transitions are necessary, but unless they are carefully managed, a considerable amount of learning time may be lost.

Distractions reduce instructional time (Doyle, 1986b; Behnke & Labovitz, 1981). Distractions may be generated by the school, students, teachers, and external influences. Effective teachers use a variety of coping techniques to keep distractions to a minimum. One of the most productive techniques is careful planning to avoid and minimize potential distractions and loss of time.

Instructional time is also reduced when teachers start class late and end instruction early. Teachers who allow interruptions are sending a message that productive use of class time is unimportant. Frequent breaks, late starts, and early endings demonstrate that learning is not a high priority. Effective teachers allocate time to learning activities, communicate the belief that learning is important, and model the importance of learning through their personal behavior.

Many teachers could improve the way they use instructional time. Student engagement varies depending on each teacher's ability to organize and maintain an efficient learning environment. Teachers need to examine their own teaching practices. They may find that they have more diversity of activities in the classroom than can be properly managed. In such cases they should reduce the variety of classroom activities to make maximum use of learning time. This is especially important when activities require different within-class groupings.

Gage and Berliner (1984) identified specific actions that teachers can take to increase ALT:

1. Establish rules and procedures that students follow without requiring teacher permission.
2. Move around the classroom and monitor student work.
3. Make assignments that are interesting and of value.
4. Keep time used for giving directions and organizing instruction to a minimum.

5. Use instructional materials (textbooks and workbooks) and avoid using games and toys.
6. Make sure that behavior management actions focus on students who are misbehaving.

Achievement is also affected by the teacher's orientation toward learning. Teachers who emphasize cognitive expectations and maintain a high percentage of ALT will usually have high achievement gains. An orientation that is both cognitive and affective leads to moderate ALT and achievement (Fisher et al., 1984). When the emphasis is on the affective, ALT and achievement tend to be low.

Effective use of instructional time is not just the responsibility of teachers. Karweit (1983) pointed out that schools can demonstrate a commitment to maximum use of available instructional time. For example they can forbid unnecessary interruptions and examine scheduling and organization to make sure that the maximum amount of school time is being allocated for instructional purposes.

Student Involvement.   Teachers need to develop strategies to increase student involvement, content coverage, and success rate (Squires et al., 1983). Students who are actively involved in learning have higher achievement than those less involved. While the degree of student involvement in most classrooms will vary widely, the instructional process has a direct effect on the level of involvement. Teachers can increase involvement by accurately preassessing students to determine if they have mastered prerequisite skills and then planning instruction using the assessment information. This will help to ensure a high success rate (Fisher et al., 1984).

Cognitive and affective entry-level characteristics of students should be considered when developing instructional plans. There is a correlation between affective measures such as self-concept and a positive attitude toward school, motivation, and involvement (Levin & Long, 1981). Other student factors to consider include age, socioeconomic status, and aptitude for the subject.

Although teachers should strive to increase student involvement in learning tasks, they should keep in mind that involvement is both overt and covert. It is not always possible to tell if quiet and somewhat passive students are actively engaged in learning tasks. Teachers have to carefully monitor the working habits of these students and the results they obtain before they can make accurate determinations about the level of engagement. Substantive interaction between teachers and students will result in higher levels of student involvement.

Levin and Long (1981) and others have identified several approaches that can be used to increase student involvement in learning tasks:

1. Keep distractions to a minimum.
2. Use clear, well organized materials.
3. Make maximum use of teacher-led group discussions (no small-group discussions without adult supervision).
4. Provide reinforcement for being on task.

5. Vary movement and communication patterns.

6. Distribute time across several activities rather than staying too long with one activity.

Perhaps the most important finding is to recognize that student involvement can be altered to improve engagement rates and academic learning time.

Routines and Interactive Decisions

Routines are recurring activities that become established within a classroom in a predictable sequence. They are "shared socially scripted patterns of behavior" (Leinhardt, Weidman, & Hammond, 1987, p. 135). They are clearly understood by teachers and students and appear to be automatic (Berliner, 1986). Planning for instruction is basically making decisions about the selection, organization, and sequencing of routines (Clark & Peterson, 1986). Teachers string together simple routines to build complex routines (Leinhardt et al., 1987). Teachers follow routines much as actors follow a script.

Once routines become nearly automatic, little effort is required to use them (Berliner, 1986). Routines reduce the cognitive complexity of the learning environment by reducing the number of separate decisions to be made, maintaining the activity flow, and making student behavior more predictable. The information load, demand for cognitive processing, and complexity of the class are also reduced. Teachers are free to concentrate on a few high-priority decisions and deal more effectively with those unpredictable elements of a task (Leinhardt & Greeno, 1986). Routines contribute to classroom order providing a continuous signal for behavior (Doyle, 1986b). Students also benefit from routines because they provide familiar conditions and more constant expectations. Students are free to concentrate on the content when the process is familiar (Leinhardt & Greeno, 1986).

Routines generally fall into three categories—management, instructional support, and teacher-student exchange (Leinhardt et al., 1987). Management routines keep the class running; they address areas such as housekeeping, discipline, and movement. Support routines serve to keep the lesson moving; these routines cover actions such as distributing and collecting papers, getting materials ready, and specifying locations for activities. Exchange routines govern interactions such as calling on students to respond, giving choral responses, and providing teacher feedback. Effective teachers develop a repertoire of routines that promote the accomplishing of goals during the common phases of each class period—entry, settling down, the lesson itself, closing out, and exit (Doyle, 1986b). Teachers teach and rehearse routines with the students. Monitoring the effect of routines is important because students can learn dysfunctional routines easily as functional routines.

Expert teachers and novice teachers differ markedly in their ability to develop and maintain functional routines (Berliner, 1986; Leinhardt & Greeno, 1986). Expert teachers are almost intuitive in maintaining routines. When they try to explain how they maintain routines, they have great difficulty. This is one reason why novices have trouble learning this skill from experts. Expert teachers use routines with clear signals to provide consistency for students. Once in place, their routines require less time, no explanation, and little monitoring. Novice teachers have not established patterned ways to accomplish recurring tasks. Their routines change from lesson to lesson and require effort and time to explain and monitor. Students are more likely to be confused because they see constantly changing requirements (Leinhardt & Greeno, 1986).

When routines are not going as planned, teachers make interactive decisions. They make deliberate choices to implement specific actions. About one third of the decisions relate to instructional strategies and procedures; very few concern the content to be taught. According to Clark and Peterson (1986), teachers make interactive decisions every two minutes. Experienced teachers' interactive decisions are strongly influenced by factors related to student learning. Effective teachers attend to more student cues and make more decisions while teaching (Gagne, 1985). They efficiently use visual scanning. This skill distinguishes expert teachers from less experienced or less effective teachers (Berliner, 1986). They note specific details of student behavior and observe the behavior in relation to other students over a period of time. They look at the behavior in a broad context and consider a number of options when responding to disruptions.

Observations of high school physical education teachers reveal how experienced and inexperienced teachers pay attention to the most informative aspects of successful performance. Inexperienced teachers' decisions are based on student interest in the activity. Experienced teachers respond to learning problems and then apply one of several alternatives; beginning teachers seem unwilling or unable to change their strategy (Gagne, 1985).

The effectiveness of interactive decisions is related to several cognitive skills (Clark & Peterson, 1986). Effective teachers make rapid judgments when a decision point is reached. They are also able to chunk or group discrete events into larger units which reduces the mass of student cues to a manageable number. Successful teachers also are able to differentiate behaviors with immediate significance from those with long-term significance. Less successful teachers, and novice teachers in particular, cannot distinguish the most important cues from those that are unimportant (Berliner, 1988). They get bogged down in details, try to make decisions about too many aspects of the classroom, and consequently lose instructional time. Making appropriate interactive decisions can improve the smoothness, momentum, and overall effectiveness of instruction.

Monitoring Student Progress

The instructional practice of monitoring student progress is positively related to student achievement (Cotton, 1988b). Monitoring involves all those actions teachers take to keep track of students' learning progress and task engagement. Figure 7–3 illustrates the role teachers play in monitoring student learning. Teachers who are effective instructional monitors attend to the behaviors of all students, not just a few. They position themselves appropriately, circulating and looking beyond individual students or a small group. They do not become absorbed with one student for too long (Evertson et al., 1984). Successful monitoring also involves getting the whole class to begin work together and then giving special attention to the slow starters.

Monitoring is beneficial to students and to teachers. Students become more responsible and teachers become better instructors. Monitoring provides information teachers can use as the basis for instructional and management decisions. Effective teachers constantly monitor the group as a whole and individuals within the group for student understanding and learning behavior. Information is gathered through monitoring and interpreted in light of student achievement and attitude. Monitoring involves both information collection and decision making (Cotton, 1988b). Smith and Geoffrey (1968) compared teachers to ringmasters as they monitor activities and control momentum and pace.

Monitoring for learning progress involves both formal and informal approaches, but the overall aim is to hold students accountable for their work. Students need to develop responsibility by participating in class and following through on assignments. To help develop accountability and responsible work behavior, effective teachers employ specific monitoring strategies. One strategy is to develop realistic and specific expectations for student work and to communicate those expectations effectively. This can be accomplished by

- Designing assignments at the appropriate level of difficulty
- Developing a late policy and ways to inform absent students about assignments
- Determining due dates and standards for neatness and form
- Providing appropriate examples and procedures for getting additional help (Emmer, Evertson, Sanford, Clements, & Worsham, 1984)

It is important for teachers to take definite and immediate action if students do not complete or attempt the assigned work. Teachers need to follow up and require that the work be completed.

FIGURE 7–3. Monitoring learning progress

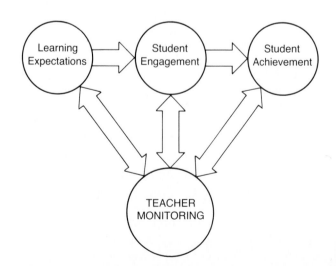

Another monitoring strategy is to employ appropriate assessment practices. Simple routines can be established for students to check their work, get feedback, and correct errors. For long-term assignments, teachers can designate interim checkpoints and due dates. If students record their own grades, they can better monitor their own progress (Worsham, 1981; Cotton, 1988a). Tests and quizzes should be graded and corrected promptly. Teachers occasionally have students check their own work or the work of classmates or use student helpers. This practice is most effective when carefully managed by teachers.

Monitoring techniques that evaluate students' understanding help increase student achievement. Learning probes can be used effectively to determine if the success rate is appropriate and to target students having difficulty. Learning probes can be used in several ways. The teacher can have students summarize the information, ask higher-order questions, use individual chalkboards or response cards, and comment on the responses of other students (Cotton, 1988b). In addition to using probes, teachers should hold periodic reviews on a daily, weekly, or monthly basis to give regular and frequent feedback. Both practices contribute to developing student accountability.

Monitoring of learning behavior is a key to maintaining a classroom management system once it has been established. Teachers must monitor systematically and consistently for adherence to rules. Effective managers are especially watchful for compliance the first few weeks of school. Appropriate behaviors need to be reinforced until the behaviors become automatic. Because some lesson formats are more demanding for monitoring than others, it is generally advisable to use whole-group formats with less complex management demands while students are becoming accustomed to the classroom, learning rules and procedures. Teacher-led activities with uncomplicated content and simple procedures are the easiest to manage. By helping students feel comfortable with the classroom environment, positive attitudes about school can be developed.

Transitions

Transitions occur between major instructional activities. They are "points in social interaction when contexts change" (Doyle, 1986b, p. 406). Transitions are required to start up new activities and to put away materials after instruction (Berliner, 1984). Estimates for the amount of class time spent in transitions range from 10 to 15 to 26% (Doyle, 1986b; Doyle & Carter, 1987; Gump, 1982). In most elementary schools, about 31 major transitions occur per day (Doyle, 1986), while in secondary schools planned transitions occur 3 to 4 times per hour (Steere, 1988). Transition times require additional attention to management because during these intervals almost double the off-task behavior of students and more corrective statements by teachers can occur (Arlin, 1979; Gump, 1982, 1987). Problems during transitions result from a loss of structure, difficulty in detaching students, saved-up tension, and delays in beginning the next segment. Effective management of transitions has a positive effect on the degree of order and student engagement (Doyle & Carter, 1987).

Minimizing time in transitions and maintaining momentum and cooperation are major concerns for teachers (Arlin, 1979; Webber, 1988). The efficiency and smoothness with which transitions are managed influences subsequent activity (Doyle, 1986). Effective teachers conduct transitions in approximately 30 seconds while less effective teachers may take from 4 to 9 minutes (Steere, 1988). It is helpful to structure transitions in three phases. First, teachers can help students close out or detach from an activity by using signals, giving advance warning, setting time limits, and being aware that students may not want to stop the activity. Second, the teacher directs the physical and psychological set-up of the next activity which may require different grouping, location, materials, and mind set. The third phase is to enter the new activity by providing an introduction and giving directions (Gump, 1982). Teachers can preplan transitions and develop routines to facilitate smooth, efficient changes in instructional activities.

Substantive Contacts

Students progress best when teachers' interactions are related to the content to be learned. Substantive teacher-student interaction promotes greater student attention or engagement, which is a prerequisite to achievement. Contacts increase engagement and contribute to a sense of academic purposefulness (Filby & Cahen, 1985). Research studies have focused on the content and length of the contacts and how the contacts are distributed. Hawley and Rosenholtz (1984) reported that effective high school teachers interact with their students at least 50% of the time. Brophy (1986c) reported impressive gains when teachers and students had a high rate of interaction. Effective teachers begin substantive interactions as soon as the bell rings.

The content of teacher-student interactions is crucial. Substantive contacts are those that are related to the content students are learning, reviewing, or attempting to master. Teachers discuss homework, give directions for assignments, or explain the structure of the content to be learned. Their actions signal that learning is the major purpose of the class. Effective teachers deliver explicit instructions that keep student errors to a minimum.

When students are engaged in guided practice, substantive contacts are made as teachers move toward students, giving more explanation, corrective feedback, and, when necessary, reteaching. It is especially important for teachers to interact and maintain contact with slower learners (Rosenshine, 1983) and those in remedial classes (Stallings, 1982).

The distribution of substantive contacts varies dramatically. Generally, the top one third of the class tend to have the majority of interactions with the teacher (Bloom, 1981). In most classrooms, high-achieving, usually more vocal students receive more contacts, longer feedback, longer wait time, and attention (Leder, 1988). Recent studies conducted in high school math classes have shown that teachers differ in the number of substantive contacts they have with students of different ability levels (Eaton, 1985). When the same teachers were observed teaching advanced math and general math classes, they used many more direct teaching behaviors with advanced students. In the general math classes, short explanations, giving a single assignment, and long periods of independent practice were more typical. Leder's (1988) study with seventh and tenth grade students found that teachers spent less time with the high-achieving students but called on them more frequently for certain interactions such as high-level questions. When teachers are made aware of their teaching behaviors, they are able to alter them and improve the substantive contacts with all of their students. All students benefit from the more frequent contact, feedback, and attention.

Substantive contacts in classes for young children in kindergarten or first grade should be qualitatively different. Feeney and Chun (1985) reported that effective teachers at this level interact more with children individually. They are more flexible in planning and timing. This helps them meet the specific needs of children. One of the teacher behaviors that increases student achievement with young children is an interest in student thinking rather than accuracy of responses.

At times substantive contacts may need to be kept to a minimum. For example, if students are expected to integrate information from several sources or carry out other high-level cognitive tasks, they may need to work without teacher intervention for short periods of time. Teacher behavior should be consistent with the instructional objectives (Brophy & Good, 1986).

Instructional Cues

Instructional cues, or "situational instructions for lesson behavior," are part of the signal system of the classroom (Doyle, 1986b, p. 407). Bloom (1981) identified instructional cues as one of the important variables that determines the quality of instruction. Instructional cues provide information about what is to be learned and what the learner is to do in the process. Cues focus student attention and are used to promote cognition (Marx & Walsh, 1988). Effective teachers use instructional cues to communicate their learning and behavior expectations. They provide cues whenever they sense students' frustration, confusion, or a lack of comprehension. Cues are also helpful in managing students and can alert students to changes in expected behavior (Doyle, 1986). The most frequent teacher cue is a signal to students to participate in the lesson appropriately (Morine-Dershimer & Beyerbach, 1987).

According to Morine-Dershimer & Beyerbach (1987), students actively process cues in a variety of ways. The rules of interaction are not static and evolve through collaboration. The flow of the interaction is constructed as it happens. Content and meaning evolve on a moment-by-moment basis (Weade & Evertson, 1988). Participants in the interaction must constantly monitor for cues to extract what is important to know and how to demonstrate knowledge. Student performance may be decreased when errors in communication occur such as when cues are incompletely signalled or when faulty cues are used. Teachers can develop cues which facilitate correct communication of their intentions (Morine-Dershimer & Beyerbach, 1987).

Cues may be verbal or nonverbal, and are received through a variety of sensory modes. Cues are generally given by the teacher in verbal form. For example, teachers tell students what they are expected to learn. They explain what they are to remember, what terms to use in speaking about a topic, or how to perform some complex cognitive or psychomotor task (Bloom, 1981). Teachers use questions as instructional cues. Students are aware that good teachers use questions to reinforce important facts or stress main ideas. Questions can be effective cues when they are appropriate and clearly related to instructional materials and learning outcomes.

Kounin and Gump (1974) identified continuity of signaling as an effective way to maintain student attention. Verbal cues need to be clear, on target, and forward moving. Effective cues focus students on the action. When students give presentations or extended answers or when teachers become involved with one responder, the momentum is slowed down. Students are not good signal givers. They repeat themselves, falter, and omit important information (Gump, 1982). Teachers must decide when the value of student input is important enough to warrant a slower instructional pace.

Students differ in their ability to learn from verbal cues. Concrete manipulation is necessary for some. Bloom (1981) stated that cues can be visual, tactile, kinesthetic, or olfactory. They can be presented as models, observations, or demonstrations. The choice depends on the age and ability of the students as well as the familiarity of the topic. Levin and Long (1981) reported that the use of a variety of instructional cues, including visual and manipulative materials, contribute to student learning. Pictures may serve as valuable cues for young students who cannot form mental images themselves, especially when the content to be covered is unfamiliar. Demonstrations and other forms of visual cues are effective when they are informative, clear, and simple.

Many instructional materials include cues. Textbooks have titles, captions, subheadings, graphs, and questions inserted at appropriate points to cue students about important facts, ideas, and processes. Films use close-up shots to emphasize important points. These study aids can be very helpful. They serve as cues by identifying main ideas and by motivating students to participate in mental rehearsal. Effective teachers alert students to these cues. When textbooks do not include study aids, teachers provide them through the use of guides or advance organizers. The use of practice materials can help students identify material to be mastered when the practice sheets are specific and clearly related to high-priority instructional objectives.

Effective cues must be clear to the students. In addition, they must bring about the reactions and responses the teacher intends (Levin & Long, 1981). Teachers sometimes use cues inconsistently, or their verbal and nonverbal cues or their words and actions do not match (Morine-Dershimer & Beyerbach, 1987). When teachers use unfamiliar terms or talk too rapidly, their cues lose clarity. When this happens, students do not perform as well as expected. Successful teachers concentrate on cues that focus student attention on important information. If cues are familiar, students can understand and respond appropriately. Effective cues relate new information to knowledge students have encountered and used before. Examples of effective and ineffective cues are listed in Figure 7–4.

Cues can differ in their strength, size, and volume. Good teachers realize that they must emphasize important cues so that students will not perceive them as just another detail in a continual stream of verbal information. When teachers make the cues more concrete or dramatic, they emphasize what is important. Teachers who are enthusiastic make positive statements about their subject. They move about, use gestures, vary their voice level, and make eye contact (Gephart, Strother, & Duckett,

Effective Cues	Ineffective Cues
Clear	Contradictory
Appeal to several senses	Appeal to one sensory mode
Maintain academic focus	Interrupt academic focus
Understood by students	Misunderstood by students
Focus on important expectations	Focus on irrelevant expectations

FIGURE 7–4. Effective and ineffective instructional cues

1981c). Another technique for increasing the strength of instructional cues is repetition. When teachers repeat a cue several times during one class or at intervals over several classes, students understand the importance of the information being presented. Timing is also important in communicating cues more effectively. Students should be able to act on cues immediately. One frequent timing error is when a teacher interrupts a student to clarify or give one last point and then does not signal the students to begin work again.

The absence of salient cues is a distinguishing characteristic of inexperienced, less effective teachers. Effective teachers signal relevant cues while less effective teachers use fewer and often contradictory cues (Weade & Evertson, 1988). Inexperienced teachers may give cues only at the beginning of instruction. More experienced teachers find ways to be creatively redundant with their cues (Rosenshine, 1983). They find new ways to explain the content to be learned and the process to be used at any point in the learning.

Pacing

The pacing of instruction is an alterable variable that has a strong influence on student learning. Pacing is the speed with which students move through the material to be learned. This includes the curriculum as a whole, curricular lessons, or activities (Brophy, 1979c). Decisions related to the pacing of instruction are powerful because they determine the amount of content to be covered. Content coverage equates with students' opportunity to learn. The relationship of pacing decisions, content coverage, and opportunity to learn is presented in Figure 7–5. Content coverage and academically engaged time are two variables that most affect achievement gains. Rosenshine (1986) cautioned that what is not taught cannot be learned. For example, up to 80% of the variance in basal reading achievement can be attributed to the pace of instruction (Berliner, 1984). Much of the variance is directly related to content covered during the school year.

Content coverage is closely associated with learning, but coverage does not necessarily equate with learning. In one study (Barr & Dreeben, 1983, in Barr, 1987),

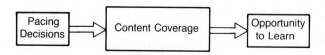

FIGURE 7–5. Relationship of pacing decisions to student learning

students learned 57 to 98% of what was covered. Other researchers have noted that curriculum goals are often too numerous to be covered fully (Porter & Brophy, 1988). Teachers generally attempt to incorporate all goals, teaching certain concepts while only mentioning others, which results in a watered-down curriculum. Tobin (1987a) made a similar finding; teachers identified topics to be covered in a certain time period and attempted to "cover the curriculum in the prescribed time whether or not learning occurred" (p. 292). The focus appeared to be on covering the content rather than developing a deep understanding of the information. Tobin further noted that if certain topics required additional time, teachers adjusted by allocating less time to the next topic. Increasing the amount of content covered has a positive effect on learning to a point, but learning may be hindered if too much content is covered too rapidly (Barr, 1987).

A related finding is that teachers also attempt to cover material already learned by students. Burns (1987) reported that students spent two thirds of the school year covering material previously mastered. For optimal learning, it is critical that appropriate learning objectives are selected and sequenced (Marliave & Filby, 1985). Teachers should carefully determine the essential, not previously mastered curriculum goals and set estimated time targets to serve as reminders. They must consciously decide how to integrate subjects and topics effectively and determine how to adjust the content.

Success Rate.   Effective teachers are able to set a pace that is appropriate for student learning. The pace should be smooth and establish the proper momentum for optimal learning. Teachers must be sensitive and responsive in matching success rates to students' individual and collective needs. A high success rate would be greater than 80%; a medium success rate would be 20 to 80%; and a low rate less than 20%. Success rate varies at different points in the learning process. During the introductory phase, more errors and effort should be expected, while at the consolidation phase students should know the material well and make few mistakes (Berliner, 1982). Brophy and Evertson (1976) noted that some level of challenge is necessary for learning to be productive. Quickly achieving a success rate of 100% would indicate a lack of appropriate challenge and limited learning.

Berliner (1982) noted that very high and very low success rates appear to affect student attitude and achievement. Optimal success rates vary with student entry-level characteristics. Squires et al. (1983) contended that students with low motivation and a high fear of failure should have over a 90% success rate while a success rate of 60% would be acceptable for students with high motivation and a low fear of failure. High success rates result in positive cognitive outcomes as well as affective outcomes including more enjoyment, more positive self-concept, higher levels of attention, and more appropriate behavior (Marliave & Filby, 1985). The influence of high success rates on affective gains may be especially important with low achievers. Student achievement and self-concept suffer in low-success situations. According to Berliner (1982), "When students spend large amounts of time in low-success experiences, their achievement is lower" (p. 210). It is recommended that students spend no more than 3% of their time feeling frustrated, yet classroom observations have shown students have low success 10% (or more) of the time. Low success rates could indicate that the material is too difficult. However, success rates are difficult to observe and analyze (Berliner, 1982).

Success rates are contextual. In general, students from low socioeconomic status backgrounds should experience a higher success rate than those from high-SES groups. Pacing in low-SES groups should be slower when students show an unwillingness to respond or when specific individuals need more monitoring and corrective feedback. Assignments should be at the right level of difficulty and, if necessary, the pace should be slowed to the point of overdwelling (Brophy & Evertson, 1976). For high-SES students, assignments that are too easy are negatively related to achievement (Brophy & Evertson, 1976). An understanding of students' backgrounds along with a careful assessment of their entry-level abilities is needed to determine an appropriate instructional pace. It is especially important to assess cognitive prerequisites for both current and future learning expectations.

Teachers must find the right match between the difficulty of the materials, the ability levels of the students, and the pace of instruction. Tobin (1984) pointed out that matching the rate of a presentation with students' capabilities ensures they will cognitively process the information. For more mature, higher ability students materials and expectations should be challenging; with less able students the material should be presented in smaller chunks and with more redundancy (Brophy & Evertson, 1976). Resources and assistance are needed to help less-able students succeed and keep them from being frustrated, especially when students are working independently. Another way to increase success rates and meet individual student needs is to use instructional subgroups.

Even though teachers are encouraged to move briskly through the curriculum, there are times when they may have to spend extra time on certain skills or knowledge areas. It is important for students in the early grades to learn basic skills because they are prerequisites for future learning. Instruction should be paced so that teachers feel certain basic skills are being thoroughly mastered. However, Lesgold (1986) pointed out that training for automaticity of basic skills is not without cost. It takes up time that could be spent in learning higher order skills. Ideally, the teacher should balance the amount of time used to teach basic skills and higher order thinking skills.

Pacing Decisions.   There appear to be dramatic differences in the pacing of instruction for groups of various ability levels. Pacing for high groups may be 10 to 15 times faster than for low groups (Shavelson, 1987b). Low groups have much less exposure to the total curriculum than do high groups. Students in lower groups have less opportunity to learn because of this limited exposure. One of the major challenges for teachers is to pace groups so that the rates of learning for all students are optimal and so that all students receive the maximum amount of exposure to the curriculum.

It is not clear how pacing decisions are made (Karweit, 1983), but these decisions greatly affect students' level of understanding and the comprehensiveness of their learning. Teachers must be aware of all the instructional influences and skillfully establish the appropriate pace. Influences on pacing decisions include the amount of time available and time of the school year, individual students' learning rates, the class size and aptitude distribution, the diversity of languages, the curriculum difficulty, and the amount of material to be covered (Burns, 1987; Karweit, 1983; Barr, 1987). Teachers can be compared to musical conductors who establish a tempo with the musicians (i.e., the students) to produce a harmonious performance (Morine-Dershimer & Beyerbach, 1987).

Teachers' expectations, theories, and belief systems also play a critical role in the pacing of instruction. Teacher expectations based on students' prior achievements affect pacing decisions, which in turn affect students' opportunity to learn (Brophy, 1979c). These expectations are often developed early in the school year and not changed throughout the year. Teachers should actively monitor student progress and adjust the pace based on how well students are currently performing, rather than on original expectations held before instruction began.

Teachers must consider the structure of the subject matter as they make pacing decisions. Subjects that require prerequisite learning and are arranged in a specific hierarchy require a high level of student mastery. In order to ensure that optimal learning does take place with subjects that are cumulative in nature, teachers have to adjust the pace of instruction. Over a period of time, an appropriate pace of instruction will have a major impact on student learning.

Instruction is either teacher paced or student paced (Posner, 1987). In teacher-paced instruction, teachers look for cues about attention and completion from individual students, subgroups, or whole groups to determine the appropriate pace (Doyle, 1986b). Many times a teacher monitors a subgroup of students, or steering group. During whole-group instruction, some teachers pace instruction for the lower ability students (usually those in the 10th to 25th percentile) and less content is covered (Burns, 1987; Doyle, 1986b; Barr, 1987). This results in a loss of learning for the more-able students. Burns (1987) also found that teachers focus their pacing on lower ability groups so that they will not lose the slower students. This creates a leveling effect with the learning of the higher ability students being depressed. In another study, Tobin (1987a) found teachers using steering groups close to the 50th percentile to gear instructional pace in high school math and science classes.

Student-paced conditions exist when the learners decide when to move ahead such as with individualized instruction, computer-assisted instruction (CAI), or programmed learning. Developing student responsibility for pacing their own instruction can improve achievement (NREL, 1984) and can result in positive task-related beliefs (Anderson et al., 1988). Among the disadvantages of student-paced conditions are increased teacher demands and instructional management problems such as record-keeping, materials preparation and distribution, and monitoring (Burns, 1987). Student involvement may not be as great in some self-paced conditions, such as when students are doing workbook assignments (Doyle, 1986b). Other studies document the advantages of student-paced conditions. Teachers are better able to accommodate individual differences in learning rates. In a study by Burns (1987), students completed more assignments than did a comparable group of students under teacher-paced conditions, and the learning of the high-ability students was not depressed, that is, the leveling effect did not occur.

Teachers base their pacing decisions on some standard of performance. They appear to move ahead when sufficient numbers of students have sufficient grasp of the material (Posner, 1987). The measure of success can be norm referenced (comparing individual student achievement to the achievement of other students) or criterion referenced (comparing achievement to a preset standard).

These studies underscore the need for teachers to recognize how they make pacing decisions and how these decisions affect student opportunities to learn. Rosenshine (1983) and others believe that teachers can effectively monitor the pace of instruction by having periodic weekly and monthly reviews. The information generated by the reviews can be used to make pacing adjustments.

 ## PRIMARY REFERENCES

Berliner, D. C. (1983). Developing conceptions of classroom environments: Some light on the T in classroom studies of ATI. *Educational Psychologist, 18*(1), 1–13.

> This article is especially helpful for elementary teachers. Common activity structures are described in terms of specific characteristics, regularities, and behaviors of teachers and students.

Berliner, D. C. (1984). The half-full glass: A review of research on teaching. In P. L. Hosford (Ed.), *Using what we know about teaching* (pp. 51–77). Alexandria, VA: Association for Supervision and Curriculum Development.

> Berliner summarizes the research on preinstruction and during-instruction factors in teaching. There is an excellent discussion of how planning decisions affect academic learning time. A diagram defining ALT is included.

Burns, R. B. (1987). Steering groups, leveling effects, and instructional pace. *American Journal of Education, 96* (1), 24–55.

> The findings of a year-long study of student-paced versus teacher-paced instruction are reported. Results concerning the number of assignments completed and the level of student learning have implications for making pacing decisions.

Cotton, K. (1988). *Monitoring student learning in the classroom* (School Improvement Research Series). Portland, OR: Northwest Regional Educational Laboratory.

> This analysis addresses effective classroom monitoring practices. Research support is presented as well as suggested instructional practices.

Doyle, W. (1986). Classroom organization and management. In M. C. Wittrock (Ed.), *Handbook of research on teaching* (3rd ed., pp. 392–431). New York: Macmillan.

Research that addresses how classroom experiences are organized, managed, and maintained is synthesized. The detailed presentation includes types of activity structures with the associated teacher and student behaviors, participation patterns, and programs of action.

Doyle, W., & Carter, K. (1987). Choosing the means of instruction. In V. Richardson-Koehler (Ed.), *Educators' handbook: A research perspective* (pp. 188–206). New York: Longman.

The authors emphasize that teachers' choices regarding the means of instruction have a critical effect on students' opportunities to learn. The chapter focuses on the many factors teachers must consider in structuring students' academic work and in organizing students for learning tasks.

Fisher, C. W., Berliner, D. C., Filby, N. N., Marliave, R., Cahen, L. S., & Dishaw, M. M. (1984). Teaching behaviors, academic learning time, and student achievement: An overview. In D. B. Strother (Ed.), *Time and learning* (Hot Topic Series). Bloomington, IN: Phi Delta Kappa.

This is a review of the Beginning Teacher Evaluation Study. Based on their findings, the authors suggest productive teaching activities and classroom conditions that promote student learning in elementary reading and mathematics.

Leinhardt, G., Weidman, C., & Hammond, K. M. (1987). Introduction and integration of classroom routines by expert teachers. *Curriculum Inquiry, 17,* 135–176.

This is a thorough discussion of how expert teachers establish and maintain instructional structure through the use of routines. Of particular interest is the observational data describing the most pervasive routines.

Levin, T., & Long, R. (1981). *Effective instruction.* Alexandria, VA: The Association for Supervision and Curriculum Development.

The focus of this work is on ALT, feedback and corrective procedures, and cues, and their powerful effect on student learning. Observation techniques and suggestions for altering teacher behavior are included.

Marx, R. W., & Walsh, J. (1988). Learning from academic tasks. *The Elementary School Journal, 88* (3), 207–219.

This is an excellent discussion of the elements of classroom work and task conditions. The authors advocate helping teachers understand the complexity of instructional tasks as a way to improve instruction.

Morine-Dershimer, G., & Beyerbach, B. (1987). Moving right along. . . . In V. Richardson-Koehler (Ed.), *Educators' handbook: A research perspective* (pp. 207–232). New York: Longman.

This chapter is a unique presentation of research findings and teachers' practical knowledge of classroom life. The ways teachers use cues to improve student understanding and increase student participation are highlighted.

RESEARCH IN PRACTICE

Finding 1: Selection of task structure is a critical instructional organization decision.

Instruction is a carefully defined and sequenced series of tasks and routines. The selection of tasks influences the learning process and determines what students will practice and learn. Determining task structure is an important planning decision. While a number of factors influence task decisions, the most important factor is how the task structure supports the achievement of learning goals. The amount of time allocated to instruction and the availability of materials and equipment also have a major influence on task structure.

Scenario. The task structures used with many writing programs are excellent examples of managing resources to achieve important learning goals. Many teachers have students work independently on writing assignments. The students are expected to develop discrete writing skills by using worksheets or similar formats. After they have mastered the skills, they are expected to compose sentences, paragraphs, and eventually write essays. Nearly all of the interaction and feedback takes place between teachers and students.

More recently developed writing programs are based on a different task structure. Students work with other students to plan, write, edit, and give corrective feedback to one another. Skills are taught as a part of the composition process. Teachers interact with students working together and give corrective feedback as needed. When this happens, several students, and at times the entire class, benefit from the teacher's comments. The task structure used with these writing programs has helped students achieve higher levels of writing proficiency and at the same time understand the importance of learning the principles and processes that are basic to effective composition. This task structure, however, requires a considerable amount of planning. Decisions about time to be allocated to the process and preparing students for new roles will have a major impact on the extent to which writing goals will be achieved.

Finding 2: Task structure influences levels of learning, student and teacher relationships, and classroom management practices.

The way students perceive the conditions surrounding an instructional task affects their behavior. Students attend to instructional tasks differently depending on the cognitive demands, the effort required, the potential for success, and the accountability measures used. Students use a number of coping mechanisms when they are unsure about their ability to meet teacher expectations. Some students become anxious when they are expected to take part in a large group discussion, while others may not want to ask teachers for help when they do not understand what they are expected to do during seatwork. These coping mechanisms can affect student performance as well as teacher and student relationships. Teachers sometimes forget, or may not be aware of, the effect that task structures have on students' attitudes toward learning. When teachers use a variety of task structures, student involvement, content coverage, and success rate are improved.

Scenario.   A foreign language teacher in a high school found that her task structure created several problems that she had not previously experienced. The teacher is considered to be an expert by her colleagues and students in the school. She has high expectations for student learning and she is very effective at helping students achieve those expectations.

The teacher regularly required her students to make written translations of phrases and short sentences. With one of her better classes, she raised her expectations and started requiring translations of essays and short stories. She had previously allowed students to work together to write the translations, but she decided with the new assignment that she would have them work independently so she could make more accurate assessments of their work.

At first the students attempted to meet the teacher's expectations. When they became frustrated with their inability to write the longer translations, they quit trying and became somewhat hostile toward the teacher. The students met informally outside of class and asked one of their peers to approach the teacher to discuss the frustrations they were experiencing. The student met with the teacher and described how the students felt and explained why they had quit trying. Needless to say, the teacher was surprised by the level of frustration and anxiety created by the new structure. After reflecting on the discussion with the student, the teacher decided to maintain her expectations but allow the students to work in pairs to write the translations. She also allotted more time to do assignments. The results were gratifying to both teacher and students. Student success rates went up, there was less frustration, and the classroom environment once again became positive.

Finding 3: There are important differences between time on task, engaged time, and academic learning time.

There is no question about the positive relationship between time and learning. Unfortunately, however, several major time-on-task studies generated inappropriate responses among some educators. The studies caused attention to be given to how many minutes students were on task or engaged in some learning activity. In too many cases, little attention was paid to what students were learning, the quality of tasks, or to what extent tasks were worthwhile. Academic learning time occurs when students are successfully engaged in materials or activities directly related to desired outcomes. Academic learning is a result of conscious decisions based on careful pre-assessment, planning, monitoring, and feedback. The quality of instructional time, rather than quantity, is the most critical variable associated with student learning.

Scenario.   Several northeastern school systems contracted with an external agency to study the amount of time their elementary students were on task. The agency sent observers to record the amount of time students appeared to be on task, or engaged in some form of learning activity. The observers recorded the time by making periodic visual scans of classrooms. When observers left the classrooms, they reported to teachers the percentage of the observation time that was time on task. For example, a teacher might be told that for the class that had just been observed the time on task was 83%. At the end of the day teachers shared their percentage grades with a good bit of caustic humor. The entire process was demoralizing to the teachers because they felt that the wrong measures were being used and that little attention was being given to student learning.

A sixth grade teacher in a different school system was faced with a situation that caused her to change the emphasis from on-task behavior to student learning. She had several students who were scoring well on standardized reading tests but who were not able to apply their knowledge when they wrote compositions or when they were engaged in content-area reading activities. She realized that in her effort to get through the curriculum, and to have the students ready for the statewide achievement tests, she was neglecting some of the higher level language arts skills and competencies. With the assistance of the school's reading resource teacher, the teacher developed a structured program to help her students develop and apply reading skills in the content areas. This approach took more time, but the teacher was able to enhance and enrich the reading and writing ability of her students. Not only did the students successfully raise their levels of learning, they also continued to do very well on standardized tests. The teacher's attention to learning rather than to time on task had important payoffs for the students and the teacher.

Finding 4: Teachers can take specific actions to increase the amount of academic learning time, which will result in improved student achievement.

Many teachers believe that they need more time allocated to the subjects they teach. This is often the case, but very few teachers can control the time available for instruction. They can, however, use their time wisely and reduce the amount of time lost to factors over which they have control. In order to increase the amount of academic learning time, teachers should be aware of how instructional time is lost. Transitions, distractions, interruptions, frequent breaks, late starts, and early class endings are among many ways instructional time is lost.

Scenario.   A high school conducted a study to identify the strengths and weaknesses of the school's curriculum and instruction programs. As a part of the study, randomly selected classrooms in each of the subject areas were observed. The observation of an English class provided some interesting insights about the use of allocated time. A member of the study team met the teacher just prior to class, asked the teacher to briefly describe what would be taking place during class, and had the teacher select where the observer should sit. The observer waited outside the classroom for the teacher, who arrived several minutes late. The teacher was unable to clearly describe his expectations for the class, but he did find a desk for the observer.

The teacher made a few informal comments to the students and then began the class about 10 minutes after the bell. After he briefly described the topic for the day, he began to describe some of the details of a shopping trip he and his wife took the previous weekend. This discussion took nearly 20 minutes. While the teacher was talking, several students quietly began doing assignments for other classes. Over one half of the allocated instructional time had elapsed before the teacher addressed the topic he mentioned at the beginning of class. There was a brief, general discussion before the bell rang. No assignment was given and the students went to their next class.

The teacher wanted to review the notes taken by the observer. He was amazed that he had used up so much time before starting the class discussion. He asked the observer to meet with him at the end of the school day to talk further about the observation data. They had a rather long discussion about actions that could increase academic learning time. The teacher was concerned enough to ask the observer for specific recommendations. They both agreed that he needed to carefully plan each lesson, that he should model appropriate behavior by being on time, and that expectations and assignments should be clearly communicated to his students. Several months later the head of the English department reported that the teacher had improved the management of his instructional time.

Finding 5: Teachers are able to make the most effective interactive decisions when classroom routines are well established.

Routines make classroom life predictable and give both teachers and students a sense of security. Over time routines become automatic, requiring little thought and attention. This reduces the level of cognitive demand on all those involved in the learning process. When efficient and effective routines have been established, there are fewer management problems and teachers are able to use their allocated time to attend to student learning needs. By focusing on learning rather than on the numerous managerial demands, teachers are better able to make appropriate interactive decisions that can improve the effectiveness of their instruction.

Scenario. Virtually all classrooms benefit when routines have been established, but it is especially important to develop routines for activity and laboratory classes. In these classes, it is possible to lose a significant amount of learning time in getting organized, making transitions between activities, and preparing to end class.

A new high school was opened in a rapidly growing suburban area. All of the teachers were able to spend time preparing for the first year of school. Because they knew they were going to have large classes, the physical education teachers spent much of their time planning the management routines they would establish and follow. For example, they decided that rather than taking roll orally they would have numbers painted on both the side of the gym floor and in the outdoor walkways for students to stand on as soon as they were dressed. This would allow teachers to quickly scan the classes and note which numbers were not covered. They would be able to know which students were absent by simply comparing the numbers with their class rosters.

The teachers also spent a considerable amount of time deciding how they would identify, train, and use student assistants. These students were identified and given a thorough orientation to their responsibilities, which included having equipment ready for each class, posting schedules and related instructional information, distributing equipment to teams, and working with students to put everything away at the end of each class.

The new school opened with the expected number of minor problems due to facilities that did not quite operate as anticipated and a number of schoolwide routines that needed to be refined as they were being implemented. Some classes seemed to take an inordinate amount of time to begin operating smoothly and efficiently. The physical education classes, however, were soon seen as models of effective management where the maximum amount of allocated time was devoted to learning.

It was interesting to observe these classes during the first few weeks of school. The first several days were spent teaching the routines that would be followed and orienting students to the facilities and instructional areas. By the middle of the second week, students were getting dressed, attendance was taken, and learning activities were initiated in a minimum amount of time. Student assistants played an important role in helping students understand how to get organized quickly and where to report for each instructional activity. Teachers were able to spend their time giving group instruction, monitoring activities, and giving one-to-one tutoring and special assistance to students. All of this was especially impressive in view of the fact that the average class size was approximately 50 students. Perhaps the most important outcome was that students had very positive attitudes about physical education which resulted in excellent attendance, participation, and achievement.

Finding 6: Careful monitoring of student progress enhances the learning of individual students as well as the entire class.

Students learn more when teachers systematically monitor their work and their involvement in instructional activities. Monitoring involves a number of teacher behaviors such as regularly scanning the class, moving about the instructional area, observing students doing seatwork, and paying close attention to homework and other class assignments. Effective monitoring is the process of gathering information for instructional decision making. Information generated by monitoring helps teachers make informed decisions about the quality and quantity of individual and group learning.

Scenario.   A number of teachers in a large high school were being observed as a part of an instructional improvement project. One of the high school social studies teachers stated, prior to an observation, that she would be moving throughout the classroom when students were given time to work on their research projects. She explained that she was convinced that careful monitoring resulted in higher quality student work.

The teacher's class pretty well followed the plan that she had outlined during the preobservation conference. She quickly took care of the beginning of class activities and engaged the entire class in a discussion about the material assigned for the day. Participation was very good and students appeared to be involved and on task. With about 20 minutes left in class, students were told that they could use the remaining time to work on their research projects. Some students worked independently on their projects while others worked in teams.

The teacher began to move about the class and monitor student work. During the first few minutes this appeared to be a very effective process and students seemed to be working diligently on their projects. With about 10 minutes to go in the class one team of students asked the teacher for some assistance. She quickly moved to the students and began to assist them with their project. She became so involved that she did not pay any attention to the rest of the class for the remainder of the period. It was not long before the students realized that she was no longer monitoring their work, so several of them began to visit quietly about upcoming social events. Others began to put their work away and read material for other classes, or just waited for the period to end.

During the postobservation conference the observer's notes were shared with the teacher. She was very pleased with the first 40 minutes of the class but unhappy with the off-task behavior of so many of the students during the last 10 minutes. She was an experienced teacher who had high expectations. She realized that she could have met outside the class period with the students who needed a significant amount of assistance. This would have enabled her to keep all of the students engaged in their work until the end of the class period. Although this may not seem like a major problem to some teachers, it is important to those who place a high value on use of instructional time.

Finding 7: A substantial amount of allocated learning time may be used for instructional transitions.

Transitions occur throughout the school day. They take place when students move from class to class and when major activities change within a classroom. Transition times are potentially disruptive and require careful managing. Teachers can control within-classroom transitions so they will be able to use the maximum amount of their allocated time to engage students in learning activities. Elementary teachers have many instructional transitions. Over a period of time most teachers become quite proficient at managing transitions effectively and efficiently. Junior high and high school teachers have far fewer class transitions so they may not be as effective at changing instructional activities.

Scenario.   An eighth grade English teacher was conducting a creative writing class. She began the class by conducting a discussion of emotionally laden words and explained how these words could have an impact on different individuals. She also explained how the words were used in creative writing. She played a record that supported the theme she was pursuing with the students. This first phase of the class took approximately 20 minutes. During this period of time students appeared to be very attentive, took notes, and asked good questions related to the discussion.

When the first phase of the class had been completed, the teacher told the students that it was time for them to work individually on their creative writing assignments. She did not elaborate on the assignment, which had been posted on the chalkboard, nor did she ask if there were any questions. The students went to work and the teacher began to monitor the classroom. She noted that one student was using the words discussed earlier to focus his writing assignment. She stopped him and told him that he was to be creative and use words other than the ones she had used as examples. Other students heard the discussion and quit working to ask her to clarify the assignment because they were also using words from the first part of class. There was so much confusion that the teacher had to go back to the front of the classroom and engage the entire class in a discussion to clarify the assignment. By the time she had finished and had gotten the students back on task, the class period was about over.

During a discussion about the class with her supervisor, the teacher quickly recognized what had happened—that she had not given clear directions and had not effectively managed the transition. This episode brought to her attention the need to plan and organize so that a minimum amount of time would be used to change instructional activities. It was not long before she reported that she was using very little class time to manage instructional transitions.

Finding 8: The quality and quantity of substantive contacts have a major impact on student learning.

Substantive contacts help to maintain academic focus and give students a sense of purpose. If the contacts relate to the curriculum, students are more apt to achieve the intended learning outcomes. If contacts are random and do not address the content to be learned, student achievement will be adversely affected. Effective teachers are aware of the positive impact of substantive contacts and manage to interact appropriately with all students.

Scenario.   A supervisor was asked to observe a kindergarten class where parents were dissatisfied with the teacher. Parents had been complaining that their children did not seem to be learning anything and believed the teacher was not able to communicate her expectations to students or parents. The parents were aware that there was a formal kindergarten curriculum that stressed language development.

The supervisor made an appointment to observe the teacher during a period of time when language development activities were expected to be taking place. When the supervisor arrived, the teacher was sitting at her desk looking at some papers while the students were playing with puzzles, blocks, and other shelf games. There did not appear to be any particular purpose or structure for the games. When students tired of a game, they simply dropped the game and started a new one. During this period there was little interaction between the teacher and students.

After approximately 30 minutes the teacher signaled that it was "table time" and gave students work sheets and materials to cut and paste. They were to cut out objects from one worksheet and paste them on another sheet that had a picture of a place where the objects would normally be found. For example, they were to cut out pictures of things normally found in a kitchen and paste them on a picture of a kitchen. While the students were doing their cutting and pasting, the teacher asked one student to come to her desk and gave him an individualized assessment. After the observation she told the supervisor that she was trying to get ahead of the testing schedule with this student. The supervisor had observed the class for over one hour during which time there were virtually no substantive contacts between the teacher and students.

The supervisor decided to visit another kindergarten class in the same building at the same time the next day. She made an appointment with the teacher to visit and observe her class. When she entered the classroom, all of the students were working in small groups. Each group had a paper sack with a number of objects such as spoons and clothespins in each sack. The teacher asked the students which objects should go together and gave them specific criteria for making their decisions. She told them that they were forming categories, and they seemed to understand the concept.

The students worked together in their groups to categorize the objects. The teacher monitored the groups, interacted with the students, and talked with them about their progress and problems. When the groups had finished, the teacher went to each group to find out how they had developed and labeled the categories. During their discussions the teacher clarified a number of points and responded to student questions. At times she explained unfamiliar words and provided examples. All of the students seemed focused on the task as the teacher guided them through this language development activity.

The supervisor had observed one kindergarten where there were virtually no substantive contacts and one where the contacts were not only numerous but helped to enrich student learning. The supervisor made a commitment to helping the first teacher plan, organize, and monitor her instruction so that student learning would be focused and purposeful.

Finding 9: Substantive contacts are qualitatively different depending on student ability, grade level, and content area.

Teachers should attempt to have numerous, high-quality contacts with students of all ability levels. They should provide contacts that are consistent with student needs and task demands. In many cases, however, substantive contacts for more-able students are different from those for students with less ability. It is sometimes difficult for teachers to interact with all students in ways that help them reach higher levels of achievement. Very often teachers depend on certain students in class to give the best answers and help to move the class along. Teachers may not even be aware that they have altered their substantive contacts to fit their perceptions of student ability levels.

Scenario.   An experienced high school social studies teacher asked to have one of her classes observed to obtain some suggestions about her teaching and interaction with her students. The class to be observed was a political science class that was open to eleventh and twelfth grade students. The ability levels of the students ranged from average to very bright. The class was organized into five discussion groups with five students in each group.

The class began with students finishing a group assignment from the previous day. During this period of time the teacher moved throughout the class monitoring the groups, but she did not get involved in their discussions. After about 20 minutes it was obvious that the groups had finished their assignments, so the teacher began a discussion with the total class. The discussion focused on the conclusions reached by each group. Although there were group leaders, the teacher called on individual students from each group. A number of students also volunteered information to be included in the conclusions. Two boys, from different groups, were the most verbal and volunteered more information than other students. As the discussion progressed, the teacher raised the level of the questions, seeking higher level thinking. The two boys actively participated in the discussion while other students became less involved. When the pace slowed and the teacher wanted to move the discussion along, she would call on one of the two boys.

During the postobservation, the teacher reviewed the sequence of events and identified students who had participated as the discussion was raised to a higher level. Although the great majority of the students participated during the initial phase of instruction, many of them did not actively participate as the discussion progressed. One entire group of five girls did not participate during the last 10 to 15 minutes of the class. The two boys increased their interactions with the teacher as others dropped out.

By the time the teacher had reviewed the class notes, she had begun to replan instruction for this class. She said that she had been aware that she was very dependent on the two boys for giving correct answers and for helping her move the class along. But she was not aware that she was allowing so many students to drop out of the interactions. She decided that she would reorganize the small groups to give them more balance in terms of student interest and ability and that she would change her position during discussion sessions to achieve better visual contact with more of the students. She said that she would concentrate on involving more of the students in higher level discussions. During a subsequent discussion with the teacher, she indicated that she was very pleased with the changes she had made and that her contacts with the students had improved. This was a case of an excellent teacher seeking feedback so that she would be even better. Her commitment to her work paid off when several years later she was named teacher of the year in her school system.

Finding 10: Instructional cues that are timely, clearly communicated, and delivered in a variety of modes have a powerful effect on student learning.

Cues communicate teacher expectations about student achievement, teacher attitudes about the material to be learned, and the importance of the teaching-learning process. Teacher cues are given through both verbal and nonverbal behavior and are received by a variety of senses. Very often nonverbal cues are as clear and powerful as verbal cues. Students differ in their ability to understand cues and, likewise, teachers differ in their ability to deliver cues effectively. In some cases students receive contradictory cues from teachers. For example, a teacher may emphasize important points to be learned and then test for entirely different information. For cues to have a positive effect on student learning, they must be consistent with learning expectations, be communicated clearly, and produce the desired student responses.

Scenario.   A middle school social studies teacher uses a number of cues to enhance the learning in his classrooms. He is always on time to class, well prepared, and enthusiastic about the subjects he teaches. Students think he is a great teacher. They enjoy his enthusiasm and are excited about going to his classes even though they know he has high expectations for student achievement.

The teacher begins each class with an upbeat discussion about what he expects to be accomplished during the class period. As he interacts with the students, he moves about the room encouraging the widest possible participation. He cues students by looking at them, encouraging them to respond, directing his attention to students who are reluctant to get involved, and calling on students to get the maximum amount of interaction. He uses a variety of responses to praise student input. If an answer is satisfactory, his response may be "Good" or "Fine." If he is really pleased with an answer he may use responses such as "That's great" or "Right on target." The students know which of his responses is the higher form of praise.

When the teacher wants to reinforce points made during a discussion, he uses the overhead projector and lists the points on transparencies. He leaves the points on the screen as he continues the discussion. Students know that he is emphasizing what he wants them to learn, so they pay special attention to what is written on the transparencies. He has used other visual devices, such as cartoons that are on transparencies, to summarize a discussion and assess student learning. This teacher's cues are an important factor in establishing a positive climate for learning. His cues are rich, varied, and consistent with his learning expectations. It is no surprise that student achievement in his classes is always excellent and in many cases better than students anticipate when they enroll in the class.

Finding 11: Optimal student success rates can be achieved when the pace of instruction is consistent with student characteristics and desired levels of learning.

Pacing decisions have a powerful effect on student learning. As teachers make pacing decisions, they are determining the amount of content to be covered and the depth of the coverage. Pacing decisions expand or limit what students can learn. If students do not have exposure to certain content, they do not have the opportunity to learn that content. Good teachers are aware of the importance of their pacing decisions and adjust their content coverage expectations to fit the characteristics of their students. They know that once active instruction begins they will need to make adjustments in the pace of the lesson depending on how quickly students can demonstrate the expected skills or understandings. Regular assessment provides accurate information for pacing decisions.

Scenario.   Several years ago an elementary teacher who was known to be one of the better teachers in her school invited her supervisor to observe one of her language arts classes. During the preobservation conference she described what would be taking place during the lesson. She planned to have 12 of her students engaged in the lesson while the others were doing seatwork. Her direct-instruction lesson would focus on identifying and using prefixes and suffixes. She described seven different activities that would be used during the 20-minute lesson. The supervisor was concerned about the number of activities planned for such a short period of time but did not express his concern to the teacher.

The teacher began the class with a discussion about what the students had learned regarding prefixes and suffixes. It was a lively discussion that involved all of the students. The pace was brisk, but all of the students seemed to keep up. Students were asked to go to a feltboard and arrange prefixes and suffixes to form words. Again, all 12 of the students were involved and moved quickly to accomplish the task. The teacher continued the discussion, and while the students were arranging the letters, she commented on their work. After the students had all been to the feltboard, the lesson continued with a short discussion about other word possibilities. Students were then invited to go to the chalkboard and write some new words using either prefixes or suffixes. Six students were at the chalkboard while the other six observed what was happening. They changed roles so that all students had an opportunity to try a new word.

The lesson ended with a game that the teacher had constructed to assess student learning. She had moved through the entire lesson at a brisk pace, but the students were able to keep up and understand what was going on. All of the students in this small-group activity had been actively engaged in the learning process. At one point the teacher did slow down long enough to encourage two shy students to take part in the discussion. Later she encouraged the two students to go to the feltboard first and demonstrate what they had learned. Her informal assessment at the end of the lesson demonstrated that the success rate was very high for the entire group. This teacher had planned and integrated her teaching activities so they would have maximum impact on student learning. She was able to make adjustments in pacing so that all students could be involved and have a positive learning experience.

Finding 12: When teachers understand the effect of their pacing decisions on student learning, they can make appropriate adjustments in content coverage.

The level of success students experience as they progress through instruction affects their attitudes toward learning and their achievement. When material is appropriately challenging, students see that their persistence pays off; they are reinforced by their efforts and are willing to continue trying. Effective teachers know their students' motivational and learning needs. They make decisions about the pacing of the instruction so that the success rate is consistent with those needs. While affective concerns are a high priority, teachers must be concerned about covering the required content. Teachers experience constant pressure in balancing optimal learning rates with content coverage.

Scenario.   Novice teachers are more likely to be unaware of the pace of their instruction than their more experienced colleagues. New teachers get so caught up in what they are teaching that they may not monitor student understanding. A first-year junior high mathematics teacher was observed introducing a unit on basic statistics to a mixed-ability class. His goal for the lesson was for the students to understand the concepts of mean, median, range, and mode. He also wanted the students to be able to compute mean scores. After taking care of the normal administrative duties, the teacher began lecturing about the four concepts. As he lectured he listed the most important points on the chalkboard. The pace was very fast, and as the teacher finished lecturing about each concept, he would ask the class, "Does anyone have any questions?" He did not wait after asking the question, nor did he scan the class to try to determine if anyone had any questions. He gave a number of cues that indicated he was in a hurry to cover the material.

After the teacher had completed the lecture, he gave the students worksheets that covered the concepts he had presented. Students were to solve the problems on the work-sheets. As the teacher monitored their work, nearly every student had questions and needed help. The students were clearly perplexed and confused and for the most part could not solve the problems without the teacher's help. The success rate in the class was very low.

After the lesson the observer shared the observation notes with the teacher. A time log was included in the notes. By analyzing the time log the teacher was able to see that he had taught all four concepts in less than 16 minutes and had not given the students an opportunity to ask any questions. The teacher was totally unaware of how little time he had spent in direct instruction and that he had not given his students adequate time to ask questions. He decided to reteach the lesson the next day. He also decided to monitor his instructional pacing and to check for student under-standing by calling on students to give them a chance to demonstrate how well they understood the concepts being taught.

Subsequent observations of the teacher indicated that he was becoming more effective at pacing his instruction and assessing student understanding. Students ex-hibited less frustration and more persistence. The teacher's behavior did not change immediately, but he gradually became more aware of the impact of his instructional pace on student learning. His heightened awareness helped him make appropriate pacing and monitoring decisions.

 ## GUIDE TO OBSERVATION, ANALYSIS, AND REFLECTION

The following activities focus on several specific areas critical to effective instruction. Teachers attend to these areas as they make decisions about organizing and managing learning tasks. Each area is appropriate for a focused observation, and you may find that several of the areas are of particular interest to you. The data collected during the observations should provide ample information for analysis and reflection.

1. Learning tasks

Observation: What are the conditions of the learning tasks?   Visit briefly with the teacher prior to the observation. Ask the teacher to describe the learners and the learning objectives (both content and process). It is important to know what learning tasks will occur during the lesson. The focus of the observation is on the structure of one or more learning activities. As you observe, briefly describe the type of activity, such as seatwork, group work, or whole-class instruction. Be sure to record the beginning and ending times for each learning task. Identify the number of students involved and how they are organized to do the work, independently or with others. Describe what the students are required to do as they participate, such as respond verbally, write answers, make a group decision, or do peer teaching. Describe the product or outcome the students are required to produce, individually or collectively, and how the product is to be evaluated.

Analysis: How appropriate are the task conditions in promoting the learning objectives for the students?   The analysis will be more productive if the teacher joins in the discussion. First, focus on the amount of effort the students had to exert in accomplishing the task. Share with the teacher your perception of the cognitive demand of the different tasks. You may want to categorize the demand as lower level, if the task required memorization or procedural application, or higher level, if the task required comprehension, making higher order inferences or applications, or forming an opinion. The teacher should confirm the level of demand since it could appear to be higher level when it actually is not. Discuss whether the level of mental processing demanded by the task is appropriate given the timing of the lesson, student needs, and prerequisite experience.

Second, focus on additional instructional task conditions. Determine if the way the students were organized to do the task was effective and if evaluation measures and feedback opportunities were appropriate. The duration of the task, the degree of teacher or student control, and the nature of the response (public or private) are other points of analysis. Together, develop ways to make the instructional task conditions more consistent with learning expectations.

Reflection: In planning learning tasks for my students, what conditions should I consider?   Focus on the level of cognitive demand, the organization, and the outcome or product required by each learning task. In determining appropriate conditions, consider your educational philosophy, the behavioral learning goals, your level of experience, student needs, the sequencing of the lesson, how the students are organized to do the work, and how much time is available to accomplish the task.

2. Use of time

Observation: *What amount of class time is allocated for instructional and non-instructional activities?*   First, decide if it would be possible or productive to observe in one teacher's classroom for several hours or to observe the same class period or specific subject lesson for several days. Keep a time log with a short description of the activity that is taking place. Be sure to record beginning and ending times for all instructional and noninstructional events.

Analysis: *Is class time allocated and used effectively to promote learning expectations?*   Review the observation record and total the amount of time spent on non-instructional activities and the amount of time spent on instructional activities. Determine if the amount of time devoted to procedural matters, housekeeping, and transitions was appropriate and if time was used effectively to promote student learning. If the time was not used well, identify areas for improvement.

Reflection: *How will I allocate available instructional time and manage it to promote student learning?*   It is important to devise ways to stay alert to how much time is spent on particular instructional and noninstructional tasks. Planning and incorporating systematic self-monitoring procedures is one way to become aware of how time is used. Look at the number of minutes given to a topic or subject over an extended period of time as well as on a specific day. It is also necessary to protect available time by minimizing transition time and time lost to distractions or behavioral disturbances; finding ways for you and your students to be better organized and prepared; and incorporating additional cues, routines, and monitoring or feedback procedures.

3. Student engagement

Observation: *What is the level and type of student engagement during instructional activities?*   Obtain a seating chart, or construct one of your own, for the students you plan to observe. You may wish to confine your observations to a group of students close to you or to one particular group of students such as a lab group, small cooperative group, or a specific workstation. Visually scan the students at regular intervals (every 1, 2, or 5 minutes, depending on the number of students) and note if the students appear to be on task and engaged or off task and unengaged. If possible, note if particular students are able to succeed or progress smoothly at the task or if misunderstanding or frustration occurs.

Analysis: *Was the level and type of student engagement appropriate?*   Decide if the students you observed were appropriately engaged in the instructional activities. You may want to look at the ratio of time spent on task to time spent off task. If students remained engaged and progressed smoothly, identify those conditions that promoted engagement and success. If students were off task and frustrated or confused, pose possible reasons for the behavior and ways to improve engagement and success.

Reflection: How will I maintain a high level of student engagement and success? Review your analysis notes and summarize your ideas about how best to promote a high level of student success and engagement. Be sure to include strategies for pre-assessment, monitoring, feedback, and establishing conditions that motivate students.

4. Routines

Observation: What instructional and management routines are evident? Although an infrequent observer in a classroom may have some difficulty identifying routines, it is possible to detect routines by keying in on those actions that appear to occur almost automatically. Describe those actions that seem to promote appropriate behavior, keep the instruction moving, and facilitate verbal interaction between the teacher and students and between students. Focus your observation on teacher and student actions that occur as the students enter and leave the class, as they settle down to work and finish up, and during the lesson itself. These events occur in all classrooms, in all grade levels, and in all subject areas.

Be sure to record the ways in which housekeeping activities, such as roll taking, lunch count, money collection, assigning make-up work, and making announcements, are handled. Note how student movement, misbehavior, or inattention is dealt with, how materials are distributed and collected, and how monitoring, providing feedback, and student participation are managed. Other routines may be evident that are unique to the subject area or grade level.

Analysis: In what ways are routines effective in making the class run smoothly? Begin the analysis by grouping the routines into categories such as housekeeping (H), student movement (SM), student behavior (SB), instructional materials (IM), teacher-student interaction (TS), student-student interaction (SS), and teacher monitoring (TM). Label each of the routines identified in your observation.

If you can, share the information with the teacher observed. The teacher might be able to help clarify what was observed and add to the list. Some of what you observed may not have appeared to be routine action. The teacher may also share any spur-of-the-moment procedures or additional procedures that were incorporated for this particular lesson.

Continue the analysis by determining which routines promoted a smooth flow to the classroom activity and to the lesson. Suggest any additional routines that might provide needed structure or address points of confusion.

Reflection: What routines will I establish in my classroom?   Reflect on your observations and analyses. Formulate some routines that would provide the necessary structure for your class(es). Briefly jot down your ideas. Be sure to address each of the following critical areas:

- Housekeeping: opening activities, attendance check, lunch count, announcements, make-up work, closing activities, clean-up, reminders (homework)
- Student movement: in and out of classroom, to and from areas within classroom
- Student behavior: ways to prevent misbehavior, ways to attend to misbehavior
- Instructional materials: storage, distribution, collection, student materials, teacher ("off-limits") materials
- Monitoring: teacher records, student records, conferences, contacts
- Interacting: responding (voluntary, nonvoluntary, choral), think time, student/student interaction

5. Instructional cues

Observation: What cues are used to signal important learning and behavioral expectations?   Focus your observations on verbal and nonverbal (including visual) cues that let students know what is important to learn and what they are expected to do. Briefly describe what the teacher says when communicating learning objectives, using questions, or giving verbal cues and what the teacher does such as signaling, using study guides, underlining or highlighting information, or using cognitive organizers.

Other nonverbal cues may include physical movement or sounds. Also give attention to the delivery of the cues (clarity, timing, intensity) and how well students receive and interpret the cues.

Analysis: Did the cues effectively communicate the learning and behavioral expectations?   Review the observation information. First, determine the ways cues were delivered. Continue by assessing the effectiveness of the delivery such as clarity, intensity, and timing. Determine if the cues were understood by the students. Suggest additional cues or improvements in the cues observed.

Reflection: What cues will I use to communicate expectations and significant information?   Decide what cues would be appropriate with your students and how they should be delivered. Effective visual cues can be especially powerful. Most cues are not complex, but some cues require some explanation. Think about how and when cues should be introduced.

6. Instructional pace

Observation: At what pace are topics covered during the lesson?   The observation should occur during a teacher-paced lesson where new information is being presented or known information is reviewed. Develop a log by recording time (in minutes) spent on each topic. Also record teacher questions and the correctness of student responses, using these symbols: **T?** for a teacher question, **+** for a correct response, **−** for an incorrect response. Record **SC+** if a student corrects an inaccurate response.

Analysis: Is the instruction paced for optimal student learning? Calculate the amount of time spent on each topic. Evaluate the appropriateness of the pace based on the amount of time given to the important concepts or topics compared to the amount of time spent on less significant material.

Determine the level of student success. Analyze student success rate by first tallying the total number of questions delivered and then the percentage that were answered correctly or appropriately. Choral responses may be considered in the total of responses. A low success rate is less than 20%; medium success is 20 to 80%; a high success is greater than 80%. Identify individual students with low success rates.

Determine if the pace was appropriate for the students. Discussion should focus on diversity within the class, the nature of the subject, the point in the learning process, teacher expectations, and the amount of assistance available.

Reflection: What factors must I consider as I pace instruction? Identify the indicators you will use in pacing instruction during a lesson. What information is critical and how will you determine if the students are with you? Is the level of success appropriate for this group at this point in the instructional sequence? How will you meet the needs of the slower students while challenging the faster students?

7. Monitoring student progress

Observation: How is student learning progress and participation monitored? As students work on assignments, concentrate on ways students are held accountable—individually and collectively—for both learning and behavior. Focus, in particular, on the teacher's physical movement around the classroom as student work is monitored. Draw a classroom map. Use lines to indicate teacher movement. Verbal or visual contacts with students can be indicated by an *X* and the length of time can be shown by adding hash marks next to the *X*.

Analysis: How effectively is student progress monitored? Review the information recorded on the map. Determine the number of students receiving direct teacher contact. Also look for repeated patterns of movement.

Assess if the monitoring was effective or ineffective. If both teacher and observer feel that monitoring was effective, identify the ways the teacher accomplished this. If the monitoring was ineffective, identify causes and suggest possible remedies.

Reflection: What monitoring practices will I incorporate in my teaching? Your observation and analysis information should suggest certain monitoring practices that would be appropriate when students are working on assignments either independently, in pairs, or in groups. Think about how and when you will get feedback about the appropriateness of the instruction and how students are progressing. It is especially important to think about ways and times to monitor student work progress when it may be necessary for you to be working with another group of students.

8. Managing transitions

Observation: How are transitions managed?   This observation should take place over an extended period of time. Concentrate on the transition periods that occur between instructional activities. Tally each transition that occurs and record the beginning and ending times. Briefly describe how the teacher closes out current activities or record as much of what the teacher says as possible. Also describe what the teacher and students do as the transition occurs and how the students are re-engaged in the next instructional activity.

Analysis: How effectively were transitions managed?   Determine the amount of time used in executing transitions and also summarize student behavior during transitions. Determine if the transitions were smooth and efficient and identify what the teacher did to facilitate them. If they were not, pose possible reasons and remedies. Make an estimate of the total number of minutes lost to transitions and compare this to the total instruction time observed.

Reflection: How will I structure and manage transitions?   For your particular teaching situation, think about appropriate ways to help students close out one activity, the level of direction they need to complete the transition, and the best ways to re-engage students in the new activity. In planning instruction, you may want to specify actions you will take to structure transition times.

 DEVELOPMENT AND RENEWAL ACTIVITIES

1. Interview several of your fellow college students or younger students with diverse interests and ability levels about the types of instructional activities they enjoy, do not enjoy, find easy, difficult, boring, or of little use. Discuss the specific reasons for their feelings and think about how this information should influence your own instruction.

2. Time is a limited resource and must be protected and used to provide high-quality instruction. Various factors influence the amount of time available for learning and the amount of time students need in order to learn. These influences may be positive (+) or negative (−), or may have minimal or no impact on learning (0). After several days of informal observation in your elementary or secondary school or college, subjectively assess the positive, negative, or neutral impact of the following influences by placing a checkmark in the appropriate column on a chart like the one below:

	+	−	0
Student absences and tardies			
Teacher absences			
District policies and practices (days available, early closings)			
School policies and practices			
General orderliness (in school and classroom)			
Class size			
Student ability			
Student interest and effort			
Quality and appropriateness of instruction			

3. If you have access to a school, observe a single child for the entire day. Focus on the ways the child is allowed to work, either independently or with others, the level of challenge involved in the work, and the amount of time spent in instructional activities (as opposed to transitions, housekeeping, and procedural activities). Summarize your findings by describing what the child's day is like. Compare that to an ideal day that is stimulating and challenging. Pose possible alternatives to what you observed and describe how your findings will influence your instruction.

4. Talk with fellow teachers, supervising teachers, or college instructors about what influences their selection of instructional tasks. Ask the teachers about the instructional formats they use most often and those they tend to avoid, and why. Try to determine what is important to the teacher, such as promoting student thinking, maintaining order, developing group processes and interpersonal relations, or fostering self-esteem by providing successful experiences. If the teacher deals with several groups of students, try to determine what adjustments are made to meet different student needs.

5. After you have observed teachers who are experienced and those who are novices, try to make generalizations about the differences in their behavior. Think about how routines were used, how cues were given (and how well they were communicated and understood), how monitoring was (or was not) used, how transitions were structured and executed, and how well the instructional pace matched student needs. If the teachers observed appeared to be withit, alert, and cognizant of the entire class, identify specific behaviors these teachers exhibited.

6. If you are not currently teaching, think through the following questions about classroom routines. Determine the procedures you will establish with your students. If you have access to students, interview several of them using these questions:

- How do you know when the teacher is ready to start the class or lesson?
- How do you obtain and put away materials and equipment?
- If you need help when the teacher is busy, what are you supposed to do?
- During lessons, how are you supposed to participate?
- What do you do with returned class work and test papers?

7. Observe a recitation or review session in an elementary, secondary, or college classroom. Focus specifically on the learning probes teachers use to determine student success and problem areas or points of misunderstanding. It might be helpful to categorize the way the probes were used. Consider these questions:

- Were the probes addressed to individual students or to the group as a whole?
- Did the students respond to teacher questions and were students involved in asking other students questions?
- Were higher order questions used?
- Did students use response cards, signals, or choral responses?
- Did the teacher give timely reviews or summarizations?

8. To learn more about monitoring, arrange to observe classes of different ability groups, in different content areas, and at different grade levels. Construct a map of each classroom before the observation begins. Focus on how the teacher monitors as students work independently or in groups. Record teacher contacts with students and how long the contacts last. If possible, describe the content of the interaction, that is, are the interactions focused on content or generally procedural?

After the observations, analyze the information to determine the distribution of the contacts. The following questions may help guide your analysis:

- Were the contacts evenly distributed or directed toward particular students (e.g., high-achieving or low-achieving students, boys or girls, those with hands raised)?
- Were some contacts prolonged?
- Which students did not receive contacts?
- Were the contacts related to the learning or predominantly procedural?
- Was it appropriate for monitoring to occur or should the students have had uninterrupted time?

9. Analyze the response format of a study guide, workbook page, or worksheet you have recently assigned (or would assign) to your students, using Walter

Doyle's categories of cognitive routes, or ways students must process the information to complete the learning task. Which of the following cognitive plans must students execute to accomplish the task?

- Reproduce verbatim (memory)
- Apply in a familiar situation (procedural)
- Comprehend by making higher order inferences, applying the learning in a new situation, paraphrasing, and so on
- State an opinion and provide a rationale

What implications does this analysis have for your instruction?

10. Several factors influence the way teachers sequence learning tasks. These include the subject matter, the specific learning objectives, and the teaching method. Talk with teachers or college instructors about the influences on their instructional decisions about sequencing.

11. Talk with your college instructor or other teachers about how they make decisions about pacing instruction. Find out how they pace instruction for the entire year or semester, for a sequence of lessons, and for a single lesson. Talk with the teachers about specific influences on their pacing decisions. Determine whether they have a specific target group of students and how they decide when it is time to move on to the next topic or take longer on the current topic. In your discussion find out if and how they integrate other topics or other subject areas.

12. After planning a lesson, reflect on the way the lesson is structured. Try to determine if the lesson is structured to help students learn the information in the least amount of time and therefore maximizes ALT. Answer the following questions:

- Are incentives either inherent in the task or material or provided by you to encourage students to be involved actively in the learning?
- Do the students have the prerequisite knowledge, skill, or experience to accomplish the objectives?
- Is this lesson appropriately sequenced within the unit?
- Is the amount of material included appropriate?
- Is the level of challenge appropriate?
- Are adequate opportunities for feedback and additional practice provided?

13. If you have access to elementary or secondary students, interview them about their perceptions of a particular learning task. Find out how much effort they plan to expend on the task (or have expended), how they know if an assignment counts, if they feel they can succeed on the task, if they feel the task is worthwhile or interesting, and so on. If you are not able to interview students, think about your own responses as a student.

14. Interview teachers or college instructors about how they deal with diversity in their classes. Focus on one group of students the instructor teaches. Ask about the diverse learning needs of the students within that group. Be sure your discussion covers such topics as how teachers adapted instruction to meet specific demands; if (and how) they group the students, for specific needs or as general work groups; if they have individualized assignments with varying levels of challenge; and if they devise different performance standards for certain students.

15. Interview teachers about their interactive decisions. Their decisions might be influenced by unexpected events that interfere with the activity flow, by student performance, involvement, interest, requests, mood, or attitude, by teacher mood or attitude, and by the availability of alternate strategies. Ask the teachers about how these various influences shape their decisions. Your discussion might also focus on the teacher's usual responses during interactions compared to modifications they make in special cases.

Instructional Delivery

8.
Providing Direct Instruction

COMMENTARY

The great majority of teachers spend a good deal of their allocated learning time using some form of direct instruction. Yet our conversations with teachers reveal some confusion about this instructional approach. In many cases, direct instruction is viewed as a one-way process of transmitting information to students. Direct instruction, however, includes several instructional modes that can be adjusted to meet specific learning needs. At a minimum, direct instruction includes a variety of lecture, presentation, and recitation formats. In this chapter we examine lecture and presentation, and in the following chapter we focus on conducting recitations and providing feedback.

Lectures and recitations have been predominant modes of instruction since the advent of formal schooling. At times, however, educators and parents have raised concern about too much teacher-controlled instruction. Advocates of experience-centered learning have often been critical of any form of direct instruction. Their views have received considerable support from those who would like to see education become more "humanistic." During the free speech movement of the 1960s, a great deal of criticism was leveled at those who lectured students rather than actively engaging them in the learning process. When educational accountability became a national priority in the 1970s, teachers were criticized for allowing students too much freedom and for not spending more time telling students what they ought to know. Because of the pressure on teachers to have their students make high test scores and the need to work within rather stringent state guidelines, direct instruction has once again become one of the most common instructional modes.

The role and function of direct instruction requires clarification. Preservice programs should help students understand when some form of direct instruction would be the most appropriate teaching strategy. Classes in preparation programs should provide students with an opportunity to observe and analyze a full range of instructional approaches. Differences between lectures, presentations, and recitations should be clearly spelled out. Student and intern teachers should have the opportunity to develop skills and understandings that are essential for using different forms of direct instruction, as well as other instructional modes. Most important, both beginning and experienced teachers should know when direct instruction is the most appropriate approach for achieving specific learning goals and objectives.

RATIONALE

Schools have traditionally operated with restricted time and resources. Curriculum demands, on the other hand, seem to be unlimited. Given these conditions, instructional methods must be practical. Teachers must operate in discrete blocks of time that usually cannot be altered. Direct instruction is a mode of instruction that fits the structure of most schools.

Learning gains are greatest in classrooms where students receive the majority of their instruction directly from the teacher. Teachers who use direct instruction are explicit about the content and skills to be learned or practiced. Teacher-directed, large-group instruction provides for a high degree of academic engaged time. When students are actively involved in academic work, the task of classroom management is simplified.

Maintaining a systematic, intensive focus on goals and objectives leads teachers to spend more time planning. Activities are chosen because they are related to achieving high-priority objectives. Planning for direct instruction includes introduction, practice, and review so that students have several opportunities to learn new material. Very little is left to chance. The direct instruction model is flexible and allows teachers to incorporate other strategies such as independent reading or writing. However, learning new knowledge or skills is planned and presented systematically.

Assessment plays an important role by providing the basic information for planning direct instruction. Prerequisite skills and knowledge are assessed and student understanding is monitored. Teachers interact with students to diagnose and correct faulty concepts during explanations. Assessment procedures give teachers information that allows them to provide individual assistance within a group structure.

Research on information processing has shown that humans are limited-capacity processors who can only process so much information at any one time. When teachers pace instruction too rapidly or present too many ideas at once, students become confused and cannot correctly grasp the information. Thus, teachers who use direct instruction divide the content into small segments so as not to overload students' working memory.

Although numerous studies have documented the effectiveness of direct instruction, some educators are concerned about the possibility that students may be more passive when this instructional mode is used. When direct instruction is conducted properly, students are not passive. They are actively involved in attending to the teacher, answering questions, listening to their peers, processing the information, and incorporating it into long-term memory. They are encouraged to apply what they have learned in meaningful ways during independent reading and writing, problem solving, and other individual learning activities.

A major goal of education is to develop the ability of students to use higher level thinking skills independently. Students must master basic skills and build an extensive knowledge base before they are able to perform at higher levels. Systematic, intensive, teacher-led group instruction is an effective method for developing the foundation of knowledge needed to think or reason in accordance with high-literacy goals.

RESEARCH SYNTHESIS

The Concept of Direct Instruction

When teachers determine the structure for their lessons, they are making critical instructional decisions. They can choose to have students work on individualized assignments, in small cooperative groups, or as an entire class. In addition, they must decide whether to use a discovery method, indirect instruction, or direct instruction. Their choices should help them accomplish specific objectives. Teachers who understand the research on different instructional modes are more apt to select the most appropriate structure for their lessons.

The term *direct instruction* has been applied to a wide range of instructional processes. For some it means the use of regimented scripted lessons that are designed to be teacher proof. For others direct instruction means any instruction given in a businesslike manner. A good working definition for direct instruction is explicit instruction with an academic focus led by teachers who interact directly with their students (Lehr, 1986; Baumann, 1988).

Explicit instruction is unambiguous, clear, and detailed. The content to be learned is not merely implied. Students are given a substantial amount of information by the teacher. The instruction emphasizes the knowledge or skills being taught. Teachers know what they want the students to learn and consequently have a distinct academic focus. The elements that make up direct instruction are illustrated in Figure 8–1.

Teachers who use direct instruction should allocate classroom time carefully and control the pace, sequence, and content of their lessons. This helps to ensure that all important content is covered and that students are working on material appropriate for them. Increased student learning is possible only when the time available for learning is used productively (Baumann, 1988; Brophy, 1979a; Kierstead, 1985). The mathematics program developed by Good et al. (1977) is an example of a direct

FIGURE 8–1. Elements of direct instruction

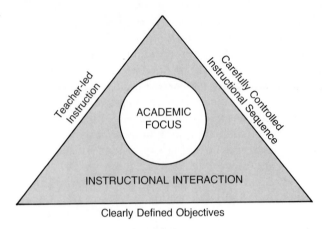

instruction program that provides guidelines for all aspects of a lesson. This program gives specific suggestions about how time is to be used for instruction, seatwork, and homework.

The direct instruction format has a strong academic focus (Lehr, 1986). Content is carefully sequenced, there is a high rate of pupil engagement, student work is closely monitored, and students receive specific corrective feedback. Direct instruction is delivered face to face by the teacher. Learning centers, instructional packets, or peers are seldom involved in direct instruction (Baumann, 1988). Workbooks, worksheets and kits may be used for practice, but students are not expected to learn new content from ancillary materials. Teachers lead, tell, and show students what they want them to learn. When students have problems, teachers explain, give additional examples, and reteach until they accomplish the learning objectives.

A Direct Instruction Model

Rosenshine and Stevens (1986) have developed a direct instruction model that includes six fundamental instructional functions:

1. Review, check previous day's work, and reteach if necessary
2. Present new content/skills
3. Guided student practice and check for understanding
4. Feedback and correctives and reteach, if necessary
5. Independent student practice
6. Review weekly and monthly (p. 379)

This sequence of instruction recognizes the importance of the teacher. Good (1979) pointed out that "the [direct instruction] model provides a plausible, practical system of instruction" (p. 58). Review and reteaching ensure readiness for new tasks. Students are assessed to see that they have the prerequisite skills before new instruction is given. This aspect of direct instruction supports the position that students are more likely to learn when new material includes information that is not too difficult (Morine-Dershimer & Beyerbach, 1987). Guided student practice provides opportunities for students to use new skills while teachers are available to give corrective feedback. Teachers using direct instruction are able to promote high success rates by pacing instruction so that students answer correctly 80 to 85% of the questions asked in class. Weekly and monthly reviews are used to maintain and reinforce the concepts that have been learned (Rosenshine & Stevens, 1986).

Appropriate Use of Direct Instruction

Direct instruction is a strategy that should be used wisely. Overuse or misuse can encourage passivity on the part of the student and may interfere with development of higher level skills. Direct instruction is most effective when teaching basic skills in the primary grades or in working with low-achieving students. The objective is to master a body of knowledge that will connect with new information in future instruction (Morine-Dershimer & Beyerbach, 1987; Rosenshine & Stevens, 1986). For example, when students develop a sight vocabulary, they learn most of the frequently used words necessary to comprehend more difficult material. For most pupils, direct instruction is an efficient way to develop basic skills in reading, mathematics, and other subjects requiring specific prerequisite knowledge. This is also true of any new skills that can be taught in a step-by-step manner (Rosenshine & Stevens, 1986). Beginning skills in cooking, carpentry, or computer use are good examples of basic skills. It is possible to learn such skills independently or by trial and error, but direct instruction can make the learning process less frustrating and less time-consuming.

Direct instruction can be effective when teaching new or difficult material (Rosenshine & Stevens, 1986). Learning world geography might seem to be an enormous task for some students. A knowledgeable teacher, however, can organize the information around major unifying concepts that provide the structure for learning complex material. Explicit instruction can provide the basic information base and the unifying concepts that will help students to be successful when they are expected to learn higher level concepts.

Students should be allowed to develop a repertoire of processes that will help them apply what they have learned (Rosenshine & Stevens, 1986). Direct instruction can be used to teach a general rule or procedure which can then be used in new situations. Many mathematics computation skills such as long division are first taught directly. Later, the skills can be used independently to solve a variety of problems. Map-reading skills may be taught through direct instruction, so that students can use the skills later in planning a trip.

Direct instruction can also be used to develop higher level thinking skills. Students may be given a label for a skill to be learned and then taught a process to use when applying the skill. Through modeling and guided practice, students can learn how and when to use higher level skills. Examples and nonexamples are provided to help develop an understanding of conditions that would be conducive for using higher level skills. Teachers can gradually withdraw their support until students are able to use new skills independently (Gersten & Carnine, 1986).

In some instructional situations direct instruction may not be the best approach. Careful consideration of the instructional goals and objectives can help teachers choose the most appropriate instructional mode. As Rosenshine and Stephens (1986) noted,

> [Direct instruction is] least applicable for teaching in areas which are "ill-structured," that is, where the skills to be taught do not follow explicit steps, or [in] areas which lack a general skill which is applied repeatedly. Thus, the results of this research are less relevant for teaching composition and writing of term papers, analysis of literature, problem solving in specific content areas, discussion of social issues, or the development of unique or creative responses. (p. 377)

Direct instruction can be used for teaching content that is well structured, but teachers should choose an inquiry or group discussion format for those areas that have less structure (Rosenshine & Stevens, 1986).

Direct instruction does not provide opportunities for learning through experience. At times students have to learn new procedures that are not clearly defined or delineated. Doyle (1983) contended that "in such cases, the only alternative is to allow students to experience content so that they can invent procedures and construct knowledge structures on their own" (p. 178). Students can be told how to make bread, but the only way they can learn how to knead the dough and form loaves is through actual involvement in the process. How much flour to use, when to stop kneading, and how long to let the dough rise can be influenced by many factors that are fully understood only after students have experienced the process.

Several researchers are cautious about the use of direct instruction for teaching higher level skills. Doyle (1983) suggested that such instruction may produce immediate effects but will not have long-term benefits or generate real comprehension and meaning. He pointed out that students may learn routines or "surface algorithms" without developing the regulatory processes necessary to use the correct procedure or have the deep understanding to choose the best path to a solution.

Lecture and Presentation

Rosenshine (1986) listed presentation of new content as one of six important instructional functions. Presentations, or lectures, are used most often to transmit knowledge from teachers to students. A lecture may last from a few minutes to a total class period. Lectures are quite effective when schools are organized around groups of students who are assigned to various classes for specific periods of time. Bourke (1986) found that more frequent use of teacher lecturing and explanation was positively associated with enjoyment and achievement.

Effective lecturing begins with an examination of several alternative methods to accomplish learning objectives. The most effective teachers know when the lecture is appropriate and use it only then. Gage and Berliner (1984) reviewed studies on the proper use of lectures and concluded that the lecture method is appropriate when

> (a) the basic purpose is to disseminate information, (b) the material is not available elsewhere, (c) the material must be organized and presented in a particular way for a

specific group, (d) it is necessary to arouse interest in the subject, (e) the material need be remembered for only a short time, and (f) it is necessary to provide an introduction to an area or directions for learning tasks to be pursued through some other teaching method. (p. 457)

Although communication of new information is a one-way process during a lecture, it is seldom an uninterrupted monologue. Textbooks and other teaching materials may be used in conjunction with the presentation. Le Clerc, Bertrand, and DuFour (1986) found that student achievement was positively associated with the use of teaching materials and questions addressed to individual students during lectures.

Expert teachers have a knowledge base that they bring to the teaching act. They know their content and are convinced that this knowledge is of value to their students. Shulman and Sykes (1986) contended that content knowledge is only a part of what makes some teachers more effective than others. Expert teachers also know ways to teach their specific content and have an understanding of student diversity and individual differences. They are able to create instructional representations that build a bridge between the sophisticated understanding of the teacher and the developing understanding of the student. Wineburg and Wilson (1988) described instructional representations as "the product of the teacher's comprehension of content and their understanding of the needs, motivations, and abilities of their learners" (p. 57). Expert teachers use this knowledge to choose just the right example, analogy, or story to illustrate each point. When a lecture is of high quality, students are able to view knowledge through a living personality, relate this body of knowledge to their lives, and develop an active interest that leads to comprehension (Gage & Berliner, 1984).

When knowledge of both subject matter and how to teach content is combined with an understanding of student diversity and good presentation skills, the lecture can be an exciting tool. Shulman and Sykes (1986) included voice, manner, and poise in a category they call "performance skills." The way teachers present content can have an effect on learning. For some time, researchers thought that teachers' use of enthusiasm during a lecture was related to affective rather than cognitive outcomes. Recent studies have shown that enthusiasm is related to achievement, especially for older students (Brophy & Good, 1986). Indicators of enthusiasm may include

rapid, uplifting and varied vocal delivery; dancing, wide open eyes; frequent demonstrative gestures; varied, dynamic body movements; varied, emotive facial expressions; selection of varied words, especially adjectives; ready, animated acceptance of ideas and feelings; and exuberant energy level. (Gephart et al., 1981c, p. 2)

Teachers can deliberately plan to use elements of enthusiasm. They can use presentation skills that will generate student enthusiasm for learning new information. They can also model enthusiasm about the content by adding statements about their own excitement and valuing of the topic (Gage & Berliner, 1984). Effective lectures and presentations, then, are a result of teachers' knowledge, their understanding of instructional processes, and their presentation skills. A summary of these three components is presented in Figure 8–2.

Content Knowledge	Content-Specific Instructional Processes	Presentation Skills
Key concepts	Best instructional sequence	Methods for improving enunciation, pronunciation, and presentation of self
Structure and organization	Examples, analogies, stories	Elements of enthusiasm
Facts, dates, details	Meaningful relationships to student lives	Elements of clarity

FIGURE 8–2. Knowledge and skills needed for effective lectures and presentations

During a lecture or presentation there may be very little student talk. Students are expected to listen, analyze information, make connections with previous knowledge, and reorganize their mental networks to incorporate new ideas or concepts. When introduction of new content is clear and properly paced, student talk is likely to be minimal. Students often ask questions when teachers talk too fast, the information is not clear, or when they want to distract the teacher.

Very often student talk during presentations in the primary grades is unrelated to the learning objectives. Student questions may relate to classroom procedures and not to the topic at hand. At the middle and upper grade levels it is more likely that student talk will be related to learning. When teachers encourage and use content-related student talk to develop an academic focus, they capitalize on a developmental characteristic of their students (Brophy, 1979c).

Elements of Effective Lectures

Effective lectures are structured to include an overview, the development of new content, and a conclusion. Cognitive psychologists have found that this type of structure helps students understand and remember what they learn (Sparks & Sparks, 1984).

Providing an overview of the content helps students see the "big picture." The overview communicates what is to be learned and a rationale for why it is important (Squires et al., 1983). In their delivery teachers stress learning objectives, basic skills, and concepts to be learned. They alert students to important knowledge that will be presented. This helps students understand the structure of the information that is to follow. Advance organizers are a form of overview that provides learners with rules for organizing a body of knowledge; they make the structure of the lecture clear (Berliner, 1987). Other types of cognitive organizers may also be used to provide a visual picture of the main concepts to be presented (Sparks & Sparks, 1984).

Berliner (1987) noted:

An organizer is not just an introduction; it provides verbal structures to aid students in fitting new information into their existing knowledge system. To "understand" is to have integrated new information into one's personal store of knowledge. Understanding is distinguished from memory by this kind of integration. (p. 260)

Gage and Berliner (1984) stressed the need for lectures to help students see the relevance of the content to their personal goals. Students pay more attention to content when they feel that it may be meaningful in their lives. Relating new knowledge to student interests and goals can be a part of the overview.

The development stage of the lecture should be used to present new knowledge or skills. Good et al. (1977) defined the development portion of a mathematics lesson as the part of a lesson devoted to increasing comprehension of skills, concepts, and other facets of the mathematics curriculum. Developmental activities include initial instruction, developing meaning of concepts or labels, and attempts to extend ideas and transfer new knowledge. Rosenshine (1983–84) found that effective mathematics teachers spend a considerable amount of time developing new content. They find several ways to present the same ideas; they are creatively redundant. A number of explanations and examples included in presentations help to improve student understanding and prepare them for seatwork and other independent learning activities.

Wineburg and Wilson (1988) found that good history teachers use lectures to help students see history as a human construction. They spend time examining the significance of what has happened, rather than simply presenting facts. Their lectures encourage students to determine what is important rather than letting the textbook do it for them. Like mathematics teachers, they use examples, analogies, demonstrations, simulations, stories, dramatic enactments, and debates. Effective history teachers are not satisfied with one way of presenting an idea; they too are creatively redundant.

The conclusion of a lecture or presentation can be used to review, summarize key points, introduce a postorganizer, or assess student comprehension through questions. Teachers may ask students for questions to help determine the need to provide additional examples or information. When teachers plan to use a series of interrelated presentations, they might use the last part of the lecture to tell students how the material just covered will relate to future lessons (Gage & Berliner, 1984). Effective conclusions remind students of important information and how this information can be useful to them.

Structuring Behaviors

Student achievement improves when teachers use structuring behaviors during presentations. Structuring behaviors include stating objectives, signaling transitions, emphasizing main points, summarizing parts, and reviewing main ideas (Brophy & Good, 1986). Structuring behaviors help students link new information to familiar knowledge. Reviewing, stressing main points, and summarizing help create redundancy and make the organization of the content more explicit. Gephart, Strother, and Duckett (1981b) stated that structuring also "offers students a chance to think about, respond to, and synthesize what they are learning" (p. 2). Nuthall (1987) found that students who are not aware that teachers are using structuring behaviors do not learn as much as students whose teachers help them to recognize why the behaviors are being used. A comparison of elements of effective lectures and structuring behaviors is shown in Figure 8–3.

Stating objectives and telling students what is to be learned and why it is important to them can improve student learning. Berliner (1987) described this behavior as "telling students in advance about what they are going to learn, what the key points to be mastered are, and what they should know at the end of an instructional episode" (p. 260). There is a positive relationship between these behaviors and student learning in both daily lessons and in units that last for longer periods of time.

Signaling transitions is a structuring behavior teachers use to let students know that one part of a lesson has ended and another is about to begin. Teachers signal transitions both physically and mentally. Mental transitions are most frequently used to signal a change in topic during a presentation. Frequent unexplained mental transitions interfere with students' ability to see relationships between relevant ideas and thereby decrease the effectiveness of a presentation.

Emphasizing main points is another method for helping students understand and remember key concepts. When teachers point out the most important features of concepts, processes, or models and make overt statements about the importance of these features, students begin to see that the information can be organized around main ideas (Sparks & Sparks, 1984). When main ideas are not identified and stressed, students may try to memorize all of the information because they cannot determine what is most important.

Review can occur at the beginning or end of a lesson. When it occurs at the beginning, it can be used to draw together several points from a previous lesson. At the end of a lesson a review will help highlight the most important points students need to remember, which in turn helps to improve their recall of the entire body of information. When instruction is clear and well structured, a review or summary may

Elements of Effective Lectures	Elements of Structuring Behaviors
Overview	**Statement of Objectives**
Learning expectations	What is to be learned
Rationale	Rationale
Cognitive organizers	
Development	**Lesson**
Present information	Emphasize main points
Use creative redundancy	Signal transitions
Use examples, analogies	
Conclusion	**Summary**
Summarize key points	Provide timely review
Postorganizers	Summarize parts
Assess learning	Assess learning

FIGURE 8–3. Comparing elements of effective lectures and structuring behaviors

be unnecessary (Nuthall, 1987). Rosenshine (1983–84) found that the use of a daily review in mathematics classes gave teachers the opportunity to assess prerequisite skills and improve student learning. In most cases, timely reviews that summarize or abstract main points can help to improve student learning.

Taken together, the structuring behaviors teachers use during a lecture or presentation give a lesson direction. Students feel that the lesson is going somewhere, and because they perceive that the information is well organized learning tends to improve (Gage & Berliner, 1984). It is not necessary to use all of the structuring behaviors during one class period. The behaviors should be used in a timely manner to focus student attention on a topic or problem and to help students organize and store information.

Care should be taken not to overstructure presentations. Soar and Soar (1976) found that an intermediate amount of structuring was best. It is probably wise to maintain a balance between student independence and teacher direction. Too much structuring occurs when teachers structure information that students could have comprehended by themselves. Students should share the responsibility for their learning (IRT, 1987b).

Clarity of Instruction

Clarity of instruction is a multidimensional factor. According to Gephart et al. (1981b), "Clarity is not a simple dichotomy (clear vs. unclear teacher behaviors); . . . it is more than a continuum (clear at one end, unclear at the other, with gradations in between)" (p. 2). Gagne (1985) identified clarity as the variable that most clearly separates effective from ineffective teachers. Effective teachers communicate objectives, directions, and content more clearly. Brophy and Evertson (1976) found clarity to be less important at the elementary level, but it is increasingly important as content becomes more complex.

Studies have shown that students evaluate their teacher's instruction on the basis of clarity, and that clarity is consistently and positively related to student achievement (Gephart et al., 1981b; Brophy & Good, 1986). Students are often dependent on oral information for the bulk of their learning. They pay more attention to information when it makes sense to them. When lectures are clear, learners have a better opportunity to understand, remember, and use the information (Chilcoat & Stahl, 1986). Students in diverse settings, ranging from junior high age to the university, report that the same teacher behaviors influence clarity. Moreover, studies of individual teachers in different settings have shown that clarity is a stable quality (Cruickshank, 1989). Teachers who strive for clarity do so regularly and their presentations are consistently clear.

Teacher behaviors related to clarity can be grouped into three main categories: substantive (factors related to the content to be learned), semantic (factors related to the way teachers use language), and strategic (deliberate use of strategies to improve learning). Teachers who communicate with clarity give careful attention to each of these areas. Figure 8–4 depicts the factors related to clarity.

FIGURE 8–4. Factors affecting instructional clarity

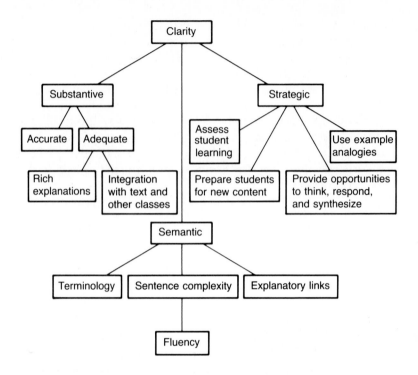

Substantive Clarity.   Teachers are responsible for communicating a body of knowledge to their students. Presentations should be accurate and adequate enough to give students opportunities to fully understand the information. Students report that clear teachers stay with topics until they understand them rather than briefly going over information and assuming the content has been learned. The use of structuring behaviors is one way to ensure that the information being presented is adequate. Providing examples, related details, and more complete explanations is another technique that can be used to ensure that content coverage is adequate. Information presented should also be relevant to the topic (Armento, 1977).

Other factors related to student understanding of content are the methods teachers use to integrate information from textbooks and from other content areas. Porter and Brophy (1988) found that the use of published instructional materials contributed to the quality of instruction. Teachers who use materials thoughtfully to accomplish important curriculum goals and objectives are more successful in fostering student learning. They use lecture time to reinterpret, expand, and explain the ideas presented in the text. Integrating instruction across disciplinary boundaries also proves to be a productive teaching behavior. Students tend to remember more of the content if learning goes beyond the immediate context.

Kallison (1986) identified specific teacher behaviors that help clarify relationships among parts of a communication. When teachers use these behaviors, they make the organization of their substantive content explicit. For example, teachers can identify a sequence for instruction that best reveals the relationships among parts of the content and use that sequence to guide instruction. Another clarifying behavior is to present a diagram or cognitive organizer of the structure of a lesson prior to instruction. Using explicit verbal statements to accentuate relationships also helps to clarify the organization of the information. These statements can be used before, during, or after instruction. Gage and Berliner (1984) referred to these statements as verbal markers of importance.

Semantic Clarity.   The semantic component of clarity refers to the teacher's ability to give information in a meaningful way. This involves choice of terminology, sentence construction, and fluency of presentation. The words teachers choose to use can add to or detract from clarity. Terminology should be precise, and concrete terms that students already know should be used to explain abstract concepts. Unfamiliar words should be clearly defined. When pronouns are used, teachers should make sure that students know their referents. Learners have difficulty comprehending messages when pronouns are separated from the words they represent (Armento, 1977). Teachers may also use explanatory links to enhance the fluency of their presentations and to help integrate ideas. Prepositions and conjunctions such as *because, in order to, if, then,* and *therefore* indicate relationships within and between sentences. Explanatory links can cue the learner that a relationship is being described (Rosenshine, 1971a).

Speaking in complete sentences, rather than in choppy phrases, is an aspect of fluency that enhances clarity. When teachers frequently interrupt their message with "uh" and "um," clarity suffers. False starts or halts, sentences that go nowhere, and mazes (units of speech that do not make sense) all interrupt the fluency of speech (Gage & Berliner, 1984).

Strategic Clarity.   Strategic clarity is the process of taking purposeful steps to make sure students are learning. Cruickshank, Kennedy, Bush, and Holland (1978) identified four strategic behaviors teachers can use to increase clarity. The first of the behaviors is to assess student learning. Teachers can actively attempt to find out if students understand the content, and if there are any misunderstandings they adjust and clarify their presentation. The second strategic behavior is to provide students with opportunities to think about, respond to, or synthesize what they are learning. Frequent use of examples is the third behavior. The fourth is to review prior work and prepare students for the next day's work. Brandt (1984) suggested that giving clear directions is an important clarifying strategy for teachers to use. Dividing a task into parts, providing directions for each of the parts, giving directions in order, and making sure that the directions are given at the appropriate time, are actions that can clarify the teacher's intentions.

Factors That Detract from Clarity.   Early studies identified vagueness and mazes as factors that detract from clarity. Vague terms indicate approximations, ambiguity, or lack of assurance (Gephart et al., 1981b). Berliner (1987) provided examples of several types of vague terms:

Ambiguous designations: *somehow, somewhere, thing*
Approximations: *about, a little, just about, somewhat, sort of*
Bluffs and recoveries: *actually, and so forth, and so on, anyway, as you know, in a nutshell, in essence, in fact, in other words, of course, or whatever, to make a long story short, you know, you see*
Error admissions: *excuse me, I'm sorry, I guess*
Indeterminate quantifications: *a bunch, a couple, a few, some, various*
Multiplicities: *kind(s) of, type(s) of*
Possibilities: *chances are, could be, may, maybe, might, perhaps, seems* (p. 263)

Harris and Swick (1985) pointed out that teachers use vague terms because they cannot recall or do not have a good understanding of the information they are presenting. When those same teachers acquire more knowledge about the content, they are able to reduce the use of vague terms. Land (1987) found negative correlations between the frequency of vague terms and the amount of content coverage. When teachers are vague, their students learn less, participate less during class, give shorter answers or contributions, and use more vague terms themselves when answering.

Teacher verbal mazes detract from learning. False starts, halts in speech, repeating the same word over and over, or using tangles of words are examples of verbal mazes. The mazes interfere with learning because explanations are not as clear and the teacher appears to be nervous or unprepared. Student learning is damaged more by the frequency of mazes than by vagueness. Land (1987) found that students will tolerate a number of mazes, false starts, or tangles. However, when the frequency increases, they decide that the teacher does not know the material.

At times teachers may include additional, unexplained content that does not appear to relate to the subject under discussion. Smith, Smith, and Staples (1982) found that adding superfluous content negatively influenced achievement and student perception of the effectiveness of instruction. Students reported that the addition of unexplained information annoyed them and made them feel less confident.

Teachers sometimes interrupt their own lessons with announcements or irrelevant material or stimuli. This deviation from the instructional focus detracts from clarity. Brophy and Putnam (1979) gave several examples of interruptions that cause teachers to deviate from their focus, such as wandering for no apparent reason, repeating or reviewing material that is understood, pausing to gather their thoughts or prepare material, and interrupting the lesson to deal with behavior problems occurring outside the group or with other concerns that could have been postponed.

Explanations

Explanations are often given during lectures and presentations. Teachers offer explanations as part of the development of new content or in response to student questions. A good explanation is much more interactive than a presentation. Teachers must elicit and respond to students' efforts to comprehend new information. The fact that teachers need to find out how students are interpreting instruction eliminates the use of questions with known answers.

Students and teachers each have an active role to play in constructing explanations that help students comprehend new information. These roles are presented in Figure 8–5. The knowledge students bring to a lesson and their schemata, or the ways they have organized their knowledge, determine to a large extent what they learn. Students play an active role in learning, mediating, and restructuring information so that it will fit into their own personal knowledge base. Duffy and Roehler (1986) contended that effective explanations are characterized by:

(a) A responsiveness to student restructuring of information;
(b) An effort to put the student in conscious control;
(c) A presentation of declarative, conditional, and procedural knowledge is conceptually accurate, explicit, and meaningful; and
(d) An attempt to assist student efforts to build understanding by sequencing and providing restructuring "hooks." (p. 212)

Berliner (1987) pointed out that "good explanations occur when instructors help students generate personal meaning, carefully communicate what to focus on, are explicit about how students should think about what they are focused on, and emphasize the most salient ideas of the content in the explanations" (p. 290).

Carefully structured explanations help teach the reasoning processes students need to understand information being presented. Teachers also use modeling to help make reasoning processes visible. They talk out loud about the way they think when they are engaged in the reasoning process. Student understanding is assessed by asking students to explain or describe the reasoning processes they have used. When student misunderstanding is evident, teachers can reexplain, remodel, or clarify what they want students to learn. Student feedback is used until teachers are satisfied with the level of understanding (Herrmann, 1988). In general, teachers monitor and shape student understanding as they generate explanations students can use to reformulate their mental networks of knowledge.

Information given during an interactive explanation should have at least three characteristics; the information should be explicit, conceptually accurate, and useful (Duffy & Roehler, 1986). There is a strong relationship between a teacher's

Teachers	Students
Give explicit information	Explain their thinking
Provide factual, conditional, and procedural knowledge	Delineate their reasoning process
Are responsive to student thinking	Tell how the process can be used
Present information that is conceptually accurate, explicit, meaningful, and useful	Restructure their knowledge base to accommodate new learning
Model the reasoning process	Apply new processes in real situations

FIGURE 8–5. Teacher and student roles in interactive explanations

explicitness, student learning from instruction, and strategic use of target skills (Duffy, Rohler, Meloth & Vabrus, 1986). The information teachers give in interactive explanations is determined through a process of eliciting and analyzing student knowledge. This process of diagnosis identifies the information students need to overcome misconceptions and form valid concepts (Roth, Anderson & Smith, 1986). In good explanations teachers are explicit about what they want students to know. They base their explanations on an accurate assessment of students' prior knowledge.

Effective explanations present key concepts that are conceptually accurate. When teachers do not have deep knowledge of the content, or when they are teaching out of their areas, their explanations may not always be conceptually accurate. Teachers must be able to explain complex concepts accurately to their students so that any misconceptions held by students can be corrected.

Students often have misconceptions that are based on their personal experience rather than on valid information. Roth et al. (1986) found that science textbooks often fail to alert teachers to the naive concepts students may bring to school. When teachers depend on information in textbooks, students may cling to their experiential knowledge. As a result, science concepts that students develop may be inaccurate. Teachers' explanations should help students contrast and compare commonsense misconceptions with scientific fact and link concepts presented in the text with what they know about the everyday world. Roth et al. (1986) suggested that teachers use scientific terms correctly, rephrase and expand the textbook, and use explanations to correct any confusion. Discussions between teachers and students should focus on understanding and applying scientific principles. Porter and Brophy (1988) studied explanations in science and concluded, "Effective teachers not only know the subject matter they intend their students to learn, but also know the misconceptions their students bring to the classroom that will interfere with their learning of that subject matter" (p. 79).

Research has confirmed that students often develop misconceptions in mathematics that must be corrected before content can be mastered. Schoenfield (1987) found that misconceptions are systematic and consistent, and are frequently the result of teaching techniques. While effective math teachers explain new content completely, novices are less likely to explain. Leinhardt (1986) asserted that explanations in mathematics should be richer or more detailed and that the explanations should have several characteristics:

1. Students should already know all of the components to be included in an explanation.
2. Teachers should make sure students have all of the prerequisite subskills.
3. Students should be told when and why to use a new procedure.
4. Understanding should be assessed, and errors should be corrected and explored until students really understand when and under what conditions to use the new procedure.
5. Explanations should be completed in one class session.

A series of interrelated lessons can be integrated so that explanations lead to independent practice, feedback, and review of the same procedure or concept.

Research in reading (Duffy et al., 1986) identified the need to provide conceptually accurate information during explanations. A process called responsive elaboration has been used to improve student understanding. After providing accurate, precise, and explicit introductory information, teachers demonstrate a specific reasoning process complete with examples and a step-by-step procedure to follow. At this point, student responses are elicited and used to assess their understanding of the process. Students are asked to tell how the process could be used in their lives. Teachers listen carefully and respond with more information. The teacher's role is to diagnose student misunderstanding and, when needed, construct a reinterpretation. Closure is used to make sure that students understood, to review, and to give students an opportunity to apply the process in a reading situation.

Effective explanations should provide students with useful information. Whenever possible, information should be given that has personal meaning for the students. When a process is explained correctly, students should be able to use it outside the school context. Failure to help students see the usefulness of information in their lives is a common problem. Gunstone and White (1981) studied first-year college students who were well grounded in physics and mathematics. They found that these students could not use their mathematics knowledge to explain observations or resolve discrepancies between their predictions and their observations. The researchers were surprised that these capable students were not able to apply information they had acquired. They concluded that teachers at all levels should pay more attention to helping students apply their knowledge to the solution of real problems. Roth et al. (1986) contended that providing experience with numerous real-world applications of new knowledge will help students transfer knowledge to situations they will experience.

Interactive explanations are advantageous because they put the student in control of processing information. Students learn to make sense out of instruction by restructuring information to fit their knowledge base. Herrmann (1988) believed that "the teacher's primary role is to teach students how to monitor their comprehension and how to fix a comprehension breakdown" (p. 24). In order to do this, teachers have to help students learn to use the same strategies experts use. During explanations teachers help shape student comprehension of a concept, idea, task, or procedure until it is congruent with the curriculum. Strategies and skills are applied in real situations, not just on worksheets. Students have an active role in their own learning and they are able to apply their knowledge to solve problems in and out of school.

 PRIMARY REFERENCES

Armento, B. J. (1977). Teacher behaviors related to student achievement on a social science concept test. *Journal of Teacher Education, 28*(2), 46–52.

This study relates teacher behaviors to learning social studies concepts. Factors that improve the clarity of instruction are discussed. The interaction of substantive, semantic, and strategic factors is stressed.

Berliner, D. C. (1987). But do they understand? In V. Richardson-Koehler (Ed.), *Educator's handbook: A research perspective* (pp. 259–291). New York: Longman.

Explaining for understanding is one major section of this chapter. Using advance organizers, prompting awareness of relevant knowledge, a model for explaining, and tips for giving better explanations are included.

Brophy, J. E., & Good, T. L. (1986). Teacher behavior and student achievement. In M. C. Wittrock (Ed.), *Handbook of research on teaching* (3rd ed., pp. 328–376). New York: Macmillan.

This chapter includes a concise discussion of active teaching and summarizes the research on structuring and clarity.

Cruickshank, D. R., & Kennedy, J. J. (1986). Teacher clarity. *Teaching and Teacher Education, 2,* 43–67.

Two decades of research on the clarity of teacher presentations are reviewed. An operational definition of clarity is given. Evidence linking clear teacher behaviors to desirable student outcomes is presented.

Duffy, G. G., Roehler, L. R., Meloth, M. S., & Vabrus, L. G. (1986). Conceptualizing instructional explanation. *Teaching and Teacher Education, 2,* 197–214.

Characteristics of the explanations of more effective teachers are identified and described. Responsive information giving, developing awareness, specific kinds of information, and devices for assisting student efforts to learn are described.

Gage, N. L., & Berliner, D. C. (1984). *Educational psychology* (3rd ed.). Boston: Houghton Mifflin.

Chapter 19 is a comprehensive review of the research on lecturing and explaining. Procedures for developing and delivering effective lectures are clearly presented and described. Chapter 24 has an excellent description of the research on recitation and structuring.

Gersten, R., & Carnine, D. (1986). Direct instruction in reading comprehension. *Educational Leadership, 43*(7), 70–78.

This article reports research findings on direct instruction and identifies factors that significantly benefit students' comprehension. Specific procedures and components of this explicit process are presented.

Good, T. L. (1979). Teacher effectiveness in the elementary school. *Journal of Teacher Education, 30*(2), 52–64.

The pattern of teaching behavior called direct instruction is described. The concept of direct instruction in this article is one of active teaching that includes articulating learning goals, assessing student progress, and frequent presentations.

Land, M. L. (1987). Vagueness and clarity. In M. J. Dunkin (Ed.), *The international encyclopedia of teaching and teacher education* (pp. 392– 397) New York: Pergamon.

This is an excellent review of recent research on teacher clarity. Research on vagueness and mazes is reported as well as clusters of other low-inference variables that facilitate learning.

Rosenshine, B. V. (1983). Teaching functions in instructional programs. *Elementary School Journal, 83,* 335–351.

A review of recent research related to structured presentations is presented. A general model of effective instruction includes instructional functions and a more complete explication of each component.

Schoenfield, A. H. (1987). A mathematician's research on math instruction. *Educational Researcher, 16*(9), 9–12.

A description of instructional strategies that can eliminate some barriers to math learning is provided. Explanation behaviors to counteract misconceptions and unproductive problem-solving techniques are included.

 ## RESEARCH IN PRACTICE

Finding 1: Direct instruction is a systematic strategy designed to teach new information, basic skills, and procedures that can be applied to different situations.

Direct instruction is an explicit instructional strategy whereby teachers interact directly with students. Teachers control the instructional process. This helps to ensure that instruction is properly sequenced and that learning objectives are accomplished. Teachers using direct instruction are also able to control the pace of their lessons and cover the desired content. If direct instruction is used to the exclusion of other teaching strategies, student involvement in the learning process may decrease. Properly used, however, direct instruction can be a powerful teaching strategy.

Scenario. A high school teacher was hired in the middle of the year to teach a computer class. He found that his students had a wide range of knowledge and ability. Some students were obviously beginners while others could complete complicated procedures. At first the teacher thought he would continue the individualized instruction format that was in place. After a few days he discovered that even the most able students needed to learn basic information and procedures. Most of these students had learned how to use computers from the tutoring of friends. They could complete some tasks, but they had no real understanding of the underlying principles and processes. Many of the procedures they used were accomplished by trial and error, and there was little consistency in their performance.

The teacher decided to begin each class period with direct instruction. He followed a sequenced, systematic program designed to develop a knowledge base with the beginners and to fill in gaps in the knowledge of more experienced students. Content was taught directly, and student understanding was systematically assessed. Teacher-directed practice of each new skill was required for all students. Independent practice time was used to consolidate skills with the beginners and for more complex applications with the more able students. Regular reviews were conducted in a whole-group setting. The more advanced students were able to help reteach those who were having a difficult time.

After a few weeks of direct instruction two of the better students asked to meet with the teacher. They wanted to see if their teacher could do something about the other computer classes in the school. These students were concerned that their friends were not getting the benefit of a structured program. They felt that the individualized approach caused students to develop bad habits that would be hard to break later on. The two concerned students had actually developed some "cheat sheets" for their friends. The sheets listed the series of steps necessary to accomplish specific procedures. On their own they were making an attempt to structure the learning for other students in the school.

Finding 2: When direct instruction is used appropriately, students are actively engaged in processing information.

Teachers know that getting students actively involved in the learning process increases the amount of information they will be able to absorb and retain. Presentations should be developed after students are carefully assessed. Teachers should take time to review the knowledge students would need to understand new information. Whenever possible, new information should be taught in small segments using concrete examples that can be applied to the lives of the students. Development of new content should be alternated with questioning, discussing, and checking for understanding. Although the instruction is teacher directed, it should be student centered and promote student learning.

Scenario.   A general science teacher was teaching a lesson about levers to ninth grade students. The lecture covered three types of levers. Vocabulary terms such as *load, fulcrum,* and *effort* were introduced, and diagrams similar to the one in Figure 8–6 were used as the information was presented.

Students in the class were quiet and seemed attentive. They did not ask questions, nor did they take notes. Toward the end of the period the teacher introduced the concept of mechanical advantage and gave a homework assignment. He explained how to compute mechanical advantage and demonstrated the process with a problem on the chalkboard.

At this point the students began to ask questions. When the bell rang, they became very frustrated. Several students announced that they would not be able to do

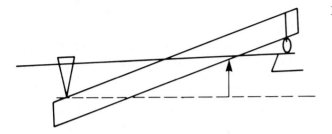

FIGURE 8–6. Levers

the homework because they did not understand how to do the problems. These were students who had not taken algebra and who did not have the necessary prerequisite skills.

The next day the teacher asked students to explain what they had learned about levers. It became clear that these students had not understood much of the information that had been presented. A good deal of abstract information had been presented without any assessment of student understanding. When asked, the students could not give a single example of how they might ever use a lever. They had not translated the stylized illustrations into meaningful examples of real machines.

The teacher retaught the lesson over a period of several days. Students were actively involved in explaining their interpretations of what the teacher presented. They made a list of levers they had seen in actual use and grouped them appropriately under each type. The breakthrough came when one of the less able students suggested that a wheelbarrow was a form of lever and defended his position by referring to his own class notes.

Finding 3: The lecture format gives teachers the opportunity to share their knowledge and relate the content to their students' lives by using analogies, examples, and related stories.

A lecture is often considered an appropriate instructional strategy for students with average or high ability levels. Lectures also can be effective with low-ability and learning disabled students. As with other students, these students need teachers who present clear, relevant information. Effective lecturers know their content, know how to adjust their lectures to meet the ability and interest levels of their students, and are able to relate the content to their students' lives. They understand that their students are diverse, and so they use appropriate examples and analogies to illustrate key points. Lectures can improve comprehension as well as provide students with essential knowledge.

Scenario.   An interesting lecture was conducted in a high school class where students were considered to have behavior disorder problems. The teacher believed that most of these students' problems were the result of negative personal experiences and chaotic lives. Nine students were assigned to the teacher's class which was designed to help them develop functional living skills.

The teacher began his lecture by referring to a chart on the board with the title "Getting Out of the House." Listed down one side were the headings "Employment," "Housing," "Food," "Transportation," and "Insurance." At the top two vertical columns were titled "Now" and "On My Own." Some sections of the grid had amounts of money entered. When class began, the teacher introduced three types of insurance. He put a graphic organizer on the board, using insurance as the major topic with medical, automobile, and life insurance subsumed underneath. He explained that they would only discuss automobile insurance during this class. He asked why having automobile insurance was important to members of the class. The answers were revealing because students mentioned their plans to get out on their own. These students were developing personal plans that would prepare them to live independently away from home. Information given during the lecture was related to the kinds of arrangements and amount of income necessary for students to live away from their parents.

As each type of insurance coverage was discussed, the teacher added words to the organizer. When the word *collision* was introduced, one young man wanted to know why the teacher used such a big word when he could have said *wreck*. He moved out of his desk, complaining about teachers who made it so hard to understand them. The teacher did not respond to this young man's challenge. Instead he calmly wrote *(wreck)* underneath *collision* and told the student that an insurance agent might not know what he meant by "wreck" insurance. The student was invited to tell what the insurance company had done when he had been involved in a collision. The young man told about the amount of money the company had paid to cover the wreck. As he finished the example, he returned to his seat.

Throughout the class period new ideas were presented, terms were explained, and costs were recorded on the chart. There was a deviation from focus when a young woman insisted that the teacher was incorrect. She said you couldn't have a collision with a deer in the winter because they would be hibernating. At least four students began to talk at once, arguing about which animals hibernate. When the teacher had restored order, he continued his lecture. Accurate information was given, many examples were used, and the students' desire to live away from home was used to maintain interest and organize information. The lecture had been productive even though the class presented the teacher with a number of challenges.

Finding 4: Teachers using the lecture format can improve students' attitudes toward learning by modeling their enthusiasm for the subject.

Enthusiasm fosters achievement. Teachers who lecture have many opportunities to enhance their presentation skills so that their lectures will be exciting. Enthusiasm can be communicated nonverbally with gestures, body language, and appropriate animation. Teachers can verbally demonstrate their enthusiasm by making positive statements about the material to be learned and the excitement they feel about presenting the information.

Scenario.   A science department head was concerned about one of the instructors in his department. The young woman came to the school with an excellent academic background. She was very well organized and had good working relationships with members of her department. In spite of this, her students, especially those in afternoon classes, were inattentive during her presentations. There was a sense of sameness about the lectures that made it hard for students to stay on task. Even students who said that they liked her as a person were making requests to transfer out of her classes.

When the teacher sat down to discuss the problem with the department head, he was able to provide her with some constructive feedback. He talked about changing her voice level, deliberately using some gestures, and letting students know how deeply she cared about science. The young teacher explained that she was not a demonstrative person by nature. Furthermore, she had been advised that a cool detached presentation would make her seem more professional.

Since both she and the department head knew that she could not change overnight, they started by planning some deliberate statements she might insert into her next lecture to communicate her excitement about the subject. She began to keep a list of adjectives that would add variety to her descriptions. Oddly enough, she found that deliberately using these words caused her to give them more emphasis as she lectured. Her classes began to take on a new excitement, and students responded by being more enthusiastic about the class.

The teacher modeled a new laboratory coat she had just been issued. She explained that it brought back many happy memories about the time she had spent in science labs. Later, during a demonstration, she stopped and said, "Hold on to your seats because this is going to amaze you!" Students grasped their seats as if they were about to be shaken out of them. She completed the demonstration with everyone clearly enthusiastic about the class.

Certainly, teaching styles should be consistent with teachers' personalities. Adjustments can be made, however, without compromising one's teaching philosophy. This teacher was able to improve her presentation skills and still stay within her own comfort zone. Little by little she had begun to relax, communicate her enthusiasm, and demonstrate that she had a sense of humor. The changes she made in her behavior were an important influence on improving her students' attitudes toward learning.

Finding 5: When specific structuring behaviors are used to develop lectures and presentations, student learning is enhanced.

It is important for teachers to structure their lectures and presentations so that students will clearly understand the learning expectations. When lessons are properly structured, objectives have been made explicit and students know what they are expected to learn. After new ideas and concepts have been introduced, they should be reviewed and summarized. Main points should be emphasized, and students should understand how the information has been organized. Students should have more than one opportunity to approach new ideas and concepts. Teachers should not move ahead until they are confident that students understand the material being presented.

Scenario.   During a preobservation conference, an English teacher told her principal that, during the class he would be observing, her students would be learning how she teaches the short story. When pressed for more specificity about learning expectations, she seemed puzzled and repeated that she wanted her students to know how she teaches the short story.

When the class began, the teacher reminded her students about the short story they had read the night before. She then gave a definition of the short story as a literary form. Following this she analyzed the story they had read in terms of setting, point of view, plot structure, and the use of a minor character as a foil. She spent 10 minutes talking about the theme of the story. After this she mentioned that she always taught the short story by examining important literary elements. She then passed out a worksheet. To complete the work the students had to define 15 literary terms. When they began to work, many hands went up. The questions asked by the students demonstrated that they did not understand what she wanted.

During the postobservation conference, the principal again asked the teacher what she had expected the students to learn. The teacher repeated that she wanted them to know how she teaches the short story. He reviewed the notes he had taken during class, pointing out the topics covered and the amount of time allotted to each topic. They looked at the worksheet to see what information was needed to complete it successfully. The principal commented that most of the time had been spent on defining literary elements and relating them to the short story students had read. This information helped the teacher realize what had happened. She could now express that she had actually wanted the students to recognize literary elements in *that* short story. She also realized that it would have helped if the students had clearly understood her expectations.

The principal and the teacher discussed additional actions the teacher could take to increase student understanding. To begin with, targeted questions could be used to find out what students already knew. In addition, structuring behaviors such as stressing main points and summarizing could be employed. As a result of the analysis, the teacher was able to improve her instruction by planning future lessons to accomplish specific learning objectives. She also decided that the deliberate use of structuring behaviors would play an important role in achieving the objectives.

Finding 6: Clarity of instruction depends on a number of teacher-controlled factors.

Effective teachers differ from less effective teachers in their ability to communicate information clearly, concisely, and accurately. Because it is critical that instruction be easily understood and remembered, adequate detail must be provided. Teachers must also convey the information fluently with carefully chosen terminology, vocabulary, and examples. Clarity is also increased when teachers employ specific strategies to assess student understanding and their ability to process new information. During clear presentations deviations from the main focus are avoided as well as the use of vague terms or extraneous content. Teachers who provide clear instruction help to improve student understanding and acquisition of new information.

Scenario.   A third grade teacher was conducting a session on writing paragraphs. This was the first time he had taught this unit. His previous experience had been at the sixth grade level, and adjusting his instruction to the third grade was a real challenge. He asked for some assistance from the language arts supervisor who agreed to observe his class and work with him. As class began, the teacher wrote the word *paragraph* on the board. The following dialogue took place.

Teacher. All right class, you all know what this word means and how important it is to write well-structured paragraphs. I've been very pleased with your sentences. Now this is the next step. Get out a pencil and paper and take a look at the paragraph that I have written on the board. There is something wrong with this paragraph and we are going to rewrite it. First, it should be in accepted paragraph form. That means that the first sentence should be indented. Also the sentences should be about the same topic. Make sure that there are no sentence fragments and that punctuation marks and capital letters are correct. I want Sally to read the paragraph out loud. Sally!

Sally. I watched the birds at the feeding station yesterday. There were three kinds of birds. When we lived in . . . in . . .

Teacher. Pennsylvania, it is a state in the East. Look right here on our political map of the United States. Notice where it is in relation to New York and the Atlantic Ocean. Close your eyes and visualize Pennsylvania. Now open your eyes and find it on the map again. Very good! Continue.

Sally. . . . Pennsylvania there were no foxes in the region. I saw three kinds of birds at the feeder. I saw cardinals, bluejays, and a mockingbird. I like raccoons better than foxes.

Teacher. That must be some feeder! Normally those three birds would not be at the feeder at the same time. The mockingbird doesn't even eat the same things. Mark, what is wrong with that paragraph?

Mark. Those birds would not all eat at the same feeder because they don't eat the same thing.

Teacher. Well, that's true, but what is wrong with the paragraph in terms of what we know about ideal paragraphs?

Mark. Nothing that I can see. It is indented, and I don't see any words that need capitals.

Teacher. No, let's go back. Read the paragraph silently. All of the sentences should be about the same topic. Good paragraphs begin with a topic sentence and have several supporting sentences and a concluding sentence. Now, who can tell me what is wrong with this paragraph?

Justin. Mr. Johnson, what do you mean, *tropic*? Like the Tropic of Cancer?

This question puzzled the teacher until he remembered that he had talked about the Tropic of Cancer the preceding day. He had no idea why the student was confused about the two concepts. He did report that this was not the first time he had experienced this kind of confusion. It took some time before he learned to use words and concepts his students could understand and to control his tendency to add extraneous information at inappropriate times. Throughout the year he reported how surprised he was by the amount of direct instruction that was necessary when introducing a new skill. To his credit, he became excited about teaching third grade and asked to stay at that grade level for another year. He was able to make the adjustments necessary to communicate clearly and effectively at the appropriate level with his students.

Finding 7: An effective explanation is a highly interactive process of assessing current student thinking and helping students acquire conceptually accurate information.

Interactive explanations help students understand new content and prevent student misconceptions. Explanations can lead to higher levels of understanding when students are actively engaged in the process. When they are, students gain ownership of the information. When explanations are properly used, students must integrate new knowledge with prior understandings and incorporate the restructured information into their personal knowledge bases. Explanations should help students acquire useful information that is personally relevant. Effective teachers are skillful and responsive in regularly assessing and shaping student understanding as they engage in explanations.

Scenario.   A fifth grade mathematics teacher was introducing a unit on multiplying mixed fractions. This had always been a difficult concept for his students, so he planned the experience carefully with a peer teacher. They made sure that their students had all of the prerequisite skills they needed. The teachers both felt that the instruction would be more effective if the pupils had mastered the times tables, so they set aside the time for students to review the times tables. Together, they discussed every aspect of the explanation of multiplying mixed fractions. Several types of manipulatives were considered. The steps of the explanation were mapped out. They planned both concrete and numerical representations for each key step of the computation. Together, they chose the mathematical problems to use. They made a list of difficulties their students had encountered in years past and planned ways to avoid similar problems. They calculated the time needed for each step of the process. The teachers knew it was important to complete the explanation in one class period.

The detailed planning paid off. Students were able to follow each step of the mathematical process. They felt less frustration, and they were able to successfully represent each step of the process numerically. When mistakes were made, students could generally explain their thinking and correct their own errors. One young man needed more help than the others. When his computation resulted in an improper fraction, he simply inverted the numerals. Since this is a common problem that had been anticipated, the teacher was able to get him to recognize what he was doing. He said, "I guess I'll have to add another step to the process—check to see if you inverted the fraction."

As class ended, one of the students asked an interesting question. She said, "That was fun, but when would we ever use it?" Both teachers realized that they had skipped an important part of the explanation. They had not planned to tell students why it is important to learn to multiply mixed fractions in real life. The following day the review began with a clear statement of the kinds of situations that require multiplication of mixed fractions. Nevertheless, the teachers felt good about the results of their collaboration and decided to work together on other presentations and explanations during the year.

 **GUIDE TO OBSERVATION, ANALYSIS,
AND REFLECTION**

Because some form of direct instruction is so often used by teachers, there are many opportunities to observe lectures and presentations. Identify teachers who are skilled in direct instructional modes and make arrangements to observe them in action. Share your observation information with them as you analyze what took place. As you reflect on your observation and analysis activities, try to determine what insights you have gained about using direct instruction.

1. Presentation or lecture

Observation: *What behaviors contribute to effective use of the presentation or lecture format?*   Make arrangements to observe a presentation or lecture class. Plan time for a preobservation conference with the teacher before the class. The following questions will help guide your discussion:

- What do you expect the students to learn from the information you will be giving today? What concepts do you plan to address?
- What sources did you use in preparing for today's class? How much of the information presented today will be new for the students?
- Why did you choose the lecture as an instructional format? How did student characteristics influence your decision?
- How does the information you will provide relate to the textbook?
- What other activities, if any, do you plan to include during today's class (e.g., reading from textbook, comprehension checks)?

Keep an anecdotal log of the lecture or presentation. Describe teacher behaviors briefly without making any value judgments. Be sure to report the main idea behind statements or organizers included in the overview or introduction. During the development part of the lecture describe the major ideas or concepts that are introduced. Note the use of examples, analogies, similes, or stories to elaborate a point.

Record the time when the teacher changes to a new topic or makes a transition. If possible, keep a record of student questions and comments during the presentation of new content. Describe the conclusion of the presentation. Note key points made in summaries, postorganizers, or assessment questions. Report any reteaching activity or additional examples.

Analysis: Was the organization of the lecture effective in helping students learn and recall the content?   Review the information from the presentation or lecture class you observed. Make a list of the topics, concepts, or ideas covered during the lesson. See if you can arrange these to show the organization of the lecture. Teachers may organize the information hierarchically, subsuming each new idea under a major concept, as in Figure 8–7. Or they may use a contrast-and-compare organization (Figure 8–8) or a cause-and-effect pattern (Figure 8–9). Other organizing principles include time order, problem-solution, and the argument pattern that presents both sides of an issue. How did the teacher make the organization or structure of the information known to the students? What structuring behaviors were used to make the organization clear? How could the structuring have been done more effectively?

Refer to your notes again. This time look at the amount of time spent on each part of the lesson. Compare the amount of time spent on each topic or objective. Talk with the teacher to see if the time allotment was deliberately planned. Try to determine if there are ways to improve the way time was used.

How effective were the examples the teachers used? Were there enough examples? How did they relate to the students' lives? Brainstorm to generate additional examples that might have been used. Did student comments provide any indication of the degree of comprehension? In what way? Work with the teacher to replan or fine tune the lecture notes for future presentations.

Reflection: How effective are your lectures or presentations?   Assess your own ability to communicate information effectively. Do you consider all factors before you choose to present explicit information to a large group? Evaluate your presentation

FIGURE 8–7. Hierarchical lecture organization

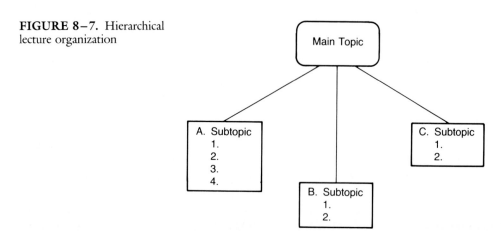

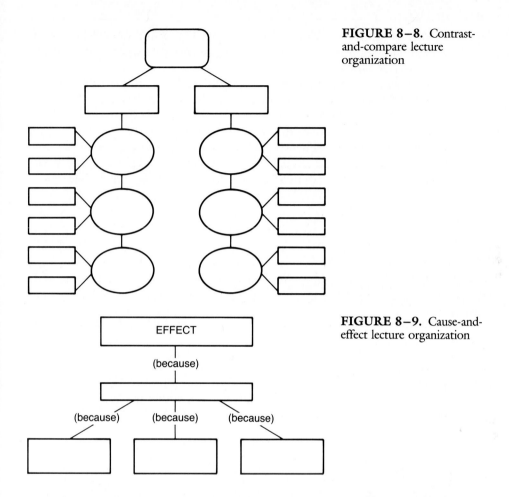

FIGURE 8–8. Contrast-and-compare lecture organization

FIGURE 8–9. Cause-and-effect lecture organization

skills. What elements of enthusiasm are a part of your teaching style? How often do you plan an introduction, development of new information, and a conclusion? What structuring behaviors do you use? Do you take the time to help your students recognize and use structuring to improve their learning? What kind of feedback have students given about the clarity of your instruction? Develop a systematic plan for improving the way you present explicit information in groups.

2. Explanations

Observation: *What elements must be present for explanations to be effective?* Talk with several teachers about lessons that involve explanations of processes or concepts in order to schedule an observation. Try to observe a class when a new concept or process is to be introduced.

Have a conference prior to the observation to find out how the teacher thinks about explanations. Questions might include the following:

- What is your role during an explanation? What is the students' role?
- Please talk about any problems you have encountered when explaining this concept or process in the past.
- What kind of knowledge base will your students bring to the explanation? Will you use any of the time to assess the adequacy of student knowledge?
- What role will textbooks or other instructional materials play?
- Please describe the sequence of instruction during this lesson.
- How long will it take to complete the explanation? How long will it take before your students can comprehend and apply what will be introduced today?

Focus your observation on the elements of the teacher's explanation. Since it is important to know how responsive teachers are to student thinking, you will need to describe the interactions. Try to keep a record of the main points teachers stress during the explanation. Note any instructional components, such as number lines or laboratory equipment, that are used. Describe examples, analogies, and stories used to illustrate a concept. Be especially careful to include statements that require explanation, restatement, or reasoning processes by students. Other important aspects of teacher behavior you may want to record are

- Stating learning objectives
- Telling students why the concept or process is important
- Assessing to make sure prerequisite knowledge and subskills are available
- Dividing the process into smaller segments or steps
- Deviating from the focus or topic
- Explaining when to use the process and when not to
- Modeling the thinking process required
- Providing teacher-directed practice

Students may be actively involved in the explanation process as well. Note any student questions, explanations, descriptions of their thinking processes, or contributions that indicate confusion.

Analysis: *How did specific characteristics of this lesson compare to the elements of effective explanations?* Review your notes on the explanation you observed. Your goal is to contrast and compare that explanation with the characteristics of effective explanations. The following chart (see Figure 8–10) can be used to organize your information.

Reflection: *How can student learning be improved through effective explanations?* If you are teaching now, think about your own explanations and monitor your behavior as you explain concepts or processes in your classroom. If you are in a

Basis of Comparison	Effective Explanations	This Explanation	Conclusion as to Similarity or Difference
Interactive			
Responsive to student thinking			
Assesses student understanding			
Explicit, useful information			
Teaches or models thinking strategy			
Challenges misconceptions			
Helps restructure knowledge base			

FIGURE 8–10. Comparison of explanations

preservice program, talk to other teachers about their explanations or reflect on the explanations you hear in your college classes. The following questions may help guide your thinking:

- How student centered are your explanations?
- Do you take time to assess student understanding?
- Are you aware of common misconceptions students have developed about the content?
- Do you address students' experientially based concepts directly?
- When students do not understand, do you give additional examples, re-explain, or clarify?
- Are you satisfied with the depth and currency of your content knowledge?
- What renewal activities might be appropriate for you?
- Are you aware of any problems related to the textbook (skimpy coverage, too many concepts, poor organization)?
- How do you plan to compensate for any problems that have been identified?
- Do you make sure that your students know how to apply their knowledge to their lives?

DEVELOPMENT AND RENEWAL ACTIVITIES

1. Choose a topic for a lecture or presentation. If you are currently teaching, choose a topic you will be able to use soon. If you are a preservice teacher, choose a subject you would like to teach. Refer to the organizational formats under activity 3 in "Observation, Analysis, and Reflection." Choose the form of organization that is most appropriate for your material. Organize your lecture by filling in the organizer of your choice with the main points you plan to make. Use the organizer to develop your lecture notes. Take time to be sure your information is current. Plan examples to use. If you are currently teaching, use your plan in class, evaluate, and note problem areas. Be sure to file your plan so you can refer to it as needed.

2. If you are presently taking a college course, you will likely have many opportunities to observe a lecture or presentation. If you are currently teaching, you may be a participant at a workshop or inservice session where a presentation is the instructional mode. Follow the suggested steps in activity 1 under "Guide to Observation, Analysis, and Reflection" in examining the organization of the information. Make an assessment as to how well the information was organized. In your opinion, what could have been done to improve the organization of the information?

3. During your next opportunity to observe a presentation at school, in class, or on television attend to the elements of the presentation that contribute to or detract from its clarity and effectiveness. Decide whether the following statements describe the presenter:

- The presenter demonstrates enthusiasm for and interest in the subject, through energy level, vocal delivery, use of gestures and movement, and facial expression.
- The presenter communicates the importance of the topic and its relevance to the members of the audience. The presenter should make it clear why attention should be paid to the information.
- The presentation uses structuring behaviors to help organize and guide listening; emphasis is given to important points, transitions are signaled, and summaries occur at appropriate points.
- The content is clearly presented; ambiguous terms and unfamiliar terms are avoided, content is well organized and focused, examples are incorporated, and complete sentences and proper grammar are used.

In critiquing the presentations of others, you'll find that the elements of effective presentations become clear. What elements will you incorporate in your presentations and what elements will you avoid?

9.
Conducting Recitations and Providing Feedback

COMMENTARY

Our classroom observations support the research finding that the recitation format is one of the most common task structures used during direct instruction. This is not surprising. When we visit with beginning teachers and talk about teaching strategies, they often tell us that they use instructional formats that they have encountered most often during their college careers. Lectures and presentations are the most common instructional modes used for large undergraduate classes, while recitations are prevalent in many of the smaller upper-division and graduate classes. Because these instructional formats are so similar, students are usually unable to define clearly what type of direct instruction is being used and if the approach used is the most appropriate for achieving learning expectations.

In addition to the conditioning teachers have experienced in their college classes, there are other reasons why the recitation format is so popular. It is one of the easiest instructional processes to manage. Students can be monitored and controlled by teachers during recitations. Also, the level of recitations can be planned to meet the learning needs of the majority of students. Teachers can make additional adjustments during recitations to enhance student learning.

Many students like to be involved in recitations. Students tend to enjoy the interaction they have with the teacher and their peers during recitation activities.

Those who do not want to participate can usually find ways to be left out of the interactions. When recitations are going well, there is a strong possibility that a number of students will receive positive feedback about their participation.

Recitations can be planned to fit rigid school schedules and organizational expectations. They can be adjusted to accommodate interruptions and student movement in and out of class. It does not take a great deal of time and effort to orient students to the roles they are expected to play during recitations.

Students receive feedback in many forms and from multiple sources. They know they will get some kind of feedback in nearly all of their school experiences. When students start going to school, they get feedback about learning expectations and their social behavior. As they continue, the sources of feedback tend to increase, depending on organizational structure and academic expectations. By the time they get to middle school or junior high, students receive feedback from several different teachers, counselors, administrators, and in many cases from extracurricular coaches and advisors.

In general, students become very accepting of the feedback they receive in school. We have found it interesting to observe extracurricular activities where feedback may seem to be very intense and often quite negative. Yet students use this feedback to improve their performance. Sometimes students are willing to accept feedback in voluntary school activities but reject the same type of feedback in a classroom.

Because feedback is such an important aspect of the recitation format, teachers should use feedback wisely and in a manner that will help to achieve performance expectations. Giving feedback should be a conscious process that is a part of a planned instructional sequence. Teachers and students should know why feedback is being given and how it supports the learning process.

RATIONALE

Because so much time is spent using the recitation format, teachers should be well versed in all aspects of the process. They should know when and under what conditions recitations will be most effective. Because a great deal of time during recitations is given to soliciting student responses, teachers should be prepared to manage the responses effectively. Teacher reactions to responses will have a powerful influence on future student responses and participation.

Although recitations are a predominant mode of instruction for many teachers, it is difficult, if not impossible, to achieve certain objectives using the recitation format. When recitations are improperly used, creativity can be stifled and there is very little chance that higher level learning can be successful. Also, recitations do not offer very many opportunities for students to engage in cooperative learning activities. It is imperative that the instructional format selected is congruent with the learning expectations.

Feedback and correctives are essential components of the learning process. Recitations provide teachers with numerous opportunities to give students corrective

VICS
or
self evaluation

and helpful feedback. When mistakes are made during recitations, students can be given immediate feedback. When students are on target, they can be given feedback to reinforce what they have learned. If students appear to be confused during a recitation, teachers can make the decision to stop and reteach to clear up any misconceptions.

When feedback is given on a regular basis, it has a powerful influence on the learning process. Teachers who use multiple forms and sources of feedback are in a position to help students make significant learning gains. Feedback given at the right time and in the proper manner helps motivate students and has a positive effect on student attitudes toward learning.

Beginning teachers may not have had the opportunity to analyze the recitation format and the feedback process. Experienced teachers tend to select the formats that have been effective for them and their students. Nearly all teachers can profit by comparing their modes of instruction to the related research. Although recitations and feedback may seem to be inseparable, there is ample research that suggests the two concepts should be examined and analyzed independently. For that reason, recitation and feedback are treated as separate entities in the remainder of this chapter.

RESEARCH SYNTHESIS

The Concept of Recitation

Dillon (1983) defined recitation as "all those episodes when teachers ask a series of questions, one after another, and students give answers in turn. Often the question-answer exchanges are short and the pace is quick, but the exchanges may also be longer and leisurely" (p. 10).

Teachers can control the opportunity to talk, alternating speaking turns with students. This interaction has been called turn taking or an initiative, response, and feedback cycle (Lehr, 1984). Teachers speak, students answer, then teachers react to students' replies. The recitation turn-taking pattern is unique to life in a classroom.

Recitation is a structured discussion that Corno (1981) described as a variation of the Socratic method. Most recitations include the whole class in a public, single-task performance. Students must recognize and comply with the social demands (when to speak) and the academic demands (getting the correct answer) that are inherent in this phase of instruction (Weade & Evertson, 1988).

Teachers usually ask "known information" questions during recitations; that is, the teacher asks questions to find out if the student knows the answer, not to get information (Dillon, 1988). In normal conversation questions are not asked unless the questioner has a need to know the information.

Recitation is the predominant mode of instruction in the primary grades and is frequently used in intermediate and secondary grades. Gage and Berliner (1984) reported that recitation accounts for about one third of the instructional time in mathematics and social studies classes. Its use is almost universal, not only in the United States but throughout the world (Gage, 1976).

Characteristics of Recitation

The recitation process involves four of the "basic verbal actions" identified by Bellack, Kliebard, Hyman, and Smith (1966). Teachers repeatedly structure, solicit, respond, and react. Researchers have noted that the pattern of interaction holds true at all grade levels. At times the teacher may ask students to read aloud or give answers to homework, but the communication pattern is the same.

Most recitations begin with teacher talk followed by student response. This process or cycle is represented in Figure 9–1. The initial phase of teacher talk may include telling students what the topic will be, how much time will be used, and whether they will need their books or other materials. Learning objectives to be accomplished may be presented at this time. Doenau (1987b) referred to this phase as the process of structuring. Silvernail (1986) pointed out that "structuring activities are the presentation of instructional frameworks and/or teacher comments which are designed to assist the learner in identifying and focusing his/her attention on the content to be learned" (p. 23).

Soliciting responses is similar to questioning except that the query does not always have to be a complete sentence. Like structuring, soliciting is an initiating move that is meant to start the question-answer cycle. Teachers may solicit student responses without speaking. They may nod or use some other nonverbal signal to have students respond. Soliciting encourages students to pay attention so that they will be able to make proper responses. The expectation is communicated that students will become actively involved in classroom interactions (Doenau, 1987a).

When teachers solicit answers, students are expected to respond. Power (1987) used the term *responding* to refer to any move students make as they try to fulfill the expectations implicit in a question or command. This is a basic move in the classroom communication process. Over 90% of the statements students make in classrooms are responding moves (Power, 1987). Dillon (1988) compared the recitation to a quiz show. There are many questions, the teacher has all of the answers, and students are expected to get the answers right.

When students fail to respond, teachers continue the interaction until an answer is produced. In this process Mehan (1979) noted, "If the reply does not

FIGURE 9–1. Recitation cycle

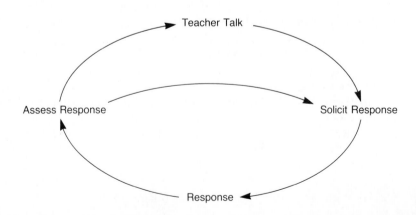

immediately appear, the teacher 'works' (e.g., prompts, repeats, or simplifies) until that reply is obtained—then the teacher evaluates the reply" (p. 287). Two factors affect student replies. First, answers are given in a public situation which creates some stress. Other students and the teacher attend to and evaluate the correctness of the responses. Another problem is knowing that teachers are often searching for one predetermined right answer known only to them and to the best students. Mehan (1979) contended that this causes students to provide trial responses that are attempts to find out which answer the teacher is seeking. These may be partial answers or tentative replies. When this happens, teachers rephrase the question, give more information, or remind the student of something they learned previously. The result is not a correct answer from students but an answer created by teachers and students out of a number of tentative tries. Again, this communication pattern is unique to recitation. Mehan (1979) noted that "students learn that interaction in school has unique features and must be kept separate from the demands of everyday discourse" (p. 291).

What teachers do after a student answers is referred to as *reacting*. Teachers can recognize, evaluate, or praise student responses. Zahorik (1987) described several types of reacting behaviors:

> Reacting behaviors can consist of direct rating, repeating the response, correcting the response, developing the response, repeating the solicitation, and ignoring the response by moving the lesson on to new areas through structuring or soliciting. In addition, reacting acts can occur in pairs or triplets such as "Good, radiation poisoning" (rating and response repetition) or "Accidents in nuclear plants are very rare. What do you think is a disadvantage, Vicky?" (correcting and repeating the solicitation). (p. 417)

How a teacher reacts to answers provides students with feedback about the correctness of their response. Dillon (1988) noted that students seldom disagree with the teacher's evaluation or ask for justification during recitation. In fact, students negotiate during the evaluation to find out what answer the teacher wants to hear and use this information to construct mutually acceptable answers. As a result, teachers often receive the answer the student thinks the teacher wants rather than a meaningful reaction to the content. Mehan (1979) concluded, "The evaluation act plays a significant role in classroom discourse. While it seldom appears in everyday discourse, it is an essential component of instructional interaction" (p. 290).

Advantages of Recitation

The success and persistence of recitation as an instructional strategy is probably due to the fact that the method has some distinct advantages for both teachers and students. Recitation fits the rigid organization of the school. It can be tailored to accommodate any amount of time and any number of students (Gage & Berliner, 1984). Teachers have limited amounts of allocated time to accomplish their learning objectives. Furthermore, this time is often interrupted by recess, lunch, and pull-out classes in the elementary grades. Secondary classes are most often scheduled for a specific time. Teachers can expand or restrict the number of recitation cycles to fit the time allocated for their classes.

Because recitation is a flexible strategy, it is appropriate for many educational objectives and for students of different types (Gage, 1976). Teachers can use recitations to perform several functions. Gage and Berliner (1984) have identified the most common of these as review, introduction of new material, checking answers, practice, and checking understanding of materials and ideas.

There are several obvious advantages for using an established process like recitation. First, everyone knows the procedure, so no time has to be used to teach new rules and routines. Teachers and students are comfortable with a format that allows teachers to concentrate on questions and student responses. It is easier to make sure that all students get a chance to participate. Because recitation is a whole-class activity, interruptions can be managed more easily so that less allocated learning time is lost. Morine-Dershimer and Beyerbach (1987) pointed out the importance of "establishing routines for dealing with inattention, interruptions, turn taking, and transitions between lessons, so that maximum time is devoted to instruction and lessons flow smoothly" (p. 229). Unfamiliar routines require more attention just to make sure that students can meet new expectations.

Second, recitations are reinforcing for teachers. They have an opportunity to interact with the students as they check student understanding and provide feedback. Gage (1976) stated that recitation "emphasizes things that only human teachers can do well, such as engage in a dialogue with students" (p. 35). Teachers feel that they are actively helping students learn. Promoting student achievement and developing positive relationships with students are two incentives that are most rewarding to teachers (Bellon, Bellon, Blank, Brian, & Kershaw, 1989).

Recitation can also promote better student attention and less student anxiety. Again, the whole-class format helps teachers keep students on task more of the time. When students are relaxed and actively engaged, the result is learning that is superior to that during seatwork (Gage & Berliner, 1984). The questions teachers ask serve as cues for students. Teachers signal important information by repeating a question several times or asking for the same information in different ways. When teachers praise or clarify an answer, they emphasize information that is important to remember. Students also get an opportunity to practice and hear other students answer (Morine-Dershimer & Beyerbach, 1987).

Factual questions can be used during recitation to give students the practice necessary to consolidate information in long-term memory. When factual questions are planned at the right difficulty level, more students can participate. Hawley and Rosenholtz (1984) stressed that opportunity for students to participate is a strength of interactive instruction. High achievers tend to participate more frequently than lower achievers. There are at least two reasons for this. Students who know the answers raise their hands more often, causing teachers to notice them. In addition, teachers tend to call on students who they think will have the correct answers. Other pupils pay attention to the answers of high achievers more often and learn from the participation of those who can be expected to know the answers (Morine-Dershimer & Beyerbach, 1987).

Anticipating participation may increase learning. Stahl and Clark (1987) found that students who were told that they would not be called on scored significantly lower on tests over the content. Those students who were told that they would be expected to participate learned more from the structured discussion even when they did not participate. Apparently, students who think they may be called on pay closer attention. Also, the covert mental activity that takes place as participants compose an answer for use may also contribute to learning.

Disadvantages of Recitation

Although recitation is an effective instructional process for some objectives, several disadvantages of this approach have been identified. Beginning teachers may depend too much on structured whole-class formats such as recitations, at least until the routines of teaching become more automatic. As teachers mature and become more secure with traditional task structures, they are in a better position to use other instructional models. Overuse of recitations can have a debilitating effect on the professional development of teachers.

Joyce and Showers (1986) suggested that teachers have become so dependent on recitations that they have difficulty learning to use other instructional models. They are so used to thinking of learning as the process of acquiring one bit of knowledge at a time through repetition that they have difficulty learning to use other instructional models. For example, prepackaged instructional materials may fit nicely with a recitation; the teacher can glance at a section and proceed with little planning. Knowledge is organized into small bits, questions are often provided in the teacher's manual, and there are frequent reviews. This results in a slow instructional pace and limited content coverage. With such materials teachers do not have to make many professional decisions before or during instruction. They simply alternate giving directions, asking for information, and providing praise and feedback (Joyce & Showers, 1986). When teachers become too routinized, they are not likely to expand their repertoire of instructional methods (Morine-Dershimer & Beyerbach, 1987).

Bossert (1977) studied teacher behaviors in several task structures. He found that teachers tended to become more authoritarian during recitations. The same teachers using a multitask structure became more democratic and flexible about controlling student behavior. The whole-class format appears to call for more authoritarian control and offers less opportunity to interact with individual students. Teachers using the recitation process may appear to be less concerned and less empathetic.

A typical turn-taking recitation restricts student talk. The students concentrate on getting the one right answer the teacher wants rather than trying to understand the purpose or importance of the lesson (Lehr, 1984). The pace of instruction and the necessity to keep all students involved contributes to a high incidence of short factual answers from students. Dillon (1983) noted:

> A question-asking style of recitation will reveal only a limited part of the students' understanding. If one of the broad goals of recitation is to provide the teacher with an assessment of the students' knowledge of the subject matter so that the next

learning activity may be planned, then a question-asking style of recitation may actually frustrate a primary goal of recitation itself. (p. 12)

When students are limited to short right answers, their thinking is also restricted. Creative answers are discouraged. Pupils whose responses are different from the expected answer are seldom given an opportunity to explain their thinking. When facts are stressed in isolation from thinking skills, students are given knowledge rather than encouraged to think about it. As Paul (1985a) stated, "Right-answer inculcation is not a preliminary step to critical thought" (p. 37). He cited twin obstacles to the development of rational learning with this approach: "(1) being told, and coming to expect to be told what to believe, and (2) being told, and coming to expect to be told, precisely what to do" (p. 39).

Good, Slavings, and Mason (1988) found that "many teachers call on low achievers less often, wait less time for them to respond, give them answers rather than try to help them improve their responses when they answer incorrectly, are less likely to praise their successes, and are more likely to criticize their failures" (p. 364). When low-ability students do answer, they are often wrong. Making mistakes in public is embarrassing, so these students may stop volunteering and responding when called on. The result is that many of these students become passive.

There are ways to improve recitations so that more students will participate and have more opportunity to use their communication and thinking skills. Morine-Dershimer and Beyerbach (1987) have suggested the following:

1. Asking questions or presenting tasks that require different levels of thinking;
2. Asking "real" questions as well as "known information" questions;
3. Recycling questions, in order to get several different correct responses to the same question;
4. Increasing wait time after asking a question so that more students can think of better responses;
5. Varying turn-taking procedures to include "joint" or "choral" responses;
6. Providing opportunities for pupil-to-pupil interaction in peer-directed study groups or peer-teaching situations; and
7. Encouraging students to discuss their thinking, by providing their interpretation of the question being asked or by describing the cognitive strategies they use in solving problems. (p. 229)

Recitations will continue to be a predominant mode of instruction for many teachers. Whenever this instructional format is used, teachers should consider both the advantages and disadvantages. In a sense the advantages are almost diametrically opposed to the disadvantages. This results in a bipolar relationship, as depicted in Figure 9–2. Most often, however, the selection of the recitation format is not so clear-cut. In some situations teachers will have to decide if the advantages outweigh the disadvantages and if there are ways that they can use recitation but minimize the disadvantages.

Advantages	Disadvantages
Fits school organization	Overused
Maximum use of learning time	Imposes instructional rigidity
Effective in controlling student behavior	Encourages authoritarian teacher behavior
Increases student participation	Increases passive behavior of low achievers
Easy to check understanding	Discourages creativity and divergent thinking

FIGURE 9–2. Recitation as a bipolar process

The Concept of Feedback

Providing feedback is a major teacher behavior. About one third of classroom interactions are teacher reacting behaviors, which usually include some element of feedback (Zahorik, 1987). Recitations play a predominant role in the delivery of feedback (Melnick & Raudenbush, 1986). Evaluative information is almost inherent in the sequence of teacher questions, student responses, and teacher reactions to student responses. Gagne (1985) suggested that student questions, comments, and responses that occur during public recitations give teachers the opportunity to provide informative feedback. Although feedback may be given as a part of other instructional formats, or in written form, Zahorik (1987) concluded that feedback seems to be most effective as a part of direct instruction.

Feedback is the process of giving information to students about the correctness of their responses. It may also include information about the quality of performance. Although feedback can be reinforcing, the informational function is the most important factor. Feedback provides a timely and accurate assessment of learning or progress (MacKenzie, 1983). The research on instruction has emphasized the importance of academic feedback.

Feedback is not the same as praise. While feedback is related to academic performance, teacher praise conveys information about a student's status in the teacher's eyes (Hawley & Rosenholtz, 1984). Feedback is usually based on academic achievement, while praise may be determined more by a student's personal qualities or the teacher's perception of a student's need for praise.

Advantages of Feedback

Extensive research has confirmed the positive effects of providing students with knowledge about the correctness of their responses and academic progress. Feedback is a type of substantive interaction that is especially powerful since it often occurs at a teachable moment. Academic feedback is more strongly and consistently related to achievement than any other teaching behavior (Fisher, Berliner, Filby, Marliave, Cahen & Dishaw, 1984). This relationship is consistent regardless of grade, socioeconomic status, race, or school setting (Hawley & Rosenholtz, 1984). Feedback is consistently related to achievement with basic skills instruction in the elementary school and with systematic instruction at the high school level (Zahorik, 1987). When feedback and corrective procedures are used, most students can attain the same level of achievement as the top 20% of students (Levin & Long, 1981). Brophy and Evertson (1974) found that corrective feedback was especially important for low-SES students and concluded that these students are more dependent on the teacher as a source of feedback than students in higher SES schools.

Feedback is positively related to student engagement rate (Fisher et al., 1984). Students who are given accurate information about the correctness and quality of their work spend more time working on academic assignments. There are two possible reasons for this. First, students who are not given feedback may believe that the teacher is not checking their work. They may not feel that they will be held accountable. Second, students who do have a source of information about their work may feel more confident about their ability to correct errors and to master the content. Contemplation of successful completion of the work may influence students to spend more time working on academic tasks. The relationship between feedback and student engagement may be consistent with Levin and Long's (1981) findings that students who received systematic feedback and correctives felt more confident and had more interest in the subject.

Self-concept of primary grade students appears to be affected by teacher feedback on school performance. Kindergarten and first grade students are most impressed by feedback about their effort and ability to follow directions, while second and third graders are more influenced by feedback about performance on specific academic tasks (Wittrock, 1986). They base their view of themselves as learners on the feedback they receive.

Credible positive feedback, given when students are doing well, can serve as a reinforcer. Most students are encouraged by information that confirms their achievement or progress. This can motivate them for future learning (Zahorik, 1987). Feedback is especially important for low achievers. These students need information about how they are doing and how much progress they are making. Good and Brophy (1974) found that, unfortunately, teachers sometimes fail to give appropriate feedback to low achievers.

The Three-Step Feedback Process

Providing effective feedback is a complex process that involves a standard of performance, information about progress (what has been learned and what is yet to be learned), and a system of corrective procedures to clear up any misunderstanding (Levin & Long, 1981). When these three elements are integrated into a total system, as presented in Figure 9–3, feedback has its most powerful effect.

Standard of Performance. Effective teachers have a predetermined standard of performance that helps them decide if their instruction has been successful. They can describe the level of performance students must achieve in order to succeed. Their description may include specific criteria, steps, or strategies. They may also provide a statement about the success rate or required degree of mastery. The standard

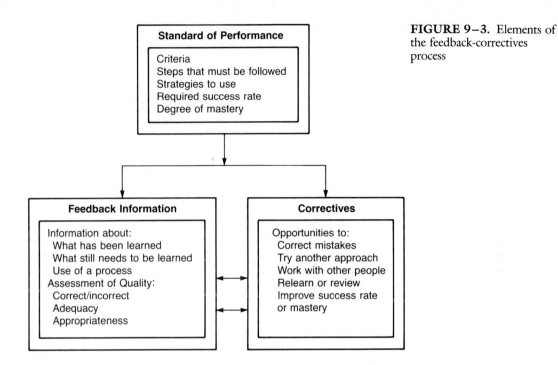

FIGURE 9–3. Elements of the feedback-correctives process

should be well defined because it is the basis for determining if a student is ready to move on. However, Levin and Long (1981) found that most of the feedback currently given is related to items on a test, not to a predetermined standard of performance.

Teachers may choose to have a single standard for all students or a varied standard that can accommodate a wide range of ability levels within the class. Teachers may choose to make the standard progressively more difficult over time. For instance, typing teachers raise their standard as students improve their skills. Standards should be practical. Setting unrealistic standards can decrease student motivation to learn. Levin and Long (1981) suggested that realistic standards can be set by determining the level of performance necessary on the current unit or task in order to be successful on subsequent units or tasks. Realistic standards should be high enough to provide a challenge for the students. Standards that are too low may communicate low expectations.

Information About Progress.   Students need to know how they are progressing. This does not mean that they need to know about the correctness of every specific item on a worksheet or test. That kind of information is too specific to be helpful. Rather, they need general feedback about what they have learned and what they still need to learn. Relating this information to a standard of performance increases the power of the feedback. Information about progress is encouraging and helps students concentrate their efforts on those areas not yet mastered. Materials and instruction can be adjusted accordingly (Levin & Long, 1981).

Teachers may believe that they need to reinforce every correct answer. Crooks (1988) reported that providing feedback on correct responses has little effect. Sparks and Sparks (1984) urged that

> praise be used in moderation. Most students need not be praised every time they give a correct answer. They do, however, need to receive feedback about the correctness of their response. Low achieving students need more support, encouragement, attention to evidence of genuine progress, and expressions of appreciations. (p. 73)

When an answer is incorrect, feedback that identifies the error in knowledge and understanding is very important. This is especially true when students make the initial response confidently and firmly. The element of surprise may cause students to pay more attention to the information (Crooks, 1988). Bloom (1981) contended that failure to receive accurate feedback about incorrect responses leads to later learning errors. Final achievement may be affected when errors are not corrected as they are made. Zahorik (1987) concluded that teacher feedback can "communicate the extent to which [students'] responses or other acts are correct, adequate, or appropriate and thereby help them to adjust and gain a measure of control over their future behavior" (p. 417).

There is one exception to the finding that feedback after incorrect responses improves student learning. When the material is too difficult and the error rates are high, students do not profit from feedback. Crooks (1988) found that students who were faced with material that was too difficult tended to try to learn all of the specific information included in the feedback. For example, they may try to learn each addition fact they missed, instead of learning how to regroup in the tens column. When error rates are high, learning tasks may seem impossible to some students.

Feedback involves more than identification and correction of errors. The most effective teachers give process feedback more frequently than less effective teachers (Zahorik, 1987). Effective teachers not only identify the incorrect portion of an answer, they help students learn a process for avoiding such errors in the future. Process feedback is especially important in performance areas. Teachers may tell students how many words they typed per minute, but they also give them information about behaviors that might be slowing them down. For example, woodshop teachers may point out the jagged edges on a finished product and describe the technique that caused the problem. LeClerc et al. (1986) studied feedback in mathematics classes and found that just saying the answer was wrong was negatively associated with achievement. Helping students understand the process so that they could answer correctly was found to be positively associated with achievement. Land and Evans (1987) studied student responses to feedback on their compositions. Students were most positive about explanations of errors, written examples of correct usage, individual conferences with the teacher, and the opportunity to rewrite. They were least positive about corrections that merely identified the type of error.

Teachers who give process feedback help students apply the learning process to similar situations (Collins, Carnine & Gersten, 1978). When students answer higher level questions confidently but incorrectly, teachers need to give detailed feedback that helps to identify the source of their errors. Students who answer questions incorrectly with low confidence may need to be given help developing or solidifying their basic concept knowledge. Teachers may need to help students learn a productive process for successfully accomplishing learning expectations. Explicit feedback on using a process or learning strategy is especially valuable with young children (Crooks, 1988).

Correctives.   Additional opportunities to correct mistakes or to improve performance are called correctives. When correctives provide a chance to relearn or improve to a preset standard, student learning improves significantly (Levin & Long, 1981). Correctives are an important element of the feedback loop, as Bloom (1981) noted: "The key to the success of mastery learning strategies . . . largely lies in the extent to which students can be motivated and helped to correct their learning difficulties at the appropriate points in the learning process" (p. 214).

Students who do not master content when it is first taught need more time to study the information to be learned. Students who do not learn from the first instructional strategy need an opportunity to try another approach. Teachers often choose correctives that involve a different learning style. They know that some of their pupils learn best when information is presented orally, while others may profit most from visual information.

Effective correctives give students an opportunity to relearn and teachers an opportunity to reteach the content. Roehler and Duffy (1981) found that teachers provide only minimal substantive assistance. Negative feedback about student performance must also include ways that students can improve. Correctives are designed to provide students with the help needed to improve their performance.

Correctives can be given in many forms. Independent students may be given the opportunity to review information on their own, while others might need to work with alternative approaches or peer assistance. For example, primary pupils who have difficulty learning sight words from flash cards often profit from repeated reading of stories that include those same words. As they read aloud to partners, working for fluency, they begin to develop instant recognition of high-frequency words (Beck, 1989).

Homework assignments based on learning objectives that students have not mastered can be used as correctives. In order to function as effective correctives, homework assignments must be corrected and students must be given feedback (NREL, 1984). Butler (1987a) stressed the use of elaborated feedback for homework. He found that homework was more effective as a corrective when teachers took the time to lead students through the process again to ensure understanding. Emphasizing improvements and successes was also found to be helpful.

Levin and Long (1981) found that small study groups of two or three were effective in grades three and above. Bloom (1981) suggested the development of a student partner system to do the correctives work. He also recommended the use of teacher aides, programmed instruction, and audio tapes or cassettes. Bloom has found that students need additional time, help, and motivation if correctives are to be effective. Working with alternative materials, peers, or aides may provide all three of the conditions necessary for effective feedback.

Types of Feedback

The type and amount of academic feedback varies with changes in instructional activities and in different lesson segments (Silvernail, 1986). Teachers may give basic or elaborated feedback to their students. Cotton (1988a) defined basic feedback as "telling students if their response is correct and, if incorrect, supplying the correct answer" (p. 3). This kind of interchange is often accomplished quickly during a recitation or as part of teacher-directed practice. Errors are corrected without interrupting the flow of the lesson.

Elaborated corrective feedback is usually longer and more detailed. Students who have answered incorrectly are given a series of rules or prompts designed to help them correct their mistakes. Cotton (1988a) commented that "both basic and elaborated feedback produce greater achievement gains than no feedback, and elaborated corrective feedback produces greater gains than basic feedback" (p. 3).

Mild positive feedback can promote student progress as long as it is directly related to an academic topic, is genuine, specific, sincere, and is initiated by the teacher (Silvernail, 1986). This kind of feedback appears to help by affirming correct responses or performances. Bender and Hom (1988) found that students may concentrate on correcting their errors. When this happens, they fail to confirm correct responses. As a result they often forget their correct answers. Posttests may show errors on items the students answered correctly on the pretest. When teachers reinforce correct responses, they help to confirm what students have learned.

Silvernail (1986) reported that positive comments given to secondary students are more effective when they are given in conjunction with a letter grade. Levin and Long (1981) found that if positive comments given with a letter grade are to be effective they must communicate what has been learned and what is still to be learned.

Another type of elaborated feedback is given in classes where students are working independently to complete a process, create a product, carry out experiments, or solve problems. Teachers observe students and give feedback about the way equipment was set up and used, the sequence of activities, number of tries, successes and failures, and the amount of time it took to carry out a performance (Stiggins, 1984).

Elaborated feedback is different from process feedback. Process feedback is given when teachers help students by providing a process for getting correct answers. For example, a teacher could direct students to the index in the textbook, then help them locate the pages where the information is discussed. Modeling the way they would find the answer by identifying key words and skimming may be helpful. Teachers who use process feedback go beyond the content of students' answers. They provide direct instruction that helps students develop a procedure for future learning.

Task engagement feedback gives students information about the acceptability of their behavior in the classroom (Zahorik, 1987). When task engagement feedback is given as a reminder to change behavior, or as a reprimand, the feedback correlates negatively with student achievement. Fisher et al. (1984) reported that there is no support for using frequent reprimands, scolding, or criticism. Instead, inappropriate behavior usually indicates a need for a change in the structure of the classroom. The assignments may be too difficult, the pace of instruction may be causing frustration, or there may be a need to review class rules and procedures. Spending class time giving corrective feedback about task engagement may ignore the underlying cause of misbehavior.

Forms and Sources of Feedback

Information about student performance can be given verbally or nonverbally. Both forms can be effective if used as an integral part of an overall instructional plan. Oral feedback is usually given in a public situation. Other students listen to and may learn from a teacher's reaction to an answer. Melnick and Raudenbush (1986) suggested that oral feedback either sustains students' right to speak or terminates the exchange. Teachers use probing behaviors to sustain students' responses when they repeat a question, rephrase it, or give clues. Giving specific positive feedback, asking the same student another question, or using student responses to make a new point are also forms of sustaining feedback since they encourage and reinforce continued participation. Using student ideas can serve as a sustaining behavior (Silvernail, 1986). When teachers acknowledge, modify, apply, compare, or summarize student ideas, students learn more. Students view incorporation of their ideas into the learning activities as a form of positive feedback.

Verbal feedback can also terminate or discourage participation. This occurs when teachers answer questions themselves, ask other students to answer, or give no feedback at all. There is some overlap between sustaining and terminating behaviors. Teachers can use specific negative feedback to sustain or terminate participation. Summarizing information previously taught can also be used to encourage further participation, or to signal that the topic has been adequately covered.

Many researchers have studied verbal feedback given by teachers as if this were the only form of feedback. Research based on classroom observations, however, indicates that much of the feedback is given in a nonverbal form. Teachers use their faces and bodies to give feedback. They nod, smile, gesture, and move about the room. Nonverbal feedback is subtle, yet most students accurately interpret such behaviors. When teachers want students to continue, they may use a hand motion that indicates, "Go on, give me more." At other times they move closer to students, maintaining eye contact. When students are on the wrong track teachers often shake their heads. This gesture is seldom misinterpreted. Students immediately review or check their work to correct an error. Melnick and Raudenbush (1986) also found that giving no feedback was a terminating behavior and classified it as nonverbal behavior.

Quizzes or short formative tests are a form of written feedback. Bloom (1981) has made use of such tests a critical part of mastery learning. Tests are used to determine what each student has learned in a particular unit and what still needs to be learned. Test scores alone do not provide high-quality feedback because the information is too general. Homework and workbooks can provide the same kind of information when they are tied to specific learning objectives and used to pinpoint learning needs.

Written comments on papers can give students excellent information about their work. Writing specific comments on papers, providing examples of ways to correct errors, explaining mistakes, or briefly identifying missing information or steps in a process can be very helpful. Although writing comments is time-consuming, the process provides the kind of specific information students need to improve. Some teachers have used video and audio tapes to provide feedback on performance. Students can get a more realistic view of their successes and problems when they review their performance with teachers who can help them analyze their work.

Teachers are the major source of information for students. Other sources include aides, peers, other students, and instructional materials. Who or what gives feedback is an instructional decision that depends on context. Teachers consider the nature of the tasks, student characteristics, and effective use of their time. Some instructional tasks are pivotal to student success. When this is the case, teachers usually feel that they need to be personally involved in providing the feedback. When the task involves drill and practice for mastery, teachers may delegate the process of providing feedback to others. Students who do not have a solid knowledge background may need to get feedback from their teachers. A final consideration is the limited amount of time teachers have to give one-on-one corrective feedback.

Aides or volunteers are often available in classrooms and can give feedback to students (Fisher et al., 1984). Teachers may choose to use aides to correct and discuss seatwork with students. Aides can also monitor individual practice, providing help as needed. This may be especially important with students in the primary grades. Other students can also give feedback. Teachers may designate one student as a resource person for another student. Both cooperative learning and process writing programs depend on peer feedback.

Students can be trained to evaluate their own work. Teachers can provide a set of criteria that can be used to judge a product or performance. Students are then given the opportunity to reflect and judge their own work. Some teachers have students keep journals to record success and progress as a form of positive feedback. These teachers are careful to define success in a variety of ways so that success is within the reach of all students (Kearns, 1988). Encouraging students to monitor and evaluate their own progress on a difficult problem or assignment is another method for developing self-regulated learners.

Instructional materials may be used to provide feedback. Programmed texts are designed so that students get immediate information about the correctness of their answers. Answer keys are provided so that students can check their responses after completing a task. Many learning centers are planned so that a self-check answer key is available. Computer programs can also provide feedback. Most of the effective programs are highly interactive, requiring students to make critical responses in almost every frame. Students are notified of errors and use the feedback provided to correct their mistakes. Drill and practice programs set time limits to beat and repeat problems that are especially difficult for students. Simulation programs imitate a real process. The computer program sets up a situation and requires students to initiate the action. Immediate feedback is provided for every move so that students immediately know the consequences of their actions (Vargas, 1986). Other programs allow students to access a memory bank and use the information stored there to write or improve a composition (Dede, 1983). All of these computer programs provide immediate feedback.

Feedback is a critical instructional process. Teachers need to be aware of the forms and sources of feedback that figure in various instructional interactions. It is important that potential sources of feedback not be overlooked. The graphic organizer in Figure 9–4 summarizes the most common types and sources of feedback.

Characteristics of Effective Feedback

The most effective teachers are clear and specific when giving feedback (Gagne, 1985). They may give feedback to one particular student or to a small group working on a common product. Most studies support the position that feedback should be evaluated in terms of the information it conveys. Students must know why they are being praised or criticized and, if criticized, how their behavior should change (Levin & Long, 1981). Sparks and Sparks (1984) noted, "A general response such as 'Good job' is not as powerful as the descriptive statement 'That answer is perfect; you listed all the steps that must be used in this problem' " (p. 73). Descriptive feedback provides objective information about behaviors or answers. Judgmental responses should be avoided. The feedback should be genuine, and should only be given if it is deserved. It is probably best for teachers to concentrate on information related to behaviors instead of what they think students intended to do.

When teachers give specific feedback they should make every attempt to be positive:

> There are several ways in which the effectiveness of feedback could be enhanced. First, feedback is most effective if it focuses students' attention on their progress in mastering educational tasks. Such emphasis on personal progress enhances self-efficacy, encourages effort attributions, and reduces attention to social comparison. (Crooks, 1988, p. 468)

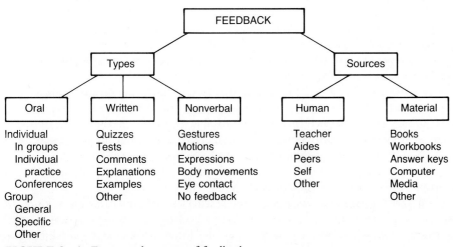

FEEDBACK

Types	Sources

Oral	Written	Nonverbal	Human	Material
Individual	Quizzes	Gestures	Teacher	Books
In groups	Tests	Motions	Aides	Workbooks
Individual	Comments	Expressions	Peers	Answer keys
practice	Explanations	Body movements	Self	Computer
Conferences	Examples	Eye contact	Other	Media
Group	Other	No feedback		Other
General				
Specific				
Other				

FIGURE 9–4. Forms and sources of feedback

Giving specific feedback should be related to student needs:

> Simple knowledge of results should be provided consistently (directly or implicitly), with more detailed feedback only where necessary to help the student work through misconceptions or other weaknesses in performance. Praise should be used sparingly and where used should be task specific, whereas criticism (other than simply identifying deficiencies) is usually counterproductive. (Crooks, 1988, p. 469)

Concerning the timing of feedback, immediate feedback has a modest advantage over delayed feedback (Kulik & Kulik, 1988). Crooks (1988) reviewed the studies on timing and concluded, "The precise timing of feedback does not appear to be too critical, unless it is delayed so long that students have little motivation to pay close attention and learn from it" (p. 457). In other words, feedback must be given while the information is still clearly relevant to the students and while there is an opportunity to correct deficiencies.

Feedback should be given early enough that it keeps students from practicing mistakes. Levin and Long (1981) found that feedback given at regular intervals reduced the number of errors and the frustration rate. Roehler and Duffy (1986) stressed the importance of immediate, spontaneous reactive-corrective behaviors whenever a comprehension error occurs during reading groups.

Effective timing depends on the learning task, characteristics of the instructional materials, and student progress in the curriculum. Feedback on student composition should be given while the work is still in progress. Cotton (1988a) found that most feedback in traditional composition was given in the form of written comments on the final product. Students tended to ignore or disregard these corrections because the work had already been graded and there was no opportunity to improve.

Feedback can be given too soon. Programmed learning materials provide instant feedback on each specific student behavior. Students are deprived of the opportunity to read carefully, find their own errors, and correct them (Crooks, 1988). Teachers may give feedback too soon during problem solving or scientific experiments. Students sometimes need to identify their own ineffective strategies. One of the best ways to counteract faulty scientific concepts is to encourage student involvement in testing their preconceptions. When they are able to see that their preconceptions cannot be supported, students are more amenable to accepting scientifically correct explanations (Clark, 1988).

Porter and Brophy (1988) found that "effective teachers continuously monitor their students' understanding of presentations and responses to assignments. They routinely provide timely and detailed feedback, but not necessarily in the same way for all students" (p. 82). Some teachers change the way they give feedback when they work with students of different age levels. Subject area specialists often work with several grade levels during the day and must vary the feedback so that it is appropriate for students' developmental levels.

Gagne (1985) has suggested that teachers should give different kinds of feedback for different kinds of knowledge. When students are trying to acquire factual knowledge, feedback should stress the way the information can be organized or elaborated. If the learning objective requires students to recognize patterns or learn concepts, feedback should help them distinguish examples from nonexamples. If students are trying to learn an action sequence, the teacher should remind them of the steps in the procedure. When an error is made, process feedback might include identification of the step in the procedure that produced the wrong answer.

Teachers sometimes vary their feedback on the basis of other factors. The ability level of students and on-task or off-task behavior appear to influence teachers. Tisher (1987) identified a tendency for low achievers to receive more terminal feedback from teachers. That is, teachers tended to cut these students short more often than they did high achievers. However, Melnick and Raudenbush (1986) studied teachers who reported giving low achievers more sustaining feedback in an attempt to maximize their chance of achieving. The teachers in this study reported that they often gave high achievers negative feedback or no feedback at all. They believed that sustaining feedback was more appropriate for low-ability students. Feedback to low-achieving students may be less contingent on behavior and more dependent on teachers' concern for success.

Teachers have reported that their feedback is influenced by whether students are on task. On-task students are given more sustaining feedback, while off-task students receive more terminating behavior or no feedback at all. These teachers felt that it was appropriate to differentiate feedback to students on the basis of their effort to get involved in learning activities. One exception to this rule occurred with low-achieving students. Teachers gave them feedback even when they were not on task. This behavior may signal that it is not necessary to be engaged to get helpful feedback, and may reduce the possibility that low-ability students will attribute success to their own effort (Melnick & Raudenbush, 1986).

Some attention has been given to the role feedback should play in summative evaluation or grading. Bloom (1981) has taken the position that formative evaluation in mastery learning should not be used to grade or judge the student or teacher. Teachers have reported that the addition of computer programs to tutor students changed traditional evaluation policies. Point systems based on the number of errors are no longer applicable when students get immediate feedback on their mistakes and can correct them (Schofield & Verban, 1988). Crooks (1988) reported several studies that found

> where evaluations count significantly toward the student's final grade, the student tends to pay less attention to the feedback, and thus to learn less from it. This effect should be reduced if students are given multiple opportunities to test and prove their achievement, with only the final evaluation counting toward their grade, as is generally the case in mastery learning procedures. Of course, one argument for counting more evaluations in grading is to improve the reliability of the grading process, but this consideration will often be less important than the benefits of evaluation for learning. (p. 457)

Many teachers find that they must give a letter grade based on demonstration of knowledge so that it can be factored into graduation requirements or appear on transcripts for college applications. The power and potential of the feedback-correctives process may not be fully realized as long as grades play such an influential role in the evaluation of student performance.

PRIMARY REFERENCES

Dillon, J. T. (1988). Discussion versus recitation. *Tennessee Educational Leadership, 15*(1), 52–61.

> This article contrasts recitation and discussion as instructional formats. Predominant speaker, sequence of talk, pace, type of questions, answers, and evaluation are compared.

Good, T. L., & **Grouws, D. A.** (1979b). Teaching and mathematics learning. *Educational Leadership, 37*(1), 39–54.

> This article summarizes the Missouri Mathematics Effectiveness Study. Key instructional behaviors that can improve learning in mathematics are described.

Lehr, F. (1984). ERIC/RCS report: Student-teacher communication. *Language Arts, 61*, 200–203.

> This report summarizes the research on turn-taking cycles. Some attention is given to the effect on cognition. The use of wait time is examined.

Mehan, H. (1979). "What time is it, Denise?" Asking known information questions in classroom discourse. *Theory into Practice, 18*, 285–294.

> Asking questions when the answers are already known is explored. This article explains the way students search for the "correct" answer when teachers ask known information questions.

Morine-Dershimer, G., & **Beyerbach, B.** (1987). Moving right along. . . . In V. Richardson-Koehler (Ed.), *Educator's Handbook: A research perspective* (pp. 207–232). New York: Longman.

> Classroom participation patterns are examined with an emphasis on students' perceptions of teachers' actions. This chapter details the question-answer sequence in the classroom and the way answers are constructed.

Power, C. N. (1987). Responding. In M. J. Dunkin (Ed.), *The international encyclopedia of teaching and teacher education* (pp. 413–416). New York: Pergamon.

> Research on responding as a basic function of verbal interaction is reviewed. The focus of this review is on covert and overt processes that occur as students respond to questions.

Zahorik, J. A. (1987). Reacting. In M. J. Dunkin (Ed.), *The international encyclopedia of teaching and teacher education* (pp. 416–423). New York: Pergamon.

> A review of research on teacher reactions that modify or rate student answers is included. The structuring-soliciting-responding-reacting cycle is explained.

RESEARCH IN PRACTICE

Finding 1: Recitation, a process of structuring classroom communication, is the predominant mode of instruction for most teachers.

Recitation is the instructional format in most classes in the majority of the nation's schools. For a variety of reasons, recitations are often stimulating and are responsible for getting students involved in the learning process. The most effective teachers are energetic and animated as they distribute questions, solicit responses, and evaluate student answers. Their students are attentive and involved. Effective recitations do not just happen, they are the result of careful planning, management of response opportunities, and sensitivity to student needs. The most important factor seems to be the caring demonstrated by teachers for their students.

Scenario.   A third grade teacher started her mathematics class by checking homework. Students were seated in heterogeneous teams of five. She then had a student helper in each team distribute small plastic bags containing replicas of coins and bills. There was an excited buzz as the money was arranged in piles on the tops of the desks. The teacher began by telling the class that she had gone to the grocery store to buy a candy bar. She showed them the candy, telling them the cost and the amount of money given to the clerk. Students immediately started rearranging their coins on the desk tops. When most of the students were finished the teacher said, "Now, let's see who gets to tell me how much change I should get back." She walked through the rows of desks looking at the coin arrangements before choosing a student. A series of questions and answers followed. Each time the teacher asked for the correct change, the names of the coins used, and the reason for choosing those coins.

The teacher then presented a story problem featuring a student in the class and a bicycle she wanted to buy. A price was given and change was manipulated at each desk. One of the answers given was incorrect, so the teacher asked the girl if she had been given the right change. The student who had given the wrong answer was asked to think again and correct the answer. All of the students had an opportunity to respond during this part of the class.

The activity changed when the teacher placed a transparency on the overhead projector. This time the problem was presented in numerals and answers were computed by adding or subtracting on scratch paper. Again, every student worked the problem and questions were addressed to various individuals. When the answer was correct, another student in the same cluster of desks was asked to tell which coins should be given as change. Two points were given if both answers were correct. When an answer was incorrect, team members helped to explain the error and one point was recorded. Each team was given an equal number of turns, and the total number of points for the teams was computed.

The teacher ended the recitation by summarizing the kinds of errors they had made and giving them a homework assignment. They were asked to talk with their parents about purchases they had made recently and the amount of change they had gotten back. Students were asked to convert the results into a story problem for their class to answer.

After class the teacher talked about how she used the "every student responds" technique during recitations to increase the opportunity to practice. She deliberately used examples about herself or her students to make mathematics more interesting and realistic. The teacher spoke about using manipulatives followed by numerical representation and then application to real life as an instructional sequence she tries to follow during most mathematics recitations. By carefully monitoring the success rate during each portion of the lesson she has been able to teach the class as one unit. The teacher said that this instructional plan, along with the group competition, helps vary the recitation and motivates her students.

Finding 2: During recitations, teachers and students are jointly engaged in developing predetermined answers to specific questions.

Teachers use the recitation format both for drill and practice as well as to check student understanding. The intent of recitations is to elicit specific answers which ought to be known by the students. When a student answers correctly, the teacher rates or evaluates the answer before moving on to the next question. Incorrect or partially correct answers present a different problem. Teachers may attempt to help students improve answers or ask other students to respond. Classroom interactions during recitations evolve and are highly dynamic and somewhat unpredictable. When recitations are done well, they are joint efforts to assess and build knowledge and can be highly effective in facilitating student learning.

Scenario.   A high school history teacher was teaching a unit on the French Revolution. Students had read the chapter in their book and listened to a lecture. Now the teacher planned to conduct a recitation. He wanted his students to compare the French Revolution to the American Revolution. He started the recitation with a question for Frank:

Teacher. Frank, which revolution came first? Was it the American Revolution or the one in France?

Frank. Actually it was the one here because I remember July 4, 1776.

Teacher. That's right, so what happened here may have had an influence on what happened in France. Alex, what did the two revolutions have in common?

Alex. They were both started by revolutionaries. Is that what you mean?

Teacher. No, I'm looking for more than that. Think about the basic causes behind what happened. What caused the people to revolt?

Frank. Well, yesterday you said there were economic problems, but that probably isn't what you are looking for.

Teacher. It is part of it, but there were other political and ideological factors. What were the American people fighting for?

Frank. Freedom, they were fighting for the right to make their own rules. That was true in France, too. They thought that they ought to make their own rules?

Teacher. Yes, each side was fighting for the right to rule themselves. Were there any differences?

Frank. The French were already ruled by Frenchmen.

Teacher. So, is that important? Does it make a difference whether you are being ruled by your own people or someone else?

Frank. It does, and it doesn't. In America, they were being governed by the British who didn't understand their problems. You said yesterday that the French peasants were being ruled by royalty. They didn't understand what it was like to be poor either. So they have that in common, but the French were revolting against their own countrymen.

Teacher. Good answer, Frank. That is the kind of thinking I want. You identified something the two revolutions had in common and then told me one way that they were different. The main point here is that the French citizens were the first to insist that people had a right to choose those who are going to govern them. They rejected their own royal class. That is important!

During this interchange Frank, with some help from Alex, played the question-answer game very well. He gave safe answers until he figured out which facts the teacher wanted. Then, by using information from the lecture he responded with the answer the teacher was seeking and was praised for its quality. In reality the teacher never got an accurate assessment of Frank's knowledge.

Finding 3: Because the recitation process is flexible and can be managed within most school structures, there is a tendency to overuse the process and limit the options for student learning.

Recitations can accommodate many common instructional purposes such as reviewing, new learning, and assessing student progress. Recitations are also adaptable to available time frames and for use with larger numbers of students. Because recitations adapt so well and because students and teachers are comfortable during these inter-actions, there is a tendency to overuse this task structure. Several negative outcomes can result from such overdependence. Teachers may become reluctant to learn and use other equally productive instructional strategies. But perhaps a more serious disadvantage is that students' thinking and creativity may be limited because of the responses required during recitations. Effective teachers plan instruction that ensures more variety in task structures and more diversity in teacher and student behaviors.

Scenario.   Recently a school superintendent asked each of his high school principals to spend one day following the class schedule of any student. They were told to keep notes and be prepared to discuss their reactions at the next administrative meeting. The reaction was exactly what the superintendent had thought it might be. Each principal had attended six 50-minute classes. Almost all of these classes were some variation of recitations. The principals reported that it was hard to remain attentive and their minds wandered. In some classes they got involved and wanted to follow up on some student answers, but there was no opportunity to do this. One administrator had been called on, given a wrong answer, and had been corrected in public. All of them spoke about the lack of variety and active student involvement. In many of the classes small-group discussions or group investigation would have been more appropriate instructional modes. One principal had been in a health class where drugs and alcohol were being discussed. The students were reluctant to share personal experiences in the large group so the teacher stopped the discussion and gave the students a writing assignment planned for the following day.

The principals concluded that recitations and discussions were being used when other instructional modes might be more appropriate. They also agreed that staff development sessions focusing on alternative modes of instruction might help teachers expand their teaching repertoires. The major goal would be for teachers to use instructional strategies that would facilitate student learning.

Finding 4: Academic feedback has a powerful influence on student achievement, engagement, and self-concept.

Giving feedback to students about their progress is a critical teaching behavior. Providing appropriate academic feedback has consistently been found to improve student achievement. In addition, feedback can significantly affect students' willingness to remain engaged in academic tasks and their confidence and interest in completing assignments. Teachers' behavior demonstrates that they are aware of the importance of academic feedback because they spend valuable time grading papers, conferencing with students, and reteaching. They do this because they understand the relationships among feedback, task engagement, and student self-concept.

Scenario. A middle school principal conducted a brainstorming session with his mathematics department to generate ideas about ways to help their students. Over and over again, the teachers mentioned helping students see that they were making progress. Another common theme was to identify the skills students needed to help them learn. When the group clustered the ideas and organized them into categories, they were surprised at the number of ideas that could be clustered under "providing better feedback." They decided that providing students with quality feedback should become a departmental priority.

One of the teachers made a list of the students in her class and did an informal assessment of their attitudes about themselves as mathematics students. After she targeted several students who seemed negative about their mathematics ability, she began systematically giving them more helpful feedback. During the explanation portion of each class she made sure that her target students participated. She asked them to talk about the reasoning behind their answers and was patient in explaining when their answers showed that they did not understand. She had developed a habit of monitoring student practice in a predetermined, row-by-row pattern. She changed this so that she moved to the target students first, making sure that they got started doing the examples correctly. Homework and tests were graded and given back with written comments. The teacher deliberately identified the parts of the problem that were done correctly as well as the errors that had been made. She altered her grading procedure so that students who had worked most of a problem right got credit for that part. Students were encouraged to ask questions. The teacher treated mistakes as opportunities, explaining that errors were the only way the class could find out what they still needed to learn.

The class was organized into small groups for problem solving. These groups were sometimes asked to write real-life problems that could be solved using a particular mathematics process. At other times the groups were asked to solve difficult problems in several different ways. Feedback was related to logical and creative thinking. The target students proved to be valuable members of the problem-solving groups. Although they had trouble with formal mathematics, they had developed creative ways of dealing with numbers in practical situations. Over a period of weeks, some of the target students began to change their attitudes. One young man said, "Hey, I'm beginning to like this stuff!" By the end of the year most of the grades had gone up and the teacher reported that it took less time to introduce new material. She was spending less time reteaching and more of the students were actively engaged in learning.

Finding 5: The most helpful feedback is based on a standard of performance, information about progress, and correctives that provide additional learning opportunities.

Providing academic feedback involves three specific steps. First, information is provided about what is expected. Setting realistic standards appropriate to ability level is important. Second, information is given about how the student is progressing. The feedback goes beyond identifying errors or inadequacies. It extends to providing information as to how errors occurred so that students understand a process for avoiding further mistakes. The third ingredient in the feedback-corrective process is giving additional assistance and opportunities to improve performance and overcome difficulties.

Scenario.   A high school science teacher taught at a school where the practice of writing across the curriculum was firmly in place. One of his course requirements was for students to write a research paper. With some help from the English department head, the teacher developed a detailed plan for the research requirement. Students were expected to begin by writing a research proposal. When the proposals were submitted, the teacher held conferences with each student. At this time he helped them evaluate their plans. Feedback was timely and appropriate correctives were provided.

The second step of the research project was to develop a working bibliography and a set of reading cards. Again, students were given feedback and assistance with the development of their projects. The teacher had developed a modified research manual to guide students in preparing standard bibliographical entries. The librarian helped identify additional sources and materials to give the students more support for their assignment.

Next, outlines were developed and evaluated. This was an important step for the students, who used feedback on their outlines to improve the organization of their papers. When students had completed their first drafts, they met with the teacher to assess their progress and receive corrective feedback. After these conferences, students were able to do their final rewriting and complete their projects.

At each step of the project students had been given specific feedback. They received partial credit toward their final grade during each conference. They were able to see the progress they were making and what they needed to do to improve. The feedback process helped all of the students complete their projects successfully and assured them of satisfactory grades. Most important, they learned a process they could use to respond successfully to future writing assignments.

Finding 6: The type of feedback given to students should be clearly related to desired learning outcomes.

Feedback should be given as quickly and clearly as possible to help students achieve desired objectives. The feedback should be consistent with the learning expectations. This means that the amount and type of feedback will vary depending on the instructional process. When students are working independently to acquire basic information, feedback needs to be different from feedback given when students are engaged in higher level problem solving. When students are involved in problem solving, creative activities, or group processes, there is no one right answer or approach. Feedback given too soon or using inappropriate criteria might be counterproductive.

Scenario. A high school political science teacher was using a process-oriented curriculum. She had her class organized into small political action committees. The groups had each been given a description of a real political action committee (PAC) as well as a brief description of their committee's activities during the previous legislative session. The class had received a copy of four bills that were about to be voted on and had examined them from the point of view of the PAC their group was representing. Their assignment was to determine the position lobbyists for each PAC would take and how they would try to influence the legislation. The groups were to reach a decision and be able to defend their positions.

At the beginning of class the teacher provided a standard of performance by reminding the students about group process skills they had learned. As each piece of legislation was introduced, a spokesperson for each group gave a report. Other members spoke about the reasoning that had caused them to develop their positions. The teacher recorded the group's points on the chalkboard, encouraging more discussion. Feedback about the correctness of the response was not given. Instead, the teacher probed for the logic behind a position, asked other groups to comment, and pointed out inconsistencies. When the activity for the day was completed, she gave each group an evaluation of its use of group processes. The evaluations included information from observations she had made during the previous day. She assessed the degree and quality of participation, willingness to listen and consider all ideas, and how the groups reached consensus.

The type of feedback given supported the learning outcomes the teacher had established. She expected the groups to learn to work together in a productive manner. The students were to use higher level thinking skills to analyze the information and to reach a conclusion. Because the feedback was consistent with her learning objectives, student performance during this instructional unit met or exceeded her expectations.

Finding 7: The impact on learning is greater when multiple forms and sources of feedback are used.

Feedback can be provided in numerous ways. It is given verbally in brief or elaborated forms. It is also conveyed nonverbally through specific actions and cues. Feedback is commonly given through written assignments, tests, quizzes, and written comments. Although teachers are the major source, feedback can come from other adults or students, from self-assessment strategies, and from instructional materials or computers. Student learning and task engagement is increased when feedback occurs in several forms and from several sources. Many teachers consciously try to keep students from becoming overly dependent on them as the only source of feedback.

Scenario.   An elementary teacher was assigned a split-level class of fourth and fifth grade students. In general, the fourth graders were successful students who worked well independently, while the fifth grade students seemed to have problems with content mastery and on-task behavior. Mathematics posed the biggest problem for this teacher because the ability span was greatest in that area. Two of the fourth graders were working well above grade level, and all of the fifth graders needed some assistance to reach grade level. There did not appear to be a common pattern to their errors. Some students needed to review multiplication and division facts, while others had no real comprehension of place value. Three of the fifth grade students were quite accurate with computation, yet they could not translate that ability into solving simple problems.

The teacher decided to work with the fourth graders as a group when presenting new skills. The fifth grade class was organized into small, short-term groups to work on common skills. There were times when some of the fifth grade students could join the fourth grade direct instruction group in order to get a fresh introduction to a skill they had missed. The teacher asked the instructional aide to check and provide feedback on all of the basic computation tasks for both groups. They planned together so that the aide was clear about the type of feedback needed. Students were asked to keep a chart of their progress on each skill. The teacher checked all student work that required application of mathematical knowledge or problem solving. She also felt that she needed to be responsible for reteaching and giving correctives. Many of the fifth grade students were given hands-on experience with concrete materials to overcome misconceptions and build an accurate knowledge base. Enrichment activities were designed for self-assessment.

During the first few weeks of school, the teacher and her aide developed procedures that helped them work as a smoothly functioning team. Students received the type of feedback and help they needed and were able to point with pride to skills they had mastered as well as higher grades on tests. Gradually, the fifth grade pupils learned skills they had missed and were able to advance to grade-level material. At this point, the teacher was able to use direct instruction to introduce new processes. She could include the two fourth grade students who were working above level in some of these sessions. Because of the organization, the teacher was also able to give students working on enrichment activities more time and attention. All students received feedback in different forms and from a variety of sources.

Finding 8: The most effective feedback is clear and specific, provided at an appropriate time, and differentiated according to student needs.

Effective feedback has several important characteristics. The content and timing must be appropriate; that is, the feedback should be objective and provide enough detail. It should also be given at a time when students will not be reinforcing errors and when improvement is still possible. Students may ignore general feedback that is directed to a group because they do not think that it applies to them. Teachers who wait too long to give feedback get the same result. Students pay little attention to comments written on their papers if the grade has already been recorded. In addition, for feedback to have the most positive impact, it should be consistent with student needs and abilities and clearly related to the learning tasks.

Scenario.   An example of effective feedback was demonstrated by two physical education teachers who were responsible for a coeducational program. The class was observed when they were introducing the front-roll progression which was the first unit in their gymnastics program. The class had been preassessed during the first session and organized into groups based on their mastery of specific subskills. Class began with an overview of the front-roll progression. The teachers stressed the role each subskill played in performing a successful handspring. A filmstrip was used to demonstrate the proper execution of initial skills.

Students moved to their stations. Beginners reported to a station with a teacher and two student assistants. They began with a very simple front roll. The teacher provided feedback so that the students knew what they were doing correctly and what needed to be changed. Those who needed help moved to a second station where student assistants were supervising individual practice. The assistants helped each person get into the proper position and reminded them of key points. The assistants demonstrated the proper techniques and in some cases showed the film loops again. When they worked with the students, they described how they used mental images to guide their movement as they went through the exercises. Students who appeared to need additional help were referred to the teacher at the first mat for more instruction. The more advanced students worked at another station with the second teacher and two student assistants. They worked in pairs and critiqued each other when they were going through the more advanced stages of the progression. The teacher worked with one pair at a time and provided constructive feedback. The student assistants demonstrated specific techniques and helped spot those who were trying new techniques.

Feedback in this class was truly differentiated according to student needs. Feedback was also specific to the skills being developed and provided in a timely manner. Because there were multiple sources of feedback, students appeared to be motivated and totally engaged in the learning process.

GUIDE TO OBSERVATION, ANALYSIS, AND REFLECTION

The following activities focus on how teachers plan and manage recitations and how feedback is provided to students during the learning process. The activities emphasize how recitations and feedback are used most effectively to promote achievement and positive attitudes in students. Each activity involves observing and sharing the information with the teachers in order to analyze what took place. When reflecting on your observation and analysis activities, try to determine what insights you have gained about conducting recitations and providing feedback.

1. Effectiveness of recitations

Observation: *What factors make recitation an appropriate instructional format?* Make arrangements to observe a class when the teacher is planning to conduct a recitation. Plan time for a discussion prior to the observation. The following questions should help you structure the conference:

- What are the learning objectives for this lesson?
- What conditions or influences caused you to choose direct instruction as the instructional format for this lesson?
- What kind of information will students be learning or practicing, such as basic skills, new or difficult material, processes for later use, or higher level thinking skills?
- Will there be a number of activities during this class, such as review, homework, and practice? Please give your rationale for using the selected sequence of instruction.

While observing the recitation keep a verbal log. Be sure to record any introductory statements that focus student attention on what is to be learned and why it is important. When the question-and-response sequence begins, write down the teacher's questions. You may find that you have to record a skeleton form of the questions, omitting words like *the* and *for*. Your notes should convey the basic focus of each question. It will be very difficult to record student answers, but you can probably briefly indicate the correctness of the response. You might want to use the symbols below to chart student answers:

Right answers	+
Wrong answers	−
Partially correct answers	+/−
No response	R R (refuses response opportunity)

Analysis: *Was recitation the most effective instructional format for this lesson?* What is the relationship between learning objectives and the recitation format? This question does not have an easy answer, since many objectives are not accomplished in a single lesson. The learning process often occurs in a developmental sequence. On a given day teachers may plan to introduce a process. As time passes, they will progress to the point where students can use the process efficiently. Figure 9–5 depicts a developmental continuum for accomplishing learning objectives.

Review the objectives for the class to see where they fall along the continuum. Recitation can be an appropriate choice for achieving the first three types of objectives. Consider other conditions and influences related to the choice of an instructional format and the kind of information students were expected to learn. Compare these types of learning objectives to determine the congruence between the level of the objective and the use of recitation as a format. Write a brief statement explaining your decision.

Reflection: *What will influence your decision to use the recitation format in a specific class?* Reflect on your experience and the classes you have observed. List the conditions or influences that would cause you to plan a recitation. Consider student characteristics, learning objectives, the kind of information to be learned, and the sequence of instruction. Also develop a list of conditions or influences that would indicate that recitation is not a good choice.

At times it will seem that no single instructional format is ideal. When this happens, teachers have to make adjustments. Refer to the previously cited suggestions for improving recitations as you plan your next recitation. If you are a preservice

Recognizes	Identifies parts or steps	Practices with help	Knows or uses independently	Applies	Analyzes	Evaluates

FIGURE 9–5. Developmental learning continuum

teacher, develop a plan for a class you would like to teach. Include a list of questions, techniques for distributing and varying response opportunity, and opportunities for student-to-student interaction.

2. Structuring and conducting recitations

Observation: *How are recitations structured and conducted?*   Plan to observe several lessons when recitations are planned. Visit briefly with the teacher beforehand to ask about the learning objectives, student characteristics, anticipated difficulties or level of readiness, the estimated time for the lesson, and sequence of events.

As you observe, note the time the recitation begins and ends. Record what the teacher says to introduce the lesson. Describe the ways in which the teacher directs turn taking, any signals or cues used to move the lesson along, and how the teacher encourages active participation. Include a description of how the teacher deals with any interruptions, distractions, inattentiveness, or digressions as well as how the teacher brings the recitation to a close.

Analysis: *Were the recitations appropriately structured and conducted?*   Review your observation notes and identify patterns or routines that help structure the recitations and engage the learners. These would include ways the teacher introduces the recitation, any cues or signals used, techniques for dealing with unexpected events or inattentive students, and how the recitation is brought to a close. Identify those techniques you feel were productive and those that did not seem to produce the desired results.

Talk with the teacher about planning and conducting the recitation. Get the teacher to discuss the strong points of the lesson as well as to reflect on the ways the recitation could be adjusted. Ask the teacher whether the learning objectives could have been accomplished using some other instructional format.

Reflection: *How will I structure and conduct recitations?*   Based on your observation and analysis activities select techniques that you want to incorporate in your teaching when structuring and conducting recitations. Decide which routines and techniques would be appropriate for you given your level of experience and your students.

3. Teacher reactions during recitation

Observation: *How does the teacher react to student responses during recitations?* Record the teacher's reactions to student responses during a recitation session. Identify the reactions using a chart that classifies them according to the following categories:

Rating the response
Repeating the response

Correcting the response
Developing the response
Ignoring the response
Encouraging the student to expand the response
Encouraging the student to explain his/her response
Providing the opportunity for another student to respond
Providing the opportunity for student to student interaction
Encouraging all possible correct responses
Extending the wait time before reacting
Other

Use hash marks after each heading to tally reactions. Since teachers often pair two or more reactions, be sure to tally each reaction.

Analysis: During recitations, do teacher reactions to student responses promote learning expectations and actively engage the students?   Analyze your observation information by totaling the occurrences of each teacher reaction. Decide which reactions were productive in helping students attain learning objectives and in keeping interest and participation high. Determine if there are some possible reactions that were not used, or not used extensively, that could have been productive. You might share your notes with the teacher and discuss why particular reactions were used and why others were not appropriate for this lesson with these students.

Reflection: What reacting behaviors will I incorporate during recitations? After observing and analyzing many recitations, you'll be more aware of the number of possible reacting behaviors. Some reactions have general application while others may be helpful with particular students. Devise a strategy that will enable you to incorporate several of the reactions in your next recitation. Gradually your range of reacting options will grow.

4. Types of feedback

Observation: What types of feedback are given?   Plan to observe two classes that are quite different. Elementary teachers could choose one basic class such as reading, mathematics, or science and a second class such as art, music, or physical education. Another selection could be a general-ability class and a special education class. Secondary teachers might choose a core curriculum class and an elective, or a class for higher track students and one for lower track students.

Sketch the classroom so that you can identify each student. You may be able to get a seating chart from the teacher. During each visit describe the type of feedback given by the teacher and indicate which students get feedback. One way to record this is to use the letter *B* for basic feedback, *E* for elaborated feedback, and *P* when the teacher is providing process feedback. Nonverbal feedback (*NV*) can also be noted. Figure 9–6 shows a sample classroom feedback chart.

   Analysis: How effective was the feedback?   Interview the teachers you observed and share your feedback chart. Have the teacher describe the feedback process. Construct a graphic organizer to depict the feedback process described by the teacher. You may want to use one similar to the one shown in Figure 9–4.
   Using your graphic organizer and your notes, describe this teacher's mental image of the feedback process.

- What types of feedback are most important? What types are missing from the discussion?
- What sources are predominant? What sources are not used?
- What role does a standard of performance play?
- What resources does the teacher feel would improve the feedback process?
- Are there sources that do not seem to be important?

Synthesize the information from your interview and compare your findings to the research on feedback.

   Reflection: How can I use feedback most effectively?   It is essential that all teachers develop skill in using feedback to promote learning. Develop a list of guidelines that you will use in planning feedback for your own teaching. You may want to organize a small group of peers to try out different forms of feedback and give each other suggestions.

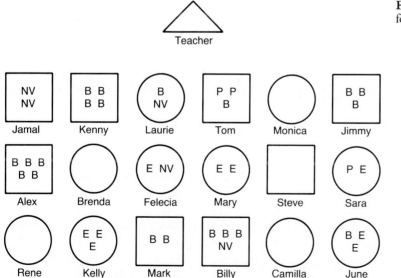

FIGURE 9–6. Classroom feedback chart

5. Feedback

Observation: *How do teachers plan to use feedback?*   Arrange an interview with a teacher to discuss the types and sources of feedback he or she uses. Use the following questions to guide your discussion:

- How do your students know the expected standard of performance?
- What types of feedback do you use most often? Why?
- What types of verbal feedback do you give your students? Consider corrective feedback during group work, individual feedback during individual practice, and more formal student conferences. What are the advantages and disadvantages of each type of feedback?
- What types of written feedback do you use? Think about quizzes, tests, and comments on homework or assignments. What are the advantages and disadvantages of these?
- What sources of feedback, other than yourself, do your students have, such as aides, peers, themselves, computers, and other media?
- What resources, such as time, personnel, and instructional materials, would help you improve the feedback you give to students?

Analysis: *How well did the feedback work as a holistic process?*   The feedback process should be planned so that all components work together. Analyze the information you obtained in the interview. After reviewing the research, answer the following questions:

- What is the relationship between the feedback plan and the teacher's learning objectives?
- What types and sources of feedback are used?
- In what ways are these choices supported by research findings?
- How do the teacher's practices reflect the findings that feedback should be specific for each student and given while students can still improve?
- How are the teacher's correctives related to the learning objectives and instructional plans?
- Are there any discrepancies between the various components of the feedback plan? If so, what are they?

Reflection: *How can I use the feedback and correctives process as an interactive unit, with each component building on and supporting progress toward mastering instructional objectives?*   Reflect on what you learned about the overall effect of the feedback and correctives process using the following questions as a guide:

- What essential elements of feedback will I use with my students?
- What ineffective elements of feedback will I try to avoid?

DEVELOPMENT AND RENEWAL ACTIVITIES

1. Arrange to observe a class. The purpose of this observation is to focus holistically on the feedback process. Be sure to review the teacher's plans so you can examine the fit between learning objectives, instruction, feedback, and correctives. Talk with the teacher prior to the observation and ask the following questions:

- What learning objectives do you have for this unit of instruction?
- Please discuss the feedback you plan to use during the current unit. What types and sources of feedback will be used?
- Will the feedback be the same for all students? If not, how do you plan to differentiate feedback? Why?
- When will students be given each type of feedback?
- What correctives will be available for students who have trouble?

During the observation keep a log that describes the feedback given in class. When possible, identify the students involved in the process. General feedback given to the entire class or group should also be noted. Describe any correctives that are used. If the students have turned in any assignments, ask to see them before they are handed back. What kind of feedback is given on the assignments?

2. If you have the opportunity to observe elementary or secondary teachers or college instructors, focus on the feedback students receive. If you have previously observed a teacher providing feedback, review the observation notes and charts you made. Develop a chart with students' names listed across the top and feedback elements on the side. If you have observed more than one class, make a separate chart for each class. Figure 9–7 shows a sample feedback chart.

Examine your notes and tally the number of times teachers reinforced correct responses, identified incorrect responses, and gave basic, elaborated, process, or nonverbal feedback. Total each column to determine the number of times each type of feedback was used. Compare the charts for different classes to see if there are any observable differences.

- Is one kind of feedback used more frequently in one class than in another?
- What factors, such as type of class, student characteristics, learning objectives, might account for the differences?
- Is there any difference in the way feedback was given to individuals or groups of students in the two classes?
- How are these differences related to student ability level, correctness of the responses, on-task behavior, or other factors?

3. Identify the influences that appear to affect the feedback that is given to different classes, groups of students, or individuals. Reflect on your experience, the interviews you have conducted, and the classes you have observed. List the influences you think may have affected the way feedback was planned or delivered. What

FIGURE 9–7. Feedback
chart

Types of Feedback	Belva	Shirley	Bobbi	Jim	Sue	Marti	Lois	Pat	José
Correct response reinforced									
Basic corrective feedback									
Elaborated feedback									
Process feedback									
Nonverbal feedback									
Other									
TOTALS									

information from your observations indicates that providing different types of feedback affects instruction and learning? If you were asked to suggest changes for these teachers, what would you suggest? Why?

4. Many college instructors use recitations in their teaching. Talk with one or several of them about the benefits of recitations. You might also ask these teachers about how they plan their recitations.

5. Reflect on your experiences as a student, presently and in previous school experiences. Think, in general, about the oral and written feedback you received from teachers and its effect on your attitude and performance. The amount and type of feedback you received in elementary and secondary situations may be different from the feedback you received as a college student. Identify the kind of feedback you feel was the most helpful, reinforcing, and encouraging and led to your increased participation and effort.

10.
Questioning and Responding

COMMENTARY

Teachers often discuss instructional concerns about classroom management, pacing of instruction, and time on task but seem to have relatively few concerns about using questions. From this we can assume one of the following: teachers are well informed and feel comfortable about their questioning techniques; questioning is not generally viewed as an important instructional process; or questioning is so interrelated to all aspects of classroom verbal interaction that it is not often viewed as a specific and discrete instructional process. We believe that the last assumption is the closest to reality.

Several influences have made teachers aware of the importance of the use of questions. A number of teacher evaluation instruments include sections on questioning. Some of these instruments indicate that the most effective teachers use many high-level questions while less effective teachers use more low-level questions. Unfortunately, this misuse (or misunderstanding) of the research often goes unchallenged. In addition to the influence of evaluation instruments, a growing number of staff development sessions on asking questions, the use of wait time, and other questioning techniques have emphasized the importance of questioning. Also, hundreds of articles and books have been written about questioning.

These influences do not seem to have had a major impact on instructional practice. Our classroom observations of both beginning and experienced teachers support the contention that the predominant form of verbal interaction is for teachers to ask students questions. Yet, it is very difficult to determine what purposes the questions serve and even how concerned teachers are about the kind of answers they are getting. In some cases, questioning appears to lack a clear purpose. Teachers have thousands of interactions with their students each day, and this makes it very difficult to carefully plan their questioning strategies. Furthermore, many teachers feel that they have not been well prepared to effectively manage the verbal interaction processes that are so central to teaching and learning.

There are other conditions that prevent teachers from having helpful information about questioning techniques and strategies. Once, when we were speaking at a statewide meeting of educators who are responsible for providing instructional leadership to their school systems, we asked the entire group how they would respond to teachers who were asking for assistance in improving their classroom questioning strategies. Very few of the participants were aware of any research or references that would be useful in responding to teachers' requests.

Not long after this meeting, we were working with teachers in a school system in a state that places a heavy emphasis on staff development. We were given a memo from a recent workshop on questioning that was sent to all teachers in the system. The memo advised teachers to wait for 20 seconds or more after each question in order to improve student responses. This is one example that causes us to be concerned about the lack of understanding about an instructional process that is the cornerstone of teacher and student interaction. We are even more concerned about the misuse and inappropriate applications of research findings.

RATIONALE

Questioning is the instructional process that is central to verbal interaction in the classroom. The questions teachers ask serve as the interface between teacher expectations and student responses. Verbal patterns in the classroom are complex. Teachers ask questions, attend to the responses, evaluate the adequacy of the answers, react to student questions, and manage the classroom. All of these actions may occur in a very short period of time. When teachers are cognizant of the research on questioning and can incorporate the findings into their practice, they are in a position to manage these complex verbal interactions effectively.

Students who attend to teacher questions and provide answers are actively engaged in learning. Recently, there has been more and more stress on the importance of raising the level of student thinking. Skillful use of questions can facilitate higher level thinking and problem solving. This requires teachers to write good questions, know when and how long to wait after questions, and resist attempts by students to reduce the cognitive demands of the task.

Participation in learning activities is a source of motivation. Students who are actively involved in instructional interactions develop more positive attitudes about learning. Affective gains have been reported when students have had more opportunities to respond to teacher questions. The gains are greater when students have a chance to think through their responses and when teachers wait for them to formulate their answers.

Observations of current practice indicate that there is a need to improve the use of classroom questions. Teachers ask many questions that seem to be unplanned and that do not stimulate thinking or motivate students to be more actively engaged in their own learning. Feedback from supervisors also may not be very helpful. When teachers are given a general recommendation about the need to improve their questions, they may not be given specific recommendations to help them strengthen this area of instruction.

Preservice programs may not deal with questioning at a level that will help prospective teachers be effective at using classroom questions. Students may have little opportunity to practice questioning in an interactive situation. They may learn to write questions at different levels but may not be given opportunities to apply the questions in real or simulated classroom settings.

Staff development programs can be effective in helping teachers improve the planning and use of classroom questions. The programs that are most effective give teachers an opportunity to practice new techniques after they have developed a thorough understanding of the research on questioning. When they put these new techniques into practice, they are given helpful feedback from observers who are also knowledgeable about the research. Unfortunately, too few teachers are involved in these types of programs.

Teachers' manuals, especially in reading, provide questions at predetermined levels. The questions, however, may not constitute a questioning strategy since they often do not provide structure or direction. Student characteristics may not be considered, and there may be little attempt to coordinate these questions with formal assessment processes. Manuals can help give direction or focus the questioning, but teachers need to be aware of their inherent limitations.

The research on questioning is extensive. The results of hundreds of studies have been reported. However, little work has been done to synthesize the work of different researchers into a unified discussion of the various aspects of questioning. Such a synthesis would give teachers a usable reference for developing and improving their questioning skills and techniques. Because questioning can have a profound influence on student learning, it is imperative for both beginning and experienced teachers to understand and be able to apply the research that can help them improve the quality of their questioning strategies.

RESEARCH SYNTHESIS

The Concept of Questioning

Questioning is a complex process consisting of the cognitive level of the question, questioning strategies, student responses, and the way teachers react to student responses. All of these factors function in concert, as depicted in Figure 10–1, when teachers use questioning effectively. Student questions and the role student questions play in improving the quantity and quality of learning are also important components of the questioning process.

Recent research on instruction has provided direction for teachers as they seek to develop and use effective questions. Much of the information on questioning has been generated by those conducting research on effective teaching. This research must be examined contextually, in terms of clarity, grade levels, instructional objectives, and content areas.

Wilen (1986) defined a question as "any sentence having either an interrogative form or function" (p. 5). This definition delineates questions from commands or nonverbal gestures that may serve classroom management functions. Questions are related to the content students are expected to learn. They focus student attention on information to be learned and on teachers' expectations about what students are to do and how they are to do it.

Questions are so prevalent in classroom teaching that it is hard to conceive of instruction without them. Researchers have studied the number of questions teachers ask and have concluded that approximately one third of classroom interactive instruction consists of teacher questions (Fisher et al., 1984). A primary school teacher may ask approximately 150 questions per hour, while elementary grade and high school teachers may ask several hundred questions per day (Gage & Berliner, 1984).

Several studies have shown that the frequency of questions is positively related to learning. A high frequency of questions often indicates that teachers are well organized and are pursuing academic goals or learning-related activities. Having a wide variety of questions that supplement lectures, recitations, and discussions also enhances learning because more students get to participate and be involved in learning activities (Good & Brophy, 1987).

Questioning often follows a predictable turn-taking cycle sometimes referred to as the initiative-response-feedback (IRF) cycle. A typical cycle involves a teacher

Figure 10–1. Questioning process

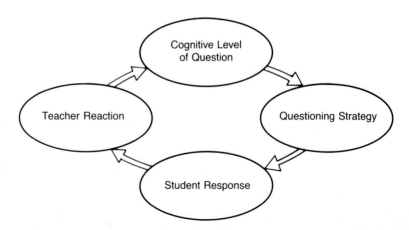

question, a student answer, and some feedback from the teacher. More than half of classroom dialogue follows this cycle (Watson & Young, 1986).

In many instances, teachers view questions as an end in themselves and not as tools to produce desired changes in student behavior. Questions should be clearly related to the learning objectives of a lesson. Yet observations of instruction often indicate a discrepancy between the objectives and the questions asked. Objectives for a lesson may require application and analysis, but the questions may only ask for a recall of facts. The question-answer-feedback cycle may be the source of the mismatch between objectives and questions. Clearly, teachers should carefully plan the questions to be asked and the interaction pattern to be developed in order to help students achieve desired learning outcomes.

Purposes of Questions

The early research on questioning was based on the assumption that questions were related to the content to be learned and to the level of thought required to answer. Current research efforts, however, focus on four main functions or purposes of questions, which are summarized in Figure 10–2: instructing, encouraging student participation, managing the classroom, and assessing learning. Findings from the work of Hunkins (1972), Wilen (1986), Brophy and Evertson (1976), Farrar (1988), Fisher et al. (1984), Morine-Dershimer and Beyerbach (1987), Ornstein (1987), and Stiggins (1986) guide the following discussion of the purposes and use of questions for instruction.

Instructional questions may focus students' thinking on one topic or a particular aspect of a topic. These questions may be at different cognitive levels. Questions that focus student thinking may

1. Orient students to content objectives, procedures, and affective aspects
2. Introduce or clarify the major concepts or ideas of a lesson
3. Consolidate previously learned material
4. Initiate a discussion based on previous learning
5. Control shifts in topics to keep a discussion on track
6. Review previously learned material

Focusing questions are usually considered to be convergent since they converge on one idea, thought, or conclusion that has been predetermined by the teacher.

Teachers also use questions that ask students to seek new ideas or information. These extension questions can be at one cognitive level or can gradually raise thinking to higher levels. They are usually divergent in nature since they encourage students to produce several answers or to consider information from different perspectives. In fact, such questions may be deliberately designed to prevent the group from converging prematurely on one point or thought. Extension questions may

1. Help students improve their oral or written responses
2. Arouse curiosity or interest

Figure 10–2. Purposes of questions

3. Act as a catalyst to student thinking
4. Encourage creative thought or imagination
5. Direct and guide inquiry, discovery, or the search for new knowledge
6. Develop student initiative or responsibility for their own learning
7. Generate guidelines for judgment or standards for evaluation
8. Help students develop strategies for learning how to learn

Creating a classroom climate that encourages student participation in discussion is another important function of questioning. Student involvement in the intellectual interchange between teachers and other students increases the level and rate of engagement in the learning process. In most cases, the larger the number of students who are involved in a discussion, the greater the impact on learning (Taba, 1966). Questions to promote student discussion should support student contributions, keep participation open to all students, and keep ideas flowing.

Using questions to manage the classroom is closely related to encouraging student participation. The function of management questions, however, is to convey a message about student behavior. Teachers use management questions to get and keep student attention and to keep the students alert. They also use them to control student behavior and maintain order in the classroom.

The role questions play in student assessment has been the focus of recent research. Teachers ask questions in a deliberate attempt to determine what students have learned. Stiggins (1986) described this as an informal mode of monitoring and assessment which is an integral part of instruction. He suggested that teachers plan questions to achieve a high level of congruence between the questions asked during class and those asked on final exams and tests. Students perceive teacher questions as cues to what they are supposed to learn and the level of thinking the teacher will require as a demonstration of their learning. Assessment questions can reveal what has been learned and the level of comprehension. The ability of students to use and apply new knowledge can also be assessed with the appropriate questions.

Assessment questions can also be used to make decisions about the pace of instruction: when to review, provide more practice, or move ahead. Questions can be used to diagnose student readiness for a new task and to determine how well prior objectives have been achieved. Student interest and motivation to learn can also be assessed with carefully structured questions.

Questioning Techniques

Questions are the dominant mode of communication in most classrooms. The more effective the questioning techniques, the greater the potential for student learning. Studies have identified several factors that influence the quality of classroom interaction and the effectiveness of instruction. These factors include the way the question is phrased, the type of question asked, the order or sequence of inquiries, and the choice of respondents. Much of the advice about questioning techniques is based on logical analysis of the strengths and weaknesses of types of questions and the effect they have on instructional goals (Good & Brophy, 1987).

The learning objectives for a lesson and student characteristics both influence the type of questions teachers use. Ornstein (1988) stated that "a good question is one that serves the instructional objective, is thought provoking, and enhances students' comments and discussion. A good teacher knows when and how to use what type of question for achieving the instructional objectives and increasing student participation" (p. 73). Participation and student responses will depend, of course, on the developmental readiness of students and their background knowledge of the subject being discussed.

When questions are not clear, a communication gap is created. Clear questions describe the specific points that students should attend to. Vague questions waste time because they can be answered in several ways, requiring the teacher to clarify or ask new questions. Asking clear questions involves skill in adapting vocabulary, sentence structure, and the difficulty level of the question to students' ability and conceptual levels (Wilen, 1986). Clear questions are stated in natural, simple language; vague terminology is avoided. Clarity also comes from conciseness. When teachers ask run-on questions or include several queries in one sentence, students can become confused. Clear questions increase the possibility of receiving appropriate responses. Clear questions are also meaningful. Using questions that relate to student lives or current situations helps to improve student understanding. By checking with students to make sure they understand the questions, teachers can determine if the questions are clear (Wilen, 1986; Ornstein, 1988).

Teachers may plan their instruction around several key questions (Wilen, 1986). Teachers prepare four or five questions related to the objectives or major ideas of the lesson. Key questions help introduce or clarify important concepts that will guide discussion. Other questions must be formulated during instruction as the need arises, but key questions provide structure and direction for a lesson.

When teachers ask questions and receive responses, they must decide whether to ask the same student another question or call on other students. Asking the same student a follow-up question is called probing. Teachers ask a series of questions of the same student to get the student to improve the quality of the answer. This helps students learn by giving them an opportunity to organize their knowledge into overt responses. It also gives the teacher an opportunity to shape the reply into a more acceptable form (Gall et al., 1978).

Studies of probing have not always completely described the behaviors the teacher can use. However, the work of Brophy and Evertson (1976), Gage and Berliner (1984), Wilen (1986) and Ornstein (1988) provides a more complete picture of probing behaviors. These behaviors include:

1. Repeating questions using different words
2. Asking a second question that pursues the implications of the first answer
3. Asking a new question
4. Asking a lower level question to review basic knowledge
5. Giving clues
6. Eliciting clarification in a nonthreatening manner
7. Using student ideas

Probing questions can be used after wrong answers to get a credible response from low-achieving students. Frequent use of this type of probing is positively related to student learning. Another advantage is that probes reduce the frequency of non-responses, which have a negative correlation to learning (Brophy & Evertson, 1974). Frequent teacher probes after unsatisfactory answers is viewed in a positive way by students. Bourke (1985) found that students saw probes as an attempt to help them get correct answers.

Researchers point out the danger of overusing probing as a questioning technique. In the early grades students either do or do not know the answer. They do not yet possess the ability to reason logically, so probing can easily become pointless pumping (Brophy, 1986b). Giving a student who has not been paying attention another chance might appear to condone inattention. There is a fine line between effective probing and a rapid series of questions that more closely resembles a cross-examination (Ornstein, 1988). When used wisely, however, probing can help to improve student learning.

Redirection occurs when the teacher calls on another student to answer a question. This may happen when the response given by the first student is incorrect or inadequate. Another use of redirection is calling on several class members to respond to the first student's original answer. In either case, the teacher redirects the question to one or more students following the first response (Gall, 1970). Redirec-

Bellock

tion seems to be more helpful when working with high- or middle-ability pupils. Students who are less academically oriented may gain more if the teacher stays with them and uses probing for an improved response.

When questions are used as teaching strategies, the order or sequence of the questions must be carefully planned. An effective technique is for teachers to ask questions, obtain answers, and carefully integrate the answers with previously learned material before they move on to the next question. This technique helps accomplish specific learning objectives (Good & Brophy, 1987). The process of sequencing questions is explored in greater depth in the section "Questioning Strategies."

Several questioning techniques have proven to be unproductive. Nonacademic questions are negatively related to achievement during direct instruction in basic skills. Asking for personal experience or opinions are examples of nonacademic questions (Rosenshine, 1983–84). Phrasing the question so that students can answer with a yes or no may also be unproductive. When yes or no responses are given, calling for an explanation of the response does promote thinking (Stiggins, 1986). Fill-in-the-blank questions that suggest or imply an answer and those that encourage guessing are other poor questioning techniques.

Repeating questions, repeating student answers, and the answering of teacher questions by teachers are practices that can detract from learning. Interrupting student responses or seeking instant closure tends to deter student thinking. Questions that are really commands also confuse students (Farrar, 1984).

Question Level

Researchers have examined the amount of mental processing required to respond to questions. The cognitive level of a question is usually described using the *Taxonomy of Educational Objectives* (Bloom, Engelhart, Furst, Hill, & Krathwohl, 1956). Other classification systems exist, but the taxonomy best represents the common factors (Gall, 1970).

Lower level questions usually call for the recall of one item of information or several facts. Higher level questions are characterized by two features. First, they require students to state predictions, solutions, explanations, generalizations, interpretations, or opinions. Second, they cannot be answered directly from the available information. The answer is not in the textbook, the teacher's lecture, or other instructional materials (Gall, 1978). The student must actively process information in some way to arrive at an answer.

Some researchers have classified questions somewhat differently. They consider questions that ask students to define terms, interpret statements, and state facts to be lower level. Questions that elicit explanations, opinions, and justifications are considered to be higher level (Bellack et al., 1966).

Recent research supports the idea that question level should be directly related to learner objectives. The popular belief that lower level questions are less effective than higher level questions has not been upheld. Achievement is related to the use of a variety of questions designed to accomplish specific purposes. For example, a pattern of factual questions, student responses, and teacher feedback has been found to be the most functional mechanism for student achievement in basic skills (Rosenshine, 1983).

Successful responding to lower level questions is a prerequisite for higher level learning. Students need a firm base of factual knowledge when they are engaged in higher level thinking activities. It is impossible to summarize or evaluate information that a person does not know or understand. When prerequisite knowledge is in memory, processing, organizing, and evaluating can take place.

Using a number of low-level questions as a form of practice is more than a way to check for understanding; it is a necessary step in the development of deeper forms of understanding (Berliner, 1987). In Bloom's study (1986) of the relationship between mastery of basic skills and complex learning, he found that certain skills and facts need to be overlearned so that conscious thought can be devoted to ideas rather than the mechanics of a process. This allows students to manipulate concepts and practice problem-solving skills.

Lower level questions can be used to provide practice, to check for knowledge of subject matter, and to assess readiness for complex or abstract thinking. Despite the concern about overuse of lower level questions, there is a positive relationship between recall questions and basic skills acquisition for low-SES students in the lower grades (Gall, 1984).

Higher level questions help students recall and manipulate information mentally. Although higher level questions do facilitate learning (Berliner, 1984), it should not be assumed that higher level questions are categorically superior to lower level questions (Brophy, 1986c). Higher level questions seem to be especially helpful in assisting students with problem-solving skills. Age and ability of the student are other factors to consider. Higher level cognitive questions appear to be more productive with older students of average or better ability (Gall, 1984).

There are other promising findings related to higher level questions. A typical student who is exposed to instruction without higher order questions scores at the 50th percentile on a test related to the lesson. If the same student engages in a lesson where many higher order questions are asked, the student performs at about the 75th percentile on the same test (Berliner, 1984).

The level of questioning should be determined by the instructional objectives and the sequence of instruction. Asking higher level questions when introducing a complex process might be counterproductive. Later on, when students have a good understanding of the concept, those same questions might be very helpful.

The number of higher level questions teachers ask has also been a focal point for the research on questioning. The findings in this area have been quite consistent. Gall (1970) concluded that teachers ask about 60% recall or fact questions and only 20% higher level thinking questions. The remaining 20% of questions concern procedural activities. In some classrooms over 80% of the questions are lower order. When teachers are aware of the problem and given assistance in improving their techniques, however, they can improve their questioning techniques. In one study, the changes made were still evident three years after the training (Berliner, 1987). Staff development programs that help teachers ask higher level questions stress patience, clarity, careful sequencing, and a slower instructional pace (Ornstein, 1987; Doneau, 1987a).

One way of examining the impact of questions is to study student responses. The belief that higher level questions elicit answers that reflect higher level thinking is widely held. Yet the research on question-answer correspondence seems inconclusive (Dillon, 1982). For example, teachers may ask what they think is a higher order question, but students give answers that consist of information from the textbook or lecture. While the answer only shows evidence of recall of knowledge, the teacher accepts the answer. According to Berliner (1984), "The odds are only about 50–50 that an analysis, synthesis, or application question will be responded to with an answer reflecting analysis, synthesis, or application" (p. 64). Teachers who classify the level of the question often do not classify the level of thought reflected in student responses.

The relationship between the level of the question and the level of thought in the answer is complex. Questions that are ranked high on Bloom's taxonomy may not require higher cognitive activity in developing an answer. One student may already know the answer and can answer from memory. Another student, not knowing the answer, may have to use higher level skills. Sometimes characteristics of the text can affect the level of thought a student uses to answer questions. If a synthesis is stated explicitly in the textbook, students can answer using memory or identification. When relevant information is mentioned in several different places in the text but is nowhere summarized or synthesized, the task becomes more difficult. If the information needed to answer is only alluded to in the text, then students must combine their background knowledge with information in the book to give an answer. This is a much more difficult task. Clearly the availability of information affects the level of thinking necessary to respond to questions (Raphael & Pearson, 1985).

Dillon (1982) has taken a different approach to research on levels of student thought. He examined teacher statements as well as questions. When teachers make declarative statements, then wait for students to respond, almost half of the responses are at higher levels. Concerning questions and statements, Dillon noted:

> The respondent to a question is implicitly instructed to supply the information and then stop; for a statement, the respondent is to accept or to reject the information preferred. A question might thus be said comparatively to circumscribe response and to delimit inquiry, and a statement to leave these open. (p. 546)

Whether the student is responding to a question or a statement does not appear to affect the length of student response. When students have time to collect their thoughts and organize information, the answers are longer. It is unlikely that students will be able to communicate the results of higher level thinking in a word or a phrase. The relationship of levels of questions to wait time and student learning is depicted in Figure 10–3. Note that longer periods of wait time are associated with the higher level questions. The length and complexity of responses are positively related to the level of thought (Cole & Williams, 1973; Lange, 1982). Regular practice in answering higher level questions results in extended replies and improved comprehension.

A relatively new area of study is the difficulty level of questions. The level of difficulty refers to students' ability to answer questions regardless of the cognitive

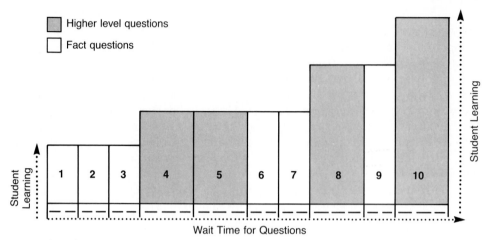

Figure 10–3. Relationship of levels of questions and wait time to student learning

level. Even recall questions may be very difficult for some students when they are first learning new material. The optimal level of difficulty varies. Students should get most of the answers correct in basic skills classes. When the level of question is too difficult, the number of nonresponses increases; teachers are faced with silence, or answers come from only the top students. On the other hand, when the content is complex and the teacher is trying to extend student thinking, questions must be challenging (Brophy & Good, 1986).

Medley and Cook (1980) related difficulty level to the socioeconomic status of students. With low-SES students it is important to ask easy questions in order to provide an atmosphere where students are not afraid to risk being wrong. High-SES students can handle more difficult questions, more wrong answers, and less prompting or help. Contextual factors such as the age, ability, and self-concept of the students determine the optimal difficulty level for questions.

It is generally assumed that teachers alone determine the difficulty of questions because they formulate them. But researchers are discovering the role students play in negotiating the cognitive demands of questions. In subtle but observable ways students try to adjust or lower the difficulty level of questions. One tactic students use to reduce the level of thinking required to answer is to depend on other students. Lower ability students restrict their output when they do not know the answer. They hesitate or give provisional replies until the more able students answer for them. Both Doyle (1983) and Tobin (1987b) found that these target students asked and answered most of the higher level questions. This reduces the level of thinking required of other students.

When tasks are risky and the evaluation criteria are unclear, students react by trying to get the teacher to give more assistance. Over a period of time, teachers relent and provide prompts or reduce the level of the question. Because this is done in public, students who could have accomplished the higher level work circumvent it and work below their ability level. These behaviors have been observed in several content areas and at all grade levels.

Wait Time

Mary Budd Rowe (1969) was one of the first researchers to study the concept of wait time. She observed that the communication pattern in classrooms often consisted of questions followed almost immediately by student answers. She noted that a rapid-fire pace did not give students time to think or process information before they had to answer. Students who took time to organize their information into a reasoned reply often found that the opportunity to answer had passed. During her study of science teachers, Rowe found that students were given approximately one second to answer before a reply was expected or another student was asked to answer. The amount of time a teacher gives a student to reply to a question has become known as wait time. When teachers have been made aware of their wait time and have been trained to increase wait time to five seconds or more, a number of benefits result:

1. Longer student responses
2. More speculative thinking and arguments based on evidence
3. More child-to-child comparing of differences and fewer teacher-centered interactions
4. More student questions
5. Opportunities for teachers to hear and think, thus a wider variety of questions asked
6. Changed teacher expectations for some students because they contributed more (Rowe, 1969)

Additional benefits of increased wait time have been identified in subsequent studies. Slower students make more contributions and teachers make fewer disciplinary moves (Lehr, 1984). Also, teachers interrupt students less often. This may account for some of the increase in the length of student responses (Tobin, 1984). In 1986 Rowe reexamined wait time in science classes. She found that increasing wait time improves the quality of student answers. Students give more complex answers, provide more logical arguments, and are willing to speculate. Some negative behaviors also decrease. The communication pattern is less teacher-centered, students reduce their competition to respond, there are fewer nonresponses, and there is a decrease in the number of students rated as poor.

Research on wait time has been extended to include what is now known as "wait time II." Wait time II has been defined as the amount of time a teacher waits *after* a student response before speaking or calling on another student. When a student answers a question and the teacher waits for three to five seconds, the speaker has a chance to continue. Other class members also have an opportunity to speak. When the teacher does not wait, students' thinking may be cut off. They do not have time to develop a complete answer or correct errors in their reply. Teachers who extend wait time II are giving their students time to think about prior answers, to formulate their own reaction, and to generate an oral answer if called on (Tobin, 1987b). Quick reactions by teachers appear to cut off student ideas and elaborations. Increasing wait time II may improve motivation. Student restlessness and inattentiveness decrease, and communication becomes more coherent. Students feel that teachers care about their responses and are not just looking for one correct answer. High-ability students report their relief at being given time to make connections, elaborate on answers, and go below the surface of ideas (Rowe, 1986). One unexpected outcome of increasing wait time is improved performance on written measures with cognitively complex items. This is true at all grade levels and is evident both in the ways students use language and in the logic of their replies (Rowe, 1986).

Waiting longer after asking a question or after a student responds is not always beneficial. The amount of wait time should vary directly with the difficulty and cognitive level of the question. Low-level questions used for basic skills drill and practice require very little wait time. When students must think and formulate original answers, a slower pace and longer wait times are necessary. Cueing students to the objective and the kind of response desired may be necessary. Some students are so used to memory-level questions that they do not realize that the teacher is looking for quality instead of speed (Good & Brophy, 1987). Increasing wait time for students who are unlikely to be able to improve their responses will not help. With low-SES students, for example, a long silence may be threatening. Another factor to consider is the flow of the lesson. Waiting too long can interrupt the continuity and momentum of the class (Brophy & Evertson, 1976).

Questioning Strategies

A questioning strategy is a deliberate series of questions designed to accomplish a specific goal. When planning a questioning strategy, teachers should consider level, sequence, the relation of each question to others in the series, and the amount of instructional time it will take to complete the strategy. Such a plan serves as a guide for the teacher and provides a framework for interaction with students. Without a strategy, a discussion often becomes a series of single questions that lacks cohesion and purposeful sequence (Wilen, 1986). The process for developing an effective questioning strategy is depicted in Figure 10–4.

The key to preparing an effective questioning strategy is developing clearly defined learning objectives. The level and sequence of questions to be asked depends entirely on the knowledge that is to be acquired and the cognitive processes necessary to respond to the strategy.

An examination of two questioning strategies demonstrates the differences between purpose and construction. Hilda Taba (1966) was one of the first researchers to propose a questioning strategy. She believed that the level of thinking is not influenced by the nature of a single question. Rather, the whole pattern of the com-

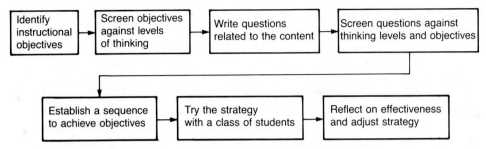

Figure 10–4. Sequence chain for developing a questioning strategy

munication, both questioning and providing information, affects the level of thought. Taba's goal was to help students with concept formation in science and social studies. In addition, she wanted students to learn to generalize, make inferences, and apply principles. All of these are high-level skills. She planned a strategy that would focus students' attention on the attributes of a concept to make sure they had the necessary prerequisite knowledge. Questions would then be asked to extend that knowledge at the same cognitive level. Finally, a series of questions would raise the level of thought so that students would use their knowledge by applying it to new situations. This strategy is hierarchical since it starts with lower level questions and gradually raises the level of thinking.

Taba's basic strategy is for the teacher to ask questions at each of the three levels to help students form valid concepts. The hands-on activities and questions related to each cognitive task at one level prepare the students for the next level of complexity and abstraction. The hierarchical nature of Taba's questioning strategy is depicted in the following outline of her work (Ornstein, 1987).

Taba's Questioning Strategy

A. Concept formation
   1. Enumerate and list.
   2. Group together.
   3. Label categories.
B. Generalizing and inferring
   1. Identify points (or information).
   2. Explain identified items of information.
   3. Make inferences or generalizations.
C. Application of principles
   1. Predict consequences, explain unfamiliar phenomena, hypotheses.
   2. Explain and support predictions and hypotheses.
   3. Verify predictions and hypotheses.

When teachers plan their questions using Taba's approach, it may take several days to complete the strategy. However, this approach leads to qualitative changes in students' thought processes (Ornstein, 1987).

Inquiry or discovery learning approaches use an entirely different questioning strategy. Teachers who use these strategies do not want to present key concepts or question to see if students have the necessary prerequisite knowledge. Instead, the learning objectives allow students to discover key concepts for themselves. The following discussion of the inquiry strategy is based on information from Joyce and Weil (1986) and Bibens (1980). Inquiry usually has three phases: exploration, invention, and discovery. Students engaged in inquiry are challenged to explore a topic. Usually the teacher presents examples or situations that are contrary to what the students know or believe. During the exploration phase, students read and collect information to verify the facts of the situation. They may ask the teacher questions. However, teachers will only give a yes or no answer; they do not provide all the needed information. The teacher does not act as a subject matter specialist, but, rather, serves as a guide or sounding board. Teachers also ask questions. These questions are usually broad, open-ended, and designed to get students to think divergently. During the exploration phase, teachers ask questions that lead students to verify facts, properties, conditions, or events, such as:

observe

inductive

1. How did you come up with this answer?
2. How did you get to this point?
3. Which factors do you consider most important? Why?
4. What other ways can you organize your information?

invent rule

During the invention phase, students consider what they have learned and try to invent a rule to encompass all the examples they have studied. The class examines the rule, testing it against the results of their investigation. They may experiment directly to test the rule. Teacher questions must keep students from forming one single hypothesis without considering alternatives. Questions or statements made by the teacher might include the following:

test rule

1. Explain how your hypothesis accounts for this example (nonexample).
2. Here's a hypothetical case; apply your rule to this case.
3. What inconsistencies do you see?

Deductive

4. Suppose your conclusion is not right. What other hypotheses might you generate?

During the discovery phase, students examine their thinking to discover the inadequacies of their rule or hypotheses. They try to modify the rule so that it can be applied more generally. In addition, they evaluate their own inquiry process so they can be more effective the next time. In this phase teachers might say or ask:

use rule to predict or classify new examples

1. Why do you think that is the answer? Review for us your line of reasoning.
2. Is there more than one right answer or rule? How do you explain that?
3. What data support each of the alternatives?

4. What kind of information was most helpful? What information was not useful?

5. Which questions that you asked were most effective? Why?

In inquiry or discovery classes, teachers must be prepared to ask heuristic questions which guide students' discovery or problem-solving approaches. They must be prepared to provide examples and nonexamples. When students use faulty reasoning, the teacher should use questions to reveal the inadequacy of their thinking. In short, the questions prod students to think for themselves (Good & Brophy, 1987). When planning a questioning strategy to encourage discovery, the level of the question is not critical. Teachers may return to lower level questions at any stage. Their decision is based on the students and the way they approach the problem.

Rakow (1986) studied inquiry sessions and concluded that "open-ended questions, extended wait time, and neutral praise stimulate students to think more divergently, to give more complete answers, and to participate in classroom discussion" (p. 17). Students do not share speculative ideas when they fear that they might be evaluated or judged.

Some of the recently developed questioning strategies are designed to help students learn how to learn. The sequence of questions is used to model a learning strategy that can be applied independently in other situations. When teachers use these strategies, their questions make cognitive processes explicit. Direct instruction and modeling provide a knowledge base for acquiring new learning strategies. Questions assess comprehension of the content and the learning processes. The work of Anthony and Raphael (1987) and Palinscar and Brown (1986) is especially useful in developing strategies that emphasize learning how to learn.

Student Answers

Studies on questioning have concentrated largely on the teacher's behavior; very little attention has been given to student responses. The studies assume that students either attend to the teacher's questions or fail to attend. Recent studies have shown that before students respond, they must mentally compose an answer. Some students are unable to organize their thoughts under stress so they do not respond or give the wrong answer (Morine-Dershimer and Beyerbach, 1987). The sequence of student behavior related to each of these options is shown in Figure 10–5. Recently, researchers have looked at how student answers affect the instructional process. In the conventional classroom, most of the student talk consists of answers to factual questions. About 90% of the responses require reproducing textbook information (Tisher, 1987). Answering is viewed as the students' major verbal task in the classroom, and students may give answers simply to satisfy the teacher with very little concern for the quality of their responses.

When questioning moves from the recall to the understanding level, the answering task involves ambiguity and risk. There may be no predetermined right

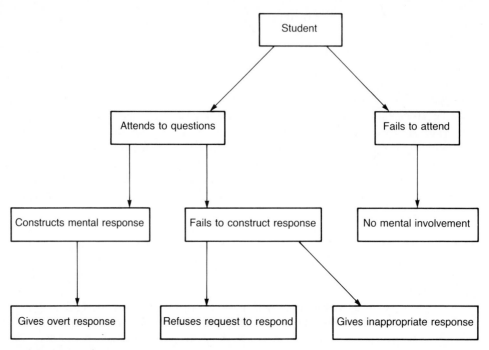

FIGURE 10–5. Student response behavior

answer and students must organize their thoughts to compose an answer and to express a complex idea. Rogers and Stevenson (1988) reported that many students found explaining, illustrating, describing, or clarifying their ideas exceedingly difficult. Answers to higher level questions are significantly longer than answers to lower level questions. These answers are more difficult to compose because they are grammatically complex. Students faced with a difficult question often restrict their answers, try to get more information before answering, or invent other strategies to circumvent the thinking processes demanded by the question (Doyle, 1983).

When students answer questions, teachers usually evaluate the responses against a set of criteria. For lower level or convergent questions there is a single criterion: correctness. Responses to higher cognitive questions should be evaluated in terms of complexity, plausibility, and clarity (Gall, 1970).

Students can learn to improve their answers. Raphael and Pearson (1985) developed processes to help students give better replies to text-based questions. They teach students to consider each question in relation to the text and their own background knowledge. Students examine each question to see if the answer is stated directly in the book in a single sentence. When this is not the case, students are taught to "think and search" to see if the answer is in the book in several sentences or in different paragraphs. They learn to locate this information and combine it in order to answer. When the answer is not explicitly stated, students learn to use their background experience to generate answers. This process is especially helpful for average and lower ability students. Teaching students to identify the source of the answer helps correct overdependence on either the text or background knowledge.

Teachers also help students answer high-level questions by modeling or thinking aloud. They make the thinking processes needed to answer explicit as they demonstrate how they themselves think about such questions. Gradually, teachers transfer the responsibility for thinking to the students, encouraging them to verbalize their reasoning or problem-solving processes.

Reacting to Student Answers

A typical communication cycle in a classroom involves a teacher question, a student response, and some type of teacher reaction to that answer. What the teacher says after a student's response may clarify, synthesize, expand, or rate the response (Gage & Berliner, 1984).

When students give responses that are partially correct or that are not stated clearly, teachers can clarify the answers themselves or use probing techniques to help students clarify their own responses. When this fails, the teacher can direct the question to another student for further development. Sometimes teachers merely repeat the question, then wait to see if the student can improve the answer. Each of these reacting moves can help clarify an answer.

Synthesizing may occur when a student gives a long detailed response, or after a series of responses. Teachers may synthesize the information themselves or ask students to do this. When the information is complex, teachers may involve the entire class in organizing the information and identifying unifying ideas or elements.

Rating a response is a very common teacher behavior. Teachers may give a direct evaluation after a student answer, or the correctness of the answer may be discussed and then praised or criticized. Some teachers rate the response and then correct it themselves. Others provide feedback about the answer and attempt to get students to make the correction.

According to Tobin (1986), "Reacting moves modify the previous discourse by clarifying, synthesizing, expanding, or evaluating what has been said" (p. 194). In addition, teachers' reactions to student answers act as signals about which answers are important to remember. Teachers who praise an answer or pursue the idea through probing give students an indication that the question is important enough to remember (Morine-Dershimer & Beyerbach, 1987).

Observers have identified differences in the behavior of teachers as they react to the responses of high-achieving and low-achieving students. Teachers may unintentionally discriminate against low-achieving students in several ways. They may praise unacceptable answers, criticize wrong answers more frequently, and fail to confirm correct answers.

Research on reacting to student responses has identified several appropriate options for teachers to consider. Wilen (1986) called these options a "response repertoire." The idea is for teachers to use reacting behaviors in a deliberate manner. Teachers evaluate a student's answer, make some judgment about that student's ability to correct or expand the answer, then choose a reaction from their response repertoire.

Joyce and Showers (1986) reported that these interactive skills are difficult for teachers to learn. Students try to steer the teacher back into a recitation mode. Challenge produces discomfort for students, so they try to get the teacher to tell them the answer. Teachers must acquire the invisible skills of processing information from students rapidly and then either constructing or delaying their reaction.

Brophy and Good (1986), Rosenshine (1983), Lange (1982), and Fisher et al. (1984) have all studied the effectiveness of specific reacting techniques. A synthesis of their work is presented in Figure 10–6.

Student Response Opportunity

Participation in class recitations or discussion is an important variable. Student achievement is positively related to responding to academic questions (Levin & Long, 1981). Students learn more if they interact with the teacher and their peers, and learning is related to the frequency of responding. Pupils who participate frequently achieve more than pupils who participate infrequently (Morine-Dershimer & Beyerbach, 1987). The reason for this is clear. Students are not passive recipients of instruction; they have to be actively involved in attending to and processing information in order to learn. Academically and socially successful students are usually actively engaged intellectually in responding to teachers' questions. The intermittent participants tend to be less successful academically (Power, 1987).

The relationship between responding and achievement is complex. Some students participate covertly. They attend to instruction, actively process the content, and mentally construct replies. Overt responses are not necessary for learning to take place. If students are shy or insecure about replying in public, attempts to increase their verbal participation can be counterproductive. Observers have documented changes in participation when instructional strategies are varied. The use of textbook-based, experience-based, models-based, or small-group activities influences the amount and type of participation. Power (1987) suggested that increasing a student's involvement may depend on the characteristics of the student, the task, and the setting.

The influence of participation on learning has led to studies designed to determine which students have the most opportunity to respond. In general, students who actively try to get a turn to respond by raising their hands are more likely to be called on. These target students get most of the response opportunities. Others who wait passively do not have as many turns.

Observers have also documented a pattern of overparticipation by high-achieving students. Many students believe that you should raise your hand if you know the answer. When teachers call on volunteers, class members who know most of the answers get to respond most often. Teachers may deliberately call on those who they think will know the answer. Tisher (1987) reported that teachers have positive attitudes toward students who volunteer and initiate other interactions. They develop an attachment to them. Students who interrupt or call out more often are rejected and get fewer turns to answer. Whatever the reason, it is clear that many students are passive, while a small number become the targets of teacher questions. Gradually,

FIGURE 10–6. Options to consider when reacting to student responses

Correct Responses

Correct, quick, firm
  Acknowledge response as correct
  Ask a new question
  Omit overt affirmation during fast-paced drills
Correct but hesitant
  Provide brief feedback
  Give specific rather than global praise
  Use praise with low-SES or dependent or anxious students
Partially correct responses
  Confirm the correct part
  Give clues or rephrase the answer
  Give the answer
  Call on another student (with secure high-SES students)

Incorrect Responses

Incorrect but careless
  Indicate that the answer is incorrect
  Correct and move on
  Give the correct answer with an extended explanation
Incorrect, showing lack of knowledge
  Rephrase the question
  Avoid pointless pumping in unsuccessful situations
  Ask a simpler question
  Reteach
  Explain why the answer is incorrect
  Explain how it can be determined from the information given
  Provide steps to follow to verify data
  Do not give the answer

No Response

Extend wait time
Wait until student asks for help
Probe
Present more information and ask again
Elicit an overt response such as "I don't know"
Supply the answer
Redirect
Ask again in a private situation for reluctant participants

Questions and Comments

Answer relevant questions
Redirect them to class
Incorporate relevant comments into the lesson
Follow up student comments with feedback
If there are many questions:
  Reteach
  Consider clarity of presentation
  Consider pace of instruction
  Reassess prerequisite skills

students adapt to expectations communicated by this pattern by volunteering less often and restricting their output when they are called on to respond (Power, 1987). This nonparticipation hinders their learning. Teachers cannot monitor these students' understanding, answer their questions, or assist them because there is so little communication about the content to be learned (Tobin, 1987b).

Some students do not choose to participate even when teachers attempt to distribute response opportunity evenly. According to Morine-Dershimer and Beyerbach (1987), there are four possible reasons why a student may not respond: "(1) the student is not attending, (2) the student is attending but doesn't understand, (3) the student understands but doesn't have the knowledge and cognitive skills to respond, (4) the student understands and has the knowledge and cognitive skills to respond but chooses not to" (p. 208). Experienced teachers are aware of all four possibilities. They know that attention is a selective, filtering process. In order for students to answer they must attend to the question and be motivated to answer. Teachers try to maintain attention by adding unexpected questions, gestures, and changes in pitch and volume, and using other strategies such as random distribution of questions (Power, 1987).

Teachers can control opportunities to respond. Some teachers act as gatekeepers, directing questions to students by name. Others are more flexible, allowing volunteers to call out the answers. Two kinds of decisions determine the pattern of participation. Teachers have to decide how to let the students know whose turn it is to answer. In addition, they have to decide on the order of respondents. There is no simple guide for making either of these decisions. Each option has advantages and disadvantages. It is important, however, for teachers to make the decisions consciously. Teachers who do not carefully consider the way they control response opportunities often create communication patterns that may interfere with learning.

There are several ways to control response opportunities. The teacher can call out a student's name first, then ask the question. Or the teacher can ask the question before choosing a respondent. When teachers ask the question first, all of the students have a chance to think about the answer, thus increasing covert participation. This appears to work very well with older students in a whole-class structure. However, with younger students in reading groups it is better to call the child's name first and then ask the question (Gage & Berliner, 1984). Another possibility is to ask a question without choosing a student to answer. This way, anyone who knows the answer can volunteer. The communication pattern created in this case is less like a recitation and closer to normal conversation. However, this pattern can create a classroom management problem if too many students answer at once. Furthermore, the more able students or attention seekers tend to monopolize answering opportunities.

One way to ensure that all students get to answer is to direct questions in a predictable, systematic procedure. Researchers have found that using patterned turns is more effective in small-group settings in primary grades. These students may feel some anxiety if they do not know when they will be called on. This may also be true when working with older students in low-SES schools. Staying with students to try to help them improve their responses reduces anxiety, builds confidence, and helps avoid undesirable competitiveness (Brophy & Good, 1986).

Patterned turns may not be as helpful with older students in large-group settings. Class size and schedules that segment instruction into blocks of time make the use of predictable turn-giving impractical. Older students may tune in only when they know they may be called on. These students are very sensitive to public failure. When the teacher uses ordered turns, students may be given a question they cannot answer correctly. In fact, using a predictable order is seldom feasible in whole-group settings. Brophy and Good (1986) found that overt verbal participation in lessons is not an important correlate of achievement in the upper grades. Thus, ensuring equal response opportunity is less crucial at this level.

There are some advantages to calling on students in a random order. Not knowing when they will be called on can help students to pay attention. Students who know they can answer the question correctly will raise their hands. When they do, most of their answers are correct and nonparticipants do not hear information that is incorrect. There are also some disadvantages in using random order. Teachers may unconsciously favor the more able students while depriving others of a fair share of the response opportunities (Gage & Berliner, 1984). Students may become aware of this pattern and make inferences about the teachers' expectations and their own ability to cope with school work.

When teachers use random order, they have to make decisions about whether to call on volunteers or nonvolunteers. Always calling on volunteers can favor the high-achieving, competitive students. In general, teachers should call on volunteers no more than 15% of the time (Ornstein, 1988). It is very important for teachers to monitor carefully whom they call on and how often they ask each student to respond.

 ## PRIMARY REFERENCES

Bibens, R. F. (1980). Using inquiry effectively. *Theory into Practice, 19,* 87–92.

> Bibens provides a good explanation of inquiry as a method of teaching. Using inquiry as a questioning strategy is encouraged in all content areas.

Brophy, J., & **Good, T. L.** (1986). Teacher behavior and student achievement. In M. C. Wittrock (Ed.), *Handbook of research on teaching* (3rd ed., pp. 328–376). New York: Macmillan.

> Chapter 12 is a review of process-product studies that link teacher behavior to student outcomes. The summary and integration of the findings is a useful section for teachers. The section on questioning includes a review of difficulty level, cognitive level, clarity of questions, selecting a respondent, wait time, and reacting to student responses.

Dillon, J. T. (1982). Cognitive correspondence between question/statement and response. *American Educational Research Journal, 19,* 540–551.

Dillon's study analyzes the teacher-student exchanges in high school discussion classes. The focus is on the cognitive correspondence between questions and answers. Dillon's findings are integrated with prior studies.

Gage, N. L., & **Berliner, D. C.** (1984). Classroom teaching: Seatwork and the recitation. In *Educational Psychology* (3rd ed., pp. 582–619). Boston: Houghton Mifflin.

Chapter 24 is an excellent review of the research on teacher questioning behaviors, types of questions, level and difficulty, wait time, directing questions, and teacher reacting behaviors.

Gall, M. D. (1970). The use of questions in teaching. *Review of Educational Research, 40,* 707–721.

In this article Gall presents a survey of the research on teacher questions used in classroom instruction. Programs for improving questioning behavior are suggested.

Morine-Dershimer, G., & **Beyerbach, B.** (1987). Moving right along. . . . In V. Richardson-Koehler (Ed.), *Educators' handbook: A research perspective* (pp. 207–232). New York: Longman.

This chapter discusses the problems teachers face as they try to cover specified content in a limited amount of time. The unique element in this research is the examination of questioning from the student's perspective. The danger of overemphasizing participation, of reacting differently to answers from lower ability students, and using questions in a routinized manner are stressed.

Rowe, M. B. (1986). Wait time: Slowing down may be a way of speeding up! *Journal of Teacher Education. 37*(1), 43–50.

This is an updated article by the researcher who first identified wait time as an important variable. Rowe reviews the research and presents new findings. The use of wait time with special needs students is examined.

Stiggins, R. J., Rubel, E., & **Quellmalz, E.** (1986). *Measuring thinking skills in the classroom.* Washington, DC: National Education Association.

Stiggins presents a framework for developing questions to measure five fundamental cognitive operations: recall, analysis, comparison, inference, and evaluation. Congruence between oral classroom questions and test questions is stressed.

Wilen, W. W. (1986). *Questioning skills for teachers* (2nd ed.). Washington, DC: National Education Association.

This booklet reviews the research findings on verbal questioning behavior and the current practices of teachers. Emphasis is on the impact of questioning practices on student thinking, achievement, and attitudes. Also included are questioning techniques, strategies, and approaches to improving questioning behavior systematically.

RESEARCH IN PRACTICE

Finding 1: Questions can serve a range of purposes including guiding instruction, managing the classroom, and influencing student achievement.

Frequent questions in classroom interactions relate positively to student learning. Teachers use questions to emphasize instructional content, focus student attention, and as catalysts to extend student thinking. Questions are also used to accomplish management functions such as keeping students alert and on task. An additional and critical purpose of questions is to monitor and assess student understanding.

Scenario.   A high school teacher working with a group of advanced placement seniors used questioning to extend the thinking of his students and to assess their understanding of the concept of imperialism. His first questions asked students to provide new examples of countries that were currently extending or expanding their control over other territories. He then asked them to imagine what might have happened at specific points in history if our country had not succeeded with its imperialist policies. Students were asked to explain and give reasons for their answers. Finally, he asked questions to evaluate or judge the policy of imperialism. These questions led students to develop some guidelines for evaluating an imperialistic move. The teacher asked if the morality of a policy could always be determined. When most of the students said, "Absolutely!" the teacher said, "I can see what you are thinking. Maybe you need to look at imperialism from two different points of view." He gave them an assignment that would help them look at imperialism from the perspective of each country involved.

This teacher had skillfully used his questions to raise and extend the level of his students' thinking. His last question also gave him good information for planning the next day's questions. He used that question to assess student understanding of an important aspect of the discussion and made an instructional decision to spend more time before moving on to new material.

Finding 2: Questioning techniques that improve student engagement include asking clear questions, probing for answers, and redirecting.

Teachers who are skillful in using the appropriate questioning techniques increase the potential for student learning. Their questions are sequenced so that students will achieve the learning objectives. Asking clear questions involves skill in adapting vocabulary and sentence structure to the ability level of the students. Teachers who are especially effective in using questioning techniques know how to probe and when to redirect questions to other students. Probing is a technique used to get students to improve the quality of their answers. To probe, teachers may rephrase questions, give more information, or ask other questions. Redirecting occurs when teachers call on other students to improve or correct answers.

Scenario.   A first grade teacher needed to use probing and redirecting with students in her low math group. She was trying to teach the students that the fraction one half should only be used to represent one of two equal parts. Some of her students continued to have difficulty with this concept. The following dialogue occurred when the teacher attempted to clarify the concept with one student:

Teacher. Jordan, look at the first two parts on the flannelboard. Are these two parts equal?
Jordan. Those aren't right (points to two unequal parts).
Teacher. Tell me more, Jordan. What's not right?
Jordan. One's skinnier and one's fatter. That's not right.
Teacher. That's true, so what can you say about these two parts of a circle?
Jordan. One's, like, big and one is, like, small.
Teacher. Think about our new word, equal (writes it on the board). Now, what can you say about these two parts?
Jordan. It's just not right, one's fatter.
Teacher. Jordan has the right idea. Who can use our new word to tell us about these two parts of a circle? All right, Mary, you try!
Mary. The two parts are not equal because the red one is bigger than the blue one. They are not halves.

In this example, the teacher got a partially correct answer, so she used the probing technique to see if Jordan could improve his response. When it seemed clear that Jordan was still confused about what equal meant, she redirected the question to Mary. As a result of this interaction she made the decision to work with Jordan individually to help him understand the concept.

Finding 3: Careful planning is needed so that the cognitive level and difficulty of questions will be consistent with teacher expectations, learner objectives, and student characteristics.

Decisions about the cognitive level of questions should be based on several factors. Lower level questions can be used to develop a knowledge base which will become the foundation for high-level information processing. Higher level questions can be asked to extend student thinking and add to the students' information base. Questions at all cognitive levels can be productive when asked at the appropriate point in the instruction. As teachers plan instruction, they should focus on developing a variety of questions that are consistent with the learning objectives and student characteristics rather than on concentrating on just using higher level questions. Failure to consider student characteristics and knowledge before asking higher level questions often results in student frustration because questions are too difficult.

Scenario.   During a preobservation conference an English teacher stated that she would be attempting to achieve higher level cognitive objectives and would use questioning as her primary instructional strategy. Students would be asked to analyze the effect of the author's choice of language and use of symbolism in relation to the theme of a poem. When the class began, the teacher presented a series of questions about the literal meaning of lines in the poem. The teacher then asked questions about some specific words and their meaning in context. It was clear that students were expected to agree with the teacher about each of these words. When a student asked if the author might have been using another meaning of the word, the teacher said, "No!" After this exchange, the teacher asked about symbolism. There were no volunteers, so she listed three symbols on the board. The teacher asked what these words suggested to the students on a personal level. Each answer was evaluated against the one right answer the teacher was seeking. For example, after a student response, the teacher stated, "No, woods is not a symbol for sleep. I'm sure the author meant woods to symbolize safety. Can you see that?" The final question was "Is hopelessness the theme of the poem?" One student said, "If you say so."

This scenario is an interesting example of the lack of consistency between the level of the questions asked and the objectives to be achieved. When the teacher rejected answers that did not agree with her interpretation, the questions were reduced to the recall level. Thus, a lesson that could have involved students in interpretation and analysis became an exercise in storing information for future reference.

Finding 4: Waiting after high-level questions and after student responses results in higher levels of achievement and improved student attitudes.

When teachers have an understanding of the research on wait time and deliberately adjust the amount of time they allow after asking questions or after getting student responses, the level of student thinking is raised. The appropriate use of wait time also affects interaction patterns in the classroom. The interactions are more like a discussion and less like an interrogation. In addition to improving student learning, extended wait time causes students to exhibit positive attitudes about learning.

Scenario.   A high school math teacher in a peer coaching program complained that participation in one of her classes had fallen way off. She said that the students had developed a real attitude problem as the work became more difficult. She was also concerned about the lack of student participation in her advanced classes. During a workshop, the teacher expressed a desire to refine her questioning techniques and use an appropriate amount of wait time.

The week after the discussion, the teacher's peer observer visited her class. He focused on teacher questions, especially what happened after questions were asked. When the teacher asked easy recall or computation questions, students volunteered answers. Most of these answers were quick, and the majority of them were correct; little wait time was needed. However, when questions were difficult or required the use of a new problem-solving strategy, a different pattern emerged. The teacher asked a question, then called on a student, expecting an immediate response. Other students were still jotting down computations and trying to work out solutions. When a response did not come quickly, the teacher became impatient, went to the board, and did the work herself. This pattern was repeated several times. In essence, the teacher was answering the hard questions herself. Some students were apparently aware of her tendency to do this and merely sat in their seats waiting for the teacher to answer her own questions.

With objective feedback from her peer observer, this teacher was able to correct the problem. She learned to wait after difficult questions and was able to recondition student expectations. She taught students to expect and use wait time. One technique she used was to monitor the class visually during wait time. This helped her read student cues so that she could adjust wait time to their needs.

The proper use of wait time can also influence teachers' attitudes about their students. An experienced second grade teacher had a rather negative attitude toward the students in her low reading group. As she began to develop a better understanding of wait time, she began to increase the time she gave students to think after asking comprehension questions. As she observed the effort her students were making, she began to appreciate how hard they were trying. When she encouraged them to take time to really think, they began to give examples from their own lives. She reported that she got to know students better and learned to respect their honest attempts to think through an answer. Her most important insight was recognizing that she had not believed they could answer difficult questions and consequently had not bothered to wait for them to think. She reported that her attitude about the students had changed; she realized that she really liked and appreciated them.

Finding 5: Developing an effective questioning strategy is a complex process that should attend to cognitive level, clarity, and the sequence of questions.

Since Hilda Taba (1966) pointed out the importance of looking at the relationships among multiple questions designed to accomplish a specific objective, there have been numerous efforts to develop questioning strategies that have a positive effect on student learning. Teachers must plan carefully to identify appropriate questions and sequence them properly within a series while also attending to the amount of instructional time available. A questioning strategy is more than simply using a series of unrelated questions. A questioning strategy is cohesive and designed to achieve a specific purpose. Inquiry learning and hierarchical approaches are two questioning strategies that can enhance student learning.

Scenario.   A high school history teacher pointed out that he did not have the time to plan his questioning strategies but that as a part of a peer coaching program he would give it a try. He worked with his coaching partner to develop a strategy that he would use during the following week. The questioning strategy allowed the teacher to present some content and ask a series of questions, then present more information and ask a new set of questions; the strategy was designed to give students opportunities to contrast and compare information that had been presented. This plan gave the teacher a sense of security because he did not have to learn new skills but only had to do a better job of planning his questions.

Both the history teacher and his peer observer were excited about what happened when the new strategy was used. Students were eager to participate and showed an excellent grasp of the concepts presented. As a result, the teacher moved on to new concepts. He was surprised that he actually saved time. His peer observer had previously raised the possibility that the teacher had a tendency to overdwell on each idea. By reflecting on this behavior he could see that he had underestimated his students. The teachers talked about the tradeoff between the planning time necessary to develop the questioning strategy and the results in the classroom and agreed that the questioning strategy had saved time. They noted that this strategy could be applied to similar situations or modified slightly to adjust to the specific needs of the students.

Finding 6: When teachers help students improve their answers, students' willingness to participate, the quality of their answers, and the level of their thinking are all improved.

Research on student answers has shown that some students do not know how to provide an answer to questions above the recall or knowledge level. Effective strategies have been developed to help students learn how to answer higher level questions. Students are taught to identify sources of information that can be used to compose good answers. They learn to use both the text and their background knowledge in formulating responses. It is important for students to learn how to use specific thinking processes. This can be accomplished by teachers modeling their own thinking. Students who are usually more confident about the adequacy of their responses are more likely to be involved in instructional interactions.

Scenario.   A student teacher had identified a student who did not know how to answer most questions and therefore was very hesitant about answering in class. The student teacher began to work with him on an individual basis. She showed him how to find information explicitly stated in textbooks as well as how to make inferences from personal experience. The student teacher also used every opportunity to review location skills such as how to use a multilevel index.

The student learned to predict words that might be in the answer so that he could skim a page after he used the index. When it became obvious that answering inference questions was a problem, the master teacher suggested working on inferences with the entire class. Both of the teachers felt that all of their students needed help in making inferences. They planned and presented a series of lessons that gave the teacher an opportunity to ask inference questions. The student who had gotten individual help was able to participate in these sessions on an equal basis. In fact, he had some advantages. At one point he said, "The answer's not there. You have to use your own experience to get the answer, but the author gives you a clue." Other students were able to learn from his comments. The lessons turned out to be a positive experience for the entire class.

Finding 7: Student questions give teachers information about comprehension, academic focus, and different levels of learning.

When students ask questions, they have opportunities to clarify misconceptions and to fill in details they have missed. Learning to ask productive questions that focus on academic concerns is a powerful learning tool. Researchers have identified teacher and student patterns that affect student questioning. For example, students in primary grade classrooms seldom ask questions related to the content to be learned. Also, the number of academic questions generated by students at any grade level is very small. When teachers encourage student questions, they are better able to assess student learning. They are also demonstrating that students should ask questions when they do not comprehend the information being presented.

Scenario.   A kindergarten teacher used her story time to help students learn to ask good questions. She showed students the cover from the picture book and read the title out loud. She then told her students to think about what they wanted to know about the story. She reminded them that the important things about a story are the people, where the story takes place, and problems that need to be solved. It was clear that she was using story grammar to give direction to this part of her instruction.

After reading the story, she reminded the students about their questions and asked them for answers. They were able to answer most of their own questions. At one point when they did not know the answer she returned to an illustration in the book. She held it out, waiting for them to examine it carefully. Everyone laughed when they realized that the answer was right there in the picture. When one child asked a question about a noise outside, the teacher reminded him that his question should be about the story. He was given another opportunity to focus his question on the story. The learning experience was enjoyable and profitable for the entire class.

Finding 8: A variety of techniques can be used to improve student participation and to manage response opportunity.

Participation in classroom interactions is motivating to students and has a positive effect on learning. Patterns of participation can be enhanced when teachers use a wide range of response options in reacting to student answers. Teachers can develop specific reacting behaviors and apply them in a deliberate manner. When teachers' reactions are appropriate, they are able to distribute response opportunities evenly, thus increasing student participation. Expanding the level of participation increases the potential for learning as students become active participants in the instructional process.

Scenario. Teachers can distribute response opportunity evenly in creative ways. A high school English teacher asks quick content-related questions as a form of roll call. She does this on days when she knows she will not have a chance to interact with students on an individual basis. She feels that her roll call questions give all of her pupils at least one chance to respond. A fifth grade teacher uses students to identify the next respondent. The teacher asks a question, then selects a student to answer. After the response, that student identifies another student to answer the next question. Other teachers use a deck of name cards to monitor the distribution of questions. After asking a question they pull a card from the deck and call on the student whose name is on the card. When the answer is given, the student's card is reinserted in the deck. These strategies have a gamelike element of suspense. When used as a change-up strategy, they can help to improve student participation.

Some teachers try to avoid rating or evaluating student answers, especially when they are asking higher level questions. They feel that rating answers limits thinking because students compete for praise instead of concentrating on the response. Techniques that have been used to avoid evaluating responses include indicating that the student who is answering still has the floor and should continue, redirecting the question to another student for completion or another opinion, and asking a question about the answer. Several of these techniques are obvious in the following series of teacher statements taken from an exchange in a high school social studies class:

> I'm looking for two things. (after an incomplete response)
> Joan, help him out. (when the student seemed to be floundering)
> That answer surprised me. I'll add it to our list.
> So, you're saying . . . ? (to encourage a student to make the main point)
> Now, contrast that with China.
> That's interesting. I wasn't prepared for that.
> Jan, I have a feeling that you are changing your position on this point.
> Why do you say that's wrong; what's your reasoning?
> So these two countries were real "buddies." In what ways?
> That's a new idea. Does it relate to any of the others? (after an answer that
>   seemed to be wrong or unrelated)
> I can see that Ben wants to talk about that. Let's hear another opinion.
> Hold on, think. Take a minute to think about Jan's answer before you start
>   attacking it.

Each of these reactions helped the teacher manage the discussion without rejecting student ideas or making some students feel that their answers were not as good as others. Students were encouraged to take time to think and expand on their responses. They were given an opportunity to explain their reasoning and to build on the ideas of others.

 ## GUIDE TO OBSERVATION, ANALYSIS, AND REFLECTION

Because questions are used extensively in instruction, there are many opportunities to observe how teachers incorporate questions. Make arrangements to observe a colleague's (or supervising teacher's) class when questions will be used. Visit briefly with the teacher prior to the observation to gain an understanding of the objectives of the lesson. While the overall focus of the observation is on questioning, to simplify you may need to attend to selected aspects of the questioning process. Try to do several focused observations. Analysis of your observation records can be done independently but is enhanced when the teacher participates. As you reflect on your observations and analyses of the questioning sessions, identify the ways questions can be used most productively.

1. Teacher questions

Observation: *What questions does the teacher ask during the lesson?* Write down the questions asked by the teacher. This may be difficult when lessons are moving at a fast pace, but record the questions as completely as possible.

Analysis: *How appropriate were the questions in promoting student learning?* Examine the questions to determine if they are directly related to the learning objectives. Look for questions that focus, extend, or assess student comprehension. Also, compare the number of content-related questions and the number of procedural or nonacademic questions. You may be able to identify several key questions or analyze the sequencing of the questions.

Identify strong points about the delivery of the questions, such as:

- Clear and concise phrasing
- Avoiding the use of yes-no questions
- Not using fill-in-the-blank questions
- Maintaining conversational tone

Examine the ways questioning promoted student learning. Suggest any possible improvements.

Reflection: *How can I productively employ questions to promote student learning?* Think about the ways questions can be used most effectively to help students achieve learning objectives and maintain an eager attitude toward learning. Synthesize what you have learned about the planning, delivery, and management of questions that you will incorporate in your own teaching.

2. Wait time

Observation: How does the teacher use wait time?   Obtain a digital watch to record wait time. Be sure to record both wait time I (how many seconds the teacher waits after asking a question before allowing a student response) and wait time II (how many seconds the teacher waits to react to student responses).

Listen carefully to the first few words of the questions. Jot down those words, noting the time as the teacher completes the question. Now record the number of seconds the teacher waits before allowing a student response. For example,

- What is. . . . (1 sec.)
- How did the first. . . . (3 sec.)
- How do the two processes differ? (2 sec.)
- Imagine if you were. . . , what would be. . . . (3 sec.)

It is not critical that you record each instance of wait time. You are attempting to document a representative sample. For the second part of the task, you need to record the number of seconds that elapse between student responses and teacher comments.

Analysis: Did the use of wait time facilitate student thinking?   Enlist the teacher's help in determining the relationship between the length of wait time and the level of processing required by the questions. The teacher can more readily distinguish lower level (recall) questions from the more complex questions. Use your observation notes to decide if the amount of wait time, both I and II, was adequate to promote student thinking.

Reflection: How can I use wait time to facilitate student thinking?   In attempting to raise the quality and quantity of student responses, devise ways to extend your use of wait time before and after more complex questions and after student responses.

3. Directing students to respond

Observation: How do teachers direct the students to respond to questions?   Record the ways teachers allow students to respond. Note what the teacher says to cue the students to respond as a group (choral responses). Also record cues that communicate expected think time. Make notes in the form of rules that seem to guide the way the class operates, such as:

- Students must be recognized by the teacher before responding.
- Called out answers are accepted.
- Students are encouraged to take risks and venture guesses.

Analysis: *How was student participation encouraged and controlled by the teacher?* Review your notes to identify the patterns of student participation. Tallies of choral, volunteer, and nonvolunteer responses will indicate the dominant ways students responded. Decide which cues that signal expected responding behavior are effective in encouraging student participation.

Reflection: *How will I control and encourage student participation in questioning?* Identify the techniques used by other teachers that you may want to use to cue student responses. Describe the ways you will manage student participation and how you can encourage more students to participate.

4. Student response

Observation: *How do students respond to questions?* Obtain a seating chart prior to the observation or draw a rough classroom diagram and identify students as they are recognized. As individual students respond, place a checkmark in the student's space. For most student responses you can also identify correct responses with a plus ($+$) and incorrect responses with a minus ($-$). Additional notes could include student hesitations, questions asked, tallies of choral responses, and instances of no response.

Analysis: *Were most students actively and successfully engaged in the lesson?* Analyze your observation chart to determine the distribution of response opportunities. Make a decision about how actively engaged individual students were in processing the questions. The chart may also provide information about the level of difficulty of the questions. Determine the appropriateness of the questions based on the pattern of correct versus incorrect answers.

Reflection: *How can I ensure that students will be actively and successfully engaged in the questioning process?* Think about the elements you will need to consider in providing opportunities for all students to be involved in questioning activities. Use your knowledge of the characteristics and needs of your students to determine the level of their engagement.

5. Teacher reaction

Observation: *How do teachers react to student answers?* Attend only to the statements and actions teachers take in reacting to student answers. It may be impossible to write the complete reaction but attempt to record key words or phrases. Or you may prefer to tally teacher reactions in the following categories:

- No visible reaction
- Nonverbal reaction
- Accepts answer
- Restates answer
- Expands answer
- Rates answer
- Probes with the same student
- Redirects to another student
- Other (describe)

Analysis: *How effective were teacher reactions in promoting student learning?* Use your notes or your tally to identify the most common reactions to student responses. Determine which reactions seem to facilitate student engagement and learning.

Reflection: *What reacting behaviors will I use to foster student engagement and learning?* Developing and adjusting a range of productive reacting behaviors is a challenge for teachers at any experience level. Think about the reactions that will be the most effective with your students, as a group or individually.

 DEVELOPMENT AND RENEWAL ACTIVITIES

1. Tape-record or videotape one of your own or one of your colleague's questioning sessions, or obtain a previously videotaped questioning session. While viewing the session, take notes on the number of questions that address each topic or step in the process being taught and the student success rate for each. Organizing your information in a chart like the one in Figure 10–7 will be helpful. Determine how many questions were addressed to each step or topic.

2. The focus of this activity is on teacher reactions to student responses. Use a videotaped classroom interaction or the tape recording from the previous activity (or

Step/Concept	Number of Questions Asked	Number of Correct Answers	Success Rate

FIGURE 10–7. Questioning chart

a new one) to identify and categorize the responses. Using the chart in Figure 10–8, classify each student response as correct, quick, and firm; correct but hesitant; partially correct; incorrect but careless; or incorrect, showing a lack of knowledge. Tally teacher reactions in each category and subcategory. When the teacher uses reactions not listed on the chart, briefly describe those behaviors.

Use the chart to summarize patterns of teacher reacting behavior.

3. The chart in Figure 10–9 depicts the questioning that occurred during a reading group. Maria began the action with a question (1?) to the teacher. The teacher then redirected Maria's question to the other students. The lesson proceeded

Answer	Teacher Reaction
Correct, quick, firm	Acknowledges response Asks new question Gives brief feedback No overt reaction Other
Correct but hesitant	Gives brief feedback Gives general praise Gives specific praise Asks new question No overt reaction Other
Partially correct	Confirms correct part Prompts Rephrases the question Gives the answer Redirects Other
Incorrect but careless	Says answer is incorrect Corrects answer, moves on Corrects, gives explanation Other
Incorrect, showing lack of knowledge	Rephrases the question Prompts Asks a simpler question Reteaches Explains why answer is incorrect Explains how to get right answer Provides steps to get answer Gives the answer Other

FIGURE 10–8. Teacher reaction chart

with questions about word identification and meaning vocabulary. Students read silently after question 11. The teacher then asked comprehension questions.

Use the key to follow the action. What patterns do you see? How do these patterns relate to the research on questioning?

4. Examine the sequence of questions reflected in the chart in Figure 10–10. Describe the patterns of interaction that occurred. Focus on student participation: when students responded, the sequence of responses, the correctness of responses, teacher reactions to incorrect or partially correct responses, student questions, and so on.

5. Use the sequence in Figure 10–4 to help you develop a questioning strategy for a specific lesson you plan to teach.

6. Using a textbook or other material, write several instructional objectives for the content to be learned. Use the general descriptions below to see if your objectives reflect the levels of thinking you desire. If necessary, rewrite your objectives to reflect all three levels of thinking.

- *Information or recall:* Students provide facts, feelings, or opinions based on past experiences or furnish information. Examples include identifying, naming, and defining.
- *Comprehension and analysis:* Students demonstrate their ability to process information. Examples include explaining, comparing, organizing, and making analogies.

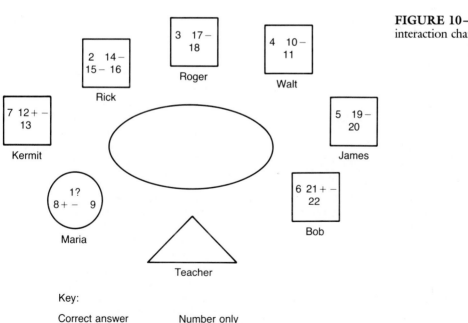

FIGURE 10–9. Activity interaction chart

Key:

Correct answer	Number only
Incorrect answer	Number with −
Partially correct answer	Number with + −
Student question	Number with ?

FIGURE 10–10. Activity interaction chart

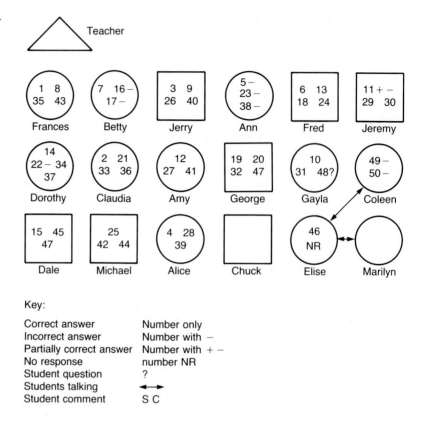

Key:

Correct answer	Number only
Incorrect answer	Number with −
Partially correct answer	Number with + −
No response	number NR
Student question	?
Students talking	◄──►
Student comment	S C

■ *Application:* Students use information or concepts in new ways. Examples include applying a principle, predicting, evaluating, and generalizing.

7. Write several questions for the objectives identified in question 5. Review your questions to eliminate any that are unrelated to objectives or are at an inappropriate level of thinking. Add questions where necessary. When you are satisfied with your questions, decide on a sequence to use during instruction. Add or rewrite questions as needed. The result should be a specific plan or questioning strategy designed to accomplish your instructional objectives. Teach the lesson following your planned strategy. Reflect on the lesson and identify any adjustments that could be made to improve future instruction.

11.
Adapting Instruction for Small Groups and Individuals

COMMENTARY

Teachers use a wide variety of task structures to help them meet the needs of their students. We have observed teachers using several different forms of small-group instruction. Although cooperative learning has become very popular in recent years, most teachers continue to use the small-group organizational structures that they have developed during their teaching careers. Both types of structure have a number of underlying principles in common.

Nearly all teachers use some form of independent or individualized instruction. Seatwork is used in virtually every elementary classroom. Students work independently while teachers instruct small groups, monitor independent work, tutor individual students, or attend to management tasks. Middle school and high school students are often engaged in some form of independent work. They work on assignments and homework during class as well as engage in silent reading and other forms of independent activity. Recently, more and more schools have computers available for different forms of individualized learning. The amount of time allocated to independent work varies with the expectations and routines established by teachers.

Other structures, such as learning centers, individual research projects, and peer tutoring are used to accomplish specific objectives and meet a wide range of student needs. The predominant task structure in the majority of classrooms, however, is whole-group direct instruction. There are a number of reasons for this. First, teachers are more familiar with whole-group instruction than they are with any other task structure. Much of the instruction they experienced as students in elementary and secondary education was some form of large-group direct instruction. This is also the most popular form of instruction in colleges and universities. It is not uncommon for students in preservice programs to attend lectures on alternative task structures without having the opportunity to gain experience in the alternative approaches.

Class size also influences teachers' preference for whole-class instruction. Although there has been some reduction in the size of many classes, most teachers still have more students than they can attend to on an individual basis. A considerable amount of research supports whole-group direct instruction as one of the most effective and efficient instructional modes. These research findings support those teachers who contend that they can be more effective if they spend the majority of their allocated time in large-group instruction. Teachers with large classes often feel that they have too many students to organize into alternative task structures. Yet this may be the most important reason for using small-group and individual task structures.

Different forms of accountability are another influence on teachers' choice of large-group instruction. Because of the recent emphasis on standardized testing, teachers know that they must cover the content that will be tested. It is much more efficient for most teachers to move their entire classes through the required curricula as a group. Very little time may be available to involve students in activities and experiences that focus on something other than specific knowledge acquisition. Some teachers have reported that when they use small groups to develop higher level thinking or cooperative problem-solving skills, they are suspected of not paying attention to the curriculum. In some cases, parents have complained that small-group work does not include enough direct instruction by the teachers and that the students are having too much fun instead of paying attention to their work.

The lack of adequate planning time is another major influence on decisions about task structure. Elementary teachers usually have very little time for instructional planning. Yet adapting instruction to meet the needs of small groups and individuals requires a considerable amount of planning. When teachers attempt to adapt instruction without being properly prepared, they are usually dissatisfied with the results and quickly return to the task structure they can use most comfortably. It is not surprising to find that many teachers assign independent seatwork in order to have the time to get caught up with their paper work and to plan future instruction. Unfortunately, students do not learn nearly as much from unsupervised seatwork as they do from carefully monitored independent learning.

Most teachers do adapt instruction to meet the needs of their students, but they are often limited by influences over which they have little control. The popularity of staff development programs that focus on successful procedures for adapting instruction attests to the interest teachers have in using instructional approaches that will meet the needs of all of their students.

RATIONALE

Teaching continues to be a complex and challenging profession. The amount of information teachers are expected to cover continues to increase at a rapid rate. This is one reason for the continued expansion of the school curriculum. At the same time, schools are under more and more pressure to prepare students for the world of work. The content demands of schooling are at an all time high.

Greater emphasis is being placed on educating all students. Mainstreaming has become an accepted practice in most schools. Schoolwide ability grouping and tracking are not always viewed as acceptable alternatives to having a general mix of students in all classrooms. Student needs in virtually all classrooms and schools are more diverse today. In some cases, personal needs must be given as much attention as learning needs. Although the personal and instructional expectations placed on teachers may seem overwhelming, strategies can be used to more effectively manage teaching and learning.

Certain preconditions are necessary before teachers can adapt instruction for small groups and individuals. Routines and procedures need to be established that provide structure and security for students and teachers. A basic instructional format should be established prior to using alternative task structures. This format is usually some form of total-class organization. Adaptations can then be made to meet the specific needs of small groups and individuals. One of the early leaders in a form of small-group instruction (known as team learning) advised teachers with whom he worked not to make instructional adaptations until they really knew their students well enough to make informed decisions. He suggested that the first six weeks of school should be used to develop the preconditions that would be the basis for alternative task structures.

Teachers should fully understand the principles and assumptions that underlie small-group and individual learning formats before making their own adaptive decisions. They should be well enough schooled in the different approaches so that they can implement them without losing valuable instructional time. Adaptations should be made to achieve specific learning goals and to give attention to the needs of all students. Strategies for carefully monitoring small-group and individual learning need to be carefully developed and implemented.

RESEARCH SYNTHESIS

The Concept of Adapting Instruction for Small Groups and Individuals

Alternative task structures are used to supplement and enhance whole-group instruction. These forms of adaptive instruction are intended to address the needs of learners both as small groups and as individuals (Walberg, 1985). The adaptations may be relatively minor and fairly easy to implement, as with tutoring or independent practice, or they may require major accommodations, as with computer-assisted instruction (CAI) and mastery learning which require special training and rethinking. No one instructional approach can effectively meet the learning needs of all students at all times.

Decisions about developing alternative task structures should be based on the teacher's background and experience, the amount of time needed, and the availability of equipment and materials. Another important consideration is the difficulty of making the adaptation. It is much easier to engage students in independent practice than it is to implement computer-assisted instruction. As adaptations are made, the amount of time available for whole-group instruction is diminished, so teachers should be aware of how they affect the larger instructional picture. Figure 11–1 shows the amount of resources needed for various instructional adaptations.

Adaptive instruction must be well planned, implemented, and monitored to achieve positive effects on student achievement and attitude toward learning. Adaptive approaches can be evaluated by assessing several critical areas. The amount of time spent on the content, the time used to manage transitions, and the effectiveness of routines should be evaluated and compared to the effectiveness of single-task structures.

Adaptive instruction must be high-quality instruction that is consistent with student learning needs. It must be relevant, worthwhile, and at the appropriate difficulty level. Instruction must provide adequate time and opportunity for students to practice and obtain feedback. Some means of holding students accountable for their learning should be incorporated into the instructional process. Because inattention to learning tasks has an adverse effect on student achievement, student involvement and progress must be regularly monitored. The effort, training, and resources required to maintain high-quality adaptive instruction must be taken into account.

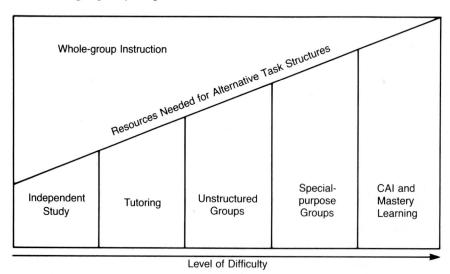

FIGURE 11–1. Effect of instructional adaptations on whole-group instruction and resources

According to Walberg (1985) adaptive instruction occurs in many forms, but effective instruction incorporates certain features. First, assessment determines student placement in the instruction. Materials and procedures are geared to students' needs and designed to allow students to progress at their own pace. Periodic evaluations provide information about student progress. Second, students are expected to assume a degree of responsibility for diagnosing their own needs, selecting learning goals, planning learning tasks, and evaluating progress. Third, alternative or supplemental activities for remediation are provided. And fourth, students not only work independently but are given opportunities to work with others in achieving their goals.

Small-group Instruction

Small-group instruction is not a specific and well-defined teaching method but a range of techniques for structuring learning relationships among students (Sharan & Sharan, 1976). Small-group instruction is designed to be supplementary and complementary to other instructional methods. It is used in a variety of organizational and instructional settings. The amount of instructional time devoted to small-group techniques and the type of small-group instruction used will vary according to the learning context, especially student and teacher characteristics. The cognitive and affective needs of students, the instructional sequence, the grade level, and the teachers' expectations all influence decisions about grouping practices.

Teachers must consider the advantages and disadvantages of heterogeneous or homogeneous grouping when they plan small-group activities. In addition, group work may have to be designed so that students can carry out the work independently because teacher assistance will not be available to all groups at once. Classroom management will be more complex if teachers engage in direct instruction with one group while monitoring the behavior of other students.

Ability Groups

The placement of students into groups with students of similar ability is a long-standing educational practice. When classes are heterogeneous with wide differences in ability, achievement, and language, teachers have found it difficult to provide suitable instruction for all of the students. Teachers often feel frustrated because they are unable to meet individual instructional and emotional needs. Students may be less cooperative and spend less time on task. In addition, unless special attention is devoted to meeting the needs of low-ability students, they may learn less in classes that have a wide range of academic ability (Evertson, Emmer, & Sanford, 1981; Hawley & Rosenholtz, 1984). Small-group instruction can be used to address these problems and serve the important purpose of reducing the variability among the learners (Thomas, 1987).

The ability range of classes is affected by schoolwide organizational practices. Ability grouping, or tracking, and mainstreaming of special education students are examples of these schoolwide practices. Class size is also an important factor because whole-group instruction is more difficult to manage when class size increases and opportunities for student input and teacher feedback diminish (Hawley & Rosen-holtz, 1984).

Teachers have found it effective to assess and group students by need before employing instructional strategies. Classroom grouping by student ability is commonly used in elementary schools but occurs less frequently in secondary classes (Doyle, 1986b). When small-group instruction has been well planned and implemented in a high-quality manner, it can be more effective than whole-group instruction (Stern & Shavelson, 1983; Brophy & Good, 1986; Karweit, 1983). Grouping students of similar ability helps teachers provide assignments that match student needs and helps them pace instruction more appropriately.

Small ability groups are productive when planning and management practices keep loss of instructional time to a minimum. Even so, instruction in these groups should be significantly superior to instruction that students would receive in the whole-group setting (Karweit, 1983). The quality of instruction students receive is what primarily affects student achievement in groups (Gamoran, 1987). In general with lower groups, the instructional pace is slower, materials involve less challenge and interest, and time allocated for instruction is less (Featherstone, 1987). Also, student achievement is negatively affected when time is lost during transitions and when groups are poorly structured. Furthermore, there is often a stigma attached to status of group membership which also negatively influences students' attitude and behavior (Good & Brophy, 1987).

group of all low ability ...

Instruction with small groups of students of similar ability can produce gains in student achievement and feelings of increased competence and motivation, but may limit students' opportunities for cooperative endeavors and for pursuing areas of interest on their own. Generally, ability grouping does not provide opportunities for students to work together as a team toward a mutual goal, to develop leadership and social skills, or to investigate relevant topics of personal interest. But if students are to develop appropriate academic and work-related behaviors, they must be given opportunities to engage in learning processes that support those behaviors. Some small-group instruction is structured specifically so that students can be more overtly engaged in the learning process by exercising decision making and a higher level of responsibility. They can study topics in depth and use higher levels of cognitive processing. Students often become caught up in the learning experiences and enjoy the interaction.

Short-term groups, designed to address skill or knowledge deficiencies, are often recommended in place of ability groups. These groups can be very productive. Students are not labeled by ability because groups are disbanded when objectives are achieved. It is important for teachers to review and adjust groups often to reflect the changing achievement levels (Ward, 1987). Planning for short-term groups is time-consuming, especially when group composition changes and new objectives are established. One productive method of meeting diverse needs is the Joplin plan, which groups students across grade levels (Slavin, 1987b). With the Joplin plan, students stay in one class most of the time but are grouped for specific subjects. Assessment and regrouping occur frequently.

Cooperative Learning Groups

Cooperative learning is not totally new but has recently become a popular instructional approach. Research support is mounting for students working together in heterogeneous cooperative learning groups toward a common goal. Students working collectively can accomplish more than students working alone (Slavin, 1987a). Students in these groups cooperate to practice and learn new material or to complete what could have been independent seatwork. Students understand that they are not only responsible for their own learning but also for the learning of their team members. Cooperative learning approaches are usually used to supplement other instructional practices. In spite of the renewed interest, Johnson, Johnson, and Holubec (1990) reported that small-group learning methods are used only 7 to 20% of the time.

Cooperative learning approaches include those developed by Robert Slavin and his colleagues at Johns Hopkins (STAD, TGT, Jigsaw II, TAI, CIRC), by Roger and David Johnson (Learning Together), and by Spencer Kagan (Co-op Co-op). The key features of these approaches are presented in Figure 11–2. According to Johnson, Johnson, and Holubec (1990), cooperative learning occurs in many forms, but the following elements are common to all approaches:

1. Positive goal interdependence
2. Face-to-face interaction among students
3. Individual accountability for mastering assigned information
4. Use of interpersonal and small-group skills

In addition, intergroup competition is used in some cooperative learning approaches and is more effective than students competing as individuals (Gage, 1986).

Researchers have examined cooperative learning in various settings (urban, suburban, rural), countries, and subject areas, at various grade levels (mainly 2 through 12), and with various objectives (lower and higher level) and student characteristics (achievement level, sex, handicap condition, ethnic background) (Slavin, 1987b). Cooperative learning has led to positive gains in achieving social and academic goals. In addition, cooperative learning helps to increase intrinsic motivation. Students enjoy the feeling of belonging and affiliation that arises in team situations (Glasser, 1986). Students also show increased positive peer contact, interpersonal attraction, acceptance, and self-esteem. The social and interpersonal skills students learn can benefit them later in adult life. This may be especially true for those students who are extremely withdrawn and isolated (Lew, Mesch, Johnson, & Johnson, 1986).

Academic gains made through cooperative learning approaches include increased achievement, deeper understanding, and retention of information. Students gain from the increased rehearsal (e.g., asking, explaining, showing) and the opportunity to practice and get corrective feedback in language that students understand and that is geared to their needs. All students may benefit from cooperative learning. Slavin (1987b) reported academic benefits for low-, average-, and high-ability students. He noted that some studies showed slightly greater gains for lows and highs.

Approach	Features
STAD Student Team Achievement Divisions (Slavin)	Structured approach Used when learning specific skills or objective information Phases are teach, team study, test, and team recognition Procedures provided for determining base scores, improvement points, and achievement awards
TGT Teams, Games, and Tournaments (Slavin)	Similar to STAD with test phase replaced by a tournament Equalization of ability occurs through bumping
Jigsaw II (Slavin)	Appropriate when learning narrative material and concepts Phases are reading with teammates, expert group discussion, team member reports, test, and team recognition All students read entire selection with each student becoming an expert on at least one subtopic Easily applied to material divided into four or five topics
Jigsaw (Aronson)	Same purpose and format as Jigsaw II but students read only one part of the material
CIRC Cooperative Integrated Reading and Composition (Slavin)	Used with the reading series Phases include basal-related activities, direct instruction in reading comprehension, integrated language arts and writing Activities are cyclical, involving teacher presentation, team and independent practice, peer preassessment, and testing
Learning Together (Johnson & Johnson)	Used with any lesson at any grade level in any subject area Not tightly prescribed but structured to ensure use of positive social skills, goal interdependence, and individual accountability Specific roles may be assigned to group members Learning and social skill expectations communicated through implementation assignments
Co-Op Co-Op (Kagan)	Used when students explore topics of mutual interest Sequence of ten steps Can occur within one session or span several sessions Teams produce a final product to share with the entire class

FIGURE 11–2. Cooperative learning approaches

All students are encouraged to do their best and the better students serve as models, not as leaders or stars (Levin & Long, 1981). According to Kohn (1987b), "Children who learn cooperatively learn better, feel better about themselves, and get along better with each other" (p. 53).

Although each cooperative learning approach has unique features, all of the approaches rely on students' ability to work together productively and to learn from one another. Most teachers do not assume that students know how to encourage and help each other; they know that socials skills must be taught, reinforced, and monitored. Johnson et al. (1990) specifically advocated teaching social skills simultaneously with academic material. Skills such as giving direction, showing encouragement, asking for help, and paraphrasing can be taught explicitly. Students should know how to use each skill and why it is important. They should have opportunities to practice and receive feedback as students incorporate the skill into their repertoires. Johnson et al. (1990) suggested assigning specific roles such as direction giver, encourager, or runner to each student to facilitate the learning of skills. The process of developing social skills is enhanced when skills are observed by teachers or students and when students are asked to determine how they can function more effectively as a group.

Evaluation of student progress in cooperative task structures focuses on both cognitive gains as well as affective development. In cooperative structures all students have access to "good grades" (Slavin, 1987b). Standards of performance as well as procedures for recognizing and rewarding group effort are established prior to group activities (Hawley & Rosenholtz, 1984). All students must be held accountable for learning, thus avoiding having one or two students do the work for teammates. Cooperative groups should be structured so that all students have equal opportunity to contribute to group scores. Using self-assessment questionnaires is another productive approach in evaluating group functioning (Cohen, 1986). Because it is important for students to value the contributions of low-achieving teammates, scores can be based on improvement over past performance. Assessing social skills also provides opportunities for all students to contribute to a group score. Every student is capable of listening to others, getting the group on task, and giving praise.

Successful cooperative learning is well planned and structured. Structures vary from informal, temporary arrangements to formal, long-term formats. Formal groups usually stay together for an extended time and meet periodically, at designated times, to accomplish clearly defined learning objectives, while informal groups may work together for a short time on a specific learning task.

Some teachers find it difficult to use cooperative learning groups. The demands of organization and coordination as well as the patterns of interaction are different from those in traditional task structures (Sharan & Sharan, 1976). When students work together, teachers have to delegate some authority and responsibility to students. Class members are responsible for some management functions such as routine checking and managing paper work. Help comes from peers more than from the teacher, and there is more student-to-student interaction. Training students to work effectively in groups, establishing new rules and procedures, and planning for group work require additional time and effort (Hawley & Rosenholtz, 1984). Teachers must actively monitor progress to ensure that students stay on task.

Problem-solving Groups

Problem-solving groups can be established for the purpose of cooperation, discovery, inquiry, or critical thinking. The specific characteristics of these types of groups are shown in Figure 11–3. An example of a cooperative problem-solving group is several students working together to solve mathematical problems and discover mathematics concepts through exploratory activities. Direct instruction may be used to help students develop computation skills, learn general problem-solving strategies, or to introduce specific mathematics strategies. During this time students solve problems that are well structured. When this knowledge base has been established, students work in pairs or groups to solve more complicated problems or problems that are poorly structured or to identify real-world problems that could be solved using a particular strategy.

Students in problem-solving groups are encouraged to identify several ways to represent a problem. They may use manipulative materials, pictures, charts, graphs, or algorithms. Together they develop several plans for finding a solution, choose the most promising approach, and carry out the steps of their plan. Simon (1986) described the benefits of using problem-solving groups in math instruction:

> Two important benefits result from pair and group problem solving. First, students are exposed to diverse thinking and problem solving approaches. Second, they develop metacognitive skills—knowledge about their own cognitive processes and the ability to use them. Metacognition, which until recently received little attention in mathematics instruction, is knowledge about the use and limitations of particular information and strategies and the ability to monitor and evaluate their use. (p. 42)

Rosenbaum, Karla, Brown, & Burcalow (1989) suggested that pupils in small groups are more motivated and stay on task longer because of peer support and encouragement. Teachers who are aware of the positive effect of the group reward

| | Type of Group | | | |
Characteristics	Cooperative	Discovery	Inquiry	Critical Thinking
Peer interaction	+	+	+	+
Solve well-structured problems	+	−	−	−
Solve poorly structured problems	+	+	+	+
Exposure to many possible solution paths	+	+	+	+
Develop metacognitive knowledge	+	+	+	+
Explore, discover key concepts	+	+	+	+
Make group decisions	+	+	+/−	+/−

FIGURE 11–3. Characteristics of problem-solving groups

students for questioning and rethinking problem-solving strategies, for helping each other understand problems, and for supporting the achievement efforts of others.

Lapp, Flood, and Thorpe (1989) suggested that cooperative problem-solving groups be used in secondary science classes to encourage student involvement and accommodate student differences. Teachers may give each group a task that involves gathering information needed by the entire class. Teams work together to arrive at an answer to a problem, and each group shares its findings with the total class. Teachers often lead a summary or synthesis session after all reports are given.

Students can be organized into groups for the purpose of discovery learning. According to Murray (1989), "The premise of discovery learning is that the information students discover for themselves will be learned easier and remembered longer than information acquired in some other way" (p. 8). Implementing discovery learning in classrooms has not been easy. Corno and Snow (1986) suggested that teacher mediation may be required. Teachers must carefully plan a series of activities for, as Simon (1986) noted, "Left alone, students are not apt to make mathematical discoveries that took the best mathematicians in history thousands of years to discover" (p. 41). Teachers who use discovery groups must create a series of problems and experiences that offer students the opportunity to explore and discover key concepts. When this is done, discovery groups can be an effective instructional approach. Simon (1986) described the responsibilities of teachers who engage in discovery learning:

1. Identify and prioritize what needs to be learned
2. Distinguish between facts, procedures, and concepts
3. Organize concepts hierarchically
4. Divide what is to be learned into appropriate increments
5. Create or adapt activities that stimulate the development of the desired concept (p. 42)

Once students are involved in discovery tasks, it is important for teachers to ask questions that encourage reflection, provide subtasks when the original problem is too difficult, and evaluate student understanding regularly (Simon, 1986).

Inquiry groups are carefully structured to promote students' problem-solving abilities. The purpose of inquiry groups is to stimulate scientific thinking, develop problem-solving skills, and provide an occasion for students to learn to ask good questions. Inquiry is conducted in a systematic manner. During the first stage students are given a problem that illustrates a principle. The teacher may provide a demonstration. Wilen and McKenrick (1989) pointed out, "A problem is central to inquiry and it should represent something perplexing to the student. Without the need for a solution to a problem, an explanation for a phenomenon, or an answer to a question there is no reason for inquiry" (p. 51). The problem the teacher presents may be a discordant event that presents a puzzling situation. Students are taught to ask questions to verify the facts of the situation, establish relationships among variables, or identify ways variables affect each other. When students question the teacher, the teacher answers only yes or no. When students ask questions that cannot be answered in that way, the teacher asks them to rephrase the question. During the second stage, students gather and verify information. They formulate hypotheses, then conduct experiments to test them. When students are satisfied that they have solved the problem, they generate an explanation. In the final stage, teachers help students analyze their thinking. They may also help students develop more effective process and content skills at this time.

Groups can be structured to promote critical thinking. Problems in social science, literature, or health cannot be solved without using critical thinking. Newmann (1988) described social studies teachers who are committed to higher order thinking:

> They applaud students who ask the unconventional question, who dare to defend a dissenting point of view. They value students who generate their own solutions to problems in their own language—written and oral. In short, they characterize good thinkers as those who generate critical discourse as they cope with the challenges of empathy, abstraction, inference, and evaluation. (p. 10)

Teachers who want to promote opportunities for critical discourse often choose small groups so that more students can actively participate in dialogue. Working in small groups, students are encouraged to question the facts, concepts, and conclusions presented in their text or other sources. They are taught to ask questions that place the information in a new light and allow them to see it from a new perspective.

Dillon (1984) suggested using issue-oriented discussion groups. Students are expected to analyze and evaluate their own opinions and those of others. Johnson and Johnson (1988) stressed the importance of controversy in helping students understand their own logic, interpretations, and positions. Three important outcomes of using controversial topics are higher quality problem solving, enhanced creativity, and higher achievement (Johnson, 1980).

One interesting technique for using controversy involves students working in groups of four that are composed of two-person advocacy teams (Johnson & Johnson, 1988). Each team is given a position on a controversial topic to research, develop, and present to the two other students. Specific conflict management skills are highlighted and discussed. The members of the group are told that they must listen carefully so that they understand the facts and rationale behind the position taken by the opposing pair. After both sides of a topic have been fully explored, the advocacy teams are told to reverse perspectives, present the opposing argument, and incorporate any additional information that would support their new perspective. In the final step, all four students are asked to come to a consensus that can be supported by the facts. This technique increases the ability of students to view issues from different perspectives and to enlarge their own views to include opposing positions. Other benefits include greater student mastery of content, higher quality decisions and solutions, creative insights, more feelings of enjoyment, and emotional commitment to solving problems.

Discussion Groups

Gall and Gillett (1980) defined the discussion method as "a strategy for achieving instructional objectives that involves a group of persons, usually in the roles of moderator and participant, who communicate with each other using speaking, nonverbal, and listening processes" (p. 99). Students are encouraged to interact with very little teacher intervention. In discussion groups the focus is on high-level cognitive objectives instead of recall and recitation of subject matter. The important differences between recitation and discussion are summarized in Figure 11–4.

Dillon (1984) added three points to this definition of discussion: more than one point of view is expressed; different points of view are examined; and the intention is to develop knowledge, understanding, and judgment. Klinzing and Klinzing-Eurich (1988) described discussion as the purposeful, systematic exchange of facts, ideas, opinions, points of view, feelings, and beliefs.

Examination of these definitions yields three main characteristics of discussion. First, classroom discussion is a purposeful, planned instructional format. Teachers choose the discussion method to accomplish specific curriculum objectives. Although knowledge may be developed, attention is also given to affective objectives. Second, discussion is a social activity that involves an exchange of information or points of view among members of a group. Teachers may serve as moderators, but they do not dominate and control the communication pattern. Third, the main purpose of a discussion is to develop, enrich, or refine understanding. Discussions are not casual conversations, formal lectures, or opportunities to check on recall of previous learning. Hyman (1987) suggested that participants must be systematic and yet creative as they amend some points and offer new ideas.

There are compelling reasons for using the discussion method. When students leave school, they will spend a good deal of time in group settings. Pinnell (1984) emphasized the fact that the business of life is conducted through discussion. Social groups, businesses, families, and churches all negotiate decisions through discussion. Success outside of school depends partly on the ability to participate in formal and informal settings. Most job-related tasks are accomplished by several

	Recitation	Discussion
Purpose	Recall or review information Build an information base Achieve mastery of subject matter	Exchange ideas and points of view Development of knowledge Enrich and refine understanding Develop and change attitudes
Speaker	Teacher is predominant speaker	Students speak more than half of the time
Sequence of talk	Teacher question, student answer, teacher evaluation	Mixture of statements and questions by both teacher and student
Pace	Brief, fast exchanges	Fewer, longer exchanges
Evaluation	Teacher evaluates	Teacher and students agree or disagree Participants justify answers

FIGURE 11–4. A comparison of recitation and discussion

people working together. The modern work place requires employees to be capable of participating in shared intellectual functions and group decisions. For example, quality circles, used in many organizations, require skill in presenting ideas, backing them up with information, linking them to the ideas of others, turning the talk to a new topic, and persuading others (Pinnell, 1984). Students who leave school without the skills necessary to work effectively in groups will be at a disadvantage in numerous situations.

Interaction with group members can lead to the development of higher level cognitive skills in content area learning. Discussion facilitates critical analysis and changes in attitudes about issues (Klinzing & Klinzing-Eurich, 1988). Paul (1985b) called for programs that develop students with a strong sense of critical thinking, who are not routinely blinded by their own point of view, and who realize the necessity of putting their own assumptions and ideas to the test of the strongest objections that can be leveled against them. Critical thinking skills are more likely to be developed in group interactions than from working alone. Discussion provides students with the opportunity to analyze a variety of positions and to test the validity of their own positions against those of others.

Problem solving is another high-level cognitive skill that is fostered by discussion. Groups generate higher quality solutions and are more committed to carrying out the solutions (Simon, 1986). Viewing problems from the different perspectives in a group increases creative problem solving (Johnson & Johnson, 1988).

Gage and Berliner (1984) saw improving the ability to speak as one of the most important purposes of discussion. Students have an opportunity to practice speaking audibly, correctly, concisely, and logically. Discussion groups can also help students clarify and improve their ability to communicate effectively in written form through group editing and feedback sessions.

Discussion fosters and maintains a positive attitude toward instruction (Klinzing & Klinzing-Eurich, 1988). Students are stimulated by the process of talking and sharing knowledge with other students, which results in motivation to learn (Gall & Gillett, 1980). Students who work cooperatively are more positive about school, subject areas, and teachers (Johnson & Johnson, 1982). Furthermore, working together helps students make more realistic social judgments about other groups (Johnson, Johnson, & Maruyama, 1983).

Teachers may need to provide an outline or discussion guide when groups are not experienced in using the discussion method. Some teachers use the logical steps of thinking developed by John Dewey:

1. Define the problem.
2. Analyze the problem.
3. Suggest solutions.
4. Examine the advantages and disadvantages of the proposed solution.
5. Check the validity of the solution. (Sharan & Sharan, 1976)

Allotting a specific amount of time for discussion helps a group determine how well the discussion is developing. They can see how much time is available for each area to be covered (Gage & Berliner, 1984). However, teachers should be open to revising the time allotment when groups are working well but have not reached consensus. Rushing may cause students to shortcut important intellectual processes.

The physical arrangement of the classroom affects the success of the discussion. Discussants should sit so that all members of the group have eye contact with one another. Teachers should develop routines for moving quickly into discussion groups. Johnson et al. (1984) referred to these skills as "forming skills."

Learning to lead a discussion is difficult because students and teachers expect group leaders to use directive questioning and a didactic style (Dillon, 1984). They are accustomed to a recitation task structure where the teacher asks questions, students answer, and the teacher reacts to the response. When teachers begin a discussion with a question, students interpret this as a recitation and wait to be called on. They are so accustomed to the unique pattern of verbal interaction in school that they may be frustrated by any departure from this format. Beyer (1984) pointed out that the kinds of language activities that appear to promote thinking (asking questions of the instructor, clarifying, expanding, and evaluating each other's responses) are systematically excluded from classrooms by traditional teaching practices.

In large groups, a teacher usually serves in the role of moderator. When there are several small groups, students serve as moderators and the teacher oversees all groups. As moderators, teachers or students introduce the topic or assignment. Hyman (1980) suggested that moderating includes mentioning important aspects of the topic, relevant issues, and significant facts. Another role moderators have is keeping the discussion open by insisting on all participants' having equal rights to participate and to state an opinion. They use supportive silence to encourage participation. Moderators keep the discussion from bogging down due to confusion, repetitiveness, or irrelevance (Gage & Berliner, 1984). They may intervene when a digression takes too long, when pauses become uncomfortable, or when errors or serious fallacies go undetected. Intervening is a matter of judgment. Teachers learn when to act to prevent disorganization.

Sometimes students take very different positions. Effective moderators learn to get temporary agreement so that other points can be covered. Moderators also analyze points of view. They may clarify, identify points of agreement and disagreement, or call for reasoning (Gage & Berliner, 1984).

Teachers analyze and evaluate discussion sessions. They may provide feedback to individual students or to the group about their contributions (Prawat, 1989). Criteria for evaluation include the logic used, correctness of facts, relevance to the topic, and points, issues, and definitions covered. Teachers may also evaluate the way students use discussion skills they have been taught as they interact with other members of the group.

Students must have a conscious understanding of their role in discussions. Much of the responsibility for effective discussion belongs to the students. Teachers can set up the opportunity for discussion, but students must work to reshape their own knowledge through interaction with other group members. When students do not assume this responsibility, teachers should remind them that they are not fulfilling their role. Gage and Berliner (1984) listed the following student responsibilities:

1. Propose their own solutions to a problem
2. Elaborate and defend against attack
3. Relate solutions to other ideas and modify them when necessary
4. Allow fellow students to evaluate their comments
5. Evaluate the comments of others
6. Ask for clarification of a point
7. Engage in cross-questioning when necessary

Students who have not been trained to do so seldom talk to each other, acknowledge the ideas of others, or ask for clarification (Gall & Gillett, 1980). Teachers can teach these discussion skills. These are usually introduced prior to a group meeting and are practiced during each discussion. Studies have shown that students who have had this kind of training use the discussion process more effectively as a learning and problem-solving tool than do untrained students (Gage & Berliner, 1984).

Individualized Instruction

During individualized instruction students generally work independently on learning tasks. In some cases all students attend to the same learning objectives, use the same materials, demonstrate mastery in the same way, but they progress at their own rate. In other individualized approaches all students address the same learning objectives but use different materials and have different criteria for success. The instructional tasks may or may not be individualized for particular students (Gage & Berliner, 1984). There are also some highly individualized approaches that allow students to select personally relevant learning objectives and use various strategies to achieve the objectives.

Current adaptive approaches have evolved from earlier, less effective attempts at individualizing instruction. The Adaptive Learning Environments Model (ALEM) and Team-Assisted Individualization (TAI) are two recent adaptive instructional methods that have produced positive achievement gains. ALEM is a highly structured, complex approach intended to assist students with special learning problems in the regular classroom. The approach was designed to avoid some of the problems associated with earlier individualized methods (Good & Brophy, 1987). It combines high-quality whole-group instruction, specific instructional interventions, and opportunities for independent inquiry and peer cooperation. Research in ALEM classrooms has yielded some promising results. Students exhibit a high rate of time on task and have many interactions with teachers rather than just with materials (Wang, Gennari, & Waxman, 1985).

TAI is an adaptive approach for teaching math in grades 3 through 6. It was developed by Robert Slavin (1985) and his colleagues at Johns Hopkins. TAI combines direct instruction by the teacher, practice with programmed materials, and team study in cooperative learning groups. Instruction by the teacher is to small groups of students who are at the same point in the curriculum. The focus is on understanding mathematical concepts. Computational practice to apply the concepts occurs independently. Students receive the needed practice based on preassessment measures that determine a student's point of entry. Students work on specific materials including instruction sheets, practice sheets, formative and summative tests, and answer sheets. Cooperative study occurs in teams of four students of mixed ability. Teams remain together for eight weeks. Within these groups, students work in pairs or triads in a prescribed fashion with teammates checking and scoring each other's work. The teacher is available to give remedial assistance. Teams are evaluated by the average number of units covered for the week plus additional points for perfect or near perfect papers.

TAI has outperformed other individual approaches and has shown significant positive learning gains (Slavin, 1985). Some problems, however, have been encountered in implementing TAI in classrooms where students have reading and behavior difficulties and are not prepared to handle the increased responsibility. Refinements are being made to ensure productive outcomes in all learning situations.

Mastery Learning

Mastery learning is a systematic instructional strategy based on the assumption that all students are capable of learning when appropriate conditions are provided (Bloom, 1981; Block, 1980). The mastery model ensures that most students will reach mastery level because learning time is flexible and each student receives targeted instruction, needed practice, and feedback. Mastery learning involves traditional group-based instruction and individualized remediation and enrichment. Instructional methods in mastery learning include well-defined and appropriately sequenced objectives, regular monitoring of student progress with structured assessments, immediate feedback about progress, criterion-referenced standards, and additional time and assistance to achieve mastery levels. Mastery learning approaches use a cyclical process involving teaching and testing. Pacing is a key component. Several important conditions distinguish mastery learning from individualized instruction, but the primary difference is pace. The pace is based on the group rather than the individual, which means that the group moves ahead together. Furthermore, the pace is determined by the teacher, as opposed to having students pace their own instruction. Mastery learning is a carefully planned strategy in which outcomes, instruction, and student characteristics are carefully aligned.

Several studies have reported positive outcomes with mastery approaches (Kulik, Kulik, & Bangert-Drowns, 1990). Achievement, retention, and amount of material covered is increased. Positive effects, however, do not appear to be uniform. They are generally larger at the elementary and junior high level than at the high school level. Positive outcomes occur in all subject areas, but larger effects have been found in language arts and social studies than in science and math (Guskey & Gates, 1986). Mastery learning also appears to work well for lower functioning students (Kulik, Kulik, & Bangert-Drowns, 1990). In addition, learning efficiency improves (Block, 1980). Individual learning rates improve, and differences between the slowest students and the fastest students decrease (Guskey & Gates, 1986). The learning time is shortened because the instruction is geared to student needs, increasing motivation. Students are more eager to learn because they feel confident of their ability to learn. (Block, 1980). Slower students may require more time early in the instructional sequence, but they will require less time later on. Positive affective gains have also been reported (Block, 1980; Guskey & Gates, 1986). Students enjoy learning more, and teachers enjoy teaching more and feel more responsibility for student learning.

Although mastery learning has been widely used, research results have been questioned and certain drawbacks noted. According to Good and Brophy (1987), reported outcomes of mastery learning are somewhat contradictory and misleading. While achievement levels in mastery classes may be higher than in traditional classes, the learning of higher achieving students may be suppressed. Although mastery learning is intended to be used with large groups of students and in a fixed time frame, time constraints can be a major problem. Finding time for correctives for slower learners while arranging enrichment activities for faster learners is a problem for many teachers. The gains can be offset by the time required for planning and management tasks. It is argued that given increased time and enhanced instruction, most students could progress cognitively and affectively in traditionally taught classes. Problems in implementing mastery learning are compounded when students are absent or transient, when the teacher-student ratio is too high, or when there are few materials. Also students with severe learning problems and major misunderstandings may require more remediation than time allows (Good & Brophy, 1987).

Tutoring

Tutoring is an individualized approach designed to provide remedial or supplementary instruction to one student or to a small group of students. The tutor may be the regular teacher, another teacher or teaching assistant, a same-age or older student, a parent or guardian, or a volunteer. Technically, a computer could be considered to be a tutor. Tutoring is applicable with all age groups and ability levels.

Tutoring has proven to be beneficial to both the learners and the tutors. For the learners, the additional assistance allows success and progress, which results in academic gains as well as improved self-esteem and positive attitudes (Medway, 1987; Gage & Berliner, 1984). For the tutors the benefits are mainly affective, including positive feelings about the experience and improved self-concept. When older students tutor younger ones, reading improvement is an additional payoff for the tutor (Medway, 1987).

Tutoring is not difficult to implement but does require appropriate structuring. A positive atmosphere and respectful interpersonal relationships are essential conditions for successful tutoring. The focus should not be on "fixing" someone else but on working together in the learning process. Tutors, especially student tutors, need to be encouraging and supportive with their partners. Also, it is probably unwise to match close friends or students who do not have a congenial relationship. All students should have the opportunity to be tutors. Although low-achieving students may need more preparation, they can benefit significantly from the experience. The interactions should be enjoyable and directly related to student needs. One advantage with student tutors is that the feedback is in language that is easy for students to understand. Many times tutors have previously experienced similar problems and can use appropriate examples and explanations. Instruction should be prescribed based on preassessment so that misconceptions and errors can be correctly addressed through additional practice. Alternative learning materials can be used. Evaluation should be based on individual improvement or measured against a preset standard.

Reading Recovery is an effective intervention program for early readers who are at risk of falling behind their cohort group (Pinnell, 1990). The program is a specifically designed set of interventions that enable low achievers to make accelerated and continuous progress. One key feature is intensive tutoring for 30 minutes each day with a highly trained tutor. The attempt is to strengthen strategies students possess so that students learn to monitor and self-correct their own reading. The ultimate goal is independence and withdrawal from tutoring. This intervention has been proven to have immediate and long-term effects.

Computer-assisted Instruction

Many educators predicted that the availability of microcomputers would cause wholesale changes in instruction. They expected microcomputers to radically alter classroom organization. They believed that computers and individualized instruction could replace teachers and group instruction. Several factors have worked together to lessen the impact of computers. The social organization of schools, traditional practices, and the way each change influences all aspects of classrooms have dampened the immediate impact of computers (Mehan, 1985). Still, microcomputers are in the schools and are having an impact on teaching and learning.

Researchers have identified some positive effects of computer use on achievement, motivation, and social interaction. Kulik and Kulik's (1983) analysis of computer-assisted instruction (CAI) showed that student test scores were raised from the 50th percentile to the 63rd percentile and students took less time to learn when using computers. Good and Brophy (1987) suggested that learning time is reduced because the machines can be programmed to expose students only to material they have not learned, eliminating the need to practice skills already mastered. Moreover, computers provide opportunities for students to respond actively and receive feedback, both of which have been shown to have a positive influence on learning. Teachers have found that they have more time for small-group and individualized instruction when students are using software to accomplish basic skills and objectives (Slaughter, 1989).

Electronic learning can affect motivation. White (1983) noted the allure of technology and the interactive nature of computer-assisted instruction. Using CAI adds novelty, giving teachers opportunities to communicate information in unique ways; for example, CAI can be combined with videodiscs or other multimedia equipment. Kulik (1983) reported that student attitudes toward the subject being taught are slightly more favorable when teachers use CAI, but their attitudes toward computers are strikingly more positive.

CAI was originally designed as a form of individualized instruction, but economic considerations have led teachers to assign two or more students to one computer. Bracey (1987a) found that these groups completed more worksheets, were more goal oriented, and outperformed other students on factual and problem-solving questions. In addition, social relationships developed in the groups. Members of the dyads assisted each other and cooperated to complete assignments. These interactions facilitated learning. As students explained their work or asked for explanations, they restructured their own understanding, were exposed to differing perspectives, and tried to find ways to resolve conflicting viewpoints (Mehan, 1985). The role of the teacher also changed. Hawkins and Sheingold (1986) found that teachers and students developed a collaborative system. Teachers used less direct instruction, spending more time demonstrating software, managing physical and social demands while students worked, monitoring or participating in computer games, and serving as resource persons.

Availability of technology does not guarantee improved learning. Computers that sit unused or that are used for purposes unrelated to curriculum goals do little to facilitate student learning. The key to student gains in CAI programs is a knowledgeable teacher who prepares and organizes a sequence of productive experiences that includes computer-assisted instruction. The limitations of CAI were summarized by Good and Brophy (1987). Access to computer instruction is limited because of the high cost of both hardware and software. After the novelty of the technology wears off, boredom may be a problem. Most of the learning modules take one to two hours to complete and address only one set of skills. As yet, systematically sequenced and integrated curriculum packages are not available for long-term instruction. Appropriate software is still hard to find, and when it is available, teachers are unclear about how to use it. Current use tends to be limited to drill and practice for remediation or enrichment. Balajthy (1988) found that computers are seldom used in most subject areas. Only 25% of third graders and 17% of eleventh graders used computers in language arts classes. Ten percent of mathematics students used computers, while only 5% used computers during science instruction.

When microcomputers first appeared in schools, they were used to keep records or grade tests. Gradually, computer literacy classes were added that stressed programming and computer operation. These classes treated the computer itself as an area of study. Programming was viewed as an essential job skill for the future and as an important aid in developing analytic and problem-solving skills. Snider (1986) noted that such classes are not the best way to use student time or resources. Improved software has made programming less essential as a job skill. Although learning programming is a form of problem solving, the skills do not transfer to other subjects. In spite of these findings, Balajthy concluded, "Most school use is for teaching programming, a surprise in light of today's almost universal disdain for teaching children to program" (p. 242).

Upchurch and Lochhead (1987) identified four ways computers can be used in classrooms: "(1) as teacher, (2) as object for programming and computer-literacy training, (3) as facilitator (e.g., word processing), and (4) as recreational device (for playing games)" (p. 159). Basically, computers can be used as an interactive instructor or as a tool to support classroom work (Hawkins & Sheingold, 1986).

Computers used in classroom instruction can serve as interactive teachers. Drill and practice, tutoring, and demonstrations are teaching tasks that can be accomplished by computers alone or in combination with other technology. Some schools have successfully used a combination of satellite dishes, computers with voice modulators, and TV monitors to teach students. This practice is often called distance learning and usually occurs when qualified teachers are not available for specialized language instruction or when a small number of students need advanced classes not available at their school.

The most common form of computer classroom instruction is drill and practice. This instructional approach provides practice almost like a workbook (Walker, 1986). Vargas (1986) found that the ability to give immediate feedback, set time limits, and repeat difficult problems made computers an ideal medium for providing drill and practice. Unlike instructional films or television, most computerized drill and practice programs keep students continually responding. Motivation may be improved in gamelike situations that provide an element of fun and allow students to compete against themselves. Since student effort is machine graded, students are able to evaluate their own progress. Hawkins and Sheingold (1986) reported that increasing speed and accuracy on previously developed skills enhances cognitive reasoning. Students who use a computer to learn basic skills to the point where they process them automatically can give more attention to solving higher level problems.

Computer tutorials are like a sophisticated textbook, since they provide information as well as questions and answers. A tutorial program focuses on new facts and skills instead of review. Basic objectives related to the content area are installed on computers. Students are pretested and enter the program at the appropriate level of difficulty. As students learn new content and respond to questions, the program assesses what students know and what they do not know and branches accordingly to new instructional segments to build new knowledge or to help correct errors. The system detects student errors, diagnoses, and corrects much like a teacher. Some interactive programs are supplemented with a database that students can use like an encyclopedia, with videotapes, or with laser discs designed to teach or reteach specific concepts (Slaughter, 1989). Neuwirth (1989) suggested that the use of intelligent tutoring systems is very promising despite the fact that the technology is not mature. Properly designed, these programs can provide information, challenge, evaluate, and remediate. Some teachers use a combination of software, TV monitors, and videodisc players to illustrate their classroom presentations. They can choose simulated experiments, laboratory exercises, or dramatic presentations whenever student answers indicate the need for another example, a demonstration, or an opportunity to apply their learning (West, 1990).

Computerized instruction can also take the form of simulations. According to Vargas (1986), "Simulations are computer imitations of processes" (p. 741). Designers of simulations try to provide environments that are as lifelike as possible. Simulation programs can be used instead of hands-on experiments. Science teachers use simulation programs as part of their study of genetics or to design molecules on the computer screen. Mathematics simulations are available for geometry, problem solving, charting, and graphing. Simulations support exploration of high-level concepts and foster cognitive engagement.

Problem-solving simulations present complex situations. The students must identify the problem, choose from a variety of possible solution paths and find a solution. There may be several equally valid answers. The computer's task is to pose a complex problem, provide a rich knowledge base, and involve students in finding a solution (Patterson & Smith, 1986). Problem-solving simulations encourage active exploration and discovery. Although these programs have been used in medicine, auto care, and accounting for some time, they have been used infrequently in schools.

One difficulty with using interactive computer software has been the lack of programs that teach more than a single concept. This situation is changing and schools have begun to purchase complex, integrated hardware and software systems commonly referred to as integrated instructional systems (IIS). Sherry (1990) described the general characteristics of IIS programs: (1) most of the instruction is done on a computer, (2) students work at individual computers or terminals, (3) the instruction includes a management system, (4) courseware spans several grades, (5) lessons are linked to a standard curriculum, and (6) revisions are available.

Computers can be used as tools to accomplish learning tasks. In the past students used typewriters, encyclopedias, and calculators as learning aids. Today, they also use the computer—for word processing, database management, and microcomputer-based laboratory probes, among other tasks.

Word processing systems have given many students more control over the writing process. Mehan (1985) found that "the screen editing and printing capabilities of microcomputer systems improved the production of students' text by subordinating the mechanical details of writing (such as producing neat script, spelling, and correcting errors) to the higher order goals of clear writing, fluency, and the flow of ideas" (p. 12).

Database management programs are like filing systems. Students use them to store and organize information on electronic note cards. They have access to commercial databases as well as those they create themselves. Database information can be used to generate and answer questions, to formulate and test hypotheses, and to evaluate the results of an inquiry. A database provides a medium for inquiry (Watson & Strudler, 1989). Some programs allow students to synchronize words, graphics, and video sequences. It is possible to create multimedia class reports by combining the computer and a videodisc.

When students have access to the vast amount of information available through databases and telecommunications, learning facts becomes less critical. It is more important for students to understand the structure of the information, so that it can be easily stored and located. Hawkins and Sheingold (1986) noted that "skills in finding, synthesizing, and interpreting information are likely to become centrally important in the educational process" (p. 47). When accompanied by effective teaching, database programs can help students analyze, interpret and synthesize information. Teachers are using this technology to support inquiry, as well as critical thinking.

Computers can be a supportive tool for problem solving or conducting experiments. Programs that allow students to enter information and display it in the form of charts or graphs can help them find alternate ways to represent and solve problems. Some science teachers conduct microcomputer-based lab projects. In these projects software and electronic probes are combined to collect data. Temperature, light, sound, and other variables can be recorded accurately by the computer over a long period of time. Young scientists are freed to concentrate on observation and analysis instead of tedious data collection (Holte, 1989).

Educators have begun to use technology more intelligently as an integral part of their instruction. Although technology is having a significant impact on instruction, it has not replaced teachers or traditional areas of the curriculum. On the role of the computer Davies and Shane (1986) concluded:

> It seems likely, as computers become even more sophisticated, and as they retrieve information even more efficiently, that there will be not a decreasing but an increasing need for reading, speaking, and writing skills. There also seems certain to be a need for expanded knowledge with respect to the content and application of the sciences. The computer and networks purvey information; they do not dispense the ability to understand or interpret this input. As a result of increased input the meaning of meaning needs to be emphasized. (p. 15)

Independent Study and Practice

Independent study projects are generally self-directed pursuits that allow students to explore academic areas of personal interest. Lawry (1987) proposed that projects be designed to relate closely to real-life, practical experiences. The aim of independent study is for students to acquire knowledge indirectly by successfully completing projects. Independent studies should be structured by specifying learning goals, tasks involved, resources needed, ways achievement would be demonstrated, and time frames. Interim checkpoints are needed for long-term projects. Teachers' involvement in planning and monitoring independent projects depends on the needs of their students.

Students in independent study projects often make use of learning centers. Learning centers are designated areas or stations that are designed to aid students in accomplishing various learning goals. Learning centers may include listening stations, materials for reading, equipment for experiments, and manipulatives for problem solving. Organization and structuring is critical to ensure maximum benefit. Additional timing and logistical decisions need to be made if several centers are used. Because students are expected to progress independently, or as a small group, the teacher needs to prepare students to take responsibility for their learning.

Independent study makes learning more personally relevant, develops student responsibility for learning, and provides opportunities for students to practice learning how to learn on their own. Learning centers provide opportunities for students to explore additional relevant aspects of the curriculum individually or collectively. Students are usually actively involved with little teacher supervision. This can increase student motivation and appropriate independent or cooperative action. When properly implemented, independent projects and the use of learning centers produce positive attitudes toward learning and address a broad range of student interests and abilities. Both approaches have a long history in educational practice with an up and down record of acceptance (Lawry, 1987; Gage & Berliner, 1984).

Independent practice provides opportunities for students to practice new skills and to increase speed and confidence. Independent practice usually occurs in the form of seatwork or homework. Because independent practice is generally unsupervised, the success rate should be high. Students should not attempt independent practice until teachers are confident that students have the prerequisite skills and knowledge (Sparks & Sparks, 1984). It is important that students do not practice errors or faulty processes. Because independent practice is a predominant activity structure, generally consuming 50 to 70% of class time (Steere, 1988; Gage & Berliner, 1984; Doyle & Carter, 1987), it is critical that it be appropriately planned, presented, and monitored.

Seatwork

An assignment given to students to be carried out without continuous teacher supervision is commonly called seatwork. Most often seatwork assignments for elementary students focus on reading and writing (Anderson, 1981). Many of the materials used are part of a basal reading or math program. Seatwork is a self-paced, passive activity in which students receive signals from materials and have little interaction with teachers. Students must depend on self-motivation to keep working. When several students are grouped for reading or math, seatwork assignments are used to keep the rest of the class occupied.

Seatwork does have some benefits for students. Student involvement in seatwork is positively correlated with achievement (Brophy & Evertson, 1976). Seatwork gives students the opportunity to practice, to try out new things they have been taught, and to repeat a task until they can do it effortlessly (Brophy & Good, 1986). Young children learn by doing, and seatwork provides repetition and practice. If the material is hierarchically organized and must be mastered to the point of overlearning, students should be able to do nearly all of the work correctly. This form of learning allows students to go on to higher level tasks.

The effectiveness of seatwork also depends on the appropriateness and interest value of the assignment. Students learn more from interesting practice at the right level. Engagement in seatwork tends to be low, waning in and out, with a "spurt" occurring at the five-minute warning (Doyle & Carter, 1987). Other factors to consider are students' willingness to persist and their reaction when they encounter a problem that they cannot do alone (Brophy & Good, 1986).

Anderson (1981) studied student perceptions of seatwork. She found that, for many students, the most important aspect of seatwork is simply "getting it done," not mastering skills or content. This attitude is more detrimental for low achievers than for high achievers. Low achievers more often face assignments that are too difficult for them. Nonetheless, they are expected to work independently and to finish in an allotted time. In order to finish on time, they find inappropriate ways to get their work done. Getting seatwork assignments that do not make sense or that are confusing is an unusual event for high achievers. When this does happen, they take actions to reduce the confusion.

Teachers can improve the way students view seatwork. They should make sure that tasks are clearly defined and communicated. Students need to know the work expectations, how to get help when they need it, and what to do when they finish

(Brophy & Good, 1986). Introductions to seatwork should address additional concerns such as why they are practicing a skill and how they will be able to use the skill in real-life situations (Roehler & Duffy, 1986).

Seatwork directions should stress content mastery. Comments indicating that students will be rewarded for finishing should be avoided (Anderson, 1981; Roehler & Duffy, 1986). Directions should include explanation, demonstration, and a check on student understanding. Assignments should be posted and, if appropriate, the steps involved should be listed (Steere, 1988). Once directions have been given, teachers should make sure that all students begin working. It may be helpful to start the first problem or item with the students. In addition, all students should begin their seatwork assignments before teachers start any small-group work. It is also important to use independent activities with flexible beginning and ending times as an adjunct to seatwork so students who finish early will not be idle (Cangelosi, 1988).

Gump (1982) suggested that teachers can improve motivation by designing seatwork tasks that students find useful, interesting, or fun. Ill-conceived seatwork assignments can lead to boredom. For high achievers, it may be helpful to emphasize the challenge. Providing challenge and variety can increase student involvement (Brophy & Putnam, 1979). Ensuring that seatwork is at the right level and has challenge and variety may require different assignments for different students. Seatwork tasks that are complex decrease engagement and are difficult for teachers to manage (Doyle, 1986b).

Students will be more productive if teachers monitor seatwork to discover their level of understanding and performance (Emmer & Evertson, 1981). Monitoring also increases student accountability (Cotton, 1988a). Student engagement rates during seatwork increase by about 10% when teachers actively circulate, ask questions, and give feedback. Substantive interaction is critical for maximum student learning (Doyle & Carter, 1987). Teacher contacts during seatwork should be short— 10 to 30 seconds (Steere, 1988). When longer contact is necessary with one student, others do not get the help they need. One suggested strategy is praise-prompt-leave (Sparks & Sparks, 1984). Teachers are encouraged to emphasize what is correct, be sure the student knows how to proceed, and then go on to another student. If there is a pattern of longer contacts, it probably means that the initial explanation was not clear, and teachers may need to stop and reteach (Rosenshine, 1983–84).

Homework

Homework is considered a form of independent practice. Homework requires that students spend time out of class practicing, reinforcing, or applying knowledge and skills as well as learning to study independently (Butler, 1987b). Homework gives students opportunities to build on what they have learned during instruction, to practice and to integrate. Homework should also help students learn how to learn (LaConte & Doyle, 1986). Homework is an integral element of the instructional process.

Relatively few research studies have focused on homework (Strother, 1984). There appears to be no strong consensus about the value of homework or specifically how it should be structured. Homework is intended to improve student achievement and promote positive attitudes toward learning. Although additional research is needed to determine the full impact of homework on student achievement, it is clear that under certain conditions homework is an effective and inexpensive way of extending learning opportunities. However, homework may be counterproductive when proper conditions are not met (Coulter, 1987).

Homework does offer several benefits. It gives teachers additional opportunities to monitor student progress and diagnose problems. Through homework, teachers can accommodate the differing learning rates of students. Slower students have additional learning time. Homework is a process that extends the school day, increases opportunities for academic engaged time, and allows for more content coverage. Homework can help students develop independence and self-discipline (Strother, 1984) since it increases responsibility and accountability (Butler, 1987b). Students who do homework improve their ability to concentrate, follow rules, and resist distractions. Through homework, teachers are able to communicate high expectations.

Cooper (1989) reported some negative student outcomes with homework, such as decreasing interest in the subject, time away from leisure activities, and parental interference. In addition, cheating or copying from others can occur. Homework appears to have variable effects. Higher ability students seem to benefit more from homework, but not if assignments are repetitive or routine. Lower ability students may profit more from supervised study rather than from independent work. Students with minimal home support may not have the same opportunities to do homework as other students (Coulter, 1987).

Homework appears to have greater benefits in some subjects than in others. Larger effects are found in reading and social studies than in other areas of the curriculum (Walberg, Paschal, & Weinstein, 1985). However, research on mathematics and science achievement also supports the positive effects of homework (Strother, 1984; Coulter, 1987). High school students benefit from homework more than junior high students, and elementary students make only minimal achievement gains (Cooper, 1989). Certain conditions must be present for homework to be productive (NREL, 1984; Butler, 1987b; Cangelosi, 1988). Teachers' homework-related behavior, which is how it is planned, presented, and monitored, is a strong predictor of student participation in homework (Coulter, 1987).

Homework assignments should relate closely to in-class work so students will see them as relevant and worthwhile. This can be accomplished by relating homework to testing and grading practices and using homework as the basis for in-class work. It is important for students to experience a success rate of close to one hundred percent on homework assignments. It is advisable to individualize homework as much as possible by matching assignments to student ability and maturity levels, although this may be burdensome to plan and manage. Homework can involve long-term projects that students have selected (LaConte & Doyle, 1986). Teachers may find it useful to develop a taxonomy of homework according to its purpose: practice, preparation, extension, or creativity (Jackson & Pruitt, 1983–84). Assignments could ask students to apply the information in a meaningful way, to supply and organize information for a subsequent lesson, to explore a topic further, or to create their own assignments.

Assignments should be simple since students are less likely to attempt complex assignments. Homework should be assigned on a regular basis, and not be seen as punishment. Teachers need to be realistic about the amount of time required to complete homework assignments. They should also communicate homework expectations to parents. Parents need to understand the purpose and importance of an assignment. They also should be responsible for providing a quiet, suitable place and scheduled time to do homework.

Homework assignments should be thoroughly understood by students (Butler, 1987b). The way the teacher communicates the assignment conveys its importance. If a homework assignment is written on the board or in a syllabus, it carries more significance than if it is given orally at the end of class. Teachers may have to help students budget their time to complete assignments and should be certain that students know the procedures to follow in doing homework assignments. Leinhardt and Greeno (1986) found that expert math teachers assign homework only after students have been successful on two in-class rehearsals, while novice teachers move rapidly from presentation to homework practice. Novice teachers also tend to use homework to finish incomplete lessons.

Monitoring homework is an important step in holding students accountable. When homework is collected and reviewed, and recognition is given for doing it, students are more likely to complete their homework assignments. Homework should be graded or checked quickly either by the teacher or by students. Feedback is essential so errors will not be repeated. Oral or written comments and scores give importance to homework. It is generally more effective to give feedback on correctness rather than on the effort to attempt the work. Feedback should emphasize progress and success. Definite policies about late or incomplete homework should be developed.

Homework has become a rather emotional issue primarily because the amount of homework required of students in this country is far less than the amount required of students in other countries. Although some critics charge that there is little payoff from homework (Barber, 1986) and that older students with jobs will not do it anyway, others contend that additional homework will at least take the place of watching more television (Hawley & Rosenholtz, 1984). In response to this issue, authorities on homework agree that schoolwide or districtwide guidelines should be established regarding the amount and type of homework (Butler, 1987b). The following general guidelines have been suggested:

- For primary students, homework should be voluntary or involve special interest projects or reading for pleasure.
- For intermediate students, homework should be assigned on a regular basis in reading and math but should not exceed one hour per night. Little or no homework should be given on weekends (only on a voluntary basis).
- For junior high students, homework should be regularly assigned but not necessarily nightly. Emphasis should be on math and reading. One hour per night is recommended with weekend homework being voluntary or for make-up.

■ For high school students, homework should be regularly assigned in all courses and should range from five to ten total hours per week. It is permissible to begin homework in class. Weekend homework should be limited to review, voluntary or make-up work. The length of the assignments should vary, but quality should be emphasized. (Butler, 1987b; Strother, 1984)

 PRIMARY REFERENCES

Alpert, B. R. (1987). Active, silent and controlled discussions: Explaining variations in classroom conversation. *Teaching and Teacher Education, 3,* 29–40.

Alpert examines whole-group discussions in high school classes in terms of the structural sequence, the content of teachers' questions, and the use of informal language. Success in using this instructional format is measured by comparing discussion to everyday conversation. Alpert identifies factors that cause students to express resistance, which leads to silence or reluctant participation.

Anderson, L. M. (1981). *Student responses to seatwork: Implications for the study of students' cognitive processing.* East Lansing, MI: Institute for Research on Teaching.

In this IRT publication, Anderson reports findings related to first grade students' cognitive processing during seatwork assignments. Implications for classroom practice are highlighted.

Block, J. H. (1980). Promoting excellence through mastery learning. *Theory into Practice, 19,* 66–74.

The article explores mastery learning and describes specific instructional practices used in Bloom and Block's mastery strategy.

Bloom, B. S. (1981). *All our children learning.* New York: Mc-Graw-Hill.

This special collection of papers written by Bloom is divided into four sections: significant research contributions and their influence on teaching and learning; relations between home and school and how this affects student academic success; developments in instruction and curriculum, specifically learning for mastery; and evaluation of student learning progress. A major concept presented is that teaching variables and processes can be altered to enhance the learning process.

Brandt, R. (Ed.). (1989–90). Cooperative learning. *Educational Leadership, 47*(4).

The primary focus for the entire issue is on cooperative learning. It includes articles from the developers of cooperative learning approaches (Slavin, Kagan, Roger and David Johnson) as well as testimonials from practitioners. It is an informative collection of articles for teachers and administrators interested in cooperative learning.

Dillon, J. T. (1984). Research on questioning and discussion. *Educational Leadership, 42*(3), 50–56.

This article summarizes the research on the use of questions in classroom discussions. Dillon distinguishes between recitations and discussions and offers suggestions for using the discussion method effectively.

Gall, M., & **Gillett, M.** (1980). The discussion method in classroom teaching. *Theory into Practice, 19,* 98–103.

This article describes the characteristics, purposes, and benefits of the discussion method and possible reasons for teachers' reluctance to use it. Ways to incorporate discussion in content area instruction are presented.

Hawkins, J., & **Sheingold, K.** (1986). The beginning of a story: Computers and the organization of learning in the classroom. In J. A. Culbertson & L. L. Cunningham (Eds.), *Microcomputers and education* (pp. 40–58). Chicago, IL: University of Chicago Press.

The authors examine the growing impact of microcomputers on learning in the classroom. Research findings related to programming and the use of computers as a tool are presented. The chapter concludes with a look at the long-term implications for instruction.

Hawley, W. D., & **Rosenholtz, S. J.** (1984). Good schools: What research says about improving student achievement. *Peabody Journal of Education, 61*(4), 15–52.

The chapter "Effective Teaching" reviews the research on general teaching processes that result in higher student achievement. Of particular interest is the discussion of small-group work (including cooperative groups), ability grouping, and individualized instruction.

Johnson, D. W., & **Johnson, R. T.** (1988). Critical thinking through structured controversy. *Educational Leadership, 45*(8), 58–64.

The Johnsons describe a discussion format that uses academic conflicts for instructional purposes. They provide a model for the use of controversy and provide a step-by-step process for involving students in using rational arguments to explore multiple perspectives on a controversial topic. The article offers a clear, concise explanation of a generic problem-solving strategy that can involve students in higher level reasoning.

Kulik, J. A. (1983). Synthesis of research on computer-based instruction. *Educational Leadership 41*(1), 19–21.

This study synthesizes evaluation studies on the impact of computer-based instruction on student learning. The author reports on how computers have influenced learning outcomes, academic attitudes, attitudes toward computers, and instructional time.

LaConte, R. T., & **Doyle, M. A.** (1986). *What research says to the teacher: Homework as a learning experience* (2nd ed.). Washington, DC: National Education Association.

> The authors emphasize that the research base on homework is limited and inconclusive but summarize what is known about the effects of different kinds of homework as well as future developments.

Wang, M. C., & **Lindvall, C. M.** (1984). Individual differences in school learning environments: Theory, research, and design. In E. W. Gordon (Ed.), *Review of research in education* (Vol. 11, pp. 161–225). Washington, DC: American Educational Research Association.

> In Chapter 5, Wang and Lindvall provide a comprehensive review of the research related to the challenges of adapting instruction to meet the needs of individual learners. Early attempts at individualizing instruction are discussed as well as more recent efforts. The focus is on designing and implementing effective adaptive practices in school settings.

Wang, M. C., & **Walberg, H. J.** (Eds.). (1985). *Adapting instruction to individual differences.* Berkeley, CA: McCutchan.

> The editors enlisted the help of respected researchers in the field to present a wide range of issues and topics related to individualized instruction. Several approaches to adaptive education are examined with an emphasis on recommendations for current practice.

 ## RESEARCH IN PRACTICE

Finding 1: Careful planning is necessary when instructional adaptations are made to address specific learning needs.

Adaptive instruction in the form of group and individualized task structures can enhance whole-group instruction. Specifically targeted learning interventions and activities can result in improved achievement and attitudes. To ensure that intended outcomes are achieved when teachers use multitask structures, numerous planning and management considerations must be given attention.

Scenario.   Several years ago a group of secondary interns were having their first teaching experience in a summer demonstration school. The school was affiliated with a major university training program. As a part of the program, guest speakers were brought in to discuss various instructional strategies. One of the presenters made a strong case for secondary teachers using small groups and decreasing the amount of time used for large-group direct instruction. The advantages of small-group work were stressed, but very little attention was given to planning and managing this type of task structure.

After hearing the presentation, one of the interns decided to reorganize his classroom immediately in the hope that he would be better able to meet the learning needs of his students. He changed the task structure without consulting his cooperating teacher or his university supervisor. During the first day in small groups, the intern gave an assignment and explained that he wanted the groups to do some reading and then discuss several questions that he posed. He expected that the groups would be able to engage in high-level discussions, and he would provide an opportunity for students to learn to work cooperatively. On the day the intern was trying the small-group structure for the first time, two nationally known educators visited the demonstration school. At the end of their visit they told the school director that they were impressed with what was happening in the school and especially with one of the classes where students seemed to be really involved in group work. They noted that there was a good bit of "learning noise" in this particular classroom.

The intern's account was somewhat different from the visiting experts'. He reported to his seminar group that he had lost complete control of the class, that the students did not stay on task, and that the small-group discussions were largely devoted to social activities that were most interesting to the students. From this experience, the intern and the seminar group learned how important it was to carefully plan when they made adaptations in their normal instructional modes. The intern teacher did use a small-group task structure on several occasions later in the summer session. Each time he used the structure he and the students became more successful in adapting to the instructional change and gaining the benefits from working in small groups.

Finding 2: Cooperative learning strategies can have a positive effect on important instructional goals.

In recent years, cooperative learning strategies have been developed, tested, and refined. The structure of cooperative learning approaches varies widely, but all are designed to promote positive goal interdependence among students. Students must work together to accomplish learning goals. A number of teachers who have been given in-depth training in cooperative learning have found that when cooperative learning is properly implemented there are academic and interpersonal benefits. Cooperative learning can be an effective instructional strategy and can be an excellent method for meeting cognitive and affective expectations.

Scenario.   A team of second grade teachers was concerned about how the students with learning disabilities were affected by being mainstreamed into the regular classrooms. The teachers had attended several staff development sessions that focused on cooperative learning. They decided that they needed to know more about cooperative learning strategies so they invited a local consultant to the school to provide them with further information and to give them an opportunity to engage in some in-depth discussions about the process. The meetings were successful and the teachers felt that they had learned enough to move ahead with their planning. Their primary goal was to provide a mechanism for socializing the mainstreamed students who were not being accepted by other students in the classroom.

After carefully planning when they would use cooperative learning and making certain that the strategies would enhance the socialization process, the teachers implemented the process. They all agreed to monitor the groups carefully and to be ready to make any corrections and adjustments that might be needed. The results were very gratifying to the teachers, and they concluded that their students had benefited from the alternative task structure. Students working in the groups provided assistance to one another while attending to their academic work. For the most part, students with learning disabilities were accepted as part of their groups and engaged in problem-solving activities. Their ideas were accepted and their interaction with peers was positive. Perhaps the most important effect was that the special students were accepted by other students both in and out of the classroom.

Finding 3: Small groups can be organized to attend to specific instructional purposes.

Teachers plan small groups to accomplish learning objectives that call for interaction among students. Problem solving, discovery learning, inquiry, and critical thinking are fostered by using small groups. Group members profit from exposure to a variety of ideas and approaches. When problems or concepts are difficult, students in groups tend to persevere longer. Peer support and encouragement help students stay on task. In discovery and inquiry groups, students create subtasks, share the work of gathering information, and trigger creative thinking in other members of the group. Students in critical thinking groups view an issue or problem from many different perspectives. They have opportunities to explain and defend ideas, to examine the ideas of others, and to use logic as they enlarge or alter their own thinking.

Scenario.   A high school teacher had a challenging situation in her advance placement history class. During instruction she liked to present a historical event, examine the causes and effects, and then contrast and compare that event with events in the modern world. A number of her brightest students seemed to view each issue the class discussed from an egocentric perspective. They read all assignments and searched the library for more information. All of these students were active participants in class discussions. The problem was that each student formed an almost unshakable opinion on each issue. During class discussions, they argued their own position and refused to consider the information or viewpoints presented by others.

One day it occurred to the teacher that her students viewed class discussion as mental combat. Using their intelligence, information, and communication skills, they were competing against one another. Many of the other students were intimidated during the interchanges. By the end of each class period, the teacher was faced with at least three polarized views of any issue. The teacher also realized that three of her students were members of the school's debate team. They knew how to research and argue a single point of view, using information and logic to persuade others.

The teacher made a major change in her instructional strategy when the class moved to the next unit. The students were organized into small study groups and were told to study a particular historical incident. Each group had to present a historically accurate view of the event assigned to them. The groups were cautioned about making value judgments or taking sides.

After the known facts had been established, groups were asked to list as many of the major players (individuals, political factions, and interest groups) as possible. Then each group was asked to describe how the major players viewed the historical event and give reasons for their points of view. The student debaters had no difficulty with this part of the assignment. In fact, they divided the task into subtasks and delegated responsibilities to other students.

When the results of this activity had been collated and presented, students were asked to identify with a particular historical person or party they had just studied. They were asked to organize their facts then make some inferences about the point of view their person or party would have based on this knowledge. Those students who had selected the same person or group met to develop a single presentation describing how that person viewed the event. This activity was difficult because two of the debaters were in the same group and had to work together to arrive at consensus. When the other two groups finished their work without difficulty, the teacher spent some time discussing the cause of the impasse in the third group.

As a culminating activity, students were assigned to new groups to consider application of what they had learned to the modern world. Each group was told to develop their ideas around a list of characters or groups. As the teacher observed the groups, she realized that the same students still tended to dominate the interaction. However, they were listening more, showing more interest in new ideas, and working in a more collaborative manner. Having to work in small groups was helping these students learn to accept the ideas of other students.

Finding 4: When discussions are properly structured and moderated, students can develop, enrich, and expand their knowledge.

Classroom discussion should be designed to accomplish specific instructional purposes. Students participate in an exchange of information or perspectives as they develop, enrich, or refine knowledge. In many cases teachers are not prepared to plan and lead discussions. They often confuse the discussion method with recitation. When teachers understand their role in structuring, limiting questions, and moderating, they find that discussions foster higher level learning, increase motivation, and improve social relationships. Students who learn to participate effectively in discussion groups develop important skills for participation in the work place and in a democratic society.

Scenario.   A middle school teacher was enrolled in a class on instructional research. When the role of discussion in student learning was reviewed, he chose this as the topic of his major paper. As he studied the topic, he shared the research with two other teachers in his teaching team. With their support, he decided to use small-group discussion during his next social studies unit. The team helped with the planning so that the experience could be integrated into other content areas. The university instructor was invited to observe the class at work.

The teacher planned to structure the discussion around the major theme of war. During the first discussion, students were asked to compile a list of the causes of wars and rank them in order from most to least influential. The teacher explained that decisions should be based on historical evidence. Students were reminded to be open-minded and sensitive to the arguments and reasoning of others in their groups.

The groups organized their desks in huddles so that they had good eye contact. There was an awkward silence once this was accomplished. Nobody seemed willing to start. The teacher walked to the front of the room and said, "You should try to be finished by 10:30 so that we can have small-group reports before the bell rings." This time one student got his group started by announcing that he would write down any influences the group offered. This seemed to break the ice and other groups decided who should act as recorder. Most of the groups were able to compile a list of influences without major difficulty.

The teacher walked around the room listening and making notes. The groups did not appear to make progress as he had expected. One group had difficulty deciding how to rank the influences in their list. The teacher approached this group and reminded them to provide support for their arguments using evidence from the past. One of the students got out a history book to find a section that discussed economic influences on the Civil War. Then others in the group got out their books to search for evidence to support their own positions. This took so much time that the groups were not ready to report at 10:30. Group reports were given and a class list of causes was compiled. The bell rang before there was time to decide on the ranking of influences in the composite list.

The teacher was not satisfied with the results of the discussion. He felt that the students had used textbook knowledge without real concern for the accuracy or coherence of their reasoning. He had been disappointed with the participation pattern in the groups. Some students spoke too often, some did not participate, and several interrupted others. None of the groups had ranked the causes in the order he had expected. He decided to start the next class by having the students evaluate their own discussions.

The following day the class talked about the way their groups had functioned. They identified the same problems the teacher had observed. This gave him an opportunity to talk about student roles in a discussion. One of the students said that she had not spoken out because she was afraid that others would find out how little she remembered about wars. Other students agreed that they felt the same way. The teacher realized that it is hard to reason logically without a knowledge base. He agreed with the students and suggested that he would give them some time to prepare for discussion groups. The next day students used class time to read about war. Students used history books, resource materials provided by the teacher, and books they had selected themselves. Group members compared notes and shared findings.

The second discussion was much more productive. Students were more willing to listen, there was a better participation pattern, and explanations were more thoughtful. One group still had difficulty deciding whether economic or patriotic influences were most important, but they were criticizing ideas instead of the people who presented them. One group moved beyond a discussion of past events when a student brought in an article from a news magazine that traced the beginnings of a conflict in the Middle East. The group used this to show that wars are caused today by some of the same economic and nationalistic influences that have caused earlier wars.

The teacher was pleased with the groups' progress and with the evidence that students were learning content from one another. Other members of the instructional team reported that the students were coming into their classes still talking about wars. The English teacher said that several students had chosen historical fiction as outside reading. When she looked at their choices, she realized that each book had a wartime setting.

Finding 5: Individualized instruction, in order to be effective, must be carefully planned, managed, and monitored and should provide for regular student and teacher interaction.

Individualized instruction serves several important purposes. With the range of diverse ability and interest levels in most classes, it is necessary for teachers to provide opportunities for students to explore areas that are personally relevant or to engage in practice that is targeted to individual needs. It is also important for teachers to provide experiences that promote the development of independent work behaviors. Students need to progress through learning tasks and become secure in their ability to succeed on their own. There are innumerable ways to adapt instruction to the needs of individual learners, but regular monitoring must occur if adaptations are to achieve the desired learning outcomes.

Scenario.   A fifth grade mathematics class was involved in piloting a new individualized program. The teacher was fortunate to have an aide who was helping her with the program. When the teacher and the aide began the program, they found that a significant amount of instructional time was being lost while students were attempting to get materials to begin their lessons. They also found that some of the students lost time waiting to have their work checked so they could move on to the next lesson. Because the class was not operating smoothly, too much time was being used for activities that did not involve substantive interactions.

The teacher and aide developed a plan to decrease the lost time and increase the amount of learning time. They began by carefully delineating their own management responsibilities. The aide would facilitate student use of materials so that the teacher would have more time to monitor student progress. The teacher began to move quickly to students who needed assistance and to help students assess their own progress. The teacher would alert the aide when she saw that a student was about to finish and needed new materials or when a student was ready to participate in small-group enrichment activities. Student movement in the classroom was kept to a minimum, and when students needed to move to group work, they did so in an efficient and effective manner. The teacher also developed cues for group alerting when she sensed there were common problems and she needed to give direct instruction to the entire class.

The teacher and aide believed that the key to success was the detailed planning that they had done to make sure they did not waste any time using this task structure. They had taken the time to instruct the students about classroom management expectations. It was not long before the students knew how the class was to progress and how to make sure that they were using their time well. The most important outcome was the success the students experienced in achieving the learning goals of the mathematics program.

Finding 6: Computers can be used as instructional tools to address a range of learning goals and objectives.

Computers are now an expected and accepted element of classroom instruction in many school settings, but many educators have been slow to accept them, and the availability of computers has been limited. Where computers have been fully and appropriately implemented, increased student achievement and favorable attitudes toward learning have resulted. Computers have created new instructional roles and have made it necessary for teachers to develop new technological skills. In addition, students have had to adjust to unfamiliar interaction patterns and become proficient at using computers to accomplish their learning tasks. Current educational thinking is positive about the potential of using computers in classrooms.

Scenario.   A high school remedial reading teacher decided that she needed to become computer literate. Although she is a midcareer teacher, she felt that it was important for her to have as many strategies as possible for individualizing instruction to meet the specific learning needs of her students. She enrolled in several computer workshops that helped her develop the computer skills and understandings she needed to function effectively with the computer equipment that was available to her.

When the teacher reached a point where she felt that she was making good progress using computers with her students, she invited her department chair to observe what she was doing and give her some constructive feedback. The teacher was using a tutorial program that gave her students opportunities for practice and reinforcement of basic grammar concepts. She was also using a program designed to develop keyboarding skills. During the preobservation conference with the department chair, the teacher shared printouts that indicated the individual performances of each student in the class. The tutorial program helped place each student at an appropriate point in the instructional sequence in order to achieve optimal success rates. The class had access to the computer lab 40 minutes per week.

During the observation the class functioned very well, even though several students from a different class were also using the lab. While the students were working with their tutorial programs, the teacher was able to spend her time working with individual students. She was able to help them with problems and reinforce their successes.

During the postobservation conference the teacher and the department chair agreed that the computer-assisted instruction was working very well. Individual student problems were easy to identify and correct, and the teacher was able to provide credible positive reinforcement. The teacher also felt that because the students had the opportunity to use the computers, their attitudes toward learning had improved.

Finding 7: Because so much time is devoted to seatwork and other forms of independent practice, teachers should take steps to ensure that the time is being used to promote and enhance student learning.

The most common form of independent practice is seatwork. During seatwork students can work at their own pace to extend or reinforce their learning. Unfortunately, many students involved in seatwork are unsupervised and very often are not actively engaged in learning activities. Seatwork, especially in the elementary grades, is often used to give teachers the opportunity to work with small groups of students. It is important for students to understand the value of seatwork assignments and how the assignments relate to the overall instructional goals.

Scenario.   A middle school science teacher was very creative in developing independent practice activities that went well beyond the typical seatwork assignments. He developed a series of learning stations that addressed the concepts that had been taught during direct instruction. Each learning station was devoted to the elaboration or extension of a key concept, and each was designed to accommodate several student learning styles. When the teacher worked with small groups of students, the balance of the class had several options. Students could review material in their textbooks and workbooks, they could go to the learning stations and work independently, they could work with a peer to review important concepts, or they could use a combination of the approaches.

The learning stations took a considerable amount of time and effort to develop, but it was not long before some students were able to help plan and organize the stations for the next science unit. Using learning stations gave class members an opportunity to enrich and deepen their scientific knowledge. Because they were tired of brief lectures followed by independent practice in the form of workbook or worksheet activities, learning stations significantly improved their attitude about the importance of learning scientific concepts. Both cognitive and affective gains were made by changing the approach to independent practice and by providing optional learning activities.

Finding 8: Under certain conditions, and when appropriate guidelines are followed, homework can be an effective instructional tool.

Both students and teachers should view homework as an important element in the ongoing instructional process. When homework is properly used, students are able to extend and reinforce learning activities that were initiated during instruction. Homework also provides teachers with additional diagnostic and assessment information. Homework yields the highest returns when teachers assess the work and give feedback in a timely manner.

Scenario. A high school mathematics teacher has carefully integrated homework assignments into her classroom instruction. She begins her classes each day by sharing with her students the answers for the homework assignments. She has the answers prepared on transparencies so they are available to students throughout the day. As students check their work, they identify which problems were difficult for them to solve. Once these problems have been identified, the teacher asks for volunteers to work on the problems and present their solutions to the entire class. The volunteers put the problems on transparencies and lead a discussion about the problem. The other students review their work and contribute to the discussion. This teacher has made homework an important element in her instructional plan.

A high school biology teacher uses a different approach to emphasize the importance of homework assignments. When his students come to class, they put their homework on their desks so the teacher can quickly review what they have done. The class assignment for the day is posted on the front chalkboard, so students can go to work while the teacher is monitoring the homework. The teacher takes less than 10 minutes to move through the class, check the assignments, and identify any problems students experienced with their homework. He begins each class with a discussion of the homework assignments in order to reinforce and clarify learning expectations. This teacher is facilitating student learning in the amount of time it takes some teachers to take roll and get class started.

GUIDE TO OBSERVATION, ANALYSIS, AND REFLECTION

Many factors influence teachers' decisions in adapting instruction to the collective and individual learning needs of students. In order to meet the diverse needs of students, numerous and varied task structures are incorporated to promote optimal learning for all students. The following activities are guided observations and analyses that focus on the preactive influences on teachers' decisions in adapting instruction and on the organization of small-group and individual task structures.

1. Adaptive instructional approaches

Observation: What approaches are used to adapt instruction to small groups of students or to individual students? The most productive observation would be one that is extended over several lessons in an instructional sequence. Prior to the observation try to find out from the teacher the specific content objectives and learner characteristics that influenced the teacher's instructional decisions. As you observe, describe the ways students are involved in learning tasks by identifying whole-group, small-group, pairs, tutoring, and independent activities. Focus on several students and record their actions. Note materials and equipment used, interactions with the teacher or other students, the level of on-task behavior or active engagement with the content, and the ways students are evaluated or their progress is monitored.

Analysis: How effective were attempts to adapt instruction to the needs of individual learners?   From your observation information, identify the ways instruction was adapted. Estimate the degree to which instruction is. adapted to individuals and groups. If students were involved in learning activities with peers, in small groups or triads or pairs, with supplementary materials or equipment, or with computers, assess how appropriate the instruction was for individual student needs. Indicators could be the level of task engagement, the amount of time spent gathering materials or gaining assistance, the level of interaction with other students or with the teacher, the students' success rate, and statements or actions that demonstrate a positive student response. It may be difficult to tell if the learners are progressing, but you should be able to make some determination of the level of difficulty or challenge and students' ability to deal with the task structure.

Reflection: What forms of adaptive instruction will you use to meet individual learning needs?   Identify the strategies you feel may be the most productive with your students (or potential students) and with specific areas of the content. Decide how you would incorporate the effective practices you observed. Suggest possible alterations in assessment, management, and monitoring to make the strategy more effective.

2. Group work

Observation: How is group work structured and implemented?   Contact a teacher who uses cooperative group work or team learning approaches and arrange an observation. Before the visit, find out what content objectives are being addressed as well as the social skill objectives. Discuss the students' prior experiences with group work and their responsibilities during the learning activities. Also discuss the teacher's methods of assessing and assigning students to groups. Find out if students have been given specific roles and if instructional materials have been structured for goal interdependence. Ask about the ways students are expected to work together and how their efforts are to be evaluated and rewarded.

During the classroom observation, draw a map noting the arrangement of groups and the placement of materials, equipment, and supplies. Focus on one group. Record student behaviors as the students work together.

Analysis: How effective was the group work in meeting students' needs?   Review your observation notes with the teacher. Based on your information, make an assessment of the degree to which the learning objectives were accomplished by the target group. Discuss the accuracy and adequacy of the group response or product. Consider the appropriateness of the task in relation to student needs. Pose possible adjustments in the assignment that might be appropriate. Think about the ways students were held accountable for the learning and for their participation. Consider possible adjustments.

Also assess the level and appropriateness of student interaction. Discuss specific student actions and statements that provide evidence of cooperative social skills. Think about the composition of the group. Would you make any changes in the assignments of those students? Also determine possible changes in structure and organization or instructional emphasis that would help the group function more productively.

Reflection: *How will I structure and implement group work in my classroom?* Reflect on the insights you gained from your observation and analysis activities as well as the discussion with the teacher. Before you implement cooperative learning in your classroom, identify the preliminary steps that would be necessary before you actually begin. It may be that you will need to read additional information, talk with teachers who use team learning, devise specific management routines, assign students to groups, arrange the room, develop instructional materials, and so on.

3. Interaction during discussion

Observation: *What interactions occurred during the discussion?* Identify teachers who use the discussion method and make arrangements to observe a class when a discussion is planned. Focus your attention on the sequence of interaction during the observation. Note the size of the group (whole class or small group). You will need to record teacher statements that structure the discussion. For example, record statements that give students information about forming into small groups, objectives or tasks to be accomplished, choosing a discussion topic, the scope of the discussion, time allocation, student roles (e.g., recorder, chairperson), and use of discussion skills.

When the discussion begins, focus on the sequence of the interaction. The following symbols may be helpful as you make notes:

T?	Teacher question
TS	Teacher statement
S?	Student question
SS	Student statement
XSS	Extended statement (two sentences or more)
TE	Evaluation statement by the teacher
SE	Evaluation statement by a student
OT	Off-topic statement or question

In addition to using the symbols try to include a few words that indicate the content of the statement or question.

Analysis: Did the interactions reflect a high-quality discussion?   Review your notes to compare this discussion with the characteristics of effective discussions. You might want to use the following categories and criteria to organize your information:

- *Classroom climate:* Discussion is open to all arguments, positions; students treat each other with respect; students encourage one another, listen well, and give others an opportunity to participate; the use of logic, evidence, and reason prevail; divergence of opinion is respected.
- *Structure:* Discussion has a clear topic and objectives; scope and limits of the discussion are known; time limits are flexible; physical arrangements accommodate discussion; students have specific roles.
- *Interaction pattern:* Teacher questions are limited; both statements and questions come from students and teacher; student-to-student interchanges are numerous; even participation is encouraged.
- *Students' roles:* Students are actively involved in giving information, asking for information or reasons, asking for clarification, evaluating information, proposing solutions, accepting feedback from others, reconciling disagreements, summarizing, and reaching consensus.

In summarizing your information, how was this discussion like a true discussion? How was it different? Was the discussion more like a recitation? In your opinion, did the differences affect the quality or outcomes of the discussion? What changes would you suggest? What evidence is there that students have been taught discussion skills? Which participants will need to change their behavior—the teacher, students, particular students?

Reflection: Is the discussion method congruent with my view of how students learn? If so, how can I establish the conditions necessary for discussion?   Think about the insights you have gained about using discussion in the classroom. Use the questions that follow to guide your reflection:

- What should influence the choice of discussion as an instructional method?
- What discussion skills should my students be taught?
- How can I sequence discussion tasks so that students learn skills *and* content?
- How will I organize the groups (e.g., whole class, heterogeneous small groups, homogeneous small groups)?
- How much structure should I provide? Will this change over time?
- How can I moderate discussions without using too many questions?
- What kinds of evaluation measures will the students and I use?

4. Independent practice

Observation: *How is independent practice used as a learning activity?*   The focus of the observation is on how independent practice is incorporated into the lesson. When the learning task is seatwork or homework, pay specific attention to how the task is introduced. Record as much of what the teacher says as possible. Describe the ways the teacher checks to see if the students understood the task. If homework is assigned, note when the instructions are given and if the assignment is written out, (by the teacher or by students, on the chalkboard, in the syllabus, or on a calendar). If seatwork is assigned, note if the students are able to proceed on their own and if they know how to get help when they need it and what to do when they have finished. Describe how the students are organized to do the work (independently, in pairs, in groups). Describe how the teacher gets the students started with the task and what the teacher does to monitor their progress. Also note evaluation measures or procedures.

Analysis: *How effective was the independent practice in promoting learning expectations?*   Determine if the assignment was clearly defined, communicated, and understood by the students. Assess how well the assignment was linked with previous or future learning and supported as relevant and beneficial. Suggest ways the assignment could have been presented more effectively. Identify the positive points about the way the independent practice was structured, monitored, evaluated, and used in current instruction. Identify any negative points and offer suggestions to make the independent practice more effective. If the students were not able to progress, think about the reasons and suggest alternative approaches.

Reflection: *How can I use independent practice to promote learning expectations?* Collect your thoughts after observing and analyzing to suggest general strategies for planning, presenting, and monitoring independent practice. Include the type of assignments that are most productive and interesting, the way they are structured, communicated, and evaluated, the way students are organized, methods for handling late or make-up work, the way students track their progress, and so on.

 DEVELOPMENT AND RENEWAL ACTIVITIES

1. Contact a teacher who uses cooperative learning or mastery learning strategies and arrange an observation at an appropriate time. After the observation, talk with the teacher. The discussion could include the following topics:

- Reasons for using cooperative learning or mastery learning
- Prior training experiences
- Preparation the students received
- Teacher's role and student's role
- Advantages or gains resulting from cooperative learning or mastery learning

- Disadvantages or negative results from the strategy (such as demands created by record keeping, classroom management, planning, material preparation, or assessment)

2. Observe students as they work on individualized assignments on the computer. Describe the type of assignment, the student's level of success, and any problem areas you observe. Talk with teachers about the use of computers and what they perceive to be the benefits and disadvantages of computer use.

3. Talk with other teachers at your grade level or prospective grade level. Find out what they perceive to be the benefits of homework assignments. Also, discuss the difficulties they experience with homework. Ask teachers to share their strategies for getting students to attempt and complete assignments.

4. Talk with several students in elementary or secondary school about their habits and feelings regarding homework. Find out:

- If they have a scheduled time and particular place to do their assignments
- If they have the television or radio on when they do their homework
- If they frequently need help and who they get help from
- If they do homework, why they do it and if not, why not
- What types of assignments are enjoyable and beneficial and what types are not

You can gain additional insights by reflecting on your own feelings about homework as a student. The information you obtain will be helpful in making homework productive independent practice.

5. Talk with teachers about their use of ability groups. Ask about their specific expectations for the different groups and their standards of performance. Talk about the criteria used to place the students in groups and when reassessments and regrouping occur. Also discuss the adjustments needed in instructional methods and materials.

6. Obtain a copy of the homework policy of your local district or school if it is available. Review the policy statements to determine if the following areas are adequately and appropriately addressed:

- Amount required per week
- Type of homework (practice, preparation, extension)
- Class time allocated to begin the assignment
- Consequences or incentives for completion
- Grading procedures (e.g., grades for trying or correctness, letter or number grades; teacher or student grading, percentage of total grade)
- Communication to students
- Communication to parents

If a homework policy has not been articulated, suggest possible guidelines for an actual or fictitious school or class. You might want to confer with several colleagues to discuss appropriate policy.

7. If you are teaching, review your seatwork or homework assignments for a recent unit of study. If you are not currently teaching but have planned a unit of instruction, examine the independent practice assignments. Categorize each assignment (or parts of the assignment) into the following groups:

- *Practice:* Applying the information in a meaningful way
- *Preparation:* Gathering and organizing information in preparation for a future lesson (to use as an advance organizer)
- *Extension:* Capitalizing on creativity or individual interests including using longer term projects or investigations of the student's design
- *Pleasure:* Generally voluntary and enjoyable activities

Decide if assignments are balanced appropriately among these categories. Suggest adjustments in the assignments so that each category is represented.

8. Talk with the appropriate person about how the students are tracked or grouped within the school (talk with the guidance counselor in a secondary school, with the principal or guidance counselor in an elementary school) and within the classroom (talk with the teacher). You may find a written statement regarding district or school policy. Try to determine the criteria used to place the students, when reviews about placements occur, when changes in placement occur, and who makes the final decision about the placement (teacher, parents, principal, guidance counselor, or student).

9. After reading extensively about cooperative learning or after attending workshop sessions or classes on using cooperative learning, plan to teach a unit, lesson, or series of lessons using cooperative learning strategies. Use the following checklist to reflect on your planning:

- Specific learning objectives have been identified. Both content objectives and process or social skill objectives have been specified.
- The cooperative learning strategy selected is appropriate in helping students achieve the learning objectives.
- Instructional materials have been developed and prepared.
- The classroom has been arranged for team activities (e.g., the arrangement of student desks facilitates moving into teams, bulletin board space is reserved for team recognition or record keeping, instructional materials are available in a specific place).
- Procedures for ranking students and assigning students into teams have been followed.
- Assessment procedures have been developed (e.g., individual student base scores, record-keeping forms, and expected standards of performance).
- If appropriate, student roles have been assigned and student responsibilities for distributing materials and record keeping have been determined.
- Ways to recognize team performance have been determined.

- Students have been prepared as appropriate to their needs (e.g., they have been instructed on the structure of cooperative learning and the importance of using positive social skills in accomplishing learning tasks, classroom rules have been developed for teamwork activities).
- Appropriate team-building activities have been planned to accustom students to working together and to emphasize the use of social skills.
- Problem-solving activities have been planned to occur after each cooperative learning activity. It is important for teachers to maintain a problem-solving attitude when trying to incorporate an unfamiliar instructional approach. It takes time for teachers and students to feel comfortable, and adjustments will be necessary.

12.
Moving to Higher Level Learning

COMMENTARY

Concerns have been expressed about the need for students to improve their standardized test scores. Teachers have been held accountable for improving test results, especially in the so-called basic skills. Local schools often publish their test scores, and comparisons are made about their relative effectiveness with other schools in the area. Some states have a statewide report card for schools based on the results of standardized tests. In recent years the U.S. Office of Education has highlighted the results of the National Assessment of Educational Progress (NAEP) as an indicator of school effectiveness. It is no wonder that many teachers have focused their efforts on improving test scores of their students. However, in many cases the tests focus on the ability of students to recall specific information and give little attention to critical thinking, problem-solving, and comprehension skills.

During the past several years many educators and citizens have become concerned about the lack of time given to teaching higher level thinking. Workshops and conferences on teaching higher level thinking skills and processes have become very popular. Participants in these conferences have heard several points of view about the most appropriate strategies to use in engaging students in higher level learning activities. Some propose that higher level thinking can be taught strictly as a process without reference to any specific content area. Others take the position that higher level thinking processes must be integrated with the content to be learned. Still others make the assumption that higher level thinking skills are needed only in subjects such as math and science.

In addition to sorting out differing opinions about how to engage students in higher level learning processes, teachers, because of the accountability movement, are under considerable pressure to prepare their students to score well on standardized tests. Thus, they may have very little time to spend on critical thinking or comprehension activities. Most textbooks are filled with specific information that is often fragmented, and give little attention to concept development. Workbooks may be composed largely of worksheets that require students to fill in the right answers rather than engage in problem-solving activities. In short, the instructional materials available to many teachers do not support or facilitate the teaching of higher level thinking skills and processes.

Many teachers have been prepared to teach for recall rather than for comprehension. They have been conditioned to seek the right answers and the specific facts to be remembered. New teachers often feel that stimulating divergent thinking in their students may create management problems. They may be concerned about losing control if students are allowed too much flexibility and creativity in the learning process. Experienced teachers have told us that they find it very difficult to break away from teaching patterns they have developed over the years, even when they know that what they are doing may be restricting student thinking and learning.

In spite of all of the challenges and organizational constraints, teachers have found ways to incorporate higher level learning strategies in their instruction. One teacher told us recently that she allocates a specific amount of time to prepare her students to take standardized tests. The balance of her time she uses to help students learn how to learn on their own, how to learn from one another, and how to develop problem-solving and critical thinking skills.

We have worked with teachers in professional development programs who have demonstrated a commitment to higher level learning. In nearly all cases the teachers have expressed a desire to develop a deeper understanding of the research on higher level learning before they attempt to apply new strategies in their classrooms. They are careful to evaluate the research in light of their practical knowledge as they experiment with new approaches. When they experience success in stimulating student use of higher level thinking skills, teachers have become even more committed to expanding their teaching repertoires to include higher level learning strategies.

Rationale

The mission of schools is shifting from preparing students for specific vocations to enabling them to participate in social, economic, and political decisions. In a complex and rapidly changing world, it is essential for students to develop critical thinking skills and to learn how to assimilate and process large amounts of information. One of the most important skills for students to acquire is learning how to learn.

The view of knowledge acquisition is also changing. Although students receive information from many sources, teachers continue to play a key role in developing the strategies students use for acquiring and processing information. Students should be expected to be active learners who can engage in a wide range of learning experiences. They should not be seen as passive, empty receptacles that can be filled with facts and bits of information.

Students of all ability levels should have the opportunity to develop higher level thinking skills. Higher level instruction should not be restricted to the more able students or to classes that are deemed to be appropriate for higher level learning, such as advanced placement courses in math and science. Students at all grade levels need to learn how to identify key concepts and use these concepts as organizing centers. They need to learn how to screen new information critically in order to determine its worth, importance, and applicability to the problems that they will be expected to solve.

Students, then, should be fully empowered to develop information processing skills so that they can successfully integrate new information with prior knowledge. They should become self-regulated learners who are able to monitor their own learning processes. As they strengthen these metacognitive processes, students' attitudes about their ability to learn will improve. This, in turn, will strengthen students' commitment to the learning process.

As schools move more and more to school-based decision making, teachers will be given greater autonomy and control over what they teach and how they teach. With this freedom will come the responsibility to develop optimal learning conditions for all students. It will be incumbent on teachers to understand and use strategies that will foster the development of learning processes that students will need to succeed in complex, rapidly changing environments.

RESEARCH SYNTHESIS

The Concept of Higher Level Learning

Engaging students in higher level learning is a complex task. Because assessing the level of thinking is complicated by the learner's prior knowledge, it is not always possible to tell the difference between lower and higher order thinking. Most scholars, however, do agree on the major attributes of higher level thinking.

Newmann (1988) defined higher order thinking by comparing it with lower order thinking:

> Lower order thinking demands only routine, mechanistic application of previously acquired knowledge; for example, repetitive exercises such as listing information previously memorized, inserting numbers into previously learned formulae, or applying the rules for footnote format in a research paper. In contrast, higher order thinking challenges the student to interpret, analyze, or manipulate information, because a question to be answered or a problem to be solved cannot be resolved through the routine application of previously learned knowledge. (p. 5)

Other experts highlight the active, purposeful, self-conscious role students play in higher level learning. Quellmalz's (1985) definition stressed involvement in purposeful, extended lines of thought that include identifying and defining terms, evaluating information, and developing self-monitoring strategies.

Lauren Resnick's (1987) definition is quoted most often by other researchers. According to Resnick:

- Higher order thinking is *nonalgorithmic*. That is, the path of action is not fully specified in advance.
- Higher order thinking tends to be *complex*. The total path is not "visible" (mentally speaking) from any single vantage point.
- Higher order thinking often yields *multiple solutions*, each with costs and benefits, rather than unique solutions.
- Higher order thinking involves *nuanced judgment* and interpretation.
- Higher order thinking involves the application of *multiple criteria* which sometimes conflict with one another.
- Higher order thinking often involves *uncertainty*. Not everything that bears on the task at hand is known.
- Higher order thinking involves *self-regulation* of the thinking process. We do not recognize higher order thinking in an individual when someone else "calls the plays" at every step.
- Higher order thinking involves *imposing meaning*, finding structure in apparent disorder.
- Higher order thinking is *effortful*. There is considerable mental work involved in the kinds of elaborations and judgments required. (p. 3)

Changes in Learning Theory

Early in the 1970s many psychologists shifted from a behaviorist to a cognitive orientation. Researchers stressed a concern for the mind and the way it functions. The cognitive approach focuses on changing learners by helping them develop more appropriate strategies. According to Resnick and Klopfer (1989), "Cognitive scientists share Piaget's constructivist view of learning, asserting that people are not recorders of information but builders of knowledge structures" (pp. 2–3). This change in learning theory has begun to have a profound influence on teaching and learning.

Behaviorists suggest that learning occurs when learners acquire associations, or bonds, between a stimulus and a response and change their behavior accordingly. Cognitive psychologists, however, believe that learning is the process of acquiring and processing new information. Brophy (1987) expressed the cognitive view of learning: "Learning refers to information processing, sense making, and comprehension or mastery advances that occur during the acquisition of knowledge or skill. Performance refers to the demonstration of such knowledge or skill after it has been acquired" (p. 41).

Snow (1989) noted that learning involves a progression from simpler to more complex comprehension of a domain. As students acquire a more sophisticated information base and more complex concepts, they must restructure and replace their old beliefs. Deep understanding often involves unlearning as much as learning. Resnick and Klopfer (1989) stated that students know something only when they receive information, interpret it, and relate it to other knowledge. Thinking and learning merge in the cognitive perspective and should not be separated.

The Role of Prior Knowledge.   Behavioral psychologists study learning by constructing tasks that are unrelated to what students already know. In this way they design experiments that are not contaminated by other factors. Cognitive psychologists, on the other hand, stress the importance of prior knowledge and design studies that examine the interaction of knowledge and learning. These studies have found that learning does not merely expand a body of interrelated facts and concepts; rather, it involves a change in the form of knowledge which sets the stage for new discoveries. Prior knowledge plays an important role in determining when students are ready to learn (Shuell, 1986).

The amount of knowledge students already possess has a major impact on learning. Information that learners have acquired, and the way it is organized, determines how students interpret tasks and what they will learn from studying tasks. They often begin their learning with misconceptions, or they make systematic mistakes. Their prior knowledge affects the way they process new information and often interferes with learning. Snow (1989) described three overlapping phases of learning:

> The accretion of new information, and its chunking, elaboration, and connection to existing knowledge; its restructuring, through which new knowledge organizations are formed, usually to replace or reformulate old concepts and relations; and, finally, the tuning or adaptation and practice of knowledge structures in particular uses. (p. 9)

Brown, Campione, and Day (1981) found that more mature students derived greater benefits from exposure to new information and experiences and needed less explicit instruction even though they did not appear to differ on their initial performance. They concluded that the superior performance of these students was related to their ability to relate new information to a rich store of background knowledge. Less mature students were often hampered by inefficient application of rules and strategies as well as an impoverished knowledge base.

Researchers have found that knowledge is content specific. Experts in mathematics, political science, or technical skills reason more easily on topics within their specialties than they do on other topics (Resnick & Klopfer, 1989). Domain-specific knowledge includes factual information, specific strategies, and an understanding of when and where to use certain facts or employ particular procedures (Alexander & Judy, 1988). Chi (1986) studied children who were engaged in classification tasks. Younger children appeared to use only observable characteristics, while older children could classify according to abstract characteristics. However, young subjects were able to organize knowledge in sophisticated, efficient ways in areas where they had a substantial knowledge base. For example, subjects who had a deep knowledge of dinosaurs were able to use abstract characteristics to categorize them. Their knowledge base allowed them to take in, order, and recall information in a more meaningful way. Resnick (1987) clarified the role of content-specific knowledge:

Even on the tasks used to assess general intelligence or scholastic aptitude, recent analyses have made it clear that much depends on specific knowledge: of vocabulary, of particular number relationships, of possible transformations of visual displays, and the like. General skills such as breaking down a problem into simpler problems or checking to see whether one has captured the main idea of a passage may be impossible to apply if one does not have a store of knowledge about similar problems—or know enough about the topic to be able to recognize its central ideas. (p. 18)

Representing and Organizing Knowledge. Students' ability to use prior knowledge in new situations is dependent on the way that knowledge is organized (Prawat, 1989). Verbal information is likely to be called into service only if it is stored in memory within well-structured, elaborated networks of meaningfully related ideas (Derry, 1989–90). Teachers who help students organize what they learn improve comprehension and recall of information. Organizing strategies can include grouping, ordering, or categorizing. Complex organizing tasks might include outlining or creating a hierarchy (Weinstein, 1983). Students who have to remember separate items may have a difficult time, while those who pay attention to organization can simplify the recall or comprehension process. Including specific instructions on how to organize information is especially important when developing higher order skills. Teachers do this verbally as they question, explain, make lesson goals explicit, and stress important points (Corno, 1981).

The term *cognitive organizer* is used to describe a variety of organizational strategies. Cognitive organizers help students learn by increasing their ability to comprehend complex information. In addition, cognitive organizers can aid "far transfer," which occurs when students use their knowledge in tasks quite unlike the original learning context. When teachers help students organize their information, they increase the students' ability to pay attention and stay on task. When the organizing strategy is presented before instruction, it serves as an instructional cue reminding students to pay attention to important facts and issues (Hawley & Rosenholtz, 1984). Learners who do this make better use of their time. They attend to key ideas and relate them to a larger context. The result is more efficient learning.

Cognition is the process of knowing or perceiving. It is almost synonymous with thinking. However, cognition carries a deeper meaning. Learners may think about a topic in a lighthearted way, merely letting ideas form in their minds. Cognition is usually associated with a seriousness of purpose or effort. Organization is the providing of structure, or an effort to provide a systematic arrangement. Researchers employ these terms together to describe a complex process that learners use to classify and store information for retrieval. Material that is organized into categories is learned faster with less chance of interference. Organizing helps students learn and retain material (Corno, 1986). Figure 12–1 shows a graphic organizer that depicts the relationship among cognition and organization to a body of information.

Students receive new information through listening, observing, or reading. Their task is to comprehend the messages and find some way to remember them at a later time. Even the most effective learners do not remember everything, nor do they recall information in its original form. They reduce and organize new information for

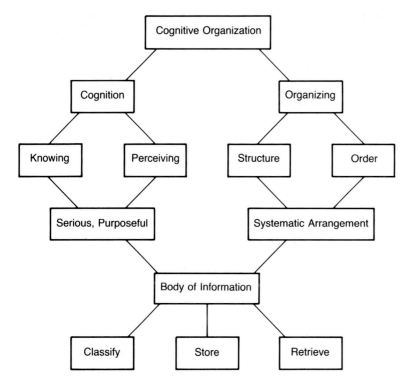

FIGURE 12–1. The relationship of cognition and organization to a body of information

later retrieval. In doing so, they actively transform the information. Transformation involves comparison, integration, rehearsal, and elaboration. Corno (1986) stated, "Classroom activities that require students to actively transform information are more demanding cognitively. This is one of the most theoretically sensible and replicated findings of instructional research" (p. 362).

Organizing involves alertness, separation, and integration. Students who are alert are curious, sensitive to teachers' cues, and are constantly deciding what is worthwhile to remember. They contrast and compare new information with their prior knowledge, separating important facts from details. Information is reduced and integrated into their previous knowledge base.

Students receive a tremendous amount of information. Attempts to remember all of it are doomed to failure. Information reduction helps to make the memory task possible. The challenge is to decide what information to remember and what to delete. Cognitive organizing helps students solve this problem through a process of categorizing. Teachers can guide students systematically through a body of information, generating categories and moving them toward an integrated view of a problem. In this way teachers model information reduction and storage processes (Corno, 1986). When the cognitive organizer is complete, it serves as a memory support, easing the burden of information processing. This is especially helpful when dealing with complex content and when working with low-ability students or those who are anxious (Corno, 1981). Using cognitive organizers helps students develop an integrated view of a body of knowledge that is organized to display and stress interrelationships, rather than a mass of unrelated facts.

Recent studies have shown that students who read or listen are involved in generating meaning that is dependent on their background and goals (Stewart, 1986). Teachers can use organizers to help students recall and use related prior knowledge. Once this knowledge base is brought to the conscious level, it becomes the basis for building new concepts. Cognitive organizers help display and organize the elements of a concept. Later on, information can be added to help students discriminate between closely related concepts.

All subject matter has structure. The structure is often most evident in the fact that some concepts subsume others (Corno, 1986). When the structure is made explicit, it serves as a conceptual anchor for learning new concepts. Cognitive organizers help teachers make the basic structure of a body of content explicit. Gage and Berliner (1984) reported that organizers help students who already have the concepts and organization bring them out of memory for use. When students understand the structure of the content, they can concentrate their memory search on the most relevant sector. According to Prawat (1989):

> Our ability to draw on previous knowledge in new situations is also very much influenced by how it is organized. According to Polya (1973), this factor is even more important than the extent of one's knowledge. A major source of the difference between experts and novices is the way the former are able to organize their knowledge in a domain so that it can be used efficiently and effectively. Some ideas serve as better organizers than others. Identifying and figuring out how to focus our instruction on these "key ideas" is one of the major challenges confronting those who want to move toward a more conceptual approach to teaching. (p. 318)

Teachers use many different kinds of cognitive organizers. Hierarchical organizers are based on subsumption theory, with more abstract, inclusive concepts serving as the basis for learning new information. Advance organizers are one example of hierarchical organizers. Examples of different types of organizers are shown in Figure 12–2. Ausubel (1963) devised the use of advance organizers for improving presentations and students' ability to learn from them. Joyce and Weil (1986) suggested that the use of advance organizers is a way to teach students to become active by looking for organizing ideas, reconciling new information, and generating organizers of their own.

Nonhierarchical organizers use different kinds of networks to illustrate interrelationships among ideas graphically. Text structure maps and semantic maps are nonhierarchical organizers. Text structure maps help students use the structure of the text as an aid to comprehension. Semantic maps are used to involve students actively in using prior knowledge before, during, and after reading. Students graphically link main ideas to words they know and related categories in an arrangement that depicts important relationships.

HIERARCHICAL ORGANIZERS

FIGURE 12–2. Types of organizers

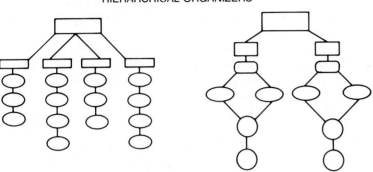

NONHIERARCHICAL ORGANIZERS

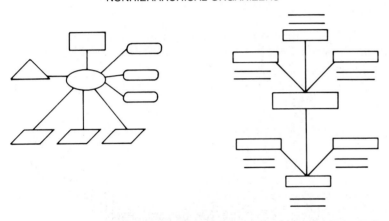

The Importance of Metacognition. Cognitive psychologists and content area experts stress the importance of metacognition. Jones (1986) defined metacognition as "thinking about what one knows and how to control one's thinking processes" (p. 9). If students are to take an active role in their learning, they must be able to plan, monitor, clarify, and revise their thinking. Cognitive psychologists have rediscovered purposiveness and consciousness as part of the motivation for learning. Paris and Lindauser (1982) identified three common threads of research on metacognition: evaluation, planning, and regulation. Evaluation occurs when learners assess their own current knowledge. Young learners are often not aware of the fact that they do not have the knowledge they need. They charge right ahead, even when they do not understand the task. Good students keep a constant check on their understanding by restructuring messages, asking questions, anticipating outcomes, and thinking about the other person's point of view. Planning occurs as students select strategies to meet the goals of the task. Teachers help students plan when they model the planning process or give feedback that highlights the utility of student plans.

Regulation of learning refers to the constant monitoring of progress toward goals and a conscious effort by students to change the way they are trying to learn.

Specific metacognitive strategies have been identified in most content areas. For example, successful math learners check their own understanding of procedures, monitor for consistency, and try to relate new material to prior knowledge (Resnick, 1987). Competent readers declare a purpose, evaluate the reading task, choose appropriate strategies, check their understanding while reading, correct comprehension failures, and reflect on the task after they finish (Paris, Oka, & DeBritto, 1983).

Teachers create metacognitive awareness in students through their teaching strategies. Their role is to help students know when their comprehension is breaking down and what to do about it (Mealey & Nist, 1989). Crain (1988) suggested modeling, attention to individual student problems, self-questioning, and the use of general and specific guides to texts as ways of promoting metacognition.

Concept Formation

Concept formation is a foundation for other higher level thinking processes (Marzano et al., 1988). Gage and Berliner (1984) pointed out the positive relationship between teachers' tendency to emphasize concepts to be learned and student achievement. Effective teachers know the key ideas in a subject matter domain. They plan their teaching around concepts that are important for students, organizing and sequencing instruction to maximize student understanding (Prawat, 1989).

A concept is a general idea of a thing or class. Educators use the word *concept* to describe the way knowledge and experiences are grouped or categorized. A collection of discrete objects or ideas is sorted mentally into classes based on certain criteria. Classes can then be stored and recalled as single concepts instead of having to remember each individual member of the group. Concept formation allows students to reduce and organize incoming information. Concepts are used to provide a taxonomy of objects or events and to describe relationships.

The mental processes necessary for concept formation have intrigued researchers for years. Many teachers are familiar with the work of Piaget and others whose studies sought age-dependent similarities in and constraints on learning (Eylon & Linn, 1988). More recently, researchers have studied the way individuals develop concepts, the influence of prior knowledge, and instructional design. Although this research has appeared under different labels (e.g., concept learning, concept formation, concept attainment) the findings have a high degree of consistency.

Most researchers have studied what Joyce and Weil (1986) called the elements of a concept: (1) the concept name or label, (2) examples or instances, (3) attributes (essential and nonessential), and (4) attribute values. They maintained that understanding a concept means knowing all of its elements.

The concept name is the word used to label a category or class of experiences. Individual members of a category may have certain differences but will have crucial common features that allow us to refer to them with one term. It is important to remember that the name represents a concept in a particular culture. Other cultures or speech communities may have different labels. Concept names are short, usually a single word plus a few modifiers. Information that cannot be stated in a few words is probably a principle, not a concept (Marzano et al., 1988). Students who have the experience base but do not know a concept name cannot comprehend instruction that depends on knowledge of the concept name. Combining direct teaching of concepts with direct teaching of vocabulary is a powerful educational tool (Marzano et al., 1988).

Tennyson and Cocchiarella (1986) listed six instructional design variables teachers can use when presenting new concepts:

1. Definition (a rule or generality that verbally states the structure of the critical attributes)
2. Expository examples (examples and nonexamples that systematically present the content in a *statement* format)
3. Interrogatory examples (examples and nonexamples that systematically present the content in a *question* format)
4. Attribution elaboration (prompting or expository instances and feedback on the critical attributes)
5. Strategy information (giving students a specific solution or strategy after they fail)
6. Embedded refreshment (making connections in memory between to-be-learned concepts and existing prerequisite knowledge) (pp. 57–60)

Other researchers (Klausmeier, 1980; Marzano et al., 1988) stressed the need to introduce new concepts at an experiential level, with concrete objects, or through simulated guided imagery. There is general agreement on the need to include these instructional variables in concept formation tasks. Textbooks usually introduce new concepts with a general definition, one example, no nonexamples, or comparison to related concepts (Marzano et al., 1988). If teachers are to teach concepts effectively, they must compensate for the inadequacy of their textbooks.

Conceptual Change

When children enter school, they have already developed preconceptions about mathematics and science based on their experience. In some cases their preconceptions provide the basis for formal instruction. Other children may have formed concepts that will be serious obstacles to instruction (Anderson & Smith, 1987). Rogan (1988) found students who believed that heat was a substance that could be added to or removed from an object. They believed it entered from the heat source and traveled throughout the objects. These students made no reference to molecular activity. Silver (1986) reported young math students who commonly used the size or frequency of numbers to decide which operation to use in solving a story problem. If there were two numbers and one was very large compared to the other, the students decided to divide. If there were more than two numbers in a problem, they added. By using these rules of thumb for solving story problems the students were able to have a fairly high success rate.

The faulty concepts students bring to class are influenced by consistent reasoning that makes sense to the students and can be traced to meaningful origins in their experience. These concepts are amazingly robust, difficult to change, and often impervious to traditional instruction (Eylon & Linn, 1988). Good and Brophy (1987) concluded that part of the problem can be attributed to the limited capacity of working memory in the human mind. Since humans can only actively manipulate about seven items at a time in working memory, they are very susceptible to information overload. Teachers may unwittingly give too much information at one time. In addition, knowledge that is already stored in memory plays an important role in how students allocate their attention. When faced with new or difficult knowledge, students tend to filter it through their preexisting cognitive structures. When their knowledge base is not accurate, learning is more difficult.

When teachers find that students have a faulty knowledge base and preexisting misconceptions, their solution may be to deliver a lecture or conduct a lecture-discussion in an attempt to correct the problem. Anderson and Smith (1987) concluded that presentations almost always include information that students have not learned or understood. The problem with most presentations arises from teachers' failure to take students' naive conceptions into account, despite the fact that conceptions serve as the organizing and interpretive framework for new information.

Researchers in several content areas have designed a new strategy to overcome the influence of preexisting faulty concepts. Use of this strategy will help students change or restructure their conceptual knowledge. Porter and Brophy (1988) described the strategy as follows:

> Conceptual change teaching strategies are based on the premise that teaching does not involve infusing knowledge into a vacuum, but instead involves inducing change in an existing body of knowledge and beliefs. Traditional instructional strategies have emphasized the facilitative role of relevant preexisting knowledge and beliefs in providing anchoring points and starting places for extending students' knowledge. Conceptual change teaching acknowledges these advantages to the extent that relevant preexisting student beliefs are accurate, but it calls attention to the fact that sometimes such beliefs constitute misconceptions that need to be confronted and changed rather than readiness factors to be reinforced and built upon. (p. 80)

Changes in conceptual networks occur even when learning proceeds smoothly without the interference of naive misconceptions. As individuals gain experience and learn, their knowledge structures change in three possible ways: (1) conceptual networks are modified, (2) concepts are sequenced or subsumed into higher order knowledge structures, and (3) new conceptual networks are created (Tennyson & Cocchiarella, 1986). Teaching for conceptual change depends on unlearning. Students must abandon their naive conceptions and adopt more scientific alternatives. Allowing students to keep their faulty concepts produces misunderstanding or rote memorization (Anderson, 1987). Teaching for concept change appears to benefit low-reasoning students in particular. Rogan (1988) found that students with higher reasoning skills seemed to be more adept at conceptual change regardless of the instructional strategy.

According to Minstrell (1989), instructional design that fosters conceptual change has three important phases:

1. A preliminary phase where teachers and students identify students' existing ideas about the concept
2. A focusing phase for students and teachers to clarify students' ideas
3. An activity or situation that challenges the students' initial ideas

During the preliminary stage, teachers present a question, picture, or activity that poses a problem. They ask students to make a prediction about the solution or outcome. Minstrell preferred the use of common everyday experiences as the basis for this phase. Having students write down their predictions is an important step. Some students later ignore their initial thinking unless it is written down. Teachers do not deny students' misconceptions at this point. Their goal is to identify and make their beliefs explicit. During phase two, teachers help students clarify their ideas. This usually takes place in a discussion. Some teachers are concerned that hearing alternative explanations will cause even more confusion. Rogan (1988) asserted that alternative explanations should be encouraged and compared for their power to explain and predict. Articulating different viewpoints helps students develop and examine their prior knowledge and does not interfere with accurate learning. Phase three involves a discrepant event, laboratory experience, or problem that is directly related to the most common misconceptions of class members. Minstrell (1989) made a strong case for choosing an experiment or problem that students would see in their everyday experience. When phenomena can be linked to everyday experiences, they are more difficult to deny. The activity makes it possible to confront preconceptions.

Good and Brophy (1987) identified four conditions that are necessary to get students to change concepts:

(1) dissatisfaction with existing conceptions must be induced, (2) the new conception must be intelligible, (3) the new conception must be initially plausible, and (4) the new conception must appear fruitful. (p. 496–497)

If conceptual change is to occur, discrepant events, experiments, and problems must be carefully chosen so that they confront preexisting ideas. They should set up contrasts between student misconceptions and accurate representations. Students should encounter these contrasts and be actively involved in explaining them. The activity must have the potential to make students dissatisfied with their current knowledge. After conclusion of the activity, teachers should help students differentiate their initial beliefs from valid knowledge. The critical elements in the conceptual change process are summarized in Figure 12–3.

One experiment or activity is not enough to overcome concepts that students have held for a long time. Minstrell (1989) noted that exposing students to key concepts in different contexts over a period of time is the only way to get students to transfer knowledge acquired in science classes to the real world. Prawat (1989) stressed helping students make connections that foster reconciliation of formal knowledge

Problem	Instructional Goals
Students bring faulty preconceptions based on informal knowledge.	Induce change in an existing body of knowledge.
Preexisting concepts are robust and impervious to traditional instruction.	Build an accurate, relevant base of knowledge.
	Build connections and links to the real world and informal knowledge.

Teacher's Instructional Plan	Student's Role
Identify current ideas and beliefs.	Articulate, examine, and clarify current knowledge.
Focus and clarify existing knowledge.	
Confront and challenge faulty knowledge.	Contrast and compare current ideas and knowledge presented or experienced in class.
Contrast misconceptions with accurate representations of the concept.	Explain differences and similarities.
Differentiate initial knowledge from valid knowledge.	Modify existing knowledge, when appropriate.
	Unlearn faulty concepts.
Point out connections and links to real life and informal knowledge.	Subsume new knowledge under valid concepts.
	Merge formal knowledge with informal knowledge.

FIGURE 12–3. Conceptual change process

with the informal knowledge they bring to class. He suggested linking key concepts and principles to physical representations, demonstrating with models, and using metaphors or analogies that demonstrate how separate concepts and rules are interrelated. For example, teachers can show students how the rules for computing the area of a triangle relate to rules for finding the area of a rectangle.

Finding time in an already crowded curriculum for instruction on cognitive change is a challenge. Currently, teachers feel that they must teach to cover the content that will be tested. The result can be a superficial coverage of a multitude of ideas. Eylon and Linn (1988) addressed this issue:

> Overall, these findings emphasize the value of integrated in-depth coverage of science topics to help students achieve the value of coherent perspectives. In-depth coverage can elaborate incomplete ideas, provide enough cues to encourage selection of a different view of a phenomenon, or establish a well-understood alternative. With superficial coverage, ideas will soon be forgotten. Furthermore, if students believe that scientific events are coherent, they will seek to integrate their ideas. (p. 263)

Curriculum developers and teachers need to reorganize their programs around a limited number of key concepts. When this is done, students will have the opportunity to develop a deep understanding or mastery of important concepts rather than simply learning many facts and details at a surface level.

Problem Solving

Many situations we encounter in our daily lives require the ability to solve problems. When children enter school, they are relatively successful at solving simple problems. Carpenter (1986) reported that very young children use informal knowledge and systems to solve problems before they have any formal instruction. Schools have traditionally included problem solving in mathematics, science, and social studies classes. More recently, solving social problems has been added to health programs. Yet many students have difficulty applying their problem-solving knowledge on standardized tests or in real-life situations. They do not seem to have the knowledge and skills to plan and organize in order to solve problems.

The Concept of Problem Solving.   Agreeing on a common definition of the word *problem* is helpful in understanding the concept. Shuell (1988) asserted that a problem exists when a person's first attempts to reach some goal are unsuccessful and there are several possible alternative courses of action that must be considered before making a decision about what to do. Problem solving is an active search for alternatives. It is goal oriented and involves mental evaluation of several courses of action and monitoring the effectiveness of the alternative chosen.

Problem solving and decision making are often used as synonyms. Brophy (1988) differentiated the two terms as they are used in social studies:

> Problem solving implies seeking explanations for observed phenomena or addressing relatively well-formed and noncontroversial questions that can be resolved by evidence alone (without having to take into account values and without necessarily carrying the process through to some kind of action based on the obtained solution to the problem). In contrast, decision making is seen as the making of reasoned choices from among several alternatives, where reasoned choices are based on judgments consistent with one's values and on relevant, sound information. (p. 42)

Effective problem solvers actively use information-processing skills. First, they develop an awareness that the problem exists. Second, they attempt to understand or comprehend the problem. Many problem solvers use pictures, charts, graphs, or concrete objects to represent the problem. Third, they may gather and organize relevant information. At this point several ways to solve the problem (solution paths) are identified. After careful consideration, one path is chosen and pursued. Effective problem solvers monitor their progress and accuracy as they carry out the steps of their plan. They are flexible enough to change when they see that what they are doing is not helping them reach a solution.

Recently researchers have classified problems as either well structured or poorly structured. Shuell (1988) defined a well-structured problem as "one in which there are clear and agreed upon criteria for determining when the problem has been solved and the information needed to solve the problem is either contained in the statement of the problem or its availability is fairly clear-cut" (p. 7). Many of the problems teachers assign in school are well structured. Often the solution path is provided by the textbook or the teacher. For example, students may merely apply a mathematics algorithm or carry out a specified series of actions to find a solution.

With poorly structured problems there are no clear-cut solutions, information may be missing, and problem statements may be fuzzy or absent. No clear criteria are available to evaluate the solutions. Many real-life problems are not neatly phrased, do not have clear problem statements, and information to solve them is not easily available. Solving these problems involves coping with ambiguity and uncertainty. Students have to use a variety of thinking processes. Because these factors cause some frustration for students, teachers seldom assign poorly structured problems.

Instructional Difficulties. Many problems students are asked to solve in school do not require the use of problem-solving behaviors. Students can solve them in a straightforward, automatic fashion (Shuell, 1988). Moreover, teachers often look for one right answer and may insist that students follow a prescribed process to reach a solution. Porter (1989) pointed out that computation skills are emphasized in math textbooks and instruction. Little time is allocated for higher order thinking skills, problem solving, or understanding mathematics as a discipline. Carpenter (1986) reported that many math teachers concentrate on procedural knowledge in an effort to help students decide what mathematical processes to use. This results in superficial analyses of the problems because few teachers take the time to link these procedures to concepts. When this happens, problem solving may be reduced to deciding whether to add, subtract, divide, or multiply. In more advanced classes such as physics, students may merely memorize the algorithm necessary to solve the problems (Tobin, 1987a). As a result, they cannot apply the procedure to solve new problems.

A related difficulty is the tendency to present problem solving as an activity that is conducted only in academic settings. Children think problem solving in mathematics is a chance to compute on paper. The task is to get the one right answer quickly, without thinking. They believe that thinking about short cuts to get the answer is cheating. Porter (1989) claimed that the use of artificial problems from textbooks is part of the problem. Students fail to see the connection between what they do at school and their daily lives, future study, or job opportunities. Perkins and Simmons (1988) made the point that students in mathematics, science, and computer programming do not tend to find problems that need solving. They have become accustomed to problems that are identified by teachers in schools and do not apply their knowledge of problems to their real lives.

Another difficulty for student problem solvers is the lack of a domain-specific knowledge base. Expert problem solvers rely on their deep knowledge of the content. This knowledge is not merely an accumulation of discrete facts but facts that are well organized around key concepts. Studies have shown that solving problems in any content area depends on prior content-specific knowledge. A person who solves mathematics problems easily might have difficulty solving problems in social science. As Doyle (1983) noted:

> Domain-specific knowledge plays a central role in problem solving and learning within a content area. Domain-specific knowledge consists not only of a well-formed semantic network of valid information in an academic discipline but also of strategies for using this information to represent (comprehend) problems, search for and select algorithms, use resources from the task environment, and evaluate the adequacy of answers. (p. 168)

Students who lack domain-specific knowledge usually resort to memorizing strategies in order to solve problems. They are often able to list the steps in a procedure, but they are unable to use this procedural knowledge. When Eylon and Linn (1988) studied problem solvers in the field of science, they found that experts organized their knowledge around general principles which they used to describe particular problems. These principles were stored in memory in meaningful "chunks" that the experts manipulated instead of working with a mass of details. Furthermore, the experts categorized problems by deciding what information was needed to reach a solution. Categorizing and manipulating chunks of information allowed the experts to work faster and more accurately.

Because schools often teach for exposure, or content coverage, students seldom have the opportunity to gain the in-depth knowledge necessary for integrating ideas, eliminating irrelevant information, and developing groups of linked concepts or principles. The result is a fragmented knowledge base that is hard to use when solving problems. Brophy (1988) recommended that social studies instruction should focus in depth on major principles and generalizations rather than give shallow coverage of a great range of topics.

Approaches to Effective Instruction. Direct instruction of general problem-solving procedures, instruction in specific processes, and small problem-solving groups are the most promising methods of promoting problem-solving skills. Figure 12–4 illustrates the steps that make up the general problem-solving process. Eylon and Linn (1988) described general problem-solving skills in the following manner:

> Procedural skills such as planning, testing, and reformulating are general to many problems. We define planning as the ability to select and order the knowledge necessary for solving a problem, testing as the ability to determine whether the plan is effective, and reformulation as the ability to modify the plan in light of information gained through testing. (p. 278)

The IDEAL method developed by Bransford and Stein (1984) is one generic procedure. Students are taught how to carry out the following steps:

1. Identify the problem.
2. Define the problem.
3. Explore possible strategies for solving the problem.
4. Act on these strategies.
5. Look at the effects of your efforts.

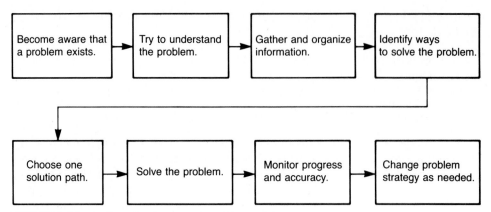

FIGURE 12-4. Steps in the general problem-solving process

General strategies work better when they are taught explicitly and the teacher models the logical thinking and problem-solving behavior by thinking out loud. Good and Brophy (1987) suggested that modeling problem solving should include the thinking that goes into choosing the general approach to use, deciding which option to take, and checking on progress. Talking about uncertainty, recovery from false starts, and using the wrong strategies may help students realize that they can solve problems even though they are uncertain about how to proceed. This is important because many students give up if the solution path is not immediately clear or if they encounter difficulty.

Teachers often present specific problem-solving strategies to their students. Eylon and Linn (1988) found that teaching specific problem-solving techniques in physics helps students overcome carelessness. Having a step-by-step process to follow may keep them from skipping a step or leaving out important information. Specific problem-solving techniques also provide a framework for organizing thought processes and work. Peterson (1988b) suggested that teachers of elementary math should promote the learning of specific strategies as early as first grade. When young children learn to use "counting on" to solve addition and subtraction problems, they should be encouraged to verbalize the strategy. Programming computers is another problem-solving activity in which students benefit from explicit teaching and modeling of problem-solving procedures.

Some cautions should be observed when teaching specific problem-solving techniques. If procedural knowledge is to be productive and meaningful, instruction must be linked firmly to a conceptual knowledge base. Young students can learn step-by-step procedures before they are ready to understand the concepts. This limits the number of procedures that should be taught (Carpenter, 1986). Newmann (1988) took the position that students should be taught problem-solving techniques only when they have in-depth knowledge of the content, information-processing skills, and attitudes or dispositions of reflectiveness. Schoenfield (1987) noted, "Instructors can teach strategies as they do other mathematical procedures, reducing them to meaningless routines. It's very easy to pervert problem solving approaches" (p. 12).

Another productive technique for problem-solving sessions is the use of small groups. Small groups can facilitate higher order learning. Explaining the reasoning process used and listening to the ideas of others promote learning for meaning and understanding and help students overcome the tendency toward rote learning. Teachers have to delegate control to group members, and this promotes independence and autonomy. In addition, students are more willing to carry out higher level executive routines such as planning and monitoring when they work together. Peterson (1988b) recommended that teachers provide opportunities for students to solve mathematics problems without teacher direction.

Developing Self-regulated Learners

Self-regulated learners use specific skills and strategies to direct and regulate their own learning processes (McCombs & Marzano, 1989). They have the academic skills that facilitate and sustain the desire to learn. Students who are self-regulated learners do not depend on teacher actions to promote their learning. They do things to ensure their own learning (Corno, 1986). McCombs and Marzano (1989) studied the way skill and will interact and jointly contribute to learning. They found that students usually develop the concept of themselves as the generator of motivation to learn. This happens naturally through normal self-development. When development of self is impaired because of repeated learning failures or other negative experiences, teachers need to intervene with the goal of helping students to learn how to monitor and guide their own learning and thinking. Corno and Mandinach (1983) found that providing too much support short-circuits self-regulated learning. When teachers provide all of the cognitive organizers, such as charts, diagrams, and marginal notes, students do not have to decide which information is important or monitor their own understanding. Without saying so the teacher has given the impression that learning is rote or associational, and does not involve problem solving or mental elaboration.

Self-concept plays a significant role in self-regulation. Students with a stable self-concept are able to view themselves as capable of controlling and regulating their own learning. Students who have poor self-concepts are often unable to internalize the knowledge and skills for self-regulation. They do not feel capable of taking control of their own learning. Teachers who realize the importance of self-concept foster development of self and a sense of responsibility before they ask students to develop self-regulation skills. They provide a positive classroom climate where young people learn to value themselves and their capabilities and where their natural tendencies to regulate their own learning can emerge (McCombs, 1988).

Self-regulation skills can help students manage their knowledge and effort so that their learning is effective, economical, and satisfying. This leads to feelings of confidence and control. When students realize that they can control their own learning, they begin to view unsuccessful learning as a lack of appropriate strategies. It is at this point in the instructional process that learners begin to use self-regulation strategies without prompting (Paris & Oka, 1986).

A first step in developing self-regulated learners is assessing students' beliefs about their own ability to learn. Recent research suggests that underachieving children lack confidence in their ability to learn. This lack of confidence affects their willingness to concentrate on new knowledge (Eylon & Linn, 1988). Children who believe that they can learn attribute their success to their own efforts, not to innate intelligence, luck, or other factors. Such students are mastery oriented (Snow, 1989). They believe that ability improves with learning so they direct their actions toward learning. Performance-oriented students believe that ability is fixed and may direct their attention solely toward getting a positive evaluation from the teacher. Driscoll (1986) offered four strategies for encouraging the belief that students can learn successfully: (1) increasing students' experience with success, (2) making sure students know the requirements for success, (3) increasing personal control over success, and (4) giving attributional feedback that connects success with personal effort and ability (p. 16).

It is not enough to teach skills and knowledge. Effective teachers must also develop in students the motivation to use them. According to Resnick and Klopfer (1989), "Substantial amounts of recent research suggest that good thinkers and problem solvers differ from poorer ones not so much in the particular skills they possess as in their tendency to use them" (p. 6). For motivation to make a difference in learning there must be an intent to learn. Intent to learn is usually influenced by an incentive or a desired outcome. Students may also be influenced by perceived blocks such as instruction that is too difficult or boring.

Volition or self-discipline is also an important part of self-regulation (Corno, 1986). Students may intend to learn but are easily distracted and do not possess the self-management or self-control techniques to get themselves back on track. Teachers must guide students toward an understanding that their attitudes affect behavior and that they have control over their attitudes. Students can *decide* to focus, to put forth the necessary energy to accomplish a task and overcome distractions. They must learn to differentiate between how they feel and a conscious decision to work at something.

Closely related to volition is the concept of effort investment. Snow (1989) found that some learners avoid any situation that requires them to put forth effort. When these students encounter failure, they lose their intent to learn. Other students appear to be action oriented, employing a variety of control strategies that help them maintain their intent to learn. Action-oriented students are willing to invest effort and persist in learning despite distractions and difficulties. When students can see how learning will help them accomplish personal goals, achieve success, and avoid failure, they usually show higher rates of task engagement.

Direct Instruction of Higher Level Thinking

Instruction in higher level thinking is a complex and often elusive process. Brophy and Good (1986) stressed that higher level skills cannot be taught by presenting simple algorithms for imitation. Yet it is clear that very few students independently develop highly sophisticated thinking skills. Although students must actively participate, recent research has emphasized the role of the teacher in promoting higher level thinking skills. Wittrock (1986) reported that teaching affects achievement only through student thought processes. Many researchers maintain that active thinking and direct instruction can be fused when teachers engage students in tasks that require higher level thinking and provide explicit instruction as the need arises. Beyer (1988) suggested three things that teachers can do to help students develop the ability to do higher level thinking; they can "make thinking the subject of instruction, focus on the key attributes of the cognitive operations that constitute thinking, and provide continued explicit instruction and guided practice in how to execute these operations in a variety of contexts for a variety of purposes" (p. 5).

Teaching Thinking Strategies.   Strategies are mental processing techniques that can be taught. When students use these techniques, learning is improved. Learning strategies are not new to educators. Historically, teachers and parents have helped young people use rehearsal strategies such as memorizing (e.g., with times tables or poetry), elaboration strategies such as paraphrasing and summarizing, and organizing strategies such as outlining and networking. Weinstein and Mayer (1986) discussed research related to learning strategies that influence the selection, acquisition, construction, and integration of new information. Most of the early research involved an experimenter and a group of students who were expected to comply with a strategy identified by the researcher. The students were often directed to learn nonsense syllables or a meaningless string of numbers. Recently, researchers have taken a different approach. Their dual goals are to teach both content and strategies (Jones, Palinscar, Ogle, & Carr, 1987). Derry (1989–90) identified three types of strategies: "(a) specific learning tactics such as rehearsal, imaging, outlining; (b) more general types of self-management activities such as planning and comprehension monitoring; and (c) complex plans that combine several specific techniques" (p. 5).

Paris, Lipson, and Wixson (1983) stressed the important role of student intention in strategy use. Students who choose a particular problem-solving strategy because it is appropriate and can help them achieve their goals are displaying strategic behavior. There is an important distinction between students who comply with an experimenter's strategy or imitate skilled behavior and self-directed use of the same strategy to enhance learning (Jones et al., 1987).

Direct instruction in using thinking strategies helps students develop awareness of and control over their thought processes. Jones (1986) defined direct cognitive instruction as "(1) explicit strategy or skills instruction, namely teacher explanations regarding what the strategy is and when, where, and how to use it as well as why it should be used; and (2) the gradual transfer of responsibility for learning from the teacher to the students" (p. 7). Mealey and Nist (1989) maintained that responsibility should move from the teacher to the student in three phases: "Initially the responsibility falls totally on the teacher. Gradually, the responsibilities are shared as the teacher and student work together. Finally, students become responsible for their own learning. It is not until this last stage that transfer occurs" (p. 485).

Teachers who use direct instruction to teach thinking strategies must recognize the need to be flexible. Higher ability students may have developed an effective strategy of their own. It would be a mistake to force them to replace their method with a new one the teacher has introduced. Any new strategy should serve as a target or guideline to be adapted or modified. There is no one right way to proceed with higher level thinking (Beyer, 1988). A review of research from various sources by Snow (1989) showed that "learners develop multiple strategies for a task and shift strategies at will during performance. It is hypothesized that flexible strategy shifting is a hallmark of able learning, whereas rigid strategies or random shifting suggests low ability and achievement" (p. 10). Teachers should plan to provide instruction over a period of time. Students' skills and strategies will grow and develop as they use them in new and more complex situations. Encouraging flexible strategy use will help set the stage for the continuing expansion of thinking skills.

The major goal of teaching thinking skills is helping students develop strategies they can use responsibly and effectively on their own (Beyer, 1988). Porter and Brophy (1988) called these strategies "learning to learn" skills. Some skills that teachers can model so students can learn to learn independently are "information processing, sense making, comprehension monitoring and correction, problem solving, and other metacognitive strategies for purposeful learning" (p. 79). Students must have an opportunity to practice these skills without too much close supervision or too much latitude. Close supervision limits student thinking. However, students may get confused when they do not have enough structure. Teachers have to deliberately monitor their use of direct instruction techniques and know when to provide support as well as when to withdraw.

One advantage of direct cognitive instruction is that students develop a vocabulary they can use to discuss their thinking. Having the right words can help learners integrate a wide range of examples under one strategy. Teachers can provide specific feedback about a student's use of a strategy. They have a shared language for discussing student mistakes. Without this shared language and a specific set of steps, teachers often just say, "Think again," or give the answer themselves (Gersten & Carnine, 1986). As tasks become more difficult and complex, students may feel that the instruction is more ambiguous and risky. Consequently, they exert pressure on the teacher to go back to familiar memory or procedural tasks. Teachers who feel anxious when this happens and resent the slowdowns may return to memory or routine assignments (Doyle, 1983). Direct instruction in higher level strategies reduces the ambiguity and risk by providing structural support and a sequential process to follow.

Baumann and Schmitt (1986) identified four steps to use when direct instruction is used to develop reading comprehension skills: (1) tell students what the reading skill is, (2) tell students why the skill is important to learn, (3) give direct instruction in skill use by modeling or demonstrating, and (4) provide conditional knowledge by telling students under what conditions the skill should be used. These four steps have also been used to teach problem-solving strategies in mathematics (Herrmann, 1986b).

Qualitative differences were found in the explanations of more explicit teachers. They made specific statements about the tasks to be learned and presented tasks as real-life situations. The immediate usefulness of strategies was emphasized. In addition, more explicit teachers included information about how to follow the mental steps in a sequence flexibly and adaptively. When students are taught both what to do and why, they can more easily apply skills to new tasks. Understanding the meaning of procedures helps students remember them longer. This reasoning process supports continued learning (Burns, 1986).

Teachers play a key role in helping students become expert strategy users as they make decisions about what content and strategies to teach, about the procedures to use in helping students learn both content and strategies, and about the timing of instruction, practice, and application (Jones, 1986). Teachers must constantly assess both student success and motivation. Most effective teachers capitalize on students' desire to get jobs done quickly and painlessly, skillfully breaking the task into steps students can accomplish until they increase their knowledge and awareness of the strategy. At that point teachers, appealing to their students' mastery disposition, begin to help them use the strategy more independently and holistically. Equipping students with strategies to learn on their own helps foster a mastery orientation (IRT, 1988b).

When to Use Direct Instruction.   Peterson (1979) maintained that the choice of direct instruction depends on the teacher's assessment of the students' sense of personal control. Students with an internal locus of control do not respond as well to direct instruction of higher level thinking. They feel that they can accomplish difficult tasks without too much structure. High-achieving, task-oriented students often have devised their own processes for attacking difficult tasks and may resent having to learn a new method. On the other hand, marginal learners do profit from explicit instruction. Sinclair and Ghory (1987) found that the concept of a planned approach to learning is difficult for marginal learners, who often do not have an internal locus of control. When they are taught to use power thinking strategies that help them talk through tasks, they develop more confidence in their ability to learn. Sinclair and Ghory (1987) noted that instruction in learning how to learn is a way of providing academic counseling and support. Teachers act as role models and guides to help marginal students accept their responsibility as learners.

Research on direct instruction in kindergarten has shown consistently positive gains when it is used as a part of a sound child development program. Carnine, Carnine, Karp, and Weisberg (1988) observed direct instruction of the higher order skills of concept attainment and application, problem solving, and translating oral story problems into equations. Successful kindergarten programs were characterized by frequent verbal exchanges. Teachers explained, modeled, asked questions to see if students understood, provided guided practice, and then asked more questions to prompt the use of specific steps in a skill or strategy.

Doyle (1983) expressed several concerns about overconfidence in direct instruction of higher level thinking. He claimed that young children can be taught to use some information-processing strategies but typically do not use them on their own or in a flexible manner. In addition, some higher level processes cannot be communicated in a way that children at lower developmental levels can understand. Many higher level processes used at the secondary level have not yet been identified.

Furthermore, direct instruction of specific skills must be accompanied by instruction in self-regulatory processes.

Other researchers suggest that the choice of teaching approach depends on the educational objectives teachers plan to accomplish. Brophy (1979a) maintained that it is not appropriate to use direct instruction for objectives, such as literary appreciation, that do not involve skill mastery. Peterson (1979) cited development of inquiry skills as an area where direct instruction would be inappropriate.

Conditions for Effective Instruction of Higher Level Skills

Teachers who want students to do higher level thinking must get them to construct their own knowledge. To achieve this outcome, they take a middle-ground approach between direct instruction and allowing student autonomy. Instruction should be focused, coherent, and negotiated in an interactive style (Prawat, 1989). Researchers have identified some practices that appear to be most productive in helping students develop the ability to do higher level thinking.

Developing a Thinking Climate.   In classes that have a thinking climate, the concept of teaching changes. Teachers are not just adults who know relevant facts and ideas. Instead, they know how to get students actively engaged in learning activities that will lead to the desired outcomes and are aware of the cognitive processes necessary to carry out each task. Effective teachers know which ideas will be difficult for students and what kinds of preconceptions or misconceptions will interfere with accurate learning. They choose the examples, subject matter, and activities that will help their students understand key ideas. Jones (1986) described the teacher as a mediator who helps students observe, activate prior knowledge, represent information, select specific strategies, construct meaning, monitor understanding, assess the use of strategies, organize and relate ideas, summarize, and extend their learning.

In classes that have a thinking climate, it is clear that the purpose of schooling and assignments is learning. Students are encouraged to do assignments because it is fun to learn. The challenge and excitement of learning is stressed. Expectations for all students are high but attainable. Cooperation and peer help is promoted. Errors are viewed as opportunities to learn, and self-evaluation is recommended. There is less concern for completing tasks, and competition is discouraged. Teachers do less routine correcting of errors and scores are not announced publicly (Marshall, 1988).

When there is a supportive learning environment, student thinking occurs frequently because the activities require thinking and teachers give students the freedom to risk thinking. They may give explicit directions that encourage challenging, questioning, inventing, and even guessing. There is frequent student-to-student interaction related to academic content. Lessons require comparing, analyzing, and judging the logic of arguments, the accuracy of hypotheses, and the adequacy of evidence. Students are actively involved in inventing and discovering relationships and making and testing inferences. Simply put, a thinking environment supports thinking (Beyer, 1983).

Making Instruction Meaningful.   The research consistently supports using teaching strategies that help learners construct or generate meaning for themselves. This statement is not as simple as it may first appear since it is hard to define meaning. Marzano, Pickering, and Brandt (1990) spoke to this issue: "Something is meaningful to a person only if it fits with his or her goals. Effective teaching involves finding ways for students to relate school knowledge to their personal goals" (p. 21). Shuell (1986) pointed out that you cannot understand a phone number because it has no meaning. From his point of view, only information that is structured or organized can be thought of as being meaningful and can be understood.

Teachers can help learners see the relationships between what is to be learned and what they already know. They can do this by using imagery, pointing out organization, providing advance organizers, introducing key word techniques, having students write summaries, using analogies or metaphors, or encouraging some motor activity to evoke vivid images. All of these techniques stimulate information processing and help students relate new information to their own memory system (Gage & Berliner, 1984). One way to help students see relationships is to organize learning around important concepts or key ideas. Instruction that is planned and sequenced around the most important ideas in a subject matter domain is more focused and coherent (Prawat, 1989).

Joyce and Weil (1986) stressed the importance of background knowledge. They assert that having essential background knowledge is necessary before meaningful learning can occur. Students must be ready to comprehend and relate to new material, not memorize it. When learners lack prerequisite knowledge, they cannot make solid connections to ideas in their cognitive structure, so they tend to memorize.

Capitalizing on Cooperation.   Much higher level thinking outside of the school setting involves a group of people working together. Intellectual work is shared and tasks are accomplished jointly. The elements of a skill take on meaning in the context of actual work. Resnick and Klopfer (1989) commented on the prevalence of cooperation:

> Most successful programs prescribe cooperative problem solving and meaning construction activities. This was remarkable because the designers of these programs had mostly begun with purely individual definitions of what they were trying to teach, and had arrived at the need for social interaction more through pedagogical trial and error than through theoretical analysis. (p. 8)

When groups of students work together, they have more ideas, propose more solutions, and spend less time on unproductive strategies. A single student, working alone, often persists in plans that go nowhere or forgets to include critical steps in a plan. Group members usually challenge ineffective strategies or monitor the progress of a plan. Heiman and Slomianko (1985) found that working in pairs forced students to externalize their thinking when they were required to think aloud and to serve as active listeners. Cooperative pairs caught errors and noticed steps that were omitted. Furthermore, they tended to edit their own unsystematic thinking as well as that of others.

Skilled thinkers in groups can demonstrate ways to attack problems, analyze texts, and construct arguments. They have the opportunity to model mental activities that are normally hidden. Resnick and Klopfer (1989) also found that students "can solve problems together that none of them could solve alone. They may help refine their knowledge and skill through criticism and shared work" (p. 8).

Resnick (1987) noted that some programs are like apprenticeships. Less experienced students work in groups, observing and commenting on the work of more skilled students. Skills are built up bit by bit, and new students participate in the easier steps. Gradually, they share more of the thinking, until they are able to carry out the entire process independently. Novices continue to work in the group until they become proficient. Resnick and Klopfer (1989) reported on cognitive apprenticeships that involve students with experts in the real world of work. These students have the opportunity to observe thinking in context rather than in contrived exercises. Brown, Collins, & Duguid (1989) also stressed the need to involve students in authentic activities in the work place. Such opportunities help students view knowledge as a tool and provide opportunities for modeling and coaching by experts.

There is some evidence that working in groups, where the members question, try possibilities, and demand justifications, may help students develop a disposition to participate in thinking. Through participation in groups, students may come to expect that thinking will take place all of the time. Marzano et al. (1990) described desirable habits of mind held by good critical and creative thinkers. They maintained that young people develop these qualities by interacting with adult role models and by consciously practicing desirable thinking habits.

Integrating Thinking and Content.   Some thinking skills programs have attempted to teach thinking skills and dispositions separately from subject matter through what has been called a general approach. Although logic can be taught in terms of relationships between variables, most of these programs depend on previously learned subject matter or controversial issues so that learners have something to think about. The primary purpose of these programs is to teach students to think critically about nonschool subjects (Ennis, 1989). Most educators who study higher level thinking do not favor a general approach. Resnick (1987) found that most successful programs are organized around particular bodies of knowledge and comprehension of knowledge in traditional school disciplines. Ennis (1989) studied the problem of expecting thinking skills to transfer from general programs to specific content area domains. He stressed the necessity of content-specific background knowledge for thinking in any content area. When content knowledge is not included in teaching about thinking, transfer is unlikely. For transfer to occur, Ennis believed, there must be sufficient practice in a variety of domains as well as instruction that focuses on transfer. Resnick and Klopfer (1989) summarized the essential linking of thinking and content:

> In this vision of the Thinking Curriculum, thinking suffuses the curriculum. It is
> everywhere. Thinking skills and subject-matter content are joined early in education

and pervade instruction. There is no choice to be made between a content emphasis and a thinking-skill emphasis. No depth in either is possible without the other. (p. 7)

 PRIMARY REFERENCES

Anderson, C.W., & Smith, E. L. (1987). Teaching science. In V. Richardson-Koehler (Ed.), *Educators' handbook: A research perspective* (pp. 84–111). New York: Longman.

> This chapter reviews the problems learners and teachers experience in science and provides a good description of teaching for conceptual change. Teacher knowledge needed for teaching science and conceptual change is described. Educators who are interested in teaching for conceptual change will find the bibliography very useful.

Corno, L. (1981). Cognitive organizing in classrooms. *Curriculum Inquiry, 11,* 359–377.

> This is still the clearest available explanation of cognitive organizing. Corno explains the nature of mental organization and reviews the research. Behavior processes that help foster reduction, organizing, and retrieval of information are discussed. The article includes suggestions for promoting cognitive organization in the classroom.

Derry, S. J. (1989–90). Putting learning strategies to work. *Educational Leadership, 46*(4), 4–10.

> This article explains mental processing techniques (learning strategies) that can improve the quality of student learning. Derry stresses the role of the learner in formulating a plan to accomplish a learning goal. He divides learning strategies into categories: providing examples, establishing conditions for use, and detecting strengths and weaknesses of verbal, procedural, and mental support strategies.

Jones, B. F. (1986). Quality and equality through cognitive instruction. *Educational Leadership, 45* (7), 4–12.

> This article reviews the conditions that led to the call for cognitive instruction and points out both the negative and positive effects of the reform movement. The concept of cognitive instruction is defined and critical attributes are delineated. Jones also defines direct instruction and explains how it should be implemented. Strategic instruction is explained, and recommendations are made for closing the gap between current and desired instructional practices.

Marzano, R. J., Brandt, R. S., Hughes, C. S., Jones, B. F., Presseisen, B. Z., Rankin, C. S., & Suhor, C. (1988). *Dimensions of thinking: A framework for curriculum and instruction.* Alexandria, VA: Association for Supervision and Curriculum Development.

> The authors have constructed a basic framework for higher level learning skills. This work is invaluable for planning curriculum and instruction.

Major sections cover thinking, metacognition, critical and creative thinking. Thinking processes and core thinking skills are defined and discussed. The final section of the book deals with the relationship between thinking skills and content instruction.

Paris, S. G., Lipson, M. Y., & **Wixson, K. K.** (1983). Becoming a strategic reader. *Contemporary Educational Psychology, 8,* 293–316.

This is the definitive work on strategic reading. Paris and his associates present a full explanation of strategies readers can use to improve their comprehension. The ideas provided are useful for students learning to read at the primary level and for those who are using reading as a learning tool at any level.

Prawat, R. S. (1989). Teaching for understanding: Three key attributes. *Teaching and Teacher Education, 5,* 315–328.

The author draws on current research to support his position that schools need to use a conceptually oriented approach for teaching. The importance of developing networks of knowledge in learning mathematics and science is highlighted. The three key attributes that Prawat has identified are: instruction should be focused, meaning should be negotiated through interaction between students and teachers, and teachers should be strongly analytic or diagnostic.

Resnick, L. B. (1987). *Education and learning to think.* Washington, DC: National Academy Press.

This pamphlet includes the most commonly quoted definition of higher level thinking. Current views on the nature of thinking, learning, and constructing meaning are discussed. Research related to improving thinking is summarized with special emphasis on embedding thinking in content area instruction. This is one of the most practical, readable treatments of the subject.

Shuell, T. J. (1986). Cognitive conceptions of learning. *Review of Educational Research, 56,* 411–436.

The author explains current psychological and educational views of thinking. Shuell describes the factors that influence changes in knowledge structures, human performance, and concept formation. The active role of learners in processing new information is a major theme. A discussion of how cognitive theories of learning have influenced research and instruction is included.

Tennyson, R. D., & **Cocchiarella, M. J.** (1986). An empirically based instructional design theory for teaching concepts. *Review of Educational Research, 56*(1), 40–71.

The authors review the research on concept formation to suggest instructional design elements that teachers can use to help students form valid concepts. Readers will find in-depth information and significant help for redesigning their instruction for a conceptual approach to learning. Educators who are interested in basing instruction on key concepts will find much to think about in this text.

RESEARCH IN PRACTICE

Finding 1: Students' prior knowledge is an important determinant of how they process new information.

Learning does not merely expand students' knowledge but involves changes and alterations of existing knowledge. The amount of knowledge students have and the way it is organized has a direct influence on the acquisition of new information. Unfamiliar content is more easily acquired when students' prior knowledge is accurate and well developed. Teachers should consider the influence that general and content-specific knowledge previously acquired by students will have on their future learning.

Scenario. A sixth grade teacher planned a lesson for his unit on map reading by referring to the teacher's manual. Because this was his first year of teaching, the teacher's manual was one of his most important instructional tools. Several practice pages were provided for duplication, so he decided to use these to teach the concept of scale. Three maps with different scales were available for use. The first page had a map of a neighborhood with streets, schools, and a park. The second page included a road map of two possible routes between cities. Page three had an airline map with lines showing flights from Chicago to several West Coast cities. Students were required to compute distances from one point to another on each map by using the scales.

When class began, the teacher explained the task and told the students that they would complete page one together. He asked the students to tell him what they knew about scales on maps. It was clear that these students knew the word *scale* only as it related to fish or weight. When the teacher probed by asking what kind of scale they would find on a map, there was silence. He tried again, asking how their parents knew how far they would have to travel between cities when they took car trips. This question elicited two answers. One student explained that little red numbers on the map showed how far it was. Another student said that his father used some kind of graph that looked a lot like a triangle with lines. Some of the students explained that their parents never talked about maps during car trips. Several reported that they never took trips.

At this point the teacher tried another approach. He pulled down political maps of the world, the nation, and their state. Students were asked to locate their state on each map and describe its size. They did this quite well and explained the size difference by saying that the map artist had to draw it smaller on two maps because there was not enough room on the paper. When the teacher pointed out the scales on each map, his students could not explain the relationship between those "little rulers" and the size of their state on the three different representations. It was clear that they had very little knowledge about map scales.

These students did not have enough knowledge to learn from the tasks the teacher had planned. He went to the board and asked students to brainstorm, giving him every word they knew that had any relationship to measuring distance. After he had a collection of words, he helped the class group them into three categories:

(1) words that are used to measure distance, (2) words that are used to describe distances, and (3) measuring devices. This activity helped the teacher find out how much his students knew about measuring distance. For example, their list of measuring devices consisted of two words, *ruler* and *yardstick*.

That night the teacher replanned the lesson. He located yardsticks and large tape measures. During the next few days, his students measured the distance from the door of their room to the front door of the school, to the end of the school property, and to the first major cross street. They drew a separate map to show how to get to each destination. Since the size of the paper remained constant, it did not take long for the class to discover that they needed to adjust the length of lines they used to represent distances on their maps. The entire class was involved in deciding on the scale they would use to represent units of length. The students started bringing maps with different scales from home. They posted the maps on a bulletin board that showed different units of measure on different kinds of maps. When the teacher finally used the practice sheets as an independent activity, the students had little difficulty completing them successfully. More important, this teacher had learned the importance of knowing the adequacy of students' prior knowledge before beginning instruction.

Finding 2: Cognitive organizational strategies can be used to facilitate higher level learning.

Students often have knowledge they are unable to use because it is not stored in memory in a meaningful way. They may have memorized a multitude of new facts at a surface level without grouping, ordering, or relating the new information to concepts they currently understand. Teachers can help students organize and store new information so they will be able to remember and use it. Some teachers model the process of information reduction and organization as an integral part of their instruction, by constructing verbal or graphic organizers that depict the structure of their topic. Others involve students in deciding how to organize new information around key concepts. Either approach helps students integrate new information in a meaningful way and helps them develop strategies for accessing their knowledge.

Scenario.   Several mathematics teachers were talking about the difficulty they had in helping their students identify common multiples as a step in the process of simplifying fractions. Two teachers described how they taught the concept. One teacher explained the sequence of instruction she used, stressing how carefully she prepared her presentation and chose problems to use as examples. In spite of all her efforts, she reported, some of her students still had trouble recognizing common multiples. The second teacher said that his students seemed able to do the problems during teacher-directed practice but had difficulty during independent practice, homework, or unit tests. A third teacher explained that she had found a way to teach her low-ability math class how to identify common multiples with less difficulty. She invited the others to observe the process in action. Two of the teachers made arrangements to observe her math class.

The teachers watched as the students explained how to use a graphic organizer to find common multiples. After placing a difficult problem on the board, the teacher drew a large circle on the chalkboard and asked individual students to give her multiples of the number 3. These were written inside the circle. The teacher then drew a second circle so that it overlapped the first one. The students then provided multiples of the number 4. These were written in the right circle. Students compared these to the numbers in the first circle. Any matching numbers were erased and written in the overlapping space of the two circles to show that they were common multiples of both 3 and 4. The same process was followed for the number 6. The multiples that were common to all three numbers were placed in the intersection of all three circles. The organizer is depicted in Figure 12–5. When the students had finished, they could identify the common multiples visually. Moreover, they had learned a process they could use to organize their knowledge.

During the independent practice portion of the class, the visiting teachers walked around the room observing students as they computed fractions. Several youngsters drew circles to identify common multiples for each problem. Others used the process only when they had difficulty. One girl used a separate page with organizers she had produced for other problems. When the same numbers appeared in a problem, she referred to her "cheat sheet." It was clear that their organizing process was helping these students learn to simplify fractions.

Finding 3: Comprehension of complex information can be improved through conscious self-monitoring of learning.

Students who take an active role in their learning are aware of their own thinking processes. They monitor their thinking in order to take control of their own learning. The purposeful, conscious control of learning is known as metacognition. Teachers can help students develop metacognitive strategies by encouraging and modeling the processes of planning, evaluating, and regulating learning. Students learn ways to assess their level of understanding. They also possess and use appropriate learning strategies. With these resources students develop the ability to monitor their learning and remediate their own comprehension problems.

Scenario.   A student teacher was upset when he corrected the first set of research papers written by his junior high students. Although several papers were adequate, the majority of the work did not meet the teacher's expectations. One student had copied sections directly from an encyclopedia. When the teacher discussed the problem with his seminar group at the university, his supervisor asked whether the problem was due to lack of writing ability or failure to understand the assignment. The student teacher reported that many of the students did not seem to be able to decide what information to collect and include in their papers. They wrote more about details than main ideas. Some papers showed a serious lack of comprehension. He said it looked as if the students were just going through the motions.

FIGURE 12–5. A
mathematics organizer for
identifying common multiples

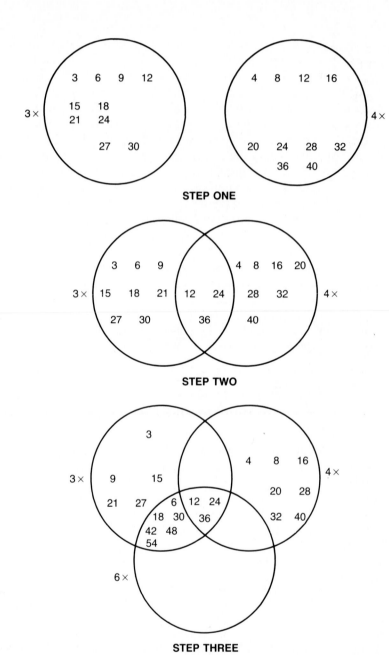

The supervisor reviewed the research on metacognition with the entire group and asked the group to help develop a plan to correct the problem. The student teacher went back to his class with renewed energy. During step one of the plan, he spent some time asking students what they thought they were supposed to learn from the assignment. This seemed like a foreign idea to the students. They reported quite honestly that they saw assignments as hurdles to get over, a price to pay for getting passing grades. The idea that they should deliberately learn something was not that important to them.

Step two of the plan was put into action as the class talked about the benefits of being able to retrieve information and communicate it to others. The teacher contributed practical, real-world examples and reasons. The following day the teacher started on step three of his plan by presenting a new research assignment. This time he helped the class develop learning objectives for the paper. Once this was completed, students talked about how they would plan their work in order to accomplish the objectives. Short individual conferences were scheduled throughout the week to help students monitor their progress and learning. When students had difficulty understanding something they were reading, the teacher tried to help them overcome the problem. By the end of the week he discerned that many of his pupils were reading nonfiction materials as if they were reading short stories. Their quick, surface examination of the material did not allow them to comprehend complex information. The students needed to adjust both their reading rate and their approach to the material. With the supervising teacher's help, he planned and introduced three text structure patterns commonly used in nonfiction: sequential or episodic, descriptive or thematic, and contrast and compare. Being able to identify the way authors organize their texts helped students understand the nonfiction material they were reading.

Throughout this process, students were reminded of the learning objectives and asked to monitor their own progress. Groups of students were organized to give feedback on outlines and first drafts. The motivation level in the class improved significantly. Both the supervisor and the teacher were pleased with the progress that was apparent when the final papers were assessed. They agreed, however, that the most important change was that students were paying attention to their own learning and were willing to monitor and evaluate their own work.

Finding 4: When instruction is designed to focus on major ideas, students are more likely to acquire key concepts.

Planning instruction around key concepts is positively related to student achievement. The rationale for this is clear. Concepts serve as organizing centers for reducing and organizing new information. Teachers who promote concept formation do not stress rote learning of isolated facts. Instead, they help students make connections between new information and important concepts within a specific knowledge domain.

Scenario.   Complex concepts are often thought to be present only in core subjects such as mathematics, science, and social studies. In today's world, this is not the case. Most curriculum areas include difficult concepts students need to acquire. For example, an auto technology teacher in a vocational school was teaching about suspension systems in different kinds of automobiles.

At the beginning of class the teacher returned the unit tests. He praised the students' work, and pointed out several common errors that he had noticed in the tests. For each incorrect statement on the test the class was asked to explain why the statement was incorrect. Most of the mistakes were related to alignment of the wheels and the effect on steering the car.

Students were reminded that they would be moving from the instructional setting into the shop on Monday for the laboratory portion of the class. The teacher stressed the fact that they would be working on cars that were driven by people who trusted the shop to do good work. He asked the students to explain the steps necessary to repair a suspension system. Students discussed starting inspection procedures by filling out the proper paperwork, followed by diagnosis and problem identification. They described several types of suspension systems and possible difficulties. One student was asked to describe a high-tech machine used in the troubleshooting process. Other students listed safety hazards for the technician working on a suspension system and explained how to avoid them.

The instructor began a series of questions related to developing a plan for repairing a suspension system. Each time he presented a physical model or enlarged photograph of a problem. Students were asked to write down the type of system and make a diagnosis of the problem. When answers were shared with the class, the instructor asked what was wrong and why the defect was important. Each time he returned to three key concepts. First, he related the mechanical problem to the alignment of the wheels. Second, he asked how the problem would affect the steering system. Last, he asked why it was important to repair the defect. When he was sure that his students could relate the information to alignment, steering the car, and safety factors, he asked how to repair the defect.

This teacher used several of the instructional design principles recommended for concept formation. He defined important terms such as *suspension system, alignment,* and *steering system.* Students could give examples and nonexamples of each concept. The teacher used questions to make sure that students knew the key attributes of each system. When they had trouble identifying parts of one of the more complex systems, the teacher elaborated by using charts and cutaway models supplied by major automotive companies. At each stage of diagnosis and planning for correction, students were reminded of checklists, diagnostic machinery, or strategies they should use. This teacher used personal experience, stories of mistakes former students had made, and humor to stress each major point. During the review, each example and story was related back to the key concepts of alignment, steering, and safety. The students had begun to master the concepts that would help them diagnose problems with suspension systems in domestic and foreign automobiles.

Finding 5: Teaching for conceptual change must provide for unlearning or reorganizing prior information as well as processing new information.

Young people come to school with a knowledge base that is the result of their cumulative experience. Some of the concepts that children have formed on their own are valid and form a solid base for new instruction. Other concepts are flawed by naive reasoning or misinformation. Students often cling to these faulty concepts because they seem logical to them. Teachers who want to help students develop valid concepts must identify existing ideas related to a concept and challenge those that are inaccurate. In these cases, learning involves unlearning. Experiences that will make students dissatisfied with their current knowledge should be planned. When young people see that an alternative explanation works better, they are willing to alter or reconstruct their faulty concepts.

Scenario. A new science program being implemented in a school system was designed to involve students in hands-on experiences. A committee of teachers, under the direction of the science supervisor, had developed classroom kits for use with each cluster of lessons. During the first year of the program, the supervisor visited classes to monitor implementation of the curriculum. As part of this effort he observed a sixth grade teacher when she was teaching a lesson on condensation and the water cycle.

The teacher introduced the kits and the task to be accomplished. Students were reminded to work cooperatively in their groups, to read directions before beginning, and to take notes on their results. With this brief introduction, students moved to their workstations. The hands-on experiment involved two empty glasses, a beaker of ice, and a bottle of water at room temperature. Each group placed ice in one glass, then poured equal amounts of water in both glasses. They followed directions to make observations at timed intervals. The teacher moved from group to group checking on progress. One group seemed quite upset because "nothing was happening." Another group thought they ought to measure the water in each glass at the end of the task.

After a time, the students reconvened as a class to discuss the experiment and their observations. The teacher polled the groups to find out what they had observed. Three of the four groups had noticed and recorded the drops of water that formed on the outside of the glass of ice water. The last group had noticed this but failed to record it because they did not think it was important. After this, each group was asked about the source of the water on the outside of the glass. Two of the four groups reported that it came from the water inside of the glass. They used the word *sweat* and compared the drops of water to sweat that comes from the inside of a human body through the skin. The third group knew that it did not come from inside the glass. The group said that they could have proved it if they had measured the water before and after the experiment. They had decided that somehow the water had melted out of the air. The teacher praised this response and explained that there is always water vapor in the air. She wrote *condensation* on the board and explained that water vapor in the air condenses when it hits a cold surface. There was no mention of the major concepts of kinetic molecular theory, states of matter, the effect of cooling and heating on the movement of molecules, or the water cycle. The hands-on task seemed to be an isolated experience, not an integral part of a carefully planned curriculum.

During the discussion students revealed serious conceptual misunderstandings. When this happened, the teacher explained why the students were wrong instead of directly challenging their faulty thinking. The science supervisor was at a loss to explain why the carefully designed program was not working. So many things had gone wrong. Some students used informal language to describe scientific concepts, while others could not grasp the importance of the phenomenon they had observed. When students suggested ways they could test their observations, they were not encouraged to do so.

The supervisor reflected about what was happening to the program. When he looked at records of attendance at staff development sessions and at the checkout list for classroom kits, he found that this teacher had not attended the training sessions designed to help teachers implement the new program. Moreover, there was no systematic pattern to her use of the classroom kits. Some weeks she did not check out any kits. The teacher had not been trained to use the program, did not have a deep knowledge of science, and implemented the curriculum incorrectly.

To his credit, the science supervisor accepted his share of the responsibility for the situation. He planned and provided additional training for teachers who had missed the initial sessions. Much to his surprise, many teachers who had attended the workshops requested permission to attend again. They, too, had encountered some problems and felt they needed further assistance. One unintended outcome of these sessions was a compilation of suggestions for adjustments, changes, and additional experiments from teachers who had used the program.

Finding 6: If students are to solve real-life problems successfully, instructional tasks must require the use of essential problem-solving behaviors.

A problem exists when attempts to reach a goal are unsuccessful and students must consider several possible alternative courses of action that might be used to reach the goal. The first step in problem solving is becoming aware of the existence of a problem. Successful problem solvers find some way to understand or represent a problem. Information is gathered and organized and several solution paths may be identified. But the process does not end there. Monitoring progress, as steps of the plan are carried out, and adjusting the plan are important problem-solving behaviors.

When instruction is carefully planned, teachers can help students learn to use general and specific problem-solving procedures effectively. Knowing how to use knowledge of subject matter and information-processing skills and having a reflective attitude are also necessary for effective problem solving. Teachers should embed problem-solving instruction in meaningful activities and encourage groups of students to investigate problems together.

Scenario.   A fifth grade teacher developed an ornithology unit for her science class. She began the unit by taking the students to the school's nature area. Several species of birds were observed during the trip. When the class got back to the room, the teacher reminded the students about the bird feeder outside their window. Together they made plans to fill the feeder and keep a record of the birds that visited the feeder. The teacher stressed the importance of careful observation. A chart was designed to record the kinds of birds observed. A collection of library books and field guides was available to help with bird identification.

Few birds came to the feeder when the food was first introduced. Gradually, a variety of sparrows began to frequent the feeder. There was a good deal of excitement when a male cardinal first appeared. One day several blue jays were at the feeder. These larger, more aggressive birds soon monopolized the feeding station. Mockingbirds and chickadees were observed in a nearby dogwood tree but never came to the feeder. The class was not happy with their attempt to attract a variety of birds. The teacher praised them for recognizing the problem and suggested that they might want to develop a plan to solve it. The students had been reading about migration and were aware that their town was on one of the flyways. They felt that they had to act quickly if they wanted to see birds that might be passing through on their way to warmer climates.

After discussing the problem and developing a plan, three small groups were formed. Group A was to visit the nature area again to see what kinds of birds were there that were not coming to the feeder. Group B was to gather more information about what birds eat. Group C began by using the reference books and taking notes. Their task was to study the behavior of the birds they saw at the feeder, keeping track of the kinds of seeds eaten by each kind of bird. The class planned to use the information to establish another feeder since the first feeder was overcrowded.

During science class the next day each group reported on its progress. Group A had reported that several birds were observed that had not used the feeder. Group B added important new information. They had found that some birds are vegetarians and eat seeds and berries only, while others are carnivorous, feeding on insects, bugs, worms, fish, and other small animals.

Group C reported that starlings had begun visiting the feeder. They had also noticed that the sunflower seeds seemed to be the favorite food for most of the birds. A small yellow seed the students did not recognize was left in the feeder each night because most of the birds did not eat it. This group had also noticed that a brown thrasher and some of the mourning doves ate seeds that fell to the ground under the feeder.

Group C had discovered that all birds don't like the same food and that the shape of their beaks is a clue to what they might eat. Yet, they still did not know how to attract a wider variety of birds. The plan was adjusted and each small group was given a new information-gathering task. Group A went to the library to find out what kind of birds might be expected to pass through their area during the next few weeks. Group B decided to gather information on the design of bird feeders that might attract birds they had seen or those migrating through. Group C was asked to visit a pet shop that specialized in bird food to find out what kinds of seeds were in packages of birdseed. They planned to find out if other kinds of food were available.

When the groups met again, they had solved several parts of their problem. They knew that they could buy a feeder that holds seeds small birds prefer; this feeder had holes and perches too small to accommodate the larger birds. They also knew that some birds prefer to eat berries and other fruit. They planned to establish different feeding stations to attract different species of birds.

When the new feeders were in place, new charts were started. It was not long before the class observed different birds using the new feeders. Their charts revealed that the birds were attracted by the variety of food that was now available. The class had been engaged in problem-solving activities that could be applied to other real-life experiences.

Finding 7: Students with a positive self-concept are more likely to acquire the skills and attitudes necessary to become self-regulated learners.

Self-regulated learners take responsibility for their own learning because they view themselves as competent learners. They have an internal locus of control that allows them to believe that they can affect what happens to them. Teachers foster these attitudes by helping students build confidence and control. While helping students build positive self-concepts is an important first step, teachers know that developing a supportive classroom climate and teaching self-regulation processes are important instructional strategies.

Scenario.   A second grade teacher met with the reading supervisor during the week before school to review records and develop plans for grouping. They were both pleased to see that the majority of the students were reading on grade level or above. Independent reading records showed that the students frequently read for information and pleasure at home and at school. Writing portfolios indicated that most of the students were able to express their ideas clearly in writing. Although they wrote about a wide range of topics, many of the student compositions related to books they had read.

The teacher talked about capitalizing on the sound foundation these students would bring to second grade. She was committed to developing independent learners. Much of her planning centered around a review of methods to promote self-regulated learning. She decided to use a whole language approach for language arts instruction.

When school started, the second grade students were organized into small heterogeneous groups. Each group was given multiple copies of a relatively easy book about dogs. The teacher started out by asking the groups to look at the pictures in their book and be ready to answer three questions:

1. What kind of book is this? (Real or make-believe)
2. What do you think the book is about?
3. Why would you read a book like this?

After the groups reported, the teacher talked about the importance of setting a purpose for reading. The class decided that books about real things should be read more carefully than story books. Because the teacher wanted to assess background knowledge, some time was spent asking questions and developing a list of things the students knew about dogs. When that list was completed, another list of things the class wanted to learn was generated. Students were told to read their books independently, helping each other with difficult words. Each group was to identify how many of the things they wanted to learn were answered in the book.

The teacher felt that she had started the class off pretty well. She wanted the children to feel confident about their ability to read, so she had given them a book at or below their independent level. She had helped them set a purpose for reading and given them a reason for concentrating on the assignment. She had plans for introducing opportunities to write about what they read and for independent reading assignments to find missing facts.

As the year progressed, the teacher taught the children how to monitor their own comprehension. Reading for meaning was stressed. Fix-up strategies were introduced when they read something that did not seem to make sense. Students learned how to use a rereading strategy first. They found that they could often fix up the problem by rereading the last paragraph carefully. A look-back technique was used when this failed. Most of the students learned to use an "Are there any clues in the story?" strategy. The teacher used these words to describe the use of context to figure out the meaning of new words.

The strategies the students learned for monitoring their comprehension served them very well throughout the year. The monitoring process helped the students take increased responsibility for their own learning. As a consequence, students became more confident about their ability to learn.

Finding 8: Direct instruction can be used to teach the vocabulary and processes that are needed to engage in higher level thinking.

Teachers can foster development of higher level thinking if they focus instruction on the key attributes of the cognitive operations that constitute thinking, model the use of thinking processes, and provide guided practice. Combining strategy instruction and use of vocabulary that describes mental processing helps students become aware of and take control of their own thinking. After teaching the specific steps of a thinking strategy and conditions for its use, teachers should gradually transfer responsibility for using the strategy to the students. Able learners have a variety of thinking strategies that they use to accomplish specific purposes on their own. Instruction in learning-to-learn strategies that integrate content area knowledge is especially beneficial for low-ability students.

Scenario.   A high school social studies teacher wanted her students to become more critical readers. She felt that the textbook presented a one-sided interpretation of historical events. Consequently, she decided to have students read different articles and essays on development of the railroad system as part of the unit on westward expansion. She chose the readings carefully, including copies of some original newspaper articles, interviews with national leaders, and research articles by modern writers. Several perspectives on the effect of the Interstate Commerce Act of 1887 and the Sherman Antitrust Law were included.

Students were assigned specific purposes for reading. They knew their individual readings would provide information other class members needed. Students were told to read, summarize their selections, and be prepared to give oral reports to the class. The teacher thought her plan would provide students with an interesting, exciting learning experience. The department head, who had helped identify some of the reading material, observed the class.

The result was disappointing. Many summaries were compilations of meaningless details or simply personal reactions to the content. The teacher and department head discovered that few of these students could summarize what they read, so they decided to teach the class a strategy for summarizing. They chose to use research on text summarization skills as the basis of the strategy.

Because she knew that there was not enough time to work with all of the articles, the teacher reviewed the reading material again. She chose and copied three articles with different points of view on the expansion of the railroad system. These three articles would be the content students would use to learn a summarizing strategy.

The first day the teacher gave the class members individual copies of one short article and asked them to read it over silently. Once this was accomplished, the teacher explained the strategy for summarizing and listed the steps on the board. During step one, students were asked to draw a circle around any information that they thought was unimportant or trivial. The teacher modeled the process talking about how she would think if she were required to do this step alone. As she proceeded through the article, she encouraged student contributions. During step two the teacher and students crossed out repetitious information. Step three involved combining a list of important individual actions into a single, broader action. The class chose a topic sentence from the selection as step four. Step five was accomplished when the class used the results of their work to write brief, concise summaries. The same five-step process was followed with the other two articles. One of these did not have a good topic sentence, so the class had to create one. For step three, they combined lists of important people in one case and causes instead of actions in the last article. Students were then given a fourth article to summarize. The teacher monitored and provided help as needed. As a final activity, the class compared the content of the articles and discussed the implications of developing trusts as a way to limit competition.

The teacher and department head spent some time reflecting on the experience. They both realized that working through the thinking strategy had taken more time than direct instruction. Moreover, they knew that the class had not mastered the process of summarizing text. There were still some students who needed reminders to complete all of the steps. Others had trouble recognizing lists that could be collapsed. Most of the students were not sure when they should choose to use the summarization strategy. On the positive side of the ledger, however, students had learned that they could follow a process to summarize text and had shown a real grasp of the material they had read. Working through the steps of the thinking strategy had helped them reduce the information by eliminating unimportant information and retaining major ideas. The teacher planned to reinforce use of the strategy during future lessons. Both teachers realized that they should be alert to the need to introduce additional higher level thinking strategies.

Finding 9: Teachers can develop an instructional climate that will enhance all levels of learning.

A positive instructional climate stresses the challenge and excitement of learning. Students know that assignments are designed to help them learn. Ritual completion of tasks just to get them done is discouraged. Teachers do not stress one predetermined answer, and students are encouraged to risk thinking. Every effort is made to promote meaningful instruction by capitalizing on relationships between what is already known and what is to be learned. Instruction is organized around key concepts that help focus learning and make it more coherent. Students work together cooperatively to learn new material, generate ideas, find solutions, and carry out complex processes. Whenever possible the class is involved in authentic thinking tasks through apprenticeships or experience in the work place. Learning to think is integrated with content area instruction, and every effort is made to integrate learning across content areas.

Scenario.   An example of developing a positive classroom climate for thinking took place in an eleventh grade unified studies class. An English teacher, a social studies teacher, and their department heads worked together to plan and carry out a unit on governance structure. They started by deciding what their goals and objectives for the unit would be. The social studies curriculum included a unit on the essential elements of the governmental process. Objectives for that unit included understanding the importance of cooperation and competition in a free enterprise system. A process objective for the unit involved developing leadership skills for accomplishing goals in a group. After some discussion, the two members of the English department decided to concentrate on two literature objectives: recognizing stated and implied themes and understanding the effect of point of view. In addition, they suggested that several objectives from their unit on discussion skills would be important.

At the beginning of the unit the teaching team divided the class into small, heterogeneous learning groups. The groups participated in some formal team-building activities. These were designed to accomplish two purposes. First, the students needed to get to know each other better in order to function as a group. Second, the activities gave students an opportunity to use the active listening and paraphrasing skills they were learning in the presentation portion of the class. Teachers pointed out the relationship between active listening, an important component of communication, and leadership. At the same time, the class began reading and discussing *Lord of the Flies*. This novel had been chosen because one of its themes is the importance of leadership. Students were given a choice of novels with similar themes as homework.

All groups had a common assignment. They each received a written description of a problem related to governance. They were to generate a hypothesis about the best way to solve the problem, plan their research, carry out the study, interpret their information, and synthesize their findings. At the end of the unit, each group would present its project to the class. The teaching team would act as judges, evaluating the projects on the basis of evidence of scholarly research, creativity, and application of leadership skills in the group.

A member of the teaching team spent some time teaching discussion skills during the first few days of the unit. The social studies teacher also introduced the leadership skills of planning, communication, conflict management, power sharing, and allocating time or resources. During group time all of the teachers monitored groups and gave feedback on the use of discussion and leadership skills. Periodic checkpoints were scheduled with each group to discuss its progress. Teachers helped by suggesting instructional resources or checking the credibility of sources. They did not enter into generating hypotheses or suggesting solutions. Part of each class was spent discussing *Lord of the Flies* and relating events in the book to the advantages of a governance structure.

One group planned to erect a tower as part of their presentation. They had developed an analogy between an effective governance structure and the construction of a strong, beautiful tower. This caused quite a stir of activity in the other groups. They began to look for creative visualizations of their own research. Several groups scheduled after-school meetings to polish their projects. Students who had artistic talent became valued members of each group. The librarian reported that one group was photographing pictures from the history collection for a slide presentation. The teaching team began to wonder if the competition element of their plan was getting out of control and started stressing the value of cooperation in their discussions with the entire class.

As the unit progressed, the teaching team videotaped portions of each class as well as their own planning sessions. They were careful to tape direct instruction of skills, group discussions, students working in the library, presentations, and even the taking of the unit test. They used these tapes as part of their evaluation of the unit. The principal was invited to attend the final summary session. This was an opportunity for all participants to reflect on their instruction and on the unified studies program. They decided they had made significant progress toward their goal of developing a positive learning climate and had achieved several important learning objectives. They were also able to identify changes they would make in future unified studies instructional activities.

 ## GUIDE TO OBSERVATION, ANALYSIS, AND REFLECTION

Many teachers incorporate instructional strategies that are effective in promoting higher levels of learning. Observing teachers as they use strategies that encourage more active processing and engagement in learning is a productive way to examine the structure and outcomes of these strategies. The following activities concentrate on several important areas such as how teachers assess students' background knowledge, communicate key concepts, and help students organize content. In addition, the activities focus on metacognitive strategies and the classroom conditions that encourage students to think and take risks.

1. Assessing prior knowledge

Observation: *What attempts does the teacher make to assess students' level of prior knowledge and the ways students are integrating new information?*   Plan to observe when the teacher is introducing new information, possibly at the beginning of a unit. Focus your observation on the amount and accuracy of prior knowledge the students possess. Also note how the teacher monitors the ways students are processing unfamiliar information. It would be helpful to visit with the teacher prior to the observation to gain information about:

- The sequence of the instruction that occurred prior to this lesson
- How this information relates to what the student should already know
- The teacher's predictions about faulty concepts or comprehension difficulties

Include in your observation data teacher questions and probes, opportunities students have to explain or to share their understanding, types of response formats, preassessment strategies (formal and informal), teacher (or student) attempts to correct inaccurate information, teacher attempts to help students reorganize information, teacher assistance in helping students elaborate or interpret information, the use of cues to emphasize major points, and teacher elaboration through the use of examples, metaphors, analogies, and organizers (e.g., outlines, charts, graphic representations, semantic maps).

Analysis: *How effective were the teacher's attempts to determine students' background knowledge and use that knowledge to help students make sense of new information?*   Before sharing the observation data, discuss the perceived level of student understanding. Encourage the teacher to share the strategies used to assess prior knowledge and compare those strategies with the ones you identified during the observation. Decide if the strategies used were sufficient to assess student's background knowledge and if additional strategies could have been used. As you look over the observation information, ask the teacher about specific attempts to help students incorporate the new information in an accurate form. Together, determine if additional attempts should have been made with specific students.

Reflection: *What strategies will I use to help students integrate new information with their prior knowledge?*   In reflecting on the lesson you observed and analyzed, identify specific strategies you could use to determine if individual students have extensive or limited background knowledge. Identify particular organizational structures, examples, and elaborations that you could use to help students restructure prior information with the new information. Specify ways students could contribute their knowledge to help other students organize their understanding of the topic.

2. Organizing information

Observation: *In what ways does the teacher attempt to help students organize information?*   Listen carefully to the introduction of new information or concepts. Record explicit statements by the teacher about relationships and connections. Examples may include:

- Stating relationships between new content and previously learned material
- Explaining connections to information from other units or classes
- Comparing or contrasting new ideas with previous information
- Using advance organizers (verbal statements of logical relationships)

Record any statements that illustrate or imply relationships and connections. Examples may include:

- Using stories that help to make the new material meaningful
- Providing analogies that make explicit comparisons between familiar and unfamiliar concepts or ideas
- Using metaphors that bridge the gap between the known and the unknown

Make notes about any verbal or graphic organizers the teacher uses to help students organize information. Examples may include:

- Providing outlines
- Using graphs, timelines, and charts
- Constructing or helping students generate cognitive organizers
- Involving students in construction of semantic maps
- Providing text structure maps

Analysis: *How effective were the teacher's attempts at organizing the information?*   Review the notes from your observation. What evidence was there that the teacher tried to help students organize new information? What attempts were made to relate new concepts or information to information already in memory? You might want to categorize the data under the following headings:

- Relationships with information learned in this class
- Relationships with major concepts in the content area

- Connections with information learned in other classes
- Examples from or connections to the real world

Look at your notes again. Did the teacher use stories, analogies, or metaphors to help organize new information? What evidence was there that the students understood the function of the figurative device used?

What verbal or graphic organizers were used? Were these provided by the teacher, constructed by the class (with teacher help), suggested by the teacher (constructed by students), or generated in small groups?

What evidence was there that students were actively involved in reducing and organizing new information? Some teachers may not help students organize information. If the new material is not difficult and students have good background knowledge, this may be a good decision. Reread your notes, mentally reviewing the class. Was there any evidence that students needed more help in organizing knowledge? Were there opportunities for promoting organization? What kind of strategy would have been appropriate at the time? If textbooks were used, examine the way the content was organized. Design a text structure or use one of the examples in Figure 12–6 to organize important information the author presented.

Reflection: In what ways can I help students organize information?   If you feel that it would be helpful, talk to the teacher about your observation and analysis. Consider the following questions:

- How can I help students recall and use prior knowledge as an aid to learning?
- How can I encourage and help students reduce, organize, and store important information in memory?
- Are some methods more appropriate or productive for this content area?
- How can I use both visual and verbal organizers to give students more opportunities to make connections?

Choose a unit you will teach in the future. Review the information students will be expected to learn. What major ideas, concepts, processes, or vocabulary will be included? What previous knowledge might students need to recall and use to learn the new material? Develop a plan to help students organize new information and integrate it with their previous knowledge. Your plan might include some of the examples provided in observation activity 2.

3. Metacognitive and self-regulated learning strategies

Observation: What evidence is there that students understand their thinking processes and have some control over their own learning?   In your discussion with the teacher prior to the observation, try to determine to what degree the teacher has

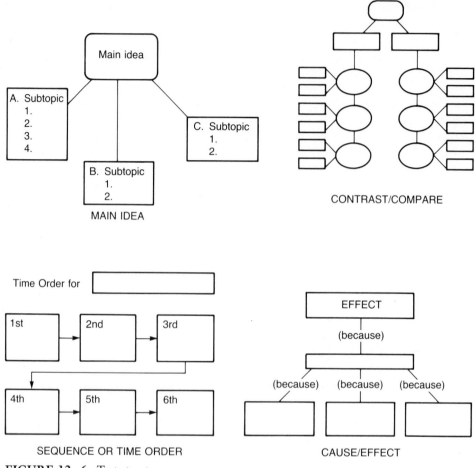

MAIN IDEA

CONTRAST/COMPARE

SEQUENCE OR TIME ORDER

CAUSE/EFFECT

FIGURE 12–6. Text structures

taught and emphasized metacognitive and self-regulated learning strategies. You might ask what strategies are especially important for these students as they learn this particular content.

As you observe, describe teacher and student behaviors that indicate awareness and use of learning strategies. Teacher behaviors you observe might include the following:

- Instruction in a specific strategy (e.g., summarizing, looking back, self-questioning)
- Giving reminders about the use of specific strategies
- Reteaching or additional instruction about the strategies
- Monitoring and providing assistance to individuals
- Providing learning aides or instructional materials that help students incorporate the strategy

- Questioning students about strategy use rather than about learning content (e.g., "How did you determine the main idea?" instead of "What is the main idea?")
- Providing students with opportunities to practice strategies and giving feedback about using them

In observing student behavior, it may be difficult to determine if students are actually using strategies (and completing the appropriate steps). If the resulting product or answer does not give you the necessary information, you may want to get some indication on strategy use by interviewing several students about what they were thinking during the learning process.

Analysis: How successful are students at understanding their thinking processes and regulating their own learning?   In reviewing your observation data, determine the level of attention given to the development and use of metacognitive and self-regulated learning strategies. If strategies are given attention, decide if they have been appropriately introduced and are being used successfully. Notice the amount of structure and control maintained by the teacher and the level of flexibility students exercise in using the strategies. Decide if the students are choosing to use the strategies independently or if they are merely complying with teacher directions.

Reflection: What metacognitive and self-regulated learning strategies are important for my students to know, and how am I going to incorporate the strategies in my teaching?   Attention should be given to student needs, their level of maturity and independence, the subject area, and the teacher's knowledge of and facility in using strategies. Since it may have been difficult to observe strategy use or to find expert teachers to help you assess this, you may want to research the area yourself or with a group of interested colleagues. You may want to find out about learning strategies that can be taught and how best to use them with your students. Identify appropriate strategies and plan ways to instruct, reinforce, and monitor those strategies.

4. Teaching key concepts

Observation: How are key concepts taught?   Make arrangements to observe a class when the teacher will be introducing new content. If possible, plan to visit with the teacher prior to the class. During the preobservation conference, ask the teacher to identify central ideas or key concepts in the content area. Try to get the teacher to explain the relationship between what will be introduced in this lesson and ideas or concepts that are central to the area of study. Ask the teacher to talk about the role of concepts in teaching and learning. Another focus of the conference should be questions about the abilities of the students and the learning objectives for the lesson you will observe. Be sure to jot down any mention of concept attainment, elements of a concept, or categorizing in the objectives.

During the observation, focus on the way concepts are taught. One way to do this is to record any statements about the elements of a concept. You will need to listen for five elements:

Deductive

1. The concept name (N)
2. Examples and nonexamples (E, NE)
3. Attributes of the concept (A)
4. A definition (D), that is, a rule or generality that states the critical attributes
5. Attribute values (V)

Other factors are important in concept formation. Be sure to describe concrete materials or representations the teacher uses. Code examples in order to differentiate between examples the teacher states (E for expository) and examples presented in a question format (I for interrogatory). When students do not understand a concept, teachers may provide a specific solution or strategy. Statements that provide strategy information (SI) should be recorded. Another important behavior is making connections between concepts and prior knowledge (ER for embedded refreshment).

Analysis: *How effectively were key concepts taught?* Review your observation information. Ask yourself the following questions:

- What evidence is there that concepts are used as a foundation for learning?
- Are students involved in mentally sorting facts or details into classes or categories?
- Does the teacher establish specific attributes or criteria for inclusion in a category? Is vocabulary instruction integrated?
- What elements of a concept are included in the instruction?
- How does the teacher use examples and nonexamples?
- How often are interrogatory examples used?
- What specific solution or strategies does the teacher provide?
- How does the teacher make connections between new concepts and prior knowledge?

Review your analysis notes and focus on the way concept formation was fostered in the class you observed. Was this class a good example of conceptual teaching? Were all elements of a concept taught (when appropriate)? Was there any evidence during the preobservation conference or the observation that the teacher believes students learn by accumulating facts over time instead of relating information to key concepts? What influence did instructional materials have on the way the concepts were taught? What opportunities were there for capitalizing on key concepts as the foundation of learning?

Reflection: *How will I teach key concepts?* Reflect on your observation and analysis activities. There is a consistent relationship between the depth of teachers' content area knowledge and their ability to use a conceptual approach to teaching. Think about the adequacy of your own knowledge base. What are the central ideas or concepts in your instructional domain? If you feel that you need to improve your knowledge base, develop a plan to make the improvement.

5. Climate for thinking

Observation: *What conditions contribute to a thinking climate within the classroom?* The list that follows includes specific indicators that suggest the classroom atmosphere is promoting student thinking. In your observation record, identify specific teacher statements and actions that relate to:

- The academic focus of the lesson
- Emphasis on cooperation
- Acceptance of errors as a sign of growth
- Emphasis on thinking and confronting misconceptions
- Reminders for students to evaluate their own work
- Encouragement to take risks
- The use of students as models and coaches

The teacher may also specifically alert students to the thinking processes required to complete the instructional tasks such as focusing, gathering information, organizing, analyzing, and evaluating. The general warmth, supportiveness, predictability, and orderliness of the classroom climate also influence student thinking. Higher level thinking requires uninterrupted, focused time.

Analysis: *How conducive were classroom conditions to promoting higher level thinking?* Assess your observation information in terms of the degree of emphasis given to thinking. Attempt to categorize the behaviors, actions, and conditions as supportive of thinking or unsupportive of thinking. An absence of supportive conditions and actions indicates a less-than-desirable state. Suggest possible behaviors, actions, and conditions that could be incorporated to give more emphasis to the importance of student thinking. If supportive conditions are present, assess their effectiveness. A variety of approaches and appropriate level of use are considerations.

Reflection: *What conditions will I establish to promote higher level thinking?* Reexamine the conditions and actions you felt were effective in establishing a thinking climate. Consider how you might best incorporate these conditions and actions in your teaching. Decide on ways you will monitor the effectiveness of your actions by identifying desired student outcomes. Remember that it is critical for you to provide ample opportunities for students to practice higher level learning skills. Therefore, it is necessary to plan instructional tasks that require a higher level of cognitive processing such as defining problems, setting goals, observing, formalizing questions, comparing, classifying, ordering, identifying main ideas, inferring, predicting, establishing criteria, and verifying.

DEVELOPMENT AND RENEWAL ACTIVITIES

1. Make arrangements to visit several classes to observe instruction of higher level thinking skills. Choose classes taught by the same or different teachers. The task is to focus on direct instruction of higher level thinking skills or strategies over a number of classes. Because direct instruction of higher level thinking is not always appropriate, observers may not see this behavior very often.

For this observation you may be able to keep an anecdotal log describing the instruction while you check off specific behaviors on a chart like the one below. You will want to start a new chart for each class.

Behaviors Used in Direct Instruction

Time	Describing the Skill	Telling Why It Is Important	Direct Instruction of the Skill	Providing Conditional Knowledge

As part of your analysis, examine the anecdotal log to see to what extent the teacher delegated responsibility for using the skill. Did the teacher assume the responsibility for use of the technique? Was responsibility shared or given to students? If students share or have full responsibility, visit with the teacher about how the skill or strategy was introduced.

How was flexibility in strategy use encouraged, supported, or discouraged? What evidence indicates that instruction in higher level learning had evolved over a number of classes so that students would gradually develop their use of the strategy? How is the vocabulary necessary for discussing thinking taught? Use your charts to assess whether the steps suggested for direct instruction of higher level thinking (see page 414) were used. Were all steps present? Which ones were omitted? How did this affect instruction?

What opportunities to use direct instruction of higher level thinking or strategies were missed? What statements or behaviors indicated that students needed direct instruction? What suggestions could you make for incorporating explicit instruction?

Review all of your observation information. Make a general assessment of how often thinking is a topic of instruction. How do you believe direct instruction in thinking could be encouraged or improved?

    2. Some teachers believe that students have to learn everything through direct instruction, repetition, and practice. When this is the case, even the most knowledgeable teachers do not organize their instruction around major concepts. Examine your own belief system. How have your past experiences and preparation affected your view of learning? Does this view influence the way you present concepts? If you would like to improve your concept instruction, you might plan to do some reading about concept formation or arrange to visit with an expert teacher who regularly organizes learning around major concepts.

    3. Choose a concept that you will have to teach in the future. Examine information presented in the textbook. Plan to alter or supplement this information so that learning will be more conceptual. If you are in a preparation program, choose a textbook that is used in your area. Colleges and universities usually have a collection of textbooks in the curriculum laboratory or education library.

    Some teachers find that hierarchical concept diagrams and concept circle diagrams like the ones in Figures 12−7 and 12−8 are helpful in concept formation. These graphic representations show the relationships between concepts. Could one of them help students visualize the concept you are trying to teach? Would you introduce the entire diagram on one day or add new elements over a series of classes? Which of the circle diagrams would best show the relationship between examples and a key concept? Use one or more to explain the elements of the concept you will be teaching.

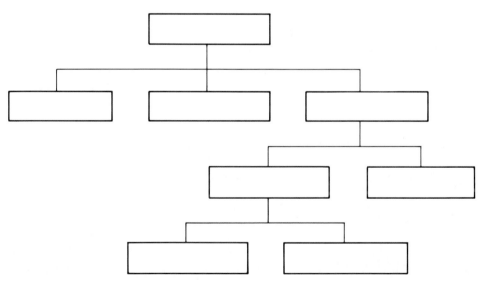

FIGURE 12−7. Hierarchical concept map

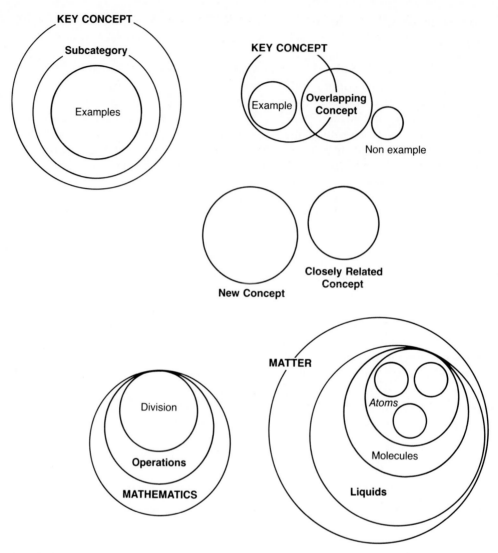

FIGURE 12–8. Concept circle diagrams

Remember that the diagram should explain the concept by showing structure, relationships, and connections.

4. If you are a student, develop a cognitive organizer for any body of content you are trying to learn. Review the graphic organizers provided in this chapter (and others) for possible formats. Be sure you have used a logical structure and one that accurately depicts the information.

Conclusion

13.

Developing and Renewing–A Career-Long Process

INTRODUCTION

Teachers choose their profession because they want to make a difference in the lives of their students. They want to feel prepared, competent, and confident of their ability to meet the needs of their students. In short, they want to feel that they are capable professionals. They strive to develop a sense of personal and professional efficacy—the feeling that they can be effective with their students. Teachers who feel that they can cause positive things to happen are more likely to create the same attitude with their students; that is, they create a sense of efficacy in their students.

Unfortunately, many of our most able teachers leave the profession. A number of reasons have been given for the exodus. Hanley and Swick (1983) cited low morale, the lack of respect and public confidence, and a sense of impotency as some of the reasons that teachers have become dissatisfied with their work. One of the important antidotes to teacher burnout and dissatisfaction is the opportunity to engage in activities that facilitate growth and renewal. Development and renewal programs need to be designed to help teachers advance their understanding of the knowledge base pertaining to teaching and learning. If the programs are to be effective, they must be conducted in supportive environments that facilitate teacher learning.

When appropriate conditions for growth are present, teachers at any stage in their professional careers can become more self-sufficient, by relying on their own competence and accumulated experience. They can become more adventurous in their approach to learning about teaching. They can develop the confidence to explore and select alternative instructional strategies. They do not have to rely on prescriptions. Instead they can apply what they learn on an individual, thoughtful basis, taking into consideration the teaching context as well as their own level of functioning. When teachers are engaged in systematic renewal programs, they do not look for one right answer; rather, they are learners seeking potential solutions to teaching problems. As Featherstone (1986) pointed out, when teachers view themselves as learners, they are in a better position to understand the learning needs of their students. They also tend to view learning as an ongoing process instead of a product (Wildman & Niles, 1987).

If teachers are expected to be committed to development and renewal, they must have some degree of autonomy in directing their own growth. As teachers develop increased efficacy, they are more likely to be motivated to engage in growth-promoting activities. As their confidence about their ability to learn increases, they will take more responsibility for their own learning (Wildman & Niles, 1987). Learning to teach is a growth process, not an event. Becoming an effective teacher is a complex task, and complex learning requires teachers to feel they have some control over their learning experiences.

The development and renewal process is a holistic, interactive activity that promotes a healthy synergism. All of the factors, conditions, and influences that are a part of the renewal process must be in harmony. A supportive, positive learning environment is essential if growth is to take place. When teachers understand the conditions and influences that can foster positive, growth-promoting experiences, they can strengthen their personal sense of efficacy.

A FRAMEWORK FOR PROFESSIONAL DEVELOPMENT AND RENEWAL

In our work with teachers we have been guided by one central assumption: teaching is a complex process, and in order to master the process systematic opportunities for renewal should be provided to all teachers. We believe that renewal is as important for the expert teacher as it is for the novice. Renewal cannot be a haphazard process. Renewal programs should be clearly conceptualized and carefully planned. The framework that serves as our reference point for designing development and renewal programs is presented in Figure 13–1. The success of the renewal process depends on a number of factors that must be considered when programs are designed: among them, teacher knowledge and experience, school influences, and external influences.

Preservice and novice teachers have a range of teaching experiences. Some preservice teachers have had earlier opportunities to teach young people in different settings such as recreation centers and church programs. Others have not done any teaching prior to their preservice clinical experiences. Even clinical experiences vary depending on college instructors and cooperating teachers. The teaching experience of teachers new to the profession will vary both in quantity and quality. And because

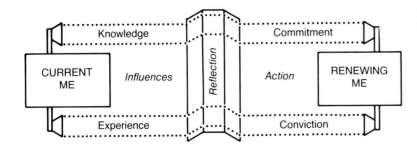

FIGURE 13–1. Framework for development and renewal

teaching contexts and responsibilities vary from school to school, experience differences may widen as teachers progress through their careers.

Teachers' knowledge bases vary as widely as their experience. Novice teachers have had coursework and seminars that emphasize various subject areas and pedagogical methods. Their knowledge of educational research will vary depending on the expectations of their instructors, their personal commitment to learning, and the available instructional materials and resources. Experienced teachers also have different knowledge levels depending on the professional development opportunities available to them and the level of commitment they have made to continuing education.

Nearly all teachers reflect on their work, making changes and adjustments that they believe will improve their teaching effectiveness. It is true that teachers have very little time to reflect during the school day, but during classes and before and after school they tend to reflect on what they have been doing and consider alternatives that may help them improve their work. If the reflection process is related only to experience and practical knowledge, options for improvement may be limited. When teachers are able to consider their actions in terms of both their practical knowledge and solid research knowledge, they have more alternatives to consider and greater likelihood of strengthening their instruction in appropriate ways.

A number of organizational and external influences affect the development and renewal actions that teachers are able to take. The resources available to make instructional changes have a profound influence on teachers' improvement plans. The school culture, or ethos, is another important influence on the change process. If there is a spirit of cooperation and collegiality in a school, teachers are more likely to have the support necessary to make important changes that will improve teaching and learning.

External influences also have an impact on teachers' development and renewal plans. State curriculum mandates may require teachers to use specific materials and allocate their instructional time in a particular way. Statewide evaluation programs may lock teachers into specific instructional processes. National and state testing programs may cause teachers to teach to the tests rather than attend to the learning needs of their students. Teachers must take into consideration both organizational and external influences prior to making changes in their instructional practices. Their development and renewal plans will depend, to a large extent, on influences over which they may have little control.

Action that takes place as a result of reflection may be the responsibility of an individual teacher, a group of teachers, or an entire faculty. Several teachers may, for example, decide that after reflecting on the level of learning in their classes they need to have their students engage in more problem solving and critical thinking. They may realize that if they are to be effective in making changes they need to learn more about fostering higher level learning. These teachers may have both the commitment and the conviction to make the changes. The actions they take, however, will depend on the organizational support they receive as they plan and carry out their development and renewal activities. When they are given the support to develop new skills and understandings and to implement necessary changes in their classrooms, their commitment and conviction will be reinforced. This creates additional enthusiasm and motivation to improve teaching and enhance student learning. The major outcome of the entire process is that teachers view themselves as renewing professionals who are more capable than ever of helping their students improve their performance. Their positive attitudes will be instrumental in creating similar attitudes in their students.

Teacher Knowledge and Experience

Teacher development and renewal is affected by organizational influences, teacher belief systems, learning modes, and prior teaching experiences. As teachers learn, their thoughts and beliefs about teaching are refined, modified, and reinforced (Hollingsworth, 1989). Their belief systems or perspectives become screens through which they make instructional decisions. Teachers learn through observing and imitating teaching, experiencing and practicing teaching skills, and attempting to integrate new knowledge and skills with their current practice. Much of their learning comes from interacting informally with their colleagues and other educators.

The most powerful influence on teacher learning is the experience that comes from teaching. As Nemser (1983) has pointed out, "The daily work of teaching shapes teachers' notions about how one becomes a good teacher" (p. 165). Much of the learning-to-teach process is, in effect, a trial-and-error method. Incorporating new strategies into teaching requires in-depth conceptual understanding and the belief that the changes will, in fact, improve student learning. New information and approaches to teaching may challenge preexisting conceptions and cause a great deal of discomfort. Before teachers change the way they do things, they must have a thorough understanding of the new information and feel that they have the skills to incorporate new ideas into practice.

Teachers acquire information about the research on teaching through both formal and informal processes. Formal processes include coursework, inservice sessions, and reading educational literature. Although the information acquired through formal processes may be excellent, teaching practice may not be altered significantly as a result of these experiences. Informal interactions with colleagues tend to be a more long-term and more important influence on teachers' professional growth (Featherstone, 1986; Nemser, 1983). The content of the interactions focuses on the everyday business of teaching such as sharing concerns and ideas, talking about students, helping each other with field trips, covering classes, and exchanging and developing materials. Informal contacts with administrators also have a significant impact on teacher growth (McEvoy, 1987). Although informal processes for sharing information may have a long-term effect on teaching practice, care must be taken to ensure that the information is grounded in credible practical knowledge or research.

A number of factors affect teachers' desire to incorporate research into practice. One primary factor is the perceived benefit in terms of student learning and attitude (Richardson-Koehler, 1987). If teachers feel that advocated changes will produce cognitive and affective progress in students, they are willing to incorporate the ideas into practice (Porter & Brophy, 1988). The worth of new ideas, research-based or otherwise, must be verified by their successful application in instructional activities. When teachers use approaches that have a positive impact on student learning and achievement, their satisfaction with teaching is increased. This satisfaction is one of the most important nonmonetary rewards that comes from teaching.

An additional factor influencing teachers' ability to act on research findings is the difficulty of fitting new ideas into existing classroom practices. Even though a practice may be based on sound research information, it may in certain situations have a negative effect on established practice. Although the negative effect may be short-term, such as student resistance to a change in a routine or procedure, many teachers may not feel the long-term benefit justifies disrupting an established practice.

Teachers' learning appears to be highly personal, self-directed, and utilitarian. Teachers, like all adults, will learn what they believe they need to know (Hammond & Foster, 1987). They will focus on knowledge they believe to be practical, concrete, and compatible with their classroom responsibilities (Guskey, 1986). The basic motivation for teacher learning is improving student achievement and, at the same time, making the work of the teacher more manageable. Not only do teachers need to understand how to translate new knowledge into practice, they must see how new approaches can be incorporated into their instructional management systems. What teachers know about managing their students will affect any changes they are willing to make in their teaching strategies.

Teachers' levels of self-esteem have an important influence on how much they are willing to learn, how flexible their thinking is, and to what extent they use new information in their instruction. Teachers who feel good about themselves are more likely to benefit from development and renewal activities than those who are insecure. According to Showers, Joyce, and Bennett (1987), "Teachers who felt best about themselves transferred nearly seven times more from the content of training than did those whose self-concepts were most precarious" (p. 82). Self-concept may play a larger role in teachers' willingness to learn than learning styles and belief systems.

The stage of a teacher's career also affects a teacher's willingness and ability to benefit from professional growth experiences. Berliner (1988) provided a framework for understanding how teachers at different career stages vary in their perceptions and interpretations of classroom events. Novice teachers may feel comfortable in classrooms largely because many of them have been students recently. Their roles and responsibilities, however, may be unfamiliar to them and cause a considerable amount of anxiety. Veteran teachers are usually comfortable with their roles and have an experience-based memory bank that they can use to evaluate new ideas and information. Development and renewal programs should take into consideration participants' background and experience, the quality and quantity of their practical knowledge, and how they feel about themselves as professionals.

School Influences

Although prospective teachers are expected to develop a basic understanding of instruction during their preservice programs, many of the essentials of teaching are learned on the job. Even though schools are the primary sites for teacher learning, most are not organized to attend to teacher inquiry and learning needs. As Nemser (1983) pointed out, "Schools have no defined structures for helping teachers learn from the everyday experience of teaching, nor have they given priority to what teachers feel are their job-related needs" (p. 163). Lortie (1975) and others contended that schools have traditionally been organized as "egg-crate structures" that isolate teachers from one another. Collegial interaction is kept to a minimum. Schedules are constructed so that there is little time for collaboration. Scarce spare moments are filled with grading, preparation, and record-keeping responsibilities. Seldom do teachers have the opportunity to observe one another's classes. According to Featherstone (1986), "The average teacher observes someone else's class only once every three years" (p. 2).

The cultural norms of schools may inhibit teacher learning. Privacy is valued by many teachers. They feel that their rights are being violated if other teachers observe them in action. For the most part, teachers keep their successes and problems to themselves (Featherstone, 1986). Through words and actions, novice teachers quickly get the message to blend in with the way things are done in their schools. The finding that novices are encouraged by colleagues to adhere to bureaucratic mandates and to maintain the status quo is well documented (Featherstone, 1986). Although some schools have introduced formal mechanisms for teacher interaction such as mentoring programs and peer coaching, there is little opportunity in most schools for teachers to learn from one another.

Little (1982) identified several conditions within effective schools that promote teacher growth:

1. Frequent and specific talk about teaching practices
2. Frequent observations of and analytic dialogue about teaching
3. Involvement in planning, designing, and evaluating curriculum materials with other teachers
4. Collegial efforts to learn new methods and techniques

Some additional conditions are necessary to ensure that schools value and enhance teacher learning. District and school leaders should communicate positive expectations about teacher growth and renewal. They should demonstrate their support by providing resources and rewards for those who engage in development and renewal activities. Teachers should be encouraged to value and respect the growth efforts of their peers. All school personnel should be expected to be involved in development and renewal activities.

Barth's (1990) vision of a good school goes beyond establishing conditions for teacher and student learning. In his view a good school is a place where everyone is learning—students, teachers, and administrators. He described schools as communities of learners and stated that:

> a major responsibility of the adults in a community of learners is to engage actively in their own learning, to make their learning visible to others in the community, to enjoy and celebrate their learning, and to sustain it over time—even (especially) when swamped by the demands of their work. (p. 513)

It is clear that Barth's "good school" would place a high priority on the conditions that promote teacher development and renewal. One of the most important conditions is teacher and administrator collegiality. The collegiality would include talking with one another about their practical knowledge as well as sharing research knowledge that could be the basis for improving practice. As colleagues, teachers and administrators would observe the work of one another and offer constructive feedback for improvement. Students would also be given the opportunity to offer feedback to improve the work of teachers and administrators. Everyone in the school would play an important role in development and renewal.

Opportunities for collegial and collaborative relationships help teachers break out of the isolation that has been debilitating to many, and which has inhibited the desire to engage in development and renewal activities. Teachers can receive a great deal of benefit from the emotional support and encouragement that comes from cooperative collegial work groups (Wildman & Niles, 1987). School conditions can be established that help provide intellectual stimulation for all of the participants. When those responsible for school leadership work actively to establish the best possible conditions for development and renewal, the motivation of the participants is unlocked, commitment to improvement is enhanced, and the conviction necessary to sustain positive action is strengthened.

External Influences

There are a number of important external influences that have an impact on teacher development and renewal opportunities. As Wasley (1989) and others have pointed out, teachers are often viewed as nonparticipants in discussions and decisions about improving professional practice. National discussions, in particular, have tended to exclude the opinions of those who will be most responsible for carrying out mandated changes.

Perhaps the most significant influence on teacher development and renewal in recent history was the so-called first wave of educational reform in the 1980s. Hundreds of pieces of legislation were passed with the aim of improving the teaching profession. The result of much of this legislation was to restrict the use of teachers' professional judgment (Darling-Hammond & Barnett, 1988). It is ironic that so many of the mandates aimed at improving teacher competence often had the opposite effect when they were enacted. Statewide evaluation programs, for example, were developed to ensure that teachers followed certain prescriptions to improve their instruction. When teachers were evaluated, they were told to include the prescribed behaviors. In many cases state and local staff development programs were organized to teach the prescriptive behaviors. Teachers and administrators were expected to attend the programs so that they could learn the behaviors and how they were to be used. Although there are a few claims to the contrary, there is no substantial evidence that the vast amount of time and resources devoted to these mandated programs had any appreciable effect on student learning. Many experienced teachers reported that their involvement was not only a waste of time, but that the time they spent in the staff development programs took away valuable instructional time. Just as important, when schools were devoting all of their development and renewal resources to complying with state mandates, teachers were not able to keep abreast of important new information and technological advances that could have helped them meet the specific needs of their students.

Second-wave reformers have focused on the control and regulation of teacher preparation and certification programs in exchange for deregulating the process of teaching. Educators are expected to systematically improve and refine educational practice so they can be more effective in meeting local needs (Darling-Hammond & Barnett, 1988). There is an expectation that schools will design their own development and renewal programs to solve local educational problems and meet the specific needs of their students.

New and emerging certification programs also influence local professional growth programs. It is relatively common for states to require teachers to continue to take courses or be involved in staff development programs as a prerequisite for continued certification. Unfortunately, too little attention has been given to whether the required work will help teachers develop competencies that will enhance their professional growth. In addition to the traditional certification requirements, alternative routes to certification have been developed and approved in a number of states. Development and renewal requirements differ, but nearly all programs require a certain number of hours of either on-the-job training and formal coursework or some combination of informal and formal program experiences that can be used for full certification. Until the certification requirements are met, teachers have little opportunity to exercise their judgment about what they need to do to improve professionally.

A number of states and school systems have enacted mentoring programs for first-year teachers. Experienced teachers are assigned, or volunteer, to mentor their novice colleagues. Some of the programs are carefully designed to give novice teachers opportunities to become familiar with a broad range of practical knowledge and to assess that knowledge in terms of research on teaching. They are given time to observe other teachers in action and to be involved in seminars that help them develop their own practical and research knowledge. Mentoring programs that are not viewed as a high priority by local school officials have not been nearly as effective in facilitating teacher professional development. In some of these programs novice teachers have little opportunity to interact with teachers who have a commitment to the development of their colleagues. These programs provide a social support system for novice teachers but have not been as effective in improving their professional competence.

Textbook adoption practices and curriculum mandates are external influences that can have a significant impact on local development and renewal programs. Because so much instructional practice is driven by textbooks and instructional materials, schools often devote a considerable amount of time and resources to their selection and adoption. In many cases only a small number of teachers are involved in these activities, but this can be a time-consuming process (Tulley & Farr, 1990). Their decisions can have a significant impact on future school staff development and renewal programs. After new materials have been adopted, time and resources are needed to prepare teachers to use them.

Changing the curriculum has the same impact on teachers as changing textbooks, especially when new programs are required by states or school systems. Several states have mandated new science and social studies curricula. The science curriculum includes a significant amount of hands-on activity. For teachers to successfully implement the new science program, they must participate in staff development programs that have been specifically designed to introduce different instructional strategies. Newly mandated social studies programs require a similar amount of time and attention in developing the understandings and skills necessary for successful implementation. Some teachers have been involved in staff development for both programs at the same time. All of their personal time and resources available for development and renewal must be used for these programs, leaving little time to meet any additional personal or professional development needs.

Standardized testing has been a dominant influence on the practices of many teachers. States and school systems have required students to take standardized tests throughout their school careers. Recently one state even mandated standardized testing for all kindergarten children. As a result of the testing requirements, many teachers invest a significant amount of their time and energy in developing an understanding of what the tests will measure and preparing their students to take the tests. Because the test scores are often publicized by the media and school leaders, teachers often feel compelled to focus on the testing programs.

Emerging developments in technology also influence development and renewal programs. The most pervasive technological influence on schools in recent years has been the microcomputer. A great deal of publicity has been given to how the microcomputer can be used to enhance student learning. A number of reservations have been expressed about the quality and availability of software and the amount of training students need to use microcomputers to improve their performance. Many schools have acknowledged that teachers are not properly prepared to help students make optimal use of microcomputer technology. Oftentimes students have been responsible for teaching other students how to make the best use of computers. To remedy this situation, staff development programs have been organized to assist teachers in developing the understandings and skills necessary to fully utilize the new technology. Many colleges have developed computer technology courses that are required for all prospective teacher candidates. A number of educators have called for more emphasis on computer technology in preparation programs, continuing updates on utilization, workshops available to all teachers, and leaves and sabbaticals for those who are expected to give leadership in this field (Davies & Shane, 1986).

Social and cultural changes also influence the continuing education of teachers. Schools are now compelled to address a number of serious social problems. Alcohol and drug abuse problems have become so prevalent that many schools have had to respond with programs aimed at reducing their use and dealing with the effects of abuse. Compounding the problem is the fact that many students do not have a stable home environment. In response, schools have had to take on more parenting and nurturing responsibilities. Dropout prevention has become a national priority for schools, the AIDS epidemic has resulted in new programs, and problems associated with teenage pregnancy are being addressed by many school systems. Schools will need to go through substantial structural changes if they are to address these and other problems of at-risk youth. Teacher roles will continue to be redefined as they address pressing social needs (Wehlage, Rutter, Smith, Lesko, & Fernandez, 1989), and teacher development and renewal programs will change accordingly.

For a number of years, workshops on teacher stress and burnout have been very popular. It is no wonder that teachers feel the need for support programs with the demands they face in contemporary schools. Several variables affect teacher stress and burnout, including negative characteristics of the organizational environment, inappropriate work demands, role conflict and role ambiguity, lack of control of time, and the lack of support for change (Brissie, Hoover-Dempsey, & Bassler, 1988). If teachers are going to be effective and maintain their commitment to teaching, they must have the time and opportunity to pursue personal development and renewal goals. Every effort should be made to help teachers achieve balance in their lives so they can be effective human beings as well as competent professionals.

REFLECTION: THE BASIS FOR ACTION

Nearly all professionals reflect on the actions they have taken and attempt to learn from their experiences. They consider the outcomes of their work and their interactions with their clients. Reflection provides insights that can lead to action, or in some cases, inaction. Reflection is the key to personal growth and renewal. It is through the reflective process that prior experience can be linked to new knowledge. This expanded knowledge can then lead to refining or improving professional practice. As the body of research knowledge expands, it is incumbent on all professionals to be aware of information that can lead to improved practice. Awareness, however, is not enough. Information should be carefully evaluated, and instructional decisions should be confirmed or modified in appropriate ways in light of relevant research.

Reflection in action is the process of making almost instantaneous decisions to change or adjust instruction as it occurs. Teachers often reflect on instructional activities as they are taking place, and as a result, make alterations in what they are doing or what they plan to do. The changes may be very subtle and appear to be intuitive. Much of the reflection-in-action process focuses on pedagogical decisions.

As Schon (1983) pointed out, the reflection-in-action process is central to the work of professionals as they deal with ambiguity and uncertainty in their work. In some ways, reflection in action is an individualized, ongoing process of professional development and renewal.

There are several factors that provide a frame of reference for reflection. First, and perhaps foremost, is the amount and level of previous teaching experience. Novice teachers may have to rely primarily on information they have acquired from their coursework and other preservice activities. Experienced teachers, on the other hand, may have a rich background of experience which provides them with a sound practical knowledge base. Practical knowledge derived from experience is the major reference point for most teachers' reflection.

New knowledge in the form of research results and theory should also play a role in teachers' reflection and change process. Unfortunately, recent research findings may not be easy for teachers to access once they leave their preparation programs. Mechanisms should be established so that teachers at all stages in their careers can stay up to date with new information that can lead to improved practice. When teachers study recent research findings and compare this information to their practical knowledge, they add a powerful dimension to the reflection process and increase the number of options they can consider prior to taking action.

Teachers engaging in the reflection process are usually careful to consider both intraorganizational and external influences and conditions that will have an impact on changes or adjustments they would like to make in their work. They know, for example, that even though certain instructional changes may benefit their students they cannot make changes that are not in harmony with the school and community culture. If changes and improvements are to be made, they must be appropriate within local teaching contexts. Contextual influences may adversely affect teachers' commitment to making needed changes and limit options for personal development and renewal.

Professional development and renewal programs should take into consideration important factors underlying individual growth and renewal. The experience levels of participants should be considered, and assessments should be made to determine the scope and depth of the participants' research knowledge. The contextual variables and external influences should be understood before development and renewal programs are initiated. Programs should provide time for participants to reflect about their experiences and the impact any new information might have on their professional practice. If programs are properly planned to take these important factors and influences into account, it is more likely that participants will have the commitment and conviction to sustain them as they improve their work.

CONDITIONS THAT FOSTER COMMITMENT TO ACTION

A number of conditions foster commitment and innovation. When conditions are positive and supportive, it is more likely that participants will have the commitment and conviction necessary to see that action plans are successful. Several of the most important conditions are discussed below.

1. The ultimate goal of development and renewal programs should be increased efficacy.

Development and renewal programs are conducted for a number of reasons. One of the most common is that a specified number of inservice or staff development days has been mandated by either state or local agencies and programs must be held on those days. These programs may or may not improve the skills and competencies of the participants.

Regardless of the reasons for providing development and renewal programs, one of the most important outcomes should be to improve participants' feelings of efficacy. As a result of being involved in the programs, participants should feel that they have become more capable in carrying out their professional responsibilities. Teachers, for example, should perceive themselves as being more effective in helping their students achieve important learning goals. When teacher efficacy is strengthened, learning environments can be developed that will improve student efficacy. Simply stated, when teachers feel more effective, both personally and professionally, they are more likely to develop the same sense of efficacy in their students. The end result is that students will view themselves as more able learners.

By focusing on efficacy, development and renewal programs provide a powerful incentive for teachers. Teachers are willing to develop and renew their skills and competencies if they are convinced the changes will have a favorable influence on the performance of their students. Properly focused development and renewal programs can provide important incentives for teachers that will strengthen their commitment to personal and professional renewal (Bellon, Bellon, Blank, Brian & Kershaw, 1989).

2. Development and renewal programs should be carefully designed to attend to high-priority needs.

All too often inservice and staff development programs are viewed by participants as a waste of their time. In too many cases they are right. This is especially true when the programs are poorly planned and do not respond to identified needs. They may be based on available speakers, current hot topics, or the special interests of a small group of teachers or administrators.

There is a considerable amount of confusion about what constitutes a bona fide need. One of the most popular forms of needs assessment is asking potential participants what type of staff development program or inservice workshop they would like to have. After everyone has been polled, the results are tabulated and the most frequent requests are identified as high-priority needs. What has really been developed is a wish list. Unfortunately, development and renewal programs designed from wish lists will, at best, attend to the affective needs of participants and may result in very little significant change in skills, understandings, and competencies that lead to improved efficacy.

A need should be seen as a discrepancy between the current state and the desired state of affairs. A number of data sources can be used to identify the discrepancies. A process for determining discrepancies and establishing priorities is shown in Figure 13–2.

Personnel evaluation programs, when properly conducted, can yield important information about both individual and group needs. Student outcome data also provide important insights about problems that need attention. Data sources that can be used to determine student needs include test scores, products of student work, informal teacher assessments, and interviews with students, teachers, and parents. Grade reports and dropout profiles may be other useful data sources. The information generated from these sources can provide a picture of current student performance.

Deciding and agreeing upon the desired state of educational programs is a challenging task. There are several approaches that can be used to determine a desired state (Bellon et al., 1990). Whatever approach is used, the views of all participant groups should be represented. Parents, students, and teachers should be expected to have a voice in establishing educational expectations. These expectations can be translated into desired levels of performance and other educational outcomes.

Goals can then be developed to reduce the discrepancies, or gaps, between current outcomes and desired outcomes. After the goals have been developed, priorities should be established. High-priority needs and goals can be used to formulate an action plan for development and renewal.

Joyce and Showers (1983) have identified the components of successful staff development programs. These components include providing the participants with a thorough grounding in the research, allocating time to discuss new information and develop a deep understanding about appropriate application of the information, having opportunities to design new strategies and practice them in a safe environment, and receiving feedback and assistance when employing new approaches during instruction. When these components are included in development and renewal programs, participants are much more likely to feel positive about being involved. The programs have been designed to meet high-priority needs and at the same time give

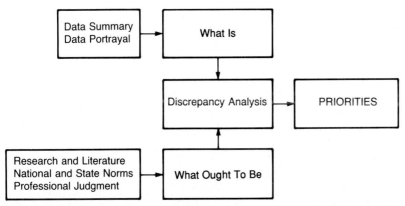

FIGURE 13–2. A process for determining needs and establishing priorities

participants opportunities to develop new skills and strategies. When this happens, personal efficacy can be strengthened and enhanced.

3. Development and renewal programs should be based on credible research.

Although this is an essential condition for all activities and programs that are intended to enhance teaching, it is a condition that may be hard to satisfy. For example, short-term programs devised quickly to respond to problems or issues may not be well researched. Other programs may be instituted to sell the participants on a new concept or approach. These may be based on what appears to be working in other school systems or what is currently popular or successful. With the constant pressure on educators to demonstrate that their schools are successful, it is easy to understand why programs that claim to be highly effective have spread.

Those who are responsible for organizing development and renewal programs must keep in mind that teachers and administrators are professionals and not technicians. Professionals are responsible for making decisions that are in the best interests of their clients (Lanier, 1982). In order to make the best professional decisions, teachers must have an in-depth knowledge of teaching and learning. They cannot depend entirely on their practical knowledge or conventional wisdom. Their important instructional decisions should reflect their knowledge of research as well as their practical knowledge. Development and renewal programs are needed to help teachers maintain an up-to-date understanding of the most credible research available. To do less is to create situations where teachers may not have the best information base for their professional decision making.

It may be easier to identify high-priority development and renewal needs than to identify research-based programs to attend to those needs. Although the quantity and quality of educational research have improved considerably in recent years, there are still too many instances where programs have been developed in the absence of any relevant research or where research findings have been inappropriately used. Professionals have the responsibility to challenge those who offer solutions to educational problems without being able to adequately describe their data sources and the contexts in which their programs have been successful. Because educational research is highly contextual, generalizations about applicability have to be carefully evaluated.

Many outstanding professionals have much to contribute to development and renewal programs in various areas of expertise. Unfortunately, in education as well as in other professions, some people market themselves so well that they are sought out by school systems to solve important educational problems. This happens even when these people do not have expertise that would stand close scrutiny. Great care must be taken to screen those who give leadership to or facilitate development and renewal programs for school systems. Decision makers should be certain that the services being provided by those from outside the schools are consistent with local needs and that their programs are grounded in credible research.

High-quality development and renewal programs must be available to all professionals. This is the most effective process for helping members of a profession stay up to date and translate their knowledge into effective practice. Great care must be taken to spend educational resources wisely. In the medical profession the term *iatrogenic* is used to describe a situation where a patient's condition is worse after treatment than before. Every effort must be made to ensure that development and renewal programs for teachers and administrators are growth promoting and not *iatrogenic*.

4. The culture of the school must be in harmony with and supportive of positive attitudes toward development and renewal.

It is difficult, if not impossible, to maintain commitment and conviction to personal and professional renewal in a culture that does not support the desire to improve performance. For example, new teachers who are left to sink or swim are not getting the organizational support and assistance that will help them to be successful professionals. Whatever success they experience will be the result of their own efforts. Experienced teachers may also find that there is little opportunity and support for them to strengthen their skills and improve their performance.

The culture of a school depends, in large part, on the leadership of the school. Schools with leaders who are committed to helping others reach their full potential are most likely to have a culture that supports development and renewal. The process of helping others reach their full potential is based on the belief that everyone can improve. This belief is the basis for a commitment to ongoing development and renewal programs.

Effective school leaders demonstrate by their own behavior that they place a high priority on development and renewal. They are models of renewal. They work to systematically improve their own performance. Because these leaders are committed to their own improvement, they tend to develop positive self-regard. They know their strengths and areas where they should improve. They know that as they improve they will have a favorable impact on their schools. This helps them to be confident and optimistic about themselves and their colleagues. As a consequence, they help others develop positive self-regard. When people feel confident that they are doing well but that they can improve, they are more willing to take risks and try new approaches than their less confident colleagues.

The leadership of a school is not vested only in administrators and supervisors. Teachers can be highly influential in establishing and supporting programs and activities that generate positive attitudes about development and renewal. Teachers and administrators can share leadership responsibilities for activities that are the basis for school improvement. When they work as a team to identify high-priority needs and design programs to attend to those needs, greater support for the programs can be generated. Teamwork and cooperation within a school will foster a culture that supports those who want to improve.

Leaders can design organizational procedures that will create and sustain the commitment to renew and improve. They can promote teamwork and collaborative activities that will generate positive attitudes about development and renewal. All participants develop such a positive climate in their schools and their work that commitment to development and renewal becomes a natural expectation for all school personnel.

5. Resources must be adequate to support development and renewal programs.

Development and renewal programs will be successful only when sufficient resources are available to support the programs. School systems are often reluctant to make development and renewal programs a high priority because it may mean shifting scarce resources away from other programs. This is a real dilemma because most school systems are underfunded and cannot provide adequate resources for all of their programs. Funding decisions have to be based on the most critical priorities. Because teachers play the pivotal role in facilitating student learning, every effort must be made to provide support for teacher development and renewal. The quality of teaching is without doubt the most significant factor in student learning.

The most costly and important resource for development and renewal activities is time. Important changes and improvements in teaching cannot be achieved through quick fixes. All too often staff development programs have been held at the end of the school day for one or two hours. Very little is accomplished, and for the most part the time is wasted. Teachers must have time to be involved in designing their own development and renewal programs. Programs must be structured to give them time to process new information, reflect on its implications, and carefully implement new ideas or strategies. It may be necessary to use time when school is not in session to plan and engage in some of the more time-consuming development and renewal activities. Care must be taken not to take teachers away from their classes so often that student learning is adversely affected by teacher development and renewal activities. But on occasion it may be necessary to use some teaching time for renewal because of the long-term benefits that will accrue to teachers and students. Each school has to be creative in addressing the problem of providing time for meaningful improvement programs.

Competent personnel are needed to provide leadership to development and renewal programs. Because time is such a precious resource, it should not be wasted by having facilitators who are not able to provide high-quality, meaningful development and renewal experiences. Care must be taken to ensure that resource personnel are well qualified to conduct program sessions and activities. The time taken to screen personnel carefully will be well spent and will help to ensure that programs will be effective.

Many development and renewal programs do not require large quantities of material and equipment. There are times, however, when equipment is essential to the success of the programs. It does not make much sense to train teachers to develop multimedia presentations when they will not have the needed materials and equipment to use in their classrooms. The rapidly expanding use of microcomputers has stimulated many workshops on computer literacy. In some cases, teachers have participated in the workshops only to find that the equipment will not be available to them in their schools or that different kinds of equipment will be used. To add to the problem, equipment may be purchased without the appropriate software. Material and equipment needs should be identified prior to engaging in development and renewal programs. Participants should be assured that resources necessary to implement new ideas and activities will be available.

ACTION PLANS TO MEET INDIVIDUAL AND GROUP NEEDS

Any number of approaches can be used to design development and renewal action plans. Whatever the approach, the plans will be successful only when the conditions discussed in the previous section have been given proper attention. When the conditions are positive and supportive, the commitment and conviction of the participants will be strengthened. The action plans described in this section range from those that are highly individualized to plans for entire school systems. The purpose, structure, and expected outcomes of each type of plan are presented. Although the action plans are representative of those used by many school systems, they are certainly not all-inclusive. They do provide, however, a sampling of development and renewal plans that have been successful.

Individual Plans

Purpose. The central purpose of most individualized development and renewal plans is to address the specific needs or aspirations of individual teachers who may be novice, mature, or expert teachers. The plans may be designed differently depending on experience, need, and context.

The development and renewal needs of individuals can be identified in a variety of ways. Self-assessment is a common process for determining improvement needs. Experienced, reflective teachers often know the areas in their teaching they need to strengthen and new approaches that they would like to know more about. Novice teachers may not have the background and experience to identify specific development and renewal needs. Preservice teachers may have their work assessed by their college supervisors, cooperating teachers, or mentors who have been assigned to work with them. It is quite likely that those assigned to work with preservice teachers can provide them with informed feedback about their teaching strengths and areas of need. School systems that emphasize formative evaluation have supervisory personnel who can provide all teachers with evaluation information that can be used for individualized improvement plans. Teachers involved in some form of peer coaching are also able to identify their own areas of strength and need.

Structure.   The structure of individualized development and renewal plans varies from those that are quite informal to those that are carefully designed and organized. One of the least structured plans is ongoing dialogue between a teacher and a supervisor, mentor, or colleague. The dialogue may focus on strategies to improve a specific area of teaching and learning, research knowledge that may strengthen certain teaching practices, or approaches that can be used to solve specific classroom problems. In some schools, mentors are assigned to novice teachers to assist them on a regular basis, orient them to district expectations, help them identify areas of need, and work with them to develop improvement plans. Other schools may use lead teachers or special-assistance teams to perform similar functions.

Experienced teachers with special needs may also be expected to work with their supervisors or an assistance team to develop and implement individual improvement plans. Peer coaching programs are usually designed to help teachers refine and strengthen current practices or implement new instructional approaches. When coaches are properly trained and the programs are carefully designed and supported, teachers have found peer coaching to be an especially effective approach to development and renewal.

Self-directed, individualized programs may be informal, but in a number of school systems mature teachers design and structure their own development and renewal plans. These plans are structured to achieve specific goals and objectives. The goals are derived from self-assessment or from formative evaluation data provided by supervisory personnel. Teachers involved in these programs are expected to keep their supervisors informed about the progress they are making toward achieving goals and to identify any assistance they may need to ensure the success of their plans. When the plans have been completed, the teachers and, in some cases, the supervisors evaluate how well the goals have been achieved and the impact on student performance.

Outcomes.   The outcomes expected to be achieved by individualized development and renewal plans will vary depending on teachers' background, experience, and need. The structure of the plans will also influence the goals to be achieved. Preservice and novice teachers may work to develop strategies that will help them to survive or manage their classrooms effectively. Teachers with special needs or problems may focus on specific areas of their teaching. Mature teachers may engage in plans that will help them refine what they are currently doing or implement new instructional approaches. The success of each of these plans must be determined by evaluating how well the goals of the plans have been achieved.

Examples.   There are numerous examples of successful individual development and renewal plans. The two described below not only made a positive impact on the teachers involved but also had a positive effect on other teachers.

An elementary classroom teacher became quite concerned about a learning disability that afflicted several of her students. She believed that there must be some way for the students to overcome the disorder. Her assessment was informal and her plan was not clearly formulated, but her goal was clear. She wanted to help these students become successful learners.

She began her plan of action by reading everything she could find about the learning problem. She consulted with specialists in the field and identified information that might be helpful. They also helped her find classes that she might take to build her information base. As she gradually became knowledgeable about the problem, she began to develop teaching strategies and materials to attend to the problem. Over a period of time she began to experience some success with the students. By personally reflecting about what worked and what did not work as well, she gradually refined and improved her strategies and materials.

Before long other teachers in the school system heard about the work this teacher was doing and the learning gains she was making. She was asked to conduct staff development sessions for other elementary teachers in the system. Over a period of time word spread, and other school systems began to contact her about providing them with some assistance. Her administrators supported her by providing substitute teachers so that she could work with her peers across the state.

The outcome of this teacher's plan went well beyond what she expected when she became concerned about her own students' performance. Her commitment to improvement and her conviction that she could make a difference made a positive impact beyond her own classroom. Her desire to learn and improve stimulated positive attitudes about renewal in many of her peers. It would be nearly impossible to measure the amount of increased teacher and student efficacy that has resulted from her work.

In a different elementary school, a lead teacher who was responsible for assisting her colleagues in elementary mathematics was dissatisfied with the problem-solving strategies presented in the textbooks. She consulted with the systemwide mathematics coordinator, who had similar concerns. The coordinator provided the teacher with information on problem solving, including reviews and position papers published by their national professional organization. The teacher's needs assessment was informal, but she found that her concern was shared by math educators across the country. The goal for her renewal plan was clear—to improve mathematics problem solving in the elementary grades at her school.

After reviewing the mathematics materials, the teacher realized that she should develop a better understanding of approaches used to promote higher level learning in all subject areas. She read widely about higher level learning strategies and attended several workshops. She began to develop new mathematics materials that incorporated problem solving and higher level learning strategies. She shared the new materials with her colleagues, and together they made some adjustments and changes to improve what she had developed. After they were satisfied with the materials, they integrated them with their current teaching strategies. Over a period of time, the teachers began to get improved results from their problem-solving activities. Meanwhile, the lead teacher organized several lessons that she could use for demonstration teaching in other teachers' classrooms.

There were several positive outcomes from this one teacher's action plan. She became very knowledgeable about problem solving and higher level learning. New materials were developed that other teachers found very useful in teaching problem solving. Teachers found that working together to address common concerns enhanced their work satisfaction and helped them sustain their commitment to improving teaching and learning.

Group Plans

Purpose. The major goal for most group development and renewal programs is to address a common concern. Several approaches can be used to identify group needs. Schools that use comprehensive personnel evaluation systems are able to identify instructional needs by analyzing classroom observation data. A number of schools regularly conduct program evaluations to identify areas of strength and needed improvement. Accreditation reports may also yield important information about aspects of programs that may need attention. It is not unusual to find that improvement needs have been identified by several teachers through self-assessment or from student performance information. Individual teachers have initiated group development and renewal programs as a result of reading current research, observing other programs in action, or involving themselves in professional associations. Information leading to group action may come from a variety of sources. When the information is credible, it can provide the stimulus for developing an action plan.

Structure. Group plans may be loosely structured with participants simply agreeing they should all work to improve their performance. Although they may be loosely structured, the success of the plans will depend on all members of the group communicating with one another and working together to achieve their goals. In some cases, group plans are carefully designed, highly structured, and systematically monitored. A number of schools provide opportunities for groups of teachers to develop improvement plans as a part of the personnel evaluation process. The teachers are expected to identify common needs and establish improvement goals. The goals become the basis for formalized improvement plans, which are submitted to the administrative staff for review and approval. After the plans have been approved, they are put into action. Periodic reports are submitted to administrators regarding the progress being made. Administrators may also observe the implementation process. At an appropriate time the plans are evaluated to determine if they have been successful. This information may also be used as a part of the teachers' performance evaluations.

Outcomes. When group development and renewal plans have been successful, there are several important payoffs. Programs or selected aspects of the programs are strengthened. In addition, individual members of the group tend to develop, refine, and enhance their skills and competencies. When one group within a school has a successful action plan, other groups are likely to be stimulated to move ahead with their own.

Examples. A social studies department chair became interested in ways to improve discussion management. She heard several research presentations about the characteristics of effective discussions which further stimulated her interest in the process. She visited with the person who had been presenting the research and asked for more information. The presenter furnished additional studies dealing with discussions and higher level learning for her to read and analyze.

After the department chair had carefully studied the research, she began to develop new instructional strategies that focused on improving discussions and critical thinking in the classes she taught. When she felt comfortable with the material and the results, she made a presentation to her social studies colleagues. When she first presented her ideas, virtually all of the members of her department pointed out that they had always engaged in classroom discussions. She noted that many of these discussions were actually presentations and recitations and did not meet the criteria for effective discussions.

After further deliberation, the entire department decided to focus on improving discussions in all of the social studies classes. The teachers worked with the department chair to identify areas in the curriculum that would be most amenable to discussion activities. Instructional strategies were then developed to facilitate student discussions in the selected areas of the curriculum.

Teachers agreed to observe one another when they were experimenting with their newly developed discussion strategies. The observations were conducted so teachers could give helpful feedback and learn from one another. It was not long before all of the members of the department reported improved student learning, as well as more positive attitudes about learning, because of the new emphasis on classroom discussions.

The need for this group activity was identified by the department chair. As a result of her insight and persistence, her colleagues began to see the same need. The purpose for using effective discussion techniques was to engage students more actively in their own learning and to raise the level of their thinking. Both informal and formal assessments indicated that the goal was achieved and the results were excellent.

Another group action plan was initiated when a group of second grade teachers were concerned about the need to enrich their language arts curriculum. They discussed their concern with the principal, who agreed that something needed to be done to improve the instruction in this area. The teachers developed a plan to make the improvements they felt would benefit their students. They presented the plan to the principal, who agreed to give them the support to put the plan into action. He also agreed that the plan and the work they would be doing would be used as a basis for their annual evaluations. They would not be expected to be involved in the regular instructional evaluation process while they were working to improve language arts instruction.

The teachers initiated their plan early in the school year by identifying library books and materials that could enrich the language arts curriculum. They also identified other books and materials that the school needed to acquire. The teachers agreed to work independently on the project but to have a regularly scheduled meeting every two weeks to discuss their progress and new assignments. The principal was invited to attend the group meetings whenever he was available. As it turned out, he was able to participate in the majority of the meetings. His presence made it easier to get approval on a number of the decisions that related to school or district policy. He was also in a position to support teachers' requests for additional resources.

The teachers soon began to feel that they not only needed to enrich the curriculum, they needed to strengthen and improve their own instruction. They became involved in a number of development and renewal activities that helped them to enact the curriculum changes more effectively. As a result of their original plan, the teachers did improve the curriculum—they developed more effective instructional strategies, and they enhanced the learning of their students. One important side effect was that they all received excellent evaluations on their work that year.

Schoolwide Plans

Purpose.   The central purpose for most schoolwide improvement plans is to make a general improvement in some aspect of school operations. Many of the processes used to identify needs for individuals and groups can also be used to identify schoolwide needs. Data obtained from the personnel evaluation process, program evaluation activities, and accreditation reports can be used to identify high-priority schoolwide needs. Other data sources can include the number of discipline referrals, dropout reports, attendance records, grade reports, and follow-up studies. Recently, many schools have organized school improvement committees that have been charged with identifying schoolwide needs. Once the needs have been identified and documented, improvement goals can be established.

Organizational changes may also lead to development and renewal programs. A number of school systems, for example, have changed from the traditional junior high school structure to some form of middle school organization. When this happens, a significant amount of development and renewal is needed for all faculty members and administrators. When the organizational changes have been supported with comprehensive development and renewal opportunities, the transitions to the new structures have been successful. Changes that are made without development and renewal support often create more problems than they solve.

Structure.   As with other development and renewal plans, the structure of schoolwide plans will vary depending on context, the personnel involved, and the needs being addressed. Many schoolwide plans are initiated with a meeting of the entire faculty. The goals of the plans are clarified and activities to carry out the goals are presented. In some cases faculties design their own improvement activities or make suggestions about the activities they feel would be most appropriate. The activities may involve entire faculties or smaller groups within the schools. Whatever structure is used, successful implementation will depend on having everyone involved and committed to achieving the goals of the plan.

Outcomes.   Schoolwide development and renewal plans have been responsible for making significant improvements in local education. Schools have been successful in addressing the specific needs of their students by focusing the efforts of entire faculties. Major organizational and instructional changes have been affected by carefully designed schoolwide plans. There are a number of other benefits when teachers and administrators work together to solve school problems. Commitment to individual improvement is strengthened, and the quality of the entire school work place is enhanced. Work satisfaction is improved because all personnel feel that their work is important and that they can bring about important organizational changes. Successful schoolwide plans can also lead to individual work satisfaction and increased personal and professional efficacy.

Examples.   The need for schoolwide development and renewal programs may be the result of a formal assessment or may be based on the concerns of a group of faculty members. Several years ago, an old elementary school was going to be closed at the end of the year, and all of the teachers and students were to be moved into a new open-space building. The teachers were told that when they moved to the new school they would be expected to work as teaching teams. When the teachers asked about a staff development program to prepare them for their new roles, they were told that nothing had been planned.

Several of the teachers had been taking a curriculum class from a professor at a local university. They talked with her about their concerns and asked her if she could help them prepare for the move. She agreed to help them develop a plan to attend to their concerns. As a result of the plan, a summer course was offered that was tailored to the needs of the teachers from this school. Although they were not required to take the course, the great majority enrolled. Those who did not were invited to participate whenever they had the time.

The entire course was designed to meet the specific needs of this group of teachers. They studied different approaches to teaming and instructional grouping. They learned how to plan together and how to work as teams. They reviewed their curriculum materials and made changes that helped them integrate their instructional strategies. By the time school began the teachers were partially prepared for their new roles. They had also begun to develop strategies to cope with an open-space building. All of them had spent their careers teaching in self-contained classrooms.

While the changeover was not completely successful, there were far fewer problems as a result of the summer program. The teachers and principal asked the professor to continue working with them throughout the school year. She agreed, and remained committed to helping the school for several years. By the end of that time it had become an exemplary elementary school. Educators from other states heard about the school and asked to visit to learn more about the educational program and to observe the teachers in action.

The teachers did not initiate their development and renewal program in order to develop an exemplary school. They were just trying to survive the first year of a major organizational change. They had the commitment and conviction to sustain them through the change and to continue to work to master their new context. They were successful because they believed they could improve their own efficacy and because they were able to find a university professor who was also committed to improving teacher performance and student learning.

Another elementary school faculty was experiencing a different problem. This faculty was dissatisfied with the amount of time that was being used for noninstructional activities. They were concerned about not covering some of the content during the year and felt they often did not have time to pursue topics in depth. The faculty and principal met to discuss the problem and agreed that one of the remedies would be to improve their long-range instructional planning. The principal and several of the teachers had been attending a yearlong staff development program that included research on planning, pacing, and the use of allocated time. As a result of their work in the program, they developed a plan for their school and presented it to the entire faculty. The faculty accepted the plan and agreed to implement it the following year.

The teachers actually began to initiate the plan during the spring of that school year. Before implementation they gathered information on noninstructional use of time. They also analyzed information about student test scores, grouping practices in the school, and the curriculum materials that were being used. They were able to get a school calendar for the following year as soon as it was officially adopted by the board of education.

The teachers and principal met for several days before the school year officially began. They established a time line for achieving their major curriculum goals. In effect they were "postholing" the curriculum. It helped them ensure that the pacing for the year would provide for adequate content coverage. The teachers from each grade level met to articulate the major curricular concepts. They also involved the librarian and other instructional support personnel to identify the materials and equipment that would be needed and to make a long-range schedule so that the support services would be available when they were needed.

The school calendar became an invaluable planning tool. Teachers were careful to note those days when there would be activities that would conflict with the normal instructional program. The principal made a commitment to keep interruptions to a minimum, and the entire faculty agreed that the highest priority should be placed on using allocated time to enhance student learning.

This plan had a number of important benefits for teachers as well as learners. New teachers received valuable insights about the planning process. They worked with their colleagues as peers and developed a sense of community. All of the teachers said they learned how to improve their planning and became much more aware of their use of time. They also developed and refined strategies to improve pacing and content coverage. The curriculum articulation was upgraded so that there were fewer gaps and redundancies. The total education program of the school was strengthened as a result of the efforts of the teachers and principal to improve their use of allocated learning time.

Systemwide Plans

Purpose.   Systemwide development and renewal programs range from one-day convocations to multiyear improvement programs. The goals for systemwide programs are as varied as the programs themselves. There is usually, however, a central purpose for most systemwide programs—they are expected to have an impact on all schools or personnel in the system.

Needs assessments for systemwide programs range from formal comprehensive processes to informal assessments made by several decision makers. Data sources for comprehensive assessments are similar to those used to identify schoolwide needs. Test information, dropout reports, and accreditation reports are commonly used data sources. School systems have also engaged in community needs assessment studies. The values and expectations of the entire community become the basis for setting improvement goals. Although these studies are time-consuming and expensive, they yield information that can guide long-term improvement activities.

The need for systemwide programs may also be defined by external sources. State and federal mandates may require local personnel to document certification requirements and other competencies. One state, for example, mandated that all new teachers should be mentored during their first year of service. School systems were expected to establish mentoring programs which would include, of course, properly trained mentors.

Systemwide organizational changes can contribute to the need for development and renewal programs. When schools are closed or new organizational configurations emerge, teachers and other personnel may have to acquire the skills and competencies necessary to be effective in new roles. In some cases the changes are so traumatic that support programs are needed to help teachers and administrators cope with new environments and expectations.

Structure. The structure of systemwide programs will vary with respect to goals, the number of participants, and the available resources. The structure may be as simple as a one-day program to orient all personnel or disseminate new information or as extensive as a multiyear program that has to be carefully planned and systematically monitored if it is to be effective. In order to be credible, long-term programs must be established in response to high-priority needs.

Outcomes. The outcomes of systemwide programs should be directly related to the goals of the programs. When goals are poorly defined, outcomes are difficult to assess. There are many potential benefits of systemwide development and renewal programs. They can help all personnel understand the problems and needs of the system. They can also be used to develop competencies that will improve teacher efficacy throughout the school system. Improvements can be made in curriculum articulation and instructional support which will benefit students in all schools. Although systemwide development and renewal programs are difficult to manage and maintain at optimal levels, they can dramatically improve educational programs. They can also help entire systems develop a unity of purpose that will ultimately benefit students in all of their schools.

Examples. Systemwide development and renewal plans are often a response to a specific concern or even a crisis in the schools. Some programs, however, have been more proactive than reactive and have focused on improving teaching and learning on a wide scale. Two such programs are presented and described in the balance of this section.

The central office administrators of one school system realized that they had an opportunity to develop a culture that would support instructional improvement in all of the schools in the system. For several years, they had conducted a program for their teachers to help them stay up to date with current research on teaching and learning. They had instituted this program because all of their teachers had been in the school system for many years. Due to declining enrollments they had not been able to employ any new teachers for over 10 years. They reached the point, however, where a number of their teachers retired at the same time, and they needed to employ at least 30 new teachers.

When the new teachers were hired, a condition of their employment was their involvement in a yearlong development and renewal program. The program started before the school year with sessions on the expectations and culture of the school system. Presentations were made on the instructional processes that were valued by the school system, including comprehensive planning, classroom management, instructional management, and strategies for involving students in their own learning. The new teachers were given the research materials that had been used in the experienced teachers' development program. The materials were reviewed and discussed at daylong meetings throughout the school year. These meetings were held on school time and substitute teachers were employed to cover the teachers' classes.

Early in the school year several sessions were devoted to the teacher evaluation process. The process was largely formative with an emphasis on ways to improve instruction. The new teachers were quite surprised that they were being prepared to receive positive, helpful evaluations. They had expected that the evaluation program would focus on rating them rather than helping them improve their performance. They soon began to see the relationship between what they were learning in the research discussion sessions and what they would be expected to do in the classrooms.

The new teachers were also given time to observe others in action. This gave them opportunities to see how their more experienced colleagues conducted their instruction. The experienced teachers also offered to advise new teachers on any of their teaching responsibilities. They were not assigned as formal mentors but served as an informal support system. By the end of the first year of the program, the new teachers had been successfully integrated into their school faculties and in most cases were performing at a highly satisfactory level.

The leaders of this school system were not willing to settle for having their new teachers find their own way into the system's culture. They created a program to promote success for their new employees rather than waiting and responding to their problems or failures. Without question the program was beneficial to the teachers and their students. The entire school system benefited from the unity of purpose that permeated all aspects of the program. Even the self-respect of the experienced teachers was enhanced by serving as role models for their new colleagues.

A larger school system faced a somewhat different problem. The supervisors and administrators identified a need that they felt should be addressed by all of the teachers and administrators. They had a considerable amount of data showing that the majority of their teachers were not keeping up to date with the research on teaching and learning. Although there were not many problems with their current classroom practices, there was little evidence that instructional decision making was based on credible research. They made the decision to design a development and renewal plan that would improve instruction in all of their schools and at the same time provide a vehicle for individual renewal.

The systemwide plan was based on a peer coaching model that had been successfully implemented in other school systems. A number of schools were selected to be in the program for the first year. The decision was made to begin with elementary schools. Each school was asked to identify four teachers to serve as lead teachers in the program. They would be expected to attend all of the training sessions, analyze research information that was presented, and make selected applications in their own classrooms. They would also serve as peer coaches to help each other develop, refine, and initiate successful instructional strategies. The principals were to attend all of the training sessions and offer support and assistance with the implementation activities in their respective schools. Principals and teachers were also expected to inform other teachers in their schools about the program, to disseminate research information, and to share the successes and the problems they encountered.

The project was highly successful the first year and was institutionalized as an ongoing development and renewal program. New schools were added each year with some schools being involved for a second year. Systemwide supervisors participated in all of the sessions so they would be aware of the information being presented and would be prepared to support and assist with instructional changes.

The school system has realized several important benefits from the program. Teachers are gradually improving their instruction by integrating research findings with their practical knowledge. A number of the peer coaches have become instructional facilitators whose role is to focus on selected areas of the research so they can provide assistance to other teachers throughout the system. The facilitators report that their self-esteem has been enhanced by being treated as professionals who have something important to offer their colleagues. As a result of the research on planning presentations, the entire school system has made comprehensive planning an instructional priority. Time has been provided at the start of the school year for all teachers to work together in their schools to develop their instructional plans for the school year. With teachers, administrators, and supervisors working together to achieve a common purpose, many of the schools are developing the characteristics of a community of learners.

LOOKING AHEAD

In this chapter, and throughout the book, we have taken the position that development and renewal must be a high priority for all teachers, from novice to expert. Our framework for development and renewal is based on the belief that reflection leads to action. Reflection is a critical activity for all those who truly want to grow and develop. But we must also look ahead, anticipate emerging needs, and be prepared to master our contexts. In short, we need to be proactive and not spend all of our time and energy reacting to the next problem or crisis.

The call for educational reform will continue in the future. Society will become even more complex and schools will be expected to solve problems that not even futurists can predict. Schools will have to become vibrant renewing organizations if they are going to survive future challenges.

Organizations, of course, can renew only when the people within them are committed to their own personal and professional renewal. To lead the way, schools will have to rely on their peak performers. Their most notable trait is that they are committed to lifelong learning (Garfield, 1986). They are individuals whose theme is: "I have done well, and I am capable of achieving much more. I am not finished yet. There is much more to me than this" (p. 20).

Adams, R., & Biddle, B. (1970). *Realities of teaching: Explanations with videotape*. New York: Holt, Rinehart and Winston.

Ainley, J. G. (1987). Equipment and materials. In M. J. Dunkin (Ed.), *The international encyclopedia of teaching and teacher education* (pp. 538–540). New York: Pergamon.

Alderman, M. K., & Cohen, M. W. (1985). *Motivation theory and practice for preservice teachers* (Teacher Education Monograph No. 4). Washington, DC: ERIC Clearinghouse on Teacher Education.

Alexander, P. A., & Judy, J. E. (1988). The interaction of domain-specific and strategic knowledge in academic performance. *Review of Educational Research, 58,* 375–404.

Allen, J. D. (1986). Classroom management: Students' perspectives, goals and strategies. *American Educational Research Journal, 23,* 437–459.

Alpert, B. R. (1987). Active, silent and controlled discussions: Explaining variations in classroom conversation. *Teaching and Teacher Education, 3,* 29–40.

Alvermann, D. E. (1981). The compensatory effects of graphic organizers on descriptive text. *Journal of Educational Research, 75,* 44–48.

Alvermann, D. E., & Hayes, D. A. (1989). Classroom discussion of content area reading assignments: An intervention study. *Reading Research Quarterly, 24,* 305–335.

Ames, C. (1985). Attributions and cognitions in motivation theory. In M. K. Alderman and M. W. Cohen (Eds.), *Motivation theory and practice for preservice teachers* (Teacher Education Monograph No. 4, pp. 16–21). Washington, DC: ERIC Clearinghouse on Teacher Education.

Ames, C., & Ames, R. (Eds.). (1985). *Research on motivation in education: Vol. 2. The classroom milieu*. Orlando: Academic.

Anderson, C. W., & Smith, E. L. (1987). Teaching science. In V. Richardson-Koehler (Ed.), *Educators' handbook: A research perspective* (pp. 84–111). New York: Longman.

Anderson, L. M. (1981). *Student responses to seatwork: Implications for the study of students' cognitive processing*. East Lansing, MI: Institute for Research on Teaching.

Anderson, L. M., & Prawat, R. S. (1983). Responsibility in the classroom: A synthesis of research on teaching self-control. *Educational Leadership, 40*(7), 62–66.

Anderson, L. M., Stevens, D. D., Prawat, R. S., & Nickerson, J. (1988). Classroom task environment and students' task-related beliefs. *The Elementary School Journal, 88,* 281–295.

Anderson, L. W. (1987). Opportunity to learn. In M. J. Dunkin (Ed.), *The international encyclopedia of teaching and teacher education* (pp. 368–372). Oxford: Pergamon Press.

Anderson, R. C., Hiebert, E. H., Scott, J. A., & Wilkinson, I. A. G. (1985). *Becoming a nation of readers: The report of the commission on reading.* Washington, DC: National Institute of Education.

Anderson, R. H. (1987). Shaping up the shop: How school organization influences teaching and learning. *Educational Leadership, 44*(5), 45.

Andre, T. (1987). Questions and learning from reading. *Questioning Exchange, 1*(1), 47–86.

Anthony, H. M., & Raphael, T. E. (1987). *Using questioning strategies to promote student's active comprehension of content area material* (Occasional Paper No. 109). East Lansing, MI: Michigan State University, Institute for Research on Teaching.

Arends, R. I. (1988). *Learning to teach.* New York: Random House.

Arlin, M. (1979). Teacher transitions can disrupt time flow in classrooms. *American Educational Research Journal, 16*(1), 42–56.

Armento, B. J. (1977). Teacher behaviors related to student achievement on a social science concept test. *Journal of Teacher Education, 28*(2), 46–52.

Aronson, E. (1978). *The jigsaw classroom.* Beverly Hills, CA: Sage Publications.

Association for Supervision and Curriculum Development (ASCD). (1986). Wiring model curriculum standards to tests may short circuit important curriculum outcomes. *Update, 28*(6), 1, 7.

Association for Supervision and Curriculum Development. (1988). Classroom management: A good start makes the difference. *Update, 30*(5), 1, 6.

Ashton, P. (1984). Teacher efficacy: A motivational paradigm for effective teacher education. *Journal of Teacher Education, 35*(5), 28–32.

Austin, J. D. (1986). Do comments on mathematics homework affect student achievement? *School Science and Mathematics, 76,* 159–164.

Ausubel, D. P. (1963). *The psychology of meaningful verbal learning.* New York: Grune and Stratton.

Balajthy, E. (1988). Results of the first national assessment of computer competence. *Reading Teacher, 24,* 242–243.

Baldwin, D. A. (1988, August). Complimentary guidelines giving and receiving positive feedback. *Piedmont Airlines,* pp. 17–21.

Bandura, A. (1977). Self-efficacy: Toward a unifying theory of behavioral change. *Psychological Review, 84,* 191–215.

Bangert, R. L., Kulik, J. A., & Kulik, C. C. (1983). Individualized systems of instruction in secondary schools. *Review of Educational Research, 53,* 143–158.

Barakett, J. M. (1986). Teachers' theories and methods in structuring routine activities in an inner city school. *Canadian Journal of Education, 11* (2), 91–108.

Barber, B. (1986). Homework does not belong on the agenda for educational reform. *Educational Leadership, 43* (8), 55–57.

Barell, J. (1985). You ask the wrong questions! *Educational Leadership, 42*(8), 18–23.

Barnes, H. (1989). Structuring knowledge for beginning teaching. In M. C. Reynolds (Ed.), *Knowledge base for the beginning teacher* (pp. 13–22). New York: Pergamon Press.

Barr, R. (1987). Content coverage. In M. J. Dunkin (Ed.), *The international encyclopedia of teaching and teacher education* (pp. 364–368). New York: Pergamon.

Barr, R., & Dreeben, R. (1983). *How schools work.* Chicago, IL: University of Chicago Press.

Bar-Tal, D. (1979). Interactions of teachers and pupils. In I. H. Frieze, D. Bar-Tal, & J. S. Carroll (Eds.), *New approaches to social problems: Applications of attribution theory.* San Francisco: Jossey-Bass.

Bar-Tal, D. (1982). The effects of teachers' behaviour on pupils' attributions: A review. In C.

Antaki & C. Brewin (Eds.), *Attributions and psychological change* (pp. 177–194). London: Academic Press.

Barth, R. S. (1990). A personal vision of a good school. *Phi Delta Kappan, 71,* 512–516.

Baumann, J. F. (1988). Direct instruction reconsidered. *Journal of Reading, 31,* 712–718.

Baumann, J. F., & Schmitt, M. C. (1986). The what, why, how, and when of comprehension instruction. *The Reading Teacher, 39,* 640–646.

Bayer, A. S. (1984). Teachers talking to learn. *Language Arts, 61,* 131–139.

Beck, I. L. (1989). Improving practice through understanding reading. In L. B. Resnick & L. E. Klopfer (Eds.), *Toward the thinking curriculum: Current cognitive research*. Arlington, VA: Association for Supervision and Curriculum Development.

Becker, H. S. (1952). Social class variations in the teacher-pupil relationship. *Journal of Educational Sociology, 25,* 451–465.

Behnke, G., & Labovitz, E. M. (1981). *Coping with classroom distractions*. Paper presented at the Annual Meeting of the American Educational Research Association, San Francisco.

Bellack, A. A., Kliebard, H. M., Hyman, R. T., & Smith, F. L. (1966). *The language of the classroom*. New York: Teachers College Press, Columbia University.

Bellon, E. C., Bellon, J. J., Blank, M. A., Brian, D. J. G., & Kershaw, C. A. (1989). *Alternative incentive programs for school based reform*. Paper presented at the Annual Meeting of the American Educational Research Association, San Francisco.

Bellon, J. J. (1985). The many roles of the skilled evaluator. In W. Duckett (Ed.), *The competent evaluator of teaching* (pp. 81–101). Bloomington, IN: Phi Delta Kappa.

Bellon, J. J., & Bellon, E. C. (1982). *Classroom supervision and instructional improvement: A synergetic process* (2nd ed.). Dubuque, IA: Kendall/ Hunt.

Bellon, J. J., Bellon, E. C., Blank, M. A., Brian, D. J. G., Kershaw, C., Perkins, M. T., Rose, T. D., & Veal, J. M. (1990). *Needs assessment guide* (2nd ed.). Nashville: Tennessee Department of Education.

Bellon, J. J., Bellon, E. C., & Handler, J. R. (1977). *Instructional improvement: Principles & processes*. Dubuque, IA: Kendall/Hunt.

Bellon, J. J., Doak, E. D., & Handler, J. (1979). *A study of school discipline in Tennessee*. Knoxville, TN: University of Tennessee, College of Education.

Bellon, J. J., & Handler, J. (1982). *Curriculum development and evaluation: A design for improvement*. Dubuque, IA: Kendall/Hunt.

Bender, T. A., & Hom, H. L., Jr. (1988). *Individual differences in achievement orientation and use of classroom feedback*. Paper presented at the Annual Meeting of the American Educational Research Association, New Orleans.

Bennett proposes model curriculum. (1988). *Education USA, 30*(21), 143.

Bennis, W. G. (1989). *On becoming a leader*. Reading, MA: Addison-Wesley.

Bennis, W. G., & Nanus, B. (1985). *Leaders: The strategies for taking charge*. New York: Harper and Row.

Berlak, H. (1985). Testing in a democracy. *Educational Leadership, 43*(2), 16–17.

Berliner, D. C. (1982). Recognizing instructional variables. In D. E. Orlosky (Ed.), *Introduction to education* (pp. 198–222). Columbus, OH: Merrill.

Berliner, D. C. (1983). Developing conceptions of classroom environments: Some light on the T in the study of ATI. *Educational Psychologist, 18,* 1–13.

Berliner, D. C. (1984). The half-full glass: A review of research on teaching. In P. L. Hosford (Ed.), *Using what we know about teaching* (pp. 51–77). Alexandria, VA: Association for Supervision and Curriculum Development.

Berliner, D. C. (1986). In pursuit of the expert pedagogue. *Educational Researcher, 15*(7), 5–13.

Berliner, D. C. (1987). But do they understand? In V. Richardson-Koehler (Ed.), *Educators' handbook: A research perspective* (pp. 259–291). New York: Longman.

Berliner, D. C. (1988, October). *Implications of studies of expertise in pedagogy for teacher education and evaluation*. Paper presented at the 1988 Educational Testing Service Invitational Conference on New Directions for Teacher Assessment, New York.

Beyer, B. K. (1983). Common sense about teaching thinking skills. *Educational Leadership, 41*(3), 44–49.

Beyer, B. K. (1987). *Practical strategies for the teaching of thinking.* Boston: Allyn and Bacon.

Beyer, B. K. (1988). *Developing a thinking skills program.* Boston: Allyn and Bacon.

Bibens, R. F. (1980). Using inquiry effectively. *Theory into Practice, 19,* 87–92.

Block, J. H. (1980). Promoting excellence through mastery learning. *Theory into Practice, 19,* 66–74.

Bloom, B. S. (1976). *Human characteristics and school learning.* New York: McGraw-Hill.

Bloom, B. S. (1980). The new direction in educational research: Alterable variables. *Phi Delta Kappan, 61,* 382–385.

Bloom, B. S. (1981). *All our children learning.* New York: McGraw-Hill.

Bloom, B. S. (1984). The search for methods of group instruction as effective as one-to-one tutoring. *Educational Leadership, 41*(8), 8–9.

Bloom, B. S. (1986). Automaticity: The hands and feet of genius. *Educational Leadership, 43*(5), 70–77.

Bloom, B. S., Engelhart, M., Furst, E., Hill, W., & Krathwohl, D. (Eds.). (1956). *Taxonomy of educational objectives: Handbook I. Cognitive domain.* New York: David McKay.

Blum, R. E., & Butler, J. A. (1987). *"Onward to excellence": Teaching schools to use effective schooling and implementation research to improve student performance.* Paper presented at the Annual Meeting of the American Educational Research Association, Washington, DC.

Boekaerts, M. (1986). Motivation in theories of learning. *International Journal of Educational Research, 10*(2), 129–141.

Borich, G. D. (1979). Implications for developing teacher competencies from process-product research. *Journal of Teacher Education, 30*(1), 77–86.

Borko, H., & Niles, J. A. (1987). Descriptions of teacher planning: Ideas for teachers and researchers. In V. Richardson-Koehler (Ed.), *Educators' handbook: A research perspective* (pp. 167–187). New York: Longman.

Bossert, S. T. (1977). Tasks, group management, and teacher control behavior: A study of classroom organization and teacher style. *School Review, 85,* 552–565.

Boucher, C. R. (1984). *Decreasing classroom conflict.* Seattle: Special Child Publications.

Bourke, S. F. (1985). The study of classroom contexts and practices. *Teaching and Teacher Education, 1,* 33–50.

Bourke, S. F. (1986). How smaller is better: Some relationships between class size, teaching practices and student achievement. *American Educational Research Journal, 23,* 558–571.

Bracey, G. W. (1987a). Computers and readiness. *Phi Delta Kappan, 68,* 243–244.

Bracey, G. W. (1987b). Reflective teachers. *Phi Delta Kappan, 69,* 233–234.

Bracey, G. W. (1987c). The social impact of ability grouping. *Phi Delta Kappan, 68,* 701–702.

Brandt, R. (1982). On improving teacher effectiveness: A conversation with David Berliner. *Educational Leadership, 40*(1), 12–15.

Brandt, R. (Ed.). (1984). *Effective teaching for higher achievement.* Washington, DC: Association for Supervision and Curriculum Development.

Brandt, R. S. (1987). On cooperation in schools: A conversation with David and Roger Johnson. *Educational Leadership, 45*(3), 14–19.

Brandt, R. S. (1988). Introduction: What should schools teach? *Content of the curriculum* (ASCD Yearbook, pp. 1–7). Alexandria, VA: Association for Supervision and Curriculum Development.

Brandt, R. S. (Ed.). (1989–90). Cooperative learning. *Educational Leadership, 47*(4).

Brandwein, P. (1981). *Memorandum: On schooling and education.* New York: Harcourt Brace Jovanovich.

Bransford, J. D., & Stein, B. S. (1984). *The IDEAL problem solver.* New York: Freeman.

Bridges, D. (1987). Discussion and questioning. *Questioning Exchange, 1*(1), 34–36.

Bridges, D. (1988). A philosophical analysis of discussion. In J. T. Dillon (Ed.), *Questioning and discussion: A multidisciplinary study* (pp. 15–28). Norwood, NJ: Ablex.

Brissie, J. S., Hoover-Dempsey, K. V., & Bassler, O. C. (1988). Individual situational contributors to teacher burnout. *Journal of Educational Research, 82,* 106–112.

Brookover, W. B. (1984). *School learning climate and student outcomes.* Paper presented at the Jackson School Management Conference, New Orleans.

Brookover, W. B., Beady, C., Flood, P., Schweitzer, J., & Wisenbaker, J. (1979). *School social systems and student achievement: Schools can make a difference.* New York: Praeger.

Brookover, W. B., & Lezotte, L. W. (1982). *Changes in school characteristics coincident with changes in student achievement.* East Lansing, MI: Michigan State University, Institute for Research on Teaching.

Brooks, D. M., & Hanks, G. (1988). Effective and ineffective session opening teacher activity and task structures. *Journal of Classroom Interaction, 23*(1), 1–4.

Brophy, J. E. (1979a). *Advances in teacher effectiveness research* (Occasional Paper No. 18). East Lansing, MI: Michigan State University, Institute for Research on Teaching.

Brophy, J. E. (1979b). Advances in teacher research. *Journal of Classroom Interaction, 15*(1), 1–7.

Brophy, J. E. (1979c). Teacher behavior and its effects. *Journal of Educational Psychology, 71,* 733–750.

Brophy, J. E. (1979d). Teacher behavior and student learning. *Educational Leadership, 37*(1), 33–38.

Brophy, J. E. (1980). *Recent research on teaching* (Occasional Paper No. 40). East Lansing, MI: Michigan State University, Institute for Research on Teaching.

Brophy, J. E. (1981). Teacher praise: A functional analysis. *Review of Educational Research, 51,* 5–32.

Brophy, J. E. (1982). *Classroom organization and management* (Occasional Paper No. 54). East Lansing, MI: Michigan State University, Institute for Research on Teaching.

Brophy, J. E. (1986a). *Socializing student motivation to learn* (IRT Research Series No. 169). East Lansing, MI: Michigan State University, Institute for Research on Teaching.

Brophy, J. E. (1986b). *Synthesizing the results of research linking teacher behavior to student achievement.* Paper presented at the Annual Meeting of the American Educational Research Association, San Francisco.

Brophy, J. E. (1986c). Teacher influences on student achievement. *American Psychologist, 41,* 1069–1077.

Brophy, J. E. (1987). Synthesis of research on strategies for motivating students to learn. *Educational Leadership, 45*(2), 40–48.

Brophy, J. E. (1988). *Teaching for conceptual understanding and higher order applications of social studies content.* Washington, DC: U.S. Department of Education, Office of Educational Research and Improvement.

Brophy, J. E. (in press). Conclusion: Toward a theory of teaching. In J. Brophy (Ed.), *Advances in research on teaching: Vol. 1. Teaching for meaningful understanding and self-regulated learning.* Greenwich, CT: JAI Press.

Brophy, J. E., & Evertson, C. M. (1974). *Process-product correlations in the Texas teacher effectiveness study: Final report.* Austin TX: University of Texas, Research and Development Center for Teacher Education. (ERIC Document Reproduction Service No. ED 091 394)

Brophy, J. E., & Evertson, C. M. (1976). *Learning from teaching: A developmental perspective.* Boston: Allyn and Bacon.

Brophy, J. E., & Good, T. L. (1974). *Teacher-student relationships: Causes and consequences.* New York: Holt, Rinehart and Winston.

Brophy, J. E., & Good, T. (1986). Teacher behavior and student achievement. In M. C. Wittrock (Ed.), *Handbook of research on teaching* (3rd ed., pp. 328–375). New York: Macmillan.

Brophy, J. E., & Kher, N. (1985). *Teacher socialization as a mechanism for developing student motivation to learn* (IRT Research Series No. 157). East Lansing, MI: Michigan State University, Institute for Research on Teaching.

Brophy, J. E., & Putnam, J. (1979). Classroom management in the elementary grades. In D. Duke (Ed.), *Classroom management* (The 78th Yearbook of the National Society for the Study of Education, Pt. 2, pp. 182–216). Chicago: University of Chicago Press.

Brophy, J. E., & Rohrkemper, M. M. (1981). The influence of problem ownership on teachers' perceptions of and strategies for coping with problem students. *Journal of Educational Psychology, 73,* 295–311.

Brophy, J. E., & Rohrkemper, M. M. (1987). *Teachers' strategies for coping with hostile-aggressive students* (IRT Research Series No. 185). East Lansing, MI: Michigan State University, Institute for Research on Teaching.

Brophy, J. E., & Rohrkemper, M. M. (1988). *The classroom strategy study: Summary report of general findings* (IRT Research Series No. 187). East Lansing, MI: Michigan State University, Institute for Research on Teaching.

Brophy, J. E., Rohrkemper, M. M., Rashid, H., & Goldberger, M. (1983). Relationships between teachers' presentations of classroom tasks and students' engagements in those tasks. *Journal of Educational Psychology, 75*, 544–552.

Brown, A. L., Campione, J. C., & Day, J. C. (1981). Learning to learn: On training students to learn from texts. *Educational Researcher, 10*(2), 14–21.

Brown, A. L., & Day, J. D. (1980). *The development of rules for summarizing texts.* Unpublished manuscript, University of Illinois, Champaign-Urbana.

Brown, A. L., & Palinscar, A. S. (1987). Reciprocal teaching of comprehension strategies: A natural history of one program for enhancing learning. In J. Borkowski & J. D. Day (Eds.), *Intelligence and cognition in special children: Comparative studies of giftedness, mental retardation, and learning disabilities* (pp. 274–326). Norwood, NJ: Ablex.

Brown, J. S., Collins, A., & Duguid, P. (1989). Situated cognition and the culture of learning. *Educational Researcher, 18*(1), 32–42.

Burns, J. M. (1978). *Leadership.* New York: Harper and Row.

Burns, M. (1986). Teaching "what to do" in arithmetic vs. teaching "what to do and why." *Educational Leadership, 43*(7), 34–38.

Burns, R. B. (1987). Steering groups, leveling effects, and instructional pace. *American Journal of Education, 96*(1), 24–55.

Butler, J. A. (1987a). *Cooperative learning: Independence High School* (School Improvement Research Series: Effective Practices in Place, Snapshot No. 1). Portland, OR: Northwest Regional Educational Laboratory.

Butler, J. A. (1987b). *Homework* (School Improvement Research Series, Close-Up No. 1). Port-land, OR: Northwest Regional Educational Laboratory.

Butler, J. A., & Dickson, K. M. (1988). *Improving school culture: Centennial High School* (School Improvement Program Research Series). Portland, OR: Northwest Regional Educational Laboratory.

Cahen, L. S., & Filby, N. (1979). The class size/achievement issue: New evidence and a research plan. *Phi Delta Kappan, 60*, 492–495, 538.

Cahen, L. S., Filby, N., McCutcheon, G., & Kyle, D. (1983). *Class size and instruction.* New York: Longman.

Calderhead, J. (1984). Classroom management. *Teachers' classroom decision making* (pp. 21–45). London: Holt, Rinehart and Winston.

Calderhead, J. (1987). *Exploring teachers' thinking.* London: Cassell Educational.

Calfee, R. D., & Piontkowski, D. C. (1987). In M. J. Dunkin (Ed.), *The international encyclopedia of teaching and teacher education* (pp. 225–232). New York: Pergamon Press.

California State Department of Education. (1980). *Report on the special studies of selected ECE schools with increasing and decreasing reading scores.* Sacramento, CA: Office of Program Evaluation and Research.

Cannella, G. S. (1986). Praise and concrete rewards: Concerns for childhood education. *Childhood Education, 62*(4), 297–298, 300–301.

Cangelosi, J. S. (1988). *Classroom management strategies: Gaining and maintaining students' cooperation.* New York: Longman.

Carin, A. A., & Sund, R. B. (1971). *Developing questioning techniques: A self-concept approach.* Columbus, OH: Merrill.

Carnegie Forum on Education and the Economy. (1986). *A nation prepared: Teachers for the 21st century.* New York: Carnegie Corporation.

Carnine, D. (1990). New research on the brain: Implications for instruction. *Phi Delta Kappan, 71*, 372–377.

Carnine, D., Carnine, L., Karp, J., & Weisberg, P. (1988). Kindergarten for economically disadvantaged children: The direct instruction component. In C. Warger (Ed.), *A resource guide to public school early childhood programs* (pp. 73–98). Alexandria, VA: Association for Supervision and Curriculum Development.

Carpenter, T. P. (1986). Conceptual knowledge as a foundation for procedural knowledge. In J. Hiebert (Ed.), *Conceptual and procedural knowledge: The case of mathematics* (pp. 113–130). London: Lawrence Erlbaum.

Carrington, A. T. (1983). Smaller classes improve reading achievement. *Phi Delta Kappan, 64,* 375.

Chall, J. S., & Snow, C. E. (1988). School influences on the reading development of low-income children. *Harvard Education Letter, 4*(1), 1–4.

Cheesman, P. L., & Watts, P. E. (1985). *Positive behavior management: A manual for teachers.* New York: Nichols.

Cheffers, J. T. F., Amidon, E. J., & Rogers, K. D. (1974). *Interaction analysis: An application to nonverbal activity.* St. Paul, MN: Association for Productive Teaching.

Chi, M. (1986). Can little children think big? *ASCD Update, 28*(2), 2–3.

Chilcoat, G. W., & Stahl, R. J. (1986). A framework for giving clear directions: Effective teacher verbal behavior. *Clearing House, 60,* 107–109.

Christenbury, L., & Kelly, P. (1983). *Questioning: A path to critical thinking.* Urbana, IL: National Council of Teachers of English.

Clark, C. M. (1986). Ten years of conceptual development in research on teacher thinking. In M. Ben-Peretz, R. Bromine, & R. Halkes (Eds.), *Advances of research on teacher thinking* (pp. 7–20). Berwyn, PA: Swets North America.

Clark, C. M. (1988). Asking the right questions about teacher participation: Contributions of research on teacher thinking. *Educational Researcher, 17*(2), 5–11.

Clark, C. M., & Peterson, P. L. (1986). Teachers thought processes. In M. Wittrock (Ed.), *Handbook of research on teaching* (3rd ed., pp. 255–296). New York: Macmillan.

Clark, C. M., & Yinger, R. J. (1979). *Three studies of teacher planning* (Research Series No. 55). East Lansing, MI: Michigan State University, Institute for Research on Teaching.

Clark, C. M., & Yinger, R. J. (1980). *The hidden world of teaching: Implications of research on teacher planning* (Research Series No. 77). East Lansing, MI: Michigan State University, Institute for Research on Teaching.

Clark, C. M., & Yinger, R. J. (1987). Teacher planning. In J. Calderhead (Ed.), *Exploring teachers' thinking* (pp. 84–103). London: Cassell Educational.

Clark, K. (1963). Educational stimulation of racially disadvantaged children. In A. H. Passow (Ed.), *Education in depressed areas.* New York: Columbia University, Teachers College.

Classroom management: A research synthesis and conference proceedings. (1980). Austin, TX: Southwest Educational Development Laboratory.

Clifford, M. M. (1972). Effects of competition as a motivational technique in the classroom. *American Educational Research Journal, 9,* 123–137.

Cogan, M. (1973). *Clinical supervision.* Boston: Houghton Mifflin.

Cohen, D. (1987). The use of concept maps to represent unique thought processes: Toward more meaningful learning. *Journal of Curriculum and Supervision, 2,* 285–289.

Cohen, E. G. (1986). *Designing groupwork: Strategies for the heterogeneous classroom.* New York: Teachers College Press.

Cohen, M. W. (1985). Extrinsic reinforcers and intrinsic motivation. In M. K. Alderman and M. W. Cohen (Eds.), *Motivation theory and practice for preservice teachers* (Teacher Education Monograph No. 4, pp. 6–13). Washington, DC: ERIC Clearinghouse on Teacher Education.

Cole, A. L. (1988). *Personal knowing in spontaneous teaching practice.* Paper presented at the Annual Meeting of the American Educational Research Association, New Orleans. (ERIC Document Reproduction Service No. ED 296 965)

Cole, R., & Williams, D. (1973). Pupil responses to teacher questions: Cognitive level, length, and syntax. *Educational Leadership Research Supplement,* 142–145.

Coleman, J. S., Campbell, E. Q., Hobson, C. J., McPartland, J., Mood, A. M., Weinfeld, F. D., & York, R. L. (1966). *Equality of educational opportunity* (Vol. 1). Washington, DC: Government Printing Office.

Collins, M., Carnine, D., & Gersten, R. (1987). Elaborated corrective feedback and the acquisition of reasoning skills: A study of computer-assisted instruction. *Exceptional Children, 54,* 254–262.

Conner, K., Hairston, J., Hill, I., Kopple, H., Marshall, J., Scholnick, K., & Schulman, M. (1985). Using formative testing at the classroom, school, and district levels. *Educational Leadership, 43*(2), 63–67.

Cooper, H. (1989). Synthesis of research on homework. *Educational Leadership, 47*(3), 85–91.

Cooper, H. M. (1983). Communication of teacher expectations to students. In J. Levine & M. Wang (Eds.), *Teacher and student perceptions: Implications for learning* (pp. 193–211). Hillsdale, NJ: Lawrence Erlbaum.

Cooper, H. M., & Baron, R. (1977). Academic expectations and attributed responsibility as predictors of professional teachers' reinforcement behavior. *Journal of Educational Psychology, 69,* 409–418.

Cooper, H. M., & Good, T. L. (1983). *Pygmalion grows up.* New York: Longman.

Corno, L. (1981). Cognitive organizing in classrooms. *Curriculum Inquiry, 11,* 359–377.

Corno, L. (1986). *Self-regulated learning and classroom teaching.* Paper presented at the Annual Meeting of the American Educational Research Association, San Francisco.

Corno, L., & Mandinach, E. B. (1983). The role of cognitive engagement in classroom learning and motivation. *Educational Psychologist, 18,* 88–108.

Corno, L., & Snow, R. (1986). Adapting teaching to individual differences among learners. In M. C. Wittrock (Ed.), *Handbook of research on teaching* (3rd ed., pp. 605–629). New York: Macmillan.

Cotton, K. (1988a). *Instructional reinforcement* (School Improvement Research Series, Close-Up No. 3). Portland, OR: Northwest Regional Educational Laboratory.

Cotton, K. (1988b). *Monitoring student learning in the classroom* (School Improvement Research Series). Portland, OR: Northwest Regional Educational Laboratory.

Cotton, K. (1988c). *Summary of research on class size* (School Improvement Research Series, Special Report). Portland, OR: Northwest Regional Educational Laboratory.

Cotton, K. (1988d). *Teaching composition: Research on effective practices* (School Improvement Research Series, Topical Synthesis No. 2). Portland, OR: Northwest Regional Educational Laboratory.

Cotton, K., & Savard, W. G. (1981). *Instructional grouping: Ability grouping* (Research on School Effectiveness Project, Topic Summary Report). Portland, OR: Northwest Regional Educational Laboratory. (ERIC Document Reproduction Service No. ED 214 704)

Coulter, F. (1987). Homework. In M. J. Dunkin (Ed.), *The international encyclopedia of teaching and teacher education* (pp. 272–277). New York: Pergamon Press.

Crain, S. A. (1988). Metacognition and the teaching of reading. *Journal of Reading, 31,* 682–685.

Critical thinking: What can it be? (1988). *Cogitare, 2*(4), 1–2.

Crocker, R. K., & Brooker, G. M. (1986). Classroom control and student outcomes in grades 2 and 5. *American Educational Research Journal, 23,* 1–11.

Crooks, T. J. (1988). The impact of classroom evaluation practices on students. *Review of Educational Research, 58,* 438–481.

Cruickshank, D. R. (1989). Applying research on teacher clarity. In L. W. Anderson (Ed.), *The effective teacher study guide and readings* (pp. 285–290). New York: Random House.

Cruickshank, D. R., & Kennedy, J. J. (1986). Teacher clarity. *Teaching and Teacher Education, 2,* 43–67.

Cruickshank, D. R., Kennedy, J. J., Bush, A. J., & Holland, D. W. (1978). A tentative resolution of teacher clarity. *The Educational Catalyst, 8*(3), 121–132.

Curwin, R. W., & Mendler, A. N. (1988). *Discipline with dignity.* Alexandria, VA: Association for Supervision and Curriculum Development.

Dar, Y., & Resh, N. (1986). Classroom intellectual composition and academic achievement. *American Educational Research Journal, 23,* 357–374.

Darling-Hammond, L., & Barnett, B. (1988). *The evolution of teacher policy.* Santa Monica, CA: Rand Corporation, Center for Policy Research in Education.

Davidson, C. W., & Powell, L. A. (1986). The effects of easy-listening background music on the on-task performance of 5th grade children. *Journal of Educational Research, 80*(1), 29–33.

Davies, I. K., & Shane, H. G. (1986). Educational implications of microelectronic networks. In J. A. Culbertson & L. L. Cunningham (Eds.), *Microcomputers and education* (The 85th Yearbook of the National Society for the Study of Education, Pt. 1, pp. 1–21). Chicago, IL: University of Chicago Press.

Davis, A., & Dollard, J. (1940). *Children of bondage.* Washington, DC: American Council of Education.

deCharms, R. (1976). *Enhancing motivation.* New York: Halsted Press.

Dede, C. (1983). Symposium: The likely evolution of computer use in schools. *Educational Leadership, 41*(1), 22–24.

Denham, C., & Lieberman, A. (Eds.). (1980). *Time to learn.* Washington, DC: U.S. Department of Education, National Institute of Education.

Derry, S. J. (1989–90). Putting learning strategies to work. *Educational Leadership, 46*(4), 4–10.

Deutsch, M. (1963). The disadvantaged child and the learning process. In A. H. Passow (Ed.), *Education in depressed areas.* New York: Columbia University, Teachers College, Bureau of Publications.

Dewdney, P., & Ross, C. (1986). Effective question-asking in library instruction. *RQ, 25,* 451–454.

Dick, W. (1987). Instructional design and the curriculum development. *Educational Leadership, 44*(4), 54–56.

Dillon, J. T. (1981a). A norm against student questioning. *Clearing House, 53,* 136–139.

Dillon, J. T. (1981b). To question and not to question during discussions: I. Questioning and discussion. *Journal of Teacher Education, 32*(5), 51–55.

Dillon, J. T. (1981c). To question and not to question during discussion: II. Non-questioning techniques. *Journal of Teacher Education, 32*(6), 15–20.

Dillon, J. T. (1982). Cognitive correspondence between question/statement and response.
American Educational Research Journal, 19, 540–551.

Dillon, J. T. (1983). *Teaching and the art of questioning.* Bloomington, IN: Phi Delta Kappan Educational Foundation.

Dillon, J. T. (1984). Research on questioning and discussion. *Educational Leadership, 42*(3), 50–56.

Dillon, J. T. (1988). Discussion versus recitation. *Tennessee Educational Leadership, 15*(1), 52–63.

DiPrete, T., Muller, C., & Shaeffer, N. (1981). *Discipline and order in American high schools.* Washington, DC: U.S. Department of Education, National Center for Education Statistics.

Doenau, S. J. (1987a). Soliciting. In M. J. Dunkin (Ed.), *The international encyclopedia of teaching and teacher education* (pp. 407–413). New York: Pergamon Press.

Doenau, S. J. (1987b). Structuring. In M. J. Dunkin (Ed.), *The international encyclopedia of teaching and teacher education* (pp. 398–407). New York: Pergamon Press.

Doty, J. (1986). *Increasing parent involvement in a first grade Chapter 1 public school classroom program.* Fort Lauderdale, FL: Nova University. (ERIC Document Reproduction Service No. ED 272 292)

Doyle, W. (1979). Making managerial decisions in classrooms. In D. Duke (Ed.), *Classroom management* (The 78th Yearbook of the National Society for the Study of Education, Pt. 2, pp. 42–74). Chicago: University of Chicago Press.

Doyle, W. (1981). Research on classroom contexts. *Journal of Teacher Education, 32*(6), 3–6.

Doyle, W. (1983). Academic work. *Review of Educational Research, 53,* 159–199.

Doyle, W. (1985). B. The knowledge base for adaptive instruction: A perspective from classroom research. In M. C. Wang & H. J. Walberg (Eds.), *Adapting instruction to individual differences* (pp. 91–102). Berkeley, CA: McCutchan.

Doyle, W. (1986a). Academic work. In T. M. Tomlinson & H. J. Walberg (Eds.), *Academic work and educational excellence: Raising student productivity* (pp. 175–195). Berkeley, CA: McCutchan.

Doyle, W. (1986b). Classroom organization and management. In M. C. Wittrock (Ed.), *Handbook of research on teaching* (3rd ed., pp. 392–431). New York: Macmillan.

Doyle, W., & Carter, K. (1987). Choosing the means of instruction. In V. Richardson-Koehler (Ed.), *Educators' handbook: A research perspective* (pp. 188–206). New York: Longman.

Drawing a blueprint for success. (1986). Washington, DC: National Foundation for the Improvement of Education.

Dreher, M. J., & Singer, H. (1989). The teacher's role in students' success. *The Reading Teacher, 42,* 612–617.

Driscoll, M. P. (1986). The relationship between grading standards and achievement. *Journal of Research and Development, 19*(3), 13–17.

Duckworth, K., Fielding, G., & Shaughnessy, J. (1986). *Relationship of high school teachers' class testing practices to students' feelings of efficacy and efforts to study.* Eugene, OR: Center for Educational Policy and Management.

Duffy, G. G., & Roehler, L. R. (1986). *Improving reading instruction through the use of responsive elaboration.* East Lansing, MI: Michigan State University, Institute for Research on Teaching.

Duffy, G. G., Roehler, L. R., & Herman, B. A. (1988). Modeling mental processes helps poor readers become strategic readers. *The Reading Teacher, 41,* 762–767.

Duffy, G. G., Roehler, L. R., Meloth, M. S., & Vabrus, L. G. (1986). Conceptualizing instructional explanation. *Teaching and Teacher Education, 2*(3), 197–214.

Duke, D. L. (Ed.). (1982). *Helping teachers manage classrooms.* Alexandria, VA: Association for Supervision and Curriculum Development.

Duke, D. L. (1987). Environmental influences. In M. J. Dunkin (Ed.), *The international encyclopedia of teaching and teacher education* (pp. 548–553). New York: Pergamon Press.

Dunkin, M. J. (Ed.). (1987). *The international encyclopedia of teaching and teacher education.* New York: Pergamon.

Dunkin, M. J., & Biddle, B. J. (1974). *The study of teaching.* New York: Holt, Rinehart and Winston.

Dwyer, E. J. (1988). Solving verbal analogies. *Journal of Reading, 32,* 73–75.

Eaton, J. (1985). There's hope for general math. *Educational Leadership, 43*(1), 91–93.

Educational Research Service. (1978). *Class size: A summary of research.* Arlington, VA: Author.

Eggen, P. D., & Kauchak, D. P. (1988). *Strategies for teachers: Teaching content and thinking skills.* Englewood Cliffs, NJ: Prentice-Hall.

Elias, M., & Clabby, J. F. (1988). Teaching social decision making. *Educational Leadership, 45*(6), 52–55.

Emmer, E. T. (1984). *Classroom management for secondary teachers.* Englewood, NJ: Prentice-Hall.

Emmer, E. T. (1986). Academic activities and tasks in first year teacher's classes. *Teaching and Teacher Education, 2,* 229–244.

Emmer, E. T. (1987). Classroom management. In M. J. Dunkin (Ed.), *The international encyclopedia of teaching and teacher education* (pp. 437–445). New York: Pergamon.

Emmer, E. T., & Evertson, C. M. (1981). Synthesis of research on classroom management. *Educational Leadership, 38*(4), 342–347.

Emmer, E. T., Evertson, C. M., Sanford, J. P., Clements, B. C., & Worsham, M. E. (1984). *Classroom management for secondary teachers.* Englewood Cliffs, NJ: Prentice-Hall.

Englander, M. E. (1986). *Strategies for classroom discipline.* New York: Praeger.

Ennis, R. H. (1989). Critical thinking and subject specificity: Clarification and needed research. *Educational Researcher, 18*(3), 4–10.

Epstein, J. L. (1981). Patterns of classroom participation, student attitudes, and achievements. In J. L. Epstein (Ed.), *The quality of school life* (pp. 81–115). Lexington, MA: Lexington Books.

Erickson, F., & Mohatt, G. (1982). Cultural organization of participant structures in two classrooms of Indian students. In G. Spindler (Ed.), *Doing the ethnography of schooling: Educational anthropology in action* (pp. 132–174). New York: Holt, Rinehart and Winston.

Evans, M., & Hopkins, D. (1988). School climate and the psychological state of the individual teacher as factors affecting the utilisation of educational ideas following an inservice course. *British Educational Research Journal, 14*(3), 211–230.

Evertson, C. M., Anderson, C. W., & Brophy, J. E. (1980). Relationships between classroom behaviors and student outcomes in junior mathematics and English classes. *American Educational Research Journal, 17*, 43–60.

Evertson, C. M., & Emmer, E. T. (1982). Preventive classroom management. In D. Duke (Ed.), *Helping teachers manage classrooms* (pp. 2–31). Alexandria, VA: Association for Supervision and Curriculum Development.

Evertson, C. M., Emmer, E. T., Clements, B. S., Sanford, J. P., & Worsham, M. E. (1984). *Classroom management for elementary teachers.* Englewood Cliffs, NJ: Prentice-Hall.

Evertson, C. M., Emmer, E. T., & Sanford, J. P. (1981). Effects of class heterogeneity in junior high school. *American Educational Research Journal, 18*, 207–218.

Eylon, B., & Linn, M. C. (1988). Research perspectives in science education. *Review of Educational Research, 58*, 251–302.

Farr, R., & Tulley, M. A. (1985). Do adoption committees perpetuate mediocre textbooks? *Phi Delta Kappan, 66*, 467–471.

Farrar, M. T. (1984). Why do we ask comprehension questions? A new conception of comprehensive instruction. *The Reading Teacher, 37*, 452–457.

Farrar, M. T. (1988). A sociolinguistic analysis of discussion. In J. T. Dillon (Ed.), *Questioning and discussion: A multidisciplinary study* (pp. 29–73). Norwood, NJ: Ablex.

Featherstone, H. (Ed.). (1986). Schools where teachers learn: Promising directions for staff development. *Harvard Education Letter, 2*(4), 1–4.

Featherstone, H. (1987). Organizing classes by ability. *Harvard Education Letter, 3*(4), 1–4.

Feeney, S., & Chun, R. (1985). Effective teachers of young children. *Young Children, 41*(1), 47–52.

Feiman, S., & Floden, R. E. (1981). *A consumer's guide to teacher development* (Research Series No. 94). East Lansing, MI: Michigan State University, Institute for Research on Teaching.

Fielker, D. S. (1987). A calculator, a tape recorder, and thou. *Educational Studies in Mathematics, 18*, 417–437.

Filby, N. N., & Cahen, L. S. (1985). Teacher accessibility and student attention. In C. W. Fisher & D. C. Berliner (Eds.), *Perspectives on instructional time* (pp. 203–215). New York: Longman.

Finley, C. D., & Seaton, M. D. (1987). Using text patterns and question predictions to study for tests. *Journal of Reading, 31*, 124–132.

First-grade reading: Who learns and who doesn't? (1987). *Harvard Education Letter, 3*(1), 4–6.

Fisher, C. W., Berliner, D. C., Filby, N. N., Marliave, R., Cahen, L. S., & Dishaw, M. M. (1980). Teaching behaviors, academic learning time, and student achievement: An overview. In C. Denham & A. Lieberman (Eds.) *Time to learn: A review of the beginning teacher evaluation study* (pp. 7–32). Washington, DC: National Institute of Education.

Fisher, C. W., Berliner, D. C., Filby, N. N., Marliave, R., Cohen, L. S., & Dishaw, M. M. (1984). Teaching behaviors, academic learning time, and student achievement: An overview. In D. B. Strother (Ed.), *Time and learning* (pp. 97–122). Bloomington, IN: Phi Delta Kappa, Center on Evaluation, Development and Research.

Flygare, T. J. (1986). Ability grouping and student achievement in elementary schools. *Phi Delta Kappan, 68*, 76–77.

Freiberg, J. J., Orth, L., Stallings, J., & Waxman, H. (1989). *Staff development: A means of teacher empowerment.* Paper presented at the Annual Meeting of the American Educational Research Association, San Francisco.

Gage, N. L. (1976). A factorially designed experiment on teacher structuring, soliciting, and reacting. *Journal of Teacher Education, 27*(1), 35–38.

Gage, N. L. (1978). *The scientific basis of the art of teaching.* New York: Teachers College Press.

Gage, N. L. (1986). *Does process-product research imply non-deliberation in teacher education?* Paper presented at the Annual Meeting of the American Educational Research Association, San Francisco.

Gage, N. L., & Berliner, D. C. (1984). *Educational psychology* (3rd ed.). Boston: Houghton Mifflin.

Gage, N. L., & Berliner, D. C. (1989). Nurturing the critical, practical, and artistic thinking of teachers. *Phi Delta Kappan, 71*, 212–214.

Gagne, E. (1985). Strategies for effective teaching and learning. In *The cognitive psychology of school learning*. Boston: Little, Brown.

Gall, M. D. (1970). The use of questions in teaching. *Review of Educational Research, 15,* 707–721.

Gall, M. D. (1984). Synthesis of research on teachers' questioning. *Educational Leadership, 42*(3), 40–47.

Gall, M. D., & Gillett, M. (1980). The discussion method in classroom teaching. *Theory into Practice, 19,* 98–103.

Gall, M. D., Ward, B. A., Berliner, D., Cahen, L. S., Wenne, P., Elashoff, J. D., & Stanton, G. S. (1987). Effects of questioning techniques and recitation on student learning. *American Educational Research Journal, 15,* 175–199.

Gambrell, L. B. (1983). The occurrence of think time during reading comprehension instruction. *Journal of Educational Research, 77,* 76–80.

Gamoran, A. (1984). *Egalitarian versus elitist use of ability grouping.* Chicago: Spencer Foundation. (ERIC Document Reproduction Service No. ED 245 821)

Gamoran, A. (1987). Organization, instruction, and the effects of ability grouping: Comment on Slavin's "best-evidence synthesis." *Review of Educational Research, 57,* 341–345.

Gamoran, A., & Berends, M. (1987). The effect of stratification in secondary schools: Synthesis of survey and ethnographic research. *Review of Educational Research, 57,* 415–435.

Gardner, H. (1983). *Frames of mind: The theory of multiple intelligences.* New York: Basic Books.

Gardner, J. W. (1965). *Self-renewal: The individual and the innovative society.* New York: Harper and Row.

Gardner, J. W. (1990). *On leadership.* New York: Free Press.

Garfield, C. (1986). *Peak performers: The new heroes of American business.* New York: William Morrow.

Garmston, R. J. (1987). How administrators support peer coaching. *Educational Leadership, 44*(5), 18–26.

Gephart, W. J., Strother, D. B., & Duckett, W. R. (Eds.). (1981a). Discipline. *Practical Applications of Research, 4*(1), 1–4.

Gephart, W. J., Strother, D. B., & Duckett, W. R. (Eds.). (1981b). Instructional clarity. *Practical Applications of Research, 3*(3), 1–4.

Gephart, W. J., Strother, D. B., & Duckett, W. R. (Eds.). (1981c). Teacher enthusiasm, a factor in stimulating student learning. *Practical Applications of Research, 3*(4), 1–4.

Gersten, R., & Carnine, D. (1986). Direct instruction in reading comprehension. *Educational Leadership, 43*(7), 70–78.

Gettinger, M. (1989). Effects of maximizing time spent and minimizing time needed for learning on pupil achievement. *American Educational Research Journal, 26,* 73–91.

Gibboney, R. A. (1989). The unscientific character of educational research. *Phi Delta Kappan, 71,* 225–227.

Gilman, D. A., & Sommer, J. (1988). *The summative evaluation: Teachers teaching teachers. A project in staff development for improving teacher effectiveness.* Terre Haute, IN: Indiana State University, Professional School Services. (ERIC Document Reproduction Service No. ED 300 353)

Glass, G. V. (1978). Standards and criteria. *Journal of Educational Measurement, 15,* 237–261.

Glass, G. V. (1987). Class size. In M. J. Dunkin (Ed.), *The international encyclopedia of teaching and teacher education* (pp. 540–545). New York: Pergamon Press.

Glass, G. V., Cahen, L. S., Smith, M. L., & Filby, N. S. (1979). Class size and learning: New interpretation of the research literature. *Today's Education, 68*(2), 42–44.

Glass, G. V., Cahen, L. S., Smith, M. L., & Filby, N. (1982). *School class size.* Beverly Hills, CA: Sage.

Glasser, W. (1965). *Reality therapy: A new approach to psychiatry.* New York: Harper and Row.

Glasser, W. (1969). *Schools without failure.* New York: Harper and Row.

Glasser, W. (1977). Ten steps to good discipline. *Today's Education, 66*(4), 61–63.

Glasser, W. (1986). *Control theory in the classroom.* New York: Harper and Row.

Glenn, B. C. (1981). *What works? An examination of effective schools for poor black children.* Cambridge, MA: Harvard University, Center for Law and Education.

Gliessman, D. H. (1987). Changing complex thinking skills. *Journal of Education for Teaching, 13,* 267–275.

Gliessman, D. H., & Pugh, R. C. (1987). Conceptual instruction and intervention as methods of acquiring teaching skills. *International Journal of Educational Research, 11,* 555–563.

Gliessman, D. H., Pugh, R. C., Dowden, D. E., & Hutchins, T. F. (1988). Variables influencing the acquisition of a generic teaching skill. *Review of Educational Research, 58,* 25–46.

Goldhammer, R., Anderson, R., & Krajewski, R. (1980). *Clinical supervision* (2nd ed.). New York: Holt, Rinehart and Winston.

Goldstein, A. P. (1989). Teaching alternatives to aggression. In D. Biklen, D. Ferguson, & A. Ford (Eds.), *Schooling and disability* (The 88th Yearbook of the National Society for the Study of Education, Pt. 1, pp. 168–194). Chicago, IL: University of Chicago Press.

Good, T. L. (1979). Teacher effectiveness in the elementary school. *Journal of Teacher Education, 30*(2), 52–64.

Good, T. L. (1981). Teacher expectations and student perceptions: A decade of research. *Educational Leadership, 38*(5), 415–423.

Good, T. L. (1983). Research on classroom teaching. In L. S. Shulman and G. Sykes (Eds.), *Handbook of teaching and policy.* New York: Longman.

Good, T. L., & Brophy, J. E. (1974). Changing teacher and student behavior: An empirical investigation. *Journal of Educational Psychology, 66,* 390–405.

Good, T. L., & Brophy, J. E. (1980). *Educational psychology: A realistic approach.* New York: Holt, Rinehart and Winston.

Good, T. L., & Brophy, J. E. (1987). *Looking in classrooms* (4th ed.). New York: Harper and Row.

Good, T. L., & Brophy, J. E. (1991). Looking in classrooms (5th ed). New York: Harper Collins.

Good, T. L., Cooper, H., & Blakey, S. (1978). Classroom interaction as a function of teacher expectations, student sex, and time of year. *Journal of Educational Psychology, 72,* 378–385.

Good, T. L., & Grouws, D. A. (1977). Teaching effects: A process-product study in fourth-grade mathematics classrooms. *Journal of Teacher Education, 28*(3), 49–54.

Good, T. L., & Grouws, D. A. (1979a). The Missouri mathematics effectiveness project: An experimental study in fourth grade classrooms. *Journal of Educational Psychology, 71,* 355–362.

Good, T. L., & Grouws, D. A. (1979b). Teaching and mathematics learning. *Educational Leadership, 37*(1), 39–45.

Good, T. L., Grouws, D. A., Beckerman, D., Ebmeier, H., Flat, L., & Schneeberger, S. (1977). *Teaching manual: Missouri mathematics effectiveness project* (Technical Report No. 132). Columbia, MO: University of Missouri, Center for Research in Social Behavior.

Good, T. L., & Marshall, S. (1984). Do students learn more in heterogeneous or homogeneous groups? In P. L. Peterson, L. C. Wilderson, & M. Halleman (Eds.), *The social context of instruction: Group organization and group processes* (pp. 15–38). New York: Academic Press.

Good, T. L., Slavings, R. L., Harel, K. H., and Emerson, H. (1987). Student passivity: A study of question asking in K–12 classrooms. *Sociology of Education, 60,* 181–199.

Good, T. L., Slavings, R. L., & Mason, D. A. (1988). Learning to ask questions: Grade and school effects. *Teaching and Teacher Education, 4,* 363–378.

Graisser, P. (1964). *How to use the fine art of questioning.* Englewood Cliffs, NJ: Teachers Practical Press.

Grant, G. E. (1988). *Teacher critical thinking.* New York: Praeger.

Green, J., & Smith, D. (1983). Teaching and learning: A linguistic perspective. *Elementary School Journal, 83,* 354–391.

Gronlund, N. E. (1985). *Stating objectives for classroom instruction* (3rd ed.). New York: Macmillan.

Grossman, P. L., Wilson, S. M., & Shulman, L. S. (1989). Teachers of substance: Subject matter knowledge for teaching. In M. C. Reynolds (Ed.), *Knowledge base for the beginning teacher* (pp. 23–36). New York: Pergamon Press.

Grossnickle, D. R., & Thiel, W. B. (1988). *Promoting effective student motivation in school and classroom: A practitioner's perspective.* Reston,

VA: National Association of Secondary School Principals.

Gump, P. V. (1982). School settings and their keeping. In D. Duke (Ed.), *Helping teachers manage classrooms* (pp. 98–114). Alexandria, VA: Association for Supervision and Curriculum Development.

Gump, P. V. (1987). Activities: Structures and functions. In M. J. Dunkin (Ed.), *The international encyclopedia of teaching and teacher education* (pp. 452–456). New York: Pergamon Press.

Gunstone, R. F., & White, R. T. (1981). Understanding of gravity. *Science Education, 65,* 291–299.

Guskey, T. R. (1986). Staff development and the process of teacher change. *Educational Researcher, 15*(5), 5–12.

Guskey, T. R. (1988). Teacher efficacy, self-concept, and attitudes toward the implementation of instructional innovation. *Teaching and Teacher Education, 4,* 63–69.

Guskey, T. R., & Gates, S. L. (1986). Synthesis of research on the effects of mastery learning in elementary and secondary classrooms. *Educational Leadership, 43*(8), 73–80.

Haertel, E. (1986). *Choosing and using classroom tests: Teachers' perspectives on assessment.* Paper presented at the Annual Meeting of the American Educational Research Association, San Francisco.

Hallden, O. (1988). Alternative frameworks and the concept of task. *Scandinavian Journal of Educational Research, 32*(3), 123–140.

Hallinger, P., & Murphy, J. (1985). Characteristics of highly effective elementary school reading programs. *Educational Leadership, 42*(5), 39–42.

Hammond, J., & Foster, K. (1987). Creating a professional learning partnership. *Educational Leadership, 44*(5), 42–44.

Hanley, P. E., & Swick, K. J. (1983). *Teacher renewal: Revitalization of classroom teachers.* Washington, DC: National Educational Association.

Hansford, B. C., & Hattie, J. E. (1982). The relationship between self and achievement performance measures. *Review of Educational Research, 52,* 123–142.

Harris, J., & Short, G. L. (1988). An introduction to the comprehensive behavior management system. *NASSP Bulletin, 72* (504), 28–35.

Harris, P., & Swick, K. J. (1985). Improving teacher communications: Focus on clarity and questioning skills. *Clearing House, 59,* 13–15.

Harvey, O., Hunt, J. D., & Schroder, H. (1963). *Conceptual systems and personality organizations.* New York: Wiley.

Hawkins, J., & Sheingold, K. (1986). The beginning of a story: Computers and the organization of learning in classrooms. In J. A. Culbertson & L. L. Cunningham (Eds.), *Microcomputers and education* (The 85th Yearbook of the National Society for the Study of Education, Pt. 2, pp. 40–58). Chicago, IL: University of Chicago Press.

Hawley, W. D., & Rosenholtz, S. J. (1984). Good schools: What research says about improving student achievement. *Peabody Journal of Education, 61*(4), 15–52.

Haynes, N. M. (1989). School climate enhancement through parental involvement. *Journal of School Psychology, 27,* 87–90.

Heiman, M., & Slomianko, J. (1985). *Critical thinking skills.* Washington, DC: NEA Professional Library.

Herrmann, B. A. (1986a). *Characteristics of verbal interaction patterns.* Unpublished paper, University of South Carolina, College of Education, Columbia.

Herrmann, B. A. (1986b). *Direct explanation of problem-solving strategies.* Unpublished paper, University of South Carolina, College of Education, Columbia.

Herrmann, B. A. (1988). Two approaches for helping poor readers become more strategic. *The Reading Teacher, 42,* 24–28.

Hiebert, J. (Ed.). (1986). *Conceptual and procedural knowledge: The case of mathematics.* London: Lawrence Erlbaum.

Hiebert, J., & Lefevre, S. (1986). Conceptual and procedural knowledge in mathematics: An introductory analysis. In J. Hiebert (Ed.), *Conceptual and procedural knowledge: The case of mathematics* (pp. 1–27). Hillsdale, NJ: Lawrence Erlbaum.

Hiller, J. H., Fisher, P., & Kaess, W. (1969). A computer investigation of verbal characteristics of effective classroom lecturing. *American Educational Research Journal, 6,* 661–675.

Hills, P. J. (1986). *Teaching, learning and communication.* London: Croom Helm.

Hines, C. V., Cruickshank, D. R., & Kennedy, J. (1985). Teacher clarity and its relationship to student achievement and satisfaction. *American Educational Research Journal, 22,* 87–99.

Hollingsworth, S. (1989). Prior beliefs and cognition change in learning to teach. *American Educational Research Journal, 26,* 160–189.

Holte, J. (1989). Technology and the science class: Going beyond the walls of the disc drive. *Electronic Learning, 9*(3), 38–42.

Houston, R. W., & Freiberg, H. J. (1979). Perpetual motion, blindman's bluff, and inservice education. *Journal of Teacher Education, 30*(1), 7–9.

Huhnke, C. A. (1984). *An annotated bibliography of the literature dealing with enhancing student motivation in the elementary school.* South Bend, IN: Indiana University. (ERIC Document Reproduction Service No. ED 252 310)

Hunkins, F. P. (1972). *Questioning strategies and techniques.* Boston: Allyn and Bacon.

Hunkins, F. P. (1976). *Involving students in questioning.* Boston: Allyn and Bacon.

Hunter, E. (1989). Three fields of research help mold the future of education. *NASSP Bulletin, 73* (515), 30–34.

Hunter, M. & Barker, G. (1987). "If at first . . .": Attribution theory in the classroom. *Educational Leadership, 45*(2), 50–53.

Hyman, R. T. (1980). *Improving discussion leadership.* New York: Teachers College Press.

Hyman, R. T. (1987). In W. Wilen (Ed.), *Questions, questioning techniques, and effective teaching* (pp. 135–152). Washington, DC: NEA Professional Library.

Iacocca, L., & Novak, W. (1984). *Iacocca: An autobiography.* New York: Bantam Books.

Imhof, H. (1989). Computers in the science classroom: The resources keep on getting better. *The Computing Teacher,* 30–32.

Institute for Research on Teaching. (1982). Do students learn from seatwork? *IRT Communication Quarterly, 5*(1), 2–3.

Institute for Research on Teaching. (1984). Seatwork can be more productive. *IRT Communication Quarterly, 7*(1), 1,4.

Institute for Research on Teaching. (1985a). Do tests and textbooks match? *IRT Communication Quarterly, 7*(3), 1,4.

Institute for Research on Teaching. (1985b). Questioning promotes active reader/text interaction. *IRT Communication Quarterly, 9*(3), 4–5.

Institute for Research on Teaching. (1986). Helping students gain greater control over their own reading instruction. *IRT Communication Quarterly, 8*(2), 2.

Institute for Research on Teaching. (1987a). Coping with hostile-aggressive students. *IRT Communication Quarterly, 9*(2), 2.

Institute for Research on Teaching. (1987b). Effective teaching: The view across IRT projects. *IRT Communication Quarterly, 9*(2), 3.

Institute for Research on Teaching. (1988a). A framework for thinking about student empowerment. *IRT Communication Quarterly, 10*(3), 1,3.

Institute for Research on Teaching. (1988b). Reinventing the meaning of "knowing" in mathematics. *IRT Communication Quarterly, 11*(1), 1,4.

Institute for Research on Teaching. (1988c). Teaching higher order thinking in social studies. *IRT Communication Quarterly, 11*(1), 1–2.

Jackson, L., & Pruitt, W. (1983–84). Homework assignments: Classroom games or teacher tools. In D. Strother (Ed.), *Time and learning* (211–215). Bloomington, IN: Phi Delta Kappa.

Jaeger, R. M. (Ed.). (1988). *Complementary methods for research in education.* Washington, DC: American Educational Research Association.

Janssens, F. (1986). *The evaluation practice of elementary school teachers.* Paper presented at the Annual Meeting of the American Educational Research Association, San Francisco.

Johnson, D. W. (1980). Group processes, influences of student-student interaction on school outcomes. In J. H. MacMillan (Ed.), *The social psychology of school learning* (pp. 123–168). New York: Academic Press.

Johnson, D. W., & Johnson, R. T. (1974). Instructional goal structure: Cooperative, competitive, or individualistic. *Review of Educational Research, 44,* 213–240.

Johnson, D. W., & Johnson, R. T. (1985). Classroom conflict: Controversy versus debate in learning groups. *American Educational Research Journal, 22,* 237–256.

Johnson, D. W., & Johnson, R. T. (1988). Critical thinking through structured controversy. *Educational Leadership, 45*(8), 58–64.

Johnson, D. W., Johnson, R. T., & Holubec, E. J. (1990). *Cooperation in the classroom* (rev. ed.). Edina, MN: Interaction Book Company.

Johnson, D. W., Johnson, R. T., Holubec, E. J., & Roy, P. (1984). *Circles of learning: Cooperation in the classroom.* Alexandria, VA: Association for Supervision and Curriculum Development.

Johnson, D. W., Johnson, R. T., & Maruyama, G. (1983). Interdependence and interpersonal attraction among heterogeneous and homogeneous individuals: A theoretical formulation and a meta-analysis of the research. *Review of Educational Research, 53,* 5–54.

Johnson, J. R. (1984). Synthesis of research on grade retention and social promotion. *Educational Leadership, 41*(8), 66–68.

Johnson, R. T., & Johnson, D. W. (1982). Cooperation in learning: Ignored but powerful. *Lyceum, 5,* 22–26.

Johnson, R. T., & Johnson, D. W. (1985a). *Staff development for the social integration of handicapped students into the mainstream.* Paper presented at the Annual Meeting of the American Educational Research Association, Chicago.

Johnson, R. T., & Johnson, D. W. (1985b). Student-student interaction: Ignored but powerful. *Journal of Teacher Education, 36*(4), 22–26.

Jones, B. F. (1986). Quality and equality through cognitive instruction. *Educational Leadership, 43*(7), 4–12.

Jones, B. F., Palinscar, A. S., Ogle, D. S., & Carr, E. G. (1987). *Strategic teaching and learning: Cognitive instruction in the content areas.* Alexandria, VA: Association for Supervision and Curriculum Development in cooperation with the North Central Regional Educational Laboratory.

Jones, V. F. (1982). Training teachers to be effective classroom managers. In D. Duke (Ed.), *Helping teachers manage classrooms* (pp. 52–68). Alexandria, VA: Association for Supervision and Curriculum Development.

Jongsma, E. (1985). Grouping for instruction. *The Reading Teacher, 38,* 918–920.

Joyce, B., & Showers, B. (1983). *Power in staff development through research on training.* Alexandria, VA: Association for Supervision and Curriculum Development.

Joyce, B., & Showers, B. (1986). *Invisible teaching skills: The orientation from theory-driven research on teaching and curriculum.* Eugene, OR: Booksend Laboratories.

Joyce, B., Showers, B., & Rolheiser-Bennett, C. (1987). Staff development and student learning: A synthesis of research on models of teaching. *Educational Leadership, 45*(2), 11–23.

Joyce, B., & Weil, M. (1986). *Models of teaching* (3rd ed.). Englewood Cliffs, NJ: Prentice-Hall.

Kallison, J., Jr. (1986). Effects of lesson organization on achievement. *American Educational Research Journal, 23,* 337–347.

Karweit, N. L. (1983). *Time on task: A research review* (Report No. 332). Baltimore: Johns Hopkins University, Center for Social Organization of Schools.

Karweit, N. L. (1988). Time-on-task: The second time around. *NASSP Bulletin, 72*(505), 31–39.

Katz, L. (1987). Preschoolers need group interaction, not performance focus. *Education USA, 29*(32), 240.

Kearney, P., Plax, T. G., Sorensen, G., & Smith, V. R. (1987). *Experienced and prospective teachers' compliance-gaining message selections on "common" student misbehaviors.* Paper presented at the Annual Meeting of the Speech Communication Association, Boston. (ERIC Document Reproduction Service No. 290 184)

Kearns, J. (1988). *The impact of systematic feedback on student self esteem.* Paper presented at the Annual Meeting of the American Educational Research Association, New Orleans.

Keeves, J. P. (1986). Motivation in theories of learning. *International Journal of Educational Research, 10*(2), 117–127.

Kennedy, J. J., Cruickshank, D. R., Bush, A. J., & Myers, B. (1978). Additional investigations into the nature of teacher clarity. *Journal of Educational Research, 72,* 3–10.

Kerr, M. M., & Nelson, C. M. (1983). *Strategies for managing behavior problems in the classroom.* Columbus, OH: Merrill.

Kershaw, C. A., Bellon, J. J., Bellon, E. C., Blank, M. A., Brian, D. J. G., & Perkins, M. T. (1990). *School based research to improve the quality of school life.* Knoxville, TN: University of Tennessee, College of Education. Paper presented at the Annual Meeting of the American Educational Research Association, Boston.

Kierstead, J. (1985). Direct instruction and experiential approaches: Are they mutually exclusive? *Educational Leadership, 42* (8), 25–30.

Kindsvatter, R. (1982). The dilemmas of discipline. *Educational Leadership, 39,* 512–514.

Klausmeier, H. J. (1980). *Learning and teaching concepts: A strategy for testing applications of theory.* New York: Academic Press.

Klein, F. W. (1978). *About learning materials.* Washington, DC: Association for Supervision and Curriculum Development.

Klinzing, H. G., & Klinzing-Eurich, G. (1988). Questions, responses, and reflections. In J. T. Dillon (Ed.), *Questioning and discussion: A multidisciplinary study* (pp. 212–239). Norwood, NJ: Ablex.

Koerner, T. F. (Ed.). (1989). School-based management. *NASSP Bulletin, 73*(518).

Koffler, S. L. (1980). A comparison of approaches for setting standards. *Journal of Educational Measurement, 17,* 167–178.

Kohn, A. (1987a, September). Art for art's sake. *Psychology Today,* pp. 52–57.

Kohn, A. (1987b, October). It's hard to get left out of a pair. *Psychology Today,* pp. 52–57.

Kohut, S., Jr., & Range, D. G. (1986). *Classroom discipline: Case studies and viewpoints.* Washington, DC: National Education Association.

Komoski, K. (1985). Instructional materials will not improve until we change the system. *Educational Leadership, 42*(7), 31–37.

Kounin, J. S. (1970). *Discipline and group management in classrooms.* New York: Holt, Rinehart and Winston.

Kounin, J. S. (1983). Classrooms: Individuals or behavior settings? (Monographs in Teaching and Learning, No. 1). Bloomington, IN: Indiana University, School of Education. (ERIC Document Reproduction Service No. ED 240 070)

Kounin, J. S., & Gump, P. V. (1958). The ripple effect in discipline. *Elementary School Journal, 59,* 158–162.

Kounin, J. S., & Gump, P. V. (1961). The comparative influence of punitive and non-punitive teachers upon children's concepts of school misconduct. *Journal of Educational Psychology, 76,* 427–441.

Kounin, J. S., & Gump, P. V. (1974). Signal systems of lesson settings and the task-related behavior of school children. *Journal of Educational Psychology, 66,* 554–562.

Kourilsky, M., & Wittrock, M. C. (1987). Verbal and graphical strategies in the teaching of economics. *Teaching and Teacher Education, 3,* 1–12.

Kronkosky, P. C. (Project Director). (1981). *Characteristics of effective inservice education.* Austin, TX: Southwest Educational Development Laboratory.

Kulik, C. C., & Kulik, J. A. (1984). *Effects of ability grouping on elementary school pupils: A meta-analysis.* Paper presented at the Annual Meeting of the American Psychological Association, Toronto. (ERIC Document Reproduction Service No. ED 255 329)

Kulik, C. C., Kulik, J. A., & Bangert-Drowns, R. L. (1990). Effectiveness of mastery learning programs: A meta-analysis. *Review of Educational Research, 60,* 265–299.

Kulik, J. A. (1983). Synthesis of research on computer-based instruction. *Educational Leadership, 41*(1), 19–21.

Kulik, J. A., & Kulik, C. (1984). Effects of accelerated instruction on students. *Review of Educational Research, 53,* 409–425.

Kulik, J. A., & Kulik, C. (1988). Timing of feedback and verbal learning. *Review of Educational Research, 58,* 79–97.

LaConte, R. T. (1981). *Homework as a learning experience.* Washington, DC: National Educational Association.

LaConte, R. T., & Doyle, M. A. (1986). *What research says to the teacher: Homework as a learning experience* (2nd ed.). Washington, DC: National Education Association.

Lambie, R. A., & Hutchens, P. W. (1986). Adapting elementary school mathematics instruction. *Teaching Exceptional Children, 18,* 185–189.

Lampert, M. (1988). *The teacher's role in reinventing the meaning of mathematical knowing in the classroom* (Research Series No. 186). East Lansing, MI: Michigan State University, Institute for Research on Teaching.

Land, M. L. (1987). Vagueness and clarity. In M. J. Dunkin (Ed.), *The international encyclopedia of teaching and teacher education* (pp. 392–397). New York: Pergamon Press.

Land, R. E., Jr., & Evans, S. (1987). What our students taught us about paper marking. *English Journal, 76,* 113–116.

Lange, B. (1982). ERIC/RCS report: Questioning techniques. *Language Arts, 59,* 180–185.

Lanier, J. E. (1978). *Research on teaching: A dynamic area of inquiry* (Occasional Paper No. 7). East Lansing, MI: Michigan State University, Institute for Research on Teaching.

Lanier, J. E. (1982). A professional role for teachers: Research and practice in teacher education. East Lansing, MI: Michigan State University, College of Education.

Lanier, J. E. (1987, August). *A professional role for teachers: Research and practice in teacher education.* Paper presented at the Southwestern Bell Invitational Conference "Restructuring Schooling for Quality Education: A New Reform Agenda," San Antonio, TX.

Lapp, D., Flood, J., & Thorpe, L. (1989). How-to-do-it cooperative problem solving: Enhancing learning in the secondary science classroom. *American Biology Teacher, 51*(2), 112–115.

Lasley, T. J. (1981). Research perspectives on classroom management. *Journal of Teacher Education, 32*(2), 14–17.

Lasley, T. J., Lasley, J. O., & Ward, S. (1989). *How effective and ineffective classroom managers deal with misbehavior.* Paper presented at the Annual Meeting of the American Educational Research Association, San Francisco.

Lasley, T. J., & Wayson, W. W. (1982). Characteristics of schools with good discipline. *Educational Leadership, 40*(3), 28–31.

Lawry, J. R. (1987). The project method. In M. J. Dunkin (Ed.), *The international encyclopedia of teaching and teacher education* (pp. 217–219). New York: Pergamon Press.

LeClerc, M., Bertrand, R., & DuFour, N. (1986). Correlations between teaching practice and class achievement in introductory algebra. *Teaching and Teacher Education, 2,* 335–365.

Leder, G. C. (1988). Do teachers favor high achievers? *Gifted Child Quarterly, 32,* 315–320.

Lehr, F. (1984). ERIC/RCS report: Student-teacher communication. *Language Arts, 61,* 200–203.

Lehr, F. (1986). ERIC/RCS report: Direct instruction in reading. *The Reading Teacher, 39,* 706–713.

Leinhardt, G. (1986). *Math lessons: A contrast of novice and expert competence.* Paper presented at the annual meeting of the American Educational Research Association, San Francisco.

Leinhardt, G. (1990). Capturing craft knowledge in teaching. *Educational Researcher, 19*(2), 18–25.

Leinhardt, G., & Greeno, J. G. (1986). The cognitive skill of teaching. *Journal of Educational Psychology, 78,* 75–95.

Leinhardt, G., Weidman, C., & Hammond, K. M. (1987). Introduction and integration of classroom routines by expert teachers. *Curriculum Inquiry, 17,* 135–176.

Lepper, M. R., & Greene, R. (Eds.). (1978). *The hidden costs of reward.* Hillsdale, NJ: Lawrence Erlbaum.

Lesgold, A. (1986). *Producing automatic performance.* Paper presented at the Annual Meeting of the American Educational Research Association, San Francisco.

Levin, J. R. (1986). Four cognitive principles of learning-strategy instruction. *Educational Psychologist, 21*(1 & 2), 3–17.

Levin, T., & Long, R. (1981). *Effective instruction.* Alexandria, VA: Association for Supervision and Curriculum Development.

Levine, H., & Mann, K. (1981). *The "negotiation" of classroom lessons and its relevance to teachers' decision-making.* Paper presented at the Annual Meeting of the American Educational Research Association, San Francisco.

Levinson, R. A., & Sanders, J. (1986). *Student engagement in learning: A psychoanalytic perspective in the development of curricula.* Paper presented at the Annual Meeting of the American Educational Research Association, San Francisco.

Lew, M., Mesch, D., Johnson, D. W., & Johnson, R. (1986). Positive interdependence, academic and collaborative skills, group contingencies, and isolated students. *American Educational Research Journal, 23,* 476–488.

Lewis, A. (Ed.). (1986). Good math teaching. *Education USA, 28,* 161–162.

Lezotte, L. W. (1986). *School effectiveness reflections and future directions.* Paper presented at the Annual Meeting of the American Educational Research Association, San Francisco.

Lindheim, E. (1982). Instructional materials: Avoiding the perils of mix and match. In D. Wallace (Ed.), *Developing basic skills programs in secondary schools* (pp. 97–104). Alexandria, VA: Association for Supervision and Curriculum Development.

Little, J. W. (1982). Norms of collegiality and experimentation: Workplace conditions of school success. *American Educational Research Journal, 19,* 325–340.

Locke, E., Schweiger, D., & Latham, G. (1986). Participation in decision making: When should it be used? *Organizational Dynamics, 14*(3), 65–79.

Lortie, D. C. (1975). *Schoolteacher.* Chicago: University of Chicago Press.

Lowe, R., & Gervais, R. (1988). Increasing instructional time in today's classroom. *NASSP Bulletin, 72*(505), 19–22.

Lucio, W., & McNeil, J. (1979). *Supervision in thought and action.* New York: McGraw-Hill.

Lysakowski, R. S., & Walberg, H. J. (1982). Instructional effects of cues, participation, and corrective feedback: A quantitative synthesis. *American Educational Research Journal, 19,* 559–578.

MacIver, D., Klingel, D. M., & Reuman, D. A. (1986). *Students' decision-making congruence in mathematics classrooms: A person-environment fit analysis.* Paper presented at the Annual Meeting of the American Educational Research Association, San Francisco.

MacKenzie, D. E. (1983). *Educational productivity and school effectiveness research: A synthesis and assessment.* Austin, TX: Southwest Educational Development Laboratory.

Maker, C. J. (1987). Gifted and talented. In V. Richardson-Koehler (Ed.), *Educator's handbook: A research perspective* (pp. 420–456). New York: Longman.

Manning, B. H. (1988). Application of cognitive behavior modification: First and third graders' management of classroom behaviors. *American Educational Research Journal, 25,* 193–212.

Maples, M. F. (1985). Three valuable constructs for classroom management. *Education Digest, 50*(9), 50–53.

Marliave, R., & Filby, N. N. (1985). Success rate: A measure of task appropriateness. In C. W. Fisher and D. C. Berliner (Eds.), *Perspectives on instructional time* (pp. 217–235). New York: Longman.

Marshall, H. H. (1988). In pursuit of learning oriented classrooms. *Teacher and Teacher Education, 4,* 85–98.

Martens, B. K., Muir, K. A., & Meller, P. J. (1988). Rewards common to the classroom setting: A comparison of regular and self-contained room student ratings. *Behavioral Disorders, 13*(3), 169–174.

Marx, R. W. (1983). Student perception in classrooms. *Educational Psychologist, 18*(3), 145–164.

Marx, R. W., & Walsh, J. (1988). Learning from academic tasks. *Elementary School Journal, 88,* 207–219.

Marzano, R. J., Brandt, R. S., Hughes, C. S., Jones, B. F., Presseisen, B. Z., Rankin, C. S., & Suhor, C. (1988). *Dimensions of thinking: A framework for curriculum and instruction.* Alexandria, VA: Association for Supervision and Curriculum Development.

Marzano, R. J., & Costa, A. L. (1988). Question: Do standardized tests measure general cognitive skills? Answer: No. *Educational Leadership, 45*(8), 66–71.

Marzano, R. J., Pickering, D. J., & Brandt, R. S. (1990). Integrating instructional programs through dimensions of learning. *Educational Leadership, 47*(5), 17–29.

Maslow, A. H. (1943). A theory of human motivation. *Psychological Review, 50,* 370–396.

Mason, J., & Osborn, J. (1982). *When do children begin reading to learn? A survey of classroom reading instruction practices in grades two through five* (Technical Report No. 261). Cambridge, MA: Bolt, Beranek, and Newman.

Massey, M. (1989). Student assessment: Slow growth toward improved measures. *ASCD Update, 31*(2), 1, 7.

Matthews, D. B. (1986). Discipline: Can it be improved with relaxation training? *Elementary School Guidance and Counseling, 20*(3), 194–200.

Mayer, R. E. (1988). *Text based questions that foster active reading strategies.* Paper presented at the Annual Meeting of the American Educational Research Association, New Orleans.

McBride, J. R. (1985). Computerized adaptive testing. *Educational Leadership, 43*(2), 25–28.

McCauley, J. (1988). Questioning techniques in the elementary classroom. *Cogitare, 2*(4), 3–4.

McCombs, B. (1988). *What is the relationship between motivation and self regulated learning?* Paper presented at the Annual Meeting of the American Educational Research Association, New Orleans.

McCombs, B., & Marzano, R. J. (1989). Integrating skill and will in self regulation: Putting the self as agent in strategies training. *Teaching Thinking and Problem Solving, 7*(5), 1–4.

McDaniel, T. R. (1986). A primer on classroom discipline: Principles old and new. *Phi Delta Kappan, 68*, 63–67.

McEvoy, B. (1987). Everyday acts: How principals influence development of their staffs. *Educational Leadership, 44*(5), 73–77.

McGee, L. M., & Richgels, D. J. (1985). Teaching expository text structure to elementary students. *The Reading Teacher, 38*, 739–748.

McKinney, C. W., Burts, D. C., Ford, M. J., & Gilmore, A. C. (1987). The effects of ordinary and coordinate concept nonexamples on first-grade students' acquisition of three coordinate concepts. *Theory and Research in Social Education, 15*(1), 45–50.

McNeil, J. D. (1984). *Reading comprehension: New directions for classroom practice.* Glenview, IL: Scott Foresman.

McTighe, J., & Lyman, F. T., Jr. (1988). Cueing thinking in the classroom: The promise of theory-embedded tools. *Educational Leadership, 45*(7), 18–25.

Mealey, D. L., & Nist, S. L. (1989). Postsecondary, teacher directed comprehension strategies. *Journal of Reading, 32*, 484–492.

Medley, D. M. (1987). Evolution of research on teaching. In M. J. Dunkin (Ed.), *The international encyclopedia of teaching and teacher education* (pp. 105–113). New York: Pergamon.

Medley, D. M., & Cook, P. R. (1980). Research in teacher competency and teaching tasks. *Theory into Practice, 19*, 294–301.

Medway, F. J. (1987). Tutoring. In M. J. Dunkin (Ed.), *The international encyclopedia of teaching and teacher education* (pp. 243–245). New York: Pergamon Press.

Mehan, H. (1979). "What time is it, Denise?" Asking known information questions in classroom discourse. *Theory into Practice, 18*, 285–294.

Mehan, H. (1985). *Microcomputers and classroom organization: The more things change the more they change each other* (Interactive Technology Laboratory Report No. 10). San Diego: California University, La Jolla Center for Human Information Processing.

Melnick, S. L., & Raudenbush, S. W. (1986). *Influence of pupils' gender, race, ability, and behavior on prospective and experienced teachers' judgments about appropriate feedback* (Research Series No. 175). East Lansing, MI: Michigan State University, Institute for Research on Teaching.

Mergendoller, J. R., Marchman, V. A., Mitman, A. L., & Packer, M. J. (1988). Task demands and accountability in middle-grade science classes. *Elementary School Journal, 88*, 251–265.

Minstrell, J. A. (1989). Teaching science for understanding. In L. B. Resnick and L. E. Klopfer (Eds.), *Toward the thinking curriculum: Current cognition research* (pp. 129–149). Alexandria, VA: Association for Supervision and Curriculum Development.

Mitman, A., Mergendoller, J., & Packer, M. (1987). Instruction addressing the components of scientific literacy and its relation to student outcomes. *American Educational Research Journal, 24*, 611–634.

Moffett, K. L., St. John, J., & Isken, J. A. (1987). Training and coaching beginning teachers: An antidote to reality shock. *Educational Leadership, 44*(5), 34–36.

Moore, D., & Readence, J. (1984). A quantitative and qualitative review of graphic organizer research. *Journal of Educational Research, 78*, 11–17.

Morine-Dershimer, G. (1986). *What can we learn from thinking?* Paper presented at the Annual Meeting of the American Educational Research Association, San Francisco.

Morine-Dershimer, G., & Beyerbach, B. (1987). Moving right along. . . . In V. Richardson-Koehler (Ed.), *Educators' handbook: A research perspective* (pp. 207–232). New York: Longman.

Moskowitz, G., & Hayman, J. D., Jr. (1976). Success strategies of inner-city teachers: A yearlong study. *Journal of Educational Research, 69*, 283–289.

Mullen, B. (1988). A self-attention perspective on discussion. In J. T. Dillon (Ed.), *Questioning and discussion: A multidisciplinary study* (pp. 74–89). Norwood, NJ: Ablex.

Munth, D. (1987). Teacher's connection questions: Prompting students to organize text ideas. *Journal of Reading, 31*, 254–259.

Murphy, J., Decker, K., Chaplin, C., Dagenais, R., Heller, J., Jones, R., & Willis, M. (1987). An exploratory analysis of the structure of homework assignments in high schools. *Review in Rural Education, 4*(2), 61–71.

Murray, F. B. (1989). Explanations in education. In M. C. Reynolds (Ed.), *Knowledge base for the beginning teacher* (pp. 1–12). New York: Pergamon Press.

National Assessment of Educational Progress. (1981). *Reading, thinking, and writing: Results from the 1979–80 National Assessment of Reading and Literature* (Report No. 11-L-01). Denver, CO: Author.

National Assessment of Educational Progress. (1985). *The reading report card.* Princeton, NJ: Educational Testing Service.

National Commission on Excellence in Education. (1983). *A nation at risk: The imperative for educational reform.* Washington, DC: U.S. Department of Education.

Natriello, G., & McDill, E. L. (1986). Performance standards, student effort on homework, and academic achievement. *Sociology of Education, 59*, 18–31.

Neely, A. M. (1986). Planning and problem solving in teacher education. *Journal of Teacher Education, 37*(3), 29–33.

Nemser, S. F. (1983). Learning to teach. In L. S. Shulman & G. Sykes (Eds.), *Handbook of teaching and policy* (pp. 150–170). New York: Longman.

Nessel, D. (1987a). The new face of comprehension instruction: A closer look at questions. *The Reading Teacher, 40*, 604–606.

Nessel, D. (1987b). Reading comprehension: Asking the right questions. *Phi Delta Kappan, 68*, 442–444.

Neubert, G. A., & Bratton, E. C. (1987). Team coaching: Staff development side by side. *Educational Leadership, 44*(5), 29–32.

Neufeld, B. (1985). Evaluating the effective teaching research. *Harvard Education Letter, 1*(3), 5–6.

Neuwirth, C. M. (1989). Intelligent tutoring systems: Exploring issues in learning and teaching writing. *Computers and the Humanities, 23*(1), 45–57.

Newmann, F. M. (1988). *Higher order thinking in high school social studies: An analysis of classrooms.* Madison, WI: University of Wisconsin, National Center on Effective Secondary Schools.

Newmann, F. M. (1990). Higher order thinking in the teaching of social studies: Connections between theory and practice. In D. Perkins, J. Segal, & J. Voss (Eds.), *Informal reasoning and education.* Hillsdale, NJ: Lawrence Erlbaum.

Nickerson, R. S. (1989). New directions in educational assessment. *Educational Researcher, 18*(9), 3–7.

Norris, S. P. (1985). Synthesis of research on critical thinking. *Educational Leadership, 42*(8), 40–46.

North Carolina State Department of Public Instruction. (1985). *Review of empirical research on the effective teaching practices contained in the North Carolina Teacher Performance Appraisal Instrument.* Raleigh, NC: Personnel Services Area.

Northwest Regional Educational Laboratory. (1984). *Effective schooling practices: A research synthesis.* Portland, OR: Author.

Novak, J. D., Godwin, D. B., & Johansen, G. T. (1983). The use of concept mapping and knowledge mapping with junior high science students. *Science Education, 67,* 625–645.

Nuthall, G. (1987). Reviewing and recapitulating. In M. J. Dunkin (Ed.), *The international encyclopedia of teaching and teacher education* (pp. 424–427). New York: Pergamon Press.

O'Donnell, H. (1985). Homework in the elementary school. *The Reading Teacher, 39,* 220–222.

Okebukola, P. A. (1985). The relative effectiveness of cooperative and competitive interaction techniques in strengthening students' performance in science classes. *Science Education, 69,* 501–509.

Omizo, M. M., Hershberger, J. M., & Omizo, S. A. (1988). Teaching children to cope with anger. *Elementary School Guidance and Counseling, 22*(3), 241–246.

Ornstein, A. C. (1987). Questioning: The essence of good teaching. *NASSP Bulletin, 71*(499), 71–79.

Ornstein, A. C. (1988). Questioning: The essence of good teaching—part 2. *NASSP Bulletin, 72*(505), 72–78.

Otto, W. (1985). Homework: A meta-analysis. *Journal of Reading, 29,* 764–766.

Palinscar, A. S., & Brown, A. L. (1986). Interactive teaching to promote independent learning from text. *The Reading Teacher, 39,* 771–777.

Palinscar, A. S., & Brown, A. L. (1989). Self regulated reading. In L. B. Resnick & L. E. Klopfer (Eds.), *Toward the thinking curriculum: Current cognitive research* (pp. 19–39). Arlington, VA: Association for Supervision and Curriculum Development.

Paris, S. G., & Lindauser, B. K. (1982). The development of cognitive skills during childhood. In B. W. Wolman (Ed.), *Handbook of developmental psychology* (pp. 330–346). Englewood Cliffs, NJ: Prentice-Hall.

Paris, S. G., Lipson, M. Y., & Wixson, K. K. (1983). Becoming a strategic reader. *Contemporary Educational Psychology, 8,* 293–316.

Paris, S. G., & Oka, E. R. (1986). Self-regulated learning among exceptional children. *Exceptional Children, 53,* 103–108.

Paris, S. G., Oka, E. R., & DeBritto, A. M. (1983). Beyond decoding: Synthesis of research on reading comprehension. *Educational Leadership, 41*(2), 78–83.

Parker, W. C., & Gehrke, N. J. (1986). Learning activities and teachers' decision-making: Some grounded hypotheses. *American Educational Research Journal, 23,* 227–242.

Parker, W. C., McDaniel, J., & Valencia, S. D. (1989). *Teaching and prompting critical thinking and public controversies.* Paper presented at the Annual Meeting of the American Educational Research Association, San Francisco.

Passow, A. H. (Ed.). (1963). *Education in depressed areas.* New York: Columbia University, Teachers College, Bureau of Publications.

Patterson, J. J., & Smith, M. S. (1986). The role of computers in higher-order thinking. In J. A. Culbertson and L. L. Cunningham (Eds.), *Microcomputers and education* (The 85th Yearbook of the National Society for the Study of Education, Pt. 1, pp. 81–108). Chicago: University of Chicago Press.

Paul, R. W. (1985a). Bloom's taxonomy and critical thinking instruction. *Educational Leadership, 42*(8), 36–39.

Paul, R. W. (1985b). The critical-thinking movement: A historical perspective. *National Forum, 65*(1), 2–3.

Pearson, D. P. (1985). Changing the face of reading comprehension instruction. *The Reading Teacher, 38,* 724–738.

Perkins, D. N., & Simmons, R. (1988). Patterns of misunderstanding: An integrative model for science, math, and programming. *Review of Educational Research, 58,* 303–326.

Perkins, D. N., & Solomon, G. (1989). Are cognitive skills context-bound? *Educational Researcher, 18*(1), 16–25.

Persano, P. A. (1990). Electronic efficiency. *American School Board Journal, 177*(7), 19–20.

Peters, T., & Austin, N. (1985). *A passion for excellence.* New York: Random House.

Peters, T., & Waterman, R., Jr. (1982). *In search of excellence.* New York: Harper and Row.

Peterson, J. M. (1989). Remediation is no remedy. *Educational Leadership, 46*(6), 24–25.

Peterson, P. L. (1979). Direct instruction: Effective for what and for whom? *Educational Leadership, 37,* 46–48.

Peterson, P. L. (1988a). Teachers' and students' cognitional knowledge for classroom teaching and learning. *Educational Researcher, 17*(5), 5–14.

Peterson, P. L. (1988b). Teaching higher-order thinking in mathematics: The challenge for the next decade. In D. A. Grouws, T. J. Cooney, & D. Jones (Eds.), *Perspectives on research on effective mathematics teaching* (Vol. 1, pp. 2–26). Reston, VA: National Council of Teachers of Mathematics.

Peterson, P. L., & Comeaux, M. A. (1987). Teachers' schemata for classroom events: The mental scaffolding of teachers' thinking during classroom instruction. *Teaching and Teacher Education, 3,* 319–331.

Peterson, P. L., Swing, S. R., Stark, K. D., & Waas, G. A. (1984). Students' cognitions and time on task during mathematics instruction. *American Educational Research Journal, 21,* 487–516.

Peterson, P. L., Wilkenson, L. C., & Hallinan, M. (1984). *The social context of instruction: Group organization and group processes.* New York: Academic Press.

Pigott, H. E., Fantuzzo, J. W., & Clement, P. W. (1986). The effects of reciprocal peer tutoring and group contingencies on the academic performance of elementary school children. *Journal of Applied Behavior Analysis, 19*(2), 93–98.

Pinnell, G. S. (1984). Communication in small group settings. *Theory into Practice, 23,* 246–254.

Pinnell, G. S. (1990). Success for low achievers through reading recovery. *Educational Leadership, 48*(1), 17–21.

Plass, J. A., & Hill, K. T. (1986). Children's achievement strategies and test performance: The role of time pressure, evaluation anxiety, and sex. *Developmental Psychology, 22,* 31–36.

Polya, G. (1973). *Induction and analogy in mathematics.* Princeton, NJ: Princeton University Press.

Popham, W. J. (1982). Basic skills and measurement basics. In D. G. Wallace (Ed.), *Developing basic skills programs in secondary schools* (pp. 105–116). Alexandria, VA: Association for Supervision and Curriculum Development.

Porter, A. C. (1989). A curriculum out of balance: The case of elementary school mathematics. *Education Researcher, 18*(5), 9–15.

Porter, A. C., & Brophy, J. (1988). Synthesis of research on good teaching: Insights from the work of the Institute for Research on Teaching. *Educational Leadership, 45*(8), 74–85.

Posner, G. J. (1982). A cognitive science conception of curriculum and instruction. *Journal of Curriculum Studies, 14,* 343–351.

Posner, G. J. (1987). Pacing and sequencing. In M. J. Dunkin (Ed.), *The international encyclopedia of teaching and teacher education* (pp. 266–272). New York: Pergamon Press.

Power, C. N. (1987). Responding. In M. J. Dunkin (Ed.), *The international encyclopedia of teaching and teacher education* (pp. 413–416). New York: Pergamon Press.

Prawat, R. S. (1989). Teaching for understanding: Three key attributes. *Teaching and Teacher Education, 5,* 315–328.

Presseisen, B. J. (1980). *Thinking skills: Research and practice.* Washington, DC: National Education Association.

Pressley, M., & Levin, J. (1982). The mnemonic keyword method. *Review of Educational Research, 52,* 61–91.

Purkey, S., & Smith, M. (1983). Effective schools: A review. *The Elementary School Journal, 83,* 427–452.

Putnam, J., & Duffy, G. G. (1984). *A descriptive study of the preactive and interactive decision making of an expert classroom teacher* (IRT Report No. 148). East Lansing, MI: Michigan State University, Institute for Research on Teaching.

Putnam, J., Roeller, L. R., & Duffy, G. G. (1987). *The staff development model of the teacher explanation project* (Occasional Paper No. 108). East Lansing, MI: Michigan State University, Institute for Research on Teaching.

Putnam, R. T. (1987). Structuring and adjusting content for students: A study of live and simulated tutoring of addition. *American Educational Research Journal, 24,* 13–48.

Quellmalz, E. S. (1985). Needed: Better methods for testing higher order thinking skills. *Educational Leadership, 43*(2), 29–35.

Raffini, J. P. (1986). Student apathy: A motivational dilemma. *Educational Leadership, 44*(1), 53–55.

Raffini, J. P. (1988). *Student apathy: The protection of self-worth.* Washington, DC: National Educational Association.

Rakow, S. J. (1986). *Teaching science as inquiry.* Bloomington, IN: Phi Delta Kappa Education Foundation.

Raphael, T. E. (1986). Teaching question-answer relationships, revisited. *The Reading Teacher, 39,* 516–522.

Raphael, T. E., & Englert, C. S. (1988). *Integrating writing and reading instruction* (Occasional Paper No. 118). East Lansing, MI: Michigan State University, Institute for Research on Teaching.

Raphael, T. E., & Pearson, P. D. (1985). Increasing students' awareness of sources of information for answering questions. *American Educational Research Journal, 22,* 217–235.

Red, C., & Shainlene, E. (1987). Teachers reflect on change. *Educational Leadership, 44*(5), 38–40.

Redfield, D., & Rousseau, E. (1981). A meta-analysis of experimental research on teacher questioning behavior. *Review of Educational Research, 51,* 237–243.

Research and Development Center for Teacher Education. (1982). *Classroom organization and effective teaching project.* Austin, TX: University of Texas.

Researchers look at teachers' thinking. (1986). *Harvard Education Letter, 2*(4), 7.

Resnick, L. B. (1987). *Education and learning to think.* Washington, DC: National Academy Press.

Resnick, L. B., & Klopfer, L. E. (Eds.). (1989). *Toward the thinking curriculum: Current cognitive research.* Arlington, VA: Association for Supervision and Curriculum Development.

Richardson-Koehler, V. (Ed.). (1987). *Educators' handbook: A research perspective.* New York: Longman.

Roberts, T. (1983). *Child management in the primary school.* London: Allen and Unwin.

Roblyer, J. D. (1985). *Measuring the impact of computers in instruction: A non-technical review of research for educators.* Washington, DC: Association of Educational Data Systems.

Roby, T. W. (1988). Models of discussion. In J. T. Dillon (Ed.), *Questioning and discussion: A multidisciplinary study* (pp. 163–191). Norwood, NJ: Ablex.

Roehler, L. R., & Duffy, G. G. (1981). Classroom teaching is more than opportunity to learn. *Journal of Teacher Education, 32,* 7–11.

Roehler, L. R., & Duffy, G. G. (1986). Helping students gain greater control over reading blocks. *IRT Communication Quarterly, 8*(2), 2.

Roehler, L. R., Duffy, G. G., Book, C., & Wesselman, R. (1983). *Direct teacher explanation during reading: A pilot study* (IRT Research Series No. 132). East Lansing, MI: Michigan State University, Institute for Research on Teaching.

Rogan, J. M. (1988). Conceptual mapping as a diagnostic aid. *School Science and Mathematics, 88,* 50–59.

Rogers, V. M. (1972). Modifying questioning strategies of teachers. *Teacher Education, 23*(1), 58–62.

Rogers, V. R., & Stevenson, C. (1988). How do we know what kids are learning in school? *Educational Leadership, 45*(5), 68–75.

Rogus, J. F. (1985). Promoting self-discipline: A comprehensive approach. *Theory into Practice, 24,* 271–276.

Rohrkemper, M. M. (1982). Teacher self-assessment. In D. Duke (Ed.), *Helping teachers manage classrooms* (pp. 77–96). Alexandria, VA: Association for Supervision and Curriculum Development.

Rohrkemper, M. M., & Brophy, J. E. (1983). Teachers' thinking about problem students. In J. Levine & M. Wang (Eds.), *Teacher and student perceptions: Implications for learning* (pp. 75–103). Hilldale, NJ: Erlbaum.

Rohrkemper, M. M., & Corno, L. (1988). Success and failure on classroom tasks: Adaptive learning and classroom teaching. *Elementary School Journal, 88,* 297–312.

Romney, D. M. (1986). *Dealing with abnormal behavior in the classroom.* Bloomington, IN: Phi Delta Kappa Educational Foundation.

Rose, T. (1984). Current uses of corporal punishment in American public schools. *Journal of Educational Psychology, 76,* 427–441.

Rosenbaum, L., Karla, J. B., Brown, L., & Burcalow, J. V. (1989). Step into problem solving with cooperative learning. *Arithmetic Teacher, 36*(7), 7–11.

Rosenshine, B. V. (1971a). Objectively measured behavioral predictors of effectiveness in explaining. In O. D. Westbury & A. A. Bellack (Eds.), *Research into classroom processes.* New York: Teachers College Press.

Rosenshine, B. V. (1971b). *Teaching behaviors and student achievement.* London: National Foundation for Educational Research in England and Wales.

Rosenshine, B. V. (1980). How time is spent in elementary classrooms. In D. Denham & A. Lieberman (Eds.), *Time to learn: A review of the beginning teacher evaluation study* (pp. 107–126). Washington, DC: National Institute of Education.

Rosenshine, B. V. (1983). Teaching functions in instructional programs. *Elementary School Journal, 83,* 335–351.

Rosenshine, B. V. (1983–84). Content, time, and direct instruction. In D. B. Strother (Ed.), *Time and learning* (pp. 128–165). Bloomington, IN: Phi Delta Kappa.

Rosenshine, B. V. (1986). Synthesis of research on explicit teaching. *Educational Leadership, 43(7),* 60–69.

Rosenshine, B. V., & Furst, N. (1971). Research on teacher performance criteria. In B. O. Smith (Ed.), *Research in teacher education: A symposium* (pp. 37–72). Englewood Cliffs, NJ: Prentice-Hall.

Rosenshine, B. V., & Stevens, R. (1986). Teaching functions. In M. C. Wittrock (Ed.), *Handbook of research on teaching* (pp. 376–391). New York: Macmillan.

Rosenthal, R., & Jacobson, L. (1968). *Pygmalion in the classroom: Teacher expectation and pupils' intellectual development.* New York: Holt, Rinehart and Winston.

Rosenthal, T. L., & Bandura, A. (1978). Psychological modeling: Theory and practice. In S. L. Garfield & A. E. Bergin (Eds.), *Handbook of psychotherapy and behavior change: An empirical analysis* (2nd ed., pp. 621–658). New York: Wiley.

Roth, K. J., Anderson, C. W., & Smith, E. L. (1986). *Curriculum materials, teacher talk, and student learning: Case studies in fifth-grade science teaching* (Research Series No. 171). East Lansing, MI: Michigan State University, Institute for Research on Teaching.

Rothman, R. (1987). Using pupil scores to assess teachers criticized as unfair: Curriculum, tests do not "align," new study finds. *Education Week, 6(36),* 1, 18.

Rowe, M. B. (1969). Science, silence, and sanctions. *Science and Children, 6(6),* 11–13.

Rowe, M. B. (1974). Wait-time and rewards as instructional variables: Their influence on language, logic and fate control: Part one—wait time. *Journal of Research in Science Teaching, 11,* 263–279.

Rowe, M. B. (1986). Wait times: Slowing down may be a way of speeding up! *Journal of Teacher Education, 37(1),* 43–50.

Rubenstein, M. F., & Firstenberg, I. R. (1987). Tools for thinking. In J. E. Stice (Ed.), *Developing critical thinking and problem-solving abilities* (New Directions for Teaching and Learning, No. 30, pp. 23–36). San Francisco: Jossey-Bass.

Rudman, H. (1980). *Integrating assessment with instruction: A review (1922–1980).* East Lansing, MI: Michigan State University, Institute for Research on Teaching.

Rutter, M., Maughan, B., Mortimore, P., & Ouston, J. (1979). *Fifteen thousand hours: Secondary schools and their effects on children.* Cambridge, MA: Harvard University Press.

Samson, G. E., Strykowski, B., Weinstein, T., & Walberg, H. (1987). The effects of teacher questioning levels on student achievement: A quantitative synthesis. *Journal of Educational Research, 80,* 290–295.

Sanford, J., Emmer, E., & Clements, B. (1983). Improving classroom management. *Educational Leadership, 40(7),* 56–60.

Sava, S. G. (1987). Holding on to student enthusiasm. *Education Digest, 52(7),* 28–31.

Saylor, J. G., Alexander, W. M., & Lewis, A. J. (1981). *Curriculum planning for better teaching and learning* (4th ed.). New York: Holt, Rinehart, and Winston.

Schmeck, R. R., & Lockhart, D. (1983). Introverts and extroverts require different learning environments. *Educational Leadership, 40(5),* 54–55.

Schmuck, R. A., & Schmuck, P. A. (1971). *Group processes in the classroom.* Dubuque, IA: Wm. C. Brown.

Schoenfield, A. H. (1987). A mathematician's research on math instruction. *Educational Researcher, 16*(9), 9–12.

Schofield, J. W., & Verban, D. (1988). Computer usage in the teaching of mathematics: Issues that need answers. In D. A. Grouws, T. J. Cooney, & D. Jones (Eds.), *Perspectives on research on effective mathematics teaching* (Vol. 1, pp. 169–193). Reston, VA: National Council of Teachers of Mathematics.

Schon, D. A. (1983). *The reflective practitioner: How professionals think in action*. New York: Basic Books.

School factors influencing reading achievement: A case study of two inner city schools. (1974). Albany, NY: State of New York, Office of Education Performance Review.

Schrank, W. (1968). The labeling effect of ability grouping. *Journal of Educational Research, 62*, 51–52.

Schrank, W. (1970). A further study of the labeling effect of ability grouping. *Journal of Educational Research, 63*, 358–360.

Schunk, D. H. (1985). Social comparison, self-efficacy, and motivation. In M. K. Alderman & M. W. Cohen (Eds.), *Motivation theory and practice for preservice teachers* (Teacher Education Monograph No. 4, pp. 22–36). Washington, DC: ERIC Clearinghouse on Teacher Education.

Schunk, D. H. (1987). Peer models and children's behavioral change. *Review of Educational Research, 57*(2), 149–174.

Schutz, W. C. (1966). *The interpersonal world*. Palo Alto, CA: Science and Behavior Books.

Seligman, M. E. P. (1975). *Helplessness: On depression, development, and death*. San Francisco: W. H. Freeman.

Shanker, A. (1990). The end of the traditional model of schooling—and a proposal for using incentives to restructure our public schools. *Phi Delta Kappan, 71*, 345–357.

Sharan, S. (1980). Cooperative learning in small groups: Recent methods and effects on achievement, attitudes, and ethnic relations. *Review of Educational Research, 50*, 241–271.

Sharan, S., & Sharan, Y. (1976). *Small-group teaching*. Englewood Cliffs, NJ: Educational Technology.

Shavelson, R. J. (1983). Review of research on teachers' pedagogical judgments, plans, and decisions. *Elementary School Journal, 83*, 392–413.

Shavelson, R. J. (1987a). Interactive decision making. In M. J. Dunkin (Ed.), *The international encyclopedia of teaching and teacher education* (pp. 491–493). New York: Pergamon Press.

Shavelson, R. J. (1987b). Planning. In M. J. Dunkin (Ed.). *The international encyclopedia of teaching and teacher education* (pp. 483–486). New York: Pergamon.

Shavelson, R. J., & Borko, H. (1979). Research on teachers' decisions in planning instruction. *Educational Horizons, 57*, 183–189.

Shepard, L. (1989). Why we need better assessments. *Educational Leadership, 46*(7), 4–9.

Sherry, M. (1990). Implementing an integrated instructional system: Critical issues. *Phi Delta Kappan, 72*, 118–120.

Sheviakov, G. V., & Redl, F. (1956). *Discipline for today's children and youth*. Washington, DC: Association for Supervision and Curriculum Development.

Showers, B. (1983). *Transfer of training: The contribution of coaching*. Eugene, OR: Center for Educational Policy and Management.

Showers, B., Joyce, B., & Bennett, B. (1987). Synthesis of research on staff development: A framework for future study and a state-of-the-art analysis. *Educational Leadership, 45*(3), 77–87.

Shuell, T. J. (1986). Cognitive conceptions of learning. *Review of Educational Research, 56*, 411–436.

Shuell, T. J. (1988). *Teaching and learning as problem solving*. Paper presented at Annual Meeting of the American Educational Research Association, New Orleans.

Shulman, L. S. (1986). Paradigms and research programs in the study of teaching: A contemporary perspective. In M. C. Wittrock (Ed.), *Handbook of research on teaching* (3rd ed., pp. 3–36). New York: Macmillan.

Shulman, L. S. (1987). Knowledge and teaching: Foundations of the new reform. *Harvard Educational Review, 57*(1), 1–22.

Shulman, L. S., & Sykes, G. (Eds.). (1983). *Handbook of teaching and policy*. New York: Longman.

Shulman, L. S., & Sykes, G. (1986). *A national board for teaching? In search of a bold standard* (A Report for the Task Force on Teaching as a Profession). New York: Carnegie Corporation.

Sigel, I. E., & Kelley, T. D. (1988). A cognitive developmental approach to questioning. In J. T. Dillon (Ed.), *Questioning and discussion: A multidisciplinary study* (pp. 105–134). Norwood, NJ: Ablex.

Silver, E. A. (1986). Using conceptual and procedural knowledge: A focus on relationships. In J. Hiebert (Ed.), *Conceptual and procedural knowledge: The case of mathematics* (pp. 181–197). London: Lawrence Erlbaum.

Silvernail, D. L. (1986). *Teaching styles related to student achievement*. Washington, DC: NEA Professional Library.

Simon, A., & Boyer, E. (1970). *Mirrors for behavior: An anthology of observation instruments* (1970 Supplement, Vols. A and B). Philadelphia: Research for Better Schools. (ERIC Document Reproduction Service No. ED 042 937)

Simon, M. A. (1986). The teacher's role in increasing student understanding of mathematics. *Educational Leadership, 43*(7), 40–43.

Sinclair, R. L., & Ghory, W. J. (1987). *Reaching marginal students: A primary concern for school renewal*. Berkeley, CA: McCutchan.

Slaughter, C. H. (1989). California's smart classrooms. *Technological Horizons in Education, 17*(1), 59–61.

Slavin, R. E. (1980). Cooperative learning. *Review of Educational Research, 50*, 315–342.

Slavin, R. E. (1982). *Cooperative learning: Student teams*. Washington, DC: National Education Association.

Slavin, R. E. (1985). Team-assisted individualization: A cooperative learning solution for adaptive instruction in mathematics. In M. C. Wang & H. J. Walberg (Eds.), *Adapting instruction to individual differences* (pp. 236–253). Berkeley, CA: McCutchan.

Slavin, R. E. (1986a). *Ability grouping and student achievement in elementary schools: A best evidence synthesis* (Report No. 1). Baltimore, MD: Johns Hopkins University, Center for Research on Elementary and Middle Schools.

Slavin, R. E. (1986b). *Cooperative learning: Where behavioral and humanistic approaches to classroom motivation meet*. Paper presented at the Annual Meeting of the American Educational Research Association, San Francisco.

Slavin, R. E. (1986c). *Using student team learning*. Baltimore, MD: Johns Hopkins University.

Slavin, R. E. (1987a). Cooperative learning and the cooperative school. *Educational Leadership, 45*(3), 7–13.

Slavin, R. E. (1987b). Small group methods. In M. J. Dunkin (Ed.), *The international encyclopedia of teaching and teacher education* (pp. 237–243). New York: Pergamon Press.

Slavin, R. E., Sharan, S., Kagan, S., Hertz-Lararowitz, R., Webb, C., & Schmuck, R. (Eds.). (1985). *Learning to cooperate, cooperating to learn*. New York: Plenum Press.

Smartschan, G. F. (1985). Final examinations as tools for instructional management. *Educational Leadership, 43*(2), 75–76.

Smith, L., Smith, D., & Staples, P. R. (1982). Effect of teacher transitions and superfluous content on student achievement and on perception of lesson effectiveness in high school English. *Journal of Educational Research, 75*, 173–177.

Smith, L. M., & Geoffrey, W. (1968). *The complexities of an urban classroom*. New York: Holt, Rinehart and Winston.

Smith, L. R. (1987). Verbal clarifying behaviors, mathematics students' participation, attitudes. *School Science and Mathematics, 87*, 40–49.

Smith, P. L., & Tompkins, G. E. (1988). Structured notetaking: A new strategy for content area readers. *Journal of Reading, 32*, 46–53.

Snider, W. (1986). Computers: A change of course? *Education Week, 6*(17), 1, 14.

Snow, R. E. (1989). Toward assessment of cognitive and conative structures in learning. *Educational Researcher, 18*(9), 8–14.

Soar, R. S. (1966). *An integrative approach to classroom learning*. Philadelphia: Temple University, College of Education.

Soar, R. S., & Soar, R. M. (1976). *An attempt to identify measures of teacher effectiveness from four studies*. Paper presented at the Annual Meeting of the American Educational Research Association, San Francisco.

Soar, R. S., & Soar, R. M. (1979). Emotional climate and management. In P. Peterson & H. Walberg (Eds.), *Research on teaching: Concepts, findings, and implications* (pp. 97–119). Berkeley, CA: McCutchan.

Sparks, D., & Sparks, G. M. (1984). *Effective teaching for higher achievement*. Alexandria, VA: Association for Supervision and Curriculum Development.

Sparks, G. M. (1983). Synthesis of research on staff development for effective teaching. *Educational Leadership, 41*(3), 65–72.

Spaulding, R. L. (1983). A systematic approach to classroom discipline. *Phi Delta Kappan, 64*, 48–51.

Spodek, B. (Ed.). (1982). *Handbook of research in early childhood education*. New York: Free Press.

Squires, D. A., Huitt, W. G., & Segars, J. K. (1983). *Effective schools and classrooms: A research-based perspective*. Alexandria, VA: Association for Supervision and Curriculum Development.

Stahl, S., & Clark, C. H. (1987). The effects of participatory expectations in classroom discussion on the learning of science vocabulary. *American Educational Research Journal, 24*, 541–555.

Stainback, S. B., & Stainback, W. C. (1989). Classroom organization for diversity among students. In D. Biklen, D. Ferguson, & A. Ford (Eds.), *Schooling and disability* (The 88th Yearbook of the National Society for the Study of Education, Pt. 2, pp. 195–205). Chicago: University of Chicago Press.

Stallings, J. (1982). Effective strategies for teaching basic skills. In D. Wallace (Ed.), *Developing basic skills programs in secondary schools* (pp. 1–19). Alexandria, VA: Association of Supervision and Curriculum Development.

Stallings, J., Johnson, R., & Goodman, J. (1986). Engaged rates: Does grade level make a difference? *Journal of Research in Childhood Education, 1*(1), 20–26.

Stanford, G., & Stanford, B. D. (1969). *Learning discussion skills*. New York: Citation.

Steere, B. F. (1988). *Becoming an effective classroom manager: A resource for teachers*. Albany, NY: State University of New York Press.

Stern, P., & Shavelson, R. J. (1983). Reading teachers' judgments, plans and decision making. *The Reading Teacher, 37*, 280–86.

Sternbert, R. J. (1987). Questions and answers about the nature and teaching of thinking skills. In J. B. Baron & R. J. Sternberg (Eds.), *Teaching thinking skills: Theory and practice* (pp. 251–259). New York: Freeman.

Stewart, A. (1986). *Principles of the design of instructional text*. Paper presented at the Annual Meeting of the American Educational Research Association, San Francisco.

Stice, C. F., & Alvarey, M. C. (1987). Hierarchical concept mapping in the early grades. *Childhood Education, 64*, 86–96.

Stiggins, R. J. (1984). *Evaluating students by classroom observation: Watching students grow*. Washington, DC: NEA Professional Library.

Stiggins, R. J. (1985). Improving assessment where it means the most: In the classroom. *Educational Leadership, 43*(2), 69–74.

Stiggins, R. J. (1986). *Lessons from the observations of classroom assessment environments*. Paper presented at the Annual Meeting of the American Educational Research Association, San Francisco.

Stiggins, R. J. (1988a). Make sure your teachers understand student assessment. *Executive Educator, 10*(8), 24–26.

Stiggins, R. J. (1988b). Revitalizing classroom assessment: The highest instructional priority. *Phi Delta Kappan, 69*, 363–368.

Stiggins, R. J., Rubel, E., & Quellmalz, E. (1986). *Measuring thinking skills in the classroom*. Washington, DC: National Education Association.

Stipek, D. J. (1986). Children's motivation to learn. In T. M. Tomlinson & H. J. Walberg (Eds.), *Academic work and educational excellence: Raising student productivity* (pp. 197–221). Berkeley, CA: McCutchan.

Stipek, D. J. (1988). *Motivation to learn: From theory to practice*. Englewood Cliffs, NJ: Prentice-Hall.

Stodolsky, S. S. (1989). Is teaching really by the book? In P. W. Jackson & S. Haroutunian-Gordon (Eds.), *From Socrates to software: The teacher as text and the text as teacher* (The 88th Yearbook of the National Society for the Study of Education, Pt. 1, pp. 159–184). Chicago: University of Chicago Press.

Strother, D. S. (1984). Homework: Too much, just right, or not enough. *Phi Delta Kappan, 65*, 423–424.

Strother, D. S. (1985). Adapting instruction to individual needs: An eclectic approach. *Phi Delta Kappan, 67*, 308–311.

Student questions in K–12 classrooms. (1988). *Harvard Education Letter, 4*(1), 7.

Swick, K. J. (1985a). *A proactive approach to discipline: Six professional development modules for educators*. Washington, DC: National Educational Association.

Swick, K. J. (1985b). *Disruptive student behavior in the classroom*. Washington, DC: National Education Association.

Swift, J. N., Gooding, C. T., & Swift, P. R. (1988). Questions and wait time. In J. T. Dillon (Ed.), *Questioning and discussion: A multidisciplinary study* (pp. 192–211). Norwood, NJ: Ablex.

Sylwester, R. (1971). *The elementary teacher and pupil behavior*. West Nyack, NY: Parker.

Taba, H. (1966). *Teaching strategies and cognitive functions in elementary school children* (Cooperative Research Project No. 2404). San Francisco: San Francisco State College.

Taba, H., & Elzey, F. F. (1964). Teaching strategies and thought processes. *Teachers College Record, 65*, 524–534.

Taba, H., Levine, S., & Elzey, F. F. (1964). *Thinking in elementary school children*. San Francisco: San Francisco State College.

Tamir, P. (1988). Subject matter and related pedagogical knowledge in teacher education. *Teaching and Teacher Education, 4*, 99–110.

Teachers' questions: Why do you ask? (1987). *Harvard Education Letter, 3*(3), 1–3.

Tennyson, R. D., & Cocchiarella, M. J. (1986). An empirically based instructional design theory for teaching concepts. *Review of Educational Research, 56*, 40–71.

Thomas, D. A. (1988). Reading and reasoning skills for math problem solvers. *Journal of Reading, 32*, 244–248.

Thomas, R. M. (1987). Individualizing teaching. In M. J. Dunkin (Ed.), *The international encyclopedia of teaching and teacher education* (pp. 220–224). New York: Pergamon Press.

Tisher, R. P. (1987). Student roles. In M. J. Dunkin (Ed.), *The international encyclopedia of teaching and teacher education* (pp. 432–436). New York: Pergamon Press.

Tobin, K. (1984). *Improving the quality of teacher and student discourse in middle school grades*. Paper presented at the Annual Meeting of the American Educational Research Association, New Orleans.

Tobin, K. (1986). Effects of teacher wait time on discourse characteristics in mathematics and language arts classes. *American Educational Research Journal, 23*, 191–200.

Tobin, K. (1987a). Forces which shape the implemented curriculum in high school science and mathematics. *Teaching and Teacher Education, 3*, 287–298.

Tobin, K. (1987b). The role of wait time in higher cognitive level learning. *Review of Educational Research, 57*, 69–95.

Tobin, K., & Espinet, M. (1989). Impediments to change: Applications of coaching in high school science teaching. *Journal of Research in Science Teaching, 26*(2), 105–120.

Tobin, K., & Fraser, B. J. (1988). Investigations of exemplary practice in science and mathematics teaching in western Australia. *Journal of Curriculum Studies, 20*, 361–371.

Tomlinson, T. M., & Walberg, H. J. (Eds.). (1986). *Academic work and educational excellence: Raising student productivity*. Berkeley, CA: McCutchan.

Trenholm, S., & Rose, T. (1981). The compliant communicator: Teacher perceptions of appropriate classroom behavior. *Western Journal of Speech Communication, 45*, 13–26.

Tulley, M., & Farr, R. (1990). Textbook evaluation and selection. In D. L. Elliott & A. Woodward (Eds.), *Textbooks and schooling in the United States* (The 89th Yearbook of the National Society for the Study of Education, Pt. 1, pp. 162–177). Chicago: University of Chicago Press.

Tursman, C. (1981). Good teachers: What to look for. *Education USA* (Special Report). Arlington, VA: National School Public Relations Association.

Ulerick, S. L., & Tobin, K. (1989). *The influence of a teacher's beliefs on classroom management*. Paper presented at the Annual Meeting of the American Educational Research Association, San Francisco.

Upchurch, R. L., & Lockhead, H. (1987). Computers and higher order thinking skills. In V. Richardson-Koehler(Ed.), *Educator's handbook: A research perspective* (pp. 139–166). New York: Longman.

Uttero, D. A. (1988). Activating comprehension through cooperative learning. *The Reading Teacher*, *41*, 390–395.

Valencia, S. W., Pearson, D. P., Peters, C. W., & Wixson, K. K. (1989). Theory and practice in statewide reading assessments: Closing the gap. *Educational Leadership*, *46*(7), 57–62.

Vargas, J. S. (1986). Instructional design flaws in computer-assisted instruction. *Phi Delta Kappan*, *67*, 738–744.

Vermette, P. J. (1988). Cooperative grouping in the classroom: Turning students into active learners. *Social Studies*, *79*, 271–273.

Vobejda, B. (1987). A mathematician's research on math instruction. *Educational Researcher*, *16*(9), 9–12.

Vygotsky, L. S. (1978). *Mind in society: The development of higher psychological processes* (M. Cole, V. John-Steiner, S. Scribner, & E. Souberman, Eds.). Cambridge, MA: Harvard University Press.

Wagner, L. (1982). *Peer teaching: Historical perspectives* (Contributions to the Study of Education No. 5). Westport, CT: Greenwood.

Walberg, H. J. (1984a). Families as partners in educational productivity. *Phi Delta Kappan*, *65*, 397–400.

Walberg, H. J. (1984b). Improving the productivity of America's schools. *Educational Leadership*, *41*(8), 19–27.

Walberg, H. J. (1985). Instructional theories and research evidence. In M. C. Wang & H. J. Walberg (Eds.), *Adapting instruction to individual differences* (pp. 3–23). Berkeley, CA: McCutchan.

Walberg, H. J. (1988). Synthesis of research on time and learning. *Educational Leadership*, *45*(6), 76–85.

Walberg, H. J., Paschal, R., & Weinstein, T. (1985). Homework's powerful effects on learning. *Educational Leadership*, *42*(7), 76–79.

Walker, D. F. (1986). Computers and the curriculum. In J. A. Culbertson & L. L. Cunningham (Eds.), *Microcomputers and Education* (The 85th Yearbook of the National Society for the Study of Education, Pt. 1, pp. 22–39). Chicago: University of Chicago Press.

Wandersee, J. J. (1987). Drawing concept circles: A new way to teach and test students. *Science Activities*, *24*(4), 9–20.

Wang, M. C., Gennari, P., & Waxman, H. C. (1985). The adaptive learning environments model. In M. C. Wang and H. J. Walberg (Eds.), *Adapting instruction to individual differences* (pp. 191–235). Berkeley, CA: McCutchan.

Wang, M. C., & Walberg, H. J. (Eds.). (1985). *Adapting instruction to individual differences*. Berkeley, CA: McCutchan.

Wang, M. C., & Lindvall, C. M. (1984). Individual differences in school learning environments: Theory, research, and design. In E. W. Gordon (Ed.), *Review of Research in Education* (Vol. 11, pp. 161–225). Washington, DC: American Educational Research Association.

Ward, B. A. (1987). *Instructional grouping in the classroom* (School Improvement Research Series). Portland, OR: Northwest Regional Educational Laboratory.

Warner, W. R., Havighurst, R. J., & Loeb, M. B. (1944). *Who shall be educated?* New York: Harper and Row.

Wasley, P. A. (1989). *Lead teachers and teachers who lead: Reform rhetoric and real practice*. Paper presented at the Annual Meeting of the American Educational Research Association, San Francisco.

Wasserman, S. (1987). Teaching for thinking: Louis E. Raths revisited. *Phi Delta Kappan*, *68*, 460–466.

Watson, J., & Strudler, N. (1989). Teaching higher order thinking skills with databases. *Computing Teacher*, *16*(14), 47–50, 55.

Watson, K., & Young, B. (1986). Discourse for learning in the classroom. *Language Arts*, *63*, 26–29.

Waxman, H. C., Wang, M. C., Anderson, K. A., & Walberg, H. J. (1985a). *Adaptive education and student outcomes: A quantitative synthesis.*

(ERIC Document Reproduction Service No. ED 263 132)

Waxman, H. C., Wang, M. C., Anderson, K. A., & Walberg, H. J. (1985b). Synthesis of research on effects of adaptive education. *Educational Leadership, 41*(1), 26–29.

Weade, R., & Evertson, C. M. (1988). *The construction of lessons in effective and less effective classrooms*. Grant No. NIE.G-83-0063. Washington, DC: Office of Educational Research and Improvement.

Webb, N. M. (1988). *Peer interaction and learning in small groups*. Paper presented at the Annual Meeting of the American Educational Research Association, New Orleans.

Webb, N. M., & Cullian, L. K. (1983). Group interaction and achievement in small groups: Stability over time. *American Educational Research Journal, 20*, 411–423.

Webber, L. D. (1988). *Transitions: Toward a grounded theory of what happens between lessons*. (ERIC Document Reproduction Service No. ED 298 083)

Weber, G. (1971). *Inner-city children can be taught to read*. Washington, DC: Council for Basic Education.

Weber, W. A. (1984). *Classroom management: An analytic-pluralistic process*. Unpublished manuscript.

Weber, W. A., Crawford, J., Roff, L., & Robinson, C. (1983). *Classroom management: Reviews of the teacher education and research literature*. Princeton, NJ: Educational Testing Service.

Wehlage, G. G., Rutter, R. A., Smith, G. A., Lesko, N., and Fernandez, R. R. (1989). *Reducing the risk: Schools as communities as support*. London: Falmer Press.

Weiner, B. (1979). A theory of motivation for some classroom experiences. *Journal of Educational Psychology, 71*, 3–25.

Weiner, B., & Kukla, A. (1970). An attributional analysis of achievement motivation. *Journal of Personality and Social Psychology, 15*, 1–20.

Weinstein, C. E., & Mayer, R. (1986). The teaching of learning strategies. In M. Wittrock (Ed.), *Handbook of Research on Teaching* (3rd ed., pp. 315–327). New York: Macmillan.

Weinstein, C. S. (1987). Seating patterns. In M. J. Dunkin (Ed.), *The international encyclopedia of teaching and teacher education* (pp. 545–547). New York: Pergamon Press.

Weinstein, R. S. (1983). Student perceptions of schooling. *Elementary School Journal, 83*, 287–312.

West, P. (1990). Videodisks gaining popularity as new instructional tool. *Education Week, 9*(17), 24.

When the student becomes the teacher. (1986). *Harvard Education Letter, 2*(2), 5–6.

White, M. A. (1975). Natural rates of teacher approach and disapproval in the classroom. *Journal of Applied Behavior Analysis, 8*, 367–372.

White, M. A. (1983). Synthesis of research on electronic learning. *Educational Leadership, 40*(8), 13–15.

Wildman, T. M., & Niles, J. A. (1987). Essentials of professional growth. *Educational Leadership, 44*(5), 4–10.

Wilen, W. W. (1986). *Questioning skills for teachers* (2nd ed.). Washington, DC: National Education Association.

Wilen, W. W. (1987). *Questions, questioning techniques, and effective teaching*. Washington, DC: NEA Professional Library.

Wilen, W. W., & McKenrick, P. (1989). Individual inquiry: Encouraging able students to investigate. *Social Studies, 80*, 51–54.

Wilkinson, L. C., & Calculator, S. (1982). Requests and responses in peer-directed reading groups. *American Educational Research Journal, 19*, 107–120.

Wilson, A. B. (1963). Social stratification and academic achievement. In A. H. Passow (Ed.), *Education in depressed areas*. New York: Columbia University, Teachers College, Bureau of Publications.

Wineburg, S. S., & Wilson, S. M. (1988). Models of wisdom in the teaching of history. *Phi Delta Kappan, 70*, 50–58.

Wise, A. E. (1988). Legislated learning revisited. *Phi Delta Kappan, 69*, 328–332.

Wittrock, M. (1986). Students' thought processes. In M. Wittrock (Ed.), *Handbook of research on teaching* (3rd ed., pp. 297–314). New York: Macmillan.

Wlodkowski, R. J. (1977). *Motivation: What research says to the teacher*. Washington, DC: National Education Association.

Wloskowski, R. J. (1986). *Motivation and teaching: A practical guide*. Washington, DC: National Education Association.

Wood, J., & Rosbe, M. (1985). Adapting the classroom lecture for the mainstreamed student in the secondary schools. *Clearing House, 58,* 354–358.

Wood, K. D. (1987). Fostering cooperative learning in middle and secondary level classrooms. *Journal of Reading, 31,* 10–18.

Worsham, M. E. (1981). *Student accountability for written work in junior high school classes*. Austin, TX: Research and Development Center for Teacher Education. (ERIC Document Reproduction Service No. ED 203 387)

Worthen, B. R. (1968). A study of discovery and expository presentation: Implications for teaching. *Journal of Teacher Education, 19,* 233–242.

Yinger, R. J. (1986). Examining thought in action: A theoretical and methodological critique of research on interactive teaching. *Teaching and Teacher Education, 2,* 263–282.

Zahorik, J. A. (1970). The effects of planning on teaching. *The Elementary School Journal, 71,* 143–151.

Zahorik, J. A. (1987). Reacting. In M. J. Dunkin (Ed.), *The international encyclopedia of teaching and teacher education* (pp. 416–423). New York: Pergamon Press.

Zimmerman, B. J., & Pons, M. M. (1986). Development of a structured interview of assessing student use of self-regulated learning strategies. *American Educational Research Journal, 23,* 614–628.

Zimmerman, B. J., & Ringle, J. (1981). Effects of model persistence and statements of confidence on children's self-efficacy and problem solving. *Journal of Educational Psychology, 73,* 485–493.

Author Index

Subject Index